INSIDERS' GUIDE® TO
CALIFORNIA'S WINE COUNTRY

Help Us Keep This Guide Up to Date

Every effort has been made by the authors and editors to make this guide as accurate and useful as possible. However, many things can change after a guide is published—establishments close, phone numbers change, hiking trails are rerouted, facilities come under new management, etc.

We would love to hear from you concerning your experiences with this guide and how you feel it could be improved and be kept up to date. While we may not be able to respond to all comments and suggestions, we'll take them to heart and we'll also make certain to share them with the authors. Please send your comments and suggestions to the following address:

The Globe Pequot Press
Reader Response/Editorial Department
P.O. Box 480
Guilford, CT 06437

Or you may e-mail us at:

editorial@globe-pequot.com

Thanks for your input, and happy travels!

INSIDERS' GUIDE® SERIES

Insiders' Guide®
to California's
Wine Country

Including Napa, Sonoma, Mendocino, and Lake Counties

FIFTH EDITION

Jean Saylor Doppenberg
and John Nagiecki

Guilford, Connecticut

An imprint of The Globe Pequot Press

Copyright © 2002 by The Globe Pequot Press
Previous editions of this book were published by Falcon Publishing, Inc. in 1998, 1999, and 2000.

Front cover photo by Jean Saylor Doppenberg
Maps by Geografx © The Globe Pequot Press

ISSN: 1539-9923
ISBN: 0-7627-2253-3

Manufactured in the United States of America
Fifth Edition/First Printing

Contents

Directory of Maps

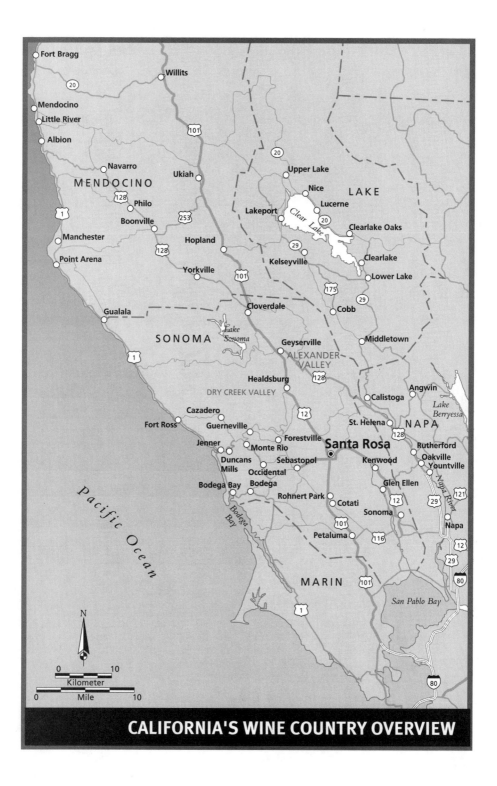

CALIFORNIA'S WINE COUNTRY OVERVIEW

NAPA COUNTY WINE TRAILS

SONOMA COUNTY WINE TRAILS

MENDOCINO COUNTY WINE TRAILS

LAKE COUNTY WINE TRAILS

Preface

Romans and Greeks knew Bacchus, the celebrated patron of wine, as a lusty god whose cult followers—made up entirely of women—held wild, ecstatic rituals. The enthusiasm of these bacchantes, as they were called, was so great that they would periodically abandon their families and head for the hills, wearing fawn skins and crowns of ivy and shouting ritual cries. They danced by firelight to the flute and tympanum and drank until they could drink no more.

Though the spirit of the California Wine Country does not exactly match that of old-style bacchanalia, it does possess a certain joie de vivre. Today, wine lovers in great numbers—and of both genders—abandon their worries and wander wide-eyed through these verdant hills and valleys.

Whether it's sampling the many exquisite vintages directly from the source or simply soaking up the sunny Mediterranean climate, our little slice of heaven here in Northern California has a distinct buoying effect. Though it may not inspire you to don a fawn skin or wrap ivy around your head, the region does have a way of teasing out one's finer qualities. Just stroll around the Sonoma Plaza or St. Helena's gingerbread neighborhoods and count the smiles.

Some visitors say our mountains and vineyards bring to mind the grape-growing regions of Tuscany; others swear we are the mirror image of Provence. We're flattered, of course, to be compared to some of the most beautiful terrain on the planet, but, as you will discover, we have an identity that is all our own. In this, the fifth edition of the *Insiders' Guide to the Wine Country*, we would like to introduce you to the many places that make our region special. We will guide you to the finest wineries, restaurants, and inns and share some of the tips and secrets that only a local would know. And it doesn't stop there. We understand that there's a lot more that you're interested in, and so we've endeavored to provide you with the most comprehensive volume about the Wine Country that you'll find anywhere.

Whether you come as a tourist or a settler, we hope you will gain insight from this book. We invite you to drop us a line about how it worked for you. And if you discovered something we missed, we'd like to know about that too. We update this guide annually, and we want it to be as accurate and helpful as possible.

Write to us at:

> The Insiders' Guide to California's Wine Country
> The Globe Pequot Press
> P.O. Box 480
> Guilford, CT 06437-0480

You can also visit us on the Web at www.insiders.com.

Acknowledgments

Books like this are not solely the work of one person. Though the author pulls the final pieces of the manuscript together and gets the credit in the end, it is not accomplished without the cooperation and assistance of scores of friends, acquaintances, and even total strangers. It's impossible to list and thank them all in such a small space, but here are several, in no particular order:

My gratitude goes to Lisa Walter of the Sonoma Valley Harvest Wine Auction for her cooperation and to Tom Fuller and Monty Sander of the Napa Valley Wine Auction for their assistance. (Thanks to all of you for a couple of unforgettable afternoons!) Kathleen Iudice at Copia took time from her strenuous schedule leading up to the opening of the museum to offer advice and supply reams of information. Fact-checker extraordinaire Bob Warden labored over the details of many listings in several chapters, and his enthusiasm for the project kept me on my toes. Thanks, Bob. My editor, Lynne Arany, deserves credit for guiding me gently through the project and keeping me focused. My sister, Jan Blanchard, was also a great help, and she lent many of her photos for use in the book. My husband, Loren, displayed quiet patience and understanding when my boxes full of research were piling up around the house.

Finally, I thank my parents, John and Gertrude Saylor, for blessing me with a lifelong curiosity for people and places and the desire to write about them. For many years, John and Gert entertained their four unruly children on a series of long automobile trips called "family vacations." It couldn't have been loads of fun for Mom and Dad, but before I reached my tenth birthday I had already hiked the circumference of Devil's Tower, waded in the Gulf of Mexico, posed for pictures in front of Mt. Rushmore, gawked at Jayne Mansfield's hot pink mansion in Hollywood, and been kissed by a cockatoo in Miami. You can't buy memories like that.

—Jean Saylor Doppenberg

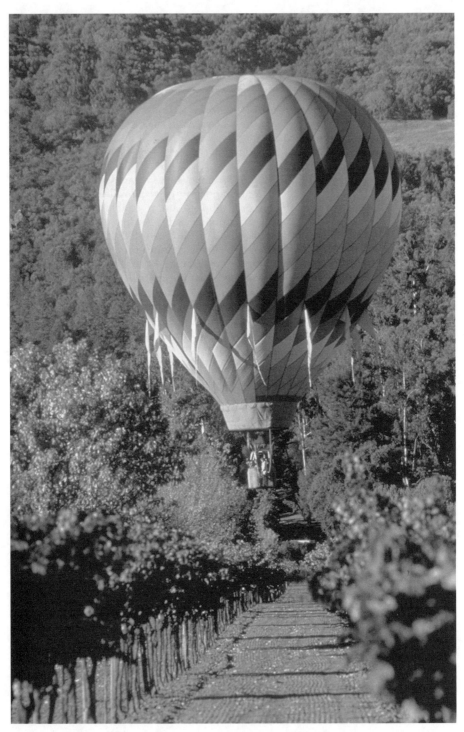

They may be full of hot air, but balloons are a popular way to see Wine Country. PHOTO: NAPA VALLEY CON-
FERENCE AND VISITORS BUREAU

How to Use This Book

Skimming through the *Insiders' Guide to California's Wine Country* is a bit like channel surfing with your TV's remote control—you flip here and there, back and forth, looking for something to grab your attention. It might be a striking image or an interesting name that leaps out and demands closer investigation.

Go ahead and chapter surf to you heart's content, and land on any page that strikes your fancy, whether it's for a restaurant, winery, or lodging listing. That's okay. Data-heavy books such as this one are designed for thumbing through. But at some point you might want to find a particular "thing" by region, so it will help to understand the book's structure.

The table of contents breaks down the chapter topics, but if any questions remain, a quick peek at chapter introductions should answer them. Beyond that, we organized each chapter geographically, more or less, with Napa County listings first, followed by those of Sonoma County, Mendocino County, and Lake County. In general, the listings for hotels, attractions, wineries, and so forth appear in order in the book as you would encounter them while driving in each region, approximately south to north and east to west. (To make the Sonoma County listings more manageable—there are scads of them—we further divided the county up into Northern, Southern, Sonoma Coast, and West County/Russian River subheadings.) Refer to the list below for the general order by town and city.

Note: We understand that many of our world-class eateries are known by name and not necessarily by their location. So we've organized our Restaurants chapter using the same geographical method explained above, then listed the restaurants alphabetically within their respective towns and regions.

Napa County

Napa, Yountville, Oakville, Rutherford, St. Helena, Angwin, Lake Berryessa, Calistoga

Sonoma County

Southern Sonoma
Sonoma, Glen Ellen, Kenwood, Petaluma, Cotati, Rohnert Park, Santa Rosa

Northern Sonoma
Windsor, Healdsburg, Geyserville, Cloverdale, Alexander Valley, Dry Creek Valley, Lake Sonoma, Westside Road

Sonoma Coast
Bodega, Bodega Bay, Jenner, Fort Ross

West County/Russian River
Sebastopol, Occidental, Forestville, Guer-

neville, Monte Rio, Cazadero, Duncans Mills

Mendocino County

U.S. 101
Hopland, Ukiah, Willits

Hwy. 128
Yorkville, Boonville, Philo, Navarro

Mendocino Coast
Gualala, Point Arena, Albion, Little River, Mendocino, Fort Bragg

Lake County

Middletown, Cobb, Lower Lake, Clearlake, Clearlake Oaks, Kelseyville, Lakeport, Lucerne, Nice, Bartlett Springs, Upper Lake

As you might have noticed, the above sequence begins with listings found in the south and east and generally moves north and west through each county. The idea is that as you drive through the Wine Country's principal valleys, beginning in the south and following the main corridors and connecting roads north, this is the order in which you will encounter things. We have the forces of volcanism and plate tectonics to thank for our topographical layout, which combined to form long rows of longitudinal valleys in Northern California (see our Flora, Fauna, and Climate chapter). Of course, it is not always so neat and tidy. Some attractions—state parks and many wineries being perfect examples—don't reside within any city limits. Hence, we placed rural items nearest their closest municipalities or squeezed them between appropriate towns in the geographical breakdown.

Having said all that, be aware that several chapters cover topics that venture beyond the Wine Country or otherwise defy a strict county-by-county organization. These include our Golden Gateway (San Francisco) and Daytrippin' chapters, which focus on more distant destinations. Likewise, the Spectator Sports chapter covers professional teams in and beyond Wine Country and is thus organized by sport. The Flora, Fauna, and Climate chapter and, to some extent, the Getting Here, Getting Around chapter deal with phenomena that have no respect for county lines and thus have their own unique breakdowns. And the Festivals and Annual Events chapter logically follows a chronological order.

And don't forget another important resource: the index. Many items are referenced several places in the book. Silverado Country Club, for instance, is mentioned in Spas and Resorts, Nightlife, and Parks and Recreation. The index reflects that.

Finally, you'll note that some material teeters on the categorical fence that divides some chapters. Take the annual Clear Lake Team Bass Tournament. Is it sports, an event, or a water activity? It's a little of all these, but we put it in the chapter called Festivals and Annual Events. We recognize that not everyone will agree with where we placed various listings, and we apologize in advance to those who believe we have misclassified their favorite place or thing. To try and mitigate the problem, we have cross-referenced information wherever it made sense, briefly mentioning a related event, activity, or locale where appropriate and referring you to the chapter where it is described in more detail.

We hope the book answers all your questions and raises a few you might not have considered. If you find anything you believe to be inaccurate or misleading, we urge you to let us know.

Area Overview

Napa County
Sonoma County
Mendocino County
Lake County

Is the Wine Country greater than the sum of its parts? Being neither mathematicians nor philosophers, we'll skip that question. However, we would like to take a small amount of space to briefly describe the municipalities and counties that make up this complex region.

Napa County

Of the four counties profiled in this book, Napa is by far the most dependent on wine and tourism and the region most associated with those two industries in the minds of visitors. Always rural in nature, Napa County has seen the rise and fall of wheat, cattle, and prunes as the dominant product. Today it is ultrapremium wine grapes—and the visitors who love them—that drive the economy.

In the last decade, Napa County's total population grew 12 percent (according to 2000 census figures), to 124,279, yet it remains the Bay Area's least populated county. Most of the residents are hard-working, average Joes and Jills, with the median household income in the city of Napa at $36,000. But we have a good share of celebrity residents, too, who earn a bit more. Property owners in Napa Valley and its environs include Francis Ford Coppola (see our Wineries chapter), Robin Williams, Robert Redford, Woody Harrelson, Joe Montana, Boz Scaggs, Danielle Steele, David Wolper, and Mario Andretti. Other household names who have shopped for homes and property here but apparently haven't signed on the dotted line (yet) include Barbra Streisand and Eric Clapton.

Even if they don't commit to buying their very own villa or vineyard, celebs (A-, B-, and even C-list varieties) flock to the area for getaway jaunts the same as you, the probably-not-world-famous visitor. Because of this growing number of high-rollers and famous faces flitting about, filmmaker/wine baron/longtime resident Coppola recently quipped to the local press that he feared Napa Valley was turning into the East Hampton of the West Coast. Be that as it may, if you should stumble upon La Streisand noshing at the Model Bakery in St. Helena, please play it cool.

The southern gateway to Napa Valley is the city of Napa, which, at about 72,500 people, makes up more than half of the county's population. Napa has several

This book doesn't pretend to teach you about wine. Instead, you get a full-bodied taste of the region known as Wine Country from an insider's view. PHOTO: SANTA ROSA CONVENTION AND VISITORS BUREAU

3

The friendly facade of City Hall in Calistoga is just one of this small town's many charms. PHOTO: JEAN SAYLOR DOPPENBERG

gracious, older districts left over from the horse-and-buggy days—the lettered streets known as Old Town, the Fuller Park area south of downtown, and Alta Heights— connected by more down-to-earth neighborhoods. It is home to most of the budget- and family-oriented accommodations and eateries in the valley and some busy, densely commercial streets that don't reflect the charm that first-time visitors might expect here.

Yet downtown Napa is slowly undergoing a major renovation that was triggered by the development and construction of Copia (see our Attractions chapter) and a $238 million flood control project along the Napa River that will take several years to complete. Where once it was seen primarily as the commercial core of the valley proper, lacking an abundance of tourist-oriented amenities, the city of Napa is becoming a destination in itself. New hotels and B&Bs have opened, many new

eateries are getting rave reviews, and the city center in general is being spiffed up and transformed. Some historic buildings are facing demolition in the flood control zone, yet others are getting multimillion-dollar makeovers. Plans for proposed hotels and other attractions are announced almost weekly, with several projects waiting for the green light so that groundbreaking can begin.

Though Napa owes much of its prosperity to the wine industry, government is the largest employer in the city. Napa is the seat of the county government, and the Napa Valley Unified School District and Napa State Hospital account for thousands of jobs. The city of Napa is also the valley's vital commercial core. As such, it is the only place in the valley where you will find McDonald's, Taco Bell, Wendy's, and other popular fast-food outlets. This is where you are likely to find "chain" businesses of other sorts, too.

To the south of Napa, just within the border of Napa County, is the county's newest incorporated town, the bedroom community of American Canyon. With a population of about 9,100, it is primarily comprised of new subdivisions, few services, and no tourist attractions.

To the north of the city of Napa is Yountville, named after Napa Valley pioneer George Yount (see our History chapter). It is a small community (population 3,000) that self-proclaims more fine restaurants per capita than any city in America—and we don't doubt it. The town is dominated by two structures: the delightful Veterans Home complex (see our Attractions chapter) that watches over the proceedings from the hill west of Highway 29; and Vintage 1870, an historic winery rescued and converted into a warren of shops (see our Shopping chapter). New subdivisions built in the late 1990s have increased the population slightly, but this is a town that caters almost exclusively, and with a lot of class, to visitors.

Oakville and Rutherford appear frequently in addresses throughout the book, but usually the reference is to nearby, countryside locales. The towns themselves are minuscule; hardly more than bulges around Highway 29. This is, however, a beautiful part of the valley—a midway sector where the mountains begin to encroach upon the valley floor. Every experienced picnicker in the region knows the Oakville Grocery Company, an unpretentious little pit stop along the highway famous for its gourmet delights. This is also the stretch of road where you will begin to come upon the showplace wineries—Robert Mondavi, Niebaum-Coppola, and so on.

When most visitors imagine the quintessential Wine Country village, they envision St. Helena—with its gingerbread cottages painted glistening white, canopied sidewalks of a thriving-yet-nostalgic downtown, pocket gardens with not a blade of grass out of place, and only three traffic lights! Though it has its peripheral subdivisions and apartment complexes, the overall look of St. Helena is defined by high-priced neatness (see our Real Estate chapter). Much of the housing is pre-

World War II and nearly all has been immaculately maintained, and the residential streets in the heart of town are lushly lined with mature trees. The north end of town is dominated by the imposing structures of the Beringer and Charles Krug wineries and the Culinary Institute at Greystone (see our Education and Child Care chapter). About a quarter of the town's approximately 6,000 residents are 65 or older, making it a popular spot for retirees with comfortable bank accounts. Due east of St. Helena is Deer Park, a small community with about 1,800 souls.

The hilltop hamlet of Angwin, up Deer Park Road/Howell Mountain Road off the Silverado Trail, orbits around Pacific Union College. The town's population tops out at about 3,100, most of them college students—a full 61 percent of the inhabitants here are under age 30. The town is so heavily Seventh-day Adventist that it's said to be one of only two in the nation where the post office delivers mail on Sunday rather than Saturday. Angwin's College Market is a richly stocked

Insiders' Tip

Duck, everyone! In 2001, Calistoga became the first place in America to install a public earthquake warning alarm system. Motion sensors in the town's firehouse can detect the first waves of a 5.0 or greater shaker, and the alarm will blare throughout the town immediately. It is intended to give residents and visitors 30 to 60 seconds to prepare themselves and take cover before The Big One hits.

The Mayacmas Mountains, which divide Sonoma and Napa Counties, serve as a spectacular Wine Country backdrop. PHOTO: JOHN NAGIECKI

supermarket with dozens of bulk bins—but no meat or liquor sections (yes, that includes wine).

To the east of Angwin, man-made Lake Berryessa figures prominently in our On the Water chapter. The settlements thereof tend to lie on the western and southern shores of the lake, especially along Berryessa-Knoxville Road. The eastern perimeter is virtually inaccessible to any vehicle. Unlike Clear Lake in Lake County, Berryessa is not encircled with hotels and restaurants. There are a few, but it is known more as a spot for vacation homes. As such, it empties out a bit in the winter.

Calistoga, the northernmost town of Napa Valley, is an iconoclastic slice of California, a burg that sees itself as "real" and unadulterated even as it supports itself almost entirely through tourist dollars, with the corner on the spa and mud bath market. As one local wag likes to describe it, "Calistoga is to pickup trucks what St. Helena is to Range Rovers." It's a place where a prominent restaurateur in a restored Queen Anne can live between an elderly Russian woman in an unremarkable 1950s cottage and an apartment complex of mostly working-class Latino families. The population hovers at around 5,200, with about 28 percent age 65 and older. Calistoga's easygoing mood can crack when the locals feel threatened by rampant development, however. PepsiCo tried to open some fast-food franchises in town a few years ago, but the citizenry hastily mobilized and ran the scoundrels out of town. That led to a bold prohibition of all new "formula" businesses. And just for the record, wine isn't the only refreshment bottled in Napa Valley: On the east side of Calistoga are two major suppliers of mineral water, Calistoga and Crystal Geyser, and some excellent beers are brewed and bottled at the Calistoga Inn.

Sonoma County

Encompassing nearly 1,600 square miles from the Pacific coast to the Mayacmas Mountains and San Pablo Bay, Sonoma County is the most populous of the four Wine Country counties. But most of the approximately 458,600 residents live in a relatively narrow corridor along U.S. 101 from Santa Rosa to Petaluma. The rest of the county—approximately 56 percent—is farmland. The farms consist of apple, peach, and plum orchards, livestock rangeland and dairy farms, and, of course, vineyards.

It's no surprise that grapes and wine are the most prized agricultural commodities, with an annual value of approximately $232 million—dairy comes in second at $95 million. Yet agricultural employment accounts for less than 4 percent of the total workforce. The services, retail trade, and manufacturing sectors by far employ the most people—approximately 62 percent. The state's Employment Development Department (EDD) expects these sectors to grow the fastest in Sonoma County over the next four to five years.

Santa Rosa is the county seat and the largest city, with a population of 147,600. In May 2000, *Forbes* magazine listed the city among the top three dynamic economic regions in the nation. The largest employers include Agilent Technologies, a spin-off company of electronics giant Hewlett Packard; aerospace and medical supplier Optical Coating; high-tech medical equipment manufacturer Medtronic; and county and state government offices. As in Napa County and the rest of California, the Hispanic population is booming in Sonoma County (currently at 15 percent). Asian peoples are the second largest minority (4 percent) followed by Blacks and Native Americans (each at 1 percent).

Santa Rosa's downtown is split in two by U.S. 101—a planning decision that many have long since regretted. To the west of the highway are multiple antiques shops and historic Railroad Square, whose sturdy buildings were constructed of locally quarried stone. To the east, especially along Fourth Street, are restaurants, coffee houses, music stores, and similar hangouts. The Luther Burbank Home and Gardens (see our Attractions chapter) are also nearby.

Due south of Santa Rosa are the residential communities of Cotati, Rohnert Park, and Petaluma. The latter is the third-largest town in Wine Country, with more than 54,500 people. The vague, down-and-out feeling of some sections of the town are counterbalanced by stately homes and Art Deco commercial palaces (such as the McNear Building). For a short architectural walking tour, stroll down Sixth Street.

A pioneer in residential growth management, Petaluma adopted a resolution in the early 1970s that regulates the number of residential allotments the city council may grant in a given year. The resolution was challenged, but the Ninth Circuit Court of Appeals and the U.S. Supreme Court upheld the plan in 1975–76.

On the southeastern edge of the county is the town of Sonoma. This small enclave of approximately 9,100 residents is largely defined by its historic sites, especially those along the town's eight-acre central plaza. There you'll find the Mission San Francisco de Solano, the Sonoma Barracks, the Swiss Hotel, and several nearby wineries within walking distance (see our Wineries, Hotels and Motels, and Bed-and-Breakfast Inns chapters). The square is a National Historic Landmark and is a great spot to relax on a sunny

Insiders' Tip

In 2001, Sonoma County was ranked No. 6 among 238 metropolitan areas in the nation in a *Forbes* magazine list of the most dynamic regional economies in America.

Learn all about grape growing at Kendall Jackson Wine Center's viticulture exhibit, in northwest Santa Rosa. PHOTO: JOHN NAGIECKI

afternoon. For a further description of the town of Sonoma, turn to our History chapter.

North of Sonoma are several tiny hamlets, including Glen Ellen and Kenwood. Tucked away from the traffic of Highway 12, Glen Ellen's Main Street is only two blocks long, so you might have to invent an excuse to spend the whole day here. One possibility is Jack London State Historic Park, just west of town (see our Attractions chapter). Kenwood is equally small, if not smaller, but no less charming. From the center of town (don't stand there; it's the middle of Highway 12), you can see the forested crests of two state parks, Annadel and Sugarloaf Ridge (see our Parks and Recreation chapter).

At the north end of the county is the town of Healdsburg, with a population of 10,700. Like Sonoma, the town has a delightful core centered around a classic town square. There you can find good food, good books, and a good dose of fine

old relics. Healdsburg is antiques central in a region gone ga-ga over old stuff.

Just a short hop north on U.S. 101 from Healdsburg is Geyserville, named for an area northeast of the town where natural steam vents from the earth. These fumaroles, as they are called, are visible from many points in the county, particularly on cool mornings. Calpine Corporation has harnessed the steam at its nearby geothermal plant, generating 850 megawatts of power. Tours of the 30-square-mile facility are available on weekends (see additional information in our Attractions chapter).

Still farther north on U.S. 101 is Cloverdale, a small, pleasant town of 6,800 souls nestled at the far end of the peaceful Alexander Valley, one of the county's prime grape-growing regions. From this point north, the coast redwoods start to take over (see "The Big Trees" in our Daytrippin' chapter), though there are still lots of grape-growing fields to be found in Sonoma's northern neighbor, Mendocino County.

The Alexander Valley south of Cloverdale offers wine tasters a more relaxed alternative to the relative bustle of Napa and Sonoma valleys. It may not have as many wineries, but it does have some good ones (see our Wineries chapter), and the traffic is comparatively light. In the spring, when winter rains have turned the hills a vivid green, the valley is especially charming—like a wee bit of the rolling Irish countryside. And in some vineyards around Cloverdale, some of the older vines are still grown in the traditional style—spaced widely and allowed to spread freely, in contrast to the trellises you normally see today.

Another smaller and similarly charming vale is the Dry Creek Valley, which lies west of Alexander Valley above Healdsburg. Here row upon row of vineyards line the rich valley floor and terraces climb up the gentle hillsides. Above the vines, thick forest overlooks the valley's western slope, while oak woodland makes up most of the sunnier eastern flank. At one time, Dry

Creek Valley extended farther to the north, but much of it was submerged when Warm Springs Dam was built in 1982. The dam gave birth to Lake Sonoma, a recreational area profiled more thoroughly in our On the Water chapter.

Finally, let it be known that there is life in western Sonoma County, despite the scarcity of wineries. Bodega Bay is the gateway to the Pacific, and it is where Highway 1 hits the coast and begins its circuitous trek northward. Much of the Alfred Hitchcock thriller *The Birds* was filmed in 1963 in both Bodega Bay and the slightly inland enclave of Bodega. The movie featured Bodega's Potter School, a one-room schoolhouse built a century before Hitchcock's cameras rolled into town.

Bodega Bay is one of the largest fishing ports between San Francisco and Eureka, and in September and October, the locals like to celebrate what they call "secret summer," when temperatures are relatively mild and the morning fog quickly disperses. The hook-shaped peninsula that shields the harbor from the open sea is Bodega Head. You can drive out on the

The historic Sebastiani Building along Sonoma's Plaza recently underwent an extensive restoration.

PHOTO: JEAN SAYLOR DOPPENBERG

shares this name with the Crimean city is located halfway between Santa Rosa and the coast (see "What's in a Name?"). Sebastopol rose to prominence on the cores of a billion Gravenstein apples—the delectable fruit that got its start here. The community has honored the revered apple by naming Highway 116, which runs through the heart of town, the Gravenstein Highway, and every summer it hosts the Gravenstein Apple Fair (see our Festivals and Annual Events chapter). It is also the only municipality in the state to currently have a Green Party majority on its city council.

Heading west and north from Sebastopol is the town of Forestville, which serves as a way station for travelers headed to the Russian River and the Pacific coast. Nearby is the all-but-forgotten town of Occidental, perched at the top of a hill in the middle of redwood country. Many know Occidental as the place for sublime Italian dinners—at Negri's and the Union Hotel (see our Restaurants chapter). It's also delightfully romantic, but what would you expect of a village whose main thoroughfare goes by the name Bohemian Highway?

Where the Bohemian Highway meets the Russian River just north of Occidental is the tiny town of Monte Rio. Here you can catch a movie at the funky Rio Theater (see our Nightlife section) before heading upriver to Guerneville (pronounced GURN-ville). This former lumber capital-cum-summer resort is sometimes referred to as the Gay Riviera, because of the large gay population that lives and weekends here.

While Guerneville is the largest town in the Russian River resort area, Duncans Mills is one of the smallest. Located about 4 miles before Highway 116 joins Highway 1, the town looks much as it did when it was the western terminus of the Northwest Pacific Railroad. A museum recalls the glory days of the beloved choo-choo, and a host of art and antiques shops and restaurants provide plenty of distractions.

headland along Westshore Road, which offers brilliant views and access to beaches and cliffs. Also on Bodega Head is the Bodega Marine Lab, a University of California field station that is open to the public every Friday from 2:00 to 4:00 P.M.

The town of Jenner lies about 7 miles north of Bodega Bay, at the point where the Russian River meets the sea. Dozens of harbor seals congregate near the town, growing fat on steelhead and other fish that migrate upriver. North of Jenner the coastal settlements are few and far between. Once the easternmost outpost of Czarist Russia, Fort Ross is now a State Historic Park (see our History and Attractions chapters).

Russian geographers will also recognize the name Sebastopol. The Wine Country town with a population of 7,700 that

Mendocino County

Mendocino County is double the size of Sonoma County, covering nearly 3,500 square miles. The population, currently at 86,200, is widely dispersed, with only a quarter of the residents living in urban areas. Most people find employment in the service sector, specifically tourism. The county's economy has historically been centered in the lumber and fishing industries, and both still have a foothold here. The Georgia-Pacific lumber company has hundreds of employees and vending and logging contracts with several hundred more people. It's estimated that the corporation annually contributes more than $60 million to the Fort Bragg–area economy. In inland areas such as the Yokayo Valley, agriculture is paramount. And because of the large holdings of public land in Mendocino County, the state parks system has become another important employer.

Hopland is a town that came by its name honestly. Awash in a field of hops in the early 1900s, it was the perfect choice as a home base for Mendocino Brewing Company, when in 1982 it became California's first brewery since Prohibition (see our Restaurants chapter). At the south end of Hopland is the Solar Living Center (see our Attractions chapter), a 12-acre site created by Real Goods, retailer of alternative energy products and services. Real Goods' 5,000-square-foot building is made of rice-straw bales, and wind generators and solar panels provide all of its electrical needs.

With a population of 15,500, Ukiah is Mendocino's largest town. It is set in the Yokayo Valley between the Coast Range and Lake Mendocino. Lumber is the chief commodity here, as it has been for decades, but Ukiah also has become the financial, business, medical, and service center not only for Mendocino County, but also for portions of Sonoma, Lake, and Humboldt counties. The town is home to many descendants of the Pomo tribe, the first inhabitants of the area.

Willits, to the north, also was kick-started during the 19th-century lumber boom, and most of the larger companies in the area are involved in manufacturing wood products. Driving along U.S. 101 6 miles south of town, look for a boulder directly across the highway from White

Small grocery stores such as this one on California Highway 1, within shouting distance of the Pacific Ocean, offer convenience for both local residents and vacationers. PHOTO: JEAN SAYLOR DOPPENBERG

What's in a Name?

Okay, Hopland and Clearlake you can figure out. But Petaluma? Cazadero? What exactly is Middletown in the middle of? And if you take your nice niece to Nice, will you be flummoxed by the pronunciation?

Borrowing from the fourth edition of the delightful and copious *California Place Names,* written by Erwin G. Gudde in 1947 and still reprinted by the University of California Press, we have compiled a partial gazetteer of Wine Country locales, with emphasis on their christenings. Besides providing a few amusing tidbits, it might give you a sideways view of California history: the Native American tribes with their complex languages and straightforward place names; the Spanish missionaries who covered so much ground as they proselytized; the feudal land grants doled out by the Mexican government, most of them later recognized by the United States; the Russian exploration along the north coast in the first half of the 19th century; and the East Coast pioneers who eventually flooded the area in search of lumber, gold, and cropland.

The whimsy we have lost over the years becomes apparent when you read Gudde's accounts of people like Dr. Edward Bale, the English surgeon who named his land grant Rancho Carne Humana. The translation is "Human Flesh Ranch," and it's now site of the Bale Grist Mill in Napa County.

Napa County

Napa. The name that eventually spread to a county, a city, a river, a creek, a slough, and a junction first pops up in baptismal records printed in 1795. It derives from the indigenous cultures that once inhabited the area, though there has been endless debate about the exact meaning. Is it a southern Patwin word for "grizzly bear," a northern Patwin variation of "house" or "tribe," or a Suisun term that nearly translates to "motherland"? We can't say. The city was laid out by Nathan Coombs in 1848; the county was named in 1850.

Yountville. George C. Yount journeyed from North Carolina to California in 1831, and five years later he received a grant for Rancho Caymus. The name Yountville appears on an 1860 map of the grant.

St. Helena. The peak that marks the border between Napa, Lake, and Sonoma Counties was called Mount St. Helena at least as early as 1851, but no one is really sure why. Most assume it was Russian explorers who dubbed the mountain, perhaps J.G. Woznesenski, who bagged the summit and left a plaque in 1841. Helena was an empress of Czarist Russia, and *Saint Helena* was the name of a Russian ship that sailed to California. The town was christened in 1855.

Angwin. This hill town was named in 1874 for Edwin Angwin, who operated a summer resort on his property on Howell Mountain.

Berryessa. Berryessa Valley was named for Jose Jesus and Sisto Berryessa, brothers who were granted Rancho Las Putas in 1843. The lake created by Monticello Dam originally was known as Monticello Reservoir, but the U.S. Board on Geographic Names adopted Lake Berryessa in 1957.

Calistoga. Sam Brannan began this resort in 1859, and he explained the name this way, according to biographer Reva Scott: "'Someday I'll make this the Saratoga of California,' I started to say, but my tongue slipped and what I said was, 'I'll make this the Calistoga of Sarafornia.'" Brannan's moniker stuck.

Sonoma County

Sonoma. Some say the name came from the Wintun word for "nose," but it's unclear whether it was in reference to a geological or facial feature. Others say it was a Miyakmah word for "town," while still another translation is "many moons." The town was founded as Zanoma in 1835, and the present spelling appeared in 1844. The county, one of California's original 27, was named in 1850.

Petaluma. Many believe that it derives from two Coast Miwok words: "peta," meaning flat, and "luma," meaning back. The name applied to a village and a low hill on the east side of what would be known as the Petaluma River. It later became part of a Mexican land grant (1834) and, of course, a city (1851).

Cotati. A land grant spelled Cotati or Cotate is dated 1844. The origin of the name is uncertain, though a Coast Miwok village north of the present town may have been called Kotati.

Rohnert Park. Incorporated in August 1962, this city was named after the Waldo Rohnert Seed Farm.

Santa Rosa. This is a popular place name throughout the state of California. Historian H.H. Bancroft lent this explanation to the naming of the creek (and later the city) in present-day Sonoma County: "the stream was named by a missionary priest who . . . captured and baptized in its waters an Indian girl, and gave her the name of Santa Rosa, in honor of the saint on whose day in the calendar this interesting ceremony was performed." The name first appears in a land grant document in 1831.

Healdsburg. The name was first applied to an outpost of the Post Office Department in 1857. It honored Harmon G. Heald, who established a trading post there in 1846.

Geyserville. Elisha Ely founded the town in 1851 and named it to advertise the nearby geothermal activity.

Bodega Bay. This long-established name is a tribute to captain Juan Francisco de Bodega, who sailed the *Sonora* into the bay in 1775. The town of Bodega was settled in 1853.

Fort Ross. Lots were drawn to choose the name of this outpost, which formed the nucleus of early 19th-century Russian activity in California. Ross is an obsolete poetic name for Russia, and its lot was selected from others placed at the base of an image of Christ.

Sebastopol. Sebastopol was the Russian city besieged by the English and French during the Crimean War in 1854. The highly publicized siege prompted no less than five California towns to adopt the name. This is the only one that bears it still. (Legend has it that when a local fight erupted, one group found itself under siege in the general store and the situation was likened to the battle in that famous city.)

Guerneville. Originally called Stumptown—for obvious reasons—the town was renamed Guerneville in 1870 after lumberman George Guerne.

Forestville. This town is at the edge of timber country, but it actually was named for its founder, Andrew Jackson Forrester, a Russian River saloonkeeper. The present spelling took hold by the late 1880s.

Cazadero. Known for redwoods and rain—it has the highest annual precipitation in the region. Cazadero is a California Spanish word that means "hunting place."

Mendocino County

Hopland. When a toll road was built on the east side of the Russian River in 1874, the tiny town of Sanel packed up and moved across the river to meet the road. The name was changed to Hopland to acknowledge Stephen Knowles' successful experiment in growing the crop there. In 1890 the California Northwestern Railroad was extended to Ukiah, and tracks were laid on the west side of the river. Back came the town. The Post Office Department restored the name Sanel, but switched it to Hopland in 1891 or 1892.

Ukiah. Mendocino County's largest city was named for a Pomo Indian village that once existed nearby. It probably means "deep valley." The town was named in 1856.

Yorkville. When a post office was established here about 1870, the settlers could not decide which of two locally prominent families to honor: the Yorks or the Hiatts. The patriarchs of the two clans finally settled it with a contest. Unfortunately, we don't know what the test was, but Richard H. York won. The loser, Elijah M. Hiatt, received the postmastership as a consolation prize.

Boonville. In the mid-1860s W. W. Boone bought the Levi and Strauss store in Kendall's City and changed the name of the town to Booneville. The "e" was some-how misplaced when the post office was established in the 1880s.

Philo. Sometime after 1868 Cornelius Prather, landowner and postmaster, called this town after his favorite girl cousin, who (probably) was named Philomena.

Gualala. Here's a bone of contention: Most anthropologists familiar with the area insist the name is a corruption of Walali, a Pomo word meaning "where the waters meet." County histories and local tradition, on the other hand, claim it's a Spanish version of Walhalla, mythical abode of slain Teutonic heroes. In any case, when the town was named in 1862 (after the river), the name giver applied the cur-rent spelling, mistakenly assuming it to be a Spanish word.

Point Arena. This cape on the Mendocino coast was sighted by Bartolome Ferrer in 1543 and called Cabo de Fortunas. By the late 18th century, the name had begun to give way to Barra de Arena, or "sand bar." The English-style Point Arena was in use by 1849.

Albion. New Albion was the name Sir Francis Drake bestowed upon northern California in the 16th century. Another Briton (and captain of the port of San Fran-cisco), William A. Richardson, no doubt had that in mind when he named the river in 1844. The town was named in 1853.

Mendocino. This moniker is almost as old as Spanish exploration of the Pacific coast. In fact, no other name for a cape has survived as many phases of real or imag-ined California geography with the same spelling and in the same location. The earli-est known reference to Cabo Mendocino is on the maps of Ortelius in 1587. The only question is after which viceroy of New Spain the protrusion was named: Don Antonio de Mendoza or Lorenzo Suarez de Mendoza. (Mendocino would be an adjectival form of the name.) The county, one of California's original 27, was named in 1850, the town in 1852. Mendocino National Forest was created as Stony Creek Forest Reserve in 1907, renamed California National Forest in 1908, and given its current name in 1932.

Fort Bragg. The military post established in 1857 honored Lt. Col. Braxton Bragg, who had won some fame in the Mexican War. Bragg soon would become a Confeder-ate general, and the town of Fort Bragg would be founded in 1885.

Lake County

Middletown. This small burg got its handle in the 1860s, when it was the stage stop halfway between Calistoga and Lower Lake.

Cobb. The town, the mountain, the valley, and the creek are named for John Cobb, the Kentuckian who built a combination sawmill and grist mill in the valley in 1859.

Clear Lake. This name dates back at least to 1851, when it appeared in the journal of George Gibbs. Before that, the Spanish called it Laguna Grande (big lake), and the indigenous people called it Kah Shoh, the Clear Lake Valley Indians' word for lake. The towns of Lower Lake, Clearlake, Clearlake Oaks, Lakeport, and Upper Lake all derive their names from their relationship to Clear Lake.

Kelseyville. When the town was established in the 1860s, it was called Kelsey Town in memory of Andrew Kelsey, the county's first white settler. Kelsey was a widely disliked character who was killed by a local tribe in 1849 in retaliation for years of mistreatment. The name was changed to Kelseyville around 1885.

Lucerne. Somebody evidently thought the shore of Clear Lake looked a lot like Switzerland's Lake Lucerne when the town (at that point, a hotel and a post office) was founded in 1926.

Nice. The community once known as Clear Lake Villas became Nice (pronounced nees) in 1927 or 1928, apparently because of the area's loose resemblance to the bluffs of the French Riviera.

Deer Lodge—it was a reputed hideout of Black Bart, the stagecoach robber who roamed the area more than 100 years ago. You probably won't catch a glimpse of Bart, but you might see a white fallow deer on Ridgewood Summit. Herds of the deer, purchased from William Randolph Hearst's San Simeon Ranch, were released here in 1949.

Highway 128 courses through the Anderson Valley, linking the tiny towns of Yorkville, Boonville, Philo, and Navarro. The valley's northern latitude and salty breezes make it appropriate for growing cool-weather grapes such as Gewurztraminer and Riesling. Anderson Valley also brings forth a healthy supply of apples and sheep, and mushrooms are gathered in the soggy forests on either side of the valley. Boonville, as you'll see elsewhere in this book, is known for its unique language, called Boontling. Here's a poem a Boonie once recited on the *CBS Evening News*:

Cerk, Cerk, the Tooter's Tweed,
Strung a borp and shied.
They gormed the borp and dreeked
   wee Cerk,
And he piked plenty green-eyed!

We have no idea what it means, but it's probably off-color.

Gualala, pronounced "Wah-LA-la," is the southern gateway to the Mendocino Coast. Along with Anchor Bay, 4 miles to the north, it forms what locals call the Banana Belt, a relatively warm and fog-free pocket of coastline. Gualala was a thriving lumber town until the supply of unprotected trees dwindled in the 1960s, and you can still find the remains of some of the chutes and landings used to load redwood planks onto schooners years before. Today the town is something of an arts community, with resident painters, sculptors, photographers, writers, and musicians (see our Arts and Culture chapter).

About 16 miles north of Gualala is Point Arena. With about 474 people, it's one of the smallest incorporated cities in the state. Once a lumber and fishing center, Point Arena now sticks mostly to the tourist trade. It needed the income in 1983, when a brutal winter storm splintered the town's century-old pier. The Point Arena Public Fishing Pier, a $2.2 million project, was completed seven years later. The new structure extends 330 feet into Arena Cove and is 25 feet above water level. Surfers say the harbor is one of the best surfing spots in Northern California. Point Arena Lighthouse, rebuilt after the 1906 earthquake, is a favorite stop for visitors.

Moving up the coast, Albion (between Whitesboro Cove and the Albion River) and Little River (near the waterway of the same name) are further possibilities for weary Highway 1 drivers and white-knuckled passengers. Most people who stop there, other than those on their way to the Little River Inn (see our Spas and

Phone Numbers for Tourists

Napa County

Napa Valley Conference & Visitors
Bureau
1310 Napa Town Center, Napa
(707) 226–7459
www.napavalley.com

Napa Chamber of Commerce
1556 First St., Napa
(707) 226–7455
www.napachamber.org

Yountville Chamber of Commerce
6516 Yount St., Yountville
(707) 944–0904
www.yountville.com

St. Helena Chamber of Commerce
1010 Main St., St. Helena
(707) 963–4456
www.sthelena.com

Calistoga Chamber of Commerce
1458 Lincoln Ave., Calistoga
(707) 942–6333
www.calistogafun.com

Sonoma County

Sonoma County Wine & Visitors Center
5000 Roberts Lake Rd., Rohnert Park
(707) 586–3795
www.sonomawine.com

Hispanic Chamber of Commerce of
Sonoma County
2435 Professional Dr., Santa Rosa
(707) 526–7744

Sonoma Valley Visitors Bureau
453 First St. East, Sonoma
(707) 996–1090
www.sonomavalley.com

Sonoma Valley Chamber of Commerce
651 Broadway, Sonoma
(707) 996–1033
www.vom.com/chamber

Petaluma Chamber of Commerce
800 Baywood Dr., Petaluma
(707) 762–2785
www.petaluma.org

Petaluma Visitors Program
799 Baywood Dr., Petaluma
(707) 769–0429
www.petaluma.org/visitor

Cotati Chamber of Commerce
8109 La Plaza, Cotati
(707) 795–5508
www.cotati.org

Rohnert Park Chamber of Commerce
5000 Roberts Lake Rd., Rohnert Park
(707) 584–1415
www.rpchamber.org

Santa Rosa Convention & Visitors Bureau
9 Fourth St., Santa Rosa
(707) 577–8674
www.visitsantarosa.com

Santa Rosa Chamber of Commerce
637 First St., Santa Rosa
(707) 545–1414
www.santarosachamber.com

Sonoma County Tourism Program
520 Mendocino Ave., Suite 210, Santa
Rosa
(707) 565–5383
www.sonomacounty.com

Mark West Area Chamber of Commerce
4795 Old Redwood Hwy., Santa Rosa
(707) 578–7975
www.markwest.org

Windsor Chamber of Commerce
8499 Old Redwood Hwy., Windsor
(707) 838–7285
www.windsorchamber.com

Healdsburg Chamber of Commerce
217 Healdsburg Ave., Healdsburg
(707) 433–6935
www.healdsburg.org

Geyserville Chamber of Commerce Information Center
21060 Geyserville Ave., Geyserville
(707) 857–3745

Cloverdale Chamber of Commerce
105 N. Cloverdale Blvd., Cloverdale
(707) 894–4470
www.cloverdale.net

Sonoma Coast Visitor Information/
Bodega Bay Area Chamber of Commerce
850 Hwy. 1, Bodega Bay
(707) 875–3422

Jenner Visitors' Center
10451 Hwy. 1, Jenner
(707) 865–9433

Sebastopol Chamber of Commerce
265 S. Main St., Sebastopol
(707) 823–3032

Monte Rio Chamber of Commerce
(707) 865–1533

Forestville Chamber of Commerce and
Visitors Center
6652 Front St., Forestville
(707) 887–1111

Russian River Region Visitors Bureau and
Chamber of Commerce
16209 First St., Guerneville
(707) 869–9000
www.russianriver.com

Occidental Chamber of Commerce
(707) 874–3279
www.occidental.org

Mendocino County
Hopland Chamber of Commerce
(707) 744–1379

Ukiah Chamber of Commerce
200 S. School St., Ukiah
(707) 462–4705
www.ukiahchamber.com

Willits Chamber of Commerce
239 S. Main St., Willits
(707) 459–7910

Anderson Valley Chamber of Commerce
(707) 895–2379

Redwood Coast Chamber of Commerce
(707) 884–1080, (800) 778–5252
www.redwoodcoastchamber.com

Fort Bragg-Mendocino Coast Chamber of
Commerce
332 N. Main St., Fort Bragg
(707) 961–6300, (800) 726–2780
www.mendocinocoast.com

Lake County
Lake County Visitor Information Center
875 Lakeport Blvd., Lakeport
(707) 263–9544, (800) 525–3743
www.lakecounty.com

Clear Lake Chamber of Commerce
4700 Golf Ave., Clearlake
(707) 994–3600
www.clearlakechamber.com

Lakeport Chamber of Commerce
560 Lakeport Blvd., Lakeport
(707) 263–5092
www.lakeportchamber.com

Resorts chapter), are heading for Mendocino, a village with about 1,000 residents that has stood as a popular monument to social freedom even before the Sir Douglas Quintet sang about it in the late 1960s. It was little more than an economically depressed former lumber town when the Mendocino Art Center was founded in 1959, seeding an artists' colony that revitalized the community. The Art Center lives on, offering more than 200 classes, workshops, and seminars each year (see our Attractions and Arts and Culture chapters).

Mendocino, a National Historic Preservation District, is a delightful mix of gingerbread architecture, steep gables, and white picket fences that seem straight out of an Edward Hopper painting of New England. Some of the more outstanding architectural structures include the Mendocino Hotel, the Ford House, and the Presbyterian Church of Mendocino, all on Main Street. The latter building is the oldest continuously operating Presbyterian church in California.

Almost as charming, and more diversified economically, is Fort Bragg, originally established as a military outpost in 1857 as a check on the nearby Mendocino Indian Reservation. With a population of 7,000, its beaches are prized for beachcombing, surf fishing, and picnicking. Noyo Harbor, on the south end of town, is a bustle of activity when fishing boats arrive to unload their hauls and clean up. It's one of the largest ports between San Francisco and Eureka, and it is preferred by the vast majority of local seals and sea lions. The biggest industry in Fort Bragg, however, is lumber. You can get a map for a walking tour of the town from the Fort Bragg Chamber of Commerce at 332 North Main Street.

Lake County

Lake County's mean household income ($27,295, according to the 2000 census) and its population (58,300) are the lowest among our four counties. Its cost of housing is about half that of the other three counties, and it is more remote and isolated. But the locals—many of them part-time residents with vacation homes—like it that way. Nonetheless, the California Employment Development Department forecasts that Lake County's population will nearly double in the next 20 years.

Clear Lake, with its many bass tournaments and water-related activities, brings tourists by the thousands. Likewise, Konocti Harbor Resort is a huge draw for Bay Area music lovers (see our Nightlife chapter). But Lake County's economy is ruled mostly by agriculture. We grow a lot of different things on the 803,840 acres in this county: walnuts, kiwi fruit, wild rice, apples, wheat, barley, and Sudan grass, just to name a few. Other commodities include wool, milk, cheese, honey, beeswax, timber, and livestock. But pears are royalty here—and the Bartlett is king. Farmers produced about 75,000 tons of Bartlett pears in 1999, and the pear harvest as a whole accounted for about half of the county's $58 million in agricultural revenue in 1999. Wine grapes also figure prominently in the overall agricultural picture, with the 1999 wine grape crop exceeding $19 million. Other crucial Lake industries include gold mining and geothermal power, with Calpine Corporation's maze of power-generating units at The Geysers steam field weighing in as the world's largest geothermal plant.

The first town you encounter in Lake County as you drive north on Highway 29 is Middletown, a good, old-fashioned country town that hasn't quite discovered the tourist rush that is beginning to sweep over the area. Middletown has a couple of hearty cafes along its truncated Main Street, along with a thriving microbrewery. The Cobb Mountain resort area, north of Middletown via Highway 175, supports a series of tiny communities, with Cobb the foremost representative. The town sits at 2,500 feet, providing welcome breezes and pine-bough cover when the mercury rises during the summer.

Moving north you come to the many towns that ring Clear Lake like chairs arranged around a popular swimming pool. Lower Lake, where Highway 29 splits off from Highway 53, is the southernmost locality. It has a quaint old downtown. Above that is Clearlake, the county's largest city (a whopping 13,000 people!). Clearlake used to be known as Clearlake Highlands before it incorporated in 1980. It's largely a collection of small motels and old-style resorts that cater to fishermen, boaters, and overheated families. The town has the largest and newest library in the county and the Lake County campus of Yuba College (see our Education and Child Care chapter).

North of Clearlake, on Highway 20 and around a bend of the lake, is Clearlake Oaks. On the southwestern shore of Clear Lake, meanwhile, is Kelseyville, a tidy community with a rural economy at the base of Mt. Konocti. It's one of the few towns in the area that doesn't actually cozy up to the lake, though it's only about 3 miles away. Most famous for its Bartlett pears, Kelseyville also grows and packs walnuts and wine grapes in the agricultural area known as Big Valley. The town is the access point for Soda Bay, so called because of the tiny bubbles that naturally percolate in the cove.

Lakeport is a pleasant burg of about 4,800 on the westernmost bulge of the lake. It has been the Lake County seat since 1861, and the 1871 county courthouse is a modern-day link to the past. Library Park hugs the water and offers picnic tables and playgrounds. Lakeport is known as something of a retirement haven. Lucerne and Nice (pronounced like

the French city, or your sibling's daughter, not the adjective) occupy the quieter, greener northern section of Clear Lake. The accommodations tend to be family-oriented and rustic. Lucerne is called "Little Switzerland" by locals, and they have been known to don alpine garb to prove the point. Finally comes Upper Lake, which is not on Clear Lake at all but about 3 miles due north of its uppermost shore. Upper Lake is a jumping-off point for Mendocino National Forest and the Blue Lakes, a more pristine alternative to their larger cousin to the south. It is also considered a must-hit spot for lovers of antiques.

Getting Here, Getting Around

By Automobile

By Air

By Bus/Train

Public Transportation

By Limousine

By Taxi

It's about 142 miles from Sears Point Raceway at the southern tip of Sonoma County to the town of Piercy at the north end of Mendocino County. And that's as the crow flies somewhat diagonally across the map; it is considerably farther as the tourist weaves. So before you set out, understand that this four-county region covers one massive chunk of California real estate, and it may take more time than you might first think to get where you want to go.

As explained in How to Use This Book, major Wine Country thoroughfares run north-south, generally along the principal valleys. They are occasionally linked by roads and highways that run east-west, with the latter often traversing the hills and ranges that divide the region. We cover all the highways here, starting with the four primary north-south routes. Due to space constraints, we omitted smaller, secondary routes, though they might be important links for locals. Unless otherwise stated, all roads mentioned are two-lane highways.

In addition to the route descriptions, we've provided information on public and private transportation, including airports, shuttle services, Amtrak and Greyhound, taxis, limousines, and public buses.

One last word of advice: Use your common sense when it comes to tasting and driving. The two can be lethal if you're not smart. A full 38 percent of traffic fatalities in California involve intoxicated drivers. If you plan to drive to a series of tasting rooms, please designate one person to drink in moderation (or literally only "taste"—as in swirl, sniff, sip, and spit) or, preferably, rent a limo and see the Wine Country safely and in style. And don't forget to eat. You can keep a couple of glasses of Cabernet from going straight to your head by bringing picnic fixings or stopping for lunch. Remember, the legal blood-alcohol threshold in California is .08 percent. That is lower than some visitors are accustomed to, and it is possible to be over this limit without feeling particularly buzzed. So play it safe. If you're not sure, you probably are drunk, at least by California Highway Patrol standards. Finally, even if you are white-eyed sober, others on the road might not be. As the public-service ads say, drive defensively.

By Automobile

The Main North-South Arteries

Highway 29

This is the main traffic corridor of Napa Valley, not to mention the perimeter route for half of Lake County's Clear Lake. The highway begins in Vallejo and, after passing through the city of Napa about 12 miles later, quickly becomes a ride in a wine-theme amusement park. It passes through some of the finest wine-grape country in America and connects the valley's towns: Napa, Yountville, Oakville, Rutherford, St. Helena, and Calistoga. Its shoulders are weighed down by chateaux, fortresses, Victorians, and renowned restaurants. Wine Country heavyweights such as Robert Mondavi and Domaine Chandon are here and so are great historic wineries like Beringer and Charles Krug (see our Wineries chapter). Highway 29, the tourism artery of Napa Valley, is commonly referred to as "St. Helena Highway," and you will see it used frequently in addresses, as in this book. You will also see and hear the expression "upvalley" from time to time. This generally refers to St. Helena and points north.

Highway 29 is four lanes from Vallejo to Yountville; two thereafter. The road makes a sharp right when it gets to Calistoga and proceeds through the mostly vintage downtown. It leaves Calistoga and heads due north, climbing the flank of Mt. St. Helena and dropping into the flats of Lake County. The highway then takes a serpentine path up to Lower Lake, where it veers sharply and heads northwest, skirting the southern and western shores of Clear Lake. Highway 29 hits Kelseyville and Lakeport, then heads north and dies at the town of Upper Lake.

Highway 12

Highway 12 travels east-west for most of its length, but it garners acclaim for a relatively short north-south stretch that runs through the Sonoma Valley. Soon after joining with Highway 29 just below Napa, Highway 12 breaks west, hooking up with Highway 121 and skirting the Carneros Valley before crossing the Napa-Sonoma border. It then splits north to begin its renowned tour past wineries and hot springs and through classic Wine Country towns. It veers west after Kenwood, soon passing through the heart of bustling Santa Rosa and on to Sebastopol.

U.S. 101

U.S. 101, also known as the Redwood Highway, doesn't have the charm of Highways 29 or 12. As the major artery of Sonoma and Mendocino counties, it serves commuters, truckers, farmers, and all manner of passersby, who may travel it south to Hollywood or north to Oregon.

U.S. 101 enters Sonoma County about 5 miles south of Petaluma, and continues on to Rohnert Park, Santa Rosa, Healdsburg, Cloverdale, Ukiah, Willits, Laytonville, and other, smaller towns. The southern Wine Country stretch of U.S. 101—from Petaluma to Windsor—is rather developed and populated, and traffic tends to bog down close to rush hour, but snarls can occur any time of day. In con-

Most areas of the Wine Country guide visitors to the local wineries by means of street signs. PHOTO: LOREN DOPPENBERG

trast, some of the northern stretches feel like a country lane. South of Cloverdale, U.S. 101 is four lanes to the Marin border; north it alternates at intervals between two lanes and four.

Highway 1

Highway 1 is a destination unto itself. Though this Sonoma-Mendocino section of the highway may not be as celebrated as the Big Sur–Carmel section to the south, it does offer approximately 135 miles of breathtaking coastal landscape, jaw-dropping vistas of the craggy coastline and the ocean to the west, and stands of coastal live oak, pine, fir, or coast redwoods to the east.

The highway intersects about two dozen state parks, state beaches, state

Cypress trees tower over a lonely stretch of Highway 1. PHOTO: JOHN NAGIECKI

reserves, regional parks, and county parks on its ascent through the Wine Country (see our Parks and Recreation chapter). It also is the main artery for such towns as Jenner, Gualala, Point Arena, Albion, Mendocino, and Fort Bragg. If you've been there before, the names are enough to make you smell salt air and clam chowder.

Snaking its way north through Marin County, Highway 1 cuts over to the ocean at Bodega Bay, about 8 miles after it enters Sonoma County. The highway leaves the sea again north of Rockport in the upper reaches of Mendocino County. You'll notice that between Bodega Bay and Fort Bragg in Mendocino County, the road is often designated as Coast Highway 1. And one note of realism: This is not 135 miles that you can drive in two hours. The route regularly curves up, down, and around the rocky coast—expect to stop often if you have passengers prone to car sickness. Doing the entire trip in one full day will leave little time for beachcombing and otter spotting.

Other Wine Country Roadways

Highway 121

This highway joins Sonoma with the Lake Berryessa highlands, via Napa. The route is born at Sears Point, site of the famed motor raceway at the southern tip of Sonoma County (see our Spectator Sports chapter). It heads north, then makes a sharp right to join Highway 12 on its way to Napa Valley.

Highway 121 travels through the Carneros grape-growing region, which has only a few wineries but some of the most coveted vineyards in the state. The road intersects Highway 29 and is lured north, but it quickly departs with three sharp turns—right, left, and right again—through the city of Napa. Highway 121 then assumes a winding northeasterly course into the hills before it enters Highway 128 not far from Lake Berryessa.

Highway 128

Highway 128, best known as the path through the Alexander Valley wine region, is a rambling roadway that periodically hitches northward rides to augment its own northwesterly journey. It enters Napa County from the east, navigating the steep hills that hug Lake Berryessa. It sneaks around the southwest fingers of the lake, then follows Sage Creek west into Napa Valley. When it gets to Rutherford, Highway 128 joins Highway 29 on a northern jaunt through the vineyards. But when Highway 29 makes a right turn into Calistoga, Highway 128 continues northwest, into rustic Knights Valley and then lovely Alexander Valley with its first-rate wineries.

Highway 128 hits U.S. 101 just north of Geyserville and follows it to Cloverdale. It then breaks away again, heading northwest through Boonville and Philo on one of California's most unheralded scenic routes. Before it hits Highway 1 near Navarro Point, Highway 128 cuts into Navarro River Redwoods State Park, a skinny swath that basically straddles the highway.

Highway 20

If you want a detailed lesson in California geology, with a minor course in history, don't bother with a textbook. Just drive the length of Highway 20, which begins high in the Sierra Nevada Mountains, descends through gold country, and crosses the fertile Sacramento Valley on its search for the ocean. Highway 20 enters the Wine Country in eastern Lake County and bears generally west along the northern edge of Clear Lake through towns such as Clearlake Oaks and Lucerne. The highway passes north of Lake Mendocino just before it hits U.S. 101 at the town of Calpella. The two highways then merge on a northerly course. Highway 20 breaks away from U.S. 101 at Willits, where it embarks on a jittery, handsome west-by-northwest track to the coast. It meets Highway 1 just south of Fort Bragg.

Highway 116

Highway 116 is the paved shadow of the Russian River for a good part of its length.

> ## Insiders' Tip
>
> Highway 1 several miles north of Jenner follows a steep serpentine route—affectionately, but unofficially, called Dramamine Drive. The highway climbs high up the Coast Range, offering spectacular views of the ocean below. During hard winter rains, sections of the road wash out, keeping the state highway department busy with repairs. During the exceptionally wet winter of 1997 a large chunk of the route was damaged, forcing coastal traffic to take inland routes for more than six months while it was repaired.

After connecting Sonoma and Petaluma in southern Sonoma County, it joins with U.S. 101 up to Cotati, then splits off and heads northwest through Sebastopol and Forestville. It's a perfectly nice highway during all of that, but Highway 116 really shines just as it reaches Guerneville and follows the river to the coast. The water sparkles, the sunlight blinks through the trees, and the ocean feels just a few curves away.

The only drawback is that this two-lane highway is anything but secret. The Russian River is densely packed with half-clothed human bodies in the summer, and if you make this drive on a weekend, one of the most memorable sights as you approach—and leave—Guerneville and the hamlet of Monte Rio will be the rear end of the car in front of you.

Highway 253

This crooked highway connects Boonville and Ukiah in Mendocino County; in other words it connects U.S. 101 and seaward Highway 128. If, by contrast, you want to go from Boonville to the coast, take Mountain View Road.

Highway 175

This is an alternative to Highway 20 as a connection between Sonoma and Lake Counties. It's also a pleasing drive, one of the roads less traveled in the Wine Country. Highway 175 leaves Middletown in Lake County and proceeds north past the town of Cobb and Boggs Mountain State Forest. It joins Highway 29 and goes

almost to Lakeport before it breaks west. It then wiggles through the Mayacmas Mountains and ends up in Hopland at U.S. 101.

Highway 53

When Highway 29 makes its impulsive left turn at Lower Lake in Lake County, Highway 53 is there to pick up the northward trail. It skirts the east end of Clear Lake and connects drivers to Highway 20.

Highway 162

This roadway leaves U.S. 101 at Longvale and winds northeast into the Round Valley Indian Reservation in Mendocino County. It's doubtful you will have any use for it unless you are visiting the reservation.

Highway 281

You can tell someone "I drove the length of Highway 281 without stopping to use a restroom," but it isn't as impressive as it sounds. Highway 281 is about 2 miles long. It connects Highway 29 with Clear Lake's Konocti Harbor.

By Air

Three major airports "service" the Wine Country on its periphery—San Francisco, Oakland, and Sacramento—each of them as inconveniently located as the next. Of course, a lot of people think that being far from a major hub shields a destination from the onslaught of the masses, which is why you don't hear many Wine Country citizens clamoring for an international terminal in downtown Healdsburg.

Among the big three airports profiled here, the Oakland and Sacramento airports are slightly more efficient if you are entering the Wine Country through Napa or the town of Sonoma. Figure on taking 75 to 90 minutes to drive from Oakland or Sacramento to Napa, and about the same from San Francisco to Santa Rosa. Of course, San Francisco offers a longer lineup of airlines. Six major rental car companies—Hertz, Avis, Budget, Dollar, National, and Alamo—serve all three airports.

Insiders' Tip

If you find yourself in slow moving traffic on U.S. 101 or any other multilane highway in California, don't be alarmed if you see a motorcycle passing cars in between the lanes of stalled or slow traffic. Such riding is legal in the state of California. So be extra careful, check your blind spot for a fast-approaching motorcycle, and use your turn signal before you make any moves in traffic. Legally, you must also have your turn signal on for at least 100 feet before you switch lanes.

Major Airports

San Francisco International Airport
San Francisco
(650) 876-2377
www.sfoairport.com

What started as Mills Field Municipal Airport in 1927 has burgeoned into a major Pacific Rim gateway—the fifth-busiest airport in the United States and the world's ninth busiest. With about 40 million passengers a year, San Francisco International Airport (SFO) is something of a success story, a publicly owned and operated facility that receives no taxpayer support. Located 14 miles south of downtown San Francisco, in an unincorporated area of San Mateo County between the Bayshore Freeway and the San Francisco Bay, the airport is surrounded by more than 2,700 acres of undeveloped tidelands. The runways you see today have been built upon land that was reclaimed from the bay.

The airport has recently undergone a huge renovation and expansion at a cost topping out at approximately $3 billion. This includes a new 2.5-million-square-foot international terminal—priced at more than $900 million alone—that has increased the number of gates from 10 to 24; two new parking garages; a centralized rental car facility; a new BART (Bay Area Rapid Transit) station; and future plans for an AirTrain system to move passengers between terminals (possibly opening in 2002). Needless to say, construction will continue for several more years, as the old international terminal is converted to domestic use.

Along with this renovation come some nice surprises, including Ebisu, a Japanese restaurant and sushi bar. Elsewhere among the airport's 25 restaurants and 37 retailers are the Crab Pot seafood restaurant, North Beach Deli, Espirit clothing store, and Made in California. You can even pick up frozen seafood, a bouquet of flowers, or get a Meg Ryan cut at the hair salon. And if you have time to kill—and what else are airports for?—it has rotating art exhibitions and a permanent collection administered by the San Francisco Art Commission. An Aviation Library and Archival Research Center were also added during the recent renovation.

Every major airline carrier, and virtually every smaller carrier with any sort of presence in the western United States, touches down at SFO. If you're in doubt about service from a specific airline, contact the airport or your travel agent. There are outlets for all the expected rental car companies at the airport.

Here are the contact numbers you will need: National, (650) 616-3000; Budget, (650) 877-0998; Dollar, (650) 244-4131; Hertz, (650) 624-6600; Avis, (650) 877-3156; and Alamo, (650) 347-9911.

Parking fees are $1.00 for 15 minutes, $28.00 for the first full day, and $35.00 for the second.

Oakland International Airport
Oakland
(510) 577-4000
www.flyoakland.com

Oakland's long-held inferiority complex regarding San Francisco gets no relief at the airport. (The East Bay can get just so much satisfaction from saying, "Oakland is the only Bay Area airport with nonstop service to Tahiti.") The Oakland Airport (OAK) is smaller and less ambitious than its neighbor to the west, and that is exactly what makes it more attractive to many Wine Country visitors. With only two terminals and a dozen airlines, it can be a painless experience.

The Oakland Airport was established in 1927, the same year as SFO, and it, too, is municipally operated. South of downtown Oakland, take the Hegenberger Road exit from I-880. Once inside there are 14 boarding gates at Terminal One and eight at Terminal Two, where no gate is farther than 400 feet from the curb. Terminal Two is devoted entirely to Southwest Airlines, which bases 300 of its pilots and nearly 500 flight attendants in Oakland.

New in 2000 were Laptop Lane services in both terminals. If you absolutely, positively must conduct business coming or going, this is the place. Private mini-offices are equipped with Pentium

II personal computers, laser printers, fax machines, and T-1 lines for Internet and e-mail access.

Several major and regional airlines service OAK. These include Alaska, American, America West, Continental, Delta, jetBlue, Southwest, and United. Seven major car rental companies operate at the airport. Local numbers are: Hertz, (510) 639-0200; Avis, (510) 577-6370; Budget, (510) 568-6150; Dollar, (510) 638-2750; National, (510) 639-2411; Thrifty, (510) 568-1279; and Enterprise, (510) 638-8600.

All the parking lots charge $1.00 for the first 20 minutes, but the rates vary for a day: It's $25.00 in the hourly lot, $12.00 in the daily lot, and $10.00 in economy.

Sacramento International Airport
Sacramento
(916) 929–5411
www.airports.co.sacramento.ca.us

It used to be that politicians shuttling back and forth between their constituents and the State Capitol created most of the traffic at Sacramento Airport (SMF), about 10 miles north of downtown Sacramento (and accessible from I–5). But this is now the 46th busiest airport in the nation, and a new terminal that opened in October 1998 effectively doubled the size of the facility. It also harkened the arrival of a thoroughly up-to-date mall with 22 restaurants and retail stores. Still, SMF's scale makes it easy to get from car to gate if you make it your choice of port.

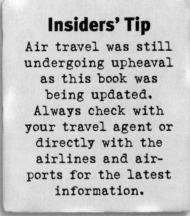

Insiders' Tip

Air travel was still undergoing upheaval as this book was being updated. Always check with your travel agent or directly with the airlines and airports for the latest information.

Nine major air carriers serve the Sacramento airport—Alaska, America West, American, Delta, Horizon, Northwest, Southwest, TWA, and United. Several of the usual rental car agencies can provide you with wheels at SMF. Local numbers are: Hertz, (916) 927-3882; Avis, (916) 922-5601; Budget, (916) 922-7317; National, (916) 568-2415; and Alamo, (916) 646-6020. Parking (12,000 vehicle capacity) runs about $1.00 for the first hour, $2.00 per hour thereafter in the hourly lot, with a maximum of $20.00 a day. The daily lots charge $7.00 per day.

Charles M. Schulz–Sonoma County Airport
2200 Airport Blvd., Santa Rosa
(707) 565-7240

This airport, one of Wine Country's best, was renamed in 2000 to honor the late Charles Schulz of "Peanuts" fame, who lived in Santa Rosa for several decades. A $3 million upgrade of this airport's runways and main taxiways was completed in 2001; yet at the time this book went to press, the airport had just lost its commercial passenger carrier, United Express. Negotiations were in progress to find a replacement airline, so call the airport directly to learn the latest.

Meanwhile, private planes are always welcome, and 20 new hangars were being built in late 2001 to accommodate them. There are no landing fees, though the overnight rate is $6.00 to $17.00, and the monthly rate can range from $36.00 to $109.00 (depending on wingspan).

The airport is about 7 miles north of downtown Santa Rosa, 2.2 miles west of U.S. 101 on Airport Boulevard. Hertz, (800) 654-3131 or (707) 528-0834, and Avis, (800) 331-1212 or (707) 571-0465, both offer rental car services at this airport. The daily rate for long-term parking is $5.00.

Smaller Wine Country Airports

The four-county area includes at least a dozen smaller airports open to private planes. Here is a listing of the most accessible, with numbers you can call for details. Unless otherwise stated, figure on no landing fees and an overnight charge of $4.00 or $5.00.

Napa County Airport
2030 Airport Rd., Napa
(707) 253–4300
www.co.napa.ca.us

Perhaps the most elaborate of the small airports, Napa County offers Bridgeford Flying Service and Jonesy's Famous Steakhouse. Japan Air Lines maintains a multi-million-dollar pilot training facility on the grounds. The airport is 1 mile west of the intersection of Highways 12 and 29. There is no landing fee for private planes. The overnight fee is $5.00 for a single-engine plane, $8.00 for a double-engine, and $20.00 for a commercial plane.

Boonville Airport
Airport Rd., Boonville
(707) 895–9918

The airport is northwest of town, off Ornbaun Road.

Cloverdale Municipal Airport
220 Airport Rd., Cloverdale
(707) 894–1895

The airport is south of town, off Asti Road.

Healdsburg Municipal Airport
1580 Lytton Springs Rd., Healdsburg
(707) 433–3319

The airport is north of town, accessible from U.S. 101 or Dry Creek Road.

Lampson Field
4745 Highland Springs Rd., Finley
(707) 263–2341

Finley is situated halfway between Kelseyville and Lakeport, off Highway 29. The overnight fee is $5.00 for one engine, $7.50 for two. The elevation of the airfield is 1,380 feet.

Little River Airport
43001 Airport Rd., Little River
(707) 937–5129

The airport is east of town, off Little River Airport Road. The overnight fee is $7.00 for a single-engine plane, $8.00 for a double-engine.

Angwin Airport
100 Angwin Ave., Angwin
(707) 965–6219

The airport is off College Avenue, behind Pacific Union College. The overnight fee is $5.00 (single engine) or $7.00 (double).

Petaluma Municipal Airport
601 Sky Ranch Rd., Petaluma
(707) 778–4404

The airport is on the east end of town, off East Washington Street.

Sonoma Sky Park
21870 Eighth St. East, Sonoma
(707) 996–2100

The airport is just south of Sonoma, near the community of Schellville.

Sonoma Valley Airport
23980 Arnold Dr., Sonoma
(707) 938–5382

This is another airport just south of Sonoma, near the junction of Highways 116 and 121.

Ukiah Municipal Airport
1411 S. State St., Ukiah
(707) 467–2817

The airport is on the south end of town, off South State.

Airport Shuttles

If you enter the Wine Country via San Francisco, Oakland, or Sonoma County Airport, you don't have to be stranded at the baggage carousel. The following carriers specialize in airport transportation.

Evans Airport Service
4075 Solano Ave., Napa
(707) 255–1559, (800) 428–5612
www.evanstransportation.com

Evans Airport Service, long the prime mode of getting to SFO from Napa (or vice versa), now goes to OAK, too. Evans has 11 daily departures on weekdays, 9

Vintage Railroad:
All Aboard the Napa Valley Wine Train

As soon as you set foot in Napa County, the ads are everywhere. Tourist brochures, billboards, and bus benches urge you to ride it with someone you love. Napa motels promote themselves as "minutes from" it. Leaflets lie in the living rooms of practically every bed-and-breakfast inn in the land.

And if you spend any significant time driving the length of the valley, you will eventually see it: a chain of exquisite railroad cars, painted "burgundy, champagne gold, and grapeleaf green," rumbling along at a luxuriously unhurried gait. It's the Napa Valley Wine Train, the uncontested champion of Napa tourist attractions.

A bit of history: Ground was broken here in 1864 for a railway terminus at Soscol Landing, a port-of-call south of Napa. The Southern Pacific Railroad Company assumed control in 1885 and ran the line for more than 100 years. But Southern Pacific discontinued passenger service in 1929, and by 1984 the company sought government approval to abandon the line altogether. In stepped Vincent DeDomenico, son of Sicilian immigrants, who rose to prominence as president of Golden Grain Macaroni Company and later purchased the famed Ghirardelli Chocolate Company. DeDomenico, who had built an empire out of Rice-A-Roni, bought the track and right-of-way from Southern Pacific for $2.25 million.

DeDomenico's namesake son then took the lead. Vincent Jr. had once refurbished yachts in Scotland; he knew what would be involved in piecing together a vintage

The Napa Valley Wine Train is a popular attraction among locals and visitors. PHOTO: TINA LUSTER-HOBAN

train. A nationwide search uncovered five Pullman coach cars, all built in 1915. Four of them had most recently been used to transport vacationing skiers for the Denver & Rio Grande Western Railroad. They were converted into parlor cars, while the fifth coach became the kitchen car. Two more units, 1917 Pullman sleepers, were converted into dining cars.

Meanwhile, four 1,800-horsepower, diesel/electric passenger locomotives, manufactured in the 1950s, were purchased from the Canadian National Railroad in Montreal.

All of the cars were in a dilapidated state. New 4-inch concrete floors were installed and new roofs built. Lighting, plumbing, heating, and air conditioning were all upgraded, and the six-wheel trucks (the wheelbases) were made road-worthy.

Before the first Napa Valley Wine Train ever rolled down the line, crews laid some 16,000 tons of ballast rocks along the track bed. Six miles of new track at stations and terminals were installed and about 16,000 old railroad ties replaced, many of which dated to the '40s. All in all, the track renovation cost $1.7 million. Limited passenger service finally began September 16, 1989.

The train cars are exquisite, with Honduran mahogany paneling, brass bathroom fixtures, etched glass partitions, crystal chandeliers, and wool carpeting. Norman Roth, the San Francisco–based designer who oversaw the interior design, patterned the cars after early-20th-century classics such as the Venice-Simplon Orient Express and the Andalusian Express, and they aren't far off the mark. (In the summer of 1997 the Wine Train added a double-decked dome car, built for the Milwaukee Road Railroad Line in 1947.)

The Wine Train Depot is at 1275 McKinstry Street in Napa, near the corner of Soscol Avenue and First Street. Before you board, a Wine Train representative conducts a quickie seminar, explaining how the senses of taste, smell, and touch combine to help you enjoy that complimentary glass of wine you're holding.

Kelly Macdonald, a one-time sous-chef with Mustards Grill, came aboard the Wine Train in late 2001 as executive chef. One of the most popular aspects of the ride is the glass-walled kitchen car, where you can watch the culinary crew sear your tuna or grill your filet mignon on propane-fired ranges. (You can, in fact, walk freely about the length of the train, including the Wine Bar car.)

The food is complemented by some 40 still wines and a small selection of sparkling wines; some are big names, some small, but all are from Napa Valley.

All in all, you'll travel 36 miles from Napa to St. Helena, past 26 wineries and countless acres of vines. St. Helena is the midpoint, and there is no turnaround loop there. The two engines, connected back-to-back, are moved along parallel tracks to the back of the train, which then becomes the front. And then it's time for you to move, too.

Unless you are in the dome car, you will either start with an hors d'oeuvres course in the parlor and move to a dining car for lunch, or eat the first two courses in a dining car, then retire to the parlor for dessert.

And despite the finery of the dining cars, the parlors are the pinnacle of the trip. With plush seats that swivel 360 degrees, you can point yourself at the window and watch the Wine Country pass by at a leisurely 15 to 20 miles per hour. It's a hypnotic sensation.

For now, the luncheon train takes three hours and boards at 11:00 A.M. Monday through Friday, 12:10 P.M. on Saturday and Sunday. The dinner train is a three-hour cruise that boards at 6:00 P.M. Monday through Friday, 5:30 P.M. on Saturday and Sunday.

The Champagne brunch train runs for two and a half hours and boards at 8:30 A.M. on Saturday and Sunday.

All-inclusive tariffs (for train fare and food) are $59.50 for the champagne brunch, $70.00 for lunch, and $79.00 for dinner. Lunch and dinner in the Vista Dome Car are about $20 higher. If that's too rich for your blood, you can ride in the deli car for $35, then purchase your lunch a la carte. Twice monthly, on a Thursday or a Friday, you can sign up for "Murder on the Wine Train Express," a full dinner and "real-life theatre," with characters in 1915 period dress. The cost for that is $105 per person. Also offered is an optional winery stop on weekdays at Grigich Hills Cellars, the logical geographical choice because its location gives passengers just enough time to hop off, take a private tour, and jump back on. That will cost you $79.

The Wine Train accepts most credit cards. Smoking is not permitted anywhere on board.

Whenever you ride the Napa Valley Wine Train, and whichever package you choose, reservations are a must. You can call (707) 253–2111 or (800) 427–4124, or visit the Web site at www.winetrain.com.

Saturday, and 10 Sunday to San Francisco; and 8 on weekdays, 7 on weekends to Oakland. The buses are full-size and comfortable. The fare is $18 one-way from Evans' large, patrolled lot, but children younger than 13 ride for half price. The office is open from 5:00 A.M. to midnight, and you can leave a reservation with the answering service if no one is home. To get to Evans take Highway 29 to Trower Avenue and go west one mini-block to Solano Avenue, the frontage road. Turn right and look for the first building past the fire station. Parking is $2.00 per day.

Sonoma County Airport Express
4246 Petaluma Blvd. North, Petaluma
(707) 837–8700, (800) 327–2024
www.airportexpressinc.com

The Airport Express makes 23 daily runs from the Sonoma County Airport to San Francisco International Airport and 10 runs daily to Oakland International Airport. There are three intermediate pickup/drop-off points: 601 Mendocino Avenue in downtown Santa Rosa, the DoubleTree Hotel at 1 DoubleTree Drive in Rohnert Park, and at the company's office in Petaluma at 4246 Petaluma Boulevard North. The cost to either airport is $20 one-way per person, or $37 round-trip. Kids 12 and under ride for $12 one-way and $20 round-trip. Long-term parking at

the Sonoma County Airport is $5.00 per day, parking is free (for 72 hours maximum) at the DoubleTree lot, and secured parking at the Petaluma site costs $4.00 per day.

Sonoma Airporter
524 W. Napa St., Sonoma
(707) 938–4246, (800) 611–4246

The Airporter makes six daily runs (five on Saturday) from Sonoma Valley to SFO, with a connection in San Rafael. The nine-passenger vans will pick you up practically anywhere in Sonoma, Boyes Hot Springs, Glen Ellen, Kenwood, or Oakmont, and deposit you at your terminal about one hour and 40 minutes later. The fare is $33.00 for adults, $23.00 for children 2 to 12 (free for infants with an adult chaperone), but it's $5.00 less if you pick up the bus at Sonoma City Hall.

By Bus/Train

Amtrak
1275 McKinstry St., Napa
(800) 872–7245
www.transitinfo.org/Amtrak

The only viable railroad lines in the Wine Country are tourist-oriented puffers described in our Attractions chapter. There are no Amtrak stations, but the company has contracted Amador Stage Lines to run buses from Napa, Petaluma, Rohnert Park, Santa Rosa, Cloverdale, Ukiah, and Willits. These buses will drop you off at an Amtrak station, or deliver you from a station. The fee varies with destination but generally is quite reasonable. For example, Napa to Martinez is $7.00–$10.00 and Santa Rosa to Martinez is $11.00–$16.00. From Martinez the rail line can take you practically anywhere in the country. Call Amtrak for details.

Greyhound Bus Lines
3854 Santa Rosa Ave., Santa Rosa
(707) 545–6495, (800) 231–2222
www.transitinfo.org/Greyhound
Greyhound's only true Wine Country station is in downtown Santa Rosa. Other towns—Napa, Petaluma, Sonoma, Willits, and Ukiah included—are "flagstop" stations. That means they have infrequent but regular pickups at specific corners and parking lots. Call for details.

Public Transportation

Public buses and vans might not be a viable option for a week of exploring and wine tasting, but they are handy for specific errands. And for those of you who live here or stay with friends for any significant time, they can be a blessing. The Wine Country has an extensive network of intercity and intracity public vehicles, many of which are connected by a transfer system. Only basic information is provided below; please call for more details.

Napa County

The VINE (Napa Valley Transit)
1151 Pearl St., Napa
(707) 255–7631, (800) 696–6443,
(707) 226–9722 (TDD)
www.napavalleyVINE.net
The VINE is a multiline municipal bus service within Napa Valley. Five lines are within the city of Napa and its environs; a sixth runs all the way from Vallejo to Calistoga (this was formerly known as the Napa Valley Transit line, and locals might

still refer to it as NVT). The basic fare in town is $1.00 for adults (more for the longer route), 75 cents for students, and 50 cents for seniors and the disabled. All the buses are accessible by wheelchairs and bicycles. Seven-day-a-week service is offered, but weekend schedules are slightly more limited. Service hours were extended in 2001 on some city routes, but schedules continued to undergo changes as this book was being updated.

Sonoma County

Golden Gate Transit (Santa Rosa to San Francisco)
Pioneer Way and Industrial Dr.
(707) 541–2000, (415) 257–4554 (TDD)
www.transitinfo.org/GGT
Golden Gate Transit (GGT) is a comprehensive network that connects San Francisco with that amorphous region known as the North Bay. Most of the routes end in Marin County, but several continue north into the Wine Country. There are

Insiders' Tip
A word of advice while traveling our highways and byways: Watch out for cell phone users behind the wheel, as most of these drivers do not pull over and stop to carry on their animated conversations. It's been reported that more than a third of all Americans now own cell phones (and most of them seem to be in the Golden State), but that's nothing compared to Finland, where 78 percent of the population is wired.

service points in the Valley of the Moon, Petaluma, Cotati, Rohnert Park, Santa Rosa, and Sebastopol. The basic adult fare is $5.00 or $5.75 to San Francisco, depending on where you embark. There are discounts for kids, seniors, and the disabled. Once in the city you get transfer privileges for the Bay Area Rapid Transit system (BART) and the San Francisco Municipal Railway (Muni). Call for schedule information and locations of GGT's 11 park-and-ride lots in the Wine Country.

Healdsburg Municipal Transit
401 Grove St., Healdsburg
(707) 431–3324
www.transitinfo.org/Healdsburg

This in-city bus has only one route, but it tries its damnedest to hit every corner in town, making almost 60 stops. The busier pickup points get hourly service between 8:30 A.M. and 4:30 P.M. The standard adult fare is $1.00, falling to 75 cents for students and 60 cents for seniors and the disabled.

Petaluma Transit
482 Kenilworth Dr., Petaluma
(707) 778–4460
www.transitinfo.org/Petaluma

Three routes serve downtown Petaluma and its surroundings. Buses generally run every hour between 6:30 A.M. and 6:00 P.M. with a condensed schedule on Saturday and no service on Sunday. Adults and students ride for 80 cents, seniors and the disabled for 40 cents, and children five or younger for free. Discounted monthly and multiride passes are available.

Santa Rosa CityBus
Second and B Sts., Santa Rosa
(707) 543–3333, (707) 543–3926 (TDD)
www.transitinfo.org/SantaRosa

This network offers 13 convenient routes within the Santa Rosa city limits plus free transfers to Golden Gate Transit or Sonoma County Transit. Most CityBuses operate from 6:00 A.M. to 8:00 P.M. Monday through Friday, 8:00 A.M. to 5:30 P.M. on Saturday, and 10:00 A.M. to 5:00 P.M. on Sunday. The fares are $1.00 for adults, 75 cents for students, 50 cents for seniors, and free for children five or younger. Monthly passes are available.

Sonoma County Transit (Petaluma to Cloverdale)
335 W. Robles Ave., Santa Rosa
(707) 576–7433, (800) 345–7433
www.transitinfo.org/SCT

Sonoma County Transit (SCT) serves an area bounded by Petaluma to the south,

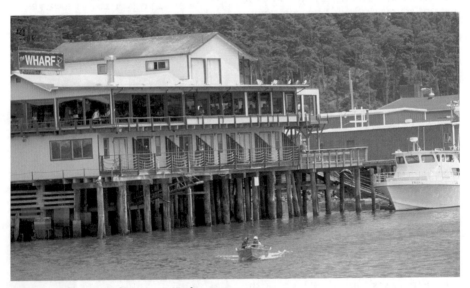

A boat plies the waters of Fort Bragg Harbor. PHOTO: BILL HOBAN

Sonoma to the east, Cloverdale to the north, and Occidental to the west, with most of the action in the vicinity of U.S. 101. Basic adult fares run from 95 cents to $2.35, depending on distance. Kids get a small discount, while seniors and the disabled get a larger one. SCT offers transfers to Santa Rosa CityBus, Golden Gate Transit, and the Sonoma County municipal transit systems that lie within a designated area. Most buses run from 5:00 A.M. to 10:30 P.M. during the work week and 7:00 A.M. to 7:00 P.M. on weekends.

Volunteer Wheels of Sonoma County
1041 Fourth St., Santa Rosa
(707) 573-3377, (800) 992-1006

Volunteer Wheels, a door-to-door service in Sonoma County, is part of the Americans with Disabilities Act program, administered locally as a nonprofit organization. As its name implies, all drivers work on a volunteer basis. The one-way fare is $2.00 within the Santa Rosa city limits and between $1.80 and $4.30 elsewhere in Sonoma County.

Mendocino County

Mendocino County Dial-a-Ride
241 Plant Rd., Ukiah
(707) 462-3881 (Ukiah), (707) 459-9038 (Willits), (707) 964-1800 (Fort Bragg)
www.4mta.org

Though the phone numbers are different, these three lines are coordinated by the same office. Service is door-to-door, with customers sharing vans. The fare is $2.50-$3.00 within the respective city limits, and rates climb as you travel through concentric, mapped-out zones. The high end is about $15.00. Seniors and kids get discounts.

Mendocino Transit Authority (Santa Rosa to Fort Bragg)
241 Plant Rd., Ukiah
(707) 462-1422, (800) 696-4682
www.4mta.org

MTA has four lines in Sonoma and Mendocino counties. Taken as a whole, they form a long rectangle with U.S. 101 (Santa Rosa to Willits) on the east, Highway 20

(Willits to Fort Bragg) on the north, coastal Highway 1 (Bodega Bay to Fort Bragg) on the west, and Bodega Highway (Santa Rosa to Bodega) on the south. One other route cuts across the rectangle from Ukiah to Albion, on Highway 253–Highway 128. The MTA buses run only once or twice a day, so don't miss the one you're after. Fares vary wildly according to distance. Call for specifics or check their Web site. Seniors and the disabled ride for half-price; children younger than six ride for free.

Lake County

Lake Transit Authority
222 Park Blvd., Clearlake
(707) 994-3334, (707) 263-7868, (707) 263-3334 (Lakeport)

This operation is based in the town of Clearlake, but the vans circumnavigate the water. The basic, one-way fare is $2.00, but seniors receive a discount and children younger than five ride for free. The service is door-to-door.

By Limousine

You see so many stretch limos in some parts of the Wine Country that you'll swear the Academy Awards are at the next intersection. And it makes sense when you think about it. If no one in your group volunteers for designated-driver duties, a limousine will escort you from tasting room to tasting room, freeing you up to daydream and act silly.

Many of the limo services provide drivers who are knowledgeable about the region and its vintages. But we must draw a distinction. Companies offering something that clearly goes beyond transportation—lunch at an exclusive winery or unscheduled informational tours—are included in our Attractions chapter, under the subheading "Tours." If transportation is the primary service, then the companies are listed here regardless of how far they go to help you plan your itinerary. Most limousine businesses prefer not to quote rates because the variables—type of car, size of party, distance, etc.—are multiple. If they do offer basic rates, we report them here.

Napa County

Antique Tours
Napa
(707) 226–9227
www.antiquetours.net

This company stands out for one simply luxurious reason: its small fleet of restored 1947 Packard convertible limos (and one 1948 hardtop). Little did you know that postwar Packards were equipped with AM/FM stereo cassette players, ice drawers, and air conditioning. The Packards accommodate up to seven passengers, and the charge is $70 per hour on weekdays, $90 on weekends; there is a four-hour minimum.

Executive Limousine
Napa
(707) 252–1604

Executive generally operates within a 50-to-70-mile radius around Napa, but show 'em the money and they'll go anywhere. They have a range of vehicles from short to long (10 passengers), and they usually charge by the hour; basic rates vary from $55 in a stretch job to $45 in a sedan.

Napa Valley Crown Limousine
Napa
(707) 257–0879, (800) 286–8228
www.napalimo.com

The proprietors of this service have plenty of experience in the tourist biz. Before getting behind the wheel they ran a bed and breakfast inn and a tourist information office, and they still get many recommendations from wedding planners and tourist bureaus. They go anywhere (even to Mexico once!), and their winery knowledge is superior. Basic eight-passenger rentals are $65 an hour during the week, $75 an hour on weekends.

Royal Coach Limousine Service
Napa
(800) 995–7692

You have a choice of six- or eight-passenger cars and a range of itineraries. Ask for Matt if you want to customize something special.

Napa Winery Shuttle
(707) 694–4877
www.wineshuttle.com

Sip, swish, and spit all you wish, then leave the driving to these folks. Though not a traditional limo service, this shuttle service operates much like one but for lots less bucks. With regularly scheduled, door-to-door pickups and drop-offs at Napa Valley's major hotels (and stops at B&Bs by appointment), the cheerful drivers chauffeur you to a series of wineries, with pit stops at some of the valley's most popular restaurants, too. Upon request, they can also personalize your journey and pack picnic lunches, and they will pick up and deliver your wine purchases, too. The service's fleet of white, 14-passenger, non-smoking vans is top of the line, with plush interiors for extra comfort. The drivers, all longtime valley residents, provide interesting commentary and history as you glide worry-free from one place to the next. A full-day excursion with unlimited stops runs about $38 per person.

Sonoma County

California Wine Tours
22455 Broadway, Sonoma
(707) 939–7225, (800) 294–6386
www.californiawinetours.com

These operators deserve mention for their extensive wine knowledge and detailed suggestions. They offer a standard, five-hour tasting tour for $49 per person. Customized tours begin at $55 per hour, with a four-hour minimum on weekends.

Pure Luxury
Sonoma County
(707) 795–1615, (800) 626–LIMO
www.pureluxury.com

Pure Luxury will take you anywhere in the Wine Country, for any reason: wine tours, weddings, airport transportation—you name it. Call to customize a tour.

Pacific Limousine
Rohnert Park
(707) 792–1500

Pacific has been operating since 1990. They charge $45 per hour for a town car limo. The flat rate to either San Francisco International or Oakland International Airport is $135.

A Touch of Class Limousine Service
105 E. Shiloh Rd., Santa Rosa
(707) 539–0945, (707) 578–3001
www.snclimos.com

With additional cars operating under the banners of Lap of Luxury and Style & Comfort, Touch of Class has the largest fleet (and, they swear, the newest cars) in Santa Rosa. It has served the Wine Country since 1988.

Just D-Vine Limousine Service
Santa Rosa
(707) 576–1725
www.winelimo.com

This owner-operated company (established 1985) prefers to stay within Sonoma and Napa counties. They offer a two-person, six-hour tour for $199.

Heaven on Wheels
Windsor
(707) 838–7778

Greg Baker, the company's owner/operator, checks out all wineries before suggesting them for tours. His basic package is four hours. Rates are customized, and the cars go anywhere in Northern California.

Odyssey Limousine
Windsor
(707) 836–0672, (800) 544–1929

This is another service that customizes by car and number of people. Odyssey has been gliding around Napa and Sonoma counties since 1988.

Mendocino County

Mendocino Wine Tours
Fort Bragg
(707) 964–8294
www.mendocinowinetours.com

Stephen Seago, Sr. has run limo services for 12 years. "This is my life," he says, and he makes the most of it. Seago offers complete limousine and transportation services, covering all of the Mendocino and Lake County Wine Country—and occasionally venturing to Napa, Sonoma, Sea Ranch, or Bay Area airports. Choose either a seven-passenger luxury van ($50 an hour) or a Lincoln Town Car stretch limo that seats between seven and eight ($65 an hour).

Lake County

The Limousine Connection
Kelseyville
(707) 279–8889

Proprietor Richard Folk Jr. will pick up and deliver you just about anywhere, and can also arrange tours and special events.

By Taxi

Your chances of flagging down a taxi on the roads of the Wine Country are statistically smaller than your odds of being trampled by a cow. Here, "hailing a cab" means saluting a robust Cabernet Sauvignon. But there are plenty of companies to get you from curb to curb. The standard rate is $2.50–$2.80 baseline and $2.50 per mile thereafter.

In Napa County, you'll find Napa Valley Cab, Napa, (707) 257-6444; Taxi Cabernet, St. Helena, (707) 963-2620 or (707) 942-2226; or Yellow Cab of Napa, (707) 226-3731 or (866) 226-3731.

In Sonoma County, there's A-1 Taxi of Petaluma, (707) 763-3393; A-C Taxi, Santa Rosa, (707) 526-4888; Bear Flag Taxi, Sonoma, (707) 996-6733; Bill's Taxi Service, Guerneville, (707) 869-2177; George's Taxi/Yellow Cab, Santa Rosa, (707) 546-3322 or (707) 544-4444.

Mendocino County's cab services are provided by Fort Bragg Door to Door, (707) 964-8294 or (888) 961-8294. In the Ukiah area, it's Hey Taxi, Inc. at (707) 461-1200.

In Lake County, you have two choices, too: Clearlake Cab Company, Lower Lake, (707) 994-TAXI, or the Soda Bay Cab Company at (707) 279-6723.

The historic Masonic building on Main Street in downtown St. Helena resembles a life-size dollhouse.

PHOTO: JEAN SAYLOR DOPPENBERG

History

Napa County
Sonoma County
Mendocino County
Lake County

Over the past few centuries, many have staked a claim to what we now know as the Wine Country. The flags of Spain, England, Imperial Russia, Mexico, and the Bear Flag Republic have all flown here, a testament to the ambition, struggle, victories, and bitter disappointments of numerous explorers and conquerors. But before all the hubbub started, the region was home to Miwok, Pomo, Mayacoma, Yukia, and other indigenous peoples. Early descriptions of their lives evoke visions of a kind of Eden, where food was abundant and the mild climate permitted a life without the burden of clothes. In 1835, General Vallejo, the Mexican military commander appointed to the Sonoma Mission, reported that the area north of San Francisco was inhabited by colonies of nude natives. In retrospect, maybe not much has changed in California.

The Gold Rush of 1849 is perhaps the most renowned and defining event of Northern California history. The accidental discovery of one tiny nugget in 1848 by James Marshall, a moody carpenter working a sawmill in the Sierra foothills, set off one of the most frenzied mass migrations in history.

California was then newly a part of the United States, having been acquired from the Republic of Mexico—a remote, sparsely populated region cut off from the United States by 1,800 miles of broiling desert and nearly impassable mountain ranges. As news of the California Eldorado spread, hordes of gold seekers stampeded West, while others sailed from the East Coast around South America's Cape Horn. Some came from as far off as Germany, England and Wales, Ireland, and China. By the summer of 1849, more than 100 vessels floated empty in San Francisco Bay, their passengers and crew having forsaken all for a chance in the mines.

Though it is often eclipsed by the tumult of '49, California's early history was not without import. Mexico (which included California) had declared independence from Spain; the Russians had established a settlement on the coast—and later pulled up stakes; and a scruffy impromptu band of 33 farmers and woodsmen had staged a rebellion in Sonoma, seizing the presidio from the Mexicans and declaring California an independent republic. The Bear Flag Republic, as it was called, existed for 26 days, after which it was admitted as a part of the United States.

Through all of this, the various settlers of the region had experimented with growing vines north of San Francisco. However, the area's potential was not fully recognized until a man by the name of Count Agoston Haraszthy arrived on the scene (see "The Father of California Viticulture" in this chapter). Not long afterward, vineyards began to stretch in neat rows to the horizons. With time, numerous wineries sprang up and the region began to slowly gain international fame as the California Wine Country.

Napa County

For 10,000 years or more, the Pomos were the undisputed occupants of the lands of the upper Sonoma and Napa valleys, on up to Clear Lake and the surrounding lands. It was their custom to settle into small groups, each of which spoke a different dialect of the same language. They lived an orderly life, with the men carrying on the outdoor work and often specializing in fishing or crafting arrowheads. Marriage was conducted in traditional fashion, and babies were the domain of the women—mothers, grandmothers, aunts, and cousins.

The Pomos lived peacefully and enjoyed a relatively easy existence compared to tribes in other regions of California. The climate was mild; the streams abounded with fish. The Pomos were the first to discover the value of the mineral and hot springs south of Clear Lake. They were also on friendly terms with the Nappa tribe to the south near the Napa River.

The first white settler in the Napa Valley was George Yount—frontiersman, hunter, trapper, and mountain man. He had left his wife and three children in Missouri in 1832 to drive mules with a pack train to Santa Fe. The job fizzled, but Yount saw no reason to return to Missouri. Instead, his restless feet took him to California's coast, where he trapped beaver for a while. He eventually made his way north in the summer of 1834 to the mission in Sonoma.

There he was welcomed with considerable enthusiasm by Padre Jose Quijas, who had been praying for someone to repair the mission buildings. It appeared that Yount was a resourceful man who could do almost anything.

In time Yount became acquainted with the Mexican commandant Vallejo, who, it turned out, also needed work done—a new roof for his hacienda. Soon Yount was turning out 1,000 shingles a day and training the mission workers to help. Yount's payment likely came via a 12,000-acre Napa Valley land grant he received, with Vallejo's help. Land was seldom given to outsiders unless they were converted to Catholicism and married into a Mexican family. Indeed, Padre Quijas did baptize Yount. But it's certain that, with a wife in Missouri, Yount couldn't marry the daughter of a Mexican landowner. Yount was content never to see his wife again. He learned years later from a passing stranger that she had divorced him.

Upon Yount's arrival in Napa Valley, he hiked up an old Indian trail leading to the top of Mount St. Helena. From there he could look across the entire valley, and he was ready to settle down. In 1836 he set about building a Kentucky-style blockhouse for himself. He got on well with the Pomos and Nappas and taught them how to help. Then he erected a flour mill and sawmill, planted wheat and potatoes, and started a small vineyard. But like most God-fearing Missourians who made their way to Napa, he believed grapes were for eating, not for making wine. Yount's name would eventually live on into future generations—the town of Yountville was named in his honor (see "Name Calling" in the Area Overview chapter).

Soon another settler appeared on the scene—Dr. Edward Bale, a young English surgeon. His marriage to a niece of Gen. Vallejo made him a Mexican citizen, and as such he was given a land grant north of Yount's. Bale established a sawmill to cut timber, and a grist mill (still standing and known as Bale Mill) to grind the settlers' grain. The mills became centers of great activity and supplied work for new settlers, but the best was yet to come for Bale. When gold diggers poured into the state, flour became a premium product, and Bale's mill was a gold mine in its own right.

Between 1836 and 1846, most Napa County land had been given away in the form of grants to citizens who had proven their loyalty to Mexico. That left little territory for overland immigrants. Sometimes the grantees sold small parcels of their land to settlers, but that was later outlawed by Mexico. The legal descriptions in some of these deeds were quite primitive and sometimes took years to untangle. Typical was the following: "Bounded on the northwest by the spring on which the grist mill stands, as far as its waters run, easterly to the main creek, thence to a high bluff on which there are two dead trees, one of which has its top broken off...."

Validation of the land grants was guaranteed by a treaty between Mexico and the United States, but long after the U.S. acquired California, tricky court cases raged on. The near-wilderness aspect of the Napa Valley changed dramatically after gold was discovered in the Sierra foothills, 100 miles east of San Francisco, in 1848. The city by the bay, which boasted a population of less than 450, was virtually abandoned in the rush to the gold fields. And although Napa was 40 miles to the north—not exactly on the direct route to the foothills—large numbers of gold seekers did wander off course and find their way into the valley, on foot or on horseback. If anyone in town had a horse for sale, the sale was quickly made. Sometimes the horse was simply stolen.

Miners also found the valley a popular wintering place when rains drowned the mines. Some stayed in the area. In two years Napa's population tripled to 450. A census two years later showed a jump to 2,116 (including 252 women). In just one decade, wilderness had transformed to populace.

City on the River

The first town in the valley, founded in 1836, was Napa City—not that it amounted to much. Until the Gold Rush there was not one house in town, only a handful of adobe huts. Hides and tallow served as the media of exchange. There were no roads and no bridges.

But soon after the discovery of gold, prosperity set in. The chief places of business were saloons, and the method of payment was likely to be gold dust. In fact, the change brought about by gold was amazing.

The only route into town, the Napa River, soon opened the region to the world. The first steamboat to make a regular run between Napa and San Francisco was the *Dolphin*, a tiny ship no larger than a whaleboat. It was a harbinger of things to come. The channel was deep, so before long bigger steamers were plying the river, transporting passengers to San Francisco and Sacramento for a $1.00 fare, lunch included. But the river's main value was for moving freight. The valley's fertile soil was producing such a profusion of fruits and vegetables that ships lined up daily at the Napa docks to load up for the San Francisco market.

In the outlying Berryessa Valley, some 30 miles inland, wheat grew so abundantly it became an international product. Ships from foreign ports arrived regularly at the Napa Embarcadero to load Napa County wheat. The river brought in industry that would last until the end of the century. Lined up along its shores were potteries, iron works, tile factories, and tanneries. The term "Napa leather" earned its own

Insiders' Tip

When you've finished touring the wineries and prefer a little exercise—and a history lesson—try walking through the historic areas of the city of Napa. To help you on your self-guided tour of the architectural splendor, pick up a copy of "Historic Walking Tours of Napa." It's available at Napa County Landmarks, a nonprofit historic preservation organization in the National Registry Historic building at 1026 First Street in downtown Napa. For more information, call the organization at (707) 255-1836.

listing in Webster's dictionary as "a type of leather resembling the original glove leather made in Napa by tanning sheepskins with a soap and oil mixture."

Many residents prospered beyond their wildest dreams, and by the 1880s Napa had achieved fame for both its charm and vast wealth. That reputation brought in the bankers, who were by no means above ostentation in the building of their great Victorian mansions. Some of those homes still stand today as an architectural reminder of other times. With all this commerce and commotion, the river became a sort of freeway, replete with snarled traffic. One wild day in January 1880, some 50 ships created the county's first traffic jam—on the river channel.

But it came to an abrupt end. Napa's river traffic was killed by a single structure—

Russia Invades California

One day, the entire North Pacific would be an "inland sea" of the Russian empire. At least that was the belief of Grigory Ivanovich Shelikhov, a principal of one of the largest Russian trading companies of the 18th century. It was, of course, not to be, but Russian colonists did establish and maintain a settlement in California in the early 19th century. Their story is one of bravery, tragedy, comedy, and even some hot romance.

It all started in 1806 when Nikolai Petrovich Rezanov, chamberlain to the Tsar, sailed into San Francisco Bay on a mission to save the Russian colonists in Sitka, Alaska, from starvation; it had been a particularly nasty winter and the supply ships just never arrived. Rezanov headed to San Francisco hoping to pry some emergency grain from the Spanish.

The Spaniards, however, were not really receiving guests. Being a little insecure about their hold on the territory, they banned foreign ships from entering San Francisco Bay. Rezanow relied on his wit and a cargo hold of ammunition and other goods to plead his case, spending six weeks bargaining with the Spanish at San Francisco. When it came time to leave, he not only had filled his ship's hull with grain but had become engaged to the commandant's teenage daughter, Doña Concepción Argüello.

While sailing north from San Francisco, Rezanov noticed that the California coast was completely unoccupied—an observation that set him thinking. Upon his return to Sitka, he informed the governor of Russian America, Alexander Baranov, of the favorable Spanish reception and, more importantly, of the stretch of vacant California land he had observed.

His task complete, Rezanov set sail for Siberia to begin his overland trek to St. Petersburg. Unfortunately, the trip would end in disaster. Somewhere on the plains he sustained a fatal injury after falling off his horse. His young fiancée in California did not receive the tragic news until two years later.

In the meantime, Baranov dispatched a team to survey possible settlement sites in California. In March 1812, 25 Russians and 8 Aleuts from Alaska arrived in California to construct a colony on a lonely bluff about 60 miles north of San Francisco. They had most of the settlement built before the Spanish even knew they had arrived.

The Spanish came to know the colony as Fuerto de los Rusos, English-speaking settlers referred to it as Fort Ross, while the Russians simply called it Ross or Colony Ross. The Kashaya Pomo, the gentle tribe that had occupied the section of coast where the fort stood, called the spot *Meteni*.

The Kashaya welcomed the Russian presence, some even choosing to work at the fort as laborers—an unusual arrangement in a region where native peoples were mostly treated as slaves. In 1821, a Russian imperial decree gave Native Americans and Creoles civil rights protected by law. Even before the decree, the Russians had respected the rights of the Kashaya, negotiating an agreement for the use of their land. According to one report, the colonists acquired permission to inhabit the area in exchange for three blankets, three pairs of pants, two axes, three hoes, and some beads.

The sheer pluck of building a fort on land ruled by the Spanish Crown must have impressed the commanders at the San Francisco Presidio. At first, they conceded to the

Russian presence, but later demanded that the colonists abandon the territory. When Mexico achieved independence in 1821, it too sent envoys to evict the Russians. Rather than feel threatened, however, the Russians tried to devise ways to say no without hurting the Mexicans' feelings. During one such visit, Kirill T. Khlebnikov, a director of the Russian colonies, was on hand to hear the demands.

Muskets blaze during Living History Day at historic Fort Ross in Sonoma County. PHOTO: JOHN NAGIECKI

He described his reaction in his journal. "I realized these were empty threats but I avoided raising objections which, even if well taken would have injured his pride and thereby interfered with our most important objective: purchasing grain."

Though the Russians had hoped to grow enough food at the California settlement to supply the Alaska colonies, they had a rough time of it and were forced to purchase food from their neighbors. The coastal lands surrounding the fort were not suited to growing crops, particularly grains. Fog and a sizable mouse and gopher population often took a substantial portion of the harvest. The colonists tried to grow a variety of crops—including grapes on vines imported from Peru—but all met with poor results.

Though agriculture was a disappointment, the local otter business was hot—at least for a time. Otter pelts commanded a high price in Moscow and became the colony's raison d'être. When the local otter population was nearly wiped out, however, the colony reached a critical juncture. Either it would have to expand inland, where land was more favorable to agriculture, or fold.

So did the Russians simply take the additional land they needed, as they had at Fort Ross? No. Times had changed. There were many American settlers who would not take kindly to an unauthorized Russian land grab. The move would not reflect well on the ability of the Mexicans to govern the area and might possibly inspire the Americans to insurrection (which did in fact happen 12 years later).

Consequently, in 1834, Baron von Wrangell, the fifth governor of Russian America, met with officials in Mexico City to obtain permission to expand the Ross Colony. The Mexicans told Wrangell that they would permit the Russian colony to expand, even granting formal rights over the existing colonies. In return, however, the Mexicans demanded that Tsar Nicholas I recognize the newly independent Mexican republic. But the Tsar, still smarting from a Polish attempt at independence, despised all republics and refused the Mexican demand.

With the failure of this last-chance effort, the Russians abandoned the settlement in 1842, never to return.

On the grounds of Niebaum-Coppola Vineyards in Rutherford stands the Chiles House, one of the oldest homes in Napa Valley, built in 1856. PHOTO: JEAN SAYLOR DOPPENBERG

a bridge built across the Carquinez Straits between Martinez and Vallejo. That allowed trucks to come into Napa Valley for the first time.

Those Amazing Hot Springs

During the 1860s it became fashionable all over the country to "take the waters." Soaking in hot mineral baths or mineral-rich mud was touted to cure virtually every known ailment. The first entrepreneur to capitalize on these bubbling springs was Sam Brannan, who had become a millionaire selling shovels and picks to miners.

Some of that wealth was spent acquiring 1 square mile of land in the northern valley. It was Brannan's vision to build an extravagant resort spa that would become a holiday retreat for San Francisco's shamefully rich. He called the place Calistoga—a combination of his fondness for Saratoga Springs and the word California. On the grounds there soon appeared a lav-

ish hotel, 25 gingerbread cottages, an observatory tower, large stables with many fine horses, a winery, and a distillery. Brannan imported great herds of merino sheep from England and silkworms and mulberry trees from China. The benefits of the hot springs, of course, were obvious and needed no further publicity.

Not one to do things in a stingy fashion, Brannan first revealed his outrageously opulent Calistoga resort to San Francisco society with a gala opening. He chartered a ship to carry his guests from San Francisco to Vallejo, where they were met by a fleet of coaches that brought them to Calistoga. For the feast, roast fowl and champagne were served indoors; outdoors was a bountiful barbecue with beer by the barrel. The guests frolicked the night away, presumably soaking away their ills—and their hangovers—the next morning in the healing waters of the spa.

But success soon slipped away from Sam Brannan. His flair for moneymaking deserted him in Calistoga, in San Francisco, and in the gold country in general. His beautiful Calistoga hotel burned. He was shot in the back by a disgruntled mill hand and harassed by his creditors. Sick and discouraged, he left Calistoga. Brannan never recovered the promise of his early youth, but he wrote a fantastic chapter in the history of Napa Valley. He died in Southern California in 1889, penniless and practically alone.

In time, another hot springs resort, Napa Soda Springs, was developed 5 miles east of Napa City and took the place of Calistoga in the fickle favor of San Franciscans accustomed to lavish living. Banked against a flower-carpeted hillside, it presented an unequaled view of Napa Valley and San Pablo Bay. A good deal of faith was put in the healing powers of "a course at the springs." According to the report of a Dr. Anderson, the waters were beneficial "in the treatment of chronic metritis and ovaritis, for Bright's disease, acid blood, and dyspepsia."

The popularity of Wine Country's hot springs and spas has endured, with a number of accommodations and other businesses still built around mineral baths, mud packs, massages, and other forms of relaxation and body therapy. See our Spas and Resorts chapter for lodging options (from world-class resorts to more modest, old-fashioned choices) and for businesses that offer walk-in spa services.

The Silver Commotion

In the winter of 1858, rumors started percolating that silver had been discovered in the mountains. In no time at all, every unemployed man had turned prospector. Most of those wielding a pick knew nothing of the characteristics of silver ledges, and outcrops of barren rock of any description were equally valued to their ignorant eyes. The commotion continued for several weeks. A local assay office was even opened, run by an assayer who gave such discouraging reports that nobody believed him. So miners instead hauled their rocks to San Francisco, where reports came back "no silver at all" or "a trace." Fortune quickly turned to folly,

and tons of shiny rocks were unloaded by the disenchanted miners to make paving material for the streets of Napa.

Of more serious import were the quicksilver mines that developed in the 1860s in the Mayacmas Mountains that separate the Napa and Sonoma valleys. Mining quicksilver, or mercury, was a hazardous process, and newspapers of the day were filled with accident stories. A typical one involved a foreman: "While inspecting a piece of ground there fell without warning a mass of rock weighing half a ton, rendering him insensible for nearly an hour." (Only an hour?)

In the 1870s, silver fever struck again. A vein of silver was discovered in the Calistoga hills, and a new town sprang up around the diggings—Silverado City. The hillsides soon were pocked with mining claims, and the city prospered briefly. The vein was short-lived, but the town's hotel and mining office became famous, for it was here that Robert Louis Stevenson brought his bride on a honeymoon.

It was a strange entourage that straggled into the Napa Valley on a warm May day in 1880—gaunt, ailing Robert Louis Stevenson; his new bride, Fanny; her 12-year-old son; and a setter-spaniel named Chuchu. They had decided to honeymoon in Calistoga, hoping to cure the Scottish author's lung problems. They arrived at the Springs Hotel, where they lived a short time in a "cottage on the green," but after a couple of weeks they located cheaper quarters. They moved into the assayer's office and the bunkhouse of an abandoned silver mine as squatters, paying no rent.

With a secondhand cookstove and a few household effects pulled up the mountain by a new neighbor who was also a squatter, they settled down for the summer, living the free life of gypsies. Here Stevenson wrote in his journal the notes that became his first literary success, *The Silverado Squatters*.

The Emergence of Fine Wine

Although Yount and Bale were the first to raise grapes in Napa Valley, it seems doubtful either had the inclination to cultivate fine wines. That distinction came to several German immigrants who arrived in the 1870s: Jacob Schram (who barbered by day and planted vines by moonlight), Charles Krug (known as the father of Napa viniculture), Jacob and Frederick Beringer (Jacob was Krug's winemaker until he built his own winery), and Gottlieb Groezinger (his winery stands as Yountville's Vintage 1870).

The 1870s marked tremendous growth in the Napa Valley wine industry. Local viticulture clubs began organizing in 1875, with Charles Krug chosen president of the largest. (A note that will come in handy: Generally speaking, we use "viticulture" when talking specifically about the science and practice of growing grapes, and "viniculture" to discuss the process of making wines.) About the same time, the Beringer brothers established their winery, complete with a cellar dug into a hillside by Chinese laborers and reinforced with stone—a feat of advanced architecture as well as masonry. Adding to the growth of the industry was an outbreak of phylloxera (a ravenous louse that eats the plant's roots) in French vineyards. Napa wineries continued to expand, with some 140 wineries producing almost five million gallons of wine.

Unfortunately, this led to overproduction. In the late 1880s growers were all feeling the pinch, and Charles Krug's vineyards and cellar went into receivership. More bad times loomed in the form of a general nationwide depression in 1890. But the blow that brought valley growers to their knees was the discovery that the dreaded, grapevine-ravaging phylloxera—for which there was no cure—had infected the vineyards of the entire area. By the turn of the century, almost every vineyard had been ruined.

Plantings of resistant varieties brought fresh hope. Viticulture looked to be getting back on track. But those bright hopes were dashed by a new cataclysm called Prohibition. For the Old World grapegrowers, who considered wine the elixir of life, the law was inexplicable madness. One Italian immigrant in Pope Valley continued selling his wine because he believed wine to be "a natural way of life." He was arrested, of course.

The plague of Prohibition lasted for 14 years, from 1920 to 1933. Some vintners survived it by making sacramental or pharmaceutical wines. But for others it would take years to build back their businesses. Still, one thing was clear: There would be no returning to wheat or cattle raising. Napa County was on its way to becoming America's premier wine region.

By 1966 wine was becoming fashionable, not only in California, but across the nation. Between 1966 and 1972 wine consumption doubled. Visitors started pouring into the area to look, sample, and buy. By the mid-'70s, there were again more than 50 wineries in operation in Napa Val-

Insiders' Tip

Though modern high-tech devices are far more efficient at "trampling forth the vintage," they lack the unique charm of older, more traditional methods, which sometimes involved a human crusher climbing buck naked inside a barrel to pounce on grapes. Such foot stompin' methods thrived in the California Wine Country until about the 1850s, when the hand crusher made its first appearance. The old days may be gone, but they're not forgotten. Each October you can see crushing done like it used to be at the Sonoma County Harvest Fair located at the Sonoma County Fairgrounds in Santa Rosa.

ley, and a new promotional technique had been developed—wine tastings. To let the public see how great the product was, vintners opened their doors and uncorked their bottles for sampling. Many offered their cellars for touring. Add to it all an outstanding showing by Napa County wines in a 1976 blind taste test against some of the most prestigious wineries in France, and the worldwide wine community began to take notice (see "California is 'Discovered' in 1976" in our Wineries chapter).

In the 1980s viticulture became a sort of dream occupation—a creative endeavor that could be both financially rewarding and personally satisfying. New wineries popped up almost overnight, many operated by individuals drawn into the field because they savored living close to the soil. Wineries started gaining public acceptance by offering extra attractions— Shakespearean plays and readings in the caves and Mozart played at eventide on expansive green lawns. Wine Country golf courses and croquet courts drew international competition. Cooking classes featured famous chefs. It all drew attention to the work of the winemaker. And along the path of progress, the city of Napa became a bedroom community for San Francisco. (Commuting isn't all bad when you have a scenic home to return to.)

Sonoma County

In 1823, a zealous young Spanish priest, Father Jose Altimira, arrived in California and established the Mission San Francisco de Solano, northernmost in a chain of missions spaced a day's journey apart along California's coast. This mission was the only one to be dedicated after Mexico overthrew Spanish rule earlier that year. In fact, not everyone in the mission hierarchy thought it was a good idea. But Altimira was nothing if not enthusiastic, and he convinced his colleagues it would be a better climate than San Francisco for the Native American converts.

Compared to other, grander missions, Altimira's was unimpressive—a flimsy wooden structure that was swept twice by fire before achieving its present, fireproof adobe state. Within six years, Altimira claimed 1,000 converts (some may have been transfers). An adobe chapel had been added, as had a number of small shops where converts could learn weaving and agricultural skills.

But the mission was doomed from the start. A decree was passed down from the Mexican government that all church properties would be "secularized" (that is, confiscated). In 1834, a young lieutenant, the aforementioned Mariano Vallejo, was sent from Monterey to seize all mission property and dispose of grain fields and thousands of head of cattle, sheep, and horses. It was outright thievery carried out under the guise of eminent domain.

The converts—turned loose to fend for themselves—were likely to have been grateful. They didn't much like Altimira, a cold and impersonal man, and they didn't care for the Spanish or the Mexicans, who were sometimes oppressive. In any case, the Mexican government had another, more serious reason to send an emissary into the territory—to discourage foreign invaders. Trappers were arriving in ever-increasing poaching forays over the Sierra Nevada Mountains, and some were staying on as settlers. And on the north coast Russian settlers had arrived from Alaska (see "Russia Invades California").

Meanwhile, young Lt. Vallejo brought his beautiful, cultured wife, Francisca Benicia, to this rough, untamed land and set up house in the abandoned mission. In one of its 37 rooms, their first daughter was born. In time, Vallejo set about creating the town of Sonoma. Using a pocket compass, he laid out an 8-acre plaza around which the town would rise. The plaza would serve as a promenade area for the populace as well as a parade ground where young soldiers could drill and practice their horsemanship skills. At the same time, Vallejo was preoccupied with developing a 66,000-acre ranch in the grasslands of Petaluma Valley, some 10 miles away. Built as a defense against intruders, the structure's walls were 3 feet thick, braced by redwood beams. It became a second home for the growing Vallejo family, which eventually numbered 15 children.

The Russian Orthodox community occasionally holds services at the historic Fort Ross chapel on the Sonoma County Coast. PHOTO: JOHN NAGIECKI

Some 2,000 American Indians (most of them transfers from the mission ranks) answered roll call daily in the courtyard before going to work making saddles and boots. These products were marketed to settlers or shipped to coastal communities as far south as San Blas, Mexico. Though it all seemed like a sustainable arrangement, trouble was brewing behind the scenes. As mentioned at the beginning of this chapter, that trouble was the Bear Flag Republic.

The Bear Flag Rebellion

"About half past five in the morning of Sunday, June 14, a group of desperados surrounded the house of General Vallejo and arrested him," wrote his sister. "Vallejo, dressed in the uniform of a General, was the prisoner of this group of rough-looking men, some wearing on their heads caps made with the skins of coyotes or wolves. . . . Shoes were to be seen on the feet of 15 or 20 among the whole lot."

The issues surrounding this drama were complex. England, France, and the United States were each vying for the California territory, which Mexico was sure to relinquish (whether by force or purchase). General Vallejo argued in favor of American rule, while his rivals, General Pio Pico of Los Angeles and General Jose Castro of Monterey, strongly preferred the English or French to the Americans. Adding to this tense situation was the unexpected arrival in Monterey of Lieutenant John Charles Frémont of the U.S. Topographical Service, a surveyor purportedly on a mission to map a more direct route to the Pacific. Frémont rode in accompanied by a contingent of 62 armed U.S. cavalry.

Frémont did not hesitate in inciting the Mexican generals, going so far as to raise the Stars and Stripes over his camp. After some fierce posturing but no real fighting, Frémont moved north to Oregon. Following his departure, rumors began circulating that the Mexicans were about to evict all Americans from California. The story incited rage among local settlers, having been lured to California by the Mexican government's promise of land. They decided to take matters into their own hands.

Thirty-three renegade malcontents went to the Sonoma presidio to dispose of the Mexicans. Along the way they hastily fashioned a flag for the new republic, made of a woman's red flannel petticoat and a length of unbleached muslin. For their emblem they used berry juice to paint on it the picture of a bear (it looked more like a pig) and the words California Republic. The ever-cordial Vallejo brought up some wine for the group, and they spent some time in convivial conversation. But in the end, he was carried off to Sutter's Fort in Sacramento, where Vallejo's friend John Sutter reluctantly jailed him.

The California Republic lasted 26 days. On July 9, 1846, U.S. Navy Lt. Joseph Revere lowered the bear flag and replaced it with the American Stars and Stripes. Vallejo was released from jail August 6. He had been away no more than a month, but in that time his horses and cattle had been stolen, his fields stripped of grain.

The New State of California

The months that followed the rebellion brought mass confusion. Nobody knew who was in charge. A group of military volunteers known as Company C from New York City's Bowery arrived. But since there wasn't much for the soldiers to do (unless they wanted to stoop to manual labor), they improved their leisure by riding spirited horses, hunting waterfowl, and staging cruel bear-and-bull fights in a makeshift stadium behind their barracks.

The discovery of gold suddenly shifted everyone's attention. Settler and soldier alike left Sonoma to the womenfolk. The village sank into stagnation. Vallejo, on the other hand, wasn't too bad off. He had seen what was coming and had hedged his bets. While serving Mexico loyally (virtually without pay), he had also taken steps to ingratiate himself to the United States. In time he actually became a California senator.

But Vallejo's plans of becoming a prominent American somehow went awry. Lawsuit after lawsuit went against him, and his land empire disappeared. He slipped deeper into debt. One by one his dreams vanished. He did manage to hold onto his Sonoma home, Lachryma Montis,

Buena Vista Winery was established more than 140 years ago by Count Agoston Haraszthy. PHOTO: RYAN LELY

and here his wife—once pampered—sold dried fruit and chili peppers for the San Francisco market. In old age, Vallejo became a symbol of the link between an idealized Mexican era and the Yankee-dominated present. In his unfailing dignity and hospitality, he seemed to personify all that was best about the past.

By the mid-1860s, Sonoma had become almost totally neglected. There were no trees, and the plaza had degenerated. A fire in 1866 destroyed much of what the early settlers had built. Some of the early pioneers responded by organizing a Pioneer Society of 340 members to revitalize the town. They planted trees, built fences, and cleaned up the plaza (appointing one member to be in charge of keeping livestock out of that area of town). Gradually the town took on a more respectable look, though the society itself fizzled out.

About 1888, many Italian immigrants came to quarry cobblestones for the streets of San Francisco. Among them was Samuele Sebastiani, who quickly recognized the possibilities for growing wine grapes. In no time at all he was supplying the demand of the growing Italian community for wine, and making a name for his winery. Today, the strong Italian influence remains in and around Sonoma, where Italian restaurants line the streets around the plaza.

One of Vallejo's mandates when he took over as commandant was to ensure that lands north of San Francisco were settled. At the time, this northern frontier was a lonesome wilderness, and Vallejo had some trouble convincing any of his fellow Californians to apply for grants. But he had plenty of relatives, so most of them fell heir to large tracts. In 1837, he convinced his widowed mother to leave her San Diego adobe and travel 700 miles to an area near Santa Rosa Creek. She packed up her nine children and seven-trunk wardrobe and built the Cabrillo adobe, the first bona fide home in the Santa Rosa Valley. In time it became the nucleus of a settlement.

Santa Rosa

In 1854, the town of Santa Rosa was little more than a trading post. A few small businesses and houses had sprung up along the creek, and the town had a repre-sentative in the state senate. That man was William Bennett, another former Mis-sourian, and his ambition was to snatch the county seat away from Sonoma. To help voters make up their minds on the issue, he hosted a big Fourth of July bar-becue attended by, according to one histo-rian, "the lame, the halt and blind if they could influence a vote." Not surprisingly the vote went in favor of Santa Rosa. At daybreak a group of Santa Rosans, fearing Sonoma wouldn't release the county records, hired a wagon and raced to Sonoma, grabbed the records, and raced back to Santa Rosa.

Reporting the hijacking, the *Sonoma Bulletin* editor wrote, "We are only sorry they did not take the adobe courthouse too . . . its removal would have embellished our plaza." Within three years, according to the newly launched *Sonoma Democrat*, Santa Rosa had grown to 100 buildings. After the arrival of the railroad in 1870, the town's population exploded to 6,000.

About this time a shy, trim New Eng-lander named Luther Burbank opened a nursery in the town and began experi-menting on flowers, fruits, and vegetables. His uncanny talent for interpreting the results of his experiments earned him the lasting title of "plant wizard" (see our Attractions chapter).

A wizard of a different sort next ap-peared in town—spiritualist-sage Thomas Harris, a man of magnetic personality and piercing eyes "like revolving lights." In the outlying area called Fountain Grove, Har-ris established the esoteric Brotherhood of New Life, a colony of communal living that separated its members from their spouses (and their cash) to await their celestial mates in another world. Harris claimed these other worlds were revealed to him during his conversations with the angels. It was left to a woman reporter to provide the impetus to drive Harris from the gates of his Eden. She joined the group long enough to write a lurid exposé that sent the preacher packing.

The infamous 1906 earthquake that leveled San Francisco also struck Santa Rosa—nearby Petaluma, Santa Rosa's then rival, escaped virtually unscathed. The courthouse collapsed, and downtown buildings suffered devastating damage. Nearly 100 people died in the rubble, but the city's spirit survived. While some resi-dents did head for other parts, many townsfolk simply rolled up their sleeves and began to rebuild. Only one minor case of looting was reported during the period. County Supervisor Tom McNamara made off with a portion of the statue of Minerva that had stood on top of the courthouse. Despite the county's requests, McNamara never returned it.

Petaluma

Before the advent of the railroads in the mid-1880s, rivers were the principal means of shipping goods inland. In the Petaluma River, steamboats—introduced to California during the Gold Rush—operated regularly during the 1850s, haul-ing wool, butter, cream, eggs, and live chicks down the twisting tidal river to San Francisco Bay. By the 1890s, Petaluma was the third-busiest waterway in the state.

But it was neither the river nor steam-boats that gave Petaluma its enduring fame. In the 1880s, it became known as the "Egg Basket of the World" when the first practical chicken incubator was invented there and marketed on a mass scale. Immi-grants from Europe thronged to Petaluma to set up hundreds of hatcheries and thou-sands of chicken-feed mills. As many as 600 million eggs per year were shipped to worldwide points. But chicken-related prosperity declined in the 1930s due to high feed costs. Leghorn hens were replaced by Holstein cows. Today the Petaluma countryside is mostly dairy land.

Jack London in Glen Ellen

Glen Ellen, 9 miles north of Sonoma, lies in an area forested with oak, madrone, redwood, and buckeye trees. Author Jack London came to this countryside in 1903 at the invitation of friends who owned the Wake Robin Lodge. There, at age 30, he met their vivacious niece, Charmian. Instantly attracted to one another, the couple spent their days riding horseback and having sprightly conversations. They were perfectly matched, adventurous individuals, and London stayed on to marry Charmian.

At first they lived at her family's lodge, but London fell in love with the land locally known as "the valley of the moon." He started accumulating property until he had a 1,500-acre tract, and here the Londons lived in a simple white house. He called the place Beauty Ranch, and it was there he wrote most of his prodigious output of books. London's success as an author had initially been spurred by the appearance of a Yukon story in *Atlantic Monthly* magazine and confirmed by publication of *The Call of the Wild* when he was 22.

Within eight years, he was America's highest paid author. In his short lifetime, he wrote 54 books, 1,300 articles, and 188 short stories, some translated into 30 languages. His house overflowed with guests—scientists, actresses, writers, and socialites. And exuberance marked just about everything London did. He took up scientific farming and designed a pigpen that gave each pig family an apartment. Later, he took a long sea voyage with Charmian on a ship he designed himself.

But London's most wondrous dream was Wolf House, his 26-room mansion, an imposing affair of redwood and huge stone blocks, with arched windows opening onto forested slopes and offering views of the entire valley. London wrote, "It will last one-thousand years, God willing." But one midnight in August 1913, billows of black smoke filled the sky as a raging fire burned out of control. The author watched silently from a nearby hill as his dream crumbled to the earth. London never quite recovered from the calamity. Three years later he died at age 40. Official cause was uremic poisoning, but rumors persisted it was suicide. The magnificent ruins of Wolf House, as well as all of Beauty Ranch, live on as a California state park.

Northern Sonoma County

The Pomo tribe lived for centuries in what is now northern Sonoma County. In 1841, Mexico granted a portion of their domain to a New England sea captain, Henry Fitch (nobody consulted the Pomos, of course), who had eloped with General Vallejo's sister. But Fitch, having received such an excellent dowry, saw no reason to live out his life in such a lonely land. He hired Cyrus Alexander to manage a ranch there with immense herds of cattle. The names of both men live on as landmarks—Fitch Mountain looms over the town of Healdsburg and to the east lies Alexander Valley, Cyrus's payment for work on the ranch.

Healdsburg itself bears the name of Harmon Heald, a disenchanted '49er who arrived on the scene in 1852 and claimed land for a town site. He surveyed the town and sold lots for $15 apiece around a central plaza. By the end of the decade, Healdsburg had a population of 500.

The town acquired a newspaper, the *Review*, after the editor of the newspaper in Sonoma, A. J. Cox, advised his readers, "the old blunderbuss has dried up." He subsequently shut down the presses and moved north to publish the paper in Healdsburg. The town lay on the road to the geysers, a tourist attraction considered "the greatest of curiosities in the state next to Yosemite Valley." To get there, tourists clung in awestruck terror within Charlie Foss's stagecoach as he careened over narrow roads and rattled over Hog's Back Ridge.

Russian River and Western Sonoma County

Called Slavyanka (Slavic girl) by Russian settlers during their tenure in California, the Russian River flows from the hilly regions above Hopland, past Cloverdale, Healdsburg, Guerneville, Duncans Mills, and finally Jenner, where it meets the Pacific. The Russians explored the length of the river basin—a territory that the

Spanish had largely ignored—initially to scout out a suitable settlement site and thereafter to occasionally chase down otter. They saw the area for what it was, a rich river valley dense with towering virgin redwood stands, bounded by fertile plains, and awash with fish. But the Russians abandoned their foothold in California before ever establishing a settlement upriver, leaving the region behind for others to exploit.

When the first American loggers arrived in the Russian River valley, they could hardly believe what they saw. The trees were enormous, some measuring as wide as 23 feet in diameter and 300 feet in height. The first sawmill opened in the valley in 1861, with others springing up soon thereafter. Stumptown, renamed Guerneville in 1870 after lumberman George Guerne, was the region's logging epicenter.

The trees offered the woodsmen a rich bounty for a time. However, around the turn of the century many had been harvested, and the mills began to close. In an effort to shore up profits, the Northwest Pacific Railroad—which had been servicing the mills—began to promote the Russian River area as a tourist destination. Urban vacationers from San Francisco and other parts were soon hopping aboard trains in droves to escape to the region—with the railroad cars rolling right onto a ferryboat for the ride across the Golden Gate. Hotels and resorts sprang up, as did bevies of summer cottages. In the 1930s, revelers boogied all night at the Rio Nido Inn to the sounds of Benny Goodman's clarinet and Ozzie Nelson's band.

Today the Russian River area has remained a popular destination site—particularly with gay and lesbian communities. It features a host of resorts and elegant B&Bs. (See our On the Water and Bed and Breakfast Inns chapters.) The intense economic boom of the late 1990s in nearby Santa Rosa and beyond also transformed the river area, bringing an influx of new residents who remodeled old summer cottages into year-round residences.

Not far from the Russian River, the town of Sebastopol got its start when

> **Insiders' Tip**
> Each year on the third Saturday in July, the staff at the Fort Ross State Historic Park host Living History Day. The event features singing, dancing, theatrical performances, period dress, gunfire, and cannon blasts. For more information, call (707) 847-3286.

Joaquin Carillo, another Vallejo relative, received the standard family land grant (this one of 13,000 acres). After American settlers overran his lands, he turned his house into a hotel.

The town—originally named Pine Grove—acquired its name in an unusual way. A fistfight had erupted in front of Dougherty's store, and the man who was getting the worst of it retreated inside, where Dougherty protected him by preventing the attacker from advancing. The Crimean War was then in progress and onlookers compared this encounter with the fight going on to England's failed attempt to capture the seaport of Sebastopol in the Russian Crimea. At the next town meeting, the locals voted to have the name thusly changed.

Another popular local name also harks back to a Russian source. Settlers at Fort Ross introduced the Gravenstein apple to the county in the mid-19th century. In 1883, Nathaniel Griffin demonstrated that "Gravs" could be grown commercially, and he was dubbed "Grandfather of the Gravenstein." The apple became popular in the county because of its exceptional flavor and early ripening. The fruit was so well liked that locals inaugurated an annual celebration—the Gravenstein Apple Festival—in 1910 in its honor. The festival continues to be held today.

Other western Sonoma towns include Valley Ford, Bloomfield, Forestville, and Occidental. The latter was first settled by Bill Howard, who had survived a shipwreck off New York, malaria in Africa, and a revolution in Brazil. He and a sawmill operator lured a railroad into the territory and after that success built the whole town of Occidental in four months. Italian woodcutters from Tuscany worked the forests, and a few opened restaurants where a traditional Italian feast could be had for two bits. Today, Occidental is still the place to go for Italian dinners; it is also a hub for artists and environmental activists. If you're feeling deficient in either of these subjects, consider a short course or workshop at the Occidental Arts and Ecology Center. Located on 80 gorgeous acres off Coleman Valley Road, the center can help you take that first step toward a new career as a blacksmith or beekeeper or learn all about landscape painting or restoration forestry.

The Sonoma Coast

For almost 60 miles along the jagged coastline, Sonoma County's Highway 1 (called "Coast Highway 1" in many locales) snakes through rangeland and small towns that lie between the Coast Range and the Pacific. Centuries ago Miwok and Pomo tribes fished these coastal waters. Later, Russians and the Aleut hunters they brought down from Alaska harvested otter here—to near extinction—in nimble kayaks called baidarkas. The hunters skillfully negotiated their small craft through the surf and swells of the rugged coastline, occasionally seeking refuge in one of the few protected coves hidden among the bluffs. Bodega Bay, near Sonoma County's southern border, was one of the few places where larger ships could safely drop anchor. It thus wasn't long before the bay became a shipping center, dispatching lumber and agricultural products to San Francisco and beyond.

Bodega Bay became famous as the site where Alfred Hitchcock filmed his classic thriller, *The Birds.* A wall-size photo at Bay View Restaurant at the popular Inn at the Tides (see our Restaurants and Hotels and Motels chapters) commemorates Hitchcock's work.

Mendocino County

Rumors of gold brought the first adventuring white pioneers to Mendocino County in the 1840s. The rumors were false, but the land itself was pleasant—a good place to settle down and raise sheep, plant fruit trees, and grow hops. Sam Orr, a Kentuckian, arrived in 1857 with his wife, along with a quantity of grape cuttings to start a vineyard. Soon another American wandered in, a prospector from the gold country named Seward. He bought some of Orr's cuttings and also started a vineyard to grow around his imposing Colonial-style house, which soon included a winery—he had clearly found success in his mining venture. Still, the valley's immediate future rested not with grapes but with hops.

By the 1890s, the Ukiah Valley had achieved modest fame for its vast hop fields. The town of Ukiah boasted two hotels, three livery stables, and ten saloons. But traffic on its dirt streets kicked up clouds of dust in summer and churned up thick mud in winter. One especially wet year a two-horse wagon sank hub-deep in the middle of Main Street.

Most incoming travelers arrived by way of Fort Bragg on a stagecoach that left at 7:00 A.M. and made a loading stop at Mendocino, before rumbling over twisty, dusty, roads to Ukiah. Along the route, the stage stopped for a meal and change of horses, with passengers arriving in Ukiah about dinnertime. When the railroad finally arrived with service to and from San Francisco, it started a tourist boom. By then the hop fields had achieved notoriety, and travelers came from hundreds of miles away just to spend a weekend in the country. A magazine travel article of the day portrayed Hopland as a bucolic paradise: "If your nerves have become supersensitive from the corrosions of city life…take a vacation among the hop fields in the gilded autumn area of California. A few hours' travel north from San Francisco and one looms upon acres of trellised hop vines and graceful, luxurious beauty delighting the eye at every turn. Pickers are at work by the hundreds."

For the hundreds of hop pickers, those trellised vines were less romantic. Pioneer Hazel Pittman recalled those days: "It was awfully hard work. We wore gauntlet gloves and still the hops would cut through with the stickers on them. You would perspire from the terrible heat and itch. But we made a penny a pound, and if you could pick a hundred pounds a day there was a whole dollar." (From *Mendocino County Remembered—An Oral History*.)

Other attractions arose to bring tourists. This was the age of the curative mineral bath, and the area boasted several. Most elegant was Vichy Springs, an upscale resort featuring such niceties as croquet, horseback rides, hunting safaris, and dancing under the stars. The water in the swimming pool was allegedly "charged with electricity and gas, a real Champagne Bath." Vichy Springs had a long fallow period, but in the late 1980s it was revived, reconstructed, and rejuvenated, and it is once again an elegant resort spa (see our Spas and Resorts chapter).

Meanwhile, in the early 1900s, grape-growing and winemaking started to become more serious. Dozens of small operations were producing wine in light volume; Zinfandel was the main product. Hardworking Italians planted grapes on the hillsides. For the most part, however, the wine industry in Mendocino County at this time involved growers shipping their fruit to other wine-producing regions for blending. Typical of early growers were the Malone family, who sold their grapes as reds and whites, with no varietal distinction.

In 1910, a census counted 5,800 Mendocino County acres in grape production, with 90,000 gallons of wine produced. Much of the activity stemmed from the arrival of the railroad, which opened up new markets. But for Mendocino County, as for the nation, wine production came to a halt when Prohibition became the law of the land. Today's wine industry is based not so much on quantity as on quality. And oenologists around the world now recognize the premier quality of Mendocino.

Anderson Valley

Walter Anderson came here in 1851 with his wife, who may have been the first white woman in these parts. Early accounts describe Anderson as a man who chose to forsake civilization and pitch his tent where the foot of man had never trod. Yet he became a wealthy man with broad acres of land and large herds of cattle. Eventually Anderson was joined by others like himself—farmers or cattlemen living on spreads that were remote from the trappings and amenities of city life. A few enterprising homesteaders tried planting grapes, but the valley's proximity to ocean temperatures 10 degrees cooler than in Ukiah meant it was not only Prohibition that killed the wine industry here, but also adverse weather.

Not until the 1960s did anyone get serious about vineyards. In 1964, Dr. Donald Edmeades, against all sensible advice, planted 24 acres of grapes. He hung out a sign, "Edmeades' Folly." Today there are a dozen small wineries in the area, mostly growing cooler-climate grapes such as Chardonnay and Pinot Noir.

The Mendocino Coast

The jagged Mendocino Coast bears little resemblance to its southern relative, that stretch of beach that's lined with sun-bathers from Santa Barbara to San Diego. Here the fog-festooned sand dunes are spotted with wild grasses, overwhelming in their lonely beauty. In springtime the hills are golden with Scotch broom, and in summer rhododendrons grow wild. Nowhere is nature more glorious.

It's a rugged coast, dotted with dog-hole ports (big enough only for a dog to turn around in), that prospered for two decades in the rush for building materials following the 1906 San Francisco earthquake. Many of these burgs have vanished or are greatly diminished. For some years, Point Arena was the largest, most active lumber port between San Francisco and Eureka. It was also a whaling station and regular port of call for passenger steamers. Today, its most impressive feature is its classic, soaring lighthouse, 115 feet up from the tip of a narrow, bleak, eroding rockbound point. It's the closest point to Hawaii on the west coast. The light tower

The Father of California Viticulture

Although many early settlers had started vineyards north of San Francisco, the first individual to recognize the area's potential for growing fine wine grapes was Count Agoston Haraszthy.

A flamboyant man who may or may not have been a true aristocrat, Haraszthy fled political turmoil in his native Hungary to seek his fortunes in America. His first endeavor in the New World was founding Sauk City, Wisconsin, where he built homes, mills, and stores; planted hops; and started a vineyard. The town remains to this day.

Once weary of that project, he headed to California along the Santa Fe Trail. He arrived at the gold fields on horseback, an Argonaut in silken shirt, red sash, and velour hat, seeking whatever opportunities might exist. Haraszthy was working as an assayer at the San Francisco mint when Gen. Vallejo heard of the man's interest in viticulture. Vallejo invited him to Sonoma in 1856, whereupon Haraszthy quickly recognized the potential of Sonoma's soil. Convinced that grapes could prosper without irrigation, he sailed for Europe and returned with 300 varieties of grape cuttings, the basis for his 6,000-acre vineyards.

This is a modern replica of Agoston Haraszthy's Sonoma home.
PHOTO: LOU ZAUNER

The winery he built was of massive stones, with cellars dug into the hillsides. For himself, he built a grand Pompeian-style villa. His fame spread quickly, and vintners from other parts of California, as well as those newly arrived from Europe, came to him for advice and for cuttings. It created something of a "grape rush" in the Sonoma and Napa valleys.

But by 1868 the count was again restless and decided to turn his enthusiasm to raising sugar in Nicaragua. He left his two sons (who had married Vallejo daughters) to run the winery business. They never saw their father again, for he vanished mysteriously in the jungle. According to legend, he fell from a tree into a river and was devoured by crocodiles.

The villa he built in Sonoma was destroyed by the passage of time, but in the 1980s, townsfolk rebuilt a replica next to the first vineyards he planted. Both are there to see today.

was built in 1870, then rebuilt after the devastating 1906 earthquake. For 36 years, it faithfully guided ships through the treacherous rocks, but today's visitors will see only seals, migrating gray whales, and cavorting sea lions.

The settlement called Elk, 18 miles north of the Point Arena light tower, used to be a lively port. The cove is heavily studded with craggy islets and tall, dome-shaped sea stacks. Steam schooners used to brave this navigator's nightmare to load lumber among the rocks.

Even before the 1906 quake, the Mendocino Coast had been turned into a lumberjack's paradise by the Gold Rush. San Francisco burgeoned into a bustling city in urgent need of lumber to build houses. At the time, the only lumber available came from the Sandwich Islands (now known as Hawaii) and was very costly. When news of the great redwood forest on the north coast trickled down, there was no holding back the tide. The history of the coast changed overnight.

Along a 20-mile stretch of coast south of the town of Mendocino are a handful of country inns with colorful histories, some perched on bluffs, others snuggled into the foothills (see our Bed and Breakfast Inns chapter). Several of the fine old structures date back to the mid-1800s. Logging had been booming in Little River for 10 years when Silas Coombs selected it as one of the best-weather ports on the coast to build a mill. The mill wasn't memorable (it burned in 1910), but the mansion Coombs built lives on as Little River Inn, one of the coast's loveliest, with gabled windows and eaves festooned with wooden scrollwork. From the porch where Silas once spotted ship arrivals, visitors now can watch the annual migration of gray whales from cold Alaska to warm mating areas in Baja California (see our Spas and Resorts chapter).

There's another historic inn nearby. Heritage House is an old Victorian farmhouse dating to the 1850s. It was an early base for smuggling both liquor and foreign laborers and once was a hideout for 1930s gangster "Baby Face" Nelson. Today, it's a leisurely retreat with a commanding view of the craggy coast.

Headstones such as this one in the Mendocino Cemetery offer a fascinating glimpse of pioneer California. PHOTO: JOHN NAGIECKI

The Village of Mendocino

The picturesque town of Mendocino lies at the mouth of the Big River, on a rocky headland overlooking a small bay. In its heyday around 1870, it was a raucous, thriving port and lumbertown, often called "Fury Town" by locals. Nearly everything in Mendocino was and is built of wood, including the sidewalks and the water towers that stand on the skyline. The settlement was initially named Meiggsville for "Honest Harry" Meiggs, a San Francisco politician and wharf owner with a weakness for speculation. The town changed its name in 1854 after Meiggs got into financial hot water and had to flee the country. He recouped his losses by building the first railroad over the Andes in South America, but his partners in Mendocino were left facing bankruptcy.

Meiggs came hot-footing to Mendocino in the first place when a Chilean barque loaded with silks and spices wrecked nearby. The captain of the ship had lost his way to San Francisco and accidentally guided his vessel straight into the rocks at Point Cabrillo. When Meiggs sent a salvage party, they found no silks but instead great forests of redwood. Meiggs, a born entrepreneur, rounded up a schooner, some mill equipment, and some partners and headed for the forested coast. Soon mills sprung up in every gulch, and mansions with leaded-glass windows rose up on hillsides filled with fine furnishings shipped around Cape Horn. Breweries, churches, and schools followed. On Steamer Day, when passengers came into port, carriages from eight hotels met ships from all over the globe.

When the forest had been cut and the mills closed down, Mendocino fell asleep and snoozed for a long while. In the 1960s, the town suddenly blossomed as a center for artists and bohemians seeking freedom of style and life on the cheap. William Zacha came up from the Bay Area to open an art gallery, then conceived the Mendocino Art Center, a rambling collection of buildings on a rise at the edge of town (see our Arts and Culture chapter).

It was this art colony that first attracted a more affluent breed of visitor, seeking escape from urban living. They came to stroll boardwalks and sniff ocean breezes. With them came a blossoming of gourmet restaurants and some uncommonly civilized inns. It is this ambience that sets Mendocino apart from other north coast villages. The fact that Mendocino looks a lot like the coast of Maine has not escaped the notice of filmmakers. Devotees of the television series *Murder, She Wrote* will recognize some "Cabot Cove" settings.

Fort Bragg

Only 8 miles north of Mendocino but seeming worlds apart, Fort Bragg is a hardworking town with a down-to-earth feel. There's the smell of sawdust in the air, and local talk often revolves around lumber or fishing. Noyo Harbor, a snug refuge just inland on the Noyo River, is the quintessential fishing port. In the predawn you can see the parade of boats heading down the river to the sea, their lights making an attractive scene.

Most visitors come to Fort Bragg to ride the California Western Railroad's Skunk Train, drawn by an old-time locomotive through 40 miles of dense redwood forest. The route from the town of Willits traverses over 31 bridges and trestles, through two deep mountain tunnels, and around sinuous switchbacks. It was a nightmare to build, and Chinese laborers did much of the work. While passenger travel is highly promoted, the Skunk—named for its coal-smoke aroma—still hauls lumber and other freight to stay in business.

Lake County

For centuries Pomo tribes lived around Clear Lake, fishing in canoes of willow poles interwoven with tules, while their women made baskets so fine they could hold water. There was plenty of obsidian for spears and tools. The Pomo bathed in the hot springs and played games on the small islands that dot the lake. Volcanic Mt. Konocti, with its eerie caves, was considered sacred ground.

The first white men at Clear Lake were probably Russian fur trappers from Fort Ross. They were followed by French-Canadian fur trappers and American mountain men. Then in 1836 General Vallejo's brother, Salvador, brought cattle and horses onto a newly acquired land grant. For the most part, Salvador ran the ranch from Sonoma headquarters, and the Pomo lifestyle was not interrupted.

But in 1847, Salvador sold out to two Americans, Andrew Kelsey and Charles Stone. They enslaved the natives, oppressed them, starved them. In desperation, two of the Pomos were hired to steal a steer, but they bungled the job. Fearing a cruel reprisal, they decided to kill Stone and Kelsey. Stone died from an arrow,

This is the house that Lillie Langtry built when she came to Lake County in the late 1880s. PHOTO: LOU ZAUNER

Kelsey at the hands of a Pomo woman whose son had been tortured. Frightened settlers called in the military from Benicia. A battle ensued and the Pomos, holed up on a Clear Lake island, were massacred, giving the name Bloody Island to the site.

The island is no more, as farmers reclaimed the marshes around it. But the name of Andrew Kelsey lives on in Kelseyville. In the early 1850s, wagon trains began arriving and settlers started raising cattle and planting fields. John Cobb, one of the first, had come from Kentucky by way of the Wabash, Tippecanoe, Quincy, and the gold mines of Placerville before finally settling down in what is now known as Cobb Valley.

By 1857, a county government had been set up in a tiny wooden courthouse, and Lakeport was on its way to being the county seat. It was assumed the key to growth was a railroad to market products elsewhere, but Lake County did grow, albeit slowly, despite the handicap of having no railroad. A number of vineyards and wineries appeared, most of them clinging to the valleys around Clear Lake, since the rest of the county was quite rugged.

But wine would not be the real attraction in the area. That would turn out to be the hot springs that bubbled up everywhere. By 1880, 100,000 people had traveled to Lake County to partake of the beneficial waters and luxuriate in the elegant hotels adjacent to the mineral springs. Posh casinos, music halls redolent with gold leaf, and formal dining rooms gleaming with silver and crystal were just some of the luxuries offered during leisure hours, while the more energetic indulged in bowling, croquet, lawn tennis, and riding.

As the fame of the resorts grew, so did the services. Hundreds were employed as servants and culinary workers, hundreds more in riding stables and on vegetable farms. Bartlett Springs could accommodate 5,000 guests, and some were notable. One year, Queen Marie of Romania sojourned for a while. Nearby Harbin Springs boasted two large hotels, 15 cottages, and springs of hot arsenic, hot iron, and sulphur with a temperature of 120 degrees (see Harbin Hot Springs in our Spas and Resorts chapter).

For generations, many faithfully vacationed at these spas not only for health benefits, but also as a gathering place for the socially elite. The undoing of this salubrious way of life was the invention of the combustion engine. With the advent of the automobile, people no longer lingered for weeks. Instead, they came for a few days and moved on to another spot. The fine old hotels degenerated, and most of them burned. It was the end of a gracious era that lasted a half-century.

The centerpiece of Lake County has always been Clear Lake, the largest natural lake in California completely contained within the state borders. But the abundance of Clear Lake had its limits. Land clearing and farming gradually released silt and nutrients into the lake, eventually causing the once-blue waters to cloud with dirt and algae. In the 1940s, gnats swarmed and had to be sprayed with DDT, resulting in the dying off of fish and fish-eating birds and animals. Today the ecological balance has been largely restored, and Clear Lake is especially popular with fishermen and campers.

Lillie Langtry in the Vineyards

Of all the rich and famous who made their way to Lake County, none was more illustrious than the vibrant, graceful Lillie Langtry—famed actress and vivacious mistress of Britain's Prince of Wales, later crowned King Edward VII. She came to Guenoc Valley in 1887, weary of the acting circuit and trying to get a divorce from her English husband. She bought a 4,000-acre ranch and intended to raise grapes and thoroughbred horses. With her was her celebrated lover, Freddie Gebhart, a wealthy horseman who had bought an adjoining 3,200 acres.

Langtry was enchanted with Lake County from the moment she came via jostling stagecoach from St. Helena at the end of the railroad line. She was intrigued by the ways of the Wild West. "We all took part in the process of corralling the different herds of cattle and the roundup of horses," she wrote. "We counted about 80 horses. My manager was in his glory and stabled about 20." Langtry had other plans for Guenoc Ranch as well. She wanted to produce wine from her own grapes and winery. She decided that no one but a Frenchman could cope with this challenge, and she engaged a capable man from Bordeaux.

The vintage that resulted never reached market. "A new law putting liquor into bond for a period spoiled the sale of those bottles with a picture of myself on the label," she complained, "and I suppose now that the country is dry my portrait still adorns the Customs." Langtry stayed at the ranch a fortnight and eagerly looked to return after completing her committed engagements. However, she never saw the ranch again, though she owned it 18 years.

When Prohibition dealt its death blow to winemaking, Lake County turned its land over to pears, walnuts, and grazing pasture. Not until the 1960s did the vineyards reappear. Now there are several top-rated wineries in operation, and one of them is Guenoc.

When Orville Magoon bought and revived the vineyards of Lillie Langtry's beloved Guenoc Ranch, he discovered old agricultural records stating that Langtry Farms had produced 50 tons of Burgundy wine in 1891. The area where Lillie's grapes grew has now been replanted and, with some additional acreage, stretches out along Butts Canyon Road. From the winery's tasting rooms that rise above a small lake, one can see in the distance the house where Langtry lived, looking almost exactly as it did when she was there. And once again the wines of Guenoc are bottled with her portrait on the label (see our Wineries chapter).

Golden Gateway

Most people who come to the Wine Country can't get enough of one thing. No, not the reserve Cabernet—though that may be true too. What they can't get enough of is time. Face it, there's just too darned much to see and do. And on top of all the delectable choices offered by these four wonderful counties, there's also San Francisco—California's emerald city by the bay—which draws and diverts everyone's attention south.

It's common knowledge that "just passing through" San Francisco generally (hopefully!) means staying at least a couple of days and nights. An icon of the American West, the City (capitalized by locals, many of whom have heard of New York) lives up to its legends. The classic old cable cars really do climb halfway to the stars (or at least as far as Nob Hill). Luminous fog does swirl around the Golden Gate Bridge, leaving its ramparts floating like the entrance to Valhalla. At eventide the golden glow of the setting sun glints from the windows of Alcatraz Island, making the old prison seem almost romantic, as errant sailors tack home against the late and misty sky. And taquerias in the Mission District, dim sum eateries in Chinatown, Italian coffeehouses in North Beach, to name just a few, make up a fascinating and tasty cultural mélange. Even the frequently chilling summer weather and traffic-snarled streets fail to diminish the multicultural excitement and avant-garde aura that pervades this town. It's a city with an irrepressible spirit, a noble grand dame on a hilltop throne, proud and resilient after the terrible earthquake of 1906 and the more recent Loma Prieta temblor of 1989.

So . . . if you had only two days in San Francisco, what places would you feel terrible if you missed? Everyone's tastes are different, but here are a few sites that most folks are sure to enjoy.

Nob Hill, at the top of California and Sacramento Streets, with its posh hotels, private clubs, and smart addresses, retains much of the glamour and gentility it possessed at the end of the 19th century, when men who had made fortunes in silver erected grand mansions for the world to envy on these unobstructed, commanding heights.

From this corner you can catch a cable car for a dashing ride down to Fisherman's Wharf. Clickety-clacking down the California Street hill, you can see straight across the bay—the ride is particularly intriguing at night. And incidentally, it's no accident that all three cable car lines cross Nob Hill. When it was invented in 1873, the cable car made Nob Hill easily accessible for the first time.

Fisherman's Wharf, with its picturesque views, pungent aromas, street performers, steaming crab pots, and fine restaurants, draws many visitors—it's all hustle and bustle during the summer tourist season. Fishing boats bob alongside the wharf, while seagulls float overhead and sea lions bask and bark on large rafts moored at the wharf's edge. Local gourmets (and commoners alike) consider West Coast Dungeness crab among the best seafood in the world. Walkaway shrimp cocktails are sold from the sidewalk, along with clam chowder and sourdough bread, and it's pleasant to nibble on a little seafood while watching the fishing boats return. Parking is available in public lots along Beach and North Point Streets. (If you crave the best seafood in town and would rather avoid the crowds at Fisherman's Wharf, get on Geary Street and drive west until you're near the ocean. Your destination is the Pacific Cafe, at 7000 Geary. They don't take reservations, but you can sip a glass of wine on the sidewalk while you wait. You won't be disappointed.)

While in the neighborhood, you might want to walk down to the Hyde Street Pier and look at the tall 19th-century ships permanently berthed there. Ghirardelli Square, a short walk uphill on Hyde Street, is one of San Francisco's most successful attempts to hang onto the transient past. Until 1964 it was a crumbling, abandoned factory that had once turned out Civil War uniforms and later served as a chocolate factory where Domingo Ghirardelli made cocoa. Steamship magnate William Matson Roth saved the old beauty from the wrecker's ball and made it a showcase—one of the most pleasurable places in the city. Within the rambling complex are a dozen fine restaurants, snug cafes, and almost 100 shops and galleries.

The Cannery, just down the street on Leavenworth, is where Del Monte once tinned fruit. Now it's a delightful and original collection of sprightly shops, art galleries, and restaurants; a place to buy French lingerie, English antiques, primitive art, and the newest in contemporary furniture. Often there's entertainment in the courtyard—small combo bands, magicians, and jugglers.

Alcatraz Island, once the end of the line and the beginning of hopelessness for federal prisoners, is now part of a national park. It can be reached by boats that leave several times a day from Pier 41 at Fisherman's Wharf. A cellblock tour gives some insight into life behind bars for men like Al Capone and Machine Gun Kelly, who lived out their days here without visitors.

Those who are curious (and not claustrophobic) are allowed to spend 60 seconds in the "dark hole" where the recalcitrant spent countless days and nights on the damp cement floors. An excellent audio tour narrated by former guards and inmates is full of fascinating anecdotes about some of the more notorious criminals, escape attempts, and the prison riot of 1946. Plan on staying at least a couple of hours on the island to soak in the history, and dress warmly. Same-day tickets are available at Pier 41 (you'll run into long lines in summer), or you can get them one month in advance by calling (415) 705-5555.

Union Square, the only green area laid out by early planners, forms the heart of the city's downtown shopping district. Posh boutiques extend a few blocks down each street as well as around the square, as do Neiman Marcus, Saks Fifth Avenue, Gucci, and Hermes.

Chinatown is just a short walk up Grant Avenue from Union Square. This "city within a city" is home to more Chinese than any other place outside of Asia. Some 80,000 San Franciscans live, work, shop, worship, and play in Chinatown. It's packed with open-air markets, a variety of bakeries, restaurants, temples, souvenir shops, and, yes, people. Grant Avenue is touristy, but Stockton Street, a block west of Grant, offers a real taste of Chinatown. Tearooms, temples, Chinese schools, and shops lining the streets offer exotic produce and delicacies such as yellow croaker salted fish, dried papaw, dried fish peel, and dried black fungus.

For a rare treat, stop for a dim sum lunch at one of the restaurants offering this unusual fare. Waitresses wheel different carts around the room, each offering a unique cornucopia of delights—some of it mysterious, all of it delicious. They call out their particular specialty in Chinese, and you order whatever you like. The challenge is making room for it all, as every one is good! (Some restaurants sell their more popular items, such as steamed pork buns, in to-go bakery-style cases for those who want to savor this delicacy on the run.)

To get a real Insider's view of Chinatown take one of the many walking tours. Among the best is Wok Wiz, operated by a long-time Chinatown native who knows its history, culture, and food customs. Call (415) 355-9657 for more information.

Between Chinatown and Fisherman's Wharf is North Beach, the Italian district of the city. Pasta, provolone, bocce, and dark, rich espresso are in abundance here, as are a wide variety of cafes, galleries, small theatres, and nightclubs. Beat poets Jack Kerouac, Allen Ginsberg, and William Burroughs chose North Beach as their principal hangout, contributing to San Francisco's international reputation as a funky, hip literary city. In 1953, Lawrence Ferlinghetti, then a struggling poet who later became a Beat legend, opened City Lights Books at 261 Columbus Avenue. It has since become one of the city's most cherished landmarks, as well as a leader among the many feisty independent booksellers that have staked their claim in the Bay Area. For the full Beat experience, wander through the little store's voluminous stacks, then take 10 steps across Jack Kerouac Alley to lift a tall, cool one at Vesuvio's Bar—a legendary watering hole that still draws the city's more colorful creative types.

If you're down in North Beach, look around you and imagine the whole place under-water. Why? Because it was. Early in the city's history both North Beach and Chinatown were awash in baywater. Landfilling extended the city's reach into the bay. Still, the sea is always near, if not in sight then in its salty smells or the sound of the sea lions or the moan of a ship's foghorn. The real place to get the feel of the Pacific is along the Great Highway. If you start at Point Lobos Avenue and the Great Highway, you can visit Cliff House, a once-famous resort area that overlooks the ocean and nearby Seal Rock. From there, the long windswept strand of Ocean Beach stretches to the great sand dunes to the south. Leave your bathing suit at the hotel, and stay out of the roiling surf, where the southbound tidal currents traveling at 12 mph have a habit of swallowing swimmers and surfers alike.

Along this highway you'll discover an entrance to Golden Gate Park, the city's great green retreat, bordered by the Great Highway, Lincoln Way, Stanyan, and Fulton Streets. When the park was built in 1887, it comprised 730 acres of dunes and 270 acres of arable land. Today, its 1,000 acres are lush with meadows, lakes, and 5,000 varieties of shrubs, flowers, and trees. Within its borders you can visit two art museums, an aquarium, a planetarium, and a plant conservatory that looks a lot like Kew Gardens in London. You can watch a polo game, gaze at buffaloes grazing, rent a bike, hear a Sunday band concert, or stop for lunch at the beautifully landscaped Japanese Tea Garden. The park also includes a nifty nine-hole pitch-and-putt golf course, possibly the best-kept golf facility in town.

When the sun begins its slow descent into the ocean and the late afternoon fog snakes its tendrils over the hills and into the bay, the city takes on a more romantic feel. San Francisco may be a sightseer's paradise during the day, but it is also a great place to spend an evening. Ease into a silky-smooth night of jazz at the New Orleans room at the Fairmont Hotel, California and Mason Streets, and also inquire as to who's playing at the velvet-gloved and sedate Venetian room there. Give an amen for some soulful gospel music at Biscuits and Blues, 401 Mason Street, or enjoy an evening of comedy at Punch Line, 444 Battery Street. One of the best comedy shows in town is the long-running Beach Blanket Babylon at Club

Insiders' Tip

Though it seems as if it's been around forever, the fortune cookie is not an ancient Asian delicacy. It was invented in San Francisco about a century ago by Makota Hagiwara, who was a gardener at the Japanese Tea Garden in Golden Gate Park.

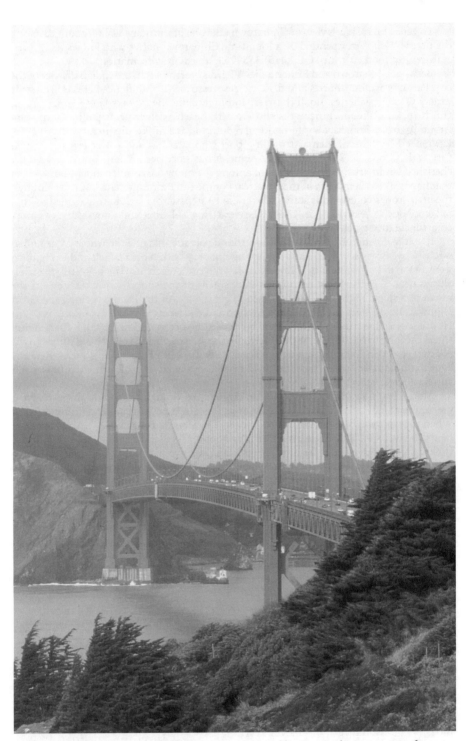

Spanning more than a mile of open water, San Francisco's Golden Gate Bridge is a must stop for any first-time visitor to the city. PHOTO: JOHN NAGIECKI

Fugazi, 678 Green Street. It's wacky, it's fun, and it's ever-changing—skewering whatever and whoever has recently shaken up our pop culture.

Of course, this listing of attractions only scratches the surface. It is said that everyone who visits San Francisco wants to come back again, and our tour leaves plenty more to see on a return trip. It would be nice, for instance, to take in the Cable Car Barn and Museum on Washington and Mason Streets to see the historic old paraphernalia and glimpse the innards of these machines in action. (Just how does that cable car work anyway?) Kids and parents alike should see the Exploratorium, Marina Boulevard and Lyon Street, which contains more than 600 interactive science exhibits.

Fort Mason is where a million good-byes were said during World War II. Now it's a regional cultural center with workshops and studios. A local delight is to walk across the Golden Gate Bridge on a Sunday and tarry on the far side for a magnificent view of San Francisco.

The city's Victorian architecture is almost as famous as its cable cars. Handsome and slightly irrational, painted brightly in all combinations of colors, these structures are certainly unique. Some of the best can be seen on Pacific Heights, particularly on these streets: Vallejo, Broadway, Pacific, Jackson, Washington, Pierce, and Scott, generally in blocks between 1600 and 3000.

Another distinctive neighborhood you might want to see is Cole Valley. This is a recently semigentrified annex to the Haight-Ashbury district, that place once filled with disaffected youth and made famous during the "Summer of Love" in 1967. Cole Valley is home to one of San Francisco's best but least-publicized cafes, Zazie, at 941 Cole Street.

Of course, there are other restaurants you may want to try during your short San Francisco visit. Pane e Vino is a well-camouflaged eating spot, tucked just below the trendy Union Street shopping zone at 3011 Steiner Street. This is a simple, well-attended Italian cafe, within walking distance of Perry's, at 1944 Union Street. More than just a sports bar or watering hole, Perry's is one of San Francisco's see-and-be-seen hangouts in the same genre as North Beach's Washington Square Bar and Grill (1707 Powell Street) and Moose's (across Washington Square at 1652 Stockton Street). Between these last two landmarks stands the cherished Italian restaurant, Fior d'Italia, at 601 Union Street and the city's definitive espresso bar, Mario's Bohemian Cigar Store, at 566 Columbus Avenue.

After your double espresso, you might get an urge to trot four or five blocks north to the corner of Columbus and Bay Street for a museum-like tour of another cathedral of sorts, Tower Records. Careful observers on this route will note they've come full circle to the end of the Powell Street cable car line, hard by Fisherman's Wharf.

After walking this far, we hope you're still warm. One thing visitors should keep in mind is that San Francisco weather is, well, unlike what you would expect. True,

Insiders' Tip

San Francisco is home to one of the world's largest gay and lesbian communities. If you want to know more about the blossoming of this colorful segment of society, take a stroll over to the city's main library on 100 Larkin Street for a look at the extensive gay and lesbian history collection. And if you are visiting in the month of June, watch for the Gay Pride Day parade, one of the city's more popular and entertaining annual events.

temperatures don't often vary outside a range of 50 to 70 degrees, summer or winter. But sometimes January and February can be the sunniest, most glorious months. On the other hand, summer can be so cold that tourists who mistakenly thought California called for tank tops and flip-flops huddle in downtown doorways to keep warm. Mark Twain reportedly once said, "The coldest winter I ever spent was a summer in San Francisco." So you may want to have that sweater or jacket handy if you're walking about. What is the best time of year to visit? Locals will tell you the most pleasant months are September and October.

Much like Manhattan and some quaint and compact European cities, San Francisco is best enjoyed by walking its many neighborhoods. Besides, driving a car in San Francisco—and then trying to park it here and there—can be an exercise in futility. But if you must drive, be prepared for the traffic idiosyncrasies you will encounter.

In negotiating the city by automobile, be aware of red-light-running fools (the city has had a spate of them), and expect traffic jams at any hour. On-street parking is virtually nonexistent—at best scarce—and those who overstay their legal welcome are subject to heavy fines and might even be clamped with "the boot," which immobilizes the vehicle. An impounded car is endless trouble to retrieve.

Fortunately there are a number of public parking facilities, one of the handiest offering underground parking is at Union Square. In hilly San Francisco, it is illegal to park a car on most hills (technically, those exceeding a grade of 3 percent) without setting your parking brake and turning the wheels into the curb. When parking uphill the wheels must be "heeled," with the inside front tire resting securely against the curb. Parking downhill, tires must be "toed"—turned in.

Complicated enough for you? We recommend parking your car when you first arrive and forgetting about it until you're ready to leave town. You'll be glad you did.

So if you only have a day or, heaven forbid, even less, and you're still wondering what to do, our advice is this: Go out and simply walk. Enjoying yourself comes easy here. It costs nothing to breathe the fragrance of a vendor's flowers on Union Square, hike up Telegraph Hill—where rowhouses climb steep slopes—take in the breathtaking view from Coit Tower at the crest, stroll through Chinatown or Little Italy, or photograph the busy fleet at Fisherman's Wharf. And don't worry, you will be back.

Flora, Fauna, and Climate

Geology
Soil
Climate
Flora
Fauna

Upon arriving in the Santa Rosa area in 1875, famed horticulturist Luther Burbank could barely contain his excitement, declaring that "this is the chosen spot of all earth as far as Nature is concerned." Many Wine Country visitors have since echoed Burbank's sentiments, inspired by the bucolic scenery and the mild Mediterranean climate. From the marshes of San Pablo Bay to the mountains of Mendocino National Forest, and from the roaring Pacific to shimmering Clear Lake, the terrain is rarely less than wondrous. Few places on the face of the planet are so blessed with natural gifts.

Every season reveals a different facet to the landscape. In spring, a kaleidoscope of wildflowers lines the roadsides. In summer, the grapevines practically beam with verdant life. In fall, the fields are quilted in bright patches of red and orange. And in winter, always wet but not too harsh, a misty and mysteriously beautiful hush descends on the hills and valleys. But that's not all. Behind the Wine Country's ever changing beauty lies a fascinating natural history. Though we can't attempt to summarize all there is to tell, we have brought together a sampling of some more salient geologic, climatic, and ecological features.

Geology

A hundred million years ago, the Wine Country area was exceptionally poor as a grape-growing region. In fact, all of it was under water. It took a lot of tectonic activity—movement of the massive plates that together form the Earth's crust—to swing Napa, Sonoma, and environs eastward onto dry land. It was all part of the succession of north-south "island arcs" that violently, if patiently, crashed into the North American continent and sent California on the way to its modern-day topography, which includes the prominent Mayacmas Mountains—which divide Sonoma and Napa and Lake and Mendocino Counties—and the steep Coast Range.

Of course, the movement hasn't exactly stopped altogether, and you can feel their effects every now and then. The renowned San Andreas system, a massive network of strike-slip faults that forms the border between the Pacific and North American tectonic plates, runs the length of Sonoma and Mendocino Counties, sometimes on the mainland and some-times beneath the sea. Several smaller, generally north-south faults lurk beneath the Wine Country, including the Rodgers Creek Fault, which caused some destruction in Santa Rosa with a 1969 quake that measured 5.7 on the Richter scale.

Things could be worse. In fact, they used to be. Much of the current four-county area was the scene of frightful volcanic activity three to four million years ago. Those eruptions, combined with unrelenting seismic activity, have given California's North Coast ranges a highly complex geologic profile. And this is of more than theoretical interest, for two of the lures that historically have drawn people to the region are direct results of geology.

The most obvious of these is geothermal activity. Sonoma and Napa Counties are pierced by fault "pipelines" that send water heated by magma 8 miles below the earth's surface percolating upward. In the Calistoga area you can pay to gawk at a burst of hot water (at the Old Faithful Geyser) or to soak in the stuff (at the many spas). And around one section of the

And because soil composition greatly affects the chemistry of a growing grape, it follows that precisely where you plant your vines has a lot to do with the quality of your wine.

The soil within a single vineyard can vary substantially. Red soil tends to produce soft wine; light, "fluffy" soils are known for hard, austere wines; and gravelly ground, which has a hard time holding water, tends to result in earthy wines. Moreover, wine made from hillside grapes usually is riskier and more robust than valley wine, because the grapes are smaller and therefore have a higher skin-to-pulp ratio. (The intense flavor is in the skin.) And some of the best vineyard soil in Napa Valley is found on the Oakville and Rutherford "benches"—broad, nutrient-rich alluvial fans that have been washed from the Mayacmas Mountains.

Of course, all of this is gross oversimplification. We provide more information on the whole business of "appellations"— slightly varied microclimates that produce grapes and yield wines with specific, refined characteristics—in our Wineries chapter, but sorting out such details is what separates a successful vintner from the rest of us guzzlers. The point is that, in a manner of speaking, the Merlot you're savoring today has been in the works for about 100 million years.

Climate

Northern California is one of five regions in the world that enjoys a Mediterranean climate, characterized by warm, dry summers and mild, moist winters. While the area's geographic location helps to shape its climate—Santa Rosa is about par with Athens on the latitude scale—local environmental influences are also important. Weather varies dramatically throughout the four counties, and you can often find a huge difference in conditions just by driving a few miles.

To understand what causes Wine Country weather, think of the Pacific Ocean as a giant climate-control device, set on MILD. In general, the farther you stray from salt water, the hotter your sum-

Sonoma-Lake County border, geothermal sites are even used to generate electricity. In fact, the Geysers steam field weighs in as the world's largest complex (19 units) of geothermal power plants, owned and operated by the Calpine Corporation.

But the peculiar North Coast geology has spawned a lot more than mud baths. The second regional drawing card with its roots in plate tectonics is the mighty grapevine.

Soil

Soils reflect the rocks they used to be, so it makes sense that an area of convoluted geology will contain many types of soil.

mers will be and the colder your winters. Temperature variations along the coast are minuscule, and river towns such as Guerneville and Napa also are fairly mild. There's only about a 5-degree differential in the usual maximum winter high temperature on the Mendocino Coast (56 degrees) and the average summer high (the low 60s). Though coastal winter nights are cooler, they don't often see temperatures drop lower than 40. There is morning summer fog and evening sea breezes.

That is in stark contrast to places such as Ukiah, Calistoga, and Middletown, where hilly terrain serves as a barrier to ocean influences. Each of these towns can be uncomfortably still and hot in August. Inland Lake County reaches upward of 100 degrees regularly in summer, and its winters can dip well below the freezing mark. On the other hand, when it's hot, it qualifies as "dry heat." Californians tend to consider that phrase a meaningless cliche, but long-suffering Midwesterners and Easterners can immediately feel the difference. A 100-degree day is a test no matter how you look at it, but the night air has a chance to cool considerably when humidity is low.

Rainfall, too, varies across the Wine Country. Cobb Mountain, in southwest Lake County, receives about 60 inches of rain a year. The Mendocino Coast gets about 39 inches, St. Helena about 34, and the Clear Lake Basin about 25. Regardless of volume, however, you can expect most of the rain between November and February, with residual storms in March and April. Summer and fall downpours are rare here.

We would be remiss if we failed to mention winter flooding in the Wine Country. Most areas are nothing worse than soggy, but the Russian and Napa rivers have overflowed their banks several times in recent years. The Russian River area, in particular, can be vulnerable to flooding (hundreds were evacuated in January 1997).

In general, spring and autumn are the best months to visit. The weather is exceptional, and there is added color from wildflowers or turning leaves. Summer temperatures in Sonoma County usually edge into the mid-80s, but the nights are still comfortable (chilly even), with the mercury falling into the 50s.

Insiders' Tip

Take a deep breath: For more than a decade, Lake County has met or exceeded standards for air quality set by the California Air Resources Board. In fact, it's the only area in the state with such a record. Those standards include levels of ozone, carbon monoxide, nitrogen, and a cocktail of other contaminants that give urban air its grimy color and aroma—and which are absent in the air over Lake County.

Flora

A flora list from the Covelo Ranger District in Mendocino National Forest alone refers to 18 different coniferous trees, 13 varieties of oak, 6 types of willow, and 6 species of manzanita. So we won't try to construct any sort of comprehensive list here—it would be voluminous. We can, however, state a few generalities.

The valley floors of the Wine Country were covered by native bunch grasses before the arrival of European settlers, but they proved to be especially sensitive to trampling by livestock. Spanish explorers,

The development of the Shasta daisy was one of Luther Burbank's renowned accomplishments. PHOTO: JOHN NAGIECKI

who carried feed grain for their horses and mules, were among the first Europeans to introduce "exotic" grasses: ryegrass, bromes, foxtail, wild oats, and the like.

Two types of ecosystem—oak woodland and chaparral—dominate the rolling hills of Napa and Sonoma Counties. It's impossible to drive along U.S. 101 or Highway 29 without noticing the stolid oak trees, but the collection includes many varieties. Coast live oaks are perhaps the most impressive, with a single tree able to spread its branches up to 130 feet. These trees prefer moist locations, such as creek bottoms and north slopes. Canyon live oaks, with their exceptionally hard wood, thrive on steep hillsides. Blue oaks like hot, dry slopes, and California black

oaks pop up on mesas with deep soil and gentle slopes.

Chaparral, made up of shrubs such as manzanita, ceanothus, and toyon, is more closely associated with the hills of southern California, but it is prevalent here too. It is an inhospitable environment for humans designed to burn—many of its plant species have highly flammable oils in their bark and the underbrush can be thorny and impenetrable.

While most of the grapes are grown at lower elevation, the Wine Country counties include a lot of mountainous, forested topography. That's especially true in the upper half of Lake County and the northeast corner of Mendocino County, which form part of Mendocino National Forest.

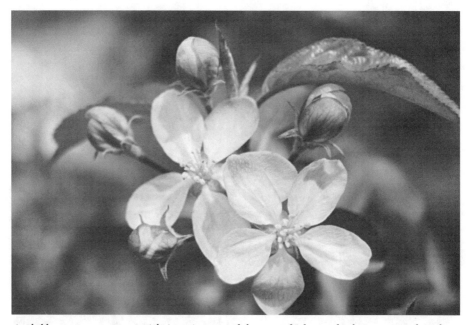

Apple blossoms are a common sight in spring around the town of Sebastopol, where an annual Apple Blossom Festival is held in April. PHOTO: JAN BLANCHARD

The standout citizen of the damp, misty Coast Range forests is the coast redwood, the tallest tree in the world. Though Mendocino and Sonoma have several preserves devoted to redwoods (see our Parks and Recreation chapter), the biggest of all are found in Humboldt County (see "The Big Trees" section of our Daytrippin' chapter). You might also stumble on a redwood in steep, darker canyons along Wine Country streams. Other dominant trees include the ponderosa pine, with its arrow-straight trunk; the Pacific madrone, whose gnarled trunk will creep 50 feet horizontally to find sunlight; and the Douglas fir, the Western Hemisphere's premier lumber tree.

No matter which Wine Country microclimate you're in, you are likely to see wildflowers if your timing is sound. Somewhere between February and June, depending on elevation and intensity of sunlight, literally hundreds of shrubs and herbs burst into bloom. The most eyecatching include the California poppy—the bright orange state flower that pops up just about anywhere—and mustard, which lays a breathtaking yellow carpet in the early spring vineyards (and inspires all sorts of reverent celebrations—see our Festivals and Events chapter). Other native wildflowers to look for include orchids, irises, monkey flowers, Indian paintbrushes, golden bushes, wild roses, lupines, violets, shooting stars, fiddlenecks, lilies, wild onions, and buttercups.

Fauna

It isn't exactly a jungle out here, but keen observers will spy a wide range of furry, feathered, or fishy creatures in the Wine Country.

Drive the scenic routes at dusk in summer and fall, and you are likely to see the omnipresent black-tailed deer nibbling scrub oak or buckbrush in the meadows. You are even more likely to see skunks, raccoons, and opossums, though it might be in the form of roadkill. They are among the most common of the region's mammals, especially in semideveloped areas. The more mountainous areas are home to all sorts of animals, including black bears, mountain lions, and bobcats, coyotes,

Distinctive abalone shells hang as ornaments around the yards of coastal homes. PHOTO: JOHN NAGIECKI

Bodega Bay, made famous by Alfred Hitchcock's The Birds, *continues to attract the feathered creatures.* PHOTO: TINA LUSTER-HOBAN

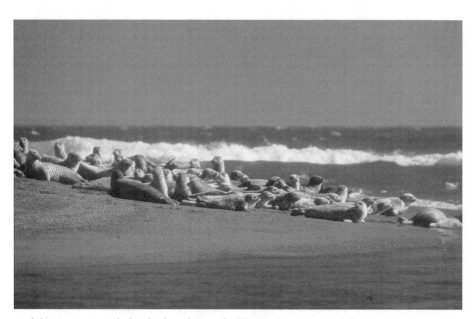

Seals love to cavort on the beach where the mouth of the Russian River meets the Sonoma County coastline. PHOTO: JOHN NAGIECKI

bats, diminutive gray foxes, porcupines, badgers, feral pigs, and even the occasional ring-tailed cat or tule elk. Many of them are nocturnal and all are elusive, but they are out there, trying to stay downwind of the humans. Once in a while, however, a bear or bobcat wanders into the eastern city limits of Santa Rosa, nestled along the western side of the Mayacmas Mountains, in search of some easy food and water. A mountain lion even startled commuters one afternoon when it strolled onto U.S. 101—a jungle of a different sort!—in the middle of the city. Though these sightings are rare, it serves to remind us that we are surrounded by wild and unpredictable beauty.

The rugged coastal areas have their own communities: seals and sea lions on the rocks; river otters in the estuaries; and gray whales offshore, migrating southward from the Bering Sea to Baja California between December and April. The nutrient-rich waters of the coastal areas also teem with a variety of benthic life, including eight species of the highly desirable—and highly endangered—abalone. River otters are found in much of the

Wine Country's freshwater. The reptile and amphibian crowd includes alligator lizards, pond turtles, king snakes, rubber boas, skinks, and the ones you need to watch out for: western rattlesnakes.

The local waterways—primarily the Napa, Eel, and Russian rivers—are dominated by anadromous fish, that is, species that travel from the sea to spawn in fresh water. The three big fish in the Wine Country (as in most of northern California) are Chinook salmon, coho salmon, and steelhead—the latter are basically rainbow trout that have learned to migrate. Most of the good lake fishing is for bass (smallmouth and largemouth) and catfish, though none of them are native sons. (See more on fishing in our On the Water chapter.)

Audubon Society chapters are active throughout the four-county region, and they have plenty to catalogue. There are swallows and swifts, American robins, and northern mockingbirds, woodpeckers and warblers, finches and flycatchers. There are at least six species of hawk and seven species of owl, including the northern spotted, that rather harmless old-growth percher despised by a generation of loggers.

Golden eagles (the nation's largest raptor, with a wingspan of up to 7 feet), ospreys, kestrels, and peregrine falcons ride the thermals along high bluffs and cliff faces. Peregrines, with a maximum flight speed of up to 275 mph, have been known to overtake small airplanes. Herons and egrets poke about in swampy spots, such as the Napa-Sonoma Marshes Wildlife Area, south of those two towns, and we've got a varied collection of ducks and geese. And if jet lag and ambitious winetasting have you feeling dehydrated and fatigued, don't fret too much about those California turkey vultures circling overhead. It's nothing personal—the hefty, red-faced scavengers are quite populous in the Wine Country.

Hotels, Motels, and Inns

Napa County
Sonoma County
Mendocino County
Lake County

Some folks love the bed-and-breakfast inn experience. Some don't. If you fall into the latter category, take heart: Not every guest room in Wine Country is swathed in Laura Ashley prints and crammed with antiques and teddy bears. In this chapter we will familiarize you with other options available for a good night's sleep. Some are full-service hotels that can be as charming and cozy as B&Bs (but with more amenities), and some are less expensive, basic motel rooms.

Our hotels reflect the dichotomy of this region: cosmopolitan, yes; metropolitan, no. Business people who come for conferences and meetings find themselves bedded down not in structures of glass and steel but in low-lying resort hotels with golf, tennis, swimming, horseback riding, and winery tours serving as relaxing options. Facilities may be ultramodern and services may match any big-city hotel, but the nation's business travelers share these accommodations with plain old tourists from all over the globe.

Other hotels in smaller towns are built to appeal to the thousands of visitors who swarm to vine land in summer and on weekends to bask in the rural atmosphere and savor the hospitality of the wineries.

Such hotels are often tucked right in the midst of vineyards. Some have a small-town, homey aura; others are posh and extravagant—and expensive. And many of those establishments with "motel" in their name offer above-average luxury.

So, contemplating this mixture of rural life and cosmopolitan airs, how do we define a hotel or motel? When is a hotel a resort? What's a country inn? How big can a bed-and-breakfast be before it becomes a hostelry?

For this chapter we define hotels and motels as structures that were built for the express intent of providing lodging. For our purposes, bed-and-breakfast inns are places with few guest rooms, places that may have started out as someone's residence. Everything else, especially anything with a staff and a dining room, is rated as a hotel or motel.

Unless we state otherwise, assume that hotels and motels take major credit cards (check when you call to see if your plastic of choice is included) and that pets are not welcome. Although California smoking laws are extremely stringent, many hotels listed provide rooms for their guests who smoke, but always inquire when calling for information. Expect that all entries will have color TV.

Hotels and motels are listed using the geographical sequence explained in our How to Use This Book chapter. We start with the Napa County accommodations, followed by those in Sonoma, Mendocino, and Lake Counties. Afterward we give agencies specializing in vacation rentals.

Insiders' Tip

Need help locating accommodations? Call Napa Valley Reservations Unlimited at (800) 251-NAPA or, within the area, at (707) 252-1985 or (707) 944-0709 or by visiting www.napavalley reservations.com. They will assist you in selecting a hotel, motel, resort, bed-and-breakfast inn, or condo, and they won't charge you a cent.

Price Code

The schedule of dollar sign symbols shown below indicates the approximate price range for a one-night, weekend, double-occupancy stay, not including tax, gratuities, or other add-on amenities such as room service or premium movie channels.

$ . . . . .Less than $70
$$ . . . .$71 to $110
$$$ . . . .$111 to $150
$$$$ . . . .$151 to $200
$$$$$ . . . . .More than $200

Napa County

Embassy Suites Napa Valley $$$$$
1075 California Blvd., Napa
(707) 253–9540, (800) 362–2779
www.embassynapa.com

In a valley where "business" usually takes the form of buying wine by the bottle and drinking it for lunch, this is as close as it comes to a high-end business traveler's hotel. A group of three-story, canary-and-burgundy buildings, the Embassy Suites offers a nice combination of corporate know-how and Wine Country charm. There are indoor and outdoor pools, wet and dry saunas, swans in the koi pond, and a soaring lobby with terra-cotta tiles and parlor chairs. Every guest unit is a two-room suite with extra pullout sofa, wet bar, and microwave. The tariff includes a full, cooked-to-order breakfast and an afternoon Manager's Reception with complimentary drinks. And if you really are here on business, Embassy Suites boasts eight meeting rooms (arranged around the Fountain Court), full conference facilities, and two-line phones with modem access in each room.

Napa Valley Marriott $$$$
3425 Solano Ave., Napa
(707) 253–7433, (800) 228–9290
www.marriott.com

If you have come to rely on the Marriott chain for its dependable accommodations, this outpost won't let you down. The 191-room hotel (including four suites) is just off Highway 29, north of the Trancas Street/Redwood Road exit. Each room has individual climate control, in-room pay movies, iron and ironing board, a work desk, and voice mail. The Harvest Cafe, specializing in steaks and California vegetables, serves breakfast and dinner; Character's Sports Bar & Grill serves lunch and dinner. For $10 extra, you can get breakfast along with your room. The Marriott also has a heated outdoor pool and Jacuzzi, lighted tennis courts, and a fitness center. And one entire level of the hotel gets down to business, with 8,500 square feet of flexible meeting space that can handle groups of 15 to 500.

Milliken Creek Inn $$$$$
1815 Silverado Trail, Napa
(707) 255–1197, (888) 622–5775
www.millikencreekinn.com

In its short life, this new "boutique inn" set on the Napa River has become one of the valley's most luxurious and popular retreats for couples wanting to get away from it all. It's only two minutes to Copia (see our Attractions chapter) and downtown Napa's restaurants, yet you will feel far removed from city life. (The property dates from the 1800s, when the old carriage house was a stagecoach stop.) More than a bed and breakfast inn, but not a hotel or a spa resort, it's in a class by itself. Once the rundown Country Garden Inn, it's a completely new environment following a million-dollar makeover. Luxurious and inviting, it's in a tranquil setting, thanks to the natural expanse of the river wherever you look. (Don't forget to wave to the kayakers.) Enhancing the grounds are gardens, fountains, Adirondack chairs, and even a waterfall and koi pond.

The innkeepers, Lisa Holt and David Shapiro, have many years of experience in the upscale hotel industry, and it shows in their attention to detail. The guest rooms are elegantly noncluttered, in what Lisa calls "British campaign" design, but these rooms have modern amenities such as DVD players (there's a lending library of 200 movie titles), well-appointed mini-bars, telephones with modem hookups, and in-room continental breakfast service. Many of the rooms come with fireplaces and genuine spa tubs, Italian linens, and terry robes. There's even a pillow menu—soft or firm, feather or foam? The Milliken Suites have private decks perched overlooking the river (and terrific sunsets). The Cottage is the most private room on the property and includes a walk-in closet, wet bar, and dining area in addition to river views. In early evening guests can sip wine in the lobby while watching David tickle the ivories on the piano (he's an accomplished jazz musician). Massage and spa treatments, along with private yoga classes, are offered on-site. Needless to say, this inn is intended for the enjoyment of couples.

Napa River Inn $$$$$
500 Main St., Napa
(707) 251–8500, (877) 251–8500
www.napariverinn.com

When the historic Napa Mill and Hatt Building were renovated along the Napa River in 2000, this spanking new hotel was the result. It offers luxury accommodations in 66 guestrooms and suites in various themes—from nautical to "California rustic" to vintage 1800s. All rooms feature large TVs, two-line data and voice ports, refrigerators, and in-room coffee. Many rooms have fireplaces, river views, and balconies. A full-service spa is nearby for use by guests, and restaurants and shops are handy right next door in the newly refurbished Hatt Market building. The room tariffs for weekends range from $225 to $500—slightly less during the week. All rooms are nonsmoking.

Wine Valley Lodge $$
200 S. Coombs St., Napa
(707) 224–7911, (800) 696–7911
www.winevalleylodge.com

South of downtown Napa, close to Highway 121, the Mission-style Lodge has 53 guest rooms. There is a heated pool in the motor court, and complimentary continental breakfast on summer weekends. Ask about the Elvis Presley and Marilyn Monroe suites, which run a bit higher in price and larger in size, each sleeping four adults comfortably. The stars stayed in these rooms at different times several decades ago—The King was making a movie nearby, but nobody seems to remember the reason Marilyn checked in.

Best Western Inn at the Vines $$$
100 Soscol Ave., Napa
(707) 257–1930, (877) 846–3729
www.innatthevines.com

Best Western offers few surprises, which is probably why it's one of America's most popular chains. The Napa version has 68 rooms, including eight suites. Two of the suites are loft-style, with a bed upstairs and living room below; others are one-level units with sitting rooms. All rooms have cable TV and refrigerators. There is a heated pool and spa, a meeting room for up to 50 people, and a 24-hour Denny's restaurant on the property. This is a non-smoking hotel.

Hawthorn Inn & Suites $$$$
314 Soscol Ave., Napa
(707) 226–1878, (800) 527–1133
www.napavalleyinns.com

One of Napa's newest hotels is this 60-room, three-story structure that focuses on comfort, with a nod to business travelers. The rooms are wired with two phone lines with voice mail and data ports, and there are irons, ironing boards, and executive chairs with oversized desks. Business services, a daily newspaper, and a board room for meetings are also available. The

Insiders' Tip

When figuring your travel budget, don't forget the occupancy tax, which varies from place to place. To take Napa County as an example, the charge is 12 percent of the bill if you are within city limits, 10 percent if you're in an unincorporated area.

deluxe suites have in-room Jacuzzis. Vacationers who like a little exercise will appreciate the hotel's swimming pool and spa, as well as the fitness center. A hot breakfast buffet is offered every morning from 7:00 to 9:00 A.M.

Napa Valley Downtown Travelodge $$$
853 Coombs St., Napa
(707) 226–1871, (800) 578–7878
www.travelodge.com

If location is everything, the Travelodge has it all. The downtown Napa locale puts you two blocks from Riverwalk, four blocks from the Wine Train depot (see our Getting Here chapter), and a few steps away from shops and cafes. The 45-room motel has a heated pool. Each unit comes with a two-line phone with a fax port, individual air-conditioning, and a big-screen TV with VCR. Movie rentals are available through the motel.

Chardonnay Lodge $
2640 Jefferson St., Napa
(707) 224–0789

The lodge offers convenient Napa centrality and beds of various proportions. The 20 rooms are air-conditioned, and they have phones and cable TV.

The Chateau $$$
4195 Solano Ave., Napa
(707) 253–9300

Somewhere between a budget motel and a major corporate hotel, The Chateau offers comfort and reliability, if not luxury. The 115 rooms are sizable, and each has a separate vanity dressing area and individual climate control. The two-story motel has six spacious suites too, with wet bars and fold-out couches. Also on the grounds are two conference centers that hold up to 500 people, and a swimming pool and spa. Kids 12 and younger stay free in the same room as their guardians.

The John Muir Inn $$$
1998 Trower Ave., Napa
(707) 257–7220, (800) 522–8999
www.johnmuirnapa.com

We can't imagine John Muir, the naturalist who wandered through the Sierra Nevada range stocked with nothing more than a pocket full of biscuits, staying here at the intersection of Trower Avenue and Highway 29. But, hey, the inn that bears his name is very environmentally conscious. Anyway, Muir might have gone for the cable TV with Showtime. The hotel is a solid midpriced choice with a courtyard swimming pool and whirlpool spa, conference room, a 24-hour front desk, and free continental breakfast. About one-quarter of the 60 rooms have kitchenettes, and some have wet bars or private spas. Children 14 and younger stay free. There is no restaurant at the inn, but Marie Callendar's is within shouting distance. The entire property is a smoke-free environment.

Yountville Inn $$$$$
6462 Washington St., Yountville
(707) 944–5600, (800) 972–2293
www.yountvilleinn.com

One of the midvalley's newest options is Yountville Inn, nestled against Hopper Creek. The rambling hotel has seven buildings and 51 bright and spacious rooms. Each unit boasts a fieldstone fireplace, French doors leading to a patio, a wood-beamed ceiling, and a refrigerator. All guests receive free continental breakfast. The inn also has a heated pool and spa, and is near the Vintners Golf Club (see our Parks & Recreation chapter). Should you be mixing business with pleasure, the elegantly comfortable Club Room facilitates groups of up to 60 people.

Napa Valley Railway Inn $$$
6503 Washington St., Yountville
(707) 944–2000

If the kids are along, you'll probably want to stay here, just south of Vintage 1870. The rooms are restored cabooses and boxcars, nine in all, sitting on original track from the defunct Napa Valley Railroad. Being train cars, the living space tends to be l-o-n-g and narrow, perhaps 8-by-40 feet. Each room has a queen bed, air-conditioning, and a private, tiled bathroom. The cars are arranged along two sides of a wooden platform, adding to the whole locomotive picture. And if you have a phobia of rectangular spaces, you can stay in the square Station House Room. Shopping and restaurants are just steps away.

Vintage Inn $$$$$
6541 Washington St., Yountville
(707) 944–1112, (800) 351–1133
www.vintageinn.com

This elegant, country-style inn is spread out on a large, landscaped lot. It has 80 units—basic rooms, mini-suites, and villas—divided between the outer court and the more protected inner court. Most have patios or balconies. All of them have fireplaces and come with a complimentary continental breakfast buffet, including California champagne. Vintage Inn offers room service, a 60-foot lap pool and hot tub, tennis courts, bike rentals in the summer, and a private limousine service. About 15 percent of the rooms are smoker-friendly, and you can even bring your dog if you don't mind plunking down the $25 cleaning fee. The inn also has executive conference facilities that can handle 20 to 200 people.

Napa Valley Lodge $$$$$
2230 Madison St., Yountville
(707) 944–2468, (800) 368–2468
www.napavalleylodge.com

If you've ever stayed at one of Woodside Hotels' Northern California establishments, you'll be keen to reserve a spot at this 55-room hotel at the north end of Yountville, which underwent a $3.5 million facelift in 2000. The new exterior incorporates classic Tuscan-style architecture, with arched loggias, iron railings, and limestone details. Woodside is known for its gracious service and amenities, and Napa Valley Lodge is right in step—from the 400-book lending library and hearth in the lobby to the free champagne buffet breakfast to the Spanish-tile double vanities, duvet bed coverings, and reproduced vintage tapestries in the rooms. About three-fourths of the units have fireplaces, and all feature a balcony or terrace with views to vineyard or pool and gardens.

Besides the pool, the hotel has a spa, a redwood sauna, and a small exercise room, and if they get your blood pumping, you can head to Chardonnay Golf Club (see our Parks and Recreation chapter), where guests receive a weekday discount on

Yountville's Vintage Inn is an elegant getaway, complete with room service, champagne breakfast buffet, lap pool, and private limo service. PHOTO: JEAN SAYLOR DOPPENBERG

greens fees. Napa Valley Lodge does brisk corporate business—not surprising when you note the hotel's two warm, well-appointed conference rooms.

Rancho Caymus Inn $$$$$
1140 Rutherford Cross Rd., Rutherford
(707) 963–1777, (800) 845–1777
www.ranchocaymus.com

If Father Junipero Serra had built a really fancy mission to impress the folks back home in Spain, it might have looked like this. Rancho Caymus, a couple of blocks east of Highway 29 on Rutherford Cross Road (a.k.a. Highway 128), carries off the hacienda motif flawlessly, from the adobe-looking stucco to the tile roof. The rough-hewn white oak and pine beams are salvaged from an 80-year-old barn in Ohio; the parota wood chairs, tables, and dressers are from Guadalajara; and the wool rugs and wall hangings are made by indigenous Ecuadorians. A central, tiled courtyard brims with flowers and small trees.

Most of the 26 units have fireplaces and a split-level layout. Five of them have kitchenettes, and about 65 percent are smoking rooms. Continental breakfast is included, and the site now includes fine dining at chef Ken Frank's La Toque restaurant (see our Restaurants chapter).

This painting by Barbara Beavers captures the beauty of the Spanish-style architecture of Rancho Caymus Inn. PHOTO: RANCHO CAYMUS INN

El Bonita Motel $$$$
195 Main St., St. Helena
(707) 963–3216, (800) 541–3284
www.elbonita.com

The old neon sign and poolside layout point to this motel's roots as a classic 1950s roadside motor hotel, but there have been upgrades galore since then. The 42 rooms are nicely furnished and painted in subdued gray-green tones. About two-thirds have microwaves and refrigerators. Some allow pets. There is a fireplace in the recently remodeled lobby, and each guest receives continental breakfast. Flowers and fountains proliferate in the lawn areas, while the pool is complemented by a sauna and a Jacuzzi.

Harvest Inn $$$$$
1 Main St., St. Helena
(707) 963–WINE, (800) 950–8466
www.harvestinn.com

The Inn's reception building, the Harvest Centre, is built to evoke the English countryside, with its corkscrewed brick chimneys and oak-paneled great room. But "rustic" this place isn't. It is a sprawling, manicured complex that specializes in (but isn't limited to) corporate functions, with conference facilities accommodating as many as 60 captains of industry. On-site catering is available through Pinot Blanc (see our Restaurants chapter). Set between Sutter Home Winery and Sulphur Springs Avenue on the southern fringe of St. Helena, and bordering a 14-acre vineyard, Harvest Inn has 54 rooms. Most of them have king beds, brick fireplaces, wet bars, and dressing vanities, and some have patio balconies. There are two heated pools and whirlpool spas on the grounds, and all guests are served continental breakfast. Most units allow smokers, and some (the ones with hardwood floors) take pets. The rates are too wide-ranging to properly classify—they go from $240 for a small room in winter to $675 for an "imperial suite" on a high-season weekend.

The Wine Country Inn $$$$
1152 Lodi Ln., St. Helena
(707) 963–7077, (888) 465–4608
www.winecountryinn.com

This hard-to-categorize accommodation does a good job of blending the comforts of a bed and breakfast with the convenience of a small hotel. The Wine Country Inn offers a full buffet breakfast, afternoon appetizers and wine tasting, distinctive rooms filled with hand-picked antiques, a large pool and Jacuzzi, a well-trained staff, and easy parking. No matter how the inn is defined, Lodi Lane, about 2 miles north of St. Helena, is hard to beat for serenity. Immediately to the east is a working vineyard; almost all of the 25 rooms have private patios or balconies that practically sit on the trellises. Most units have fireplaces, and some even have private hot tubs. The Wine Country Inn is still a family operation, founded by Ned Smith in 1975. Son Jim Smith runs the place now. Ned's widow, Marge, did most of the quilt work, and his daughter, Kate, did much of the decorative painting. The hotel, popular with honeymooners, caters to adults rather than to families with children.

The Inn at Southbridge $$$$$
1020 Main St., St. Helena
(707) 967-9400, (800) 520-6800

This upscale St. Helena hotel, which opened in November 1995, looks something like a winery with its earth tones and creeping vines. The resemblance is no coincidence, as architect William Turnbull Jr. is known for his winery design. The Inn at Southbridge has 21 ample rooms (only two smoking units), each with a vaulted ceiling, fireplace, sisal-style carpets, and down comforter. French doors open onto a private balcony overlooking the courtyard. The rooms are set up for corporate clients, each having dual phone lines and a fax/modem port. The inn has a lap pool and a full-service health club with steam, weights, and stationary bikes. Guests also enjoy (paid) access to Meadowood resort's recreational facilities—the establishments are co-owned (see our Spas and Resorts chapter for more on Meadowood). The restaurant Tomatina shares space with The Inn at Southbridge (they'll provide room service), and Merryvale Winery is just across the parking lot (see our Wineries chapter).

Hotel St. Helena $$$$
1309 Main St., St. Helena
(707) 963-4388, (888) 478-4355
www.hotelsthelena.com

This restored hotel in the heart of downtown is quintessential St. Helena: immaculate, charming, and not cheap. It was an upscale hotel when it was built back in 1881, but soon deteriorated into a second-floor flophouse over the local Montgomery Ward. Now it has recaptured and redefined its glory. At ground level are shops and a flowery arcade, plus a wine and coffee bar in the lobby. Upstairs are 18 antique-filled rooms painted in combinations of subdued tones: burgundy, mauve, chocolate, dark tan, and pale gold. Four of the rooms share two baths; the rest have private bathrooms, some with old clawfoot tubs. There is a sitting room at the top of the stairs and a TV-equipped solarium overlooking the arcade. A large continental breakfast is included in the price. Occupancy is restricted to two guests unless you rent the spacious Lillie Langtry Suite for $375 per night. Don't bring your cigarettes—this is a non-smoking property.

Calistoga Inn $
1250 Lincoln Ave., Calistoga
(707) 942-4101
www.calistogainn.com

For a no-frills (okay, maybe a couple of frills), ambiance-thick stay in Calistoga, try the Inn, an old Western-style hotel that dates back to 1882. The 18 second-floor rooms, connected by a creaking wood-floored hallway, sit over a restaurant and microbrewery/bar (see our Restaurants and Nightlife chapters). Each room has a sink and a queen or king bed, but there are central, shared bathrooms and showers, and no in-room TVs. At $75 (midweek) and $100 (weekends), including continental breakfast, these are the cheapest tourist digs in town. What's more, the Inn never has more than a one-night minimum stay, a rarity in these parts.

Mount View Hotel $$$$
1457 Lincoln Ave., Calistoga
(707) 942-6877, (800) 816-6877
www.mountviewhotel.com

This is the closest Calistoga comes to the Ritz-Carlton. The Mission Revival building, now a National Historic Landmark, was constructed in 1919 and served the area for years as the European Hotel, haunt of literary bigwigs and first ladies. (It is said that Mrs. Herbert Hoover planted the roses in the garden.) An elegant lobby takes you to either the hotel, Mount View Spa, or Catahoula Restaurant; all three are run separately and catalogued separately in this book. Mount View Hotel has 32 rooms, suites, and cottages, the latter being detached units (with private Jacuzzis) out by the pool. The other rooms are on the second floor, and some have antique furnishings. Continental breakfast is delivered to your room. The wide range of tariffs runs from $130 to $250, so inquire about specifics. No smoking is allowed anywhere on this property.

Hotel D'Amici $$$$
1436 Lincoln Ave., Calistoga
(707) 942–1007
www.rutherfordgrove.com/hotelpage

If Calistoga had luxury apartment suites, they'd look something like this. Hotel D'Amici is downtown, perched on the second floor of a 1936 building once known as Green Hotel. (The "secret door" is just to the right of the restaurant entrance.) The hotel has four spacious, well-appointed rooms, two of which share a balcony over Lincoln Avenue, making them coveted spaces during the Fourth of July and its Silverado Parade (see our Festivals and Annual Events chapter). All have private baths and kitchenettes. For now, children are welcome, but you might call ahead to make sure. The owners are the Pestonis, who run Rutherford Grove Winery. You pick up your keys there (1673 Highway 29 in Rutherford) and get a complimentary wine tasting. You also get a bottle of Rutherford Grove Chardonnay in your fridge at the D'Amici.

Comfort Inn $$$
1865 Lincoln Ave., Calistoga
(707) 942–9400, (800) 228–5150
www.callodging.com

Only in Calistoga would the Comfort Inn have a mineral water swimming pool and whirlpool tub. It also has a sauna and steam room. Each of the 55 rooms (including a two-room suite) features HBO and individual temperature control; most are in the functional style Comfort Inn is known for. Continental breakfast is included in the price.

Stevenson Manor Inn $$$$
1830 Lincoln Ave., Calistoga
(707) 942–1112
www.callodging.com

This motel is affiliated with Best Western. Stevenson Manor has a pool, a sauna, and a gazebo-sheltered central courtyard. The 34 rooms are done in subdued shades of green and burgundy. Four have private whirlpool baths, and seven are warmed by fireplaces; all of them are equipped with refrigerators, microwaves, and coffeemakers. Guests of the inn receive a 10 percent discount at the nearby Calistoga Village Inn & Spa (see our Spas and Resorts chapter). All rooms are nonsmoking.

Sonoma County

Southern Sonoma
El Dorado Hotel $$$$$
405 First St. West, Sonoma
(707) 996–3030, (800) 289–3031
www.hoteleldorado.com

On the northwest corner of Sonoma Plaza, the El Dorado has had a checkered history as a government office, college, winery, and hotel. Salvador Vallejo built the adobe between 1836 and 1846; subsequently, it was occupied by Bear Flag Party members (see our History chapter) as well as Gen. John C. Frémont during the opening days of the Mexican War. Today its 26 rooms have an Old World aura of casual elegance. It's definitely the right choice for those who really want to revel in the plaza's historical ambiance. Some rooms face the plaza with balconies that give a view of the city below. Other rooms face onto a garden courtyard and overlook flowers and trees. Continental breakfast is included in the room rate.

The hotel's Piatti Restaurant offers fine Italian cuisine.

El Pueblo Inn $$
896 W. Napa St., Sonoma
(707) 996–3651, (800) 900–8844
www.elpuebloinn.com

Built of adobe brick, it is the classic L-shaped motel of the 1950s. El Pueblo has been in the same family since it was built in 1959 and is now run by the original owners' daughters. With a large, heated swimming pool, a new spa, and a grassy, shaded garden area around the 38-room complex, it is an excellent location for either families or singles. Cribs are available, and there's a coffeemaker in each room, plus cocoa for the kids.

Sonoma Hotel $$$$
110 W. Spain St., Sonoma
(707) 996–2996, (800) 468–6016
www.sonomahotel.com

Situated on the northwest corner of Sonoma Plaza, this fine old hotel was originally a town hall built in the 1880s. Rooms are furnished with antique furniture and one, the Vallejo Room, has a bedroom suite of carved rosewood once owned by Gen. Mariano Vallejo's family (see our History chapter). All rooms are furnished in keeping with the 19th century, and all have been given names to match their decor—Bear Flag room, Yerba Buena, and Italian Suite. In one of the rooms, author/poet/actress Maya Angelou holed up to write her third novel. All 16 rooms have private baths and air-conditioning. Breakfast of fresh pastries, coffee, and juices is served in a quaint foyer that retains the original fireplace and stained glass windows.

Best Western Sonoma Valley Inn $$$$$
550 Second St. West, Sonoma
(707) 938–9200, (800) 334–5784
www.sonomavalleyinn.com

This hotel is of recent origin (built in 1987), but it has been designed in California Mission-style architecture to match the ambiance of the town's early Mexican heritage. One of its great assets is its location: It's only two blocks from the city's plaza (see our Shopping chapter), yet away from city hubbub with rooms that face onto an inner courtyard. You park your car outside your room, motel-style, yet your view is of the swimming pool, spa, gazebo, and fountain. Most rooms have patios or decks for outdoor privacy. The spacious rooms feature either a fireplace or a Jacuzzi bath. Open the refrigerator in your room, and you'll find a complimentary bottle of wine. Children 12 and younger stay free. A laundry room is available, and continental breakfast is delivered to your room.

Best Western Petaluma Inn $$
200 S. McDowell Blvd., Petaluma
(707) 763–0994, (800) 297–3846
www.bestwestern.com

Surrounded by two shopping centers, this Best Western on Petaluma's east side is right off U.S. 101. The motel is about 1 mile from the city's historic downtown area and the quaint Victorian homes of the west side. It's also about 2 miles from the Petaluma Village Factory Outlet stores (see our Shopping chapter). The 75 guest rooms are pleasantly furnished, and the amenities include coffeemakers, hair dryers, iron/ironing boards, two phone lines, and a data port. A small meeting room can accommodate 40 persons. There's a Carrows restaurant and lounge onsite, too.

Quality Inn $$
5100 Montero Way, Petaluma
(707) 664–1155, (800) 228–5160
www.lokhotels.com

Built in 1985, the hotel comprises seven clustered Cape Cod-style buildings nestled amid landscaped grounds and redwood arbors planted with grapes. Its 111 rooms include 36 with in-room spas and four two-room suites with private spas. The outdoor pool is surrounded by a large sundeck with a sauna adjacent. Its location near Adobe Creek Golf Club and its Robert Trent Jones-designed track makes it appealing to golfers (see the Golf section of our Parks and Recreation chapter), and shoppers will be glad to know it's the closest inn to Petaluma Village Factory Outlet Mall (see our Shopping chapter). A full continental breakfast is served.

Doubletree Hotel $$$$
1 Doubletree Dr., Rohnert Park
(707) 584–5466, (800) 222–TREE
www.doubletree.com

Set on 22 acres between two golf courses, the hotel evokes Sonoma County's Spanish heritage with tiled roofs and arched windows. For business travelers, the Doubletree offers every convenience and amenity necessary for successful meetings and full conferences, including 17,000 square feet of conference space; it's also conveniently located near U.S. 101 and offers express bus service to San Francisco airport. But those on business will also find, as do great numbers of tourists, that it's a very enjoyable resort, with 245 luxurious guest rooms and suites, a restaurant, a pool and Jacuzzi, and live entertainment. At the adjacent Sonoma County Wine and Visitors Center, there's ample opportunity to sample the best local wines.

Vineyard Creek Hotel, Spa & Conference Center
170 Railroad Sq., Santa Rosa
(707) 528–4542, (888) 920–0008
www.vineyardcreek.com

This brand new hotel in downtown Santa Rosa was scheduled to open its doors in spring 2002. (Prices for rooms and spa services had not been set before this book went to press.) The $30 million property with Mediterranean-inspired architecture and courtyards was built in a unique fashion: Its foundation is a combination of concrete and 2,000 plastic tubs, a revolutionary technique that allows the adobe clay soil of our region to expand and contract with the changing seasons. On top of those tubs are 155 plush rooms with upscale amenities and the extra touches business travelers appreciate: T1 lines and dual-line speaker phones with voice mail and complimentary domestic and international newspapers. Some rooms have fireplaces and whirlpools; all have deluxe mini-bars. Room service is available from the on-site restaurant, Buster's Roadhouse, and you can get an in-room massage treatment, too. Facials, massages, bodywork, and treatments of many types are offered, including a warmed river-rock massage.

If you've come to do business, this is the place. The 21,000-square-foot conference center is the largest in the area, with a multitude of meeting rooms, big and small. All this, and it's a two-minute walk to Railroad Square's restaurants and antiques stores.

Flamingo Resort Hotel & Fitness Center $$$
2777 Fourth St., Santa Rosa
(707) 545–8530, (800) 848–8300
www.flamingoresort.com

Lush landscaping makes this resort hotel very appealing, both as a vacation spot and as a business center offering conference facilities for 600 people. For both the harried executive and the tourist, there's plenty of physical activity available, including a heated Olympic-size pool, Jacuzzi, tennis courts, a lighted jogging path, basketball and volleyball courts, and table tennis. Also available for a modest fee is the Montecito Heights Health & Racquet Club. The Flamingo's golf package makes good use of the nearby Fountaingrove course, as well as other top Wine Country tracks. The 170 rooms are luxuriously appointed with elegant furnishings—some rooms also have copy machines and refrigerators.

Fountain Grove Inn $$$$
101 Fountaingrove Pkwy., Santa Rosa
(707) 578–6101, (800) 222–6101
www.fountaingroveinn.com

In harmony with the natural environment, the Fountain Grove Inn's design is all redwood and stone, sweeping low across historic Fountaingrove Ranch, the estate of famed Japanese wine baron Kanaye Nagasawa. The lobby, too, is far from ordinary, dominated by a large redwood sculpture of the legendary horse, Equus. Utmost restraint and understated elegance mark the inn's 125 rooms, which are almost Oriental in their simplicity. All rooms have separate dressing alcoves, double closets, and work spaces with modern dataports for traveling executives. The inn's pool, waterfall, and spa offer a charming view of the historic Round Barn, which sits atop a small nearby hill. Guests gather in the restaurant each morning for a generous buffet

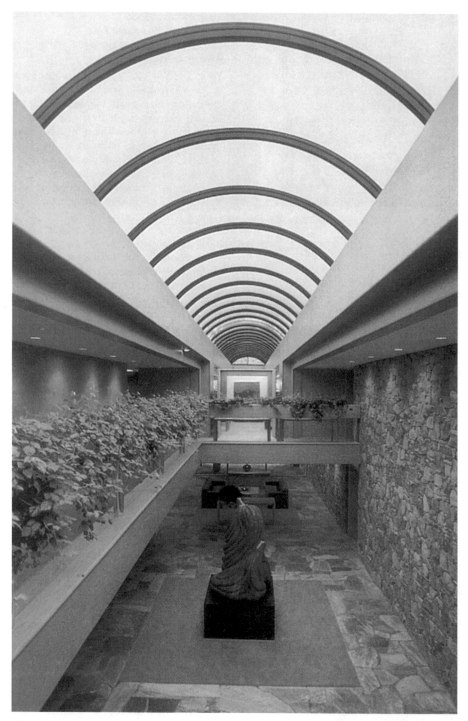

Stunning architecture characterizes the Fountain Grove Inn in Santa Rosa. PHOTO: FOUNTAIN GROVE INN HOTEL AND CONFERENCE CENTER breakfast. The inn's restaurant, not surprisingly called Equus, carries out the theme, with the legendary horse etched in glass and redwood carvings (see our Restaurants chapter).

Sonoma County Hilton $$$$
3555 Round Barn Blvd., Santa Rosa
(707) 523-7555, (800) 445-8667
www.hilton.com

Just off U.S. 101 north of downtown Santa Rosa on 13 acres of Fountaingrove Ranch, this hotel has let stand the historic landmark known as the Round Barn to mark its entrance. This chalet-style hotel has 246 rooms and suites and boasts many amenities, including a state-of-the-art in-room phone system, business center, the award-winning Harvest Grill restaurant, an outdoor patio with a panoramic view of the Santa Rosa valley, a Junior Olympic-size swimming pool, and an on-site workout facility.

Vintners Inn $$$$
4350 Barnes Rd., Santa Rosa
(707) 575-7350, (800) 421-2584
www.vintnersinn.com

Your first vision at Vintners Inn may make you feel as if you've dropped into a charming European village. From the French country decor to the arched windows and wrought-iron railings, the hotel exudes Old World atmosphere—a group of three red-roofed buildings is arranged around a plaza and fountain, surrounded by 45 acres of vineyards. Many of the oversized rooms in this Provence-inspired inn have fireplaces, exposed-beam ceilings, and pine furniture, some of which dates back to the turn of the century. Ground-floor rooms have patios; second-floor suites have balconies with vineyard or courtyard views. On the premises is John Ash & Company, a nationally acclaimed restaurant serving some of the best cuisine in Sonoma County. Its wine list won the Sonoma Harvest Fair Sweepstakes Award three years running (see our Restaurants chapter).

Courtyard Santa Rosa by Marriott $$$
175 Railroad St., Santa Rosa
(707) 573-9000, (800) 354-7672
www.marriott.com

Right on the edge of historic Railroad Square, this Marriott hotel has close access to enough antiques shops to delight any collector looking for bargains or the unusual. All the standard amenities are available in this 138-room inn. Kids will love the swimming pool, spa, and in-room movies, and adults may wander down for cocktails between 5:00 and 10:00 P.M., or to any of the wonderful restaurants located within walking distance. Kids younger than 12 stay free. There are wheelchair-accessible rooms.

Hotel La Rose $$$$
308 Wilson St., Santa Rosa
(707) 579-3200, (800) 527-6738
www.hotellarose.com

A quaint and romantic hotel in Santa Rosa's historic Railroad Square, Hotel La Rose was reconstructed in 1985 and designated a National Historic Landmark. The

Santa Rosa's Railroad Square is home to the Hotel La Rose, a charming building with National Historic Landmark status. PHOTO: JEAN SAYLOR DOPPENBERG

hotel is graced with a charming English Country interior decor that belies the fact that this is a very modern hotel. The four-story hotel has elevator access to its 29 nonsmoking rooms, and the carriage house, added in 1985, has 20 additional guest rooms (seven are designated for smokers) built around a lovely courtyard. A 1998 remodel included marbled bathrooms and a spa. One of the hotel's great assets is its proximity to the restaurants in Railroad Square.

Northern Sonoma

Hotel Healdsburg $$$$
25 Matheson St., Healdsburg
(707) 431–2800, (800) 889–7188
www.hotelhealdsburg.com
The biggest thing to pop up in Healdsburg in quite some time is this three-story, 55-room, $21 million luxury hotel that overlooks the quaint plaza in central Healdsburg. Big, because it rises grandly on the west side of the plaza (and will forever change the small-town feel of the town square, some locals fear). Nonetheless, it began attracting lodgers as soon as it opened, and business has been brisk.

The rooms all feature oversized bathrooms with walk-in showers and soaking tubs, French doors opening to private balconies, wood floors with Tibetan rugs, bathrobes and fine linens, and the usual modern amenities for business travelers. Even more luxurious suites are available (there's six of them), if that's your pleasure. Room service is offered from the Dry Creek Kitchen (see our Restaurants chapter) and breakfast is delivered to your door. The lobby features a grappa bar, the garden has a 60-foot pool, and there's a cardio-fitness room for a quick workout. All this and a spa, too! You can get pampered to your heart's content here, from massages to

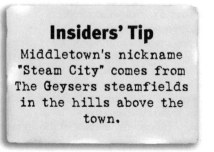

Insiders' Tip
Middletown's nickname "Steam City" comes from The Geysers steamfields in the hills above the town.

facials to a couples room with a soaking tub for two.

Duchamp Hotel $$$$$
421 Foss St., Healdsburg
(707) 431–1300, (800) 431–9341
www.duchamphotel.com

This contemporary European-style hotel, which opened in 2000, is made up of 10 cottage suites that are all truly unique, with artist Marcel Duchamp as the inspiration and the namesake. Unlike any lodgings in Wine Country, six of the rooms are poolside and creekside "villas" that are nearly spartan in their luxurious opulence. The four "artist cottages" are named Man Ray, Mirô, Picasso, and Andy Warhol. The latter, once a small house, is now a tasteful salute to Andy's genius and style. All the rooms feature modern amenities, fireplaces, down comforters on king-size beds, and fabulous bathrooms with spa showers (the Warhol room has a sunken Japanese soaking tub, too). The complimentary breakfast will start your day off right, and the 50-foot pool and heated Jacuzzi beckon after wine tasting and sight-seeing.

Owned by Pat and Peter Lenz, who were vintners on Long Island before they moved to California, the hotel's design was created by Pat, a sculptor. No less than *Conde Nast Traveller* magazine proclaimed the Duchamp as "one of the world's top 25 new hot hotels." It's a great location, down a quiet side road off the main thoroughfare through Healdsburg, yet an easy two-block walk to the shops and restaurants on the town's plaza. This is a non-smoking property that is unsuitable for children. English, German, and French are all spoken here.

Best Western Dry Creek Inn $$
198 Dry Creek Rd., Healdsburg
(707) 433–0300, (800) 222–5784
www.drycreekinn.com

The distinguishing factor here is this motel's outstanding location for wine touring in the beautiful Dry Creek Valley. The 102 rooms (including some "executive mini-suites") are pleasant, in the standard motel style, but the bonus is a view of the valley's vineyards from most of the units. A continental breakfast is included. There's a pool, whirlpool, and exercise room.

Travelodge/Vineyard Valley Inn Motel $$$
178 Dry Creek Rd., Healdsburg
(707) 433–0101, (800) 499–0103
www.travelodge.com

Built in 1992, this is not your ordinary Travelodge. The Vineyard Valley Inn Motel has 23 rooms and suites that blend into the Wine Country setting, while still providing all the modern amenities that seasoned travelers have come to expect. Rooms are furnished with two double beds or one queen. A two-room suite is available with wet bar, refrigerator, and entertainment area.

Geyserville Inn $$$
21714 Geyserville Ave., Geyserville
(707) 857–4343, (877) 857–4343
www.geyservilleinn.com

This is a new hotel, situated at the north end of the town of Geyserville and surrounded by vineyards. The location is ideal for visiting any number of wineries, as well as hitting the bike trails that crisscross this rural countryside. It's also close to Lake Sonoma (see our On the Water chapter). The 38 rooms have a Wine Country feel, decorated under the direction of a local interior decorator in shades of vineyard green and the russet colors of autumn. Rooms are graced with various amenities—for example, patios or balconies and fireplaces—and guests can enjoy the swimming pool and spa. A continental breakfast is served each morning.

Sonoma Coast
Bodega Bay Lodge Resort $$$$$
103 Coast Hwy. 1, Bodega Bay
(707) 875–3525, (800) 368–2468
www.woodsidehotels.com

Luxurious and intimate on eight landscaped acres, the lodge overlooks wildflower-covered dunes, protected marsh- lands, the Pacific Ocean, and the gentle surf of Doran Beach. While it's close enough to enjoy the sound of the surf, the wood-shingled lodge is sheltered from coastal winds. All 84 spacious guest rooms have fireplaces, private balconies, and original artwork. Many feature vaulted ceilings, spa baths, refrigerators, wet bars, and coffeemakers. The 5,000-square-foot conference center is impressive, with high, arched ceilings supported by thick beams of polished oak. The Duck Club Restaurant can be counted on for imaginative cuisine. Complimentary wine is served in the late afternoon. An 18-hole Robert Trent Jones-designed golf course is next door at Bodega Harbour Golf Links (see our Parks and Recreation chapter).

Inn at the Tides $$$$
800 Coast Hwy. 1, Bodega Bay
(707) 875-2751, (800) 541-7788
www.innatthetides.com

Six coastal acres with natural landscaping surround this inn, which is actually an enclave of 12 separate lodges that appear to be part of the rumpled hills and tawny headlands. Each of the 86 guest quarters overlooks Bodega Bay, home port for one of the coast's most productive fishing fleets. Amenities include a heated indoor-outdoor pool, spacious spa, soothing sauna, and luxurious logo bathrobes. A continental breakfast is served, and gourmet cuisine is featured in the Bay View Restaurant & Lounge (see our Restaurants chapter).

Fort Ross Lodge $$
20705 Coast Hwy. 1, Jenner
(707) 847-3333
www.fortrosslodge.com

Just north of historic Fort Ross State Park (see our History and Attractions chapters), the lodge is situated above a sheltered cove where seals lounge on rocky outcroppings. There's plenty of space in the guest rooms to stretch out and relax, or you can unwind in the hot tub and sauna. The 22 rooms are decorated in natural tones and hues. There's a barbecue on each deck and a country store across the highway. Children younger than 12 are free. Intimate, secluded suites are available for adults only. And the lodge now offers a private two-bedroom home.

Salt Point Lodge $
23255 Coast Hwy. 1, Timber Cove
(707) 847-3234
www.saltpoint.com

This is a well-maintained, older motor lodge, with 16 rooms. Situated on a knoll overlooking the ocean, Salt Point Lodge includes a restaurant with a full bar. Lovely gardens surround the place, and it's open year-round. There are TVs and VCRs in the rooms, but no phones. Besides the nearby beaches, there are miles of hiking trails to explore.

Sea Ranch Lodge $$$$$
60 Sea Wall Dr., Sea Ranch
(707) 785-2371, (800) 732-7262
www.searanchlodge.com

On bluffs above the Pacific, this lodge features one of the best ocean vistas in the Wine Country. All but one of its 20 rooms face the sea, and cozy window seats offer front-row viewing for spectacular sunsets. If you're in need of a peaceful getaway, this is the place. Not far south of the Mendocino County line on Highway 1, the Sea Ranch development is composed of vacation homes and permanent residences. Rooms are walled in knotty pine, and the aura is rustic. Hiking trails along the bluffs are well marked, and you can follow them down to the beach. A challenging 18-hole golf course is available, and there's a restaurant. Some units have fireplaces, and family units are available. All are luxuriously appointed.

West County/Russian River

Fife's Resort $$
16467 Hwy. 116 East, Guerneville
(707) 869-9500, (800) 734-3371
www.fifes.com

Among the most popular gay resorts on the Russian River, Fife's features 15 forested acres of towering coast redwood. The resort offers cabins that range from the basic one-room variety to an elegant two-bedroom, two-bath deluxe version with fireplace and hot tub. The restaurant at Fife's includes a fine selection of continental dishes with fresh local vegetables and house-made desserts. The resort's signature dish is linguini with fresh salmon caper cakes. Other amenities include a pool, gym, and bar. The resort is also walking distance to downtown Guerneville, where you can peruse the antiques shops, have coffee at a local cafe, or dance the night away at Club FAB (see our Nightlife chapter).

The Brookside Lodge Motel $$
14100 Brookside Ln., Guerneville
(707) 869–2470, (800) 551–1881
www.sonic.net/welcome

A charming family resort located at the edge of Guerneville's Korbel vineyards and bordered by Fife's Creek, the Brookside offers 36 newly redecorated spacious rooms, some with their own patio and kitchen. Amenities include a pool, sauna, Ping-Pong table, and satellite TV. The lodge also offers one- and two-bedroom cottages, some of which have a private hot tub and spectacular Wine Country views.

Cazanoma Lodge $$
1000 Kidd Creek Rd., Cazadero
(707) 632–5255
www.cazanomalodge.com

Spectacularly situated on 147 acres of giant redwoods in western Sonoma County, Cazanoma Lodge is a charming vacation retreat just a short drive from the Russian River and the coast. Two spacious, comfortable cabins have wood-burning fireplaces, contemporary kitchens, and baths. Three suites and one room in the main lodge overlook the lodge's cascading waterfall, trout pond, and two creeks. The restaurant features Bavarian specialties (sauerbraten, hasenpfeffer, and roast duck) and American cuisine. The lodge is open March through November.

Mendocino County

U.S. 101

Days Inn $
950 N. State St., Ukiah
(707) 462–7584
www.daysinn.com

Yes, it's a chain, but the rooms are spacious and luxuriously decorated; the inn is comfortable and convenient, and the staff is professional. This Days Inn has 54 units, a swimming pool, and a restaurant. It offers free local calls, and pets are welcome. Breakfast is included in the nightly rate.

Discovery Inn $$
1340 N. State St., Ukiah
(707) 462–8873

This is the largest of Ukiah's motels, with 177 units, two heated pools, four indoor spas, and a conference room. A workout room is a recent addition, and guest laundry facilities are available. Complimentary breakfast is included. A small, unique park filled with carved redwood figures—a bear, a shark, a man—surrounds an attractive fountain.

Baechtel Creek Inn $
101 Gregory Ln., Willits
(707) 459–9063, (800) 459–9911
www.baechtelcreek.com

An attractive two-story hotel built in 1992, Baechtel Creek Inn has 46 rooms, a heated swimming pool, spa, and conference rooms. Baechtel Creek runs right past the inn, providing considerable entertainment for kids and grown-ups by attracting such wild creatures as rabbits, squirrels, deer, and an occasional turtle. This is a nice, clean place to stay in a town that doesn't see all that many visitors.

Mendocino Coast

Breakers Inn $$$$$
39300 Coast Hwy. 1 South, Gualala
(707) 884–3200, (800) BREAKER
www.breakersinn.com

The 24 oceanfront rooms at the Breakers are designed to offer spectacular panoramic views of the dramatic coast through large picture windows and spacious decks. Enjoy incredible ocean sunsets and the sound of waves crashing on the shore. In winter and spring, the deck provides a front-row seat to the migration of gray whales. Each room is individually decorated in the theme of a country or state in a seacoast region, highlighting locations such as Cape Cod, Ireland, and Japan. All rooms except the three garden rooms feature decks, fireplaces, wet bars, and ocean views, and deluxe continental breakfast is included each morning. The Luxury Spa Room is near a picture window so you can soak and enjoy the view.

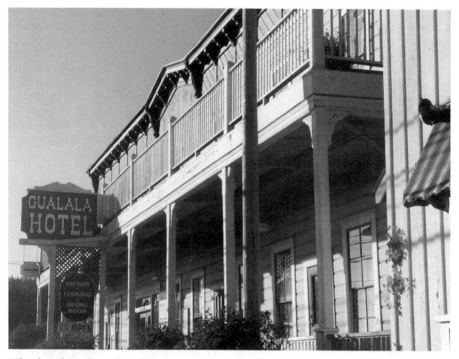

What do Jack London and Fred MacMurray have in common? Both are among the famous patrons of the historic Gualala Hotel. PHOTO: JOHN NAGIECKI

Gualala Hotel $
39301 Coast Hwy. 1 South, Gualala
(707) 884-3441

Built in 1903, the Gualala Hotel weathered nearly a century of Pacific sun and storm. Yet the building's classic facade looks much the same as it did a hundred years ago, when travelers waited on its deck for the coastal stage to arrive. Five of the hotel's 19 rooms boast a beautiful ocean view and private bath—the remaining rooms share hall baths in the European style. Though some of the individual accommodations are a bit cramped, a large central sitting room, complete with sofas and a wood-burning stove, offers plenty of space to snuggle up with a good book or to enjoy a board game. A restaurant and saloon are on the premises—the latter features a mahogany bar where you can sip your favorite vintage or brew, while drinking in the local color. Several walls of the saloon are adorned with pictures of past patrons—both famous and obscure—all proudly holding up some

monstrous fish or game animal that they had bagged nearby.

Greenwood Pier Inn $$$
5928 Coast Hwy. 1 South, Elk
(707) 877-9997
www.greenwoodpierinn.com

Perched atop a high bluff overlooking the sea, the Greenwood Pier Inn is a quiet, meditative spot, resplendent in colorful flower gardens. The inn's 12 rooms are located in several architecturally interesting buildings, such as the Cliffhouse, Garden Cottage, and North and South Sea Castles. The latter pair indeed resemble castle towers, and each has a tub in the uppermost level—perfect for soaking your weary bones while scanning the horizon for whales. The Lighthouse Suite in the main house has a cupola that offers an even more lofty perspective on the mighty Pacific beyond. Other inn amenities include fireplaces, private decks, nearby hiking trails along the bluffs, and in-room therapeutic massage. Dining is available at the Greenwood Pier Cafe, and a country store and garden shop carry a variety of horticultural, decorative, and New Age items.

Albion River Inn $$$$
3790 N. Coast Hwy. 1, Albion
(707) 937–1919, 800) 479–7944
www.albionriverinn.com

Six miles south of Mendocino, Albion River Inn occupies a prime oceanfront spot on 10 secluded acres of gardens and ocean bluffs. Guests are quartered in 20 cliff-side, New England-style rooms for two, most in duplex arrangements and all with spectacular ocean views. All have fireplaces and private decks, and many have a spa tub or tub for two. A full breakfast is included in the adjoining restaurant, which shares the view.

Hill House Inn $$$$
10701 Palette Dr., Mendocino
(707) 937–0554, (800) 422–0554
www.hillhouseinn.com

You'd swear you were on the New England coast. The recently constructed Hill House Inn captures the essence of the coast of Maine in the spectacular and unspoiled land and sea along California's scenic Highway 1. Forty-four guest rooms feature brass beds with comforters, lace curtains, elegant wooden furnishings, and the convenience of private baths. Hill House not only attracts vacationers but also caters to seminars and small conferences, with rooms designed to accommodate up to 100 people. A chapel is available for wedding ceremonies.

Heritage House $$$$
5200 Coast Hwy. 1, Little River
(707) 937–5885, (800) 235–5885
www.heritagehouseinn.com

Sprawling across 37 private acres of pristine coastline, Heritage House is a classic country inn, opened in 1949 and still maintained by the same family. A total of 64 accommodations are mainly grouped in clusters of two, three, or four private rooms under a common roof, which imparts a cottagelike feeling. One of the favorites is the sumptuous Carousel set of suites, housed in a secluded building

Perched high above the Pacific, the Greenwood Pier Inn could be mistaken for a Zen Buddhist retreat.

Hill House is one of Wine Country's picturesque lodgings found near or along California's scenic Highway 1. PHOTO: LOU ZAUNER

offering unobstructed ocean views, huge decks, and elegant furnishings. The Water Tower suite includes a spiral staircase leading to a sleeping loft. But the most requested rooms were built for the filming of the movie *Same Time Next Year*, which was written while author Bernard Slade stayed at the inn. Dining at Heritage House is a world-class experience (see our Restaurants chapter). The inn is closed from November 25 through December 14.

Stanford Inn by the Sea-Big River Lodge
$$$$$
Coast Hwy. 1 and Comptche-Ukiah Rd., Mendocino
(707) 937–5615, (800) 331–8884
www.stanfordinn.com

This elegantly rustic lodge has so many diversions that guests will find all they need here. A firm believer in preserving the health of our environment, owner Jeff Stanford offers guests bicycles for local transport and a fleet of canoes and kayaks for paddling up Big River. His terraced gardens are tended organically and are so prolific he donates produce to the local senior center. Besides that, he also keeps grazing llamas, horses, and a few cats. Jeff serves vegetarian dishes in the Ravens restaurant, along with organic wines. Hors d'oeuvres are available in the evening, champagne with breakfast.

The site is stunning, sloping from a high meadow down to the sea. And the 33 accommodations have all the amenities expected of the finest hotels—wood-burning fireplaces, down comforters, ocean views, decks, refrigerators, VCRs. Some have kitchens. There's a heated indoor swimming pool and group Jacuzzi/ sauna.

Mendocino Hotel **$$$$**
45080 Main St., Mendocino
(707) 937–0511, (800) 548–0513
www.mendocinohotel.com

The venerable, 121-year-old Mendocino Hotel is an opulent Victorian jewel named "best small hotel in Northern California" by *Focus* magazine. Guests register at a teller's cage from an old Kansas bank and congregate for drinks in a front parlor replete with antiques, leaded windows, and Oriental rugs. The historic section offers suites with balconies overlooking the Pacific as well as rooms with shared baths in the European style. The garden suites, across the courtyard, are fully modern but still maintain the Victorian decor. Look for lots of solid wood paneling, leaded glass, brass, and walls papered in period fabrics in the 50 rooms in the main hotel and the garden suites. An elegant dining room features California cuisine and an extensive wine list. The Garden Cafe is open in the daytime, as is the Garden Bar. The Lobby Bar operates in the evening. Advance reservations are almost mandatory during the summer months.

Anchor Lodge Motel $
32260 N. Harbor Dr., Fort Bragg
(707) 964-4283
www.wharf-restaurant.com

Located in the heart of Noyo Fishing Village, Anchor Lodge has been a focal point for visitors and locals for more than 40 years. You can't get much closer to the water without being in it. There are 18 rooms here, and guests have their pick of four options: economy (two persons), waterfront (two persons), or an apartment with kitchen for two or four persons.

Anchor Lodge operates in conjunction with The Wharf Restaurant and Lodge, which features fresh fish, steak, and prime rib.

Harbor Lite Lodge $
120 N. Harbor Dr., Fort Bragg
(707) 964-0221, (800) 643-2700
www.harborlitelodge.com

This rustic redwood motel has balconies that overlook Noyo River and its fishing fleet. If you're awake in the early dawn, you can see the lights of the fleet as boats head out for the day's fishing, stretching in a colorful parade out to sea. In late afternoon, the parade reenters the harbor. The lodge has 79 comfortable rooms, some with wood-burning stoves. A meet-

ing center for business or educational conferences has two large rooms accommodating 30 and 50 people, respectively. Complimentary coffee, tea, and cocoa are served in the lobby each morning.

North Cliff Hotel $$$$
180 N. Main St., Fort Bragg
(707) 962-2500
www.fortbragg.org

This is Fort Bragg's showiest hotel, perched at the entrance to Noyo Harbor. From your private balcony you can watch the fishing boats go out to sea in the morning, and then wave to them when they return at night—it's that close to the waterway. With all rooms facing the ocean, the views are mesmerizing (bring binoculars for scanning the horizon)— even as you take the waters in your private spa tub next to the window. All rooms have fireplaces, mini-refrigerators stocked with juice and water, microwaves, and plush bathrobes. A continental breakfast is left at your door each morning. Not all rooms have the spa tubs, but most rooms have king beds. Rooms with two queen beds are also available.

Hi-Seas Inn $$
1201 N. Main St., Fort Bragg
(707) 964-5929, (800) 990-7327
www.callodging.com

All 15 of the rooms here have a full ocean view. Just slide back the big glass door that leads to the deck. Between the deck and the ocean is a two-acre lawn. And right behind the Inn is a 10-mile hiking trail that goes through Fort Bragg and back into the nearby hills. Each room has a coffeemaker, and the Inn has a microwave everyone can use.

Pine Beach Inn & Suites $$
16801 N. Coast Hwy. 1, Fort Bragg
(707) 964-5603
www.pinebeachinn.com

You can walk to a beach and cove from this 50-room hotel, which is on 12 acres of landscaped grounds in a majestic setting of redwoods. The beach is secluded, the private path is paved, and you'll enjoy breathtaking views all the way down to the mighty Pacific, as it thunders in against the high rocks and cliffs. The rooms (nine are suites) are large, decorated with fine furniture, and comforters and pillow shams adorn the beds; 24 of the units have ocean views. If you're in the mood for tennis, championship courts await, offering the chance to lob into the clear blue skies. From April through October the on-site restaurant features broiled steaks and fresh local seafood.

Seabird Lodge $$
191 South St., Fort Bragg
(707) 964–4731, (800) 345–0022
www.seabirdlodge.com
One of the best-known features of this 65-room motel is a continuing package special that includes passage on the Skunk Train. The train, of course, travels between Fort Bragg and Willits (see our Attractions chapter), and most visitors find an overnight stay in Fort Bragg to be a favorable option. The package deal may vary (it seldom does), but it usually includes two nights lodging, two Skunk Train tickets, breakfast each morning, and dinner one evening at your choice of three restaurants.

The Seabird will also shuttle you to and from the depot. The lodge has an indoor pool and hot tub, and there is a restaurant right next door.

Super 8 $
888 S. Main St., Fort Bragg
(707) 964–4003, (800) 206–9833
This inn offers affordable accommodations, a convenient location, and old-fashioned hospitality. The 53 rooms have cable TV and private phones, and there is a full-service restaurant on the premises. Staff will be delighted to give a rundown on all the unique natural wonders to be explored in the vicinity—Mackerricher State Park, for instance, or Glass Beach or Pudding Creek Headlands—as well as family activities available on sea and on land.

Vista Manor Lodge $$
1100 N. Main St., Fort Bragg
(707) 964–4776, (800) 821–9498
www.callodging.com

Located at the north end of Fort Bragg, about a mile from downtown, this Best Western motel features 55 units. There's an indoor heated pool, complimentary continental breakfast, and a coffeemaker in every room. All rooms have ocean views, and a nearby tunnel dips beneath Highway 1, giving you about five minutes to walk to the beach.

Lake County

Cobb Village Inn Motel $
16595 Hwy. 175, Cobb
(707) 928–5242, (800) COBB–MTN
$
Tucked into the pines at about 3,000 feet, this quiet motel starts to look pretty good in the wilting days of August. Cobb Village has 19 rooms, 5 with kitchenettes and 3 with whirlpool tubs, feather beds, and VCRs. The office, a rich source of local information, is open from 9:00 A.M. to 9:00 P.M. The motel is across the road from Cobb Meadows Golf Course (see our Parks and Recreation chapter) and within walking distance of a pizza parlor, a fish-and-chips pub, and a breakfast cafe. Don't bother looking for the address—Cobb Village is at the intersection of Highway 175 and Golf Road.

Travelodge $
4775 Old Hwy. 53, Clearlake
(707) 994–1499, (888) 515–6375
www.travelodge.com
Highway 53 used to meander through downtown Clearlake before a bypass was built to the east; the old route is still called Old Highway 53. Where it intersects Lakeshore Drive, about a block and a half from Redbud Park, you'll find the Travelodge. It has 31 rooms, all of which come with cable TV and air-conditioning. There is a swimming pool, a spa, and individual power hook-ups for boats. Ask about their commercial and senior rates.

Best Western El Grande $$
15135 Lakeshore Dr., Clearlake
(707) 994–2000, (800) 528–1234
One of the biggest motels in Lake County, El Grande has 67 rooms, including 23

suites. Each of the suites comes with a refrigerator, and in the sitting room there's a second TV and phone—even a hide-a-bed. Inside you'll find an atrium and a full-service restaurant and bar, not to mention a sitting pool. Outside are a hot tub and spa. It's only 1½ blocks from the lake.

Highlands Inn $
13865 Lakeshore Dr., Clearlake
(707) 994–8982, (800) 300–8982

This waterfront motel offers comfortable rooms, all with a view of Clear Lake. There's a private beach and pier and fax accessibility for business travelers.

Lake Point Lodge $
13470 E. Hwy. 20, Clearlake Oaks
(707) 998–4350, (800) 900–4350

You get a lot for your dollar at this 40-unit motel in Clearlake Oaks. Half the rooms have king beds, half have two queens, and all come with cable TV and continental breakfast. The lodge also has four suites with whirlpool tubs and microwave ovens. There is a swimming pool in back and a restaurant and cocktail lounge on-site.

Bell Haven Resort $$
3415 White Oak Way, Kelseyville
(707) 279–4329, (877) 279–4329
www.bellhaven.com

If the perimeter of Clear Lake is getting too commercial for you—it does start to feel like a sandy circus midway sometimes—it may be time for Bell Haven. The Woosters offer the sort of doting attention you expect at a bed and breakfast inn. Their woodsy resort has nine cabins; size varies, but all have kitchens. It also offers a hot tub, free kayaks and, in the summer, free El Toro sailboats. Within walking distance are a hamburger joint and a market with full deli. Call to ask about weekly vacation rates.

Kelseyville Motel $
5575 Seventh St., Kelseyville
(707) 279–1874, (800) KV–MOTEL
www.kvmotel.com

Just blocks from either Highway 29 or Kelseyville's Main Street, this small motel is a convenient choice. Each of the 16 rooms has individual heat and air, color TV with cable, a refrigerator, and a microwave. Three rooms have kitchenettes, and you might talk them into accepting your beloved pet.

Soda Bay Inn $
3397 Live Oak Ln., Kelseyville
(707) 279–4722
www.sodabayinn.com

Seven housekeeping units make up the Soda Bay Inn, complete with linens, dishes, silverware, and cooking utensils. Outdoor furniture and barbecue grills are yours for the asking, and there's swimming from the private pier. You can even fish from the private dock whenever you like. Boat rentals and launching are nearby. This inn closes for winter.

Creekside Lodge $
Hwys. 29 and 281
(Soda Bay Rd.), Kelseyville
(707) 279–9258, (800) 279–1380

Though not on the shores of Clear Lake, this small, 14-room motel is conveniently located and a good alternative when all the rooms at Konocti Harbor Resort are sold out. (The resort is a short distance away.) There's a convenience store next door and restaurants nearby. Most of the single-story rooms—all with queen beds—are nonsmoking, but pets are usually allowed.

Anchorage Inn $
950 N. Main St., Lakeport
(707) 263–5417

Right on the lake and just a few blocks from Library Park, the Anchorage has 34 air-conditioned rooms with cable color TV. The motel has a pool, sauna, Jacuzzi, a barbecue area, and a pier and boat-docking facilities in a sheltered cove. In addition to the standard rooms, the inn has apartment-like one-bedroom suites and sizable two-bedroom suites with grand living rooms and writing tables. The suites are a bit pricier.

Starlite Motel $
5960 E. Hwy. 20, Lucerne
(707) 274–5515

If you wind up on the less populated side of Clear Lake, the Starlite has 22 rooms, a swimming pool, and picnic area. Each room comes with air-conditioning, cable TV, and a small refrigerator. Pets are sometimes accommodated. The motel is just across the highway from the water.

Super 8 Motel $$
450 E. Hwy. 20, Upper Lake
(707) 275–0888, (800) 800–8000

You get what you pay for at the Super 8, and that's enough to convince some weary travelers. Four of the 34 rooms come with spa tubs. There is a swimming pool and hot tub on the premises.

Pine Acres Resort $$
5328 Blue Lakes Rd., Upper Lake
(707) 275–2811
www.bluelakepineacres.com

Just off Highway 20, about halfway between where it leaves the shore of Clear Lake and where it meets U.S. 101 to the west, are the Blue Lakes, two skinny, steep-sided troughs fed by natural springs. Pine Acres is on Upper Blue Lake. It offers 11 rooms and cabins, some with two double beds and a full kitchen, some with queen beds and a small refrigerator. It also has roomy deluxe units. Smoking is allowed in most of the cabins, and pets are allowed everywhere for an $8.00 fee. Babies stay free, while children ages two through 10 incur a $2.00 per night

charge. The resort has a private beach, a fishing dock, a small store (including a bait-and-tackle shop), and boat rentals.

Vacation Rentals

Napa County

Napa Valley Cottages
(707) 963–5343
www.vineyardcottages.com

This service specializes in placing couples in rented cottages located on private estates, with short- and long-term rates available. Rates run from $175 to $750 per night, depending on the cottage you choose. But calling them "cottages" may be an understatement. For instance, the carriage house at the six-acre Bella Costa Sorrento estate is a secluded, two-story brick structure built in 1865. Upstairs are two bedrooms with their own bathrooms; the living room, kitchen, and dining room are downstairs. A private hot tub is hidden outside in the trees.

Sonoma County

Russian River Vacation Homes
14080 Mill St., Guerneville
(707) 869–9030,
(800) 310–0804 (in California),
(800) 997–3312

Since 1975 this firm has provided a large selection of vacation rental homes throughout western Sonoma County at nightly rates ranging from $145 to $450; weekly rates from $550 to $1,600.

Russian River Getaways
14075 Mill St., Guerneville
(707) 869–4560, (800) 433–6673
www.rrgetaways.com

This friendly rental company would like you to "experience getaway heaven in your very own home away from home." All the homes they offer are first-class, with many choices in size, location, and amenities. Picture yourself in a cozy hideaway for 2 in the redwoods or rendezvous with your family or friends in a beach house that sleeps 18. Or you might prefer an

Rams Head Realty
1000 Annapolis Rd., Sea Ranch
(707) 785–2427, (800) 785–3455

More than 120 vacation rentals are offered from two-night stays to multiple weeks at a rate of $100 to $300 per night. Sites are available in the meadows, in the forest, or on the oceanfront. The most desirable oceanfront sites offer grand vistas and the dramatic crashing of the waves.

Mendocino County

Coast Getaways
10501 Ford St., Mendocino
(707) 937–9200, (800) 525–0049
www.coastgetaways.com

If you're looking for a romantic studio for two or a large house that will hold your whole family, this service can match you up with one of more than 30 homes along a 20-mile stretch of the Mendocino County coastline from Albion to Cleone. Choose from oceanfront studios or bungalows nestled in the redwoods, with hot tubs or without—whatever appeals to you. Like the properties themselves, the fees are all over the map, but you can count on a two-night minimum of about $350 for a studio home for two in a secluded wooded setting, to the poshest and largest pads (oceanfront, five-bedroom) for eight or more people reaching more than $900.

Mendocino Coast Reservations
1000 Main St., Mendocino
(707) 937–5033, (800) 262–7801
www.mendocinovacations.com

Here you'll find listings of the finest in weekend and vacation lodging, from cozy cottages to oceanfront estates. Some are right in the village of Mendocino, some on the coast, some in the forest. In July and August, a three-day minimum is imposed. A wide range of rental fees varies due to weekly or weekend occupancy, time of year, size, and property amenities. A three-day, two-night visit during high season ranges from $328 for a studio in the village to $1,080 for a house with an ocean view and a hot tub.

elegant lodge with a dramatic river view in the wine-tasting region. Many houses are dog-friendly, and there's only a two-night minimum. Prices range from $125 to $750 per night, $600 to $4,500 per week.

Sea Coast Hide-a-Ways
21350 N. Coast Hwy. 1, Jenner
(707) 847–3278, (800) 937–7546

You have a choice here of oceanside vistas or seclusion among the redwoods. Hot tubs and fireplaces are featured, with boat rentals available at Sea Coast's Timber Cove boat landing. Prices range from $195 to $650 for two nights and $545 to $1,900 weekly, with midweek discounts available.

Lake County

Lake Vacation Rentals
1855 S. Main St., Lakeport
(707) 263–7188
www.clearlakevacations.com

Homes of any size and type—this reserva-tion service has 'em all. There are condos and estates, and everything in between, and most are right on the water. Prices range from $125 to $400 a day for homes with one to six bedrooms, and many have spas and their own docks.

Bed-and-Breakfast Inns

Napa County
Sonoma County
Mendocino County
Lake County

Spying the gilded sign, you pull into the long driveway and park under a 200-year-old oak, pine, or redwood tree. A heavy brass knocker hangs on the polished wood door, just beneath the leaded-glass window. The door opens and the innkeeper greets you like an old friend.

Inside, the parlor brims with an assortment of antiques—an oak secretary, a walnut rolltop desk, a marble fireplace. The only sound is the tock-tock-tock of a grandfather clock.

You amble down a parqueted hallway to find that your bedroom has a name. Inside is a four-poster bed complete with tasteful accents. A gentle breeze ruffles the lace curtain; drawing it aside you look out to the private rose garden and its grapevine arbor. Later you'll have wine and cheese in the parlor, and tomorrow you will enjoy a hearty breakfast while chatting with a broker from Los Angeles and a history professor from Toronto.

Such is the experience at many bed-and-breakfasts. Unlike modern hotels and motels, these inns are a throwback to a time when lodgings were small and homespun, offering travelers more of a social experience than isolated anonymity. For many, they are part of a perfect vacation experience. If you love B&Bs, you've come to the right place— Wine Country is bed-and-breakfast heaven.

In selecting inns for this chapter, we looked for places that make you feel as though you are sleeping over at someone's home, or at least in their separate guest quarters. But we also included a wide range of styles and choices, from Napa's top-of-the-line Blue Violet Mansion to Hopland's pleasant and affordable Thatcher Inn. Unless you read otherwise in this chapter, you can expect a few things about each of the listed inns. They have rooms with private bathrooms but no television sets; the bedrooms have lovely full- or queen-size beds; they do not allow pets or any indoor smoking; they accept major credit cards; and they usually serve full breakfast.

Though we do consider breakfast to frequently be part of the standard package, we did not consider it to be a defining criterion. Why? Because anybody can offer breakfast. For example, the Comfort Inn in Calistoga provides continental breakfast. Does that make it a B&B? Absolutely not. In contrast, the cozy Hideaway Cottages a few blocks away offers no breakfast. Does that make it a hotel? No again. You will notice that just about all of the inns we include were converted from private residences, while practically all of the hotels, motels, and spas featured in our other chapters are newly built.

What about kids? Most places do not want to forbid kids. In fact, current California law apparently won't let them make any such prohibition. However, the innkeepers acknowledge that many of their guests are attempting, above all else, to get away from children for a couple days. Also, a house of steep, hardwood staircases and fragile antiques might not be the best place for your toddler. So, in general, assume that bringing the children along is not a good idea.

So there you have it. We've tried our best to call 'em like we see 'em here, but understand the line is often quite fine.

Price Code

Please refer to the dollar-sign code below for tariffs. Rates are for double occupancy on a weekend in high-season (generally May through October). Most inns offer significant discounts for off-season or mid-week stays. Note that prices do not include taxes, gratuities, or services that are considered "extra."

$ . . . . .Less than $120
$$ . . . .$121 to $150
$$$ . . . .$151 to $180
$$$$ . . . . .More than $181

Napa County

The Blue Violet Mansion $$$$
443 Brown St., Napa
(707) 253–2583, (800) 959–2583
www.bluevioletmansion.com

The Blue Violet Mansion won the Reader's Choice Award in 1996, outdistancing inns from all over North America. It isn't hard to see why. Every detail is celebrated with a flourish here, from the in-room Port (complimentary) and rack full of wine (pay as you go), to the brass door frame salvaged from the Bank of Italy, to the iron front gate reproduced to match the original. The Queen Anne Victorian home was built in 1886 by Emanuel Manasse, executive at Sawyer Tannery and pioneer of patent leather production. Manasse's trade is evident in a most distinctive feature-embossed leather wainscoting that runs through much of the house.

The Blue Violet Mansion has 17 rooms on three floors. Each of them has a king or queen bed and a modem jack. Two ground-floor rooms are equipped with Murphy beds, making them ideal for upscale corporate meetings. And upstairs is the Camelot Floor, four rooms painstakingly hand-painted in trompe l'oeil fashion. Book the Royal Suite and sip your wine from Arthur and Guinevere silver goblets. On the one-acre grounds you'll find a heated swimming pool, a spa, an herb garden, and roses. And at the back of the mansion is Violette's, a French restaurant serving a seven-course prix fixe din-

ner for $75 per person. Extra guests are welcome—for an additional $75 ($50 for children five and under).

Churchill Manor Bed & Breakfast Inn $$$$
485 Brown St., Napa
(707) 253–7733
www.churchillmanor.com

In the heart of the Fuller Park Historic District is a grandiose, three-story Second Empire mansion built in 1889 for local banker Edward Churchill. With close to 10,000 square feet of space (and that doesn't even include the full basement or the pillar-supported, three-sided veranda), it was said to be the largest domicile in Napa Valley for decades. The interior is essentially unaltered. There are four grand parlor rooms with beveled and leaded glass and redwood moldings and fireplace frames. Old political cartoons and Victorian prints line the hallways.

The ten guest rooms, nine of which are on the second and third floors, are filled with massive cherry armoires and desks, and some of the claw-foot tubs are "in the European style"—they sit fetchingly in a corner of the bedroom. Other units have oversized tubs with two-person showers. You get a full breakfast in the dining room, plus complimentary wine and cheese (and fresh-baked cookies) in the afternoon. Play croquet in the side garden, borrow a tandem bicycle, or just stroll around the acre of grounds and toast the fat wallet of Edward Churchill.

Cedar Gables Inn $$$$
486 Coombs St., Napa
(707) 224–7969, (800) 309–7969
www.cedargablesinn.com

Chances are, you've never seen a house like this one. Designed by British architect Ernest Coxhead in 1892, it's an immense, brown-shingled home that you might expect to find on an estate in England's Cotswolds. In fact, the feeling here is decidedly masculine, making it a logical choice for not-better halves who begin whining when they hear the expression "bed-and-breakfast." Cedar Gables' six guest rooms are sizable and brimming with period antiques. The Churchill

Chamber, originally the master bedroom used by Edward and Alice Churchill, has a walnut-encased whirlpool tub to match the fireplace. Several of the rooms have old coal-burning fireplaces, converted to gas. Breakfast is served either at the long, formal dining room table or cafe-style in the adjacent sun room. Cedars, palm trees, and a cork oak shade the house in the summer.

Inn on Randolph $$$$
411 Randolph St., Napa
(707) 257–2886, (800) 670–6886
www.innonrandolph.com

This modest, tasteful inn is on a quiet street in a neighborhood of historic homes. The main house, an 1860 Gothic Revival Victorian, has five rooms with seasonal themes (the fifth is called Equinox). Spring, for example, boasts intricate flowers painted on the walls and ceiling, and Autumn features a handcrafted bentwillow canopy bed. Five more expensive rooms are in the newly refurbished 1930s cottages. All of the cottages and some of the main-house rooms have gas fireplaces and two-person whirlpool tubs; some have private decks. Roses line the front walk, and the gardens are flanked by a common deck, a gazebo, and hammocks. The Inn on Randolph serves a full breakfast, and in-room massage can be arranged upon request.

The Beazley House $$$$
1910 First St., Napa
(707) 257–1649, (800) 559–1649
www.beazleyhouse.com

The checkered past of this house took a happy turn in 1981 when Jim and Carol Beazley turned it into Napa's first bed-and-breakfast inn. On a row of rambling turn-of-the-century mansions, it was originally built for local surgeon and politician Adolph Kahn in 1902, but he and his wife divorced and left the area seven years later. Subsequent owners included the Hanna Boys Center and San Francisco jetsetter Joan Hitchcock, who reputedly had an affair with JFK and for a fact had seven husbands.

The Beazley now has 11 rooms, 6 in the main house and 5 in the carriage house. The latter are large units, each with a fireplace and two-person spa tub. Our vote for best room (and, without question, best value) is the Sun Room, a bright and nostalgic corner with a two-sided balcony and a 6-foot soaking tub. Full breakfast is

Eleven comfortable rooms comprise the Beazley House, Napa's first bed-and-breakfast inn. PHOTO: JEAN SAYLOR DOPPENBERG

served in the formal dining room. Children are permitted, and pets are assessed on a case-by-case basis.

Candlelight Inn $$$$
1045 Easum Dr., Napa
(707) 257–3717
www.candlelightinn.com

In the tradition of all good bed and breakfast inns, the Candlelight, an English Tudor style mansion with 10 guest rooms, will pamper you with four-poster beds, French doors, private balconies, and a three-course breakfast. The Garden View room has a private entrance and deck, with—you guessed it—views of the garden and 30-by-60-foot swimming pool. Other rooms look out on the surrounding hills, and several rooms have Jacuzzi tubs for two and marble fireplaces. All rooms have TVs and phones. Giant redwoods create shady areas along the banks of Napa Creek.

Hennessey House $$$$
1727 Main St., Napa
(707) 226–3774
www.hennesseyhouse.com

Adjacent to the Jarvis Conservatory on the fringe of Napa's turn-of-the-century downtown, Hennessey House is an Eastlake-style Queen Anne built for Dr. Edwin Hennessey, one-time mayor of the town, in 1889. The 10 rooms (6 in the main residence, 4 in the carriage house) are air-conditioned, and most have canopy, brass, or feather beds. Some have clawfoot or two-person whirlpool tubs in the bathroom, and the carriage-house rooms have fireplaces.

Breakfast has been known to feature delights such as blueberry-stuffed French toast or basil-cheese strata. A hand-painted, stamped tin ceiling shelters the dining room. In the evening you can enjoy wine and cheese by the garden fountain. Hennessey House offers discounts on the Wine Train, golf, hot-air balloon rides, and in-room massage.

Arbor Guest House $$$$
1436 G St., Napa
(707) 252–8144
www.arborguesthouse.com

In the Napa neighborhood appropriately known as Old Town, the Arbor Guest House is a pretty, whitewashed Colonial with a porch swing in front and a shady garden in back. The house is compact, but the rooms—three units upstairs, two more in the original Carriage house—manage to be ample. Two of them have spa tubs, three have fireplaces, and the main-house rooms are cooled by a reliable cross-breeze (and air-conditioning, if things get serious). Breakfast is served in the dining room or the garden or, if you're staying in the carriage house, it is brought to your door with prior notice.

La Belle Epoque $$$$
1386 Calistoga Ave., Napa
(707) 257–2161, (800) 238–8070
www.labelleepoque.com

In 1893 Napa's leading hardware dealer built this splendid Queen Anne for his infant daughter, who died shortly thereafter. Tragic origins aside, La Belle Epoque beams with class: multi-gabled dormers, Oriental carpets, divans, marble-topped dressers, and radiant stained

The Old World Inn in Napa is a Victorian-era structure painted in pleasant pastels and surrounded by flower gardens. PHOTO: JEAN SAYLOR DOPPENBERG

busy Jefferson Street (where it meets Calistoga Avenue). The inn is touched up in mellow pastel blue, rose, peach, and mint—colors inspired by Swedish artist Carl Larsson—and the interior walls bear hand-lettered quotations, most of which could be filed under the heading "Be Kind to Strangers." And they do practice what they preach.

You'll receive a complimentary carafe of local wine upon arrival, evening hors d'oeuvres such as smoked salmon or Moroccan eggplant on sourdough bread, and a late-night buffet of chocolate treats. Of course, you get a full, hot breakfast in the dining room. Some rooms have canopied beds; some have claw-foot tubs. Others have fireplaces and private Jacuzzis. There is also an outdoor Jacuzzi shared by all guests of the Old World Inn.

Brookside Vineyard Bed & Breakfast $$
3194 Redwood Rd., Napa
(707) 944–1661

There isn't much traffic on shady Redwood Road other than the folks trekking back and forth to the Hess Collection Winery. Anyway, with seven acres of land, Brookside offers plenty of room for sequestering. Tom and Susan Ridley's homey spot is full of images and relics true to the house's Mission style, including a long, pew-style bench in the entranceway. The three ground-floor guest rooms are off a long hallway, and each opens onto the garden. About half the acreage is devoted to vineyard, and visitors have been known to join the autumn crush. Elsewhere, fruit trees, California poppies, and Douglas fir Christmas trees abound, and a path descends to a creekside clearing. (At least it's creekside when Redwood Creek is flowing.) Brookside has a swimming pool, and the largest bedroom has a dry sauna. The Ridleys accept personal checks. No credit cards.

glass, much of it transplanted from an old church. The inn has six rooms, with all the cozy alcoves and claw-foot tubs you would expect. You get your full breakfast in the formal dining room or on the garden patio. Innkeeper Georgia Jump serves evening wine and appetizers in the wine cellar.

The Old World Inn $$$$
1301 Jefferson St., Napa
(707) 257–0112, (800) 966–6624
www.oldworldinn.com

This 1906 Victorian isn't as noisy as you might think, despite being situated on

La Résidence $$$$
4066 St. Helena Hwy. North, Napa
(707) 253–0337, (800) 253–9203
www.laresidence.com

Is La Résidence a hotel disguised as a bed-and-breakfast inn or a B&B masquerading as a hotel? Does it matter when you're sitting in the elegant, sun-infused dining room at a table for two, eating a three-course breakfast from the fixed but ever-changing menu? La Res, as it is called, is a nice surprise within shouting distance of Highway 29. The 16 rooms and 4 suites, divided between the 1870 Gothic Revival mansion and the newer French Barn, are decorated in French Provincial style. Most include working fireplaces and patios or verandas. The inn sits on $2^{1}/_{2}$ acres of heritage oaks, pines, and fledgling vines. There is a swimming pool, a separate Jacuzzi, and a small meeting room for up to 15 people. Smoking is prohibited in all rooms, and the place isn't really set up for children.

Oak Knoll Inn $$$$
2200 E. Oak Knoll Ave., Napa
(707) 255-2200
www.oakknollinn.com

The land around Oak Knoll Inn is part of Napa County's agricultural preserve. Businesses such as this are not allowed. Fortunately for its guests, the inn was here in 1984, before the prohibition. In effect, it has a virtual monopoly on 360-degree vineyard views. There is a big wooden deck outside the rooms, so you can spend all day looking at the Chardonnay and Merlot grapes before they head to Rutherford Hill, Beaulieu, or Trefethen, which is just down the road. Oak Knoll Inn has four units, each with a fireplace and private entrance. There is a heated pool and spa for common use. The place is known for its breakfasts; on one recent morning it included baked pears in cognac sauce, baked herbed eggs, and fresh muffins. But mostly the inn is renowned for the incredibly detailed itineraries that owner Barbara Passino customizes and prints out for guests. This is not a good option for couples with children.

Maison Fleurie $$$$
6529 Yount St., Yountville
(707) 944-2056, (800) 788-0369
www.foursisters.com

In the middle of Yountville (but a block away from most of the traffic) is this French-style country inn. The 100-year-old main building has 2-foot-thick stone walls, terra-cotta tile, and a gas fireplace in the brick parlor. Two other structures—the Old Bakery (a working bakery in the 1970s) and the carriage house—bring the total number of rooms to 13. Units range from $115 to $260 per night. You get a gourmet breakfast (or breakfast in bed if you'd rather) and a jar of homemade cookies in the lobby. There is a swimming pool, spa tub, and mountain bikes for guest use. Maison Fleurie is part of Four Sisters Inns, a group of nine bed-and-breakfast establishments, most of them on the California coast.

Bordeaux House $$$
6600 Washington St., Yountville
(707) 944-2855, (800) 677-6370
www.bordeauxhouse.com

A mixture of new (1980) and old (1895) structures, this inn is a bit of a bargain for this neck of the woods. In the heart of Yountville, it is surrounded by lovely trees and gardens, and the world-class restaurants and shops of the whole town are within easy walking distance. (The French Laundry is just steps away, in fact.) The inn's newer, main building has five guest rooms with fireplaces and private patios or decks. Modern amenities are provided in each room; all have private exterior entrances. The Old Water Tower, overlooking the garden, is about 15 steps up and down. The inn's reception area is where you can enjoy your morning buffet breakfast and late afternoon Port and munchies.

Burgundy House Inn $$$
6711 Washington St., Yountville
(707) 944-0889

Yountville's main drag may not be the place you'd expect to find an Old World country inn, but Burgundy House has the requisites. It's a durable cube with 22-inch-thick walls, hand-hewn posts and lintels, and lace curtains. Built as a brandy distillery in the 1890s from local fieldstone and river rock, it has also been a winery, a hotel, an antiques warehouse, and, now, a five-room inn. Buffet break-

The tiny but tony Burgundy House Bed & Breakfast on Washington Street in Yountville began life as a brandy distillery. PHOTO: JEAN SAYLOR DOPPENBERG

breakfast in the morning, appetizers and wine, usually poured by a local winery, in the afternoon. Tapestries and polished antiques abound, and paintings are hung with brocade.

The rooms are lovely but not huge—five have private baths; two share a bath. The observatory serves as the TV room. While taking advantage of the 360-degree panorama, you might pop in a video of *Wild in the Country,* an Elvis Presley romp filmed at the Ink House in 1960. The inn also offers 18-speed bicycles and an antique pool table in the basement. A steep staircase makes this an iffy choice for families with kids.

Shady Oaks Country Inn $$$$
399 Zinfandel Ln., St. Helena
(707) 963–1190
www.shadyoaksinn.com

The buildings are full of history at Shady Oaks, but it's the two acres of outdoor space that really sell the inn. The towering oaks are indeed shady. On one side of the house is a working walnut orchard; on the other are grapevines. And in back, a twisted 100-year-old wisteria vine protects the patio. Shady Oaks offers two suites (each with private entrance) in a two-story, stone structure that operated as a winery from 1883 to 1887. Three more rooms are found in John and Lisa Runnells' 1920s, Craftsman-style home. Each unit features its own small collection of antiques; particularly lovely are the beds, such as the brass and ivory king-size in the Winery Retreat. Three of the rooms have fireplaces, and the Sunny Retreat has an adjoining second bedroom.

Afternoon wine is served on the patio. Champagne breakfast, meanwhile, is a splendid affair likely to entail eggs Benedict or Belgian waffles served in elegant style. Besides advice on restaurants and attractions, they can usually set up private tours at lesser-known wineries. Please note that children are not recommended here.

La Fleur Bed and Breakfast Inn $$$$
1475 Inglewood Ave., St. Helena
(707) 963–0233
www.lafleurinn.com

fast is served in the "distillery" or outside on the rose garden patio. Children older than 12 are permitted.

The Ink House $$$$
1575 St. Helena Hwy. South, St. Helena
(707) 963–3890, (800) 553–4343
members.aol.com/inkhousebb

If you have driven the length of Highway 29 a few times, you have no doubt taken notice of this remarkable house, a wedding-cake Italianate Victorian with a wraparound porch and third-floor crow's nest. Built by Theron H. Ink in 1884, it's now a seven-room bed-and-breakfast inn where the highway meets Whitehall Lane. The Ink House has a formal parlor and dining room for guests. You get a full

This is a classic Wine Country inn—an 1882 Queen Anne Victorian with vineyard views, on a quiet road in the heart of Napa Valley. Up a steep, curving staircase you'll find the guest units. All have private bathrooms. Four have old-fashioned tubs; four have fireplaces. The wonderfully bright Vineyard Room has a big balcony hanging over the vines. (La Fleur actually owns a vineyard and makes two Petite Sirahs, a dry and a Port.) The inn is across the highway from V. Sattui (see our Wineries chapter) and next door to Villa Helena Winery, where guests are accompanied for special tours. A large buffet breakfast is served in the solarium or outside on the porch, depending on the weather. No credit cards.

Glass Mountain Inn $$$$
3100 Silverado Trail, St. Helena
(707) 968-9400

Glass Mountain was named for its large deposits of obsidian, also known as "black glass." That obsidian is evident in the dining room of the Glass Mountain Inn, where guests can peer into a wine cave dug by Chinese laborers (originally for perishables, not Pinots) in the late 1800s. The house, with its wood shingles and steepled roof, isn't nearly as old as the cave. The inn has three large rooms with private baths, each room with individual strengths—the queen bed in the Mountain View Suite is framed by five arched windows; the Garden Suite has an oversized, oval whirlpool tub; and the Treetops Suite has a claw-foot tub and a private deck. Guests are greeted with a full breakfast each morning. Bring the children; they are welcome.

Cinnamon Bear Bed & Breakfast $$$$
1407 Kearney St., St. Helena
(707) 963-4653, (888) 963-4600

The name accurately describes this inn at the corner of Kearney and Adams Streets in bucolic St. Helena. From the handmade quilts and floral wallpaper to the braided rugs to the army of antique teddy bears, it all adds up to cuteness. The ample, shingled Craftsman bungalow was built in 1904, a wedding gift for Susan Smith from her father. The man Susan married, Walter Metzner, later was mayor of St. Helena for 20 years. His former abode has been fabulously restored. Cinnamon Bear inn has three second-floor

The third-floor observatory of The Ink House near St. Helena offers a spectacular 360-degree vista of the surrounding mountains and vineyards. PHOTO: JEAN SAYLOR DOPPENBERG

guest rooms, two with queen beds and one with a king. Proprietor Cathye Ranieri is a chef, so you can expect a complete and well-executed breakfast (on the porch if the weather is nice). Children 10 and older are welcome.

The Ambrose Bierce House $$$$
1515 Main St., St. Helena
(707) 963–3003
www.ambrosebiercehouse.com

Ambrose Bierce was a novelist, a poet, an essayist, a cartoonist, and a noted misanthrope. He wrote *The Devil's Dictionary* before disappearing in Mexico in 1913. The 1872 Victorian home he left behind in St. Helena bears his name and offers visitors three lovely rooms and a covered balcony tucked next to a grand redwood tree. The entire inn was recently remodeled. The Ambrose Bierce Suite, secluded on the second floor, has a private sitting room (with a television) that can be converted into a second bedroom. The Lillie Langtry Room is painted in lavender and white, while the Eadweard Muybridge Room is awash in deep blue and white. All three have plush, raised beds; stools are provided to help you make your way up under the covers.

Like its sister bed-and-breakfast,

> ## Insiders' Tip
> If you want a bed-and-breakfast experience without the legwork, here are a couple groups that will help you select one. B&B Style covers our entire four-county area-reach them at (800) 995-8884 or (707) 942-2888. Wine Country Reservations is oriented toward Napa and Sonoma valleys; their number is (707) 257-7757.

Shady Oaks Country Inn (see write-up in this chapter), Ambrose Bierce House is guided by the Runnells family. John and Lisa serve a full champagne breakfast in the morning, premium wine and cheese in the evening. Each guestroom is equipped with a crystal decanter of Port. Relax to classical music in the parlor, or soak in the home's hot tub. Parents, please note that children are not recommended here.

Forest Manor $$$$
415 Cold Springs Rd., Angwin
(707) 965–3538, (800) 788–0364
www.forestmanorbandb.com

Six miles into the forest above St. Helena is this magnificent property with 20 acres of wooded trails and a huge 54-foot swimming pool. The six rooms are named for writers; the two honeymoon suites are the William Shakespeare and the Ernest Hemingway. All of the rooms have refrigerators and robes, and most have king beds, fireplaces, and Jacuzzis. A full gourmet breakfast is included in the tariff.

Scarlett's Country Inn $$$
3918 Silverado Trail, Calistoga
(707) 942–6669

A "country inn" can sometimes mean a suburban cul-de-sac and a large rose garden. But Scarlett's is the real thing, a bucolic acre midway between Calistoga and St. Helena, where guests share space with friendly dogs and chickens. Scarlett Dwyer has lived on the property since 1965 and has run the inn since 1981. Her house is a former chicken-processing building. The early-century farmhouse, meanwhile, now holds two of the three guest units—the Gamay Suite and the Camellia Suite, which actually can be opened into a full house for larger parties. Each room boasts a separate entrance, a queen bed, a TV, a microwave, and a fridge. But the outdoor space is the big selling point here: a hammock, a tree swing, an aviary with finches and canaries, a lush fig tree, a pine-protected swimming pool, and spa. Guests can choose the time and place for their full breakfast—and you know where the eggs are from. Note that Scarlett's does not accept credit cards, though personal checks are all right. The inn is just south of Wermuth Winery.

Christopher's Inn $$$$
1010 Foothill Blvd., Calistoga
(707) 942–5755
www.chrisinn.com

This inn proves the old adage that you can't judge a booking by its cover. The owner, an architect, joined an 80-year-old house with two cottages to make one large building. It's nice enough from the outside, but doesn't hint at the luxury held within the 22 rooms. Laura Ashley prints, exquisite antique desks, fresh flowers, and high, open ceilings—it's a tasteful experience. Some newly added rooms have private Jacuzzis. Breakfast—yogurt, baked cobbler, etc.—is delivered to your door. For those who must conduct a bit of business while relaxing in splendor, there are two small conference rooms with fax accessibility, and modem ports are available in most rooms.

Christopher's also has two voluminous flats in back, facing onto Myrtle Street, that sleep as many as five people. Children are allowed at the inn.

Wine Way Inn $$$
1019 Foothill Blvd., Calistoga
(707) 942–0680, (800) 572–0679
www.napavalley.com/wineway

This bed-and-breakfast inn, opened in 1979, was the first in Calistoga. It's right next to Calistoga's busiest intersection, and owners Cecile and Moye Stephens want you to know up front that there is some street noise. Nonetheless, from the solid oak front door with etched glass to the patchwork quilts in each second-story room, the Stephenses have managed to create a pleasant environment in their circa-1915 home. In addition to the five interior rooms, the Calistoga Room is a detached unit—it's out by the multitiered deck that backs up to a wooded hillside. The breakfasts alternate daily between sweet and savory, with specialties such as frittata and tomato omelettes. And for no extra charge, George the dog will perform stupid pet tricks (including the critically acclaimed "Burning Building") while you enjoy your complimentary wine and snacks in the afternoon.

Falcons Nest $$$
471 Kortum Canyon Rd., Calistoga
(707) 942–0758
www.falconsnestbb.com

The view is the attraction here. Sitting well above the valley floor, the many decks surrounding this inn offer spectacular panoramas of terraced vineyards and mountains. The seven-acre estate is nearly a mile off Highway 29 along a forested road. All the rooms have queen beds, private entries, and private baths. A Jacuzzi is available on the lower deck, and it makes an ideal spot for watching hawks and gliders circling overhead. A full breakfast is served each morning.

The Elms $$$$
1300 Cedar St., Calistoga
(707) 942–9476, (800) 235–4316
www.theelms.com

A.C. Palmer, the first circuit judge of Napa and Sonoma Counties, went to France for his honeymoon sometime around 1870, and he and his bride returned to Calistoga with two important items: designs for a new home and a small number of elm seedlings. The house lives as The Elms, shaded by the now-towering trees. Without a doubt, it is one of the most impressive homes in the valley. Palmer ran a lumber yard just across the Napa River, and The Elms is full of richly detailed, hand-hewn wood. It's also brimming with antiques—mostly French—thanks to the current owners.

The inn has four rooms in the main house. Two of them face Cedar Street, while another (the one in which Audrey Hepburn once slept) gazes upon pretty Pioneer Park. At the rear of the property are three rooms in the refurbished carriage house, including the Honeymoon Cottage, a large unit with a two-person shower and views to the river. Five of the rooms have fireplaces, and all seven come with a TV, plus Port and chocolate. The Elms is not a good choice for those with children.

La Chaumiere $$$$
1301 Cedar St., Calistoga
(707) 942–5139, (800) 474–6800
www.lachaumiere.com

What grabs you first is the garden, an explosion of ferns and flowers surrounding a tall pine in front of the house. La Chaumiere is a small, picturesque house with a pitched roof and an arched window that looks across the street to Pioneer Park. There are two well-appointed rooms in the house (one has a sitting room in addition to the bedroom), plus a detached cabin in the rear. The bathrooms are part of the attraction—one has antique lavender-and-black tile work, the other has a mirror framed by an old billiards cue-rack.

The log cabin, built in 1932, isn't exactly the kind Abe Lincoln grew up in. The whole-timber redwood uprights and crossbeams are complemented by touches of comfort, including a wood stove, a fireplace built of petrified wood, and a large kitchen. The outdoor common areas include a flowery patio and a treehouse built around the trunk of a redwood. You get a full breakfast in the morning, plus wine and cheese in the afternoon and Port in your room. La Chaumiere is just a block off Lincoln Avenue.

Scott Courtyard $$$
1443 Second St., Calistoga
(707) 942–0948, (800) 942–1515
www.scottcourtyard.com

This small, six-suite bed-and-breakfast on the corner of Fair Way and Second Street tries for neither Victorian splendor nor designer finery. The hallmarks at Scott are service, comfortable outdoor space and, if you want it, privacy. Each unit has a sitting room, bedroom, and private bath; some have kitchen facilities. Children are allowed in some rooms, but are not really encouraged. Air-conditioning is provided in all rooms. There is a latticed courtyard, a pool and hot tub, a small aviary full of flitting finches, and an artist's studio that inspired guests are allowed to use. (Local artists sometimes lead seminars there.) Breakfast, served in the bistro-style dining room or on the patio, tends to get rave reviews, with dishes such as banana-walnut pancakes and Thai chicken sausage.

Hideaway Cottages $$$
1412 Fair Way, Calistoga
(707) 942–4108
www.hideawaycottages.com

If you want a classic bed-and-breakfast experience without the breakfast, try this establishment on peaceful Fair Way. Look for the hedges and palm trees in front of a two-story gingerbread house. In back are 17 recently renovated cottages facing onto a landscaped courtyard. Many of the rooms have full kitchens. Hideaway, an affiliate of Dr. Wilkinson's Hot Springs (see our Spas and Resorts chapter), has a large mineral pool and Spa Jet tub.

Wisteria Garden Bed & Breakfast $$$
1508 Fair Way, Calistoga
(707) 942–5358
www.bbinternet.com/wisteria

This circa-1910 Colonial Revival cottage, about halfway between Lincoln Avenue and the fairgrounds, takes its name from the 100-year-old wisteria vines that drape over the carport. Behind the house is an old valley oak that shades the two guest rooms. Both units have private baths, gas fireplaces, air-conditioning, refrigerators and microwaves, cable TV, and VCRs. Continental breakfast is served on weekends. While Wisteria Garden does not have an on-site pool, guests receive complimentary passes to take the plunge at a local spa. Children are permitted and pets might be, too—state your case to Carmen Maib, the innkeeper. The inn offers substantial, even negotiable, savings for midweek stays.

Brannan Cottage Inn $$$$
109 Wapoo Ave., Calistoga
(707) 942–4200
www.brannancottageinn.com

About 130 years ago, this spot had row upon row of one-story white bungalows, all with five-arched fronts, intricate gingerbread gable boards, wraparound porches, and scalloped cresting. Now only one of them remains on its original site, and it's a six-room inn. (Two of the rooms are out back in the carriage house.) The look of the place—the 11-foot ceilings, oak floors, and ceiling fans—whisks you right back to the days of Sam Brannan and his stay-rich schemes (see our History chapter). Each unit has a queen bed and a refrigerator. Full buffet breakfast is served in the dining room or on the patio. Children 10 and older are accepted, but the inn won't take credit card reservations over the phone.

Cottage Grove Inn $$$$
1711 Lincoln Ave., Calistoga
(707) 942–8400, (800) 799–2284
www.cottagegrove.com

In stark contrast to the trailer park that occupied this space for many years, the Cottage Grove is decidedly high-end. That's appropriate, because long before the trailer park this was the promenade area of Brannan's Hot Springs Resort, the spa that gave birth to Calistoga (see our History chapter). The grove of Siberian elms was planted by Brannan in the 1850s, and today they form an effective visual barrier to the traffic of Lincoln Avenue.

Each of Cottage Grove's 16 private cottages has a wood-burning fireplace (and a basket of wood on the porch), a CD stereo system, TV and VCR, air conditioner, private bath with two-person Jacuzzi tub, Egyptian cotton towels, and an ironing board. Each has a theme, too, like the Music Cottage, the Audubon Cottage, and the Fly Fishing Cottage. Continental breakfast and evening wine and appetizers are served in the common room. The owners allow children age 12 and older.

Culver Mansion $$$
1805 Foothill Blvd., Calistoga
(707) 942–4535, (877) 281–3671
www.culvermansion.com

Proprietor Jacqueline LeVesque has done a magnificent job of renovating this circa-1875 Victorian mansion to make it homey and inviting. The six guest rooms are nicely furnished with comfortable McRoskey mattresses, hand-made in San Francisco, and as Jacqueline explains it, "the choice of the Queen of England for a wonderful night's sleep!" There's a private pool, spa, and sauna out back, and a full breakfast is included in the tariff. The resident feline, Eddie, will make you feel right at home while you enjoy the sweeping views from the old-fashioned veranda.

The Wayside Inn $$$
1523 Foothill Blvd., Calistoga
(707) 942–0645

This split-level, Spanish-style home, built in the 1920s, is more like something you would expect to see in an older Los Angeles neighborhood, but it seems right at home in Napa Valley. The living room has rough beams and a wood fireplace. The back yard is densely shaded by trees—a dogwood, English walnut, a loquat, and at least a dozen others. The three guest rooms are distinctly furnished and cooled by ceiling fans. One of them, the

Camellia Room, has sole use of the home's original master bathroom; some people don't like having to step out into the hallway, but the impeccable sea-green tile work makes it worth the three extra strides. If you are journeying at night, look for the oversized wreath, twinkling with white lights, in the arched window of the front room.

The Pink Mansion $$$$
1415 Foothill Blvd., Calistoga
(707) 942-0558
www.pinkmansion.com

Alma Simic was a colorful character. She was the last owner and longest resident to live in this stately home, and she had eclectic tastes in decorating, with a mixture of Victorian and Oriental influences. Fortunately for visitors, the current owners have made certain that Alma's sense of style remains intact. The six guest rooms are elegant and tasteful, and most have views. The Master Suite and Honeymoon Suites are large—900 and 800 square feet, respectively—and feature king beds, two-person Jacuzzis, and private decks and sitting rooms. By the way, the mansion has been pink since the 1930s.

Bear Flag Inn $$$$
2653 Foothill Blvd., Calistoga
(707) 942-5534, (800) 670-2860
www.bearflaginn.com

Just northwest of the intersection of Highway 128 and Petrified Forest Road, this five-room bed-and-breakfast is a renovated farmhouse built in the 1930s. Purportedly, it was on this very site that Peter Storm constructed one of the flags used for the Bear Flag Revolt in 1846. The Bear Flag Inn sits on three acres, surrounded by vineyard and meadowed hillside. Four rooms are in the two-story house; the cottage is a detached unit with a sitting room. All have private baths, queen beds, robes, cable TV and VCRs, and air-conditioning. There is a swimming pool and an outdoor hot tub for guests. A full breakfast is served, with wine and appetizers in the afternoon. The house was recently refurbished.

Foothill House $$$$
3037 Foothill Blvd., Calistoga
(707) 942-6933, (800) 942-6933
www.foothillhouse.com

One of Calistoga's most renowned B&Bs sits in a woodsy setting on the northwest outskirts of town. Fountains and cascades lend a soothing air, and views to Mount St. Helena help to keep you oriented as you sit in the arbor or Jacuzzi. The interiors are impeccable—with hand-picked antiques and handmade quilts complementing the Laura Ashley designs—and as expansive as you are likely to find. Each room includes TV and VCR, CD player, refrigerator, and fireplace or wood stove. Three of the four have whirlpool tubs. Each has its strengths, but the Quails Roost, a detached cottage just up the hillside, is clearly the palatial unit. The owners, Gus and Doris Beckert, call this their "event room." Quiet and private, the Quails Roost has a full kitchen and a washer/dryer setup; guests have been known to rent it for a week and go into hiding. (If you are bringing children, please book the Foothill Cottage.) Doris, trained as a chef, oversees breakfast and the afternoon "wine appreciation hour."

Hillcrest B&B $$$
3225 Lake Co. Hwy., Calistoga
(707) 942-6334
www.bnbweb.com/hillcrest

From Highway 29 (a.k.a. Lake County Highway) as it begins to wind up Mt. St. Helena, look for the twin stone pillars and drive to the end of the rutted quarter-mile driveway. The owner, Debbie O'Gorman, is the great-great-granddaughter of Senator Tubbs, who constructed Chateau Montelena on the valley floor (see our Wineries chapter), and this property has been in her family since 1860. Debbie is happy to open her family photo albums—with century-old pictures—to show the old wineries of the region. Views from the house, especially from the big-paned windows of the living room, are superb.

The mood here is extremely casual. Guests come and go as they please and are often left with a free run of the premises. Hillcrest has a fishing pond, hiking paths, a swimming pool and outdoor Jacuzzi, and a barbecue area. There are six rooms—three have private bathrooms and balconies, one has a bathroom but no balcony, and two share both bath and balcony. All of them have fireplaces. Children and dogs are accepted. Credit cards are not, but you can write a personal check.

Sonoma County

Southern Sonoma

The Cottage Inn and Spa $$
302 First St. East, Sonoma
(707) 996-5220, (800) 944-1490
www.cottageinnandspa.com

Located on a quiet street a block off the plaza, The Cottage invites visitors into its courtyards, which include fountains and a seating area. A nearby six-person hot tub is available to all guests. Five of the six rooms open onto the courtyards, five have their own private outdoor spaces, and five include fireplaces. The studio room has a cathedral ceiling.

Thistle Dew Inn $$$
171 W. Spain St., Sonoma
(707) 938-2909, (800) 382-7895
www.thistledew.com

This is a prime location for Wine Country visitors. Just a half-block off the Sonoma Plaza, the Thistle Dew puts guests within walking distance (or biking distance, if you want to borrow from the inn's stable) of fine restaurants, shops, wineries, and historic sites. The living room invites guests to sit by the fireplace, read a book, or work on a jigsaw puzzle. The six guest rooms manage to provide a feeling of seclusion and privacy in spite of the fact that the inn is on a busy street on the edge of downtown. Breakfast is served in the dining room looking out on Spain Street. All rooms have private baths, and some have whirlpool baths or ornamental fireplaces.

Victorian Garden Inn $$
316 E. Napa St., Sonoma
(707) 996-5339, (800) 543-5339
www.victoriangardeninn.com

It's a farmhouse built in 1870, but it's only blocks from the downtown plaza.

The wraparound porch with wicker chairs could make you believe the past is present. But it's the gardens that make this inn unique. Lawns and paths wind through the trees and along the creek, with occasional spots to sit and contemplate.

The four guest rooms—one in the main house and the rest in a century-old water tower—have private baths and are elegantly decorated. Woodcutter's Cottage is a private retreat with a fireplace, clawfoot tub, and garden view. Breakfast is served in the dining room, on the patio, or in your room. A three-night minimum stay is required on weekends.

Trojan Horse Inn $$
19455 Hwy. 12, Sonoma
(707) 996-2430, (800) 899-1925
www.trojanhorseinn.com

Rebuilt after a tragic fire in 1990, this inn has turned into a charming B&B decorated with English and French antiques, a fact you'll especially appreciate if you join other guests for complimentary wine and hors d'oeuvres between 6:00 and 7:00 P.M. Each of its six rooms has a different theme, decorated individually. Especially popular is the room called Grape Arbor, boasting a fireplace and double Jacuzzi, but all rooms are furnished with antiques of the 1880s era, when the original house was built. Children older than 12 are welcome with advance notice, but be advised: This inn is recommended in the book *Best Places to Kiss By in the Bay Area*. A full breakfast is served along the lines of French toast or banana pancakes, lemon chicken sausage, fresh fruit, and Starbucks coffee.

Above the Clouds $$$$
3250 Trinity Rd., Glen Ellen
(707) 996-7371, (800) 736-7894
www.sonomabb.com/abovetheclouds.htm

The mountain road called Oakville Grade (up Trinity Road on the Sonoma side) straddles the Mayacmas Mountains that rise between the Sonoma and Napa valleys. Trinity Road sprouts from Highway 12 about 8 miles north of the Sonoma Plaza, and winds through thickets of manzanita and scrub oaks for 3 miles before reaching Above the Clouds bed-and-breakfast inn. When the fog rolls through the Sonoma Valley, this inn lives up to its name. It's a secluded mountain retreat that surveys forests and catches the sunset. Three guest rooms are furnished with antique iron or brass beds, and each has a private bath, queen bed, down comforters, and lots of pillows. Robes are provided for those who want to take advantage of the swimming pool and Jacuzzi spa. A gourmet breakfast is served. Two-night minimum is required. You should book well in advance. The inn is closed from mid-November to February.

Beltane Ranch $$$
11775 Hwy. 12, Glen Ellen
(707) 996–6501
www.beltaneranch.com

The place has an exotic—even romantic—past. The land was first settled in 1882 by Mary Ann "Mammy" Pleasant, whose exploits as a madam to San Francisco's upper crust (plus suspicions of a possible homicide in her posh establishment) had led to alarming headlines. It was said she conducted black magic sessions too. But Mammy had another side: She became known as "the western terminus" of the Underground Railroad, making frequent trips to the South to secretly help thousands of Blacks escape to Canada.

Beltane Ranch's architectural style suggests Deep South, with a stylish veranda set off with an elaborate gingerbread railing. But the Ranch's recent past is more mundane. In the 1920s it was the bunkhouse for a turkey ranch. Inside are six guest rooms (including one cottage), each with an individual outdoor entrance. The rooms are rustic but cozy, furnished with antiques. The 1,600 acres include a working vineyard, and the owner is happy to tour the grounds with you and explain what viticulture is all about. The grapes are sold to Kenwood Vineyards (see our Wineries chapter).

A full breakfast is served, and it may include omelettes and homemade scones served on your own veranda or in the garden. This is a popular lodging place, and reservations are definitely recommended

A large swimming pool at the Gaige House Inn in Glen Ellen keeps guests cool during the Sonoma Valley's warmest days. PHOTO: GAIGE HOUSE INN/RICHARD JUNG

during the harvest season of August through October.

Gaige House Inn $$$$
13540 Arnold Dr., Glen Ellen
(707) 935–0237, (800) 935–0237
www.gaige.com

An elegant Italianate Victorian, restored from its original 1880s construction and recently refurbished, Gaige House Inn has a prime location at the edge of the village of Glen Ellen in the heart of Wine Country. It has six guest rooms and one suite in the main house, and eight garden rooms with outside entrances. The signature room is the Gaige Suite, a spacious sunny room with large windows on three sides and a wraparound deck overlooking the garden. You'll awake in your four-poster bed and step into a bathroom that's larger than most bedrooms. The creekside setting includes a large swimming pool and Jacuzzi. A formal breakfast is included, as are afternoon hors d'oeuvres and beverages.

Glenelly Inn $$$
5131 Warm Springs Rd., Glen Ellen
(707) 996–6720
www.glenelly.com

This is one of the few Wine Country bed-and-breakfast inns that was actually built as an inn. Visitors of the 1920s and '30s came by railroad and basked in the sun on the inn's long verandas. The long verandas are still there, now with wicker chairs to provide a perch to watch the sun set over Sonoma Mountain. Each of the eight rooms has a private entrance. They are furnished in a country motif, with antique furniture and Scandinavian down comforters. The Jack London Room has a sleigh bed and wood-burning stove, and all rooms have claw-foot tubs and antique sinks. An outdoor spa is set amid native landscaping. In the morning, a full breakfast is served in the common room by a large cobblestone fireplace. It's a great experience, with hot entrees, homemade bread and muffins, fresh fruit, and fresh-squeezed orange juice.

Tanglewood House $$$
250 Bonnie Way, Glen Ellen
(707) 996–5021
www.tanglewoodhouse.com

On a quiet country road a mile from Glen Ellen, Tanglewood House is a retreat occupying more than an acre of park-like, secluded gardens. Only one room is available—a large luxurious suite that occupies an entire wing of this lovely house. It has its own private entrance and patio and a spacious sitting room with fireplace, cathedral ceiling, and color TV. A magnificent pool is available to guests, and there is a full breakfast in the morning.

Cavanagh Inn $
10 Keller St., Petaluma
(707) 765–4657, (888) 765–4658
www.cavanaghinn.com

There's a feeling of turn-of-the-century elegance here that few modern houses achieve. It was built for lumberman John Cavanagh in 1902, a time when his company was known for providing some of the finest rare heart-redwood available. His house paneling shows he picked the best of what he had for his residence. The mansion's four bedrooms are furnished in Victorian style, though one of them has a special addition Cavanagh wouldn't believe—a tub with a whirlpool ready to froth with bubble bath.

There's a three-bedroom cottage beside the main house, built for two Cavanagh sisters. Bedrooms here are less formal, furnished with wicker, and two of the three rooms share a bath. Owners Ray and Jeanne Farris tell guests they can park their cars and forget them—the inn is within walking distance of most everything they'll want to visit, including Petaluma's historic district with its antiques shops. Jeanne's love of cooking shows in her breakfast offerings. A typical morning might include pears in butterscotch sauce and fluffy scrambled eggs topped with crab and seafood sauce.

Goltermann Gardens & Country Inn $$$
1000 Skillman Ln., Petaluma
(707) 762–1761

In northwest Petaluma's Leghorn Valley, Goltermann Gardens is a romantic country retreat. This rural farmhouse estate, set on more than seven acres, was once home to 10,000 white Leghorn laying hens. The Goltermanns have turned the family farm into an elegant inn. Lush landscaping with mature trees, lawns, and a lake allows you the freedom to enjoy fishing, horseshoes, croquet, and hiking. Five spacious suites that include king or queen beds, fine linens, and elegant bathroom fixtures offer an opportunity to enjoy a relaxing, pampered stay. This is also a popular site for romantic weddings and receptions, with a wisteria-covered pergola as a dance pavilion. A two-day minimum is required. This is a fabulous property that's not so easy to categorize.

The Gables Inn $$$
4257 Petaluma Hill Rd., Santa Rosa
(707) 585–7777, (800) 422–5376
www.gablesinn.com

Built in 1877 at the height of Victorian Gothic Revival architecture, this home was built with 15 gables rising above some unique keyhole-shaped windows. There are seven rooms in the main house, five up a mahogany staircase, and two accessible to disabled guests, some of which include fireplaces, and all of which share central air-conditioning. Each room is furnished in unique decor that displays its history and character; each has a claw-foot tub in its private bath. An adjacent cottage is furnished with a kitchenette, TV with video library, stereo, woodstove, two-person whirlpool tub, and private phone/data port. A lavish country breakfast is served. A large sundeck looks out across acres of country just outside Santa Rosa.

Melitta Station Inn $
5850 Melita Rd., Santa Rosa
(707) 538–7712, (800) 504–3099
www.melittastationinn.com

Once this was a busy railroad station; before that it was a general store and post office. Today it's a warm inn with six guest rooms (five if the two-room suite is occupied) furnished with antiques and folk art. The inn's former life is evident in its unique plank flooring and hand-sawed fir boards with the sawyer's strokes still well-marked. The style here is American antique, with lots of collectibles to admire. The setting is part of the charm: The inn is surrounded by state parks, hiking trails, and biking opportunities. A full buffet breakfast is served by the wood-burning stove in the large sitting room on the balcony.

Pygmalion House $
331 Orange St., Santa Rosa
(707) 526–3407
www.bedandbreakfast.com

It was built in 1880 down near Railroad Square, where Santa Rosa had its beginnings. Now this Queen Anne home has been restored to a bed-and-breakfast inn of five rooms, all with private baths featuring showers and claw-foot tubs. It's furnished with pieces that include Gypsy Rose Lee antiques and memorabilia. Decorated in the European style, the parlor has a fireplace, TV, and telephone. There's a private garden and parking behind the inn. A hearty breakfast and afternoon treats are served.

Insiders' Tip

If you can't decide between two or three bed-and-breakfast inns, call each and ask a few questions. Make a difficult request. Tell them you're coming from Oakland and your car can't make left-hand turns. In short, quickly try to gauge their friendliness and helpfulness. After all, those two measures are likely to mean the difference between a happy stay and a mixed one.

Northern Sonoma

Country Meadow Inn $$$
11360 Old Redwood Hwy., Windsor
(707) 431–1276, (800) 238–1728
www.countrymeadowinn.com

This inn is a farmhouse from the 1890s in a setting of grape arbors, vegetable gardens, fruit trees, and terraced flower beds. This is not your granddad's farmhouse; it's elegant and charming with private baths, whirlpool tubs, and air-conditioning. Outside there's a tennis court and swimming pool. Yet the farming influence is not forgotten: breakfast abounds with fresh eggs, preserves made from homegrown fruits and berries, and fresh baked breads and pastries. Five romantic, country-style guest rooms are furnished in antiques or wicker; three have fireplaces and one has a whirlpool. The Garden Suite is a truly romantic hideaway with a separate sitting area. Weekend stays require a two-night minimum.

Belle de Jour Inn $$$$
16276 Healdsburg Ave., Healdsburg
(707) 431–9777
www.belledejourinn.com

This inn's hilltop setting is on six acres and looks out on rolling hills. The farmhouse, a single-story Italianate built around 1873, is the residence of the innkeepers, and it is here guests enjoy a hearty breakfast. Guests are quartered in five white cottages, all with fireplaces and some with decks. Each cottage is its own country experience. The Caretaker Suite, for instance, has a king-size, canopy bed and a fireplace in the sitting room. There's a sunny studio atelier room with a high, vaulted ceiling, and the grand Carriage House that has everything, including views and tub for two.

Camellia Inn $$$
211 North St., Healdsburg
(707) 433–8182, (800) 727–8182
www.camelliainn.com

The inn is overtaken by blooming camellias from November to May, hence the name. Built in 1869, the house served at one time as Healdsburg's first hospital, and in fact, the room you rent might have been the lab. There have been a few other incarnations since then, but the Lewants (Ray, Del, and daughter Lucy) run a friendly and efficient operation with nine rooms. As a plus, the Camellia Inn is just two blocks from historic Healdsburg Plaza and its chic shops and boutiques. When you return to your room from your excursions you might recuperate from the rigors of shopping in your whirlpool tub for two, light up the gas fireplace if you're chilly, and have a lovely night's sleep in your four-poster bed. The Camellia Inn includes a family suite—unusual in an industry largely geared toward couples.

Breakfast is served buffet style, with a selection of entrees and breads that will keep your energy up until noon (maybe later). Sometimes it's quiche or breakfast custard, and it's always accompanied with fruit, cereal, sourdough toast, and homemade jam. Bon appetit!

George Alexander House $$$
423 Matheson St., Healdsburg
(707) 433–1358, (800) 310–1358
www.georgealexanderhouse.com

This historic house was built in 1905 by George Alexander, the 10th child of Cyrus Alexander. Cyrus was the first settler in the north county, and Alexander Valley is named for him (see our History chapter). There are four rooms in this lovely inn, which has "gone upscale" in the last couple of years under its energetic new owner, Don Krohn. The Alexander room has a fireplace and bay windows, while the Back Porch has a private entrance with a deck, wood-burning stove, and whirlpool tub for two. If you're hungry for a hearty breakfast, you'll be happy to see such menu items as ricotta pancakes with sauteed apples. Two spacious parlors are available to guests, as is the sauna in the new garden. Stay two nights (a minimum on weekends) and get a bottle of wine.

Grape Leaf Inn $$
539 Johnson St., Healdsburg
(707) 433–8140
www.grapeleafinn.com

The seven elegant guest rooms in this 1900 Queen Anne Victorian are a perfect backdrop for romance. Each room is named for a wine varietal, and all are lushly furnished with iron beds, armoires, and warm oak accents. The four upstairs rooms will put you in a honeymoon mood with tubs for two. Most luxurious is the Chardonnay Suite, with cedar wood walls and stained-glass windows. In the evening you can enjoy a glass of wine with a tray of cheese and bread. Grape Leaf Inn is near shopping, restaurants, wineries, golf, tennis, fishing, ballooning, and canoe rentals. After a busy day about town and country, you can relax on the front porch. Breakfast is served in style in the dining room. The inn is known for its daily wine tasting presentation, offering seven varietals.

Haydon Street Inn $$
321 Haydon St., Healdsburg
(707) 433–5228, (800) 528–3703
www.haydon.com

In a quiet residential area within walking distance of Healdsburg's historic plaza, this Victorian inn has eight charming guest rooms. One of the most popular is the Turret Room, tucked into the slope of the roof, with a step-down entrance to the sleeping level. Each of the other rooms is distinctively different in decor, from iron bedsteads and handmade rugs to French antique furnishings. Six of the guest rooms are in the main house, a 1912 Queen Anne structure, and two are in the adjoining two-story Victorian cottage. The Garden Room has two walls of plantation-shuttered windows overlooking the garden. All rooms have private baths; those in the cottage also have double whirlpool tubs. If breakfast is your idea of the right start to the day, this is your place. You can get fired up for a full, energetic Wine Country adventure with scones slathered with orange butter, frittatas, croissants, French toast, quiches, fresh-baked breads, oven-roasted potatoes, meat side dishes, plus an aromatic house-blend coffee. When guests return from their ramblings, they'll be greeted with a snack treat to tide them over to dinner.

Healdsburg Inn on the Plaza $$$$
110 Matheson St., Healdsburg
(707) 433–6991, (800) 431–8663
www.healdsburginn.com

The front entrance is unpretentious enough, but it opens onto a handsome art gallery. A staircase leads to the 10 antique-filled rooms—most with fireplaces, all with private baths, some with whirlpool tubs for two. Once a Wells Fargo building, the inn now rates high on the luxury scale. A solarium in the roof garden is the common area where guests meet for breakfast and afternoon refreshments, when wine and fresh buttered popcorn, coffee, tea, and a bottomless cookie jar are available.

Honor Mansion $$$
14891 Grove St., Healdsburg
(707) 433–4277, (800) 554–4667
www.honormansion.com

The architecture, decor, and surrounding gardens give this inn a feeling of turn-of-the-century grace. You can almost imagine women in ankle-length frocks carrying on polite conversation with gentlemen in tennis sweaters as they stroll along the garden path. Its eight guest rooms are furnished with antiques and feather beds, and each has a private bath. The place has a fascinating history, and the innkeeper will be glad to regale you with the life of the Squire Butcher family over a breakfast of home-baked pastries and gourmet entrees.

Madrona Manor $$$$
1001 Westside Rd., Healdsburg
(707) 433–4231, (800) 258–4003
www.madronamanor.com

Tucked away in the lush Dry Creek Valley, Madrona Manor is an estate for which adjectives like elegant and majestic were invented. Originally built in 1880 by business tycoon John Paxton, Madrona Knoll Rancho, as it was then called, became one of the grandest showplaces in all the valley. Today it stands as a wonderful exponent of a bygone era of grandeur and refined taste. The Manor's accommodations include 21 rooms in four buildings on eight acres of wooded and manicured grounds. Seventeen of the rooms have fireplaces, and eight have a balcony or deck. A buffet-style breakfast is included. Need more elegance? World-class gourmet dining can be enjoyed each evening in a romantic candlelight setting (see our Restaurants chapter).

Midnight Sun Inn $$
428 Haydon St., Healdsburg
(707) 433–1718
www.midnight-sun.com

Somewhat different from many bed-and-breakfast inns, Midnight Sun is decorated in a modern country style, with almost no antique decor. The linens are top-of-the-line, as are the beds and mattresses. There are three guest rooms in the main house: "Juliet's Balcony" invites a second-story stroll across the entire front of the house. Inside, there's a canopy bed to stretch out in. The other two rooms are the Enchanted Garden Room and the Safari Room. The latter has jungle-patterned sheets and mosquito net for atmosphere. There's also a cottage in the back yard; it has a Wine Country theme and is said to be the most romantic room of all. Both the Garden Room and Juliet's Balcony have Jacuzzis for two.

Villa Messina $$$
316 Burgundy Rd., Healdsburg
(707) 433–6655
www.villamessina.com

The setting is unbelievable, with a 360-degree view of three exquisite valleys—Alexander, Dry Creek, and Russian River. The Italian villa-style inn was built in 1986 on top of the foundation of a former water tower. The inn's five guest rooms are furnished with antiques, and the floors are carpeted with Oriental rugs. All have private baths, plus TVs, VCRs, and phones. Some have Jacuzzis or fireplaces. For breakfast the chef prepares such treats as fresh-squeezed orange juice and blueberry pancakes with bacon. He also bakes his own breads. There is a swimming pool and hot tub. Kids are discouraged, but babies are okay.

Hope-Bosworth House $$
21238 Geyserville Ave., Geyserville
(707) 857–3356, (800) 825–4233
www.hopeinns.com

Driving down Geyserville Avenue, you'll have no trouble instantly recognizing the Hope-Bosworth House—it's the Queen

Along Healdsburg's Plaza is the aptly named Healdsburg Inn on the Plaza, which offers 10 antique-filled rooms and a rooftop solarium.
PHOTO: JEAN SAYLOR DOPPENBERG

Anne with the picket fence covered with "roses of yesteryear" varieties that were popular when the house was built in 1904. George Bosworth picked out the pattern for his home from a "pattern book" and had it constructed entirely of heart redwood.

All the rooms are a step into the past. The original oak-grained woodwork is evident everywhere, from the sliding doors in the hallway to the upstairs bedrooms. Polished fir floors and antique light fixtures enhance the period furnishing. At 9:00 A.M. a country breakfast is served in the formal dining room and includes fresh fruit, egg dishes, homemade breads and pastries, and coffee or tea.

Hope-Merrill House $$$
1253 Geyserville Ave., Geyserville
(707) 857–3356, (800) 825–4233
www.hopeinns.com

In its former life, it was a stagecoach stop of the 1870s. Now it's an enchanting inn, listed on the Sonoma County Landmarks

Register. Anyone interested in architecture will recognize the squared-off look of Eastlake Stick Style, popular between 1870 and 1885. J.P. Merrill, who was a land developer, saw to it he had the best of everything for his house, and he built it entirely of redwood. The Inn has eight rooms with charming names like Bachelor Button, Peacock, and Carpenter Gothic, all with queen beds and private baths. Four rooms have fireplaces, two have whirlpool baths and one has a sitting room. Please note the restored Victorian hand-screened wallpaper—it's stunning! Breakfast is superb, served in the dining room. There's a swimming pool.

Abrams House Inn $
314 N. Main St., Cloverdale
(707) 894-2412, (800) 764-4466

A restored 1870s Victorian, Abrams House Inn offers four guest rooms, one of them a special suite with a four-poster bed and private porch. There are also three parlors, two with TV and VCR, the other a library/game room. A wicker-decorated upper deck gives a lovely view of a rose garden, gazebo, and a deck with a hot tub. And for those who simply must bring business with them, there's a fax machine and copier available. Breakfast is ample (to put it mildly), and in the evening you can enjoy a decadent dessert with Abrams House's own specially blended hot cocoa.

Mountain House Winery and Lodge $$
33710 Hwy. 128, Cloverdale
(707) 894-5683
www.mtnhousewinery-lodge.com

In its former life, Mountain House was a stagecoach stop and inn, flanked by a barn and some outbuildings. Now this 1890s-era homestead has been converted to a bed-and-breakfast inn, operating in conjunction with Mountain House's newly established winery. Accommodations at Mountain House include three suites (all with fireplaces) at the top of the winery building, three suites in the inn, and four cottages next to a lake, three of them one-bedroom and one two-bedroom—a great bonus for families.

There is a spa too.

In the morning, you can look forward to quiche or other hot breakfast specialties and fruit in season. This is a great place to get married or to have a conference, if that's your inclination. The banquet room and tasting room (with full kitchen available to caterers) provides a grand background for either occasion.

Vintage Towers Inn $$
302 Main St., Cloverdale
(707) 894-4535, (888) 886-9377
www.vintagetowers.com

Mining executive Simon Pinchower had an unusual idea when he asked an architect to design a Queen Anne house in 1913. He wanted three towers, all built in different shapes—one round, one square, and one octagonal—so his house would be different than its neighbors.

Pinchower is long gone, but his legacy has given travelers a fine way to find their way to Vintage Towers Inn. Each of the three tower suites has its own sitting area, sleeping quarters, and private bath. Three of the other five rooms also have private baths, and two share a conveniently located bath. The wide front veranda's porch swing is a pleasant place to relax after a day of touring the countryside. A hearty breakfast can be expected.

West County/Russian River
The Inn at Occidental $$$$
3657 Church St., Occidental
(707) 874-1047, (800) 522-6324
www.innatoccidental.com

This is the type of romantic getaway where you can just be together surrounded by the forested hills of western Sonoma County. Owner Jack Bullard is a lifelong collector of fine art and antiques, and each of the 16 rooms is decorated with meticulous care in a theme related to a specific piece of art. The effect is that of a gallery with beds. All rooms have a private bath, one room has wheelchair access, and all but one have fireplaces and decks. Several units have double spa tubs and views to the courtyard. A full breakfast is included.

The Farmhouse Inn $$
7871 River Rd., Forestville
(707) 887–3300, (800) 464–6642
www.farmhouseinn.com

In 1878 it really was a working farm, with a row of cottages off to the side for the workers. Now it's a country inn by the side of the road, and the workers' cottages have become charming private guest rooms with amenities the farm workers never dreamed could exist. All the rooms have jetted spa tubs, CD players, TV/VCRs, personal saunas, refrigerators, fireplaces, feather beds, luxurious linens, and European-style "rain" showerheads. Full concierge services are offered, as well as on-site massage and facials, which can be enjoyed poolside.

The Inn was set to launch a special series of "culinary adventures" for guests beginning in spring 2002. These three-day excursions will provide an up close and personal look into winemaking, a chance to pick your own vegetables for your evening meal, or visits to artisan cheesemakers, oyster farms, and more. Call the Inn for more details.

In addition, there's an events center on-site, where business affairs and weddings can be held. The facility and gardens can accommodate 300 guests.

Ridenhour Ranch House Inn $$
12850 River Rd., Guerneville
(707) 877–1033, (888) 877–4466
www.ridenhourranchhouseinn.com

Louis Ridenhour came to this land in 1850 and began farming 940 acres of land along the Russian River. This house, however, was not built until 1906. What guests find today is a large living room overlooking redwoods, and eight guest rooms, each with a private bath. One of them, Hawthorne Cottage, has a fireplace and cozy window seat. Korbel Champagne Cellars is within walking distance (see our Wineries chapter), and the Russian River is five minutes away by foot. Breakfast is ample.

Applewood Inn $$$
13555 Hwy. 116, Guerneville
(707) 869–9093, (800) 555–8509
www.applewoodinn.com

The main house at the Farmhouse Inn & Restaurant along Sonoma County's River Road was indeed once the hub of a working farm in the late 1880s. Today the property is a luxurious country inn. PHOTO: FARMHOUSE INN & RESTAURANT/JOHN SUTTON

Sixteen stylish rooms and suites fill three multistory Mediterranean-style villas set among apple orchards and redwood trees. Each is individually decorated, romantic, and formal, yet familiar—like the home of a wealthy great-aunt you may have visited. This is no stuffy Victorian museum piece; it feels like a private home. The newer rooms have fireplaces, sitting areas, private verandas or decks, and either couples showers or Jacuzzi baths for two. The common area is centered around a huge stone fireplace. A new restaurant seats 50 (see our Restaurants chapter). The kitchen, once reserved for breakfast, now offers dinner Tuesday to Saturday.

Fern Grove Cottages $
16650 Hwy. 116, Guerneville
(707) 869–8105
www.ferngrove.com

A small, quaint village of 22 romantic cottages, Fern Grove Inn provides a stylish country atmosphere and a base for exploring the back roads of the neighborhood. Cottages range from spacious one-bedroom suites to intimate guest rooms with sitting areas. All have a refrigerator; some have fireplaces, spas, or TVs. Stroll the gardens, swim in the pool, feel romantic in general! The buffet breakfast features homemade pastries. The shops of downtown Guerneville are in walking distance.

Mendocino County

U.S. 101 $
Thatcher Inn
13401 U.S. 101 South, Hopland
(707) 744–1890, (800) 266–1891
www.thatcherinn.com

It stands like a sentinel of the past—the hotel you've seen in a hundred Western movies, elegant as it was the day it was built in 1890. A carpeted stairway leads from the lobby to the 20 rooms on the two floors above, which are richly furnished and individually decorated with brass and iron beds and period furnishings. The handsome bar lounge is straight out of *Gunsmoke*. But if the decor is of yesteryear, the amenities are strictly modern (as in bathrooms and air-conditioning). Thatcher Inn sits in the heart of Mendocino wine country, close to redwood forests and hiking trails. An outdoor pool provides the background for patio dining, and it's here that breakfast is served, weather permitting. The dining room also serves dinner (see our Restaurants chapter).

Fetzer Valley Oaks Bed & Breakfast $$
13601 Eastside Rd., Hopland
(707) 744–1250, (800) 846–8637
www.fetzer.com

Located in the Fetzer Vineyards complex of tasting room and organic gardens is a charming 10-room bed-and-breakfast inn, housed in the ranch's original carriage house. Each room is beautifully ap-

pointed and features panoramic views of the surrounding vineyards (or organic gardens) from a private patio. The interiors are country casual, with overstuffed chairs pulled up to large coffee tables in the sitting rooms. All guests enjoy continental breakfast and access to a secluded pool. Two master suites have whirlpool tubs in their oversized bathrooms, separate bedrooms, large sitting rooms, and small kitchens. (For more on the Fetzer complex, see our Wineries chapter.)

Highway 128
Anderson Creek Inn $$
12050 Anderson Valley Way, Boonville
(707) 895–3091, (800) 552–6202
www.andersoncreekinn.com

This inn is a rambling ranch house set on 16 acres at the junction of two creeks, with views of the hills beyond. Each of its spacious and spotless five rooms offers a different view and feeling, and each has a private bath, king bed, and complimentary bottle of local wine. Two rooms have fireplaces, and one has a Franklin stove. The friendly family livestock includes llamas, sheep, horses, and a goat. Come in March and see the newborn lambs! Breakfast is a special event and is served in the courtyard, weather permitting.

Pinoli Ranch Country Inn $$
3280 Clark Rd., Philo
(707) 895–2550

This is the place for total peace and tranquillity. The inn is nestled on 100 acres with incomparable views of the entire Anderson Valley. Guests can cycle around the quiet country roads, ride horses, or visit some of the dozen or more wineries in the area. The inn has three guest rooms, two with private baths. But the real draw here is the great outdoors. One recent entry in the guest book: "A real plus is that it is so far off the road." A country-style breakfast is served, and well-mannered children are welcome.

Mendocino Coast
Whale Watch Inn $$$$
35100 Hwy. 1, North, Anchor Bay
(707) 884–3667, (800) 942–5342
www.whale-watch.com

Whales swim by to get a closer look at this stylish inn, perched on a cliff's edge 5 miles north of Gualala. This charming complex of five buildings is set on two acres of woods and gardens. There are 18 rooms and suites, most with whirlpool tubs and all with fireplaces, private decks, and awesome views of the rocky coast. The inn's decor slants toward contemporary rather than traditional, elegant instead of woodsy. Romance is the calling card here. Televisions and telephones have been banned from all rooms. Leave the laptop at home, and be prepared for some serious creature comforts. Breakfast is hearty: fresh seasonal fruits, freshly baked pastries, and an entree that changes daily, all delivered to your private deck.

Wharf Master's Inn $$
785 Port Rd., Point Arena
(707) 882–3171, (800) 932–4031
www.wharfmasters.com

When Point Arena bustled with sailors hauling lumber and fish to supply California's Gold Rush, the wharf master had only to step onto his porch to make sure all was proceeding in an orderly fashion in the harbor below. The view is much more peaceful these days. The 120-year-old Victorian and several newer buildings together form the Wharf Master's Inn, an accommodation that is hard to pigeonhole. All of the 23 rooms have feather beds, private baths, and TVs, and most have fireplaces and spa tubs. A continental breakfast is served.

Glendeven $$$
8205 Hwy. 1, North, Little River
(707) 937–0083, (800) 822–4536
www.glendeven.com

Named for a Scottish grand estate, Glendeven consists of 10 rooms in three separate buildings, one containing an art gallery. The gallery is a showplace for 10 local artists and craftspeople. The central building was a farmhouse from 1867 until the late 1930s. The mood is of casual elegance. It's light and spacious, and all rooms have private baths and most have fireplaces. Wine and hors d'oeuvres are served by the fireplace in the sitting room, to the tinkling music of the baby grand. Breakfast is generous and will be delivered to your room should the fancy strike.

Rachel's Inn $$
8200 Hwy. 1, North, Little River
(707) 937–0088, (800) 347–9252
www.rachelsinn.com

Rachel's Inn borders 2,160-acre Van Damme State Park and its wooded hills sloping toward the sea (see our Parks and Recreation chapter). It opened in 1984 after a massive remodeling job, and the results are striking. The inn is surrounded by informal gardens and century-old cypress trees. Cliffs overlooking the ocean are just a stroll away. A lane behind the inn leads to the beach. Each of the 10 rooms is tastefully appointed but also different from the rest. The morning meal is also unique. Rachel is a gourmet cook whose breakfasts show why she is so highly regarded for her culinary skills.

Seafoam Lodge $$
6751 Hwy. 1, North, Little River
(707) 937–1827, (800) 606–1827
www.seafoamlodge.com

The lodge has eight separate buildings offering 24 guest accommodations and a conference center. A forested hillside provides the backdrop for the lodge, which is perched on six acres of coastal gardens and pines above the inlet of Buckhorn Cove. Guests can look forward to panoramic ocean views and breathtaking sunsets from every private room. You'll have a front-row seat to the unfolding drama of sea and sky. Some rooms have kitchens, some have fireplaces, and all have VCRs. Two spas let you enjoy the outdoor space. The Crows Nest Conference Center, with its magnificent ocean view, will accommodate up to 50 guests— perfect for business meetings, seminars, family reunions, and wedding receptions. A continental breakfast is delivered to your room each morning. Pets and children are welcome.

Stevenswood Lodge $$
8211 N. Hwy. 1, Little River
(707) 937–2810, (800) 421–2810
www.stevenswood.com

There could scarcely be a more enchanting setting than this lodge enjoys, surrounded on three sides by 2,160 acres of Van Damme State Park forest. Leave your room and it's a short walk to the ocean, Fern Canyon, and the headlands. The mood here is decidedly upscale, with nine one-bedroom suites and one guest room (with handicapped access) that overlooks the gardens. All the room options have beckoning views, cozy wood-burning fireplaces, spacious private baths, and stocked honor bars. Breakfast is a gourmet delight to remember, and there is now an on-site restaurant.

The Victorian Farmhouse $$
7001 N. Hwy. 1, Little River
(707) 937–0697, (800) 264–4723
www.victorianfarmhouse.com

How charming is this bluff-top house south of Mendocino? Thomas Kincaid, the commercial master of "picturesque," chose it as the subject of his painting, *Home Is Where the Heart Is, #2.* Your heart could definitely end up here, on a two-acre parcel bordered by a creek on the south. The house was built in 1877 by John Dennen, whose grandson would later buy Pullen Farm and turn it into Heritage House (see our Spas and Resorts chapter). The Victorian Farmhouse does not have an ocean view; however, Buckhorn Cove—a public beach that feels quite private—is a five-minute walk. There are four rooms in the old structure, and six more split between two separate buildings. Seven of the units have fireplaces; two have double spa tubs. A full breakfast is served in-room, and co-owner Jo Bradley will cater to your dietary needs, adding to an overall feeling of attentive comfort.

Elk Cove Inn $$$$
6300 S. Hwy. 1, Elk
(707) 877–3321, (800) 275–2967
www.elkcoveinn.com

Secluded high atop a bluff overlooking nearly a mile of coastline, the Elk Cove Inn captures the essence of peace and tranquility. Built in 1883 as an executive guest house for a lumber company, this beachfront retreat offers the quintessential "room with a view." Massive windows

bring dramatic, panoramic views and the unspoiled beauty of the outdoors to each of the 14 large accommodations (six rooms, four cottages, and four luxury suites). A trail leads down to the beach, and an outdoor hot tub leads to tranquility. A multicourse gourmet breakfast is served daily in the oceanfront dining room.

Harbor House $$$$
5600 S. Hwy. 1, Elk
(707) 877–3203, 800–720–7474
www.theharborhouseinn.com

The main building of this inn was built in 1916 by the Goodyear Redwood Lumber Company as an executive residence and for the lodging and entertainment of company guests. Situated on a bluff overlooking Greenwood Landing, Harbor House is a sanctuary for relaxation and privacy that is reminiscent of a leisurely, romantic era.

The 10 guest rooms reflect the decor of those bygone days. A path descends the bluff, with benches placed along the way to a private beach below. A sumptuous breakfast and four-course dinner are included in the price. Products are all from local sources. In addition to home-grown vegetables, the cuisine includes naturally raised meats and cheeses from nearby farms. Rooms in the main building and adjacent cottages are individually heated and have private baths.

Sandpiper House Inn $$$
5520 S. Hwy. 1, Elk
(707) 877–3587, (800) 894–9016
www.sandpiperhouse.com

In 1916 when the house was built, Elk was a bustling harbor, where schooners loaded with redwood set sail for the San Francisco market. This house was also built by Goodyear Redwood Lumber Company. The gray, shingled inn is decidedly unpretentious, though it was then one of the finest homes in town. It's when you step inside that you realize its classic elegance. Coffered ceilings and raised panel walls typify the craftsmanship of the era. Its five rooms are tastefully appointed in the style of a European country inn, decorated with antiques, comfy chairs, fresh flowers, and down comforters. All have private baths. Look forward to breakfast served on a lace tablecloth that's brightened with a bouquet of fresh flowers.

Fensalden Inn $$$
33810 Navarro Ridge Rd., Albion
(707) 937–4042, (800) 959–3850
www.fensalden.com

Once a Wells Fargo stagecoach way station, Fensalden rests on 20 tree-lined, pastoral acres on a majestic ridge crest. At this 400-foot elevation, the ocean and meadow views are spectacular. The inn's eight rooms are divided between the main house, the water tower house, and a separate bungalow, with three common rooms in the main building. One is a guest's office, one a parlor, and the third is the Tavern Room, a namesake common for way stations in the raucous Old West lifestyle. (If you can't sense the history, check out the bullet holes that pock the original ceiling.) In the evening, wine and hors d'oeuvres are served in this room, while guests chat and view the sunset over the Pacific. In the morning, a gourmet breakfast is also served there. There's a minimum two-night stay on weekends. Retreats, seminars, meetings, and weddings are invited.

Brewery Gulch Inn $$$$
9401 Coast Hwy. 1, Mendocino
(707) 937–4752, (800) 578–4454
www.brewerygulchinn.com

The owner of this inn, Arky Ciancutti, bought the 10-acre property in 1977, then a few years later turned the original farmhouse into a small B&B. When he learned that a huge amount of virgin-growth redwood, cut a century earlier, had been discovered deeply buried in silt nearby, he found his inspiration to build a new inn. This "guiltless" redwood, mineralized by time, encompasses the major building blocks of this structure, crafted from 100,000 board feet of the nearly petrified redwood. The property was once home to a successful dairy and a brewery—hence the name. Now it's the gardens that dominate the scenery, with thousands of blooming flower bulbs amid ponds and

streams, and a two-acre woodland garden with more than 600 rhododendrons and a thousand delicate ferns.

The 10 luxurious guest rooms feature ocean views, leather club chairs, fireplaces, phones, CD players, and TVs. Some have Jacuzzi tubs for two, as well as private decks. A gourmet breakfast is served (try the caramelized banana and praline pecan pancakes), and an evening wine hour is offered at the special tasting bar. There's also a library with a large selection of books and CDs and a telescope and binoculars for gazing at the stars or watching for whales. This nonsmoking property is aimed at couples seeking quiet romance.

Agate Cove Inn $$$
11201 N. Lansing St., Mendocino
(707) 937–0551, (800) 527–3111
www.agatecoveinn.com

Agate Cove Inn was built as a farmhouse in 1860, and for the past few decades it was a comfortably funky inn with spectacular views. With breakfast cooked on an antique wood-burning stove, its current incarnation still feels like a farmhouse. The views are still breathtaking too. But recent renovations have added some glamour to Agate Cove's farm-princess image. Many of the eight cottages and two farmhouse units feature oversize tubs and showers for two, fireplaces, and huge beds with down comforters. Still down-home, however, are those breakfasts—hearty meals served with an unobstructed floor-to-ceiling view of the headlands and the waves crashing against the rocks.

Blair House $$
45110 Little Lake St., Mendocino
(707) 937–1800, (800) 699–9296
www.blairhouse.com

This is perhaps the best-known home in Mendocino, because millions of people have seen it watching the TV show *Murder, She Wrote*. The show's producers used the exterior of Blair House as Jessica's Cabot Cove home. The house was built in 1888 for Elisha Blair, a railroad worker who graciously loaned money to his fellow workers, then turned his loan business into a career as a financier. The extensive use of virgin, clear-heart redwood, now prohibitively expensive, is probably what has kept the house so well-preserved. Four guest rooms are equipped with plush queen beds and handcrafted quilts. Angela's Suite is a two-room suite with 10-foot ceilings and bay windows that offer a view of both the village and ocean. Three other guest rooms share a large bathroom in the hall. Breakfast is now served on-site. Two-night minimum on weekends.

Inn at Schoolhouse Creek $$
7051 Hwy. 1, North, Mendocino
(707) 937–5525, (800) 731–5525
www.schoolhousecreek.com

The amenity guests appreciate most about this coastal inn is its eight surrounding acres of outdoor space, replete with tall cypress trees and an open meadow. The east end of the property leads to Schoolhouse Creek itself, and for beach-goers, Buckhorn Cove is a short walk to the south. The staff here marvels at how the inn has managed to preserve the feeling of what Mendocino and environs were like 25 years ago. The Inn offers 15 accommodations—nine freestanding cottages, two suites, and four units in a small lodge. Some have ocean views. There's nothing new or high-tech here-an aspect that appeals to repeat visitors. Families are welcome, and dogs are allowed in some rooms. The Inn has a hot tub on the property, situated at the top of the meadow and with a sweeping ocean view.

John Dougherty House $$$$
571 Ukiah St., Mendocino
(707) 937–5266, (800) 486–2104
www.jdhouse.com

Historic John Dougherty House, built in 1867, is one of the oldest houses in Mendocino. The main house is furnished with country antiques of the 1860s. Two guest rooms are in the main house, six more are in the adjoining cottages or historic water tower. All are individually decorated, accented with dried flower wreaths and fresh flowers from the garden. The Captain's Room has a private veranda. Upstairs, the First Mate's Room has hand-stenciled walls and antique pine

furniture. Some rooms have four-poster beds and village views (the two newest units boast spectacular vistas); most have a small refrigerator and a wood-burning stove; four now feature jet tubs. Breakfast is served by a crackling fire in the New England–style keeping room.

Joshua Grindle Inn $$
44800 Little Lake Rd., Mendocino
(707) 937–4143, (800) 474–6353
www.joshgrin.com

Situated on two acres, this lovely home was built in 1879 by Joshua Grindle, who came from Maine to get into the booming lumber business and stayed on to become the town banker. The house features unmistakably New England–style architecture, and the decor of the inn is a reflection of the same early-American heritage. There are five rooms in the main house, two in the cottage and three in the water tower. Some have views of Mendocino and the ocean; others have wood-burning fireplaces. All have well-lighted, comfortably arranged sitting areas and private baths. Breakfast is a time to enjoy a delicious morning meal as well as conversation with other guests around the circa-1830 pine harvest table. Every morning offers a new treat, as the menu constantly changes. (The owners have pro-duced a cookbook of breakfast menus.) The inn has received many honors, including *Focus* magazine's Inn of the Year award.

Nicholson House $
951 Ukiah St., Mendocino
(707) 937–0934, (800) 962–0934
www.nicholsonhouse.com

Nicholson House, built in 1905 and located in the heart of Mendocino, was home to three generations of Nicholsons until 1976, when it was converted to an apartment and office building. Now it's a bed-and-breakfast, preserving much of the history and charm of the original house. There are seven plush rooms in all, and throughout the property guests can enjoy great views of the coast. For the more reflective, there's a pond.

Sea Gull Inn $
44960 Albion St., Mendocino
(707) 937–5204, (888) 937–5204
www.mcn.org/a/seagull

Built in 1878, one of Mendocino's oldest standing houses is also one of its oldest continuous inns. The Sea Gull began welcoming tourists in the 1960s, and Marlene McIntyre has been the sole proprietor since 1986. (A resident with roots, she managed the Sea Gull Restaurant and Cellar Bar for 20 years before that.) The Sea Gull Inn is a cozy place with a profuse flower garden, a holly tree shading the front porch, and a resident feline named Dottie. It has nine rooms, some of which offer hints of ocean blue from the windows. All have private bathrooms, though the unit known as The Shed does not have bathing facilities. (The Shed also happens to be a great bargain at $49 per night.) Two rooms accommodate children. One of those is The Barn, a funky, self-contained structure with a private deck and a secondary sleeping loft. This is the only unit with a television. Continental breakfast might include offerings from the Mendocino Cookie Company.

Sea Rock Inn $$
11101 N. Lansing St., Mendocino
(707) 937–0926, (800) 906–0926
www.searock.com

You might quibble with the Sea Rock's designation as a bed-and-breakfast inn. The inn's 14 units are spread among a complex of buildings, and the breakfast is a continental buffet. You will not, however, argue with the view. Every room has an ocean vista, on a continuum that ranges from "peek" to "spectacular." And the grounds include benches perched atop the bluffs, crashing waves, and barking sea lions far below. The Sea Rock comprises six private cottages, four deluxe suites, and four rooms in the refurbished Stratton House. Each unit also is equipped with private bathroom, queen bed, cable TV, VCR, telephone, hardwood furniture, fine linens, and down pillows. Many have feather beds and/or Franklin fireplaces. Some have whirlpool tubs, and two rooms have an ocean view from the tub. Children are permitted under close supervision. The Sea Rock Inn is about a half-mile north of Mendocino.

Whitegate Inn $$$$
499 Howard St., Mendocino
(707) 937–4892, (800) 531–7282
www.whitegateinn.com

The framework for this bed-and-breakfast inn is an elegant house dating from 1883. A cobblestone path bordered with primroses leads to a terrace and gazebo. Restored in splendid style, the house is furnished with a collection of French, Italian, and Victorian antiques. Award-winning gourmet breakfasts are served on bone china and sterling silver and include such offerings as caramel-apple French toast or eggs Florentine. Seven lovely bedrooms with private baths provide comforts from fireplaces to cable television. Guests receive a welcome basket and are invited to a wine and cheese serving at 5:00 P.M.

Annie's Jughandle Beach Inn $$
Gibney Ln. and Hwy. 1, Fort Bragg
(707) 964–1415, (800) 964–9957
www.jughandle.com

This five-room Victorian-style inn built in 1883 sits midway between Mendocino and Fort Bragg and is the only lodging along that stretch of Highway 1. Guests enjoy private baths, spa tubs, fireplaces, and, in some rooms, ocean views. Jean LaTorre and his wife Shannon like to use the phrase "Louisiana hospitality and cuisine with the country charm of the Mendocino coast." Shannon, the chef, is the one from Louisiana, so meals at the Jughandle Inn tend to have a Cajun flair. The place overlooks the Jughandle State Preserve, and footpaths lead down to the ocean. There's access to plenty of hiking trails nearby, and in the springtime visitors can watch the whales right from the inn during breakfast—and all through the day.

Country Inn at Fort Bragg $
632 N. Main St., Fort Bragg
(707) 964–3737, (800) 831–5327
www.beourguests.com

Inside this 1890s residence, innkeepers Bruce and Cynthia Knauss' intention is to transport you back to "the carefree turn-of-the-century." The sloping ceilings, decorative wallpaper, and inviting fireplaces are part of the journey. Each of the eight rooms has its own theme, such as "Granny's Attic," with its clothing niche, walnut wainscoting framed by redwood molding, and old-fashioned bathtub. The Country Inn is a short walk from the beach and features a full breakfast, free newspaper, and afternoon wine and cheese.

The Grey Whale Inn $$
615 N. Main St., Fort Bragg
(707) 964–0640, (800) 382–7244
www.greywhaleinn.com
The first bed-and-breakfast in Fort Bragg, the Gray Whale has gathered a coterie of longtime admirers who come back time after time for the ambiance and cozy comforts of its spacious guest rooms. Twelve rooms on the first and second floors offer various amenities—some have gas log fireplaces, some have views of the coastline, some are in French country style, and one has an antique sleigh bed. Two rooms in the penthouse have private sundecks; one has a double-size Jacuzzi. All rooms have private baths. The recreation room has a pool table and VCR. Breakfast is lavish.

Lodge at Noyo River $$
500 Casa Del Noyo, Fort Bragg
(707) 964–8045, (800) 628–1126
www.noyolodge.com
The lodge overlooks Noyo Harbor, and suites are particularly spacious, with a solarium-style parlor and bedrooms with king or queen beds, window seats, and plenty of fluffy pillows scattered about. Most have fireplaces. There are seven guest rooms and suites in the main lodge (one is said to be haunted!) and nine in an adjoining modern building. All rooms have private baths, down comforters, and first-class bathroom amenities. In the evening you can watch pink sunsets over the handsome Noyo bridge, then wake up in the morning to the far-off barking of harbor seals. A sumptuous breakfast is served in the wood-paneled dining room.

Old Stewart House Inn $
511 Stewart St., Fort Bragg
(707) 961–0775, (800) 287–8392
www.oldstewarthouseinn.com
Stewart House is Fort Bragg's oldest, a pre-Victorian erected in 1876. The proprietors bill it as the perfect spot for families or honeymooners. A third-story deck overlooks the ocean. All six of Stewart House's rooms have a European flair. The most formal, the Queen Anne Room, has a gas fireplace and a bathroom with a big soaking tub. (There's a Jacuzzi tub room below the main house.) An outside cottage has a Greek theme. The carriage house is more of a family unit, with bunk beds for the kids, a minikitchen and a separate room for mom and dad. Need another family amenity? Stewart House sits right across the street from the depot where the Willits–Fort Bragg Skunk Train arrives and departs. A two-night minimum is required on weekends.

Lake County

Backyard Garden Oasis $$$
24019 Hilderbrand Dr., Middletown
(707) 987–0505
www.jnb.com/~bygoasis/
The three cottages at this inn nestled in the Collayomi Valley are clean and well furnished with king beds, skylights, patio doors onto private decks, TVs and VCRs, refrigerators, coffeemakers, and air-conditioning. There's a hot tub on-site, and certified massage therapists will work over your over-stressed body (with prior reservations). All cottages have private phones with modem ports. A full country breakfast is included and served in the main house, where the view is terrific.

Willow Oak Plantation $$$$
20650 Hwy. 29, Middletown
(707) 987–9000, (800) 856–4454
www.willowoakplantation.com
Gone With the Wind comes to Lake County! From the highway, this sprawling Greek Revival plantation home looks only a wee bit like Tara. In fact, it was built in 1980, but it's based on plans found in the basement of a parish courthouse in Louisiana,

and its Southern antebellum architecture is a rare sight in Wine Country. Four suites are available, and a full Southern breakfast is served at 9:00 A.M., but other times can be accommodated. Complimentary wine tasting, hors d'oeuvres, and other goodies are dished out on Friday and Saturday evenings.

The grounds around the house include a 100-year-old oak tree and a hammock under a backyard willow. (Smoking is allowed only outside and on the porches.) Adding to the amenities are a heated pool and Jacuzzi, library, exercise room, and billiard room. The property sits north of Middletown and far enough off the highway to be buffered from the sounds of traffic. These accommodations are unsuitable for children.

Forbestown Inn $$
825 N. Forbes St., Lakeport
(707) 263–7858
www.innaccess.com/fti

It's hard to miss this inn, which takes up the full half-block between Eighth and Ninth Streets in downtown Lakeport. The two-story farmhouse and carriage house were built in 1863 for Lake County purveyor Henry McGee, whose son became the first Superior Court judge in San Francisco. The landscaping is immaculate; the four rooms welcoming, full of country antiques. Some have private bathrooms, some don't. You get refreshments in the afternoon and a full breakfast made to order anytime you want it (within reason). One major improvement to McGee's property: a swimming pool for guest use.

Arbor House Inn $$
150 Clear Lake Ave., Lakeport
(707) 263–6444
www.arborhousebnb.com

Who says Lake County lacks refinement? The Arbor House Inn, a late-1800s Victorian about a block and a half from Clear Lake, has five tastefully appointed rooms, each with a unique set of antiques. Each unit has a private Jacuzzi tub (some are doubles), a king or queen bed, a TV, and an outside entrance with porch. Outdoors you'll find a spa and cottage gardens with a koi pond. The three-course breakfast is a winner, and guests receive complimentary wine and cheese in the afternoon. They even throw in complimentary use of their paddle boat on the lake. As of now, they have no problem with children, but pets are a no-no.

Kristalberg Bed & Breakfast $$
715 Pearl Ct., Lucerne
(707) 274–8009
www.kristalbergbb.com

Clear Lake is the largest natural body of water within the boundaries of California, and you can see practically every drop of it from this hilltop inn between Lucerne and Glen Haven. Set in oak woodland, Kristalberg offers 200-degree views and a contemporary Cape Cod house. Two of the three guest rooms face the lake, and one of those is a master suite with early American furnishings, a whirlpool tub, and a balcony. The full breakfast stresses organically grown foods straight from the garden. Ask about bringing children, and while you're at it ask about off-season discounts. (Your hosts speak English, German, Spanish, and French.) Pearl Court is off of Bruner Drive, about a half-mile from Hwy. 20.

Featherbed Railroad Company $$$
2870 Lakeshore Blvd., Nice
(707) BR-GUEST, (800) 966–6322
www.featherbedrailroad.com

Here's the perfect site for a training session: nine old Santa Fe or Southern Pacific cabooses converted into guest rooms. The oldest car, the Mint Julep, is about 70 years old. Each room has a feather bed and a TV/VCR, and six of them have two-person Jacuzzi tubs. There is a swimming pool on the grounds, and if that's too tame you can go jump in Clear Lake, which happens to be right next door. Full breakfast is served in one of three locations: in the dining room of the hosts' house, on the veranda or, upon request, in your cozy railcar.

Spas and Resorts

Napa County

Sonoma County

Mendocino County

Lake County

Day Spas

Sam Brannan had no idea that when he proclaimed his new health resort "the Calistoga of Sarafornia" (after several glasses of wine) way back in the 1860s, he had unleashed a monster. The hot water that naturally percolates through various portions of the Wine Country is the active ingredient that started the spa craze in Sam's day, but it's the scenery and generally hedonistic atmosphere that allow it to thrive today. Well, that and unlimited quantities of rich volcanic ash just below the surface, which constitute the main ingredient in the legendary mud baths that attract visitors by the thousands.

Some of the nation's finest full-service resorts are here—heavyweights like Meadowood and the Sonoma Mission Inn—and most of them revolve around mud, steam, massaging fingers, and the like. You can find variety though. Silverado Country Club is the favorite of golf nuts, and the Little River Inn sings the siren's song of the Pacific coastline.

Don't feel priced out of this chapter when you see all those dollar signs. Many of the spas that greeted sore-kidneyed travelers in the middle of the last century are alive today, most of them just as charming and service-oriented as they were decades ago. Outpaced at their own game by the corporate entries, they have become a second tier of options for you. Places such as Dr. Wilkinson's offer a wide range of relaxation facilitators, but at a lower level of luxury—and price.

Now about that mud. The uninitiated may have a few questions. Yes, the mud is hot, thick, and heavy (it is typically a mixture of volcanic ash, white clay, peat moss, and hot mineral water), warmed to a temperature of about 106 degrees. And yes, it is sanitary, in case you were wondering. After each use the tubs are refreshed with scalding mineral water at a temperature that kills any and all germs. When the water is drained and the mud cools, it's ready for the next bather.

The one-hour bath procedure varies among spas but in general goes something like this: You are immersed and swathed in the gooey mixture up to your neck for about 12 minutes. Attendants watch closely and pamper you with cold water and cloths soaked in soothing oils. When it's time to emerge from the mud, you pull yourself out of the ooze with the help of the attendant and paddle across the floor to a hot mineral water shower to thoroughly rinse off. This can be followed by a mineral Jacuzzi bath and five minutes in a eucalyptus steam cabinet. After steaming, you might retire to a private room and be covered with light sheets for a brief nap. After that, the choice is yours: massage, salt scrub, mini-facial, foot reflexology, or a combination of many additional indulgences. Your imagination is limited only by your wallet.

Yes, a mud bath will leave you relaxed and detoxified. Your skin will be refreshed and cleansed, and those with chronic aches and pains may find it deliriously soothing. Then again, it's not for everyone.

A word about what you will find in this chapter: Most of these facilities offer amenities and services above and beyond a standard, pleasant lodging—a full-service spa with mineral pools, massage, and so on—places that will rub you, wrap you, soak you, and give you a bed to rest your new body. Many have accommodations, a restaurant, and multiple activities. In other words, places where you can spend two or three days without needing to leave the boundaries of the property. Considering that pampering the bod is the goal of these establishments, smoking is frowned upon or prohibited at most of these facilities. But it doesn't hurt to ask. The unspoken assumptions in the following listings are these: All rooms have private bathrooms; children are welcome, but pets are not; and major credit cards are accepted. Several walk-in spa facilities are also included in this chapter.

Whichever you choose, we guarantee you will leave happier and more forgiving of this world than when you arrived.

Price Code

For room prices, refer to our dollar code below. Rates are for double occupancy on a weekend night in high season (generally May through October). Most spas and resorts offer discounts for off-season or mid-week visits. The tariff usually includes use of facilities such as tennis courts and gyms, if there are such things, but you will pay separately for spa services. The dollar code does not reflect taxes and tips.

$ . . . . .Less than $80
$$ . . . .$81 to $120
$$$ . . . .$121 to $160
$$$$ . . . .$161 to $200
$$$$$ . . . . .More than $200

Resorts

Napa County

Silverado Country Club & Resort $$$$$
1600 Atlas Peak Rd., Napa
(707) 257–0200, (800) 532–0500
www.silveradoresort.com

It is hard not to be impressed by this mega-resort at the base of Atlas Peak. For one thing, it's big. Silverado comprises 1,200 acres and 280 cottage suites—every one of them a deluxe accommodation with living room, wood-burning fireplace, full kitchen and a private patio or terrace. Most of the hubbub is centered around the two 18-hole, Robert Trent Jones Jr.-designed golf courses. But there is a slew of additional activity, including mountain-bike rentals, eight swimming pools, jogging trails, 17 plexi-paved tennis courts, and a 16,000-square-foot spa and gym. Check-in and concierge service is in the circa-1870s Colonial mansion, originally owned by Civil War Gen. John F. Miller. There you'll also find a conference center with 12,000 square feet of flexible meeting space (including a 5,200-square-foot grand ball-

room) and a fully staffed catering and conventions department. Dining options include the Bar and Grill for breakfast and lunch and either Vintner's Court or the Mesquite-influenced Royal Oak for dinner (see our Restaurants chapter).

Villagio Inn & Spa $$$$$
6481 Washington St., Yountville
(707) 944–8877, (800) 351–1133
www.villagio.com

Here's an inn inspired by the colors and architecture of Rome and Tuscany. The images of nine Roman goddesses are in abundance to give this property a mythical atmosphere, complete with fountains, vineyards, and gardens galore. The inn is comprised of 112 rooms in two-story clusters of buildings; 26 of these are mini-suites. Each room comes equipped with fireplace, refrigerator, welcoming wine, TV, terry robes, and the usual modern amenities. Daily continental champagne breakfast is included; afternoon tea, coffee, and cookies are also served. Outside are two heated pools and two tennis courts.

The 3,500-square-foot spa features 10 treatment rooms where your epidermis will be delightfully recharged. They can do it all here: facials, massage, body scrubs, body wraps (including a grapeseed polish), and a Vichy shower treatment, too. Treatment packages include the Juventas (goddess of rejuvenation) at $230 and the Juterna (goddess of the healing waters) for $190.

Auberge du Soleil $$$$$
180 Rutherford Hill Rd., Rutherford
(707) 963–1211, (800) 348–5406
www.aubergedusoleil.com

What began as a restaurant in 1983 has blossomed into one of the Wine Country's most exclusive resorts, nestled among 33 acres of olive trees and chaparral. The whole operation exudes brightness and health, with terra-cotta tile floors, fresh bouquets, natural wood and leather furnishings, and Mediterranean color schemes. The 31 guest rooms and 19 suites all have private terraces, fireplaces, down comforters, and stereo CD systems. The sizable bathrooms have double sinks and huge tubs under skylights.

The recreational opportunities include three tournament-surfaced tennis courts, a swimming pool, a whirlpool tub, and an exercise room. There is a sculpture garden and three separate facilities for meetings, receptions, or special occasions. The Auberge du Soleil restaurant is profiled in the Restaurants chapter. The spa services are an attraction in their own right. You can get a facial, a body wrap, or a scalp treatment and choose from a variety of massage styles. The spa also delves into Ayurvedic treatments (a holistic approach developed in India some 5,000 years ago), yoga, and somatics, based on "neuromuscular retraining principles." Auberge du Soleil is not really geared for children younger than 16.

Meadowood Napa Valley $$$$$
900 Meadowood Ln., St. Helena
(707) 963-3646, (800) 458-8080
www.meadowood.com

In the 1800s, Chinese laborers harvested rice in the small valley known as Meadowood. (The 800-foot tunnel they built still drains the valley during heavy rains.) The full-service, Relais & Chateaux estate that now graces the area would have been beyond the wildest dreams of those immigrants. There are 85 suites, lodges, and cottages, spread among 250 acres and often tucked into the hillside scenery. All accommodations feature high-beamed ceilings, heated bathroom floors, private porches, and down comforters. If you're feeling active, choose among two pools, a whirlpool, saunas, seven tennis courts, two championship croquet lawns, a nine-hole golf course, and a 3-mile hiking trail. The Health Spa features a dizzying array of fitness classes, personal training, yoga, skin-care treatments, salt treatments, and body wraps.

Meadowood's staff of resident experts includes a wine director who leads Friday night wine receptions and a croquet pro—one of only two in America. The resort also has five private conference and event rooms with a total reception capacity of 200. Accommodations start at $375 and go up to nearly 10 times that: The lodges top out at $3,500. Yes, that's for one night. (See the Meadowood listing in our Restaurants chapter for even more decadence.)

White Sulphur Springs Resort & Spa $$$
3100 White Sulphur Springs Rd., St. Helena
(707) 963-8588,
(800) 593-8873 in Calif. and Nev.
www.whitesulphursprings.com

California's oldest hot-springs resort (established in 1852) retains its 19th-century charm, thanks to a laid-back management style and an idyllic setting. Take Spring Street west from downtown St. Helena; soon the town ends, but the road keeps going until you're tucked into a forest of redwood, fir, and madrone. White Sulphur Springs has gone by many names—the least impressive being Bob's Steak House—and survived under numerous owners, including, in succession, the Methodist Church Conference, the Northern California Zionist Youth Commission, and the Sanatana Dharma Foundation.

The 330-acre resort now has 37 rooms—14 in the Carriage House (shared baths), 14 in The Inn (private baths), and nine creekside cottages. There is a warm (85 to 92 degrees) sulphur pool fed by a natural spring, and you can smell it anywhere in the main residential area. Children are okay in the cottages. The spa treatments involve massage therapy and aroma/thermo therapy, including herbal facials, mineral mud wraps, seaweed wraps, and herbal linen wraps.

Silver Rose Inn & Spa $$$$
351 Rosedale Rd., Calistoga
(707) 942-9581, (800) 995-9381
www.silverrose.com

The Silver Rose is building a reputation as the top-of-the-food-chain spa in the northern Napa Valley. The setting is quite pleasant—a quiet road just off the Silverado Trail, about a half-mile south of Calistoga. The inn has a total of 20 rooms divided between two buildings, Inn on the Knoll and Inn on the Vineyard. Most units face onto vines and, beyond that, the rocky Palisades. (Some have vines planted right outside the windows.) Each room is themed, e.g., the gold-accented Cleopatra Room and the Art Deco-inspired Hello Hollywood.

Guests are free to make use of the Jacuzzi, tennis courts, putting green, and wine bottle-shaped swimming pool, and breakfast is served in the tiled dining hall. There is also a state-of-the-art conference room. The spa services include massage, body and facial treatments, various water treatments, hydrotherm massage, and herbal body wraps (some available in-room). Prices range from $50 for a reflexology session to $249 for a three-hour-plus, all-purpose body reclamation project. Most of the Silver Rose's king beds can be split into twins to accommodate corporate retreats. No children younger than 15, please.

Dr. Wilkinson's Hot Springs $$$
1507 Lincoln Ave., Calistoga
(707) 942–4102
www.drwilkinson.com

This has been a Calistoga institution since John Wilkinson opened his spa in 1952. And "the works"—mud bath, facial mask, mineral whirlpool bath, steam room, blanket wrap, and half-hour massage—is still the most popular package (though it now costs $99.00, rather than the original $4.50). Doc is a local legend who once served as the town's mayor. Often as not this fit octogenarian can be found prowling the town's streets, serving as a walking billboard for his health treatments. Dr. Wilkinson's has 43 rooms, some with kitchens, all with refrigerators and private bathrooms. Rooms in the adjacent five-unit Victorian are slightly more expensive. Individual spa services start at $49 for a half-hour massage. Children must be 14 or older to take a mud bath. Doc also offers an on-site salon where you can get facial and skin-care treatments or select from a wide range of related products.

Indian Springs $$$$$
1712 Lincoln Ave., Calistoga
(707) 942–4913
www.indianspringscalistoga.com

If this collection of teal-and-white buildings evokes the heyday of the recuperative spa, it's appropriate. Indian Springs is on land that was once part of Sam Brannan's inspired attempt to make this town the Saratoga of the West. The bathhouse and Olympic-size swimming pool date to 1913, and most of the bungalows were built in the 1930s. The property has a scattering of squat buildings (most units are duplexes) and open vistas. In addition to the 17 studio and one-room units, Indian Springs offers the Merchant Bungalow, a three-bedroom, two-bath suite that sleeps six and goes for $500 a night. The spa services include 100-percent volcanic ash mud baths starting at $75, mineral baths with a full massage for $140, facial or body polish treatments, and combinations thereof.

Calistoga Spa Hot Springs $$
1006 Washington St., Calistoga
(707) 942–6269
www.calistogaspa.com

Considering Calistoga Spa's services, excellent in both quality and quantity, this has to be considered something of a bargain. The spa is a block off Lincoln Avenue, set next to the old Gliderport runway and behind the Depot and other commercial buildings (on the site of the old Roman Olympic Pool). All 57 rooms come with kitchenettes (all the basics provided except an oven), air-conditioning, and cable TV; two suites have full kitchens. Guests are free to use the small but well-maintained gym (the only one in Calistoga) and four naturally heated mineral baths that range from 83 to 105 degrees. And then there is the typical lineup of spa services: mud baths, mineral baths, massage, and steam-and-blanket combos. Prices start at $16 for a basic steam-and-blanket; a mud dunk, mineral bath, blanket wrap, and one-hour massage go for $92. Calistoga Spa also has a conference room that accommodates as many as 40 people.

Roman Spa $$$
1300 Washington St., Calistoga
(707) 942–4441, (800) 250–2457
www.tales.com/romanspa

The Roman Spa is a straight-up motel, but you can get pampered next door at Calistoga Oasis Spa. The two establishments have the same owners, though they're run separately. Roman Spa, just a block from downtown Calistoga, has lily ponds; a large, heated outdoor pool; an indoor, hydro-jet therapy pool; and outdoor hydro-jet and Finnish-style saunas. The 60 rooms include everything from a single with a queen bed to a family suite with two full rooms. About a third of the rooms have kitchen facilities, and there are five smoking rooms. They do not take credit card reservations over the phone here; you'll need to send a check or show up in person.

Golden Haven Hot Springs $$
1713 Lake St., Calistoga
(707) 942–6793
www.goldenhaven.com

This is a comparatively affordable spa in a quiet section of Calistoga. The exterior is nothing special, but the rooms are clean and full of conveniences, including air-conditioning, color TV, and refrigerators. There is wide variation in price. For instance, a room with one queen goes for $59 on a Wednesday in April, while a king bed with a private Jacuzzi goes for $149 on a weekend. Children are allowed on weekdays only. All the soothing spa treatments are there if you want them. The lineup features mud baths (including private rooms for couples), herbal mineral baths, herbal facials, and massage. Those fees range from $45 for a half-hour massage to $159 for a mud bath, hour massage, and herbal facial package. Golden Haven also promotes a "European body wrap" guaranteed to take off 6 inches of unsightly fat. Guests use the swimming pool and hot mineral pool free.

Calistoga Village Inn & Spa $$$
1880 Lincoln Ave., Calistoga
(707) 942–0991
www.greatspa.com

Another of the town's older (post-World War II) spas, the Village Inn is a long row of whitewashed bungalows along the northern reaches of Lincoln Avenue, just before it hits the Silverado Trail. There are plenty of reasons to be semiclothed here: a swimming pool, a wading pool (children are welcome), a Jacuzzi, and a dry steam room. Among the numerous spa treatments are mud baths, massage, salt scrubs, facials, foot reflexology, and body wraps. The inn also offers 16 different types of mineral baths, including the aromatic seaweed bath, Dr. Singha's mustard bath, and the Moor mud baths. A package known as The Ultimate features a mud bath, salt scrub, mini-facial, and one-hour massage for $185. Guests of the inn receive a 10 percent discount for all the above. The Village Inn has two conference rooms, 42 guest units, and a restaurant, Illerhues, that serves up robust German cuisine for dinner.

Sonoma County

Sonoma Mission Inn & Spa $$$$$
18140 Sonoma Hwy., Boyes Hot Springs
(707) 938–9000, (800) 862–4945
www.sonomamissioninn.com

The style is Spanish-influenced early California, a sprawling pink building with red tile roof, arcade, and bell tower. Lobby decor features heavy Spanish furnishings, grouped around a massive fireplace, where guests sip late-morning coffee on Sunday while reading the San Francisco *Chronicle* or the *Wall Street Journal*. It would be no surprise to see a Hollywood star or world leader—Mikhail Gorbachev and Liz Taylor have stayed here. The health and fitness program reads like a Jane Fonda workout—aerobics, aromatherapy, body sculpting, yoga, herbal wrap, seaweed sauna, and steam room. It goes on from there. To recharge after all this activity, two great restaurants—Sante, in the main building, and the nearby Big 3 Diner—both offer low-calorie cuisine (see our Restaurants chapter).

The Inn itself has a colorful history. The first spa was built in 1860 by an eccentric doctor who burned it down after a tiff with his wife. But it was rebuilt and by the 1890s San Francisco society journeyed north by rail and auto to "take the waters." The present inn dates to 1927, when it took shape in the style of a California mission. In 1985, a total renovation brought

The Sonoma Mission Inn and Spa, located in the Sonoma Valley, is an upscale resort with its own natural hot springs and a celebrity clientele. PHOTO: TINA LUSTER-HOBAN

70 new rooms and a conference center. The hot springs, however, lay dormant, lost in the earth until 1993, when the legendary waters were brought back to the surface from 1,100 feet below the Inn. And today, this spring water is the water that fills the two pools and whirlpools.

MacArthur Place $$$$$
29 E. MacArthur St., Sonoma
(707) 938–2929, (800) 722–1866
www.macarthurplace.com

One of the newer spa resorts in Wine Country, MacArthur Place began its life as a 300-acre horse and cattle ranch with vineyards. The two-story Victorian house dominating the former Burris-Good ranch was built in the 1860s. Constructed with wooden pegs and square nails, the house was home to David Burris and his family of nine children. Burris was also a banker; he founded Sonoma Valley Bank, still in business today, in the corner library on the home's first floor. Five generations of the Burris family lived on the property until Howard and Jane Good bought it in 1971.

It became a luxury destination in 1997, when it was transformed into a 64-room hotel with full-service spa and a steakhouse restaurant called Saddles (see our Restaurants chapter). New cottages were also added and the gardens and landscaping generously enhanced and upgraded to include a swimming pool and whirlpool. Ten of the rooms are in the original stately home; the inn's 29 newest suites are luxuriously appointed with fireplaces, wet bars, flat-panel TVs with DVD players, and king beds.

The Garden Spa lives up to its name, using the herbs, flowers, and fruits grown on the property in its treatments. Most of the massages, facials, body polishes, and mud wraps (with grapeseeds) run about $100; a Lomi Lomi massage, practiced by Hawaiians for centuries, will set you back about $200. Several "signature" treatments, also about $200 each, utilize rose petals, grapefruits and oranges, and essential oils.

The Lodge at Sonoma $$$$$
1325 Broadway Ave., Sonoma
(707) 935–6600 (lodge),
(707) 931–2034 (spa)
www.thelodgeatsonoma.com,
www.raindancespa.com

Sonoma is a spa town, and this new world-class facility helps keep the town's reputation for hot water and luxurious body scrubs intact. The 182 spacious guest rooms are nicely appointed with fireplaces, balcony or patio, two-line phones, cable TV, and complimentary breakfast in the restaurant, Carneros (see our Restaurants chapter), or in-room.

Hot mineral waters flow right beneath the property, so the Raindance Spa is the perfect source for therapeutic bathing treatments. There are outdoor soaking and watsu therapy pools, and underwater massage is offered. The full-service spa offers a dizzying array of massages, skin care treatments, body wraps, facials, and an assortment of "kurs"—a series of treatments using mineral water, algae, therapeutic mud, and essential oils and herbs to detoxify and hydrate your overstressed bod. Prices range from about $95 for facials to $295 for a kur treatment. A full-day spa indulgence, with lunch too, costs about $475; a half-day is $275.

The Kenwood Inn $$$$$
10400 Sonoma Hwy., Kenwood
(707) 833–1293, (800) 353–9663
www.kenwoodinn.com

Intimate in scale with a peaceful, Old World charm, the Kenwood Inn offers the ambiance of an Italian country villa nestled in the heart of Sonoma Valley. The Inn, which has 12 private suites around a central courtyard and fountain, is situated on a secluded hillside facing more than 1,000 acres of sloping estate vineyards. The suites contains feather beds, down comforters, European antiques and lush fabrics, private baths and fireplaces. A complimentary bottle of wine greets guests on arrival. Breakfast is served either in the dining room or at outdoor tables in good weather. A full-service spa pampers guests and day visitors alike with different therapeutic massages, 11 special skin-care treatments and spa body treatments—such as clay and chamomile, seaweed body wrap—and ancient Ayurvedic body purification rituals. Half-day spa experiences are available, including the popular couples "together-ness massage," as well as the Faccia Bella facial. Spa treatments are priced individually.

Huckleberry Springs Country Inn and Spa $$$$
8105 Old Beetle Rd., Monte Rio
(707) 865–2683, (800) 822–2683
www.huckleberrysprings.com

Located in a secluded 56-acre redwood and madrone forest in the hills above the lower Russian River, Huckleberry Springs is an adults-oriented facility that caters to honeymooners or those looking for a quiet romantic retreat. The accommodations consist of four comfortable and very private cottages, each with their own personality and charm. Therapy comes in the form of a spring-fed hot tub and massage cottage, where $75 buys 75 minutes of shiatsu massage—facials are also available. A restaurant is on the premises, serving meals on Saturdays and by arrangement on other days ($35 prix fixe). The resort is open March through December; call ahead for reservations and directions.

River Village Resort $$$
14880 River Rd., Guerneville
(707) 869–8139, (800) 529–3376
www.rivervillageresort.com

This newly renovated resort features 17 cottages clustered around two swimming pools, a hot tub, and two large decks in a courtyard on the edge of town. Owners Gary and Donna Klauenburch have lived in the area for more than 20 years and together have created a charming little getaway that offers a wide range of rejuvenating and relaxing therapies. Services include Swedish, deep tissue, reflexology, and aromatherapy massage as well as salt scrubs, mud wraps, full facials, and herbal body wraps. The resort also features nutrition and diet counseling—from an herbalist and certified nutritional consultant and diet counselor. The location also affords relatively easy access to the nearby Russian River, where you can swim, canoe, kayak, or just bask in the sun.

Mendocino County

Orr Hot Springs $$$
13201 Orr Springs Rd., Ukiah
(707) 462–6277

The hot spring waters bubble up from the earth into a redwood tub and spill over into the swimming pool below. The spa has had a checkered history and at present could only be described as rustic. The first bath house was built in the 1850s and is now used as a dormitory. A 14-room lodge and three cottages serve as the main buildings today. During the 1970s the 26-acre hot-springs facility became a kind of commune. Today, the situation is informal; you can bring a picnic lunch and store it in the communal kitchen. Besides the basic facilities (some of which have half-baths), camping is also an option. Day-use is another option. Another informality: Clothing is optional.

Vichy Springs Resort $$$$
2605 Vichy Springs Rd., Ukiah
(707) 462–9515
www.vichysprings.com

Named after the world-famous springs first discovered by Julius Caesar in France, the waters of Vichy Springs bubble up from deep within the earth and are virtually identical in chemistry to those of the French namesake. Available in abundance for bathing and swimming, the waters are naturally warm and effervescent (dubbed "champagne baths"), filled with minerals and energy renowned for healing and restorative qualities. Also restorative and soothing is the idyllic parklike setting of the resort—the oldest continuously operating mineral springs spa in California. Opened in 1854 and now a California Historical Landmark, it was a favorite retreat of Mark Twain, Jack London, and Presidents Ulysses S. Grant, Benjamin Harrison, and Teddy Roosevelt. Today, the resort is restored and renovated to tastefully combine its historic charm with modern comfort and conveniences. More contemporary visitors have included Wavy Gravy and Patch Adams.

Twelve individually decorated rooms with private baths have been created from the ancient, broken-down former facilities that date to the 1860s. (Five creekside rooms were added in 1997.) These are so attractive that the company that supplied the paint brings people to Vichy Springs to have a look. There are also four cottages with kitchens, bedrooms, and living rooms. Two of them were built in 1854 and are the oldest standing structures in Mendocino County. The third was built in 1997, the fourth in 1999. Just steps away from the accommodations are the renovated indoor and outdoor bathing tubs, therapeutic massage building, and mineral-water-filled, Olympic-size swimming pool. Offered at varying rates are therapeutic massage, Swedish massage, and herbal facial. Day visitors are also welcome to use the pool, baths, and the property.

Little River Inn $$$
7751 Hwy. 1, North, Little River
(707) 937–5942, (888) 466–5683
www.littleriverinn.com

Built in 1853 by Silas Coombs, a lumberman from Maine, this classic coastal resort once was the Coombs' family home. It is now run by the great-grandchildren, who keep the flavor of the past while expanding for the future. Eucalyptus trees, planted as a windbreak for the Coombs' orchard, now shelter a golf course. The wisteria-covered front porch of the original home, where Silas once spotted ocean freighters, now beckons guests into the dining room. In the music room, someone may be tickling the ivories on the Emerson square grand piano, which survived its trip around Cape Horn in 1850. The inn has a long tradition of hosting Hollywood celebrities—Joan Fontaine and a crew of 40; Jonathan Winters, who provided impromptu entertainment; Ronald Reagan, who sprawled on the floor to illustrate football plays. (All rooms are non-smoking.)

The inn's Third Court Salon and Day Spa offers classic European facials, aromatherapy wraps, and a host of other body treatments, hydration skin treatment, and massage. Reservations are

From the porch of the Little River Inn on the Mendocino Coast, Silas Coombs watched for ships coming in to the lumber mills. PHOTO: LOU ZAUNER

required year-round. There is no charge for children younger than 18. Sunday brunch and dinner are served.

Sweetwater Spa & Inn $$$
955 Ukiah St. (spa), 44840 Main St. (inn), Mendocino
(707) 937–4140, (800) 300–4140
www.sweetwaterspa.com

The Sweetwater complex takes up most of the two blocks between Ukiah and Main Streets in the village of Mendocino, and that's not all. Besides the 22 units downtown, the company has six rooms in Little River and the cozy Redwood Cottage, a popular lodging about five minutes east of Mendocino.

For 14 years Sweetwater has maintained one of the premier massage staffs in Northern California. They offer a full range of massage and bodywork options, including the ever-popular Sweetheart Special—stay two nights in any room, book two massages, and receive a $15 discount. Sweetwater also has hot tubs and

sauna, with prices that vary according to privacy and tub size. Kids are welcome.

Lake County

Konocti Harbor Resort & Spa $$$
8727 Soda Bay Rd., Kelseyville
(707) 279–4281, (800) 660–LAKE
www.konoctiharbor.com

Most people know Konocti Harbor as a premier concert venue for post-40 rockers (see our Nightlife chapter), but there's a lot going on here even after the last drum beat. The resort has 100 acres of lakefront property and 250 guest accommodations that range from basic rooms to apartment suites to beach cottages to fully equipped VIP suites. Many, but not all, of the rooms have views of Clear Lake. The price spectrum is wide, so call for more information. Basic rooms are $69 every night of the year; deluxe rooms with balconies vary in price according to season, but expect $119 on in-season weekends; Jacuzzi suites with fireplaces are $259.

Guests with children, take notice. Konocti Harbor caters to kids with its Kids Club, a supervised activity session for children 4 to 13 during big concert nights. While mom and dad boogie in the Classic Concert Showroom or the Amphitheater, the kids are entertained for up to six hours with games, movies, arts and crafts, and other distractions. Daytime hours are available during summer; inquire when you call to book a reservation.

Konocti Harbor bustles with activity. There is a tennis complex, a gym, two swimming pools, two wading pools, shuffleboard courts, horseshoe pits, sand volleyball courts, and a softball field. And because the lake is primary among attractions, the resort has a 100-slip marina, a launch ramp, and a certified boat repair shop. It also offers a rental fleet (ski boats, Waverunners, etc.) and, believe it or not, a bass fishing pro. Konocti's Dancing Springs Spa features massage, herbal wraps, loofa treatments, facials, manicures, and more. If you must mix business and pleasure, the meeting facilities can handle groups from 10 to 700. The on-site restaurant serves breakfast, lunch, and dinner daily.

Harbin Hot Springs $$
P.O. Box 782, Middletown
(707) 987–2477, (800) 622–2477
www.harbin.com

Legendary among latter-day hippies, New Age shamans, and women who run with wolves (or swim with fishes), Harbin is a nonprofit retreat and workshop center set on 1,160 unencroached acres north of Middletown. Here you can let your hair, and practically everything else, hang down without inhibition. The guest accommodations range from camping ($30 per weekend night for one adult) to dormitory lodging ($55 per person) to rooms with shared baths ($115 for two) to rooms with full, private baths ($165) to cabins ($195). Harbin's health treatments include various forms of massage—from Swedish to acupressure—facials, aromatherapy, and "watsu," a form of warm-water massage developed at the retreat. You don't have to leave the compound for meals, either.

The Stonefront Restaurant, open for breakfast and dinner, prides itself in using organic vegetarian ingredients, and there are two cafes and a health-food store. The group facilities handle conferences and events for parties of 14 to 300, including

With Mt. Konocti rising high in the background, Konocti Harbor Resort on Clear Lake beckons to boaters to throttle down and enjoy a tall cool one. PHOTO: LOREN DOPPENBERG

scheduled workshops on topics such as relationships and meditation. Alcohol and drugs are not permitted on the premises, and meat, fish, and poultry are not allowed in guest kitchens. Children are allowed only to camp and are relegated to daytime pool use. From Big Canyon Road about a mile north of Middletown, go west on Harbin Springs Road for 2 miles.

Day Spas

Along with the destination spa resorts, you also have the option of luxuriating at one of several day spas. Spend a few rejuvenating hours sunk neck deep in mud, or enveloped in a stress-relieving hydro wrap, or soothed by the skilled hands of a masseuse and then be on your way. Here are just a few of the many possibilities.

Napa County

Mount View Spa
1457 Lincoln Ave., Calistoga
(707) 942–5789, (800) 772–8838
In the Mount View Hotel building (see our Hotels and Motels chapter), but run separately, this spa is the ultimate in luxury. The tasteful furnishings, personalized service, waffle-weave cotton robes in the dressing rooms—they all combine to set a mood of elegant decadence. Mount View offers five types of massage, from Swedish to reflexology; customized whirlpool baths with additives such as fango mud, mineral salts, powdered milk whey, and herbal bath oils; and body wraps. The latter include the herbal linen wrap, the stress-relief hydro wrap (a warm, aloe vera-based gel), and the Enzymatic Sea mud wrap, which is painted over your entire body like a dusky leotard. All of it is performed in private rooms. The massages cost $40 (for 25 minutes) to $95 (for 85 minutes). A bath treatment followed by a 55-minute massage runs $85; add an herbal wrap and a 25-minute basic cleansing facial and pay $170.

Lincoln Avenue Spa
1339 Lincoln Ave., Calistoga
(707) 942–5296
www.lincolnavenuespa.com
Set in an old stone building in the heart of town, this spa is an upscale companion to Golden Haven Hot Springs (see our Spas and Resorts chapter). Lincoln Avenue specializes in the easygoing Swedish/Esalen style of massage, with rates ranging from $45 for back, neck, and shoulder work to $99 for a full body massage and a foot reflexology treatment. The mud treatments ($55) are longtime favorites too. Lie for an hour on a steam table while wearing a suit of herbal mineral body mud (with 34 herbs), sea mud (with kelp), or mint mud. If you're not allowed to play in the mud, try on the herbal wrap. The spa also does facials and acupressure "facelifts." Packages are available, of course, such as the Ultimate Pamper Package, a four-and-a-half-hour slice of heaven that costs $259.

Lavender Hill Spa
1015 Foothill Blvd., Calistoga
(707) 942–4495, (800) 528–4772
www.lavenderhillspa.com
This intimate retreat bills itself as "A Garden Spa for Couples," and, indeed, the verdant grounds in back of the bathhouses are a suitably romantic spot for postmassage reverie and sweet talk. Inside, Lavender Hill offers elegant trappings and a warm staff. Choose from four basic bath treatments: volcanic mud bath, seaweed bath, herbal blanket wrap, or aromatherapy mineral salt bath, all of which come with a facial mask and light foot massage. Other options include la stone massage, therapeutic massage, and foot reflexology. Prices range from $55 for a basic half-hour massage to $165 for a bath treatment with one-hour massage and mini-facial. The spa's owner produces his own line of ultrapure products, Quan Yin Essentials, which can be purchased on the premises.

The Calistoga Massage Center
1219 Washington St., Calistoga
(707) 942–6193
www.calistogamassage.com

The Massage Center is for connoisseurs of massage. They offer deep tissue and sports massage, shiatsu, Thai, and esoteric methods called cranio-sacral and Jin Shin. Select a mode and a duration—it's $45 for 30 minutes, $80 for an hour, or $125 for 90 minutes. (Swedish/Esalen-based massage is a little less expensive, running $40, $70, and $100.) The center also offers massage for two ($130 for an hour each), massage instruction for couples ($240 for three hours), foot reflexology ($80 for an hour), herbal facials ($70 an hour), and various combinations of the above. Add a computer stress management massage for $55. Ask about discounts for students, seniors, upvalley residents, and anyone visiting Tuesday through Thursday.

Sonoma County

Osmosis Enzyme Bath and Massage
209 Bohemian Hwy., Freestone
(707) 874–1108
www.osmosis.com

Named the best day spa in America by *Travel & Leisure* magazine, Osmosis features a Japanese enzyme bath comprised of fragrant cedar fiber, rice bran, and more than 600 enzymes. The action of the enzymes produces a special quality of heat that improves circulation and metabolism and cleanses skin pores and beautifies the skin. Massage treatments include Swedish/Esalen method and many others. If you like, you can have your massage outdoors under a pagoda near Salmon Creek. The enzyme bath is $75, with massage $150. Osmosis is located off Highway 12 in the small town of Freestone, about halfway between Sebastopol and Bodega.

A Simple Touch Spa
239 Center St., Healdsburg
(707) 433–6856
www.asimpletouchspa.com

This lovely little spa in downtown Healdsburg offers aromatherapy baths, massage, facials, and body treatments. One of the specialty baths features detoxifying fango mud made from dehydrated volcanic ash. The body wraps include fragrant herbal or rose-petals—the latter wrap involves painting the body in rose whey and then wrapping it in a heat blanket—to the more common remineralizing seaweed wrap. Several special packages are available that range from $70 for a bath and half-hour massage to the deluxe package for $210, which includes a bath, salt scrub, one-hour massage, herbal facial, and rose petal wrap.

Camping

Napa County
Sonoma County
Mendocino County
Lake County

Prefer to end your day sipping Chardonnay by campfire light? Then you'll appreciate the wide variety of Wine Country campgrounds and RV parks. Here you can have the best of both worlds: relaxing under the stars at night and visiting wineries and other attractions by day, And don't worry, you can walk into practically any restaurant or winery, no matter how lofty the reputation or shiny the brass, in a clean T-shirt and a pair of Levi's and suffer not even a downward glance from the hostess.

Once you're in the tasting room, no one can tell the campers from the four-star hotel guests (unless you blow your cover by offering the manager a s'more).

If you desire more in the way of outdoor adventure, many campgrounds afford ample opportunities for backpacking, hiking, and fishing. Campgrounds in northern Mendocino County are generally among the most remote and primitive, where nary a wine taster is likely to be found. And then there is the plethora of breezy lakeside sites in Lake County. You can consider them the compromise choice between the wild and the tame.

If we don't say otherwise, assume that each campground has piped, potable water, a desirable part of any outdoor experience. If it doesn't, arrange to bring or pump your own. And please note that some of the listed sites are part of the region's state parks. In those cases we have provided all the basic camping information here, but for a more thorough description of the park, you should turn to our Parks and Recreation chapter.

To pitch your tent or park your RV, expect to pay anywhere from $12 to $25 nightly, depending on the location and the degree of development. (State park camping fees range from $8.00 to $12.00 per night.) Senior rates are also offered in many places, while some of the more primitive campgrounds are free.

Napa County

Napa Town & Country Fairgrounds
575 Third St., Napa
(707) 253-4900

Your chances of spotting a deer or a black bear aren't good here but you won't be far from your morning cafe latte. The fairgrounds are just off Third Street in Napa, as it approaches the Silverado Trail. There are about 75 motor-home spaces, a group campground for 15 to 500. On-site are restrooms and showers, and close by are a laundry and a market. Pets are permitted on leashes. Note that Town & Country is closed to campers for the latter half of July and most of August.

Pleasure Cove Resort
Wragg Canyon Rd., off Hwy. 128,
Lake Berryessa
(707) 966-2172

This family-oriented campground is one of five around Lake Berryessa. Pleasure Cove has 105 sites for tents or motor homes, 20 of them with water and electrical hookups. The wheelchair-accessible sites have picnic tables and fire pits, and there are restrooms, showers, ice, a restaurant and bar, propane, and groceries. Pleasure Cove also has a boat ramp if you're prowling for trout.

Spanish Flat Resort
4290 Knoxville Rd., off Hwy. 128,
Lake Berryessa
(707) 966-7700

Another possibility for a recreational jaunt to Berryessa is Spanish Flat, which has 120 campsites for tents or motor homes, a few of them with partial hookups. Picnic tables, fire pits, flush toilets, and showers are provided. The hosts also have complete marina facilities, a boat launch, and rentals. A laundry and a restaurant are a short drive away.

Bothe-Napa Valley State Park
Hwy. 29, south of Calistoga
(707) 942–4575 (info),
(800) 444–PARK (reservations)

While a million or so industrious tourists whiz by on Highway 29, you can lay next to your tent and look up at the boughs of oaks and pines or at the stars of the Milky Way. The park has a first-rate campground along Redwood Creek, with 9 tent-only sites and 50 for tents or RVs up to 31 feet long. You get picnic tables and fire pits, toilets, and showers. Wheelchairs can be used here, and pets are allowed (campground only). There is a spring-fed swimming pool, where you can take the plunge for $1.00 (free for children). There are blackberries for the pickin' in summer. (For more on Bothe-Napa Valley State Park, see our Parks and Recreation chapter.)

Napa County Fairgrounds
1435 N. Oak St., Calistoga
(707) 942–5111

If you're going to pick a municipal campground, you could do a lot worse than Calistoga's. The scenery is nice, you can walk to restaurants and spas, and right next door is Mt. St. Helena Golf Course (see our Parks and Recreation chapter). There are about 60 drive-through campsites with electrical hookups, plus a small grassy area for tents.

Restrooms, showers, and propane are available, but campfires are not permitted. Pets are allowed on leashes. The campground is closed from mid-June through mid-July as the grounds are prepared for and cleaned up after the Napa County Fair (see our Festivals and Annual Events chapter).

Lower Hunting Creek
Knoxville-Devilshead Rd., Knoxville
(707) 468–4000

This is one of the Wine Country's least-known campgrounds and, because of its isolation in the uppermost northern tip of Napa County, that isn't likely to change anytime soon. Located about 17 miles north of Lake Berryessa near the small community of Knoxville, Lower Hunting Creek has only five sites for tents or RVs, but it does have picnic tables, fireplaces, shade shelters, and vault toilets. Pets are permitted on leashes. Be forewarned that the campground is popular with off-road enthusiasts and hunters. From Berryessa-Knoxville Road, turn west on Devilshead Road and drive for 2 miles. A map of the area is available from the Bureau of Land Management at the number listed. There is no charge for camping here.

Sonoma County

Southern Sonoma

Sugarloaf Ridge State Park
2605 Adobe Canyon Rd., Kenwood
(800) 444–7275
www.parks.sonoma.net/sugarlf.html

This locale in the Mayacmas Mountains has 50 campsites for tents or motor homes up to 24 feet long. There is piped-in water and restrooms. In 1996, Sugarloaf Ridge State Park became the home of the largest observatory in the western United States that is completely dedicated to public viewing and education. Hiking is the main recreation at this popular state park (see our Parks and Recreation chapter). Pets are okay.

Insiders' Tip

To reserve a campsite in one of California's state parks, you must go through the Reserve America booking service at (800) 444-PARK. Reserve America will add a one-time $7.50 surcharge to any reservation; get more details at www.reserveamerica.com.

Spring Lake Park
Newanga Ave., Santa Rosa
(707) 539–8092

A group camping area and 30 family campsites (4 for tents only) at Spring Lake Park have centrally located restrooms and shower facilities. Also available are 200 picnic sites, barbecue pits, a bikeway, a hiking trail, and equestrian trails. No electricity is available at this campground, which is open all week during the summer (the week before Memorial Day until the week after Labor Day) and weekends only during the winter. Please reserve at least 10 days in advance during high season. It's $5.00 for an extra vehicle and $1.00 for a dog, which must be vaccinated (and you must have the paperwork handy).

Northern Sonoma

Windsorland RV Trailer Park
9290 Old Redwood Hwy., Windsor
(707) 838–4882
www.gocampingamerica.com/windsorland/index.html

There are 66 sites here, with 56 full-hookup, pull-through sites. Windsorland also features a laundry, playground, a small store, showers, and restrooms. A pool is open seasonally. The park is open all year, and night registration is available.

KOA Kampground
26460 River Rd., Cloverdale
(707) 894–3337
www.koakampgrounds.com/where/ca/05275.htm

This campground has 152 campsites (50 for tents), plus a swimming pool, recreation hall, store, minigolf course, stocked fishing pond, ball courts, and horseshoe pits. Located 1 mile from the Russian River on a hill overlooking the Alexander Valley, the Cloverdale KOA is open all year. There are also 14 Kamping Kabins for two (with no water or electricity).

Lake Sonoma–Liberty Glen
3333 Skaggs Springs Rd., Lake Sonoma
(707) 433–9483
www.parks.sonoma.net/laktrls.html

Eleven miles northwest of Healdsburg, off Dry Creek Road, this Lake Sonoma park offers more than 17,000 land and water acres. Lake Sonoma facilities include a visitor center and fish hatchery (see our Kidstuff chapter), with 118 campsites available for tents or RVs up to 50 feet. There are 2 group sites for up to 50 campers (advance reservations required). In addition, there are 15 boat-in/hike-in primitive campgrounds around the lake, and a privately operated marina that

Vista Point, north of Irish Beach, gives visitors a unique look at the Pacific Ocean. PHOTO: BILL HOBAN

offers boat rentals and a launch ramp. Piped water, flush toilets, solar-heated showers, and a sanitary disposal station are available in the developed area.

Sonoma Coast

Doran Park
Doran Beach, 1 mile south of Bodega Bay
(707) 875-3540
www.sonoma-county.org
Park facilities include 125 sites for RVs or tents, 10 tent-only sites and 1 group camping area for tents only. There are tables, fire rings, and a trailer disposal site. What to do? Try fishing, beachcombing, clamming, boating, and picnicking.

A boat ramp and fish-cleaning station are available. There's an extra charge of $5.00 per vehicle and $1.00 per dog.

Stillwater Cove Regional Park
22455 Hwy. 1, approx. 15 miles north of Jenner
(707) 847-3245
www.sonoma-county.org
This 210-acre park is comprised of open meadow and coastal forest with spectacular ocean views from Stillwater Cove. There is also half-mile trail leading to the historic one-room Fort Ross Schoolhouse. Twenty-three campsites serve most campers (large RVs and trailer campers should contact the park office to ensure that their vehicle will fit) and there is a hike-in/bike-in area. Facilities include pay showers, flush restrooms, and day-use parking. Sites are available on a first-come, first-serve basis.

Salt Point State Park
25050 Hwy. 1, approx. 20 miles north of Jenner
(707) 847-3221
www.parks.sonoma.net/coast.html
This 31-site campground offers picnic areas, hiking trails, diving, horseback trails, and the beautiful, adjacent Kruse Rhododendron State Reserve (see our Parks and Recreation chapter). It's open all year, but there are no RV hookups. Piped water and flush toilets are available. In early winter this is headquarters for local abalone divers.

Insiders' Tip

Planning to snuggle up before a campfire? Many Wine Country stores sell firewood, as do private campgrounds (gathering firewood is generally not permitted). But remember that during the dry summer months campfires are often prohibited in some areas due to grass or forest fire danger. Check your campground bulletin board for details.

Gualala Point Regional Park
Hwy. 1, 0.5 mile south of Gualala
(707) 785-2377
www.sonoma-county.org/develop/parks/
The 195-acre park is located near the coast, adjacent to the Gualala River. The overnight camping area is across the highway from the park's day-use facilities, and it contains tables and stoves. Water and restroom facilities are nearby. Recreation options for day-use or overnight campers include fishing, bike trails, hiking (one trail beside the bluff is especially good for birdwatching), and picnic areas. It's open all year and offers 19 family campsites for tents and motor homes up to 28 feet, 7 hike-in/bike-in campsites, and a trailer sanitary station. There's plenty of beachcombing to be done.

West County/Russian River

Village Park Campground
6665 Hwy. 12, Sebastopol
(707) 823-6348
Village Park is open from May 1 to October 31 for overnight or weekly stays.

Forgot your corkscrew? The Stewart's Point General Store near Salt Point State Park on the Sonoma Coast is where campers fill their essential—and some not so essential—needs. PHOTO: JOHN NAGIECKI

Laundry facilities, and restrooms with showers and hot water are offered, and children and pets are welcome.

River Bend Campground
11820 River Bend, Forestville
(707) 887–7662
www.campgrounds.com/ctpa/ca/regions/nc /39riv.htm

Eleven miles from U.S. 101, off the River Road exit, this campground has 65 sites, 35 with full hook-ups. Canoe rentals, volleyball, barbecue pits, and basketball courts are among the amenities. Other features include flush restrooms, hot showers, groceries, teepees for rent, and a huge Paul Bunyan statue. It's open all year.

Faerie Ring Campground
16747 Armstrong Woods Rd., Guerneville
(707) 869–2746

Tucked away on 14 acres near Armstrong Redwoods State Park (see our Parks and Recreation chapter), this campground features 44 campsites—33 for tents, 4 full hookups—in either a sunny or shady location. Hot showers and flush toilets are available. It's near the Russian River, 1.8 miles north of Highway 116, and it's open all year. Faerie Ring also has a popular adults-only area. Pets allowed. No credit cards.

Schoolhouse Canyon Campground
12600 River Road, Guerneville
(707) 869–2311

This camping option lies adjacent to a 200-acre wildlife sanctuary, with tent and RV sites set in the redwoods. Hot showers, fishing and swimming along the nearby Russian River, hiking, and nature trails are among the attractions. It's open April through October.

Mendocino County

U.S. 101

Manor Oaks Overnighter Park
700 E. Gobbi St., Ukiah
(707) 462-0529, (800) 357-8772
www.mendonet.com/places/noframes/
camplist.htm

There are 53 motor-home spaces (15 of which are drive-through) with full hookups. Picnic tables, fire grills, restrooms, showers, and a swimming pool are provided. A laundry and ice are available, and right next door are the tennis courts and barbecue facilities of Oak Manor Park. Leashed pets are allowed in the campground. Manor Oaks is open year-round.

Quail Meadows Campground
23701 N. Hwy. 101, Willits
(707) 459-6006

Most of the 49 motor home spaces here have full or partial hookups, and there is a special section for tents only. Amenities include patios, picnic tables, restrooms, showers, and a sanitary disposal station. A laundry, propane, ice, and TV hookups are available. Pets are allowed on leashes.

Willits KOA
1600 Hwy. 20, Willits
(707) 459-6179
www.mendonet.com/places/noframes/
camplist.htm

There are 18 sites for tents only and 50 RV spaces (27 of which are drive-through) with full or partial hookups as well as 12 cabins. Piped water, flush toilets, showers, picnic tables, playground, swimming pool, and sanitary dump station are provided. And that's just the beginning. The Willits KOA has hiking trails, fish pond, petting zoo, minigolf, an arcade, weekend barbecues, and even seasonal horseback riding. A grocery store, laundry, and RV supplies are available, too. Pets are allowed on leashes.

Highway 128

Hendy Woods State Park
18599 Philo-Greenwood Rd., Philo
(707) 937-5804
www.mcn.org/1/mendoparks/hendy.htm

> ## Insiders' Tip
>
> Camping in one of the more remote spots of Mendocino National Forest, it's highly tempting to bend down to that crystal-clear stream for a drink. Don't do it. The fresh water of California is often populated by a protozoan called *Giardia lamblia*. You probably won't die if you take in *Giardia*, but you'll wish you could. It results in severe abdominal cramping and diarrhea that can last for weeks. So be safe and boil your water or pump it through a filter. (Water purification tablets do not kill *Giardia*.)

The park campground offers 92 sites for tents or RVs up to 35 feet long, including 4 wheelchair-accessible sites. Piped water, flush toilets, hot showers, a sanitary disposal station, picnic tables, and fire pits are provided. A grocery store and a propane gas station are available nearby. Pets are permitted. (For more on Hendy Woods State Park, see our Parks and Recreation chapter.)

Paul M. Dimmick Wayside State Camp
Hwy. 128, 6 miles east of Hwy. 1
(707) 937-5804
www.mcn.org/1/mendoparks/pmd.htm

Located about 6 miles inland from the Pacific Ocean, this campground features 30 sites for tents or RVs up to 35 feet long (no hook-ups). Restrooms, fireplaces, and picnic tables are provided, and pets are permitted, but there is no potable water. The nearby Navarro River is the highlight here. In summer it's a spot for swimming or canoeing; in late winter, the river gets a fair steelhead run. The state camp is open year-round.

Mendocino Coast

Manchester State Park
41500 Kinney Rd., Manchester
(707) 937-5804
www.mcn.org/1/mendoparks/manchst.htm

Bordered by large sand dunes, this popular state campground offers 46 sites for tents and motor homes up to 30 feet long. It also includes a 40-person group site and 10 environmental camps. Most sites have piped water, chemical (nonflush) toilets, picnic tables, and fireplaces. The campground has a sanitary dump station. No pets are allowed. (For more on Manchester, see our Parks and Recreation chapter.)

Insiders' Tip

The Wine Country is home to a potent species of poison oak that produces a prolonged nasty rash in susceptible individuals. The best rule is to simply stay away from brushy undergrowth and immediately wash your skin if you suspect contact. Also, check your campground bulletin board for a description and illustration of what the plant looks like.

Van Damme State Park
Hwy. 1, 3 miles south of Mendocino
(707) 937-5804
www.mcn.org/1/mendoparks/vandam.htm

Van Damme offers quiet rain forest groves and great ocean views, with 70 campsites for tents or motor homes up to 35 feet long. There are also 10 primitive campsites reached by a 1.7-mile hike, plus a group camp that accommodates 50 people. Piped water, flush toilets, a sanitary disposal station, hot showers, picnic tables, and fireplaces are provided in the main campground. A grocery store, laundry, and propane are available nearby. Pets are permitted. (See our Parks and Recreation chapter for more on Van Damme State Park.)

Russian Gulch State Park
Hwy. 1, 2 miles north of Mendocino
(707) 937-5804
www.mcn.org/1/mendoparks/russian.htm

Set near some of California's most beautiful coastline, this park offers 30 campsites for tents or RVs up to 30 feet long—as well as several hike-in/bike-in sites. There is also a wheelchair-accessible site and a 40-person group site. Piped water, hot showers, flush toilets, picnic tables, and fireplaces with cooking grills are provided. Pets are permitted. The campground is open April through October. (For more on Russian Gulch, see our Parks and Recreation chapter.)

Jackson State Forest
State Department of Forestry,
802 N. Main St., Fort Bragg
(707) 964-5674

Pick up a camping permit and campground map at the Department of Forestry's Fort Bragg offices. There are 18 separate campgrounds scattered throughout this large state forest, with as few as 2 or as many as 24 campsites each. Open to both tents and RVs, this is a primitive area with no piped water available, but pit toilets, picnic tables, and fireplaces are provided. Pets are permitted. Two equestrian campgrounds are available (check that campground map). There is no fee at any of the campsites in this state forest. The

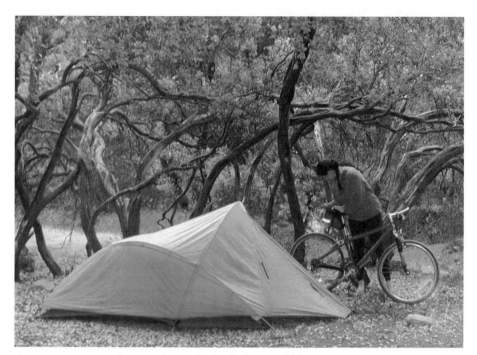

Some state campgrounds reserve sites specifically for hikers and bikers. PHOTO: JOHN NAGIECKI

surrounding redwood forest is an amazing attraction. (See our Parks and Recreation chapter for more on Jackson State Forest.)

Mackerricher State Park
24100 Mackerricher Park Rd., Fort Bragg
(707) 937–5804
www.mcn.org/1/mendoparks/macker.htm

There are 11 hike-in/bike-in campsites (for up to four people) and 143 sites for tents or motor homes up to 35 feet long—but no hookups—at this beautiful coastal park 3 miles north of Fort Bragg on Highway 1. One site is wheelchair-accessible. Piped water, hot showers, flush toilets, a dump station, picnic tables, and fireplaces are provided. Pets are permitted. (Mackerricher State Park is further detailed in our Parks and Recreation chapter.)

Fort Bragg Leisure Time RV Park
30801 Hwy. 20, Fort Bragg
(707) 964–5994

The wooded setting is a highlight here for RV campers. There are 82 sites for tents or RVs, many with full or partial hookups. Restrooms, picnic tables, satellite TV, fire rings, coin-operated hot showers, and a sanitary disposal station are provided. A laundry is available, and pets are allowed on leashes.

Lake County

Loch Lomond Park
Hwy. 175
(707) 928–5044

Off Highway 175 on the northern slopes of Cobb Mountain is Loch Lomond, a peaceful campground with about 20 RV or tent spaces. They have picnic tables, fire grills, restrooms, and showers, and a swimming pool and store are across the road.

Shaw's Shady Acres
7805 Cache Creek Way, Clearlake
(707) 994–2236

Cache Creek is a small stream that pours out of Clear Lake, and at least three privately owned campgrounds are set along it. Shaw's has 13 sites for tents or RVs—6 able to squirrel away any money? Your problems are solved! This park is actually on an island in the marshy area between Clear Lake and the town of Clearlake Oaks, just off Highway 20. (Don't worry, the road is elevated.) M&M has 37 spaces, flush toilets, showers, and a boat ramp. Boat rentals and a market are just down the street.

Edgewater Resort and RV Park
6420 Soda Bay Rd., Kelseyville
(707) 279-0208, (800) 396-6224
www.edgewaterresort.net

Edgewater is one of the higher-quality campgrounds around Clear Lake, in terms of both atmosphere and amenities. It boasts more than 150 trees of 19 varieties on the grounds. The resort has 61 spaces. Some of them work better as tent spaces, some are more appropriate for RVs, though the proprietors will mix and match as necessary. Here you'll find picnic tables, fire grills, restrooms, showers, a volleyball court, horseshoe pits, a clubhouse, a general store, a swimming pool, and laundry facilities. There's also a long fishing pier, a boat ramp, and a beach. You can even rent a boat here, and in the summer you might catch a musical event. Pets are allowed on leashes. Big groups are encouraged.

Clear Lake State Park
Soda Bay Rd., near Kelseyville
(707) 279-4293 (info),
(800) 444-PARK (reservations)

There are actually four separate campgrounds within the 565-acre park: shady Cole Creek; Kelsey Creek, which is right on the water; and Upper and Lower Bay View, nice ridge-top spots. Not all of them are open through the winter. The park is popular with boaters, anglers, and those wanting nothing more active than staring at the herons in the tules while sipping a cold drink. All together, Clear Lake has 147 campsites for tents or motor homes, plus a few primitive hike-in/bike-in sites. There are plenty of picnic tables, fire grills, restrooms, and showers, plus a grocery store and a laundry. Some sites are accessible by wheelchair. (For more on Clear Lake, see our Parks and Recreation chapter.)

RV and 2 tent sites on the waterfront, 5 tent sites under the walnut trees. You'll find picnic tables, standing barbecues, restrooms, showers, and a laundry. Need more? How about a swimming pool, a rec patio, a beer-and-wine bar, and a market. Oh, and if you want your recreation right out on the creek, they have a pier, boat ramp, fishing supplies, and boat rentals. North of Lower Lake on Highway 53, turn west at the Old Highway 53 turnoff; make a left on the frontage road and drive a quarter-mile to Shaw's.

Funtime RV Park
6035 Old Hwy. 53, Clearlake
(707) 994-6267

One of the southernmost campgrounds on Clear Lake, Funtime is just north of Lower Lake. The resort has 25 sites for tents and 40 for motor homes. It has flush toilets, showers, a recreation room, a swimming and wading pool, a laundry, and a grocery store. Of course, it offers boat rentals and a pier for anglers.

M&M Campgrounds
13050 Island Dr., Clearlake Oaks
(707) 998-9943

Have you promised your spouse a trip to some exotic island but just haven't been

Kelly's Kamp
8220 Scotts Valley Rd., west of Upper Lake
(707) 263-5754

Just far enough removed from Clear Lake that it avoids much of the traffic, this campground is on Scotts Creek, close to the Blue Lakes. Kelly's has 75 sites for tents or RVs, plus picnic tables, fire grills, flush toilets, showers, a laundry, and a small camp store.

Holiday Harbor RV Park
3605 Lakeshore Blvd., Nice
(707) 274-1136

Alongside Highway 20 in the town of Nice, Holiday Harbor has a full-service marina, a boat ramp, and reliable bass fishing. It also has 30 RV spaces with full or partial hookups. The park is equipped with picnic tables, restrooms, showers, a rec room, and a laundromat.

Pine Acres Resort
5328 Blue Lakes Rd., north of Upper Lake
(707) 275-2811
www.bluelakepineacres.com

See our Hotels and Motels chapter for a full description of Pine Acres. Note here, however, that the resort also has 32 spaces for motor homes, most with full or partial hookups. The facilities include picnic tables, flush toilets, showers, and a grocery store. Some of the campsites are on the shore of Upper Blue Lake, and Pine Acres has the requisite moorings, boat ramp, fishing supplies, and boat rentals.

From Upper Lake, go 6 miles northwest on Highway 20, turn left on Irvine Street, and proceed two blocks. Turn right on Blue Lakes Road.

Bear Creek Campground
Bear Creek Rd., north of Upper Lake
(707) 275-2361

This camp site is secluded, untrampled, and picturesque, set at about 2,000 feet, at the confluence of Bear Creek and Blue Slide Creek (just past the Rice Fork of the Eel River). There are 16 sites for tents or motor homes, plus picnic tables, fire pits, vault toilets, and access to hiking trails—but no piped water, so lug your own or bring a purifier.

Make no reservations, pay no fee. Pets are permitted on leashes. From Upper Lake, drive 17 miles north on Elk Mountain Road, then make a right onto Bear Creek Road and proceed another 8 miles. The grounds are closed to campers from mid-October through the end of April.

Middle Creek Campground
Elk Mountain Rd., north of Upper Lake
(707) 275-2361

Among the campgrounds in the mountains of northern Lake County, this one is the closest to the towns of Clear Lake (about 8 miles north of Upper Lake). Middle Creek is at an elevation of about 2,000 feet, where the West and East forks of the Eel River come together. There are 12 sites for tents or small RVs, plus picnic tables, fire pits, and vault toilets. Water is on the gravity system. You can bring a pet if it is leashed. Middle Creek, popular with dirt bikers, does not take reservations. From Upper Lake, drive north on Elk Mountain Road (Forest Service Road 1N02).

Insiders' Tip

Coin-operated "pay showers" provide hot water for as long as you have quarters to feed the machine (generally 3-5 minutes for 50 cents). State and county campgrounds frequently work on such an arrangement, but do not also provide a way for you to obtain the needed change. In short, make sure you have a supply of quarters on hand if you want to avoid having to brave an icy shower.

Lower Nye
Rice Creek Rd., north of Upper Lake
(707) 275–2361

This is a good starting point for a backpacking trip into the rugged Snow Mountain Wilderness. Lower Nye sits on the periphery of that protected area, at 3,300 feet on Skeleton Creek. The tiny campground has six sites for tents or motor homes, with picnic tables, fire pits, and vault toilets. There is no piped water, and it is closed from mid-September through April. There is no charge for camping. From Upper Lake, go 17 miles north on Elk Mountain Road, veer right on Bear Creek Road, and drive another 7 miles. Turn left on Rice Creek Road and proceed 14 miles to Lower Nye.

Sunset Campground
Potter Valley-Lake Pillsbury Rd.,
east of Potter Valley in Mendocino County
(707) 275–2361

Largest of the five public and private campgrounds set around scenic Lake Pillsbury, Sunset has 54 sites for tents or RVs. It also has picnic tables, fire pits, and vault toilets. You can angle for trout on the northeast rim of the lake or jump on the nature trail that begins near the campground. A boat ramp is close at hand. Reservations are not accepted. Lake Pillsbury is accessed via Potter Valley-Lake Pillsbury Road.

Fuller Grove
Simmons Rd., east of Potter Valley
(707) 275–2361

Another option for Lake Pillsbury visitors, Fuller Grove has 30 spots for tents or motor homes. You get picnic tables, fireplaces, vault toilets, and access to a nearby boat ramp if you want to get on the water. Pets are permitted but must be kept under control. From the Eel River Information Kiosk at Lake Pillsbury (follow the signs and you can't miss it approaching from the west), proceed 2.2 miles to the lake shore, make a right, and drive another half-mile.

Restaurants

Napa County
Sonoma County
Mendocino County
Lake County

What can we say about the food in Wine Country that has not already been well documented elsewhere? We're beginning to think we should reclassify our region as "Wine and Food Country" because the cuisine in many cases threatens to outshine the wine. In fact, we've found that many visitors don't come here for the wine at all. They come for the experience of dining in world-class establishments, and the wine is a really nice bonus. If you've ever wielded a knife and fork in these parts, you know why.

Several Wine Country restaurants seem to consistently show up on the "top" lists in a variety of gourmet and travel magazines. They achieve this lofty distinction by inventing some of the most delectable dishes imaginable. For instance, just look at what a few of them can do with a single chicken: Wine Spectator Greystone Restaurant will spit-roast it with toasted orzo, olives, preserved lemon, and sun-dried tomatoes; Celadon will roast it Indian-style, with ginger and red curry, and serve it with saffron-basmati risotto; Compadres will turn it into arroz con pollo; Catahoula will take that little sucker and roast it with tasso potatoes and garlic-lemon escarole; Pacifico Restaurante will add chayote and potato and bury it all with mole sauce; the Calistoga Inn will marinate it in lime and crust it with Jamaican jerk sauce; and Auberge du Soleil will redefine it as rosemary-roasted petite poulet with artichoke-eggplant ragout.

To no one's surprise, this region has become something of a magnet for chefs, more so since the opening of the Culinary Institute of America's "campus" north of St. Helena (see our Education and Child Care chapter). The marriage of food and wine—utilizing the finest fresh ingredients grown locally, including the wine grapes and much of what is presented on your plate—has turned the area into a prime destination for foodies.

Note that this chapter is organized a bit differently from the rest. It still follows our geographical method of listing Napa County first, followed by Sonoma, Mendocino, and Lake Counties. But to make it easier to locate that famous greasy spoon you read about in *Bon Appetit* magazine, restaurants are listed alphabetically within their respective regions and cities.

As you read these entries remember that, unless we say otherwise, you can count on certain things: The restaurant serves beer and wine but does not have a full bar, it accepts major credit cards, it is wheelchair-accessible, and it takes reservations. Most of the upscale restaurants do not have children's menus, but the down-home places do.

Lastly, most restaurants here define their dress code as "classy casual," "snappy casual," or, most often, "Wine Country casual." What that basically means is to look well groomed. Tuck in your shirt, or change it if you just dumped half a glass of Pinot Noir on it. Other than that, it is unlikely you'll be underdressed. Even the highest-rated establishments tend to allow Levi's, collarless shirts, and even shorts and shoes with no socks in the summer. And that, some say, is one of the coolest things about dining here.

Price Code

Refer to this price code as you peruse our Restaurants section. The dollar figure refers to the average price of two entrees only—no appetizers, no dessert, no drinks, no tax or gratuity. We don't actually expect you to eat that way—or forego the tip!—we just wanted to keep the calculations simple.

$	Less than $18
$$	$19 to $25
$$$	$26 to $35
$$$$	More than $35

Napa County

City of Napa

Alexis Baking Company $$
1517 Third St., Napa
(707) 258–1827

What began as a wholesale bakery has become one of Napa's coolest hangouts, whether you're eating lunch or light dinner or just sipping oak-roasted coffee and contemplating the always-engaging art on the walls. ABC puts together a variety of salads, soups, and specials, changing the lineup daily. The gorgonzola cheeseburgers and the focaccia sandwiches go over big, but it's the fresh baked goods that have inspired the most loyalty. Save room for a piece of chocolate-caramel cake or apricot-pistachio cake, or just pig out on muffins and cookies. The Baking Company is open seven days for breakfast and lunch, carrying the lunch menu through dinner on Thursday and Friday. No credit cards.

Bistro Don Giovanni $$$
4110 St. Helena Hwy. South, Napa
(707) 224–3300

Damn it all, we just can't avoid the word. Giovanni Scala's restaurant is "romantic." The subdued earth tones, the unpolished wood and the tiles, the vineyard views, the high ceilings, the fireplaces in and out—your date will be putty in your hands. Just make sure you can still concentrate on the food. Donna Scala does the cooking, favoring regional Italian dishes and tossing in a bit of Provence. The pan-seared salmon filet with buttermilk mashed potatoes is excellent, as is the grilled portobello mushroom appetizer. Side dishes not to be missed are the sautéed spinach with garlic or the house-marinated Mediterranean olives. The restaurant is also noted for its risottos and pastas. Don Giovanni is open seven days a week for lunch and dinner. The menu changes daily, and there is a full bar.

Celadon $$
1040 Main St., Ste. 104, Napa
(707) 254–9690

In Napa Valley, you'll be hard-pressed to find better quality for your dollar than you get at this bright creekside cafe in the rear of the Main Street Exchange (next to the Opera House). Celadon, painted in the pale greens and blues implied by the name, has a long slate counter and an open kitchen. Start with bruschetta, followed by a truffle- and honey-glazed pork chop or braised Algerian-style lamb shank. Celadon also has a well-conceived wine list, with 10 by-the-glass choices. It's open for lunch Monday through Friday and dinner Monday through Saturday. Seating is "upon arrival"—i.e., no reservations.

Cole's Chop House $$$
1122 Main St., Napa
(707) 224–6328

When Greg Cole, who also owns Celadon nearby, opened this classic American steakhouse in 1999, it was an immediate success. As its name implies, this is where one goes to get red meat—in huge portions. The menu's pricier steaks include the 21-day Chicago dry-aged New York strip or porterhouse, and a two-inch-thick Black Angus filet mignon. For non-carnivores, there's plenty of fish and even a short stack of portobello mushroom caps.

Housed in a restored historic building dating from 1886, the restaurant, with dining rooms on two levels, features stone walls and a wood-beamed ceiling. The cozy booths are set with white tablecloths and copper-beaded lampshades over candles. It's elegant and masculine at the same time. Another draw here is

Insiders' Tip

Smoking is no longer permitted in California restaurants. However, a few Wine Country establishments have set up separate smoking rooms mainly for the enjoyment of cigar afficionados.

the great old bar, where you can belly up for a classic Manhattan, martini, or a cosmopolitan. Not surprising is the varied assortment of bold Napa Valley Cabernets on the wine list. Dinner is served Tuesday through Sunday, accompanied by live jazz on weekends.

Foothill Cafe $$$
2766 Old Sonoma Rd., Napa
(707) 252-6178

"People are scared to come in sometimes," chef/owner Jerry Shaffer says of his small, 40-seat restaurant in southwest Napa. That's because Foothill Cafe sits in a nondescript little strip mall, an unlikely venue for a locally adored restaurant. Enter the cafe and your faith will be rewarded with food that relies heavily on fresh local produce and a hickory smoker in the kitchen. Nightly specials accent favorites such as baby-back ribs, seared ahi tuna with wasabi and ginger dipping sauce, or roasted free-range chicken breast with creamy polenta. The decor is frenetic, thanks to Shaffer's repeated excursions to Baja California. Foothill Cafe is open for dinner from Wednesday through Sunday.

Julia's Kitchen $$$$
500 First St., Napa
(707) 265-5700
www.copia.org

Named for Julia Child, who was one of the first diners when it opened its doors inside Copia (see our Attractions chapter), this eatery promises to be a food lover's destination restaurant for some time to come. With about 20 tables and an open, active kitchen led by executive chef Mark Dommen, the decor is almost industrial-like, with a concrete floor and split pea soup-green accents on the walls and chair cushions. Instead, the frills and the presentation are saved for the food, which is pleasing to the eye and the palate.

Start with a first course of sunchoke risotto with hazelnuts, garlic chives, and Parmesan cheese; or opt for the grilled quail with chanterelle mushrooms, foie gras, and herb vinaigrette. With your tastebuds thoroughly spoiled, move on to a second course of steamed Thai snapper with enoki and shiitake mushrooms, scallions and mushroom consommé—unless you prefer seared dayboat scallops with pancetta, potato puree, and chanterelle mushrooms surrounded by a Port wine reduction sauce. For dessert, dig into the chocolate bread pudding (made with devil's food cake, not bread) or the caramel pear.

As you would expect from a restaurant inside a center for wine and food, the wine list is ample, running about 10 pages. The service is professional, caring, and friendly without being cloying. The acoustics keep the racket level high, so it's not the sort of romantic place where you can whisper sweet nothings. But if you prefer a lively, bustling atmosphere—with an international clientele all around—you'll feel right at home in Julia's Kitchen.

You can dine at Julia's without paying admission into Copia; the restaurant is open for lunch and dinner in summer and for lunch only in winter. Needless to say, reservations are a must.

La Boucane $$$
1778 Second St., Napa
(707) 253-1177

Though now in his 70s, the indomitable Jacques Mokrani shows no signs of slowing down. "My skills improve every day," says the Algerian-born chef/restaurateur. By now his La Boucane, housed in a 120-year-old Victorian, is a Napa Valley landmark. There is a white tablecloth, a red rose, and silver utensils on every table. Classical music strums in the background. And out comes the classic French cuisine: a Chilean sea bass Bretonne appetizer; lobster bisque; classic escargot; onion soup Lyonnaise; crisp roast duckling with orange sauce for two; and, if you're smart, one of Mokrani's renowned soufflés.

La Boucane's wine list sticks exclusively to Napa Valley. And remember what it says at the bottom of the menu: "We will prepare any dish upon request, providing we have the ingredients on hand." And if "on hand" means he has to run across the street to Safeway, the chef says, then so be it. The restaurant is open for dinner every night but Sunday.

Old Adobe Bar and Grille $$
376 Soscol Ave., Napa
(707) 255–4310

Old Adobe's name is more authentic than you might guess. The dining room is housed in the second-oldest intact adobe building in Northern California, constructed in 1840. The 3-foot-thick walls and exposed rafters in the dining room are original, and the murals depicting Mexican village life were painted in the 1920s. Old Adobe serves up variations of Mexican standards but really specializes in steaks and prime rib, adding daily fresh fish and pasta specials. The restaurant does dinner seven days a week and lunch Monday through Friday. It also offers Sunday brunch. There is a full bar.

Pairs Cafe $$$
4175 Solano Ave., Napa
(707) 224–8464
www.pairscafe.com

This is the same Pairs that once resided in St. Helena. Brothers Craig and Keith Schauffel have increased the size of their restaurant, from 50 to 150 seats, and moved it south, but the focus of the food remains the same: California cuisine with an Asian twist. The idea at Pairs is expressed in the restaurant's name: to pair food and wine to the advantage of both. Each dish on the menu, even appetizers, comes with a varietal recommendation. For instance, Chardonnay is suggested for the lemon-fried calamari, Sauvignon Blanc for the vegetarian spring rolls, and Merlot for the grilled rosemary lamb chops. The new location features private dining rooms, an outdoor patio with water gardens, and an open kitchen and dining bar. This restaurant was experimenting with a cabaret dinner series and live music on weekends as this book was being updated.

Pearl $$
1339 Pearl St., Ste. 104, Napa
(707) 224–1552
www.therestaurantpearl.com

Proprietors Nickie and Pete Zeller have created a comfortable bistro with soaring ceilings and lots of geometric artwork to ponder as you enjoy fresh oysters served in a multitude of ways. There are soups, pizzas, sandwiches, and chicken and beef dishes with Mexican, Italian, and even Asian influences. Try the triple-double pork chop with an apple-dijon brine, or a New York steak with blue cheese and roasted garlic butter. The wine list includes several obscure Napa Valley labels. Open Tuesday through Thursday for lunch and dinner; closed Sunday and Monday.

Piccolino's Italian Cafe $$
1385 Napa Town Center, Napa
(707) 251–0100
www.piccolinoscafe.com

Food has always meant comfort to Joe Salerno, who grew up stirring pots and making sausage with his extended Italian family in upstate New York. Salerno now does his best to create fond memories at Piccolino's, his unpretentious, child-friendly restaurant in downtown Napa. The cafe offers fresh fish dishes, house-made sausage, and four types of pizza. The pasta entrees are highlighted by the colorful fettuccine Calabrese, with its multitude of simple ingredients; and the lasagna, a family recipe that employs a light ricotta shipped in from the East Coast. Lasagna and spaghetti are available in immense family-style portions. The wine list is primarily Napan, though it does include a small line of Italians. Piccolino's is open daily for lunch and dinner, plus brunch on weekends. See our Nightlife chapter for information on live music.

The Royal Oak/Vintner's Court $$$$
Silverado Resort, 1600 Atlas Peak Rd., Napa
(707) 257–0200
www.silveradoresort.com

Two separate restaurants are housed in The Mansion at Silverado. To the left of the main lounge is Vintner's Court, larger and more formal, with stolid, oak-sided walls and lots of glass. To the right is the more rustic Royal Oak, with its open beams and open kitchen. Vintner's Court serves fresh California cuisine with Mediterranean and Pacific Rim influences—for example, seared Chilean seabass with mango and jicama or Sonoma foie gras with endive, citrus relish, and honey vinaigrette. The Oak is more traditionally American, with big steaks and filet of salmon. Peter Pahk is executive chef for both restaurants. Both offer full bar service. The Royal Oak is open seven days a week for dinner. Vintner's Court is open Wednesday, Thursday, and Saturday for dinner off the menu, Friday night for seafood buffet, and Sunday morning for brunch. The 2-inch-thick waffles have inspired all sorts of devotion.

Tuscany $$$
1005 First St., Napa
(707) 258–1000

Another popular new restaurant opened its doors in downtown Napa recently, specializing in—you guessed it—the cooking of northern Italy. Start with a traditional minestrone with a bevy of vegetables and pancetta. Follow that with risotto con quaglia, featuring walnuts and a touch of gorgonzola cheese topped with two roasted quail. Classic cannoli is the perfect finishing touch. The menu also includes pizzas from the wood-fired oven and rotisseried rabbit, veal, pork, and chicken. The open room features high ceilings and earthy colors, and a wine bar is separated from the dining room by a low partition. There's a counter with stools where you can watch the chefs preparing such fare as a halibut steak with roasted red and golden beets on the side. Open daily for dinner.

Yoshi-Shige $$$
3381 California Blvd., Napa
(707) 257–3583

Good sushi restaurants are hard to find north of San Francisco. One of the best is Yoshi-Shige, now in business more than a decade, with Japanese decor and a menu of more than 60 sushi items, not to mention entrees such as chicken teriyaki and shrimp-and-vegetable tempura. The sushi dishes range in price from $3.50 to $8.50, so how much you

> ## Insiders' Tip
> After an early dinner in downtown Napa, enjoy something completely different: Saturday Night Opera, when vocalists from around northern California take turns on stage at the Jarvis Conservatory, 1711 Main Street. For $15 you get two hours of stellar operatic vocal performances on the first and third Saturdays of every month. To book your seats, call (707) 255-5445.

spend depends on how much you are willing to devour. Yoshi-Shige serves sake in addition to its beer and wine. It's open for lunch and dinner every day and night except Monday.

Yountville

Bistro Jeanty $$$
6510 Washington St., Yountville
(707) 944–0103
www.bistrojeanty.com

Philippe Jeanty became head chef at Domaine Chandon a year after it opened, and over the next 20 years he turned it into a world-class restaurant. There was much local hand-wringing when Jeanty flew the coop in 1997. But his comfortable, two-room bistro opened in April of 1998 and quickly occupied a niche that, Philippe explains, is part Paris, part French countryside. You won't find a single pasta on this small menu, no Caesar salad or hamburgers. Instead, be on the lookout for lamb tongue and potato salad, beef tournedos in black pepper

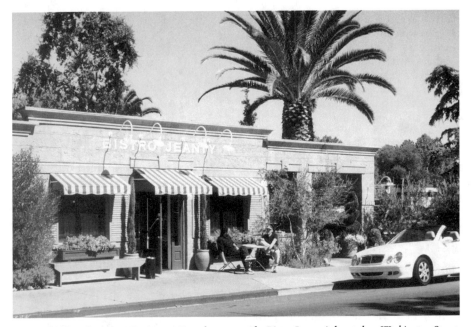

A casual eatery that's part Paris, part French countryside, Bistro Jeanty is located on Washington Street in Yountville. PHOTO: JEAN SAYLOR DOPPENBERG

cream sauce, cassoulet, and mussels steamed in red wine. The setting is just as authentic, with French furnishings and paintings by Guy Buffet. And the color of the walls? Dijon, of course. Bistro Jeanty is open for lunch and dinner seven days a week. It has a full bar; the staff calls the giant rooster that sits atop it "Philippe."

Bouchon $$$
6534 Washington St., Yountville
(707) 944–8037
If you're looking for a place to have a late-night dinner, here's one of the few gourmet delights in Napa Valley that will serve you till the wee hours—closing time is 2:00 A.M. The fare here is classic French bistro ("bouchon" is the local term for "bistro" in Lyon, France.) But it's typically not the trendy stuff; instead, it's classics like mussels mariniéres and leg of lamb with flageolet beans. The appetizers can include terrine of foie gras and an extensive raw seafood bar. The sweets run to crème caramel or tarte Tatin. The wine list is terrific and the prices are down to earth.

The atmosphere is lively and loud, but

that's part of the charm. The dining room is furnished with a zinc-plated bar and antique lighting fixtures, and the music is typically jazz from the 1930s. There's also al fresco dining. Because it keeps late hours, Bouchon is a favorite with local winemakers and staff from other restaurants. Open for lunch and dinner daily.

Brix $$$
7377 St. Helena Hwy., Yountville
(707) 944–BRIX
www.brix.com
Grilled rare ahi tuna with tomatillo crème fraîche, chanterelles, and purple potatoes? Grilled salmon with sesame mustard sauce, crisp salsify, red chard, and pickled shiitakes? Hoison grilled rack of lamb with pearled barley, radicchio, and mint oil? What do you call this? "Asian fusion" if you're Brix, the restaurant just north of Yountville. Brix is surrounded by 10 acres of vineyard and a couple of acres of olive trees; one dining room wall is all glass, revealing the restaurant's herb garden. They have a full bar, including what the *San Francisco Chronicle* called an "Academy

Award-winning wine list." Brix is open for lunch and dinner, seven days a week.

Compadres Mexican Bar & Grill $$
6539 Washington St., Yountville
(707) 944-2406

Mexican fare is more than appropriate here, on a portion of the land grant deeded to Salvador Vallejo by the Mexican government in 1838. Compadres is a sprawling, 165-seat restaurant with both indoor and outdoor seating. There is depth to the Margarita list, which includes what *San Francisco Focus* magazine once ordained the best Margarita it had sampled. The food is wide-ranging, too, with traditional Jaliscan carnitas, seafood tacos, daily fish specials, and at least eight types of enchilada. Compadres is open seven days a week for breakfast, lunch, and dinner.

Domaine Chandon $$$$
1 California Dr., Yountville
(707) 944-2892
www.dchandon.com

Parked against the hills west of Yountville, Domaine Chandon sits amid century-old oaks and the winery's own vineyards. The atmosphere is elegant, immaculate, and trés français. The menu changes weekly but returns to a few of chef Robert Curry's favorites, such as smoked trout or salmon, foie blond pâté, caramelized scallops, and local lamb. Domaine Chandon is open for dinner every night except Monday and Tuesday. It's open for lunch seven days a week. Note that reservations here should be booked well in advance.

The French Laundry $$$$
6640 Washington St., Yountville
(707) 944-2380
www.sterba.com/yountville/frenchlaundry

What does Yountville have that Manhattan and Los Angeles don't? How about the best chef in America? That's what the prestigious James Beard Foundation called Thomas Keller in May 1997. In fact, this restaurant received its third James Beard Award in 2001. Keller's restaurant is at the corner of Washington and Creek

Insiders' Tip

The French Laundry in Yountville came under fire in the media recently for being as hard to get into as Fort Knox. It's become far too exclusive (*n'est-ce pas?*), and dinner for four can run into the hundreds of dollars. Their reservations policy also infuriates many, and their phone line is constantly busy (they claim to get as many as 400 phone calls daily requesting reservations). Our advice? Keep trying!

Streets in Yountville, in a century-old fieldstone house that was once, indeed, a French steam laundry. The French Laundry has been elevated to almost mythical status among foodies, many of whom have never come close to eating here, possibly because it's so difficult to procure a reservation. If you do make it in, congratulations. But be prepared for a very pricey experience (a recent dinner for four—including wine and gratuity—came to $800). It's a prix fixe menu only: $80 per person for a five-course vegetarian offering; $105 for a more robust five-course meal; or $120 for the nine-course Chef's Tasting Menu. Keller, though a devotee of traditional French principles, is also known for his whimsical takes on common meals, like "macaroni and cheese" that turns out to be butter-poached Maine lobster with creamy lobster broth and Mascarpone-enriched orzo, or "coffee and doughnuts" that are, in fact, fresh-

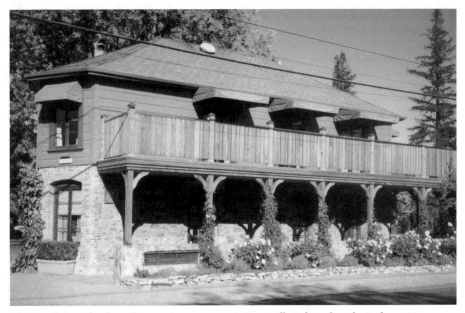

The French Laundry, housed in a unique structure in Yountville, is legendary for its fine cuisine. PHOTO: JEAN SAYLOR DOPPENBERG

baked cinnamon-sugared doughnuts with cappuccino semifreddo. The French Laundry is open for dinner seven days a week and lunch from Friday through Sunday.

Mustards Grill $$$
7399 St. Helena Hwy., Yountville
(707) 944-2424

Roadhouse meets fine dining at Mustards Grill. The restaurant is situated on Highway 29, and the casual dining room looks onto a beautiful swath of the Napa countryside. But the real action here is in the kitchen. One of the most consistently popular restaurants in the valley, Mustards is also one of the oldest, established in 1983.

The menu changes seasonally, but classics like Mongolian pork chops (marinated, grilled chops with braised cabbage and garlic mashers) and hanger steak are available year-round. Everything is made from scratch here—don't miss the house-made ketchup served with paper-thin onion rings. The menu tends toward creatively reinvented American classics, with daily fish specials providing the haute end of the cuisine. After dessert (most impressive is the lemon tart with 6-inch-high

> ## Insiders' Tip
> Mustards Grill, north of Yountville on Highway 29, is an almost-guaranteed good time and great meal, as so many diners have learned over the years. The only problem is securing a reservation on short notice. Remember, then, that the restaurant stays open between lunch and dinner. You should consider a light lunch, a light late "supper" and a prodigious Mustards dinner at 3:00 P.M.

brown-sugar meringue), you can order a cigar and retire to the smoking patio. Mustards has a full bar with "way too many wines" and is open for lunch and dinner seven days a week.

Napa Valley Grille $$$
Hwy. 29 at Madison St., Yountville
(707) 944–8686
www.calcafe.com/napavalleygrille

Like most chefs in Wine Country, new chef Gina DeCew (formerly of Spago), dishes up a changing menu that uses a number of seasonal ingredients produced locally. The menu was being revamped as this book went to press, but expect great things from Gina, who has created memorable meals for the stars of Hollywood.

There are as many as 750 wine selections to choose from here, including rare and older vintages. The dining room looks out onto vineyards, and the exhibition kitchen adds interest. Lunch and dinner is served daily, with brunch on Sunday.

Piatti Restaurant $$$
6480 Washington St., Yountville
(707) 944–2070
www.piatti.com

Dwelling on the Mediterranean end of Italy, the Piatti menu is filled with fresh herbs and seafood. Chef Peter Hall offers daily pizza, pasta, and fish specials. Some things remain constant, though, like the pappardelle "fantasia": wide saffron ribbons with shrimp, arugula, fresh tomato, and spicy lemon-wine sauce. The spice-rubbed rotisserie chicken is another favorite. Piatti has osso bucco and live music every Wednesday. The dining room is warm, with stucco walls, handpainted murals, white pine, and fireplaces. The restaurant has a full bar (with many Italian wines) and is open for lunch and dinner seven days a week.

Rutherford

Auberge du Soleil $$$$
180 Rutherford Hill Rd., Rutherford
(707) 963–1211
www.aubergedusoleil.com

Before Auberge du Soleil the inn, there was Auberge du Soleil the restaurant. It's known as one of Napa Valley's premier eateries, not just for the food but for the remarkable vistas from the dining terrace. The dining room is in theme with the entire resort—rustically classy, with thick cedar columns, rough-timbered ceilings, fireplaces, and French doors. Chef Richard Reddington joined the restaurant in 2000 and has been transforming the menu from merely adequate to outstanding. His new cuisine has included marinated raw yellowfin tuna with baby beets, radish slices, and Meyer lemon oil; and Florida red snapper with sliced almonds and capers in cauliflower puree. As with several other high-end restaurants in Wine Country, Auberge switched to a fixed price menu: The four-course dinner without wine is $75 per person. (Lunch choices might include grilled calamari with chick peas, red peppers, and lemon oil.) The restaurant is open for lunch and dinner seven days a week, and it has a full bar.

La Toque $$$$
1140 Rutherford Rd., Rutherford
(707) 963–9770
www.latoque.com

French-inspired with occasional Asian influences—that's one way to describe this elegant restaurant recently listed among the Top 20 in America by *Wine Spectator* magazine. The decadent five-course prix fixe menu whipped up by chef Ken Frank changes with the seasonal ingredients available locally, and can include fresh corn polenta with English peas and chanterelles for an appetizer, followed by chicken Ballotine with crayfish and black truffle; or a wild striped bass with spinach, Cabernet, and roasted red marble potatoes. But La Toque goes one step further in its pursuit of excellence with its annual truffle menus, when fresh white truffles come into season for a few months in the fall. (At about $1,000 per pound, they are generally used as a supplement to the prix fixe menu.) When white truffle season slows down, out come the first black truffles. Season permitting, the black truffle menu options are available from January through Valentine's Day.

Located at the Rancho Caymus Inn, La Toque's dining room is intimate, with a huge stone fireplace. Patio dining is also available.

Rutherford Grill $$$
1180 Rutherford Rd., Rutherford
(707) 963-1792

This restaurant is easy to spot by the large Phoenix date palm trees swaying in front. It's a casual "neighborhood" roadhouse that offers American comfort food in big portions. Their mashed potatoes are legend and make a yummy accompaniment to the rotisserie chicken, steaks, burgers, and prime rib offerings. (Start your meal with the Maytag blue cheese chips.) The decor is warm, with redwood walls made from old wine barrels. The huge outside patio is a great place to watch Wine Country visitors hurrying by on the highway. More than 100 Napa Valley wines are offered, with at least 30 available by the glass. Open daily for lunch and dinner.

St. Helena

Beau Vine $$$$
1347 Main St., St. Helena
(707) 968-9666

The playful name suggests steak, and there's lots of that on the menu. But what makes this restaurant a standout is its North and South American cuisine and that of Australia and New Zealand, whipped together by chef Max Duley. Yes, there is kangaroo on the menu (rubbed with roasted garlic, grilled, and served with plum and tomato chutney—ask for it on the rare side), as well as billabong yabbies. There's squash soup from Brazil and chicken and beef entrees from Argentina. The wine list is heavy on South American and Australian selections, and more than 30 are available by the glass. Dare we say it: Beau Vine is divine. Breakfast is served daily (a jazz brunch is featured on weekends); and dinner is seven days a week.

Gillwoods Restaurant $$
1313 Main St., St. Helena
(707) 963-1788
1320 Napa Town Center, Napa
(707) 253-0409

You have to get up pretty early in the morning to beat the locals to Gillwoods, St. Helena's favorite breakfast spot. It's casual, intimate, and filled with good cheer and caffeine. The big draw always has been the scrambles—eggs and cream cheese mixed with various ingredients. (Our personal favorite: the salmon scramble with capers.)

The restaurant is open for breakfast and lunch seven days a week and does not take reservations. Gillwoods has a second location in Napa Town Center. The menu is the same there, except it includes dinner on Friday and Saturday nights. Reservations for six or more are accepted in Napa.

Green Valley Cafe $$
1310 Main St., St. Helena
(707) 963-7088

Small, cozy, and reasonably priced (i.e., exactly what you don't expect in St. Helena), Green Valley Cafe is the perfect place to sup before or after a film at Cameo Cinema. If you don't make reservations, you'll probably wind up at the counter. No matter where you sit, you will be treated to Delio Cuneo's northern Italian cuisine. (Cuneo was born near

Portofino.) Green Valley offers daily fresh-fish specials, but otherwise sticks to a simple, well-executed menu. Locals tend to gravitate toward the lasagna (with tomatoes, ham, mozzarella, and basil), the braised lamb shank with polenta, or the melanzane-eggplant topped with tomato and bechamel sauces and Parmesan cheese. The wine list is a mix of Napa Valley and Italy. Green Valley Cafe is open for lunch and dinner from Tuesday through Saturday.

The Restaurant at Meadowood $$$$
900 Meadowood Ln., St. Helena
(707) 963–3646
www.meadowood.com

Chef Steven Tevere had big shoes to fill at Meadowood, when chefs Didier Lenders and his wife, Pilar Sanchez, moved on to other culinary pursuits. But Tevere is holding his own, with dishes like the terrine of Sonoma Moulard and Muscovy foie gras and the rack of lamb served with herbed potatoes and eggplant puree. Begin your meal with sweet corn flan or roasted eggplant soup; finish it with a raspberry soufflé or strawberry-rhubarb crisp.

And the wine list, by the way, is phenomenal. Sticking exclusively to Napa Valley, it represents nearly all of the county's wineries. And if that isn't enough, there is the dining room itself—a comfortable pastel room overlooking the resort's manicured golf course. The Restaurant at Meadowood has a full bar, and is open for dinner seven nights a week, plus Sunday brunch.

Miramonte Restaurant and Cafe $$$
1327 Railroad Ave., St. Helena
(707) 963–1200

And now for something completely different: Food of the Americas, as envisioned by owner Cindy Pawlcyn, of Mustards Grill and Fog City Diner fame. The place is bright and fun, yet tastefully furnished, and the flavors of North and South America are nicely fused here in hearty portions at reasonable prices. Wrap your mouth around a Cuban pork tinga torta or a rabbit tostada, or if you're really hungry, try

Insiders' Tip

The Culinary Institute of America in St. Helena hosts an annual "Service—You Deserve It" celebration to honor the servers, bussers, and other staff of Napa Valley hospitality businesses. Wine for the event is donated by local vintners, and the CIA staff cook up a great meal as a tribute to these hardworking folks.

the short ribs braised in chiles and bittersweet chocolate. Satisfy your thirst with a Caiparinha (Brazil's national drink), or choose from more than 100 different labels of wine from Chile, Argentina, and Mexico—along with California and Oregon selections. Cap off the meal with Mexican chocolate cake. Stop in just about anytime—the restaurant is open daily for lunch and dinner (until 10:00 P.M. on weekends).

Model Bakery $
1357 Main St., St. Helena
(707) 963–8192

You'd think it was a film set if those whiffs of fresh-baked bread didn't call you from the kitchen. The look is perfect for a small-town bakery, with a black-and-white checkerboard floor, ceiling fans, display windows and bench seats overlooking the sidewalk, and oversized wall mirrors at either end of the room making the place look twice as big as it is. The Model Bakery makes scones, croissants, danishes, bagels, and at least a half-dozen types of muffins. The repertoire includes six or so daily breads, plus regular daily specials. They bust loose on Friday with five specials: whole wheat, seeded, oatmeal, sour rye, and pumate-basil. The bakery also sells juices, soups, and prewrapped sandwiches and, as you would guess, coffee and espresso drinks. It's open every day but Monday.

Pinot Blanc $$$
641 Main St., St. Helena
(707) 963–6191

German-born restaurateur Joaquim Splichal and his original Los Angeles restaurant, Patina, have garnered just about every food award imaginable. Over the last decade Splichal and his wife, Christine, have opened six other L.A.-area eateries and one notable Napa Valley relative: Pinot Blanc, a country bistro on the south side of St. Helena. The always-creative pasta, fish, and meat dishes are complemented by a plat du jour. Monday it might be Bellwether Farms spring lamb with potato, fava beans, and truffle oil; Sunday it could be braised pig with herb-mustard spaetzle and red cabbage. Their fall menu features wild game, and the Liberty duck breast with celery root puree and fresh huckleberries is heavenly. This is hearty food in big proportions. Off the dining room are three private rooms for special events and wine tastings, and the outdoor patio is a lush garden with a stone fountain and fireplace. Pinot Blanc is open seven days a week for lunch and dinner and features a full bar.

Roux $$$$
1234 Main St., St. Helena
(707) 963–5330

You'll pay a bit more for your meal here, but nearly everything created by chef Vincent Nattress is phenomenal and unforgettable. French-trained, he offers a fixed price, four-course tasting menu in addition to the nightly menu selections. Count on choices like delicious foie gras or scallop with artichoke appetizers, Muscovy duck with spaetzle, organic free-range chicken on braised escarole, and asparagus with morel mushrooms. The dining room is nothing to write home

about, but there's a small wine bar and a courtyard patio for enjoying your meal when the weather is warm. It's dinner only here for the time being, Tuesdays through Saturdays (closed Sundays and Mondays).

The Spot $
587 St. Helena Hwy. South, St. Helena
(707) 963–2844

So you've sampled roasted eggplant with Sonoma goat cheese and now you're ready for a plain old hamburger. This place will hit the Spot. The local hangout serves breakfast, as well as hamburgers, pizza, and assorted fried foods at lunch or dinner. Don't expect gourmet eats here, but it's fun and you can sit outside under the palms on a warm day. If you have youngsters on board, they will feel right at home.

Taylor's Refresher $
933 Main St., St. Helena
(707) 963–3486

If all fast food was this delightful then, well, the rain forest would be getting turned into cow pasture at an even faster clip. Retired traveling salesman and pharmacist Lloyd Taylor opened the Refresher for business in 1949. It's now owned by the Gott family, who spruced it up—but managed to retain the quaint atmosphere—in 1999. Taylor's cooks up lunch and early dinner seven days a week. The menu includes burgers, hot dogs, tacos, salads, and fountain treats. There are nice picnic grounds behind the eatery.

Terra $$$$
1345 Railroad Ave., St. Helena
(707) 963–8931
www.terrarestaurant.com

In St. Helena, "off the beaten track" means anything off Main Street, and Terra qualifies. It sits one block away in a historic landmark, a hardy fieldstone foundry constructed in 1884. The open redwood-beamed ceilings in the two dining rooms give you the feel of a Tuscan villa. Chef Hiro Sone's one-page menu aims for southern France and northern Italy, though he admittedly takes a few geographic twists and turns. Two appetizers should give you an example of what to expect: the fried rock shrimp with organic greens and chive-mustard sauce and the terrine of foie gras with Belgian endive, walnuts, and Fuji apple salad. The most popular main course might be the broiled, sake-marinated sea bass with shrimp dumplings in shiso broth. Terra is open for dinner every night except Tuesday.

Tomatina $
1020 Main St., St. Helena
(707) 967-9999

If tourists ever had a reason to complain about St. Helena, it was probably about the lack of inexpensive food. Tomatina, occupying the south half of the Inn at Southbridge (see our Hotels and Motels chapter), effectively bridged the gap when it opened in 1996, with Tra Vigne's Michael Chiarello serving as executive chef. Because of this, the restaurant has become popular with local families. You order cafeteria-style, but servers bring you the food and drink. The Napoli-inspired thin-crust pizzas are recommended, as are the piadine—pizza crust removed from the big, wood-burning brick oven and topped by a selection of salad mixes and dressings. On hot days, the lemonade, simple syrup mixed with lemon juice and soda water, is irresistible. Tomatina is open for lunch and dinner seven days a week. The restaurant does not take reservations.

Tra Vigne $$$
1050 Charter Oak Ave., St. Helena
(707) 963-4444

Chef Michael Chiarello (see previous listing) scrambled to the top of the Napa Valley food chain on the strength of this cozy trattoria in St. Helena. The stone building is an old landmark, and Tra Vigne has become a contemporary one. The regional Italian menu encourages grazing, with a host of interesting small plates, pastas, and pizzas to complement the meats and fish. The restaurant is open for lunch and dinner seven days a week. There is a full bar and a wine cellar stocked with Italian reds and whites, plus a good selection of Californians.

One of the most popular restaurants in St. Helena is Tra Vigne, with award-winning regional Italian. cuisine. PHOTO: JEAN SAYLOR DOPPENBERG

Wine Spectator Greystone Restaurant **$$$**
2555 Main St., St. Helena
(707) 967–1010
www.ciachef.edu/rest

Don't worry, eating at the Culinary Institute of America's restaurant doesn't make you a guinea pig for fresh-faced chefs-in-training. Remember, this branch of the CIA focuses on continuing education. Because most of the students are signed up for short study programs, it isn't practical to hire them for the kitchen. So the staff is quite professional.

Chef de cuisine Pilar Sanchez, formerly of Meadowood, focuses on first-course small bites that she calls "temptations," which are designed to be shared by all at the table. These might include mussels steamed in Fritz Winery Melon, torchon of foie gras, or oxtail roulade. Second-course selections could be wild mushroom lasagna or a grilled pork chop with sage spaetzle, apples, braised escarole, and whiskey sauce.

Try not to dribble while craning your head around the dining room, with its cement floor and stone walls lightened by blues and yellows. Greystone has a full bar. It is open seven days a week for lunch and dinner. Tuesdays and Wednesdays from mid-January through March are reserved for Winter Evenings in Wine Country, a series of special food and wine events.

Calistoga

All Seasons Cafe **$$$$**
1400 Lincoln Ave., Calistoga
(707) 942–9111

If you read the food-and-wine magazines, you've probably been introduced to All Seasons. It has been profiled in *Gourmet, Wine Spectator,* and *Appellation,* among others, and its high standards haven't faltered a bit over more than 16 years of operation. Mixing the quaint and the luxurious, the cafe has a wine bar that makes use of a truly exceptional wine list—it ranges far beyond the valley and is especially deep in Pinots and Zinfandels. The menu changes often here, but you can expect "seasonal California" dishes along the lines of grilled rib-eye steak with Cabernet glaze and creamy horseradish

sauce; or English pea risotto with asparagus, spring garlic, tomato, and mushrooms. The chef is Kevin Kathman, who came from The French Laundry. All Seasons is open for lunch and dinner daily.

Brannan's Grill **$$$$**
1374 Lincoln Ave., Calistoga
(707) 942–2233
www.brannansgrill.com

The Calistoga culinary scene got a major shakeup in March of 1998, when Brannan's Grill opened at the town's central intersection (Lincoln Avenue and Washington Street). It's physically arresting both inside and out, with refinished trusses and ironworks (all original to the 1911 building, long used as a motor garage) and storm windows that open onto Lincoln in warm weather. Most notable is the bar, a mahogany Brunswick design that was shipped around the Cape in the late 1800s. The food is regional American, decidedly carnivore. Try the grilled hanger steak with potato leek gratin and roasted portobello mushrooms or the blue cheese and walnut-crusted filet mignon. Brannan's has a full bar. It's open seven days a week for lunch and dinner in high season, but lunch is Friday through Sunday in the winter. If you enjoy the experience, you might also consider eating at Checkers, Brannan's less formal sister restaurant just down the street at 1414 Lincoln.

Cafe Sarafornia **$$**
1413 Lincoln Ave., Calistoga
(707) 942–0555

Calistoga's most popular breakfast spot playfully incorporates the other half of Sam Brannan's legendary malapropism: "I'll make this the Calistoga of Sarafornia." The busy, sun-infused dining room has a central counter and sidewalk booths. Regulars swear by the cheese blintzes, the Brannan Benedict (two poached eggs with guacamole, bacon, and Cajun cream on toast), the chicken-apple sausage, and the Wildcat Scrambler (three eggs scrambled with mushrooms, Italian sausage, spinach, and choice of cheese). The burgers are good at lunchtime. The cafe does not take reservations, which makes it easy to spot on Sunday morning—it's the place with the line out the door.

Calistoga Inn & Restaurant $$$
1250 Lincoln Ave., Calistoga
(707) 942-4101
www.napabeer.com

The Inn is a popular place any time of year, but business really booms in the summer, when dining moves to the delightful creekside patio. (The meat is even grilled outside, over hardwood.) Rosie Dunsford, that Jill of all trades—in addition to being innkeeper and executive chef, she was a recent Calistoga city councilwoman—serves up regional American cuisine. The marinated Australian lamb sirloin, the Jamaican jerk half-chicken, and the tri-tip sirloin finished with blue cheese butter are all winners. There are fish specials too. The Inn is open for lunch and dinner every day of the year but Christmas. The restaurant has a full bar, including an extensive wine list and its own line of beers.

Calistoga Roastery $
1631 Lincoln Ave., Calistoga
(707) 942-5757

This place must be doing something right: Half the inns and restaurants in the vicinity boast about serving Roastery coffee. Owners Clive Richardson and Terry Rich roast almost 20 varieties of beans—sometimes right on the spot in a preserved 1919 Probat roaster, the oldest of its kind in the nation. If the regular house coffee isn't exciting enough for you, there is a selection of espresso drinks, frappes, and ice cream mochas, not to mention iced teas, Rocket Juices, and Italian sodas. Yes, there are fresh-made baked goods too: bagels, croissants, scones of various stripes, banana bread, granola, and more. The Roastery opens at 6:30 A.M. every day and doesn't close its doors until 6:00 P.M. It's an atmosphere designed for lounging, so bring a newspaper. No credit cards.

Catahoula Restaurant & Saloon $$$
1457 Lincoln Ave., Calistoga
(707) 942-2275
www.catahoularest.com

You can praise the food at Catahoula, just don't call it Cajun. Chef/owner Jan Birnbaum hails from Baton Rouge (the catahoula hound is the state dog of Louisiana), but he admits to taking creative liberties with his native cuisine. Birnbaum cooks up wonderful gumbos, but the menu also includes interesting combinations such as a pork porterhouse steak with red-eye gravy and "soft sexy grits" or grilled lavender squab with Calvados figs and garlic spinach. Dessert is an event here. How about a chewy molasses cookie and chicory-Kahlua ice cream sandwich with fresh peaches? The wood-fired oven dominates a dining room that manages to be elegant though decorated with industrial-looking "found art." Both restaurant and saloon are housed in the historic Mount View Hotel building (see our Hotels and Motels chapter). Catahoula serves dinner nightly and breakfast, lunch, and dinner on weekends. There is full bar service.

Hydro Bar & Grill $$
1403 Lincoln Ave., Calistoga
(707) 942-9777

In a town where the sidewalks sometimes roll up at dusk, the Hydro is the restaurant that doesn't sleep. It offers dinner until 11:00 P.M. on weekdays and midnight on weekends, then greets you for breakfast the next morning. (It's closed only for lunch on Thursday.) Bright and roomy in an old brick building, this is an affordable complement to its sister restaurant across the street—All Seasons Cafe. Hydro does daily fish specials and top-notch hamburgers, and we hear that the fried calamari is some of the best around. Few can resist the lasagna with—deep breath—goat cheese, Fontina, spinach, roasted red peppers, mushrooms, caramelized onions, oven-dried tomatoes, roasted garlic, and spicy tomato sauce. The full bar has 20 carefully selected microbrews. They don't take reservations here.

Napa Valley Ovens $
1353 Lincoln Ave., Calistoga
(707) 942-0777

If that bite of almond croissant tastes familiar, maybe you had its twin for breakfast yesterday. The Ovens supplies numerous Napa Valley restaurants, markets, and bed and breakfast inns with bread products. The lineup is as formidable as it is divine. There is garlic rosemary bread, calamata olive bread, and perhaps 10 more varieties on a given day. The owners make everything from scratch, putting almond flour in the marzipan and imported French butter in the flakier-than-thou croissants. Napa Valley Ovens serves espresso drinks and coffee, including an iced version in the summer. The sunny, colorful bakery is open daily from 7:00 A.M. until 3:00 P.M. in the heavy season; it's closed on Tuesdays in the winter. No credit cards.

Pacifico Restaurante Mexicano $$
1237 Lincoln Ave., Calistoga
(707) 942-4400

Calistoga isn't your typical small town, so why should Pacifico be your typical Mexican restaurant? Instead of mountain ranges of rice and beans, the kitchen cooks up traditional specialties from Jalisco, Veracruz, and Oaxaca. The restaurant is especially noted for its fish dishes, such as grilled fish tacos with avocado tomatillo salsa or camarones a la diabla-sautéed prawns with garlic, onion, arbol chilies, and lime.

There is a full bar, and the Margaritas won't let you down. Pacifico is open seven days a week for lunch and dinner. It's also popular for Saturday and Sunday brunch. (The morning favorites are Huevos Benito and Huevos Pacifico, Mexican eggs Benedict with a mulato chili hollandaise.) The restaurant takes reservations for parties of seven or more.

Soo Yuan $
1354 Lincoln Ave., Calistoga
(707) 942-9404

On what do you base your dining experience? If friendly service and a cozy family atmosphere are paramount, you will have a hard time beating Soo Yuan.

The Fang family opened its first restaurant in Taipei in 1974, and they have operated in Calistoga since 1985. The tried-and-true favorites include the pepper-sauce spareribs, the asparagus with prawns, and the mu shu pancakes. If you can't reach a decision, go for the multicourse Soo Yuan Special Dinner. Soo Yuan is open daily for lunch and dinner.

Wappo Bar & Bistro $$$
1226 Washington St., Calistoga
(707) 942-4712

One of the few Calistoga restaurants not found on Lincoln Avenue, the compact Wappo Bar is easy to miss—and that would be a big mistake. The scene is fairly informal and always gratifying, especially in the summer when the arbor-protected brick patio takes center stage. The inside features copper-topped tables and a wine bar with redwood interior; in the warmer months, ask for a table next to the fountain outside. (They have live music there on Sunday evenings.)

Signature dishes include the chili relleno with walnut pomegranate sauce; a paella of chorizo, rabbit, prawns, clams, and mussels; and the Chilean sea bass with Indian spices. And ridiculous as it sounds, you have to try the table water here—"marinated" with citrus, cucumber, and mint, it is highly addictive. The Wappo Bar is open for lunch and dinner six days a week (closed Tuesdays).

Sonoma County

Sonoma
The Big 3 Diner at Sonoma Mission Inn $$$
18141 Sonoma Hwy., Sonoma
(707) 939-2410, (800) 862-4945
www.sonomamissioninn.com

This is a great place for breakfast—the eggs Benedict with rosemary potatoes will draw you back here time after time. Since this is connected to the Mission Inn Spa (see our Spas and Resorts chapter), the menu also includes dishes for the calorie-watcher that are equally good—especially apple oat cakes with walnuts and crème fraîche. Lunch and dinner are also served each day, with a fine wine list and full bar. Service is friendly but not intrusive.

Sante at Sonoma Mission Inn $$$$
18140 Sonoma Hwy., Sonoma
(707) 938–9000, (800) 862–4945
www.sonomamissioninn.com

If you're ready to go upscale, walk to the main building of the Inn for a Sunday brunch overlooking the pool, or have lunch or dinner in an ambiance that has country-club class—elegant but not stuffy. This is a spa, after all (see our Spas and Resorts chapter), so there are two types of cuisine here: the spa menu for those who really are here to get healthy (a four-course, prix fixe meal for $50), and the menu for those who must have their foie gras and crème brûlée (also $50 for four courses). Executive chef Toni Robertson trained at the Les Près d'Eugenie Resort near Toulouse, France, so he knows a thing or two about creating healthy spa chow, and he uses the restaurant's new tandoori oven to produce low-fat poultry and whole fish entrees. The award-winning wine list features 300 selections from Napa and Sonoma vineyards. Reservations are recommended for dinner. The Sante is open daily.

Carneros at The Lodge at Sonoma $$$$
1325 Broadway, Sonoma
(707) 935–6600
www.carnerosrestaurant.com

This restaurant can be found within the hotel/spa complex The Lodge at Sonoma (see our Spas and Resorts chapter), but you needn't be a guest at the lodge to enjoy dining here. Executive chef Brian Whitmer has developed some interesting dishes that change with the seasons, as do the menus of many Wine Country restaurants. Here are a few examples of what you might expect to find: wood oven-roasted whole fish with baby artichokes, horseradish pappardelle with short rib ragu, rotisserie ribeye with caramelized shallots, and Sonoma lamb offered with braised fennel or slow-roasted with tomatoes and lemon thyme. The atmosphere is relaxed and casual. It's open for breakfast, lunch, and dinner daily.

Della Santina's $$
133 E. Napa St., Sonoma
(707) 935–0576
www.sterba.com/sonoma/santina/

This is an intimate, no-frills Italian trattoria-pasticceria that faces onto the main street, but the food is authentic Italian prepared from recipes inspired by owner Dan Santina's grandmother. All dishes are made from scratch, using a rotisserie to contain the flavors of all the herbs and spices used in such dishes as locally raised chicken, rabbit, and duck. The menu offers traditional northern Italian dishes such as lasagna bolognese, pressed squab, and all sorts of antipasti. One of the best entrees—maybe the best in all of Wine Country—is pollo allo spiedo, a traditional Italian roast chicken. Della Santina's serves lunch and dinner every day. Because the restaurant is small, reservations are advised.

Depot Hotel Cucina Rustica $$$
241 W. First St., Sonoma
(707) 938–2980
www.sterba.com/sonoma/depot/

Located in a historic stone building a block from the plaza, this was once a hotel, but it is now a delightful restaurant serving northern Italian cuisine. It's owned by chef Ghilarducci, who does wonders with such dishes as ravioli al bosco (shiitake mushrooms and herbs sauteed with white wine and shallots) and hand-stuffed tortellini. One of the real delights of the restaurant is its garden, with Roman fountain and poolside dining. Vegetarian dishes and heart-healthy choices are also offered. The wine list is strictly from the Sonoma and Carneros valleys and has won *Wine Spectator* magazine's Award of Excellence several times. Lunch is available Wednesday through Friday and dinner is served Wednesday through Sunday.

The General's Daughter $$$
400 W. Spain St., Sonoma
(707) 938–4004
www.thegeneralsdaughter.com

It could win a contest for "prettiest little restaurant in the county" hands down.

Erected in 1864 for Gen. Vallejo's daughter (hence the name), the house had been standing dilapidated and unappreciated for years until Suzanne Brangham undertook its renovation in 1994, transforming it into a first-class restaurant. The place is gorgeous, set in lush landscaping with an interior decor of antiques and lively murals (the Honduran mahogany bar is a standout). Lunch is served on the wide front porch in fair weather. The food is traditional Californian. For lunch, you might want to try the jambalaya with blackened prawns, sausage, chicken, tomatoes, and baby spinach. Or consider the warm peach tart Tatin with a ginger crème anglaise for dessert. Lunch and dinner are served daily, with brunch on Sunday.

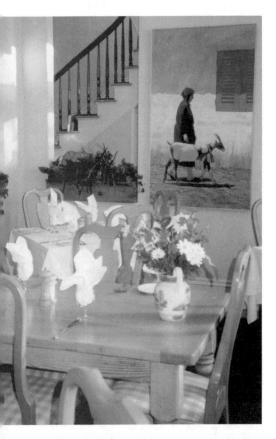

The General's Daughter restaurant is in a home built in 1864 for General Vallejo's daughter.

PHOTO: THE GENERAL'S DAUGHTER

The Girl & the Fig $$$$
110 W. Spain St., Sonoma
(707) 938-3634
www.thegirlandthefig.com

The name conjures up a sensual experience that's slightly naughty. Perhaps it's because the food is sinful, the service attentive, and the decor awash in pastels. On the ground floor of the Sonoma Hotel on the Plaza, The Girl & the Fig promises and delivers country-style Provençal-inspired cuisine. Figs figure prominently in some of the dishes, especially the signature fig salad with goat cheese, pancetta, pecans, and arugula. Several cheese cart and charcuterie selections are offered (a goat cheese sampler, for instance), mushroom ragout, and ravioli of butternut squash, raddichio, and blue cheese. The owner, Sondra Bernstein, emphasizes local seasonal produce, so the menu selections will vary. Also a nice touch in a town that rolls up the sidewalks early: a late dinner menu from 9:30 to 11:00 P.M. on Fridays and Saturdays.

La Casa Restaurant $$$
121 E. Spain St., Sonoma
(707) 996-3406
www.lacasarestaurant.com

In a town dedicated to Italian cuisine, La Casa's smashing Mexican food is as welcome as a breeze in the heat of summer. The ambiance is as close to authentic as you can get north of the border, with Mexican woven leather chairs and a tiled bar. The nachos are sensational here, the salsa and chips addictive. The food is so memorable that La Casa is often the first place former residents head for dinner when they return to the area for a visit. For a view of the Mission and Barracks (see our Attractions chapter), ask for a window seat. Or choose to eat outdoors on the patio facing onto El Paseo de Sonoma courtyard. La Casa's thin, crisp tortilla chips and salsa are now available at the upscale Sonoma Market grocery. Fiesta hour (from 4:00 to 6:00 P.M. Monday through Friday) is extremely popular among the locals, thanks to the ambiance and the great Margaritas.

Ristorante Piatti $$$
405 W. First St., Sonoma
(707) 996–2351
www.piatti.com

You enter Piatti from either the El Dorado Hotel lobby or the door on West First Street. Either way, you'll soon be enveloped with the marvelous aromas from the open kitchen at the back of the dining room. Alfresco dining is also available amid the trees on the gorgeous patio courtyard off the dining room. While you're looking over the menu, you'll be served fresh breads with a saucer of olive oil, balsamic vinegar, and garlic dipping sauce. As for the menu, it features the best of Tuscany pastas, pizzas and grilled meat and fish. Piatti is the winner of numerous Sonoma Valley restaurant awards. A full bar features select Sonoma Valley wines at lunch and dinner seven days a week.

Saddles $$$$
29 E. MacArthur St., Sonoma
(707) 933–3191
www.macarthurplace.com

Within the classy MacArthur Place hotel and spa (see our Spas and Resorts chapter), this restaurant exudes a rustic, bunkhouse feel, because it's in the original barn on the property. It has a cowboy motif—with real saddles made into chairs in the lobby and the wait staff in denims—but don't expect beans and boiled coffee here. What you will find is plenty of red meat and fixins, primarily Midwestern corn-fed, mesquite-grilled USDA prime beef. For lighter appetites, there's salmon, ahi, and chicken entrees. Start your meal with the cornmeal onion rings—a crunchy, tasty bit of heaven. The wine list runs about 70 labels strong and there's a Martini Bar that offers 14 different oversized libations. Saddles is open daily for lunch and dinner, with a weekend brunch to boot.

The Swiss Hotel $$$
18 W. Spain St., Sonoma
(707) 938–2884
www.sterba.com/sonoma/swiss/

It's a wonderful old building—a remarkably preserved adobe that was once the home of Gen. Vallejo's brother, Salvador, who built it in 1850. He didn't live there long; a year after Salvador moved in the sheriff put it up for sale to pay Salvador's debts. It became "The Swiss" when a stagecoach operator bought it and changed the name. Today it is easily recognizable by the Swiss flag flying over the door.

For decades the restaurant was patronized largely by local families who came for the generous family-style Italian dinners. The barroom was a hangout for locals as well, who came to meet and greet friends. It even drew a few celebrities: Herb Caen is said to have tippled there, as have Tommy Smothers, Jim Corbett, and even the late Charles Kuralt.

The menu is a bit upscale from the days of the massive Italian feasts, but the pastas are still served al dente, and the pizzas are turned out of wood-burning brick ovens. It's open daily for lunch and dinner.

Zino's Ristorante $$$
420 First St. E., Sonoma
(707) 996–4466, (800) 339–4466
www.zinosrestaurant.com

The place has the look of an intimate Italian bistro, housed in a historic building made from stones quarried nearby. It's owned by Zino Mezoulin, a native of Algeria, whose Italian specialties have proved so popular with locals that for the summer months he has opened an outdoor dining room bordering on El Paseo de Sonoma courtyard. If you like seafood, try the linguine in Zino's special putanesca sauce or the linguine con vongole—it's made with lots of clams, broth, and cream. Zino's is open for lunch seven days a week and dinner every night but Monday. A bar is available, and an extensive wine list offers wine by the glass or bottle.

Glen Ellen

Garden Court Cafe & Bakery $$
13875 Sonoma Hwy., Glen Ellen
(707) 935–1565
www.gardencourtcafe.com

This is a small, 10-table cafe on the side of the road, but on any given weekend day, there are as many people outside waiting to get in as there are inside eating. Breakfast is the big draw here, with eggs Benedict in three varieties leading the popularity list and a variety of omelettes following close behind. The cafe is open for breakfast and lunch seven days a week, and dinner is served on the second Wednesday of each month.

The Girl & the Gaucho $$$$
13690 Arnold Dr., Glen Ellen
(707) 938–2130
www.thegirlandthegaucho.com

No, you're not seeing double. Sondra Bernstein owns two restaurants in the Sonoma Valley: the one described in the Sonoma listings, and this one, which moved into the space previously occupied by that fig girl. They are a few miles apart in distance and even further apart in cuisine. Gaucho is all about South American culinary experiences. There are small plates (tomatillo guacamole and fried yucca or jicama and quinoa slaw) and large plates (grilled ribeye, roasted swordfish, half-chicken), all with a Latin flavor. Make a meal of several small plates, or choose a large plate selection with side dishes influenced by Spain, Mexico, Chile, Argentina, or Brazil. For your ears there's Latin American jazz and salsa music; for your eyes there's an eclectic collection of art from Latin countries. Open daily for dinner.

Glen Ellen Inn Restaurant $$$$
13670 Arnold Dr., Glen Ellen
(707) 996–6409
www.sterba.com/ge/inn/

Set inside a Cape Cod–style cottage, this tiny restaurant delivers one delight after another. Stenciled grape leaves trim the ceiling, and white linens and candles grace the tables. You have three choices of where to eat—the indoor dining room, the sun porch, or the patio. The chef learned his skills in New York and uses local ingredients to cook with a French accent. Particularly impressive is the Voodoo Jambalaya—prawns, bay shrimp, chicken, sausage, and honey-smoked ham simmered with cayenne, vegetables, and tomato sauce on a bed of basmati rice. Yes, this is a chef who can hold his own

with the finest. The desserts are truly decadent. If you can manage two, go for the Bailey's Irish Cream mousse scented with chocolate and the French vanilla ice cream rolled in toasted coconut and drizzled with caramel sauce. The restaurant is open for dinner every night except winter Wednesdays.

Kenwood

Kenwood Restaurant $$$$
9900 Sonoma Hwy., Kenwood
(707) 833–6326
www.sterba.com/kenwood/restaurant/

The parking lot is always full—a sure sign of the restaurant's well-deserved popularity. The chef makes an extraordinary bouillabaisse, using seafood from Bodega Bay in a flavorful broth. His roast duck, using local fowl, is crispy on the outside, tender inside. And his prawns in succulent sauce with puff pastry are sheer inspiration. *Gourmet* magazine recently voted this one of the top 20 restaurants in the entire Bay Area. One of the real pleasures of dining here is the opportunity to drink in the exquisite view as the late-afternoon sun hits the peaks of Sugarloaf Ridge. The scene is particularly rewarding from the deck. The wine list is acclaimed for featuring the best wines produced in Kenwood (bar drinks are also available). Lunch and dinner are served Wednesday through Sunday.

Petaluma

McNear's Saloon and Dining House $$
23 N. Petaluma Blvd., Petaluma
(707) 765–2121
www.mcnears.com/index.htm

It's friendly, funky, and great fun. Every square inch of the walls is covered with historic memorabilia and old photographs, including old sleds, skis, street signs, flags, and banners. The name McNear looms large in Petaluma history, stretching back to 1856 when John McNear came to town, creating a business empire and becoming the first owner of the McNear Building. The goal of the present-day owners is to provide a meeting, eating, and entertainment spot for locals and fun-loving visitors. Barbecue is the house specialty, with an extensive menu to back that up; the saloon is well stocked. The dining room is large, but the sidewalk cafe in front is the popular place to sip espresso on Sunday morning. Mc-Near's is open for lunch and dinner every day of the week, plus breakfast on Sunday.

River House $$$
222 Weller St., Petaluma
(707) 769-0123
www.the-river-house.com

River House, which opened in October 1997, offers the charming architectural setting of an 1888 Queen Anne Victorian.

The plan from the beginning was to have a full-service restaurant with banquet rooms featuring American cuisine and using mostly Sonoma fresh produce and local wines. Because "American cuisine" covers a lot of territory, a new segment of the country is to be featured each month—Lousiana Cajun cooking one month, New England seafood cuisine the next. Dinner is served daily, brunch on Sunday. Lunch is served Sunday through Friday.

Twisted Vines $$$
16 Kentucky St., Petaluma
(707) 766-8162
www.twistedvines.com

This is something a little different—a combination wine shop and restaurant. The local restaurant reviewer gives it five stars, for both food and wine. Fresh fish is flown in from Hawaii every day, and mahi mahi is one of the most popular features on the menu. They take pride in using only the best ingredients, including the local poultry, which they transform into their special, half-roasted chicken. You can select a wine off the racks to enjoy with your food (paying only retail plus a $5.00 corkage fee), or you can buy it by the glass.

It's a tiny place, so it's best to call ahead. The restaurant is open for lunch and dinner Tuesday through Saturday. Look for it in the Lanmart Building.

Volpi's Ristorante $$$
124 Washington St., Petaluma
(707) 765-0695

> # Insiders' Tip
> Wine lists can be confusing if not intimidating at times, with many obscure labels from boutique wineries unfamiliar to the average diner. Don't hesitate to ask a restaurant's sommelier for help in making your selection. These wine experts can recommend a good, reasonably priced bottle to complement your meal.

There's a lot of Old World charm in this place run by the Volpi family; it's been on the local scene since 1925—in a building that was once a speakeasy. This is family-style dining in an unhurried atmosphere. The cuisine is Italian, created by chef Glen Petrucci, who specializes in homemade pastas, veal, and seafood. The fully stocked bar serves tavern and restaurant patrons. If you're up to it, you can listen to live accordion music Friday and Saturday evenings. Lunch is served Wednesday, Thursday, and Friday; dinner Wednesday through Sunday.

Santa Rosa

John Ash & Co. $$$$
4330 Barnes Rd., Santa Rosa
(707) 527-7687, (800) 421-2584
www.sterba.com/sro/johnash/

John Ash is no longer there, but the cuisine he created carries on, with each entree made a masterpiece of taste, texture, color, and design. Nothing here is ordinary. The fare is "Wine Country cuisine," i.e., California cuisine using only the freshest produce from local farmers

Infidels in the Kingdom:
A Guide to Wine Country Brewpubs

Do you prefer ambers and blacks to reds and whites? Do you put more stock in a drink's head than its legs? Is the born-on date more important than the vintage? Does your mouth water when you hear a bottle go pssshhh instead of pop?

If the answers are yes, you're not as lost as you think you are. The microbrew craze has taken root, even here in Wine Country. About 20 microbreweries and brewpubs reside in our four-county area, and the number seems to grow every few months. The stereotype has the groomsmen heading to the brewpub while the bridesmaids gather at the winery, but the reality is that you're likely to see the same sort of people (maybe even the exact same people) at the two sorts of tasting rooms. Beer lovers and wine lovers both tend to be taste-bud-dominated devotees of the good life. And as you'll see below, beer critics can heave those heavy adjectives just like wine critics.

To help us get a handle on "California Beer Country," we turned to Thomas Dalldorf, editor and publisher of *Celebrator Beer News,* a tabloid-format journal of suds in America (and beyond). Dalldorf and his staff reviewed some of their favorite pubs for our guide—not every microbrewery in Wine Country, but a representative few. They stress that the brewers not reviewed would be likely to score just as highly.

Also, note that our space limits forced us to truncate these reviews; amazingly, the folks at *Celebrator* can and do go into even more exhaustive detail when talking about their favorite thing. If you like *Celebrator*'s bent, you can call (800) 430–2337 for information on distribution and subscriptions. Now pass those pretzels, please.

Third Street AleWorks
610 Third St., Santa Rosa
(707) 523–3060
www.thirdstreetaleworks.com
Experience can make all the difference, and at the Third Street AleWorks in Santa Rosa, it shows. Third Street AleWorks showcases both the experience of the owners, who were formerly associated with the Good Earth restaurants, and brewer Grant Johnston, formerly with Marin Brewing Company. The result is a comfortable and inviting pub atmosphere highlighted by a selection of innovative and fiercely traditional styles of ale.

"Here, I'm really mixing American flavors with British flavors," said Johnston, a disciple of English brewing methods. "I want to get away from that whole West Coast thing. You're not going to find any dry-hopped pale ales coming out of this brewery."

The AleWorks Rye Ale, a popular seller, is surprisingly light in color, with a distinctive rye malt character from less than 20 percent rye in the mash. The American Wheat Ale is an unfiltered example of the style, with a round flavor, dry finish, and light hop character. Its companion, the American Dark Wheat, was one of the pub's first beers when it opened in March 1996 and is one of Johnston's old homebrew recipes.

The AleWorks Mild Ale is an outstanding example of the style, one not often found in America's microbreweries. This copper-colored ale is based on the milds of northern England, a style that is often called a "session beer," due to the ability to have several pints over a late-night chin-wag without being completely anesthetized.

Seasonal beers include a blackberry ale, which is released during the summer, a smoked beer in the fall, and a barley wine for the winter.

AleWorks occupies an almost ideal location in downtown Santa Rosa, across from a major parking garage and at the entrance to UA Cinema 6, one of the busiest movie theaters in the county. The decor combines bright corrugated metal and dark wood to create a relaxing and slightly funky interior. The two-story, open interior space is highlighted by a round silo-like area near the front door, a hanging bicycle and antique Olympic rowing scull, and historical pictures of the city. The second floor has billiards and long picnic-style tables overlooking the main dining area.

The reasonably priced menu includes a selection of interesting appetizers, salads, sandwiches, burgers, and pub specialties such as pasta and barbecue beer shrimp.

Bear Republic Brewing Company
345 Healdsburg Ave., Healdsburg
(707) 433–BEER
www.bearrepublic.com
Bear Republic is in the clock tower building across from Healdsburg's historic plaza. The 5,000-square-foot brewpub unfolds beneath high ceilings. Amid brass trim and warm woods, its bright windows look out to the patio. The wall behind the bags of grain and the malt mill sparkles with a vibrant mural of scenic Healdsburg, while colorful cycling jerseys decorate another wall.

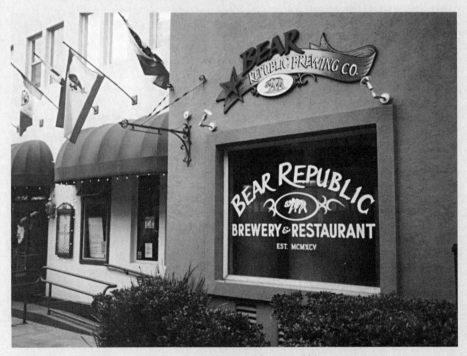

Good beer and fine food are the hallmarks of Bear Republic in Healdsburg. PHOTO: JEAN SAYLOR DOPPENBERG

Bear Republic Brewing Company was conceived by Richard R. Norgrove and his son, Rich, in 1994. The younger Norgrove was operations manager of Salsa Cycles in Petaluma (a small but revered mountain bike manufacturer) when his first beer of note—Red Rocket Ale—garnered a cult-like following in biking circles. Richard and Rich's ride has since been successful and meteoric.

The clientele at Bear Republic is a pleasant surprise, a vivid cross section of folks. Sleekly attired businessmen—ties loosened, sunglasses perched by their beer mugs—mix with laborers in dusty blue jeans at the copper-topped Honduran mahogany bar. Families cluster around big round tables. A group of twenty-somethings, some with strategic body piercing and tattoos, quaff Bear Republic brews alongside a smattering of seniors and couples.

The fast-paced kitchen at Bear Republic enlivens and expands on traditional pub offerings. The most popular beer continues to be the house IPA, but there are others worth noting. Red Rocket Ale is Richard's flagship brew, using a blend of Northwest hops for a full-bodied, caramel brew the color of terra-cotta gemstone. All Bear Republic's microbrews are aged three weeks before tapping and are available to go in 5-gallon kegs and 1-gallon reusable boxes. Rich also features one beer on tap from a local guest microbrewer, as well as homemade root beer and cream soda for the kids.

Mendocino Brewing Company
13351 S. U.S. 101, Hopland
(707) 744–1015
www.mendobrew.com

Hopland, as the name implies, was a major area for hop cultivation until the 1950s, when changes in climate and a shaky local economy forced farmers to sow pear trees and grapevines (see our History chapter). So it's a fitting locale for Mendocino Brewing Company, the oldest microbrewery in California. Established in 1983, after the close of the New Albion Brewery, the beers originally were sold only on draft in the tavern or over-the-counter in 1.5-liter magnums. The world's first 42-pound six-pack soon became legendary but could not allow the company to meet its increasing demands.

Standard six-packs began rolling out of the facility in 1987. In 1994 the company was one of a select few small manufacturers to be accepted on the Pacific Stock Exchange. More recently, the company opened a new 80,000-barrel-a-year brewhouse 12 miles north of Hopland in Ukiah.

Red Tail Ale, the brewery's best-known label, is full, malty, complex, and dry; Blue Heron Pale Ale is delightfully hoppy and crisp; Peregrine Pale Ale is soft, fruity, and assertive; Black Hawk Stout is roasty, dry, and rich with a full body. Seasonal offerings include the Yuletide Porter, a ruby, dry, and slightly spicy brew; and Springtide Ale, golden, spiced, and refreshing, with different spices used each year.

The pub is inside a 100-year-old brick building once known as the Hop Vine Saloon. An outdoor beer garden (featuring trellised hops), a dart room, and a stage for musical acts complement the tasty bill of fare and cozy atmosphere.

Anderson Valley Brewing Company
17700 Hwy. 253, Boonville
(707) 895–2337
www.avbc.com

Imagine that it's 1873 and you're a sheep rancher working hard under the blazing sun. Nothing sounds better than a chilly brew to celebrate the end of another strenuous day. If you are lucky, you live in the heart of Anderson Valley, because the Buckhorn Saloon has just been opened for business!

A new Buckhorn Saloon exists today—on the same site the original saloon stood 125 years ago—along with the Anderson Valley Brewery, established in 1987 by Dr. Kenneth and Kimberly Allen. The 10-barrel brewhouse located beneath the saloon is now emerging from the back burner on the heels of the company's recent expansion operation. A 15,000-square-foot production facility has been erected a mile away and includes a 30-barrel stainless steel brewery. A new brewhouse opened in summer of 1998.

As for Anderson Valley Brewing's product, the Boont Amber Ale is smooth and copper-colored with a rich caramel malt flavor. Poleeko Gold is a crisp, golden pale ale with a flowery hop nose and dry finish. Barney Flats Oatmeal Stout is a silky smooth, rich potion with traits of chocolate and toffee. High Rollers is a sparkling, tangy wheat beer, and Deep Enders Dark is a roasty, robust porter with complex roasted coffee notes and a good length.

The brewery started bottling six-packs in 1997. The Buckhorn Saloon offers a full menu of tasty dishes, an outdoor beer garden, and a unique gift shop.

North Coast Brewing Company
444 N. Main St., Fort Bragg
(707) 964-3400
www.northcoastbrewing.com

When a historic building—used as a church, mortuary, and college—became available in the heart of old Fort Bragg in 1988, Mark Ruedrich, Joe Rosenthal, and Tom Allen grasped the opportunity and opened the North Coast Brewing Company Tap Room and Grill. The operation has recently expanded to produce 15,000 barrels a year in a 17,000-square-foot facility across the street from the restaurant, which houses the original 7-barrel brewery.

Red Seal Ale is a copper-red pale ale with a generous hop quality and perfect balance. An unfiltered golden summer quencher, Blue Star is a wheat beer especially tasty with a lemon slice. Acme Pale Ale is a golden rendition of an 1861 California classic, and Acme Brown Ale is nutty, with a good malt character. Scrimshaw Pilsner is crisp, light, and spicy, while Old No. 38 Stout is dry with smooth, roasty chocolate and coffee flavors. And last but not least, Old Rasputin Russian Imperial Stout is a fruity, richly complex brew with toffee connotations and a warming effect on the finish.

North Coast also produces seasonal ales, all available in bottles. Visitors can savor the beers fresh at the restaurant, which also sports an eclectic menu with an emphasis on local ingredients.

The rundown of other Wine Country brewpubs and microbreweries includes Downtown Joe's, 902 Main Street, Napa, (707) 258–BEER; Napa Valley Brewing Company, 1250 Lincoln Avenue, Calistoga, (707) 942–4101; Dempsey's Ale House, 50 E. Washington Street, Petaluma, (707) 765–9694; Lagunitas Brewing Company, 1280 N. McDowell Street, Petaluma, (707) 769–4495; Moonlight Brewing Company, P.O. Box 316, Fulton 95439, (707) 528–2537; Powerhouse Brewing, 268 Petaluma Avenue, Sebastopol, (707) 829–9171; Russian River Brewing Company, 13250 River Road, Guerneville, (707) 887–2294, Stumptown Brewery, 15045 River Road, Guerneville; and Mount St. Helena Brewing Company, 21167 Calistoga Highway (Highway 29), Middletown, (707) 987–2106.

Outdoor dining is a staple in Wine Country. Here, people lunch near the waterfront along the Petaluma River in Petaluma. PHOTO: TINA LUSTER-HOBAN

and local goat cheeses—the signature dish is the Dungeness crab cakes. A recent redecoration has made this delightful restaurant more alluring than ever. From the Spanish stucco exterior to the works of art that grace the restaurant walls, the atmosphere is warm and inviting. Large, arched windows give an open airy feeling to the dining room. The wine list is one of the best, with a good selection sold by the glass. John Ash & Co. is adjacent to Vintners Inn, a Provençal-style hotel arranged around a central plaza and fountain, all set in a 45-acre vineyard (see our Hotels, Motels, and Inns chapter). The restaurant and bar are open for dinner seven days a week, but John Ash & Co. does not serve lunch on Monday.

Equus $$$$
101 Fountaingrove Pkwy., Santa Rosa
(707) 578–6101

Because this is the restaurant for Fountain Grove Inn (see our Hotels and Motels chapter), the decorating theme is horses and honors Equus, the legendary horse.

The chef creates both classic favorites and imaginative dishes that surprise with their originality. The menu changes with each season, and one lovely dish to try is grilled Hawaii Walu with grilled vegetables and pancetta/parsley mashed potatoes. You may choose to sink into a spacious booth or dine center stage under the coffered mahogany ceiling. In the lounge, you can sip cocktails and listen to romantic music played on the grand piano. Take time to examine the Gallery of Sonoma County Wines, a display of nearly 300 premium wines, chosen personally by each winery's own winemaker. Lunch is served from Monday through Friday and dinner is served daily.

La Gare French Restaurant $$$
208 Wilson St., Santa Rosa
(707) 528–4355
www.sterba.com/sro/lagare/

La Gare has been voted "most romantic" and "best restaurant" by *The Press Democrat* newspaper. *The Bohemian* also has awarded La Gare its "best restaurant" award for the past five years. Tucked away near Santa Rosa's historic Railroad Square, it's a favorite of the locals, who come for hearty, country-style, traditional French cooking. Romantic it is, with the lace curtains, soft lighting, and stained glass. It is one of the few places in Wine Country that you are offered (gasp!) French wines. La Gare ("railway station") is open for dinner Wednesday through Sunday.

Lisa Hemenway's Restaurant $$$$
612 Terrace Way, Santa Rosa
(707) 526–5111
www.sterba.com/sro/hemenway/

The atmosphere is cozy and romantic, with the warm, intimate feel of a European bistro. Lisa Hemenway was a protege of John Ash and has traveled six of the seven continents to add to her cuisine knowledge. You might want to try her bouillabaisse with rouille or hamburger stuffed with herb cream cheese. Meals are hearty here. All are made with fresh, locally grown ingredients. There's a daily fish entree, freshly caught, along with daily pasta and salad specialty. Don't miss the perfect orange-currant scones! There is a full bar and award-winning wines. Lisa's is open for lunch and dinner every day but Sunday.

Mixx $$$
135 Fourth St., Santa Rosa
(707) 573–1344
www.sterba.com/sro/mixx/

Billed as an American bistro, the atmosphere here is intimate and elegant without being stuffy. (Julia Child has even dined here.) Chef Dan Berman takes an ethnic melting-pot approach to California cuisine, shaping it into Cajun, Indian, Italian, and straight Californian. One house specialty is ravioli, but Berman also does wonderful things with fish. Berman's wife is responsible for the desserts. Dinner is served nightly except Sunday; lunch is offered Monday through Friday.

Omelette Express $
112 Fourth St., Santa Rosa
(707) 525–1690
www.sterba.com/sro/omelette/

If you happen to be walking around Santa Rosa's Railroad Square on a weekend morning, you'll see as many people on the sidewalk waiting to get into this restaurant as there are patrons inside. The menu lists 48 different varieties of the humble omelette—both plain and fancy, including vegetarian and seafood. None costs more than $9.00. The choices for lunch include two dozen "Pullman Car" sandwiches. You might want to bite into the Hot Express Special—grilled onions, mushrooms, melted jack and cheddar cheese, served open-face on dark rye. It's open seven days a week and most holidays.

Healdsburg
Bistro Ralph $$$$
109 Plaza St., Healdsburg
(707) 433–1380

Bistro Ralph offers a somewhat formal, but unstuffy, atmosphere, featuring American country French cuisine. The place is plain enough, with white-linen-covered tables lined up along one wall in an arrangement reminiscent of earlier San Francisco Italian restaurants. The food is prepared with an imaginative touch and fresh ingredients. Chef-owner Ralph Tingle can be seen at the farmer's market Saturday mornings, selecting from the seasonal bounty of vegetables that will be on his menu that night. He follows the Farm Trails map to find the best in meat vendors and duck farms as well (see our Close-up on Farm Trails in our Shopping chapter). The smoked salmon starter with an unusual focaccia pastry is a good choice. Enjoy a bottle of local wine or beer with your meal or the specialty of the house: a dry martini. The Bistro is open for lunch and dinner on weekdays and for dinner only on weekends.

Dry Creek General Store $
3495 Dry Creek Rd., Healdsburg
(707) 433–4171

It's an old-time grocery store that looks like it's been there forever, but if you've been cruising the Dry Creek vineyards for hours and your tummy says it's picnic time, you'll love the simple, delicious homemade sandwiches and salads, the

Omelette Express in downtown Santa Rosa's Railroad Square is where the locals go for breakfast. PHOTO: JEAN SAYLOR DOPPENBERG

wine selection, and the gourmet food section. Take your purchases to any one of the many wineries in the area, buy yourself a bottle of their best, and settle in for a beautiful picnic. Recently purchased by the Gallo family, the store is open seven days a week, from 6:00 A.M. to 6:00 P.M. The bar adjacent to the store is open from 3:00 to 8:00 P.M. weekdays and 3:00 to midnight weekends.

Dry Creek Kitchen $$$$
317 Healdsburg Ave., Healdsburg
(707) 431–0330
www.hotelhealdsburg.com
Maybe you've heard of Charlie Palmer. He was named New York City's best chef in 1997. His restaurant ventures include Aureole, with locations in New York and Las Vegas; Alva American Bistro in Manhattan; and Charlie Palmer Steak at the Four Seasons Hotel in Las Vegas. Now he's brought his award-winning way with cuisine to Wine Country, in the restaurant of

the new Hotel Healdsburg (see our Hotels and Motels chapter).

Charlie hired Mark Purdy to lead the kitchen here, and Mark follows Charlie's approach of presenting American cooking with European influences and doing it spectacularly with a hearty heaping of locally grown organic produce. Expect fabulous flavors and presentations around duck, salmon, beef—to name a few—and appetizers and desserts to die for. There's also a fixed price seven-course tasting menu. To accompany your meal, you're sure to find just the right vino among the eight-page wine list. The dining room is delightful, with soft lighting, fine art, and views of the leafy Healdsburg Plaza. Lunch is served until 3:00 P.M. daily; dinner begins at 5:00 daily and lasts a bit later than most places—10:00 P.M. on weekdays and 10:30 weekends.

Felix and Louis's $$$
106 Matheson Ave., Healdsburg
(707) 433–6966

Located on Healdsburg's charming downtown square, Felix and Louis's offers fine Italian cuisine in a large, often bustling, dining room. If the tables are all taken, grab a stool at either the fully stocked bar or the counter overlooking the wood-fired pizza ovens. Chefs turn out extraordinary pizzas here, topped with the familiar pepperoni and bell peppers or the more exotic caramelized onion and gorgonzola. Open for dinner every night and Saturday and Sunday for brunch and lunch.

The Geyser Smokehouse $$
21021 Geyserville Ave., Geyserville
(707) 857-4600

If you get the munchies while wine tasting in Alexander Valley, this is a good place to take a load off. It's popular with the local population, as well as the winery and vineyard workers. Chef-owner Jeff Mall (Zin Restaurant in Healdsburg) opened this Texas-style barbecue emporium to offer more family-style fare such as sandwiches, burgers, salads, and chili, but you can count on these items being jazzier than at the usual barbecue joint. The priciest thing on the menu is $17.95 (a full slab of pork ribs), but most of the dinners average about $11.00; lunch sandwiches top out at 10 bucks. There is a full bar, with eight beers on tap and a decent selection of wine by the bottle or glass. The Smokehouse is open daily for lunch and dinner.

Healdsburg Bar & Grill $$
245 Healdsburg Ave., Healdsburg
(707) 433-3333

Is it a restaurant, or is it a bar? It's both, and the proprietors handle the food and drink equally well. The cuisine isn't gourmet or snooty, but it's well above the standard fare you might expect. There's an adequate wine list, too, with many available by the glass. For dinner, choose from a blackened snapper sandwich, lamb chops, or salmon sautéed with radicchio and coarse grain mustard sauce. (The kids have their own menu here, but when dinner is done, it's 21-and-over only.) Top off your meal with crème brûlée or mousse, then stick around for the live entertainment (see our Nightlife chapter) and be

> ## Insiders' Tip
> The Dry Creek General Store west of Healdsburg, in business for more than a century, was purchased by winemaker Gina Gallo in 2001. Despite worries from residents that Gallo money might ruin the down-home gathering spot, Gina said she plans to continue running the rustic old structure as a store, deli, and neighborhood bar—just as it has been for decades.

prepared to do some dancing. The atmosphere is friendly and upscale, and there's an outdoor patio when the weather turns warm. Hotel Healdsburg is just steps away.

Lotus Thai Restaurant $$
109-A Plaza St., Healdsburg
(707) 433-5282

Here's where Bangkok meets Healdsburg. Open for lunch and dinner six days a week (excluding Monday), the chef has managed to strike a near-perfect balance between authentic dishes of Thailand and the tastes and desires of Californians. His is arguably the most succulent chicken satay with the best peanut sauce north of the Golden Gate. It's a neat, clean, and well-lit storefront restaurant. Service is unobtrusive and adequate. If you're looking for dessert, try the crispy and sweet fried banana.

Madrona Manor $$$$
1001 Westside Rd., Healdsburg
(707) 433-4231
www.madronamanor.com

Nestled on a wooded knoll surrounded by lush vineyards, Madrona Manor is a majestic sight, its mansard roof rising three stories into the treetops (see our Bed-and-Breakfast Inns chapter). The dining room is opulent, the atmosphere romantic. New chef Jesse Mallgren has livened up the fare here a bit, and he specializes in New California cuisine, using the freshest produce and ingredients available in Sonoma County. He might create an appetizer of crab with ruby red grapefruit, avocado, arugula, and pancetta vinaigrette; and an entree of roast venison loin with carrots, leek risotto, nectarine-rosemary brochettes, and vanilla sauce.

A fixed price menu is offered daily and two gourmet tasting menus as well. There's also an extensive a la carte menu Sunday through Thursday. Monthly wine-makers' dinners are also featured, when diners can meet Sonoma County winemakers and enjoy a meal that's been prepared especially to complement each wine varietal. It's open daily for dinner, but prior to eating, you might want to stroll through the delightful eight-acre gardens. Long story short: Madrona Manor is everything you love about Wine Country.

Manzanita $$$$
336 Healdsburg Ave., Healdsburg
(707) 433–8111

Healdsburg just keeps adding superior restaurants to its list of attractions, and here's another. Manzanita opened in the spring of 2001 with standard Wine Country menu selections such as cassoulet and roast sea bass—California cuisine with European influences. But what chef Bruce Frieseke has created is an outstanding example of what makes a restaurant great: food with flair, combined with terrific service in pleasant surroundings. The first-course options are exceptional—baked black mussels, a truffled beet salad, carrot soup—and the entrees include grilled rabbit set off with polenta, sweet cooked prunes, and black chanterelle mushrooms. There's a small wine bar, and the wine list is impressive. Dinner is served Wednesdays through Sundays until 10:00 P.M.

Ravenous $$$
420 Center St., Healdsburg
(707) 431–1302

Once a tiny restaurant next to the Raven Theater, with just a few tables and many people milling about outside waiting for those coveted tables, Ravenous has moved up in the world. It's now a full-size restaurant not far from the old place, and the food is better than ever. Chef Joyanne Pezzolo serves generous portions of amazing cuisine that defies categorizing. You can order Liberty duck legs that are steamed and roasted, presented atop noodles, and accompanied by grilled white and black eggplant; or choose the beef brisket braised in red wine. It comes with potato fritters and tasty vegetables, too. It's dinner only here, Wednesdays through Sundays.

Zin $$$$
344 Center St., Healdsburg
(707) 473–0946

Why name a restaurant after a wine varietal? Why not? Zin delivers great food and offers lots of great Zinfandels, too. Much of the cuisine is created to be enjoyed with Zinfandel and with an all-American accent. You might find St. Louis-style ribs one night and roasted chicken with polenta on another night. Chefs Jeff Mall and Scott Silva call their cuisine "New American"—updating classic American dishes with more interesting flavors and imagination. The dining room is simple, with big bouquets of flowers, soothing paintings, and large glass windows that look out onto Center Street. You can get dinner here every night but Tuesday and lunch on weekdays (except Tuesday).

Sonoma Coast

Bay View Restaurant $$$$
800 Hwy. 1, Bodega Bay
(707) 875–2751
www.innatthetides.com

Bay View is part of Inn at the Tides, one of the most relaxing hostelries at Bodega Bay (see our Hotels and Motels chapter). The restaurant features a menu that changes weekly and goes well beyond the local catch. Look for grilled ahi tuna on the menu, bouillabaisse, scaloppine of veal, duck breast, and rack of lamb. Cocktails are served in the lounge, a romantic setting as the sun goes down over the Pacific. The restaurant is open for dinner Wednesday through Sunday.

Lucas Wharf Restaurant & Bar $$$
595 Hwy. 1, Bodega Bay
(707) 875–3522
www.lucaswharf.com

This is a cozy, romantic place, with a vaulted ceiling and a fireplace to warm you when the weather cools (as it often does on this coast). Seafood will never be fresher than it is here, for this is a commercial fishery that supplies grocers and the public with fresh Pacific catch. The chef's special of the day is based on the best of the day's catch—salmon, halibut, crab, calamari, and oysters. Bask in the glow of the setting sun while you enjoy your meal or watch sea birds cavort as fishermen deliver their bounty at the pier. Lucas Wharf is a great place to pick up fresh cracked crab or custom-smoked fish. The restaurant is open for lunch and dinner seven days a week. Fresh crab season is mid-November through June, and fresh salmon season is mid-May through September.

River's End Restaurant $$$$
11048 Hwy. 1, Jenner
(707) 865–2484
www.sterba.com/bodega/river

From its position on a bluff where the Russian River flows into the Pacific, River's End has an extraordinary view. Menu offerings here have left local seafood far behind and moved on to upscale comfort foods with a European flair. Here you can have beluga caviar for an appetizer, whiskey-marinated lobster for the fish course, and roasted rack of lamb filled with oysters for the entree. For those without wallets fat enough for such a meal, the house specialties sound almost as exciting—say, beef Wellington or medallions of venison. Either way, it's open for breakfast, lunch, and dinner, Friday through Sunday.

The Tides Wharf & Restaurant $$$
835 Hwy. 1, Bodega Bay
(707) 875–3652
www.innatthetides.com/tideswharf.com

If it looks familiar, it's because you saw it in Alfred Hitchcock's film, *The Birds*. If you didn't see the movie, you can get a taste of the action through a poster on the wall. Aside from the renown that has come from Hitchcock and Tippi Hedren fending off birds, the restaurant has earned its own fame as the long-standing favorite of regulars who have been popping in since the place was a one-room affair. From a seat at the window, you can watch kids, grandparents, and lovers dropping their lines to catch fish or snag a crab, and wait for the commercial fishing boats to come in and dump their loads. A very nice lunch can be made of the special seafood chowder, some sourdough bread, and a glass of Chardonnay. The restaurant is open every day for breakfast, lunch, and dinner, and it offers full bar service. You might want to pick up some cracked crab in the marketplace as you leave, if it's in season. If not, get a bag of saltwater taffy!

West County/Russian River

Alice's Restaurant $$$
101 S. Main St., Sebastopol
(707) 829–3212

This small, cozy restaurant—with comfortable upholstered chairs and fresh flowers on every table—is friendly and inviting, and the food is among the best in town. The chicken Caesar salad is excellent, and we like the sound of fresh pumpkin rigatoni with grilled chicken-apple sausage, sautéed Mayan sweet onions, and sugar snap peas in nutmeg cream sauce. North Coast labels predominate on the wine list, many available by the glass. Alice also serves locally produced Ace Pear Cider, and her desserts are made on the premises with Ghirardelli chocolate. Another plus: Alice's is open every day from 9:00 A.M. to 9:00 P.M., with dinner beginning at 5:00 P.M. So enjoy late lunch, early lunch, or just stop in for a glass of wine at the counter anytime.

Don't let the "Wall Street" facade of Alice's Restaurant fool you. Though it's housed in a former bank building in Sebastopol, it's a cozy bistro with friendly service. PHOTO: JEAN SAYLOR DOPPENBERG

Applewood Inn & Restaurant $$$$
13555 Hwy. 116, Guerneville
(707) 869–9093
www.applewoodinn.com

Snuggled among the redwoods of Pocket Canyon near Guerneville, Applewood Inn is famed for its sophisticated meals. It's one of those special places you want to keep to yourself, but you can't stop talking about it. The fire-lit dining room serves 60 at individual candlelit tables with windows facing the redwoods on three sides. The restaurant does wonderful things with a crisp duck breast with sage, roasted sweet potato, and Bosc pears. But whatever you choose, save room for the Silician layer cake with ricotta, chocolate, and hazelnut sherbet. Applewood is open for dinner Tuesday through Saturday.

The Blue Heron Restaurant and Tavern $$$
Moscow Rd. at Hwy. 116, Duncans Mills
(707) 865–9135

Redwood forests give way to grassy hills at the town of Duncans Mills, a tiny outpost on one of the main thoroughfares to the coast. The Blue Heron is a popular watering hole in these parts. It features a full bar as well as a charming dining room. The gourmet entrees include Asian-style barbecue spareribs, drunken snapper (marinated in a ginger-garlic sauce), and shiitake mushrooms and spinach cannelloni. Complementing the food is regular entertainment, including a dinner show series from September to May and free live music on the outdoor patio on Sundays during the summer. Call for reservations and a schedule of upcoming acts. Open for dinner everyday except Monday, and open for lunch on the weekends.

Chez Marie $$$
6675 Front St. (Hwy. 116), Forestville
(707) 887–7503
www.chezmarie.com

Chez Marie offers a cozy, unpretentious atmosphere, exceptional food, a glowing fireplace on cool nights, and French country-kitchen and Mardi Gras decor. Chef Shirley Palmisano and her partner Angie Lewis named their establishment after their mothers, May and Mary, and together they have created a gem of a restaurant that would make any mom proud. Thursday through Sunday the restaurant features Cajun-Creole dishes done in an authentic New Orleans style—the chef's hometown—and French-continental cuisine. The rotating menu includes such items as escargots, cassoulet, bouillabaisse, lamb chops, étouffée, and gumbo. From the homemade bread served hot from the oven to the elegant desserts, all items are prepared to order. The outdoor patio, which borders the restaurant's herb and flower garden, offers a charming setting in which to enjoy a meal.

Chez Peyo $$$
2295 S. Gravenstein Hwy., Sebastopol
(707) 823–1262
www.sterba.com/chezpeyo/

A charming restaurant in a beautiful garden setting, Chez Peyo features the cuisine of the French Basque nation. Its name comes from the owner, Pierre Lagourgue—"Peyo" is Basque for "Pierre." While Lagourgue relies heavily on traditional French cooking with its grand sauces, he has also turned to what he terms California-French, using fresh herbs and lighter sauces. Produce is garden fresh, utilizing baby greens and baby spinach for salads. Fresh fish and seafood figures frequently on the menu, one of the most popular dishes being baked mussels. But for a real treat, one must try Peyo's paella, made in the Basque fashion with mussels, clams, shrimp, scallops, linguica (a Basque sausage), chicken, and ham tossed with saffron rice. It's sensational. So is the appetizer of baked brie and garlic—the aroma pulls you into the restaurant even if you are only passing by. Peyo's is open for lunch and dinner Wednesday through Sunday and serves a Sunday brunch.

The Farmhouse Inn $$$
7871 River Rd., Forestville
(707) 887-3300
www.farmhouseinn.com

The bed and breakfast service has now been expanded to include dinner, and the Farmhouse restaurant is open to visitors as well as guests. The dining room seats no more than two dozen, but the chef does a terrific job on a varied menu of fish, beef, pasta, and poultry. The entrees include sea bass sautéed with sweet pepper, scallions, and an orange sauce. Save room for dessert because the chocolate pecan pie is the best you'll ever taste. Open for dinner Thursday through Sunday (see our Bed-and-Breakfast Inns chapter).

Negri's $$
3700 Bohemian Hwy., Occidental
(707) 823-5301

It's a toss-up whether the hungry folks of Sonoma County head first for Union Hotel or Negri's—they're both terrific purveyors of great Italian meals. Negri's has been cooking pasta since 1940. Its fame is well-established, as is the expertise of the family that has been running the place

since it opened. A family-style meal starts out with a tureen of minestrone that's so popular people come in to buy it by the bucket. The pasta list is long, including vegetarian spaghetti, penne, and homemade ravioli. After that, if you choose, you can order some of their other specials, such as deep fried calamari, grilled red snapper, and prawns—wash it down with a drink from the fully stocked bar. Open for lunch and dinner every day.

Sparks $$
16248 Main St., Guerneville
(707) 869-8206

California is vegetarian heaven, and this small but hip gourmet eatery serves extraordinary fare that seems sinful, but it's not. Like San Francisco's renowned Millennium Restaurant, the menu is 100 percent vegan, meaning absolutely no animal products. Instead of slathering butter on your whole-grain roll, take a dab of a delightful spread made from carrots and zucchini pureed with olive oil. Owner/chef Alex Bury studied at New York's avant-garde Culinary Institute of America, and it shows. Even ruthless carnivores will enjoy such dishes as the rich, smokey "sausage" and potatoes (made with protein-rich wheat gluten), the polenta torte (made with layers of spinach and tomato polenta and a garlic-tofu ricotta), or the tempeh vegetable loaf. Add a glass of local organic wine and it's the quintessential California experience. Open for breakfast, lunch, dinner, and weekend brunch; closed Tuesdays.

Stella's Cafe $$$
4550 Gravenstein Hwy. North, Sebastopol
(707) 823-6637

Set in an unassuming building in outer Sebastopol, Stella's Cafe is where locals go to enjoy a revolving menu of creative delicacies, whipped up by chef-owner Greg Hallihan. Items such as the steamed half artichoke stuffed with a scoop of purple-black niçoise olive tapenade, the hearty lentil-carrot soup, the forest mushrooms in a rich wine sauce, or the pan-roasted chicken with truffled mashed potatoes—not to mention the mocha crème brûlée and other luscious desserts—keep this place packed to the gills on most nights. If you are too stuffed for dessert, buy a Gravenstein apple pie to-go at Mom's Apple Pie Shop, a Sonoma County institution, located right next door. Open Wednesday through Monday for dinner, and lunch on Sunday.

Sweets River Grill and Bar $$
16251 Main St., Guerneville
(707) 869–3383
www.sweetsrivergrill.com

In the mood for grilled ostrich fillet, venison tenderloin, or a little Cajun alligator sauté? Then head for Sweets River Grill in the heart of downtown Guerneville, just a few miles from Korbel Champagne Cellars. Along with these more exotic items, Sweets features more familiar fare, including New York steak, herb-roasted chicken, and citrus-glazed pork tenderloin. The outdoor patio is shaded and pleasant, and the dining room is highly informal but still elegant. The wine cellar offers a good selection of local vintages, and the fully stocked bar can shake up your favorite libation. Open for dinner every night, lunch Monday through Friday.

Topolos $$$
5700 Gravenstein Hwy. North, Forestville
(707) 887–1562, (800)–TOPOLOS
www.topolos.com

You can dine indoors or outside on the patio here. Either way, the food is Greek, and it's very good. If you go for lunch, you can sample a little of several of their favorite items on a special combination plate—spanakopita, polenta, moussaka, and dolmathakia. Outdoor dining is on a patio that seats 100. It's broken up into different areas by a wisteria arbor and a fountain and is covered with a shade cloth so it can be used on sunny days. This is also a winery (see our Wineries chapter), so the wines served are made right on site. Open for lunch and dinner seven days a week and for brunch on Sunday.

Union Hotel Restaurant $$
3731 Main St., Occidental
(707) 874–3555
www.unionhotel.com

It seems like the Union Hotel dining room has been there forever, housed in a building that goes back to 1879. It's not been around quite that long, but the same family has run it since 1925. The great fame of the place comes from the huge portions of pasta that are served family-style—it's known far and wide for the heaping helpings. It's a custom that was first established by Bill Howard, who settled in Occidental in the 1870s and opened a dining room to feed the wood cutters who came from Tuscany to work the forest (see our History chapter). The portions remain outsized, and the family really knows how to cook pasta. But there are other great items on the menu, chicken cacciatore for one. The establishment has its own bakery and makes great croissants and muffins to serve in its cafe. The restaurant is open for lunch and dinner every day, serving family-style meals and drinks from the saloon.

Mendocino County

U.S. 101

North State Cafe $$
263 N. State St., Ukiah
(707) 462–3726

The logo says it all: "A Casual Experience in Fine Dining." The atmosphere here is that of a fine restaurant, without being too dressy—somewhere between tank tops and neckties. The fare, known as "California Italian," features fresh local ingredients.

The building was the Palace Hotel 100 years ago, but the Palace caught fire and has been rebuilt across the street. Still, when the staff goes down to the wine cellar, some of the traces of the fire are visible among the concrete foundation partitions.

Ukiah is not a town with a heavy influx of tourists, and the Cafe's clientele is estimated to be about 95 percent local—much of the patronage coming from the staff at the nearby courthouse. The Cafe is open for lunch Monday through Friday from 11:00 A.M. to 2:00 P.M., and for dinner Wednesday through Saturday from 5:00 to 9:00 P.M.

Thatcher Inn $$
13401 U.S. 101 South, Hopland
(707) 744–1890, (800) 266–1891
www.thatcherinn.com

The Grand Dining Room offers a casual-yet-elegant ambiance that's immediately evident as you enter this Victorian-era room for dinner Wednesday through Saturday. The walls are decorated in dark green shades, and the dining room chairs are padded in rich rose hues to match the maroon carpeting. It's truly a scene from the 1890s. In true Western style, the chef turns out a great steak, which goes well with the local Fetzer wines. If you prefer, you can order a single-malt Scotch whiskey from the informal Lobby Bar, which is home of one of the largest collections of single-malts in the West. Dinner is served from 5:00 to 9:30 P.M. (See our Bed-and-Breakfast Inns chapter for more on Thatcher Inn.)

Valley Oaks Deli $
Fetzer Vineyards, Hwy. 175
and Eastside Rd., Hopland
(707) 744–1250
www.fetzer.com

This gourmet deli is in the visitor center of Fetzer Vineyards (see our Wineries chapter) and offers an extraordinary selection of fresh salads and sandwiches, all made daily with organic vegetables, fruits, and herbs grown in Fetzer's adjacent Bonterra Garden. You might like to try a grilled vegetable sandwich on focaccia with jambalaya pasta salad. For dessert, go for a cappuccino and the "devil's triangle," if you're a chocolate lover. If you are on your way to a picnic, Valley Oaks will supply you with a special gourmet bag lunch, created to fit your needs. The deli is open daily from 9:00 A.M. to 5:00 P.M. and adjoins the tasting room—you may want to pick up some of Fetzer's best and take it all out to a table on the patio.

Mendocino Coast

Albion River Inn Restaurant $$$$
3790 N. Hwy. 1, Albion
(707) 937–1919
www.albionriverinn.com

A spectacular ocean view, California cuisine, and an award-winning wine list combine to make this an especially romantic dining place. There's seafood, sure, but lots of other options, too, such as roast tenderloin of pork with a raspberry and shallot glaze, pan-roasted grouper with rock shrimp and tomatoes, or oven-roasted quail wrapped in honey-cured bacon and marinated with a burgundy vinegar.

Dinner is served nightly seven days a week: 5:30 to 9:00 P.M. Monday through Friday, and 5:00 to 9:30 P.M. Saturday and Sunday. Piano music Friday through Tuesday nights adds to the allure of Albion River Inn. Reservations are essential. (See our Hotels and Motels chapter for more information on this inn.)

Heritage House $$$$
5200 N. Hwy. 1, Little River
(707) 937–5885, (800) 235–5885
www.heritagehouseinn.com

The dining room is opulent, the ambiance elegant. Quite simply, dining at Heritage House is a world-class experience. Chef Velasquez (named one of America's 10 best new chefs by *Food and Wine* magazine) uses only the freshest local ingredients and premier quality foods, personally selected for his seasonal menus. His pan-seared, fresh Pacific Coast ahi is a sure-shot choice. The view from the dining room is of the spectacular Pacific. On sunny days, visitors may enjoy breakfast on the oceanview deck. Breakfast and dinner are served daily (reservations are advisable for dinner), and brunch is a weekend regular. Heritage House is closed from January 2 through mid-February. (See our Hotels and Motels chapter for more on Heritage House.) There is a full bar.

The Ledford House Restaurant $$$$
3000 N. Hwy. 1, Albion
(707) 937–0282
www.ledfordhouse.com

If you've ever been to Provence, in southern France, you'll recognize the style and ambiance of this restaurant. The expansive windows look out on the Pacific. Add candlelight and music and you've got the basis for a most romantic evening. The food is Mediterranean, and the menu changes monthly. Regulars are rack of lamb, steak, Pacific salmon, and a selection of vegetarian entrees. But you might want to be adventurous and try the tiger prawns flamed in vermouth for dipping in a smoky hot-and-sweet mustard sauce. Dinner is served Wednesday through Sunday from 5 P.M., and reservations are advisable.

Little River Inn $$$$
7750 N. Hwy. 1, Little River
(707) 937–5942
www.littleriverinn.com

Unlike most coastal restaurants, the menu here is not partial to seafood, but leans to classics like leg of lamb filet, Cornish game hen, and grilled pork chops. Salads are made from locally grown lettuces and greens. Desserts too may feature local items—don't fail to leave room for the ollalieberry cobbler. The restaurant at Little River Inn is open every day for breakfast and dinner and also offers Sunday brunch. (For more on the inn, see our Spas and Resorts chapter.)

Pangaea Cafe $$$
250 Main St., Point Arena
(707) 882–3001
www.pangaeacafe.com

Walls are lined with paintings by local artists, giving the small restaurant a feeling of serenity. The food is distinctive, based on the chef's long experience living in other parts of the world (the Middle East, Portugal, Spain), and a changing menu reflects the global influence. Breads are baked fresh in a brick oven every day. Mendocino County wines are featured, often from small, offbeat wineries that don't get much attention. When it comes to desserts, you've hit the culinary big time with the chocolate cake with brandied cherries. Pangaea is open for dinner Wednesday through Sunday.

Mendocino Village
Cafe Beaujolais $$$$
961 Ukiah St., Mendocino
(707) 937–5614
www.cafebeaujolais.com

It was once a Victorian farmhouse, then at the edge of town. But the town has expanded and engulfed the farm. The ambiance inside is not overwhelming—two dozen well-spaced tables occupy a rather plain room. But the food! It's been praised by restaurant critics for more than two decades and remains something of a legend in Mendocino. Borrowing from France, Italy, Asia, and Mexico, the menu features local produce and free-range poultry as much as possible. Entrees run from sturgeon with truffle sauce, for example, to boneless veal roast. One of the most popular features is the posted Country Menu, with a fixed price of $25 for the entire dinner, including dessert. During good weather, there is the option of dining on the large deck out back, which faces onto a beautiful garden. Another option: Call and ask what the menu is for the evening, pick up the entire meal at the "call window," and dine in your hotel room. An array of breads baked on the premises in the wood-fired brick oven not only serves the restaurant, but also can be purchased by non-diners. Dinner is served nightly.

MacCallum House Restaurant $$$$
Grey Whale Bar & Cafe
45020 Albion St., Mendocino
(707) 937–5763
www.maccallumhousedining.com

Daisy MacCallum's 1882 Victorian house is one of the earliest of Mendocino's lumber era. If it looks familiar to you, it may be that you've seen it in a magazine. It always seems to appear in the "perfect picture" of the village of Mendocino. Now a bed and breakfast inn, the MacCallum House has a dining room open to the public, and the Grey Whale Bar & Cafe offers cafe fare served at friendly prices on the sun porch or parlor. The dining room is more formal, warmed by a stone fireplace. The menu emphasizes fresh local seafoods and organic produce from neighboring farms. You might consider grilled portobello mushrooms or pan-seared duck breast. Dinner is served nightly, and a Sunday brunch is available after 11:00 A.M. The restaurant is closed from the first of January to mid-February.

Mendocino Hotel Restaurant & Garden Room $$$
45080 Main St., Mendocino
(707) 937–0511
www.mendocinohotel.com

Perhaps it's the graciousness of the hostess, or maybe it's the welcoming decor of this Victorian dining room, but somehow just being here is a pleasant experience. California cuisine is the specialty, and it is influenced considerably by local seafood. Service is warm but not intrusive. The Victorian Room is open for dinner Sunday through Thursday from 6:00 to 9:30 P.M., and Friday and Saturday from 6:00 to 10:00 P.M. Breakfast and lunch are available in the Garden Room, a large, airy room with a skylight ceiling that really was a garden at one time. (See our Hotels and Motels chapter.)

The Moosse Cafe $$$
390 Kasten St., Mendocino
(707) 937–4323
www.theblueheron.com

Take a seat on the deck, relax, and gaze at the sea, then order some delicious food—maybe an eggplant sandwich or smoked salmon pâté. If the weather is inclement, the indoor cafe is warm and casual and the service agreeable, with beer and wine available. For the most part, the menu features fresh regional ingredients in its selections. Open seven days a week for lunch and dinner.

955 Ukiah Street Restaurant $$$$
955 Ukiah St., Mendocino
(707) 937–1955
www.955restaurant.com

Located in what was once an artist's studio down a garden path next door to Cafe Beaujolais, this may be one of the major reasons visitors from California and the rest of the country like to come to this coast. The enduring fame of the town of Mendocino is irrevocably connected to the palates of a few thousand visitors, who know good restaurants when they find them. And the word is out that 955 Ukiah Street is one of the best on the Mendocino Coast. Basing its fame less on elegance per se than on memorable meals,

the restaurant offers a wide-ranging menu and uses local products whenever possible. Options include steaks, roast duck, lamb, and pasta. The restaurant is open everyday but Tuesday from 6:00 P.M.

Fort Bragg

Egghead's Restaurant $$
326 N. Main St., Fort Bragg
(707) 964–5005

It's known as the local's favorite, and yes, the locals do brag that there are no better omelettes or eggs Benedict in the entire United States. Beyond that, Egghead's features some 40 varieties of crepes, specialty pancakes, and waffles for breakfast. For lunch, there are creative salads, unusual sandwiches, and many unique vegetarian treats. The restaurant is distinguished by another feature: a yellow brick road that runs from the front door to the kitchen (here it's known as Oz). A collection of photos and theater bills on the wall along the row of booths shows Dorothy, the Cowardly Lion, the Tin Man, and the rest of the Wizard cast. Egghead's is open seven days a week.

Gardens Grill $$$
Mendocino Coast Botanical Gardens
18220 N. Hwy. 1, Fort Bragg
(707) 964–7474

The Grill's setting is unsurpassed; it's located in the spectacular Mendocino Coast Botanical Gardens—47 acres of blooming rhododendrons, azaleas, heather, and 100 other plants native to the area, with the Pacific as a backdrop (see our Attractions chapter). You can dine indoors in the light-filled dining room or outside on the deck overlooking the lush coastal landscape. The specialty here is grilled steak, seafood, and vegetarian selections. Open for lunch Wednesday through Saturday from 11:00 A.M. to 2:30 P.M. and for dinner Thursday through Saturday. There's also a Sunday brunch from 10:00 A.M. to 2:30 P.M.

The Rendezvous $$$
647 N. Main St., Fort Bragg
(707) 964–8142
www.rendezvousinn.com

California continental-style seafood, poultry, veal, and steak are served in cozy, comfortable surroundings in one of Fort Bragg's classic early homes. Chef Kim Badenhop studied under master chefs in Switzerland and France, and much of the food served at the Rendezvous reflects the labor-intensive European style of cooking. Seasonality is important to him, and his menus reflect this—in winter he works with wild game and Dungeness crab; in summer, fresh vegetables and king salmon figure strongly on his menu. Dinner is served Wednesday through Sunday, and reservations are advisable.

The Restaurant $$$
418 Main St., Fort Bragg
(707) 964-9800

Like the meeting place of the friends on television's *Seinfeld*, this place is simply called The Restaurant, and it has been for the past two decades. The walls are covered with the paintings of local artist Olaf Palm, and the owners—chefs Jim and Barbara Larsen—make everything on the menu except the bread. They offer light meals such as grilled polenta with mozzarella and sautéed mushrooms, and they serve a delightful chicken piccata cooked in fresh lemon and white wine sauce. But whatever you eat, save room for the desserts because they're memorable—especially the tiramisu, an Italian concoction of sponge cake, cream cheese, espresso, and bittersweet chocolate. The Restaurant presents live jazz on Friday and Saturday. It's open for dinner Thursday through Tuesday and for Sunday brunch. Reservations are recommended for Sunday brunch.

Wharf Restaurant $$$
32260 N. Harbor Dr., Fort Bragg
(707) 964-4283
www.wharf-restaurant.com

The Wharf is a favorite spot for both locals and travelers, as it has been for more than 40 years. Relax as you enjoy a cocktail or specialty of the house, watching the boats bring in the catch of the day. The chef's pride is the menu of fresh seafood, with steaks as an alternate. Open for lunch and dinner seven days a week.

Lake County

Mt. St. Helena Brewery & Restaurant $
21167 Calistoga St., Middletown
(707) 987-2106
www.mtsthelenabrew.com

As microbreweries go, this one has lots of gold and silver medals to show for its trouble. They make good brews for washing down the standard pub fare, from chili and onion rings to a pleasing selection of salads and pastas to house specialties of the red meat variety. The pizza menu is impressive, and there's even stir-fry and Thai noodles for vegetarians. Beer is king here, not wine, but the vino offerings are predominantly from Lake County wineries. The restaurant is open daily.

Park Place Restaurant $$
50 Third St., Lakeport
(707) 263-0444

This pleasant bistro emphasizes fresh, local produce and casual taste. It's just a couple blocks from Clear Lake—from the deck you can see the water and, behind it to the southeast, Mount Konocti. Park Place makes its own pasta daily—one reason its tortellini and ravioli dishes are so popular. The gorgonzola bread and Mediterranean pasta salad, meanwhile, are more than a meal in combination. The restaurant is open for lunch and dinner seven days a week.

Robert's French Restaurant $$
16170 Main St., Lower Lake
(707) 995-3569

In one of those only-in-California sort of stories, chef Robert Ayme became something of a local hero in 1999 when he generously fed about 100 exhausted and hungry firefighters who were battling an out-of-control grassfire not far away in a remote region of Lake County. When he put out his offer to feed them for free, the food was rushed to the firelines. You can bet those were the best-fed firefighters in California.

Inside the restaurant, Robert serves up elegant presentations of prime rib, oysters, seafood, and wild boar. In general, the restaurant is open Wednesday through Sunday for lunch and dinner (closed

Monday and Tuesday), but call ahead to make certain.

Sicilian Country Steakhouse $$$
5685 Main St., Kelseyville
(707) 279–0704

There is so much of southern Italy at this downtown Kelseyville restaurant that you'll feel like driving up on a motor scooter, wearing no socks. The menu includes baked zitti, fresh ravioli and tortellini, and four kinds of gnocchi. You also will find a number of veal and chicken dishes, not to mention some of the best steaks around. Oh, and don't forget the robust cioppino alla Siciliano. Ask about the children's menu. Sicilian Country Steakhouse is open for dinner seven nights a week in the summer, closed Monday and Tuesday in the winter. There is a full bar.

Sunflower Chinese Restaurant $
14521 Lakeshore Dr., Clearlake
(707) 994–1268

Exotic it isn't, but it's hard to beat the Sunflower for dependable, Western-friendly Szechuan and Mandarin cuisine. All the favorites are here: beef with broc-coli, sweet-and-sour pork, Mongolian beef, etc. They'll withhold the MSG upon request. It's a clean establishment with a view of Clear Lake, and the restaurant has a full bar. It's open for lunch and dinner every day but Sunday.

Tee Room Restaurant $$$
Buckingham Golf & Country Club,
2855 Eastlake Dr., Kelseyville
(707) 279–1140

You don't have to be a weary golfer, or even a guest of Konocti Harbor Resort (only five minutes away, see our Spas and Resorts chapter), to eat here. You just have to be a devotee of the Southwestern cuisine chef Lauretta Bonfiglio developed at her former restaurant, Lauretta's, in Aspen, Colorado. The Tee Room has a small menu with dishes such as herb-rubbed rack of lamb in a Zinfandel and garlic sauce and grilled filet mignon in a brandied mushroom sauce. The dining room offers nice views of the golf course and looming Mount Konocti. It's open for dinner Wednesday through Sunday in the summer and Wednesday through Saturday in the winter.

Nightlife

Though most towns around here start rolling up the sidewalks after sundown, there are a number of popular music venues and dance hot spots to keep your toes tapping well into the night. Napa and St. Helena have a few options, and the downtown areas of Petaluma and Santa Rosa can be relied upon for several good shows on the weekend. Guerneville, too, gets lively in the summer, especially in the town's thriving gay bars. And Lake County's Konocti Harbor Resort is always kicking up its heels in an environment dedicated to mixing music with water sports.

So, if after eating gourmet meals and drinking wine all day you are still looking for more decadent fun, here are a few Wine Country music halls, bars, and clubs where you can look for after-hours entertainment. Some of the smaller establishments don't collect a cover charge, but many do. In general, expect to pay from $2.00 to $5.00 to watch local talent, more if someone of greater renown is taking the stage. Guidelines for pricier show tickets are given in the listings.

The bar and club listings are followed by movie theaters in the four counties. Check a local newspaper for more up-to-date information.

We don't want to nag about this too much, but one thing bears repeating, especially in this chapter: Please observe the same common sense about drinking and driving that applies anywhere. California's legal blood-alcohol threshold is a stringent .08, so taking to the road after more than one drink can be expensive and embarrassing, as well as extremely dangerous. If you need a taxi, consult our Getting Around chapter.

Bars and Clubs

Napa County

Downtown Joe's
902 Main St., Napa
(707) 258–2337
www.downtownjoes.com

This riverside microbrewery offers a variety of rock, pop, and blues bands every Thursday, Friday, and Saturday. Sunday evenings are for karaoke, and Tuesdays are open-mike night.

Silverado Country Club & Resort
1600 Atlas Peak Rd., Napa
(707) 257–0200
www.silveradoresort.com

A classy joint indeed, Silverado features jazz piano from 5:00 to 9:00 P.M. on the patio terrace, Wednesday through Saturday. On Friday and Saturday nights the soloist is followed by a band that plays from 9:00 P.M. to 1:00 A.M. The regular act of late has been the five-piece Paul Martin Band.

Hemphill's Lounge
3385 California Blvd., Napa
(707) 255–9744

Your chances of spotting Drew Barrymore are practically nil at this little hideaway, but you can try karaoke on Thursday night (9:00 P.M. to 1:30 A.M.) or listen to pop music on Friday and Saturday (9:00 P.M. to 2:00 A.M.).

Piccolino's Italian Cafe
1385 Napa Town Center, Napa
(707) 251–0100
www.piccolinoscafe.com

On Friday and Saturday evenings, this centrally located restaurant provides jazz accompaniment, perhaps spiced with a little R&B or salsa. Hours are generally 5:00 to 9:00 P.M.

Violette's at the Mansion
443 Brown St., Napa
(707) 253-2583, (800) 959-2583

At the rear of one of Napa Valley's finest inns (see our Bed and Breakfast chapter) is a charming French restaurant, and its Friday- and Saturday-night performances—classical guitar, jazz, blues, or even harp—have become quite popular. Reservations definitely are required. Dinner seating is at 7:00 P.M., and the price of $85 per person includes a seven-course prix fixe meal. Dessert seating—$40 per couple for a sampler—is at 8:30.

Pacific Blues Cafe
6525 Washington St., Yountville
(707) 944-4455

This popular restaurant and watering hole sits right outside the east entrance of the Vintage 1870 shopping complex. In addition to serving what they call "Maverick American" cuisine, they spice things up with live blues on Saturdays in summer from 5:00 to 8:00 P.M.

Ana's Cantina
1205 Main St., St. Helena
(707) 963-4921

This tropical-themed Mexican restaurant heats up from 9:30 P.M. to 1:30 A.M. most Friday and Saturday nights, with a stream of bands that run from Latin-Mediterranean to jazz to rock to reggae. Wednesday and Sunday are karaoke night. Thursday is open-mike night.

1351 Lounge
1351 Main St., St. Helena
(707) 963-1969
www.1351lounge.com

A small club with a capacity for packing 'em in, that's 1351. It's usually live blues or rock on weekends, and there's always a cover charge. Acoustic singer-songwriters can be found there on the occasional weeknight.

Calistoga Inn & Restaurant
1250 Lincoln Ave., Calistoga
(707) 942-4101
www.calistogainn.com

The bartender slings Napa Valley Brewing Company beers here, and every Saturday from 8:30 to 11:00 P.M. (and often on Tuesdays and Fridays), live music fills the small oblong bar. The material varies but tends toward intimate, singer-songwriter stuff. Wednesday is open-mike night.

Hydro Bar & Grill
1403 Lincoln Ave., Calistoga
(707) 942-9777

Calistoga's late-night eatery is a perfect spot for everything from swing music to rock 'n' roll.

Sonoma County

Murphy's Irish Pub
464 First St. East, Sonoma
(707) 935-0660

This pub keeps sleepy Sonoma awake, usually every Thursday through Sunday night. The genre is hard to predict. It could be blues one night, traditional Celtic the next. Or it could be folk ballads followed by a melodious string ensemble. There is no cover, but expect a two-pint minimum.

Copperfield's Cafe
140 Kentucky St., Petaluma
(707) 762-8798
www.copperfieldscafe.com

Sonoma County's hippest bookstore chain goes one step further at this Petaluma branch, laying down folk music on Wednesday nights.

Kodiak Jack's
256 Petaluma Blvd. North, Petaluma
(707) 765-5760
www.kodiakjacks.com

With so many cowboy boots stomping at one time here, we hope Jack's foundation is structurally reinforced. On different nights, there is West Coast swing dancing, two-step, line dancing, "beginner couples," power country, and honky-tonk. You can take lessons every night. There's a restaurant (Sundance Steakhouse) with cuisine to match the country theme. Call for cover information.

Mystic Theatre & Dance Hall
23 Petaluma Blvd. North, Petaluma
(707) 765–6665

Not as big as Konocti Harbor, not as polite as the Luther Burbank Center, the Mystic Theatre might be the Wine Country's coolest venue. Built in 1911, it's a vaulted, double-decker palace that wouldn't be out of place on the Sunset Strip. Much of the music is classic rock of all shades and tones, from Warren Zevon to Tower of Power, Richard Thompson to Tommy Castro, Emmylou Harris to Todd Rundgren. A few years back, Van Morrison even recorded one of his live albums here. Stand-up comedy passes through from time to time, featuring jokers like Will Durst. Tickets generally range from $15 to $30.

Tradewinds
8210 Old Redwood Hwy., Cotati
(707) 795–7878
www.tradewindsbar.com

This small club has music most weekend nights. Expect a lot of blues and R&B, and watch for Derek and the Aces, the roots-rock band that used to be regulars here.

A'Roma Roasters and Coffeehouse
95 Fifth St., Santa Rosa
(707) 576–7765

Come down to Railroad Square on a Friday or Saturday night for live music and a hot cup of chai or joe. A'Roma does a lot of folk music, plus some world beat, jazz, and blues. Shows start at 8:30 P.M.

The Old Vic
731 Fourth St., Santa Rosa
(707) 571–7555

If you want to pretend you're in England, it's easy to do at this downtown Santa Rosa watering hole. Friday nights are generally for spotlighting local bands of the thrashy and loud variety with names like Stump Removal Kit; Saturdays are for British-style dinner theater that leans to the silly. At least 17 imported lagers, ales, and stouts are available, and the pub food is nearly authentic English: bangers and mash, mushy peas, shepherd's pie—you get the idea.

Last Day Saloon
120 Fifth St., Santa Rosa
(707) 545–2343
www.lastdaysaloon.com

This is the northern outpost of the venerable San Francisco nightclub that's been rocking the Bay Area for nearly 30 years. On a busy corner in Railroad Square, Last Day is 8,000 square feet of music, Bloody Marys, and food, too. DJ music is provided three nights a week, with weekends dedicated to live music of all kinds—you're likely to hear Motown or disco, funk or new wave. Owner David Daher draws on his three decades in the music business to bring in some terrific acts that might have previously overlooked Santa Rosa on their tour itineraries. Recent legends appearing in the main music room have included Elvin Bishop and members of the Grateful Dead. Sunday night is generally reserved for showcasing local rock bands. DJ nights usually carry a $5.00 cover; tickets for live shows can range from $10 to $20, depending on whether the artist is a household name. There's also a full menu of decent pub grub, and it's served until midnight—a nice bonus for late-night revelers.

Flamingo Resort Hotel
2777 Fourth St., Santa Rosa
(707) 545–8530
www.flamingoresort.com

Sure, it's a hotel bar, but it's better than most. Count on soul and rhythm & blues bands on the weekends, and DJs spinning discs during the week. The dance floor is one of the best around, and it's always packed with hoofers of all ages.

The Cantina
500 Fourth St., Santa Rosa
(707) 523–3663

Generation Next moves to its own beat at the Cantina, in the heart of downtown—upstairs from the restaurant of the same name. Thursday is college night during the spring and summer. Fridays and Saturdays (when they charge $2.00 and up), you get a mix of top 40, R&B, disco, house, and Latin beats.

Dance Central
3535 Industrial Avenue, Santa Rosa
(707) 545–6150

If you don't know how to dance, but want to learn, or if you are a rising star looking to improve your style, then this is the place for you. You can take lessons almost every night, and get to practice afterward during the nightly open dance parties. Tuesday it's ballroom dancing, Wednesday it's West Coast swing, Thursday is salsa night, Friday brings on the big bands and the Lindy, Saturday is variety night, and Sunday is West Coast swing. Call for prices and details.

Sweetriver Saloon
248 Coddingtown Center, Santa Rosa
(707) 526–0400
www.sweetriver.com

Seating a comedy club in the middle of a mall should provide a lot of grist for the comics. Sweetriver makes you laugh every Friday and Saturday night, starting at 9:00 P.M. The cover is $7.00 (no joke).

Healdsburg Bar & Grill
245 Healdsburg Ave., Healdsburg
(707) 433–3333

Nightlife improved significantly in this sleepy burg when HB&G opened its doors. Expect live bands on weekends, usually rock-and-roll from established local groups such as the Remedies or the Pulsators. Occasionally, the owners pull out all the stops for a Sunday evening show with renowned artists such as Dan Hicks or Coco Montoya (with tickets in the $20 to $25 range).

Bear Republic Brewing Company
345 Healdsburg Ave., Healdsburg
(707) 433–2337
www.bearrepublic.com

Another microbrewery that offers music (see our Restaurants chapter Close-up), Bear Republic often has entertainment on Thursday and Friday nights. It might be blues; it might be surf music; it might sound like heaven after a couple of pints.

Jasper O'Farrell's
6957 Sebastopol Ave., Sebastopol
(707) 823–1389

O'Farrell's keeps Sebastopol busy every night of the week—mostly blues, some rock, some soul, some original songwriting, and even the occasional Celtic group. Tuesday is open-mike night. It's very eclectic and very local.

The Powerhouse Brewing Company
268 Petaluma Ave., Sebastopol
(707) 829–9171

This brewpub-cum-night spot offers a mix of local as well as national talent, heavy on the blues. Sometimes there is no cover. Other times, the cost can be as much as $12 for acts such as the Nervis Brothers, those New Orleans boogiers.

Main Street Station
16280 Main St., Guerneville
(707) 869–0501
www.mainststation.com

When Guerneville gets a little too hot, duck into the Station for some cool, breezy jazz. The Benny Barth Jazz Trio on Tuesdays have been regulars lately. Other hipsters blow in and out on Thursdays, Fridays, and Saturdays.

Rainbow Cattle Company
16220 Main St., Guerneville
(707) 869–0206

It celebrated its 20th anniversary in October 1999, but the Cattle Company hasn't slowed down a bit. It's still where the Russian River's gay clientele gather for loud, uninhibited fun. The club has a DJ on Friday and Saturday nights and holidays.

Club FAB
16135 Main St., Guerneville
(707) 869–5708
www.fabpresents.com

Proclaiming itself as the largest gay dance club north of the Golden Gate, Club FAB is housed in an old cinema in downtown Guerneville. Since opening its doors in 1998, it has quickly become the most happening scene along the Russian River. When there's not a name act playing, the DJ revs up dancers Friday and Saturday nights with foot-tapping rhythms.

Mendocino County

Greenwood Pier Cafe
5926 S. Hwy. 1, Elk
(707) 877–9997
www.greenwoodpierinn.com

If you find yourself in the village of Elk, south of Albion on the rugged Mendocino coast, you might be surprised to hear the sound of guitar chords floating on the breeze. They will lead you to Greenwood Pier Cafe, which has music every Friday and Saturday from 7:00 to 9:00 P.M.

Patterson's Pub
10485 Lansing St., Mendocino
(707) 937–4782
www.mcn.org/a/pattersons

Beer and tall tales are paramount at Patterson's, but the pub also keeps your sports appetite satisfied with four TV sets. Live music is featured on occasion, though it is rare. Look for the old London cab in the driveway. Patterson's is open daily.

The Caspar Inn
14957 Caspar Rd., Caspar
(707) 964–5565
www.casparinn.com

It's a long way from San Francisco, but Caspar Inn has the same type of colorful rock-and-roll history as the Fillmore. This old (1906) roadhouse-style inn has been in business since Caspar was a booming logging town, and many a big name has stepped through its doors and onto the stage (Mose Allison, B.B. King). Today you can expect karaoke on Wednesdays and such diverse musical concoctions as Afro-Cuban salsa and cowpunk on weekends. Bonnie Raitt reportedly comes in now and then (she lives nearby) and just hangs out, singing along with the jukebox. Cover charges range from $5.00 to $10.00.

Headlands Coffeehouse
120 E. Laurel St., Fort Bragg
(707) 964–1987
www.headlandscoffeehouse.com

This is the epicenter of local culture in Fort Bragg, a hipster java joint where there's almost always something interesting to listen to as you stay wired. Sunday is classical music night: maybe a string trio, maybe a guitar-and-flute combination. On Friday there is usually a jazz piano trio. Beyond that you're most likely to encounter jazz or acoustic singer-songwriter stuff.

Lake County

Konocti Harbor Resort & Spa
8727 Soda Bay Rd., Kelseyville
(707) 279–4281, (800) 660–LAKE
www.konoctiharbor.com

In a few short years, Konocti Harbor has managed to place itself among the top music venues in Northern California. In fact, the resort's Joe Mazzola Classic Concert Showroom was recently named by *Performance Magazine* as "America's No. 1 Small Concert Venue." The resort actually has several different sites for performance. The Konocti Field Amphitheater, which operates between May and October, puts you under the stars for major concerts. This lakeside amphitheater seats 5,000, all within 200 feet of the stage. It pulls big acts, some contemporary, some revived. The lineup has included the likes of Wynonna, Vince Gill, Styx, the Doobie Brothers, Ringo Starr, the Pretenders, and Tim McGraw. Tickets usually range from $29 to $49.

Predating the amphitheater was the Classic Concert Showroom, a 1,000-occupancy dinner theater with two VIP balconies and tiered seating. The showroom tends to show stars of yesterday or acts more appropriate to an intimate setting. Like who? Like Ray Charles, Eddie Money, Tanya Tucker, and Bill Cosby. These tickets are in the $35 to $60 range, more if you include buffet dinner. But wait, there's more. The Full Moon Saloon, right next to Clear Lake, has live entertainment Fridays and Saturdays year-round, and seven days a week from June through Labor Day. The saloon has indoor and outdoor seating and a sizable dance floor.

Movie Theaters

Napa County

Napa CineDome 8
825 Pearl St., Napa
(707) 257–7700

Cameo Cinema
(occasional art movies)
1340 Main St., St. Helena
(707) 963–9779

Sonoma County

Sebastiani Theatre
(historic building; occasional art movies)
476 First St. East, Sonoma
(707) 996–2020

Sonoma Cinemas
200 Siesta Way, Sonoma
(707) 935–1234

Rohnert Park 16
555 Rohnert Park Expressway West,
Rohnert Park
(707) 586–0555

Sonoma Film Institute
Sonoma State University, Darwin Theater,
1801 E. Cotati Ave., Rohnert Park
(707) 664–2606

Airport Cinema 8
409 Aviation Way, Santa Rosa
(707) 522–0330

Rialto Cinemas Lakeside
551 Summerfield Rd., Santa Rosa
(707) 539–9770

UA Cinemas 6
620 Third St., Santa Rosa
(707) 528–8770

Roxy Stadium 14
85 Santa Rosa Ave., Santa Rosa
(707) 522–0330

The Raven Film Center
415 Center St., Healdsburg
(707) 433–5448

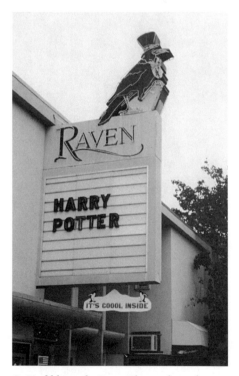

In Healdsburg, the Raven Theater shows first-run movies, but also presents live concerts occasionally. PHOTO: JEAN SAYLOR DOPPENBERG

Clover Cinemas
121 E. First St., Cloverdale
(707) 894–7920

Sebastopol Cinemas
6868 McKinley St., Sebastopol
(707) 829–3456

Rio Theater
20396 Bohemian Highway (Hwy. 116),
Monte Rio
(707) 865–0913

Mendocino County

Noyo Theater
57 E. Commercial St., Willits
(707) 459–0280

Ukiah 6 Theatre
612 S. State St., Ukiah
(707) 462–6788

Arena Theatre
214 Main St., Point Arena
(707) 882–3020

Coast Cinemas
167 S. Franklin St., Fort Bragg
(707) 964–2019

Lake County

Clearlake Cinema
3380 Washington St., Clearlake
(707) 994–7469

Lakeport Auto Movies
(drive-in)
52 Soda Bay Rd., Lakeport
(707) 263–5011

Lakeport Cinema 5
52 Soda Bay Rd., Lakeport
(707) 263–4215

Wineries

A Taste of Each Region
Wineries to Visit
Wine Shops

This is the chapter that gave us the excuse to create this book in the first place. In our little galaxy, the wineries are the sun around which all of our other attractions seem to orbit. And just as the grape varietals we grow here are dramatically different from one another, so too are the wineries that produce them. If you take time to drop in at more than a few, you'll discover each place has its own special story to tell.

Ideal grape-growing conditions have made Napa, Sonoma, Mendocino, and Lake Counties famous for producing an infinite variety of world-class wine. Some of the most valuable cropland on the continent can be found here—and prices for premium vineyard land continue to spiral upward.

More than 400 million gallons of juice are gently squeezed from grapes each year, bottled, and set aside to age as wine. But it takes marketing to turn wine into cash, so most wineries want visitors to stop in, look around, taste the product, buy it, and keep on buying it.

So when you visit Wine Country, set aside at least a day or two for a sampling of the region's wineries. On the outside, they can range from rustic barn-like structures to grand estates resembling castles. On the inside, you are warmly welcomed by genial guides and tasting room hosts who will gladly explain the mysteries of the craft, reminisce about vintage years, and share hopes for this year's crop.

Whatever you do, please refrain from rushing through Wine Country. There's nothing to be gained from sprinting between tasting rooms. Take the time to learn about the winery, the winemaking process, and especially its people. Usually they are as mellow and unhurried as the wines themselves.

A Taste of Each Region

So . . . with more than 600 wineries within the four counties, where does one begin? First, we'll give you a taste of what separates our coverage area from the rest of the winemaking areas of California and the world—qualities that have given our region the undisputed title of California's Wine Country. Next, we'll provide a brief overview of the wine and wineries of each of the counties in our coverage area. Then comes the part where you get to pick and choose: detailed listings for more than 120 individual producers throughout Wine Country.

Despite the number of wineries here and the number of acres under viticulture, it's interesting to note that Wine Country's grape harvest represents only a relatively small contribution to California's total wine production. The annual grape harvest of Sonoma County adds up to a minuscule 4 percent of the state's total volume, about the same as neighboring Napa County. This deceptively small percentage stands in stark contrast with the lofty reputation Wine Country's vintages have deservedly attained.

There are scores of wineries here, but they are not the oil-refinery-scale tank farms of the jug wine, bulk business. With a few exceptions, nearly all our wineries are small- to medium-sized operations, often family-owned. This is as good a reason as any to visit—you will nearly always find a tasty vintage to call your own personal discovery. One of Napa Valley's winemakers captured Wine Country philosophy: "The people I deal with are all happy people; wine is a happy product." Perhaps the region's most memorable quality, at any time of year, is its warm and welcoming spirit.

But there's more to the great wines produced in this region, and it doesn't all have to do with the smaller operations and intense attention to detail—these are things you might find in some other locations, too. What we have that cannot be reproduced are the unique marriages of land and climate. Pour yourself another glass of your newly discovered favorite red, and read on about the climatology of fine wines.

Understanding Appellations

Understanding appellations is this simple: The quality of the grapes is the key to the quality of the wine. Where grapes are grown makes up almost 80 percent of the characteristics of a specific wine. The mellow in your Merlot? The zest in that Zinfandel? The panache of a particular Pinot Noir? It all can be traced back to the grapes, the climate that fostered their growth, and the soil from which they emerged.

Areas with hot days, warm nights, and deep, peat-rich soils might be good for growing corn and other vegetables (and even table grapes), but they produce wine grapes that are too high in sugar content and, therefore, not good for creating fine wines. A cooler, dryer climate and the volcanic soils so common in Napa, Sonoma, Mendocino, and Lake Counties lead to the production of ultrapremium wines.

Within this four-county area, there are also many microclimates. Each of these areas has specific characteristics that affect the wine grapes grown there. In the wine industry, these special growing regions are called "American viticultural areas" (AVAs). Around here we refer to them as "appellations," a French word you will run into frequently in this guide, but which is not used officially by the Bureau of Alcohol, Tobacco, and Firearms (BATF), the agency of the federal government that monitors these things. How important is the term "appellation"? Some grapes grow better in one appellation than in another. Also, the same grape varietal grown in one appellation may produce a wine that is distinctly different from one made with the same grade of grapes grown in another appellation. A Merlot grown in Carneros, for example, produces a wine that is complex, with some light and soft fruit flavors; the same grape grown in the Dry Creek appellation may bring about a wine with a full, robust character that is bursting with flavor.

There are 12 AVAs in Sonoma County alone, and another 14 in Napa County. Additionally, the two counties share one—the aforementioned Carneros, a cool region bordering San Pablo Bay at the southern reaches of both the Napa and Sonoma valleys. At first, it may sound to the novice as if the wine snobs are splitting hairs. But the differences in the wines from different appellations (and different winemakers within the same appellation), when tasted side by side, are distinct and remarkable.

Appellations also are important economically. A wine labeled with a certain appellation name must be produced using a minimum of 75 to 85 percent of grapes from that region. For example, a "Sonoma Valley" Zinfandel must take at least 85 percent of its Zinfandel grapes from the Sonoma Valley AVA. Such distinctions add value to the wine and raise the shelf price. By comparison, a Zinfandel with the appellation "California" on the label means that the grapes could have come from anywhere in California. These wines often are produced with grapes from less-prestigious growing areas such as the San Joaquin Valley, where the long, hot summers allow production of massive quantities of grapes that are used primarily for jug wines and the so-called "fighting vari-

Where'd That Come From?

Wines labeled with a certain appellation name must be produced using a minimum of 75 to 85 percent of grapes (depending on the varietal) from that specific region. Below are the recognized appellations (American viticultural areas) of the four counties in Wine Country. Note that the North Coast AVA is a broad one, applying to wines from several different counties including Napa, Sonoma, Mendocino, and Lake.

Napa County
Atlas Peak, Chiles Valley, Diamond Mountain, Howell Mountain, Los Carneros, Mount Veeder, Napa Valley, North Coast, Oakville, Rutherford, Spring Mountain District, St. Helena, Stags Leap District, Wild Horse Valley, Yountville

Sonoma County
Alexander Valley, Chalk Hill, Dry Creek Valley, Knights Valley, Los Carneros, North Coast, Northern Sonoma, Rockpile, Russian River Valley, Sonoma Coast, Sonoma County Green Valley, Sonoma Mountain, Sonoma Valley

Mendocino County
Anderson Valley, Cole Ranch, McDowell Valley, Mendocino, Mendocino Ridge, North Coast, Potter Valley, Redwood Valley, Yorkville Highlands

Lake County
Benmore Valley, Clear Lake, Guenoc Valley, North Coast

Sources: *Appellation* magazine; Mendocino Wine Growers Alliance; Lake County Visitor Information; Bureau of Alcohol, Tobacco and Firearms; The Wine Institute

---

etals" (wine industry jargon for lower-priced varietals).

The generally dryer and cooler microclimates of Napa, Sonoma, Mendocino, and Lake Counties produce fewer grapes, but they are of a much higher quality for making fine wine. Grapes from these regions are more expensive (often as much as four to five times higher per ton), and they are in high demand.

Of course, grapes are not the only element that goes into making a fine wine. The object of the winemaker's craft—a blend of skill, experience, science, art, taste, and inspiration—is to take the special qualities of certain grapes and maximize their potential. Without getting too high-falutin' about it, a tour of Wine Country can include the dimension of a search for the perfect blend of the region's finest grapes and the winemaker's skill.

Napa County

When people hear the words "California Wine Country," they first think of Napa, where the wines have been established as the yardstick by which other American vintages are measured. Even the French have taken notice of this world-famous source. Compared to Europe, however, where vineyards have flourished for centuries, Napa Valley is still in its infancy. Yet it has grown quickly, and with about 240 wineries, it is believed to be the world's most densely concentrated winery region. Because of this, there is some concern that traffic and crowds will destroy the bucolic landscape, particularly in summer when tourist count is high.

Motorists who know the region well are inclined at such busy times to abandon the main highway through the valley, Highway

A newly restored vineyard stands ready for replanting outside Clos Pegase Winery south of Calistoga.

PHOTO: JEAN SAYLOR DOPPENBERG

29, and turn onto the Silverado Trail, which runs parallel to the east. From there, they can cross over, using any of several connecting lanes that bind the two north-south roads. Silverado Trail is a delight in itself, winding between meadows and wooded slopes to the east and vineyards to the west. Its slight elevation produces some striking vineyard panoramas, eminently suited to photography. (For more on negotiating the byways of Wine Country, see our Getting Around chapter.)

Napa boasts so many tasting rooms it is almost impossible to classify them as a group. They range in style from quaint to elegant, sparse to cluttered, disarmingly casual to alarmingly commercial. But beyond atmosphere and physical trappings, the valley's tasting rooms provide the makings of a truly unique wine experience. In these pockets of hospitality you will find an abundance of wines rivaling any in the world.

Those with a nose for business and an affinity for columns of numbers will appreciate these digits: The wine industry in Napa Valley accounts for about $4 billion (yes, billion) of the $33 billion California wine industry. Approximately 6.3 million cases of wine were produced in Napa Valley in 1998, and 103,526 tons of grapes were grown and crushed in 1999. The total value of the Napa County grape crop in 1999 was $222 million. That's how important wine is to our overall economy.

At its widest, Napa Valley is no more than 3 miles across. It is 27 miles from north end to south end, framed on both sides by hulking mountains. Most of the valley's two million annual visitors come to see its 35,000 acres of groomed vineyards—some newly replanted, some ancient, with gnarled vines that stand like regiments of old soldiers. They come to sip the nectar of the gods; to luxuriate in handsome, turn-of-the-century bed-and-breakfast inns; and to further excite their palates in some of the finest gourmet restaurants in America. Visitors also learn something more: Wineries are great places to find some unexpected entertainment. Musical events are a feature at several wineries—Sunday jazz at Domaine Chandon, for instance (see our Arts and Culture chapter). St. Supéry's guided tour includes a look at a Victorian home restored as a living museum of the late 1800s. At Sterling Vineyards, an aerial tram lifts passengers high over the valley floor to a wine tasting deck affording an unequaled view of Napa Valley's upper reaches.

Food-and-wine pairings are staged in several wineries, and many have picnic grounds that give new meaning to the great outdoors. Artesa has a charming museum with some 17th-century winemaking casks and paraphernalia from its home country of Spain. And several wineries have elegant and eerie caves open for exploring (see the Close-up in this chapter).

CLOSE-UP

Getting Your Bearings

The California Welcome Center, a handsome, 43,000-square-foot building overlooking lovely Roberts Lake next to the Doubletree Hotel just off U.S. 101 in Rohnert Park, is a great place to get more information about the Wine Country and other regions of the state. The California Division of Tourism established the center in 1995 to help visitors plan their stay and get a sense of the length of time it requires to move from one locale to another. Along with the maps and brochures, there's an interactive kiosk at the center with audiovisual information and a knowledgeable staff to answer questions and make suggestions.

This is also the information center for the Sonoma County Winemakers Association, and visitors may be surprised to find a selection of some 200 different wines to sample. A demonstration vineyard outside the building tells the story of how grapes become wine, and visitors can walk through a small vineyard featuring several different varieties of wine grapes and even sample the grapes if the season is right. Extending from the building and overlooking the lake is a large deck, complete with tables and chairs. During good weather, umbrellas come out on the tables, and guests enjoy their picnic lunches, receptions, or brunches in a relaxed setting.

The California Welcome Center in Rohnert Park is a great stop for first-time visitors who want to get a feel for the region and collect maps and information. The vineyard outside offers an upclose look at how wine grapes are grown. PHOTO: JEAN SAYLOR DOPPENBERG

Sonoma County

The Napa and Sonoma valleys are separated by the Mayacmas Mountains, but much more distinguishes these two prime grape-growing regions. Napa, which enjoyed early prestige as a wine growing region, is often considered the glitzier cousin of the more down-home Sonoma. Yet, beneath Sonoma's rural charm is an elegance and sophistication that you can sample in both the wine and local culture.

But when people say they are going to visit "Sonoma," just which Sonoma do they mean? Are they talking about Sonoma County—one-and-a-half times the size of Rhode Island? Or are they referring to the smaller Sonoma Valley, Jack London's famed "Valley of the Moon," where Count Agoston Haraszthy fathered the California wine industry? Maybe they simply mean the town of Sonoma, the historic little pueblo nestled in the southeast corner of the county, and site of the state's last mission. (See our History and Area Overview chapters for more on all these incarnations of Sonoma.)

Sonoma County is home to at least 12 distinct wine-growing appellations and shares a 13th, Carneros, with Napa County. Saying that a wine comes from Sonoma doesn't really say enough to those who know their wines. There are differences—sometimes subtle, sometimes dramatic—among the same types of wine produced by different Sonoma County vintners in different appellations.

With the exception of the bluffs overlooking the Pacific and the cool redwood forests, grapes grow in almost every corner of Sonoma County. Major grape-growing areas include the Russian River, where ocean fog makes the climate ideal for Pinot Noir and Chardonnay and for an exceptional Sauvignon Blanc; Los Carneros, where wind and fog from San Pablo Bay create conditions that produce intensely flavored Pinot Noir and Chardonnay; Sonoma Valley, whose many microclimates are suited to many grape varieties; Alexander Valley, known for its Cabernet Sauvignon and Sauvignon Blanc; and Dry Creek Valley, where the wines have been earning much publicity and numerous gold medals of late.

The handsome, green countryside of the middle Russian River Valley is one of the county's largest viticultural areas, subject to heavy rainfall and considerable fog. White grapes predominate, and some wineries produce popular sparkling wines.

Thousands of acres of vines bask in the north county's rumpled hills and river bottomlands. Wineries range from small, family-operated enterprises where bottle labels still are applied by hand, to huge corporations where ageless winemaking skills are blended with computerized technology. Several years ago, seven small wineries got together to create the Russian River Wine Road, an informational program to tell the public about their scenic and uncrowded wine region. This pamphlet is available at many locations in the

Insiders' Tip

Some of Wine Country's back roads beckon bicycle enthusiasts, particularly the two-lane country roads of the Dry Creek and Alexander valleys in Sonoma County. Quail scurry across the paths, and swallowtail butterflies enjoy roadside tastings of their own. Caution is required, though, for the roads are narrow and curves frequent. In Napa County, Silverado Trail is ideal for bikes—the road is level, and a multitude of small side roads invite exploration. (See our Parks and Recreation chapter for more on bicycling in Wine Country.)

area, including the visitors bureaus in Healdsburg and Guerneville.

Some wine experts have been calling Sonoma County "a work in progress," though others beg to differ. Regardless of how you look at it, it is true that Sonoma's image is evolving. One current development in the winemaking fraternity of Sonoma County has been the relatively quiet genesis of E. & J. Gallo's Sonoma Series. Convinced that Sonoma is the place to grow the world's finest wines, the Gallos have been quietly accumulating hundreds of acres during the past 20 years. They are now one of the county's largest landowners, owning approximately 6,000 acres— about 3,000 of them currently planted in grape vines. Headquartered near Healdsburg, Gallo does not offer wine tasting (hence, no listing). The driveway entrance has a simple sign that reads PRIVATE PROPERTY, in English and Spanish.

Enough of background, let's get down to practicalities. If you have only one day to tour Sonoma County, you can't go wrong if you start in the Sonoma Valley. It is the closest of the premium wine-growing regions to San Francisco, only 45 minutes from the Golden Gate. Your tour might well begin with a stop at the Sonoma Valley Visitors Bureau (which is also the office of the Sonoma Valley Vintners and Growers Association) on Spain Street. It's next to the Sonoma State Historic Park headquarters, across the street from the lovely central plaza in the town of Sonoma (see our Attractions and History chapters). For an easy mix of shopping and browsing and wine tasting, walk around the square before taking a free trolley 3 blocks east for a winery tour and tasting at Sebastiani Vineyards.

If you are eager for some serious wine tasting, there are more than a half-dozen small- to medium-sized wineries within a 15-minute drive of the plaza. These include Ravenswood, known for its excellent Zinfandels; Buena Vista, which also has a tasting room on the plaza; Gundlach Bundschu; and Bartholomew Park Winery (all are listed in this chapter). If you are headed south to San Francisco from the town of Sonoma, you will travel through the Carneros region with its many wineries. Stop in at Viansa (which also has an outstanding deli) and Cline Cellars. If you are able to visit and taste the wines of even half the places mentioned, you will have had a full and enjoyable day. The big-name producers in the county include Sebastiani, Glen Ellen, Clos du Bois, and Korbel, but don't neglect the smaller wineries: Benziger, Kenwood, Foppiano, Hop Kiln, Martinelli, and so on.

Besides the wine itself, touring Sonoma County offers the sheer pleasure of driving along winding roads with views of vineyards and farms that alternate between the dramatic and the sweetly rural. From some mountaintops and parts of the Carneros district at the southern border, the skyline of San Francisco is visible on clear days (and nights).

Mendocino County

While not as well known as Sonoma or Napa, Mendocino County is gradually getting the word out about the Anderson Valley's extraordinary wines—originally an area of orchards and sheep and cattle ranches. Discovered during the 1970s as a fine growing area for wine grapes, this rolling land, drained by the Navarro River, has quickly become braided in long rows of Pinot Noir, Chardonnay, Gewurztraminer, and Zinfandel.

To prove to the world that Anderson Valley is the finest but least recognized Pinot Noir–producing region in the country, vintners there held the first annual "Pinot Noir Weekend" in May 1997 and promised annual renewals. Participating wineries offer vineyard and winery tours, a look at the history of growing Pinot Noir, and lots of tastings from both barrels and bottles.

If anyone deserved to be called the grandfather of Mendocino wine success, it would be Adolph Parducci. From Prohibition times until the end of the 1960s, Parducci Wine Cellars in Ukiah was one of the few—and at times the only—wine producer in the county. Parducci launched his operation in 1918, when fear of Prohibition was driving everyone else out of the business. He bought some casks, a crusher, and some elementary equipment and began making wine in an old barn in Cloverdale. He survived the Prohibition years in part because the law allowed home winemakers to have 200 gallons of "juice" for their own use.

By 1927 Parducci had pulled together enough money to buy some land in Ukiah Valley (now fondly called the Home Ranch) and planted 100 acres of grapes. From that time on, he and his four sons tended the vineyards, harvested the grapes, and built a winery. With the repeal of Prohibition in 1933, they opened a small tasting cellar in the basement of their home. Soon the charming family winery became a favorite stopping place for tourists. They'd sample from the spigot, have their jugs filled, and watch as the Parducci label was pasted on the bottle.

Another major player in Mendocino County wine is Fetzer, just off U.S. 101 in Hopland. In the 1950s, Bernard Fetzer bought vineyards in the Redwood Valley that had been established a century earlier by gold miner Anson Seward. Some of the vines actually dated back to Seward's earlier planting. During the next 10 years, Fetzer experimented with some Bordeaux-type varietals with considerable success, selling his Cabernet Sauvignon and Semillon wines by air freight to home consumers all over the country. The Valley Oaks Ranch, purchased by the Fetzer family in 1984, is now their headquarters.

If Parducci and Fetzer are the most easily recognized names, by no means do they stand alone. There are more than 35 other wineries in the Mendocino County area, producing an abundance of award-winning vintages. Of the county's 2.25 million total acres, just 14,000 acres are planted to vineyards—25 percent of that acreage is certified organic. Mendocino's wine regions are divided into six valley areas, each noted for the different varieties of grapes produced under slightly different climatic conditions. In the southeast areas of Sanel and McDowell valleys look for the wines of Fetzer, Milano, McDowell, Jepson, and Duncan Peak. Ukiah Valley lies farther north along U.S. 101, and it's here that some of the county's largest and oldest vintners make their home. Look for Hidden Cellars, Dunnewood, Parducci, Alam-

bic, Fremont Creek, Mendocino, Whaler, Domaine St. Gregory, and Zellerbach.

The Redwood and Potter valleys—the northern frontier of California's commercial grape-growing territory—are home to Redwood Valley Cellars. The Anderson Valley, featuring some of the most pleasingly quaint countryside in the state, is where you'll find Navarro, Husch, Greenwood Ridge, Christine Woods, Lazy Creek, Brutocao, Yorkville, Handley, Roederer, Claudia Springs, and Pepperwood Springs.

Lake County

Although agriculture has been the mainstay of Lake County's economy for decades, only some 7,000 acres are devoted today to wine grapes. Still, the wholesale value of the county's 1999 grape crop exceeded $19 million, nearly as much as the county's other big crop, pears. The prevailing varietals grown in this region include Cabernet Sauvignon, Merlot, Zinfandel, Chardonnay, Gewürztraminer, and Sauvignon Blanc.

Yet, for the relatively small number of acres, Lake County wines win plenty of coveted awards, and production of these premium varietals is expected to double in the next few years. You find some of the most respected names in the wine industry here, including Wildhurst, Guenoc Estate, and Steele. This is also the home of Roumiguiere Vineyards, primarily grape growers but also the producers of a downhome but delicious—and very limited availability—table wine called Bob's Really Good Red. Unfortunately, Roumiguiere has no tasting room for visitors. Fortunately, those of us who live in Wine Country can usually pick up an inexpensive bottle of Bob's at our neighborhood supermarket.

Certainly wineries are not new to the region. The first vineyard in Lake County was planted in 1872 near Lower Lake, and by the early 1890s as many as 36 wineries were producing award-winning wines within the county's borders. Prohibition put a stop to much of the activity, but by the 1960s production was once again on the upswing.

Lake County has one unique feature

most wine-growing regions don't: Guenoc Valley was the first single vineyard/single proprietor appellation established in the United States, and Guenoc Estate sits right in the heart of it. It was established in the late 1800s by famed actress Lillie Langtry, who brought in an expert winemaker from Bordeaux to oversee production. The home Lillie built is still on the property and is the site of many fundraisers and special events.

Wineries to Visit

With some 600 wineries to choose from in the four counties, you may wonder where to begin. To make your decision easier, we have not listed those that limit their hospitality to "appointment only." All the wineries we include are open regularly to the general public, although some do require appointments for tours. Complete, exhaustive lists of all wineries are available at the California Welcome Center or the Napa Valley Wine Library at 1492 Library Lane in St. Helena.

Nearly all Napa Valley wineries charge a fee for tasting—anywhere from $3.00 to $10.00—and these amounts can fluctuate depending on the wines being poured. (Reserve wines and library wines, if offered, can run a bit higher still.) The good news is, sometimes you get to keep the logo glass, and in most cases, the tasting fee can be applied toward the purchase of a bottle. Tasting in other counties is generally complimentary.

Wineries that produce sparkling wine (champagne) serve by the glass, and there is always a charge, with a couple of exceptions: Korbel Winery in Sonoma County has stated they will never charge to taste their product, and Frank Family Cellars south of Calistoga also pours gratis.

The list of wineries that follows only scratches the surface of the possibilities. You will no doubt find new favorites of your own as you tour the area. As done throughout the book, we arrange the winery listings in the geographical sequence explained in our How to Use This Book chapter. We begin with Napa County

wineries, followed by those in Sonoma, Mendocino, and Lake Counties.

Napa County

Domaine Carneros
1240 Duhig Rd., Carneros
(707) 257–0101
www.domaine.com

This imposing winery was inspired by the Louis XV-style Chateau de la Marquetterie in Champagne, country estate of the Taittinger family, which founded Domaine Carneros in 1987. The atmosphere is elegant and trés française, with a looming portrait of Madame de Pompadour in the main lobby. You can enjoy your beverage ($6.00 to $10.00 per glass, with complimentary hors d'oeuvres) in the salon or on the patio, which is swept by breezes off San Pablo Bay. Domaine Carneros offers three types of sparkling wine (Brut Cuvée, Blanc de Blancs, and Brut Rose) and its Famous Gate Pinot Noir. Free winery tours are at 11:00 A.M., 1:00 and 3:00 P.M. during the week, and hourly from 11:00 A.M. to 4:00 P.M. on weekends. On dry Friday mornings at 11:15, the winery offers vineyard tours that explain layout, planting techniques, and vine care. Cost of the vineyard tour is $10 and includes a tasting. Domaine Carneros is open daily from 10:30 A.M. to 6:00 P.M.

Carneros Creek
1285 Dealy Ln., Carneros
(707) 253–WINE

San Franciscan Francis Mahoney started a trend in 1972 when he established the first winery in Carneros after the repeal of Prohibition. Carneros was little more than lonely cattle land then, but its Bay-cooled hills are now coveted by grape growers. Carneros Creek is a modest, homey facility, with arbor-covered picnic tables in back that offer a view to magnificent Artesa. The winery's reputation is steeped in Pinot Noir, which still makes up 85 percent of its production. (It also produces Chardonnay.) The winery is open from 10:00 A.M. to 5:00 P.M. daily, and tours are by appointment. The tasting fee of $2.50 applies to purchase.

Holy Merlot, Batman!

Some of the wine-aging caves in Wine Country are so spectacular—with their chandeliers, velvet couches, artwork, and antiques—even millionaire Bruce Wayne would feel right at home. The tomb-like stillness of others may put you in mind of Poe's "The Cask of Amontillado"—minus the bones. Some caves swallow up entire wineries, such as Napa Valley's Jarvis Winery, carved into the Vaca Range some 1,000 feet over the valley floor. It is built entirely into the mountainside, and all winemaking functions take place underground.

But one thing is certain—more and bigger wine caves are on the way.

Many wineries have taken advantage of what nature left behind five million years ago: volcanic formations ideal for sculpting underground aging caves. The natural coolness of the rock maintains a temperature of 58 to 65 year-round, with humidity levels at 90 percent or above.

Napa Valley's first wine "caves" were actually tunnels excavated in the 1870s for Schramsberg Vineyards and a couple of decades later for Beringer Winery. Chinese laborers did most of the work, and these underground passages are still in use today for the wine-aging process.

Caves are now an essential part of winemaking at many wineries, and excavating bigger and longer tunnels and caves is becoming a more common component of the business plan in Wine Country. But caves don't just open up in the hillsides—they must be made. And that takes money, manpower, and lots of evil-looking machinery.

The "roadheaders" that typically crunch the rock are 32-ton behemoths with massive drilling heads that can carve out a tunnel 18 feet wide and 13 feet high in just one pass. Multiple passes are required for larger caves. The process requires patience, as it can be agonizingly slow. Some days the drills may make a dent of only 2 feet, depending on the soil type. When the rock just won't give, especially if big boulders are standing in the way, dynamite charges are set.

The cost of digging a tunnel is in the vicinity of $65–$120 per square foot, depending on complexity and frills—not unlike the expense of erecting an above-ground building. Similarly, caves must adhere to the same codes and restrictions—and earthquake standards—as regular buildings. Caves have become such a popular alternative to above-ground storage that the companies who do the drilling and the blasting—a rare breed, indeed—are booked for years to come.

In general, cave construction goes something like this: The roadheaders chew up the rock, the debris is moved out (and usually recycled in some fashion), and "shotcrete"—a mixture of cement, pea gravel, and sand—is liberally applied several inches deep on the tunnel walls and ceilings to keep out excess moisture. Steel frames are placed around entryways and exits. More shotcrete is heaped on. Electrical wiring is installed, then hidden by more shotcrete. The coating is then waterproofed and the cave is ready for barrels and visitors—usually in that order.

Some caves remain spartan and basic, while others get the Batman-meets-Baroque treatment.

In addition to the expanded storage space for aging wine, the caves hold a fascination for most visitors, and they make an exotic location for special events such as weddings and wine auctions. The aroma of oak and wine fermenting together adds

The 32,000 square feet of caves at Kunde Estate Winery & Vineyards perform double duty—storage for approximately 6,000 barrels of wine and a spacious tasting and dining room used for special events.
PHOTO: KUNDE ESTATE WINERY & VINEYARDS

drama and a heightened sense of privacy and exclusivity to what might otherwise be a ho-hum affair.

On the practical side, caves save wineries a bundle in air-conditioning costs, and the naturally high humidity discourages the water from evaporating from the barrels as it transpires alcohol into the air. That means the barrels stay fuller and more productive for the three years, on average, they are stacked underground.

The aforementioned Jarvis Vineyards facility is truly unique. Costing $20 million to construct over five years, it's the only winery in Napa Valley—and perhaps the world—where the wine is made completely in caves. The grapes are brought from the vineyards and taken underground into the 45,000-square-foot facility for crushing and fermenting. They will not be exposed to daylight again. The nectar is mixed, the barrels are stored, and the wine is bottled—all in the caves. This underground engineering phenomenon has more than 4 miles of tunnels and features a man-made river and waterfall to pump up enough humidity to rival a rain forest. One of the special events rooms is made entirely of quartz crystal and can accommodate up to 150 people. The winery is open for tours by appointment only; call (707) 255-5280 to inquire about visiting.

Other Napa Valley wineries with sensational caves to behold include Pine Ridge on Silverado Trail and Rutherford Hill on Rutherford Hill Road. Both offer daily cave tours that are well worth the effort.

When Pine Ridge began its cave construction in 1988, they struck gold in the process. An old gravel streambed was unearthed, revealing shiny flecks of the precious ore, which the owner had fashioned into a ring for his wife. The overall size of the Pine Ridge caves is a half-mile, or about 32,000 square feet. The floors of the caves were specifically built slightly cockeyed, so the wine rests at the proper angle for aging. Special events rooms and a kitchen are interspersed among 3,000 oak barrels. Leftover stone from the excavation was recycled to build the rock walls throughout the winery's picturesque vineyards.

At Rutherford Hill Winery, tunnels, galleries, and passageways extend for nearly a mile, with more than 8,000 barrels of French and American oak stacked neatly in rows.

The caves at Clos Pegase Winery feature an extensive kitchen and a raised stage for special events. Even 12th- and 13th-century antiques are on display in specially designed cavities. The intent was to create a fully functioning wine-aging facility that also resembles an ancient museum. Mission accomplished.

Jumping to Sonoma County, one of the best spots for cave-dwelling is Kunde Estate Winery & Vineyards. On the mountainside just a short walk from the tasting room, the cave doors open to reveal a long entryway that invites visitors to mosey back to the dining room and take in the aroma and ambience of the fermenting wine. This cave gained some notoriety a few years back when it was rented as part of the high-profile $1 million Wine Country weekend wedding extravaganza of an Academy Award–winning actress and her movie director fiancè. Though the locals still talk about that glitzy weekend—and the fabulous time had by all at the lavish cave wedding dinner—the marriage didn't age as well as the wine and ended shortly thereafter.

Other notable wine caves worth visiting are located at Steltzner Vineyards, near Napa, (707) 252–7272; Truchard Vineyards in Napa, (707) 253–7153; Stag's Leap Winery on the Silverado Trail, (707) 944–1303; Cuvaison Winery near Calistoga, (707) 942–6266; Vine Cliff Winery, between Yountville and Oakville, (707) 944–2388; Buena Vista Winery in Sonoma, (707) 933–1266; and the champagne caves at Gloria Ferrer near Sonoma, (707) 933–1931. It's always a good idea to call ahead to inquire about a cave tour, especially at the smaller wineries.

Artesa Winery
1345 Henry Rd., Carneros
(707) 224–1668

For a moment, if you can, forget Artesa's rich history and its world-class champagnes. Forget the 270-degree views of the Carneros hills and the small on-site museum with its 500-year-old wine casks. Those factors are more than enough to recommend Artesa, but the physical presence of the winery takes precedence. The building was designed by Barcelona architect Domingo Triay. Dug into the top of a hill, with native grasses planted over its sloping walls, it looks like a half-unearthed Mayan ruin—until you get inside, where the breezy central atrium and reflecting pools are nothing but modern elegance. Artesa is owned by Codorniu, one of the world's biggest producers of champagne, or cava. The Raventos family has been making wine since the 16th century (a Codorniu married a Raventos in 1659) and making methode

champenoise sparkling wine since 1872. The Napa outpost bottles three varieties, including the limited Reserve Cuvée, and you can try them for $4.00 to $6.00 per glass. It also offers Chardonnay, Cabernet Sauvignon, and Pinot Noir ($8.00 for six tastes). There are two free tours daily, and reservations are recommended. Artesa is open from 10:00 A.M. to 5:00 P.M. daily.

Monticello Vineyards
4242 Big Ranch Rd., Napa
(707) 253–2802, (800) 743–6668
www.silveradotrail.com

Proprietor Jay Corley is a big fan of Thomas Jefferson. So big, he named his winery Monticello and built a small-scale "Jefferson House," patterned after the founding father's Virginia mansion, to serve as the company's offices and culinary center. It's a pretty setting on Big Ranch Road, which heads north out of Napa city about halfway between Highway 29 and the Silverado Trail. There is a vivid rose garden and a shady picnic area called The Grove. Monticello makes Cabernet, Chardonnay, Merlot, Pinot Noir, champagne, and, weather permitting, a late-harvest Semillon. Monticello is open from 10:00 A.M. to 4:30 P.M. daily. Tours are at 10:30 A.M., 12:30, and 2:30 P.M. during the summer, by appointment otherwise. You can taste for $4.00.

Trefethen Vineyards
1160 Oak Knoll Ave., Napa
(707) 255–7700
www.trefethen.com

When Capt. Hamden McIntyre built the Eshcol winery in 1886, the three-story, wooden, gravity-flow architectural design was standard. Grapes were crushed on the third floor, fermented on the second, and stored at ground level. Today the old Eshcol building is the centerpiece of Trefethen Vineyards, and it's the last gravity-flow winery building in Napa Valley. Trefethen is a throwback in another way too: All of its grapes come from the surrounding vines, making it the valley's largest contiguous vineyard under single ownership. There are 600 acres of Chardonnay, Cabernet Sauvignon, Riesling, and Merlot plus gardens, walnut trees, and oaks. It was Eugene Trefethen, an executive for Kaiser (the massive construction firm responsible for, among other projects, Hoover Dam and the San Francisco-Oakland Bay Bridge), who bought the estate in 1968. His son, John, and John's wife, Janet, started the winery five years later. Trefethen is open from 10:00 A.M. to 4:00 P.M. daily. Tasting is complimentary, unless you opt for the Reserve package—four wines for $5.00.

The Hess Collection
4411 Redwood Rd., Napa
(707) 255–1144
www.hesscollection.com

The "collection" is a stunning assemblage of modern art (see our Arts and Culture chapter). The Hess is Donald Hess, the Swiss millionaire whose holdings include Valser St. Petersquelle, one of Switzerland's most popular mineral waters. Hess doesn't do anything halfway. In 1986 he leased Mt. LaSalle Winery, the Christian Brothers' original Napa Valley home, and set about renovating the 1903 bastion halfway up craggy Mount Veeder (the southernmost peak in the Mayacmas Mountains). The result is magnificent. Hess keeps it simple as far as the wines go, with Chardonnay and Cabernet Sauvignon, bottling both under The Hess Collection label and a second, lower-priced label called Hess Select. Hours are 10:00 A.M. to 4:00 P.M. There is a $3.00 tasting charge, and you can also ask to sample Valser, the aforementioned mineral water. Hess now owns some 900 acres on Mount Veeder and, since 1996, half of Glen Carlou, one of South Africa's best-known wineries.

Clos Du Val
5330 Silverado Trail, Napa
(707) 259–2200
www.closduval.com

Clos Du Val is French in more than name only. Founder John Goelet is descended from a distinguished Bordeaux wine merchant family, the Guestiers, and president/winemaker Bernard Portet is a sixth-generation vintner from the same French region. They crushed their first Napa Valley harvest together in 1972, and their ivy-covered, stone tasting room opened in 1983. It is open from 10:00 A.M. to 5:00 P.M. daily, and the tasting charge is $5.00 per person (refunded with purchase). Clos Du Val now produces seven wines, including its signature Reserve Cabernet Sauvignon. Almost as much as for its vintages, the winery is known for the series of whimsical, wine-related illustrations it commissioned from famed graphic satirist Ronald Searle in 1977. Tours are given by appointment, and you can picnic on the grounds.

Chimney Rock Winery
5350 Silverado Trail, Napa
(707) 257–2641, (800) 257–2641
www.chimneyrock.com

At the foot of the hills east of the Silverado Trail—including the outcrop from which it draws its name—is Chimney Rock, a stately white structure of Cape Dutch style, cloaked (in the summer) or picketed (in the winter) by a row of poplars. Ask if you can see the wine cellar, where resides a faithful reproduction of the Ganymede frieze depicting the gods' cup bearer atop a fierce eagle. The winery makes Fume Blanc, Chardonnay, and Cabernet Sauvignon. The tasting fee is $3.00, and the hours are 10:00 A.M. to 5:00 P.M. daily. Tours are by appointment.

Stag's Leap Wine Cellars
5766 Silverado Trail, Napa
(707) 944–2020
www.cask23.com

Stag's Leap founder Warren Winiarski was a liberal arts lecturer at the University of Chicago, but his destiny should have been clear: In Polish, "winiarski" means "from wine" or "winemaker's son." Founded in 1972, Stag's Leap was a little-known family winery until 1976, when it outshone the best of French Bordeaux in the famous Bicentennial tasting in Paris (see Close-up, "California is 'Discovered' in 1976," in this chapter). Since then it has been a Napa Valley landmark. The winery produces several types of wine, red and white, under both its own label and Hawk Crest, a line of accessible, reasonably priced wines crushed at other facilities. Its reputation, however, is staked upon Cabernet Sauvignon, especially the versions made from the Stag's Leap and Fay vineyards, including the world-renowned Cask 23. The winery is open from 10:00 A.M. to 4:30 P.M. daily. There is a $5.00 charge for tasting (you get to keep the glass) and free beverages for the designated driver. You can picnic in the shade of oaks. (Note: Stag's Leap Wine Cellars is not to be confused with Stags' Leap Winery or the Stags Leap District, all of which get their name from the rock outcropping that overlooks the scene.)

Pine Ridge Winery
5901 Silverado Trail, Napa
(707) 253–7500, (800) 575–9777
www.pineridgewinery.com

The pines aren't only high on the ridge. There is a grove of them surrounding the picnic area, making for a cool experience on a hot Napa day. Owner-winemaker Gary Andrus has been growing grapes since 1978. Pine Ridge currently produces Chardonnay, Chenin Blanc-Viognier, Cabernet Sauvignon, Cabernet Franc, Malbec, and Merlot. You can taste current releases for $5.00, sample five limited releases for $12.00, or enjoy two reserve reds for $10.00. Tours begin at 10:15 A.M., 1:00 and 3:00 P.M. and should be booked in advance. If you can't fit one of those into your schedule, investigate the Pine Ridge Demonstration Vineyard adjacent to the winery. It displays various combinations of rootstock, clone, and trellising apparatus—all you need to distinguish your Geneva double curtain from your traditional French double guyot. The winery is open 11:00 A.M. to 5:00 P.M. daily.

Steltzner Vineyards
5998 Silverado Trail, Napa
(707) 252–7272
www.steltzner.com

Dick and Christine Steltzner started making wines for bulk sale in 1977, and they opened their Silverado Trail winery in 1983. (The current structure was built in 1992.) Steltzner is noted for its reds, as are all labels within the Stags Leap appellation. Its wines include Cabernet Sauvignon, Claret, and a South African varietal called Pinotage. Steltzner is open 10:00 A.M. to 4:30 P.M. Monday through Saturday and noon to 4:30 P.M. on Sunday. Tasting is $3.00, and tours are by appointment.

Silverado Vineyards
6121 Silverado Trail, Napa
(707) 257–1770
www.silveradovineyards.com

This is no Mickey Mouse winery, despite ownership by Walt Disney's daughter, Diane Disney Miller, and Diane's husband, Ron Miller. (Walt's widow, Lillian, died in 1997.) It isn't a '90s-style corporate takeover, either, as the Millers are longtime Napa Valley denizens. Silverado offers great views above the Trail and a winery crafted of native stone and redwood. It made its reputation with Chardonnay but probably is best known these days for its estate-grown Cabernet Sauvignon. Tastings in the 5,000-square-foot room are

$7.00 for estate wines and $10.00 for three reserve wines. Silverado is open 10:30 A.M. to 5:00 P.M. daily, but tours are by appointment and take place at 11:00 A.M. and 2:00 P.M. on weekends.

Robert Sinskey Vineyards
6320 Silverado Trail, Napa
(707) 944–9090, (800) 869–2030
www.robertsinskey.com

This is another multigenerational operation, with founder Robert Sinskey, M.D., having passed the reins to his son, Rob. Sinskey Vineyards, which has been crushing grapes since 1986, is known for tackling Merlot and the tricky Pinot Noir, grown in the winery's Carneros vineyards. ("Heathens in the land of Cabernet," as they describe themselves.) Winemaker Jeff Virnig also creates small quantities of a half-dozen other varieties, including a Stags Leap District Claret and a Pinot Blanc. The cathedral-like winery combines Napa Valley stone and California redwood. There is a $5.00 fee for tasting (keep the glass), and you just might get a nibble from the Vineyard Kitchen. Tours are by appointment. Robert Sinskey is open from 10:00 A.M. to 4:30 P.M. daily.

Domaine Chandon
1 California Dr., Yountville
(707) 944–2280
www.dchandon.com

Domaine Chandon, child of world-renowned Moet-Hennessy, is a trendsetter. It was California's first French-owned winery (established in 1973), and the first to use the Champagne varietal Pinot Eunier in sparkling wine. It welcomes visitors to Le Salon, an open, terraced, cafe-style tasting room where you get samples ($8.00 for three cuvées, $12.00 for five) and complimentary hors d'oeuvres. Chandon's renowned tours run every hour (on the hour, except for opening and closing times), and they pretty much tell you everything you need to know about fermentation, aging, riddling, and disgorging. The scenic winery produces several types of sparkling wine plus brandy and pear liqueur. It recently completed a makeover of the entrance, tasting area,

Insiders' Tip

"Tours by appointment. No picnic facilities." You'll see those words a lot during your Wine Country stay—in this book, for instance. But as Dick Steltzner of Steltzner Vineyards points out, many newer wineries have to say that—it's standard verbiage in the use permits now issued by the County of Napa. (Older wineries retain the rights stated on their original permits.) What does it all mean? Only that it never hurts to ask. "By appointment" can mean inquiring five minutes before taking a tour. And wineries without official picnic grounds have been known to turn a blind eye to small groups bearing baskets of cheese.

and a downstairs retail store, and much of the grounds. Summer hours are 10:00 A.M. to 6:00 P.M. Monday and Tuesday, 10:00 A.M. to 8:00 P.M. Wednesday through Sunday; winter hours are 10:00 A.M. to 6:00 P.M. daily. See our Restaurants chapter for information on Chandon's exclusive eatery, or call the phone number listed to inquire about upcoming musical events.

Goosecross Cellars
1119 State Ln., Yountville
(707) 944–1986, (800) 276–9210
www.goosecross.com

Goosecross Cellars likes to refer to itself as a microwinery, and the feeling is unquestionably intimate on this lonely lane

California is "Discovered" in 1976

In 1976, it was a rare vintner who hung up a sign and opened a tasting room in Napa Valley. Who would stop, except to use the restroom? Still, le vin de Californie had its fans, and one of them was Steven Spurrier, an Englishman who had become one of Paris' most influential wine merchants. His Cave de Madeleine wine shop was highly regarded, and the courses offered at his Academie du Vin were standard curriculum for the French Restaurant Association's chefs and sommeliers.

That spring, Spurrier had visited dozens of wineries in Napa and Sonoma Counties and tasted scores of labels. He then proceeded to go out on a limb by proposing a blind taste test matching the best of France against the best of the United States. Many of Spurrier's chosen vintages had not even been tasted outside of California, much less on the East Coast, and some were barely known outside the Bay Area.

And yet on May 24, 1976, on a patio of the Hotel Intercontinental in Paris, six California Pinot Chardonnays (as they were called at the time) stood ready to butt bottles with four white Burgundies, and six California Cabernet Sauvignons stared down four Bordeaux reds.

The nine assembled judges were the crème de la crème in their line of work. Each jurist held before him or her a score card and, like some character from *Les Miserables,* a hard roll with which to clear the palate between entries. The judges were immediately able to distinguish between wines from either side of the Atlantic—or so they thought.

"That is definitely California. It has no nose," one judge proclaimed after downing a Batard Montrachet '73. Yet another judge, upon learning that the wine he had just given a mere 14 points (out of 20) was the revered Mouton Rothschild, quickly re-evaluated the wine's "finish" and changed his score to 18.

When all of the whites had been evaluated, the top-rated Chardonnay was a 1973 made by Chateau Montelena. It was everything the French deplore in a wine. Not only were the grapes picked from young vines, it was a blend of fruit from two different districts—blatant disregard for France's strict appellation code.

Still, the mood remained jovial when the white results were announced, for it is red wine that courses through the heart of French culture. Then came the shocking news: The number-one Cabernet was a 1973 from Stag's Leap Wine Cellars.

For the moment, Napa Valley occupied the highest point on the global landscape of wine. And the news couldn't have been more timely for the California wine industry, which was in the early stages of the region's most severe drought of the 20th century.

When news of the tasting reached Miljenko Grgich, then the winemaker at Montelena and now co-owner of Grgich Hills Cellar, at first he was confused; he wasn't aware his wines had been entered in a contest. And yet Grgich was not surprised. "We had the grapes, the cooperage, the art of winemaking, and the money" to stay apace with France's best, he explained.

Meanwhile, one prominent French grape grower characterized the event as a direct attack on his nation's wine industry. And no less than Baron Philippe de Rothschild phoned one unfortunate judge to ask, "What are you doing to my wines? It took me forty years to become classified as a premier grand cru!"

Two weeks later, word began to circulate among vinophiles about the competition, and *Time* magazine ran a short recap entitled "Judgment of Paris," a playful reference to the Greek legend in which Aphrodite was rewarded for her beauty. Brief as the article was, it touched off a frenzy. Wine stores and collectors swarmed Montelena and Stag's Leap in search of the victors. At the Wine and Cheese Center in San Francisco, a man lunged through the door of the sedate tasting room and pleaded, "Have you got any Montelena?!" A shop in New York received 400 calls in one day.

Nobody in Napa Valley got rich right away, but a small snowball had begun to roll down the slope of popular consciousness. California wines were about to enter a new age. In the mid-1970s producers earned about $150 million a year from non-jug wines; today it's more like $2.5 billion. Wine economist Jon Fredrikson calls the Paris tasting "a major turning point in consumers' attitudes" and a factor in the subsequent "staggering revolution in vineyard technology."

Apparently, the Smithsonian Institution agrees. In May 1996, the Smithsonian's National Museum of American History created a display to document the Paris tasting. One bottle each of Stag's Leap Wine Cellars' 1973 Cabernet Sauvignon and the Chateau Montelena 1973 Chardonnay are now part of the Institution's permanent collection.

Don't look for any similar competitions among the French and Americans in the near future. California wines have moved far beyond the point of having to prove themselves to anyone—even to the likes of a Baron Rothschild.

off the Yountville Cross Road. The winery was established in 1985 by college buddies David Topper, the CEO, and Geoff Gorsuch, the winemaker. ("Goosecross" is an Old English derivation of Gorsuch.) The Cellars are open 10:00 A.M. to 5:00 P.M. daily. They produce Chardonnay and Cabernet Sauvignon, in quantities that barely surpass 7,500 cases a year. If you have some free time Saturday from 11:00 A.M. until about 12:30 P.M., sign up for the acclaimed Goosecross Wine Basics class, a hands-on crash course designed to remove the "snobbery and mysticism" from grape appreciation. The free class includes a full tour of the vineyard and winery.

Cosentino Winery
7415 St. Helena Hwy. South, Yountville
(707) 944–1220
www.cosentinowinery.com

Mitch Cosentino crafts a variety of wines and sells them in an affable, low-key setting right next door to Mustards Grill (see our Restaurants chapter). Cosentino's Meritage reds stand out, as do his Merlots and Zinfandels. He also is no stranger to dessert wines. The winemaker prides himself on his "punched cap fermentation" process, a traditional, labor-intensive technique that involves continually dunking the floating grape skins (the cap) into the juice during fermentation. The $5.00 tasting charge applies to purchase, and you get a souvenir glass too. Cosentino is open 10:00 A.M. to 5:30 P.M. daily.

La Famiglia di Robert Mondavi
1595 Oakville Grade, Oakville
(707) 944–2811
www.lafamigliawines.com

You can call this one "The Winery Formerly Known as Vichon." Robert Mondavi purchased the facility in 1985, when it was five years old, and changed the name in 1997. It is now dedicated to the "First Family's" lineup of Italian varietals, including Sangiovese, Barbera, and Nebbiolo. The winery features an Italian marketplace and tasting room (free tastings) with lots of gift items, Tuscan ceramics, cookbooks, food, and clothing. Enjoy your wine and cheese in the shaded picnic area before embarking on the 2:00 P.M. tour offered daily. The views of the valley from the steep Oakville Grade are fabulous. The winery is open from 10:00 A.M. to 4:30 P.M.

Silver Oak Cellars
915 Oakville Cross Rd., Oakville
(707) 944–8808, (800) 273–8809
www.silveroak.com

Wine & Spirits' 1996 poll of restaurants determined that Silver Oak produced the most popular Cabernet Sauvignon in America. Their secret? Do one thing and do it well. Silver Oak is all Cabernet, all the time. The winery even follows a specific routine for all its vintages: For example, they use 100 percent Cabernet Sauvignon grapes and they ferment the wine for at least 30 months in American oak barrels. Silver Oak was founded in 1972 by Ray Duncan and Justin Meyer, who had recently abandoned his post as the Christian Brothers' Napa Valley winemaker. His company has two winery sites: one in Napa Valley at the site of the Oakville Dairy, and another in Alexander Valley in the old Lyeth Winery. The Oakville facility has a tasting room in an impressive masonry structure. It is open 9:00 A.M. to 4:00 P.M. Monday through Saturday. There is a $5.00 tasting charge, but the Shott souvenir glass is far superior to the usual handout. Tours are by appointment only, and because the tasting room can get swamped on summer Saturdays, the winery suggests arriving early or calling ahead on those days.

Robert Mondavi Winery
7801 St. Helena Hwy. South, Oakville
(707) 226–1395, (888) RMONDAVI
www.robertmondaviwinery.com

Here it is, the Yankee Stadium of American wineries, with Bob himself playing the part of Babe Ruth. More than any other individual, Robert Mondavi is credited with educating the world about the virtues of California wine. His innovations are prolific. He took a disregarded varietal known as White Pinot, changed the fermentation, and released it as Chenin Blanc; sales quintupled the next year. He almost single-handedly popularized Sauvignon Blanc by producing a drier version that he renamed Fume Blanc. Mondavi still actively promotes the industry, but sons Michael (president and CEO) and Timothy (wine grower) run the winery.

Robert Mondavi Winery is known for its wine-and-food programs, art exhibits (displayed in the Vineyard Room), and jazz and classical concerts. But most of all, it is known for its tasting tours. The most popular is the Vineyard and Winery Tour, offered several times daily at $10 per person. Other tours concentrate on educating visitors on the wine-growing and wine-making processes; these are in-depth, three- or four-hour tours that cost from $35 to $95 per person (including a picnic or sit-down luncheon) and require advance reservations. Tastings are available in three different rooms, including the new To Kalon Room, with historical photographs of the valley on display. Mondavi is open from 9:00 A.M. to 5:00 P.M. May through October, and 9:30 A.M. to 4:30 P.M. from November through April.

Opus One
7900 St. Helena Hwy. South, Oakville
(707) 944–9442
www.opusonewines.com

When Robert Mondavi and Baron Philippe de Rothschild announced their joint venture in 1979, it created quite a stir in the wine world. But it also added credence to what the French had recently discovered: California wines are among the best in the world. Though the Baron died in 1988, the business went forward and groundbreaking on this architectural masterpiece took place in 1989.

As you might expect from such a team of wine royalty, this is an elegant winery that produces one pricey product. Opus One is a big red wine—a blend that's predominantly Cabernet Sauvignon—that sells for $140 per bottle. You can try this hearty drink for $25 a taste in the winery's Partners' Room, which is open for visitors from 10:30 A.M. to 3:30 P.M. daily. A concierge greets you at the door and ushers you to the tasting room. Calling ahead is strongly recommended, as this show-place is frequently booked for private functions. One tour is offered per day, by appointment only, at 10:30 A.M.

Turnbull Wine Cellars
8210 St. Helena Hwy. South, Oakville
(707) 963–5839, (800) 887–6285
www.turnbullwines.com

Publisher Patrick O'Dell bought Turnbull Wine Cellars in the spring of 1993. The winery is just north of the Oakville Cross Road, and its vineyards are primarily contained within the Oakville Viticultural Area. Turnbull's production is about 10,000 cases per year, with most of it in Cabernet Sauvignon, along with Merlot, Syrah, Sauvignon Blanc, and Sangiovese. The facility, which features a collection of Ansel Adams prints, is open daily from 10:00 A.M. to 4:30 P.M.; tours are by appointment. The $5.00 tasting charge is refunded toward the purchase of wine.

Oakville Ranch Winery
7850 Silverado Trail, Oakville
(707) 944–9500

This group has been making wines since 1989 but has been in the hospitality business only since August 1996, when it purchased a 100,000-case facility on the Silverado Trail. (Oakville Ranch produces only about 4,500 cases per year; the site is also rented for custom crush.) The winery bottles under two labels: Oakville Ranch Vineyards, made 100 percent from estate fruit, is the premium line ($5.00 for tasting), while Oakville Ranch Cellars ($3.00) is a group of less expensive wines made from purchased grapes and sold only from the tasting room. The estate vineyards are at 1,000 feet, the highest in the Oakville appellation. Oakville Ranch produces many types, including award-winning Cabernets, fine Chardonnays, and Robert's Blend, a Cabernet Franc and Sauvignon composition named for Robert Miner, the winery's late founder and also a founder of Oracle Corporation. Oakville Ranch is open daily from 11:00 A.M. to 6:00 P.M. from April through October and 11:00 A.M. to 5:00 P.M. November to March. Tours are by appointment.

St. Supéry Vineyards & Winery
8440 St. Helena Hwy. South, Rutherford
(707) 963–4507, (800) 942–0809
www.stsupery.com

More than its intriguing historical setting and its rich lineup of wines, St. Supéry is known for its Wine Discovery Center. You can wander through the display vineyard and the exhibit gallery (the SmellaVision display is a "must-see") or sign up for a free guided tour. French businessman Robert Skalli's establishment is the only major winery to grow most of its grapes in isolated Pope Valley, beyond the hills to the east of Napa. St. Supéry (named for a previous owner of the property) has a lengthy list of wines, with all the standards plus surprises such as a dessert Moscato and a Zinfandel Rosé sold only at the winery. Skalli also produces kosher Chardonnay and Cabernet under the Mt. Maroma label. (Former Israeli Prime Minister Benjamin Netanyahu reportedly gushed over the stuff at a White House visit.) There is a $5.00 charge for sampling, but the glass is equivalent to a lifetime pass to the tasting room. The facility is open daily from 9:30 A.M. to 6:00 P.M. April through October and 9:30 A.M. to 5:00 P.M. November to March.

Peju Province Winery
8466 St. Helena Hwy. South, Rutherford
(707) 963–3600, (800) 446–PEJU
www.peju.com

Everything may look familiar as you head into Peju Province, as Herta Peju's prolific flower beds have been photographed for numerous garden magazines. Husband Tony sticks to winemaking, and his Cabernet Sauvignon has been winning awards. (He also makes Chardonnay, Cabernet Franc, Colombard, Merlot, a dry rosé and, occasionally, a late-harvest Chardonnay.) The Pejus opened their French Provincial-style facility in 1991 and produce about 15,000 cases a year. You can taste for $3.00, which applies to any purchase; tours are self-guided. Open daily from 10:00 A.M. to 6:00 P.M.

Niebaum-Coppola Estate Winery
1991 St. Helena Hwy. South, Rutherford
(707) 968-1100
www.niebaum-coppola.com

Yes, it's that Coppola, a winemaker almost as long as he has been a film-maker. Francis and his wife, Eleanor, purchased a lavish Victorian and prime acreage in 1975, then discovered the story behind the locale. The house was built in 1881 by Gustave Niebaum, a Finnish sea captain who founded Inglenook, perhaps the most respected winery in California before corporate raiders used the name to sell jug wine. Enchanted by the history, Coppola used the substantial profits from his film *Bram Stoker's Dracula* to reunify Niebaum's original estate in 1995. The purchase included the original chateau, which the director renovated (check out the staircase made from exotic Belizean hardwoods). It now houses the tasting room and a museum of wine and film. Coppola's five Oscars stand at attention on the second floor, along with the Don's desk and chair from *The Godfather,* an authentic Tucker automobile, costumes from the aforementioned *Dracula,* and other memorabilia from his work in film. Niebaum-Coppola releases several wines under the Francis Coppola Family Wines label, but is best known for Rubicon, its Cabernet Sauvignon-Merlot-Cabernet Franc Meritage that is made to last 100 years. Niebaum-Coppola is open daily from 10:00 A.M. to 5:00 P.M.; tours are conducted daily at 10:30 A.M. and 2:30 P.M. There is a $7.50 charge for tasting,

and you get to keep the glass. Designated drivers get free beverages.

ZD Wines
8383 Silverado Trail, Rutherford
(707) 963-5188
www.zdwines.com

ZD might be last on the alphabetical list, but it has been first elsewhere, such as the Los Angeles County Fair, where the 1996 Chardonnay was named Best of Class. And the label is clearly bipartisan—it has been served at the White House during three presidential administrations. This is a true family affair. Norman and Rosa Lee deLeuze cofounded the winery, and their three children have taken up the cause—Robert as winemaker, Brett as marketing director, and Julie as administrative director. ZD got its start in Sonoma County in 1969, then moved to Napa a decade later. Today it makes primarily Chardonnay, Pinot Noir, and Cabernet Sauvignon. Tasting is $5.00, which is refundable toward purchase. ZD is open from 10:00 A.M. to 4:30 P.M. daily, and tours (maximum 15 people) are by appointment.

Mumm Napa Valley
8445 Silverado Trail, Rutherford
(707) 942-3434, (800) 686-6272
www.mummnapavalley.com

The setting in Mumm's tasting salon is one of the most soothing in the valley, with a long wall of glass that faces uncluttered vineyard. (It's definitely the place to bring a date.) You can buy a glass of champagne for $3.00 to $6.50 or a "taster" of three samples for $7.50. Their Pinot Noir and Chardonnay are available only at the winery for tasting. They offer tours of the winery on the hour; the last stop is the photo gallery, which is reason enough to make a pilgrimage (see our Arts and Culture chapter). Mumm Napa Valley was launched in 1979, a co-venture between G. H. Mumm of France and Joseph E. Seagram and Sons of New York. The winery currently bottles three Bruts—Blanc de Blancs, Blanc de Noir, and Brut Prestige—and a vintage sparkler, DVX, its prestige cuvée. It is open 10:30 A.M. to 6:00 P.M. daily from April to October and 10:00

A.M. to 5:00 P.M. daily from November through March.

Beaulieu Vineyard
1960 St. Helena Hwy. South, Rutherford
(707) 967-5230
www.bvwine.com

The oldest continuously producing winery in Napa Valley? It isn't Charles Krug or Beringer. It's Beaulieu, which was founded by Georges de Latour in 1900 and survived Prohibition by turning out sacramental wines. By 1940 Beaulieu might have been the nation's most famous winery, a status no doubt aided by de Latour's recruitment of young, Russian-born enologist Andre Tchelistcheff, who was more or less the Luther Burbank of the wine industry. The current director of winemaking, Joel Aiken, has pioneered new cellaring and vine management programs, and he oversees a lengthy list of varieties. The Napa Series is made up of Cabernet Sauvignon, Chardonnay, Pinot Noir, Sauvignon Blanc, Zinfandel, and Merlot; the Signet Collection includes everything from Viognier to Pinot Gris. (The Georges de Latour Private Reserve Cabernet, hunted by collectors, remains BV's benchmark product.) Tasting is $5.00, or for $18.00 you can sample five of Beaulieu's top-tier wines. Beaulieu is open from 10:00 A.M. to 5:00 P.M. daily, with tours every hour between 11:00 A.M. and 4:00 P.M.

Grgich Hills Cellar
1829 St. Helena Hwy. South, Rutherford
(707) 963-2784
www.grgich.com

The Grgich is Miljenko Grgich. The Hills, you might be surprised to learn, is a reference not to the rugged terrain around Rutherford, but rather to Austin Hills of the Hills Bros. coffee family. Hills added his business acumen to Grgich's winemaking skills back in 1977, and they have been making tasty wines ever since. Grgich Hills is known for its buttery, creamy Chardonnay, though it also produces Sauvignon Blanc, Zinfandel, Cabernet Sauvignon, and a late-harvest dessert wine. Visitors may purchase library wines, which are available only at the winery. Two by-appointment tours are offered daily: 11:00 A.M. and 2:00 P.M. on weekdays, 11:00 A.M. and 1:30 P.M. on weekends. Tasting costs $3.00 on weekends, and that includes the glass; it's free during the week. Grgich Hills is open 9:30 A.M. to 4:30 P.M. daily.

Villa Mt. Eden Winery
Conn Creek Winery
8711 Silverado Trail, St. Helena
(707) 963-9100
www.stimson-lane.com

You can break two bottles of wine with one stone here. The Silverado Trail tasting room houses Villa Mt. Eden and Conn Creek, sister wineries owned by Stimson Lane Vineyards of Woodinville, Washington. Villa Mt. Eden is descended, however tenuously, from Mt. Eden Vineyards, established in 1881 as the 11th bonded winery in Napa Valley. It now produces seven basic varietals, including Cabernet Sauvignon, Chardonnay, Zinfandel, and Pinot Noir. Volume increased after the recent purchase of more than 400 vineyard acres, 237 in the Stags Leap area and another 192 in Monterey County. There is no tasting fee, hours are 10:00 A.M. to 4:00 P.M. daily, and tours are by appointment. Conn Creek bottles a tiny amount of reserve wines, primarily Cabernet and a Meritage.

Beaucanon Winery
1695 St. Helena Hwy. South, St. Helena
(707) 967-3520

If this built-in-1987 winery looks like it was transported from Bordeaux, with its vaulted ceilings and unpartitioned interior, it's no accident. Beaucanon is owned by the de Coninck family, which owns some 15 chateaux in France. Siblings Louis and Chantal de Coninck run the California operations, bottling Chardonnay, Cabernet Sauvignon, and Merlot under two lines, Beaucanon Napa Valley and La Crosse Napa Valley. There is no tasting charge. Beaucanon is open daily from 10:00 A.M. to 5:00 P.M.

Franciscan Oakville Estate
1178 Galleron Rd., Rutherford
(707) 963–7111
www.franciscan.com

This is part of the spreading Franciscan Estate empire, which also includes Mount Veeder Winery and Quintessa in Napa County, Estancia in Sonoma and Monterey, and Veramonte in the Casablanca Valley in Chile (the homeland of owner Augustin Huneeus). Outside the winery, which is right off Highway 29, you'll encounter the Rutherford Bench, a tongue-in-cheek reference to a local geologic feature. Inside the newly renovated visitor center you can taste wine from Franciscan and Mount Veeder. It's $4.00 for a basic tasting, $7.00 for reserve wines, and either applies to any purchase. Operating hours are 10:00 A.M. to 5:00 P.M. daily. Franciscan specializes in Cabernet Sauvignon, Merlot, and Cabernet Franc, with all the grapes for Magnificat (a Meritage blend) coming from its 240-acre estate in the heart of the Oakville appellation. It also sets itself apart through its experiments in "wild" yeast fermentation, using the native yeast of each vineyard to help ferment those particular grapes. The winery's Cuvée Sauvage Chardonnay is 100 percent wild yeast, barrel fermented.

Rutherford Hill Winery
200 Rutherford Hill Rd., Rutherford
(707) 963–7194, (800) MERLOT–1
www.rutherfordhill.com

Rutherford Hill produces numerous varietals (including a Zinfandel Port), but the name has become nearly synonymous with Merlot. It's also known as one of the most pleasant places to visit, with picnic grounds amid shady oaks and olive trees, and stunning views of Napa Valley. (Because of its popularity, you might think about calling ahead to reserve a table.) The winery was founded in 1976, then purchased by wine importer and buyer Anthony Terlato in 1996. Rutherford Hill's wine caves are said to be some of the most extensive in America, with nearly a mile of tunnels, galleries, and passageways. The caves are the main fea-

The new tasting room and visitor center at Franciscan Oakville Estate is an impressive sight along Highway 29 in Napa Valley. PHOTO: JEAN SAYLOR DOPPENBERG ture of the tours given three times daily during the week (11:30 A.M., 1:30 and 3:30 P.M.), and five times on weekends (add 12:30 and 2:30 P.M.). Normal tasting is $4.00, and you leave with the glass; or you can pay $8 for the reserve tasting. Regular hours are 10:00 A.M. to 5:00 P.M. daily.

Rutherford Hill hosts a regular "Blending in the Caves" class for small groups to learn the basic principles of making wine. In fact, you get to create your very own blend to take home in a bottle. It's offered by reservations only, so call ahead to inquire about dates.

Raymond Vineyard & Cellar
849 Zinfandel Ln., St. Helena
(707) 963–3141, (800) 525-2659
www.raymondwine.com

Proprietors Roy Jr. and Walter Raymond get their last name from their father (Roy Sr.) and their winemaking skills from both sides of the family tree. Their mother was the former Martha Jane Beringer, granddaughter of the famed Jacob Beringer. The family played an active part at Beringer until 1971, when they established this winery. Now Roy Jr.'s son Craig and Walter's daughter Krisi have joined the team. Raymond has a strong reputation for Chardonnay and Cabernet Sauvignon, though it also bottles Sauvignon Blanc, Merlot, and Pinot Noir. It produces under four distinct brands: Amberhill, Raymond Estates, Raymond Napa Valley Reserve, and Raymond Generations. The winery's Napa Valley vineyards are supplemented by a large Chardonnay plot in Monterey County, on the Central Coast. All told, Raymond owns more than 500 acres. Tasting is free, though you can request a library wine for $2.50. The facility is open from 10:00 A.M. to 4:00 P.M. daily, but tours are by appointment.

Milat Vineyards
1091 St. Helena Hwy. South, St. Helena
(707) 963–0758, (800) 54–MILAT
www.milat.com

This is another intimate, family-run winery, 2 miles south of St. Helena. The Milats have been growing and selling grapes to Napa Valley wineries since 1949, and in 1986 they finally decided to affix their own label. Brothers Bob and Mike Milat (with wives, Joyce and Carolyn) wear all the hats. Milat bottles Chardonnay, Chenin Blanc, Zinfandel, Cabernet Sauvignon, and a blush table wine called Zivio, selling the bulk of their production from the tasting room. Milat is open 10:00 A.M. to 6:00 P.M. daily. The $2.00 tasting fee includes a souvenir glass or wine credit.

V. Sattui Winery
1111 White Ln., St. Helena
(707) 963–7774
www.vsattui.com

If you have made a few trips to Napa Valley, you probably know V. Sattui as the place with all the picnickers. It's a favorite for itinerant eaters, primarily because of an ample, shady picnic area and well-stocked deli featuring homemade items. Daryl Sattui is a fourth-generation winemaker, the great-grandson of Vittorio Sattui, who founded the business in 1885. Daryl's current wine list is immense, with two Chardonnays, two Johannisburg Rieslings, two Zinfandels, four Cabernet Sauvignons, and many others, all of them sold exclusively at the winery. V. Sattui offers self-guided tours and does not charge for tasting. The winery is open daily from 9:00 A.M. to 6:00 P.M. in summer and 9:00 A.M. to 5:00 P.M. in the winter.

Whitehall Lane Winery
1563 St. Helena Hwy. South, St. Helena
(707) 963–9454
www.whitehalllane.com

As wineries go, this one is a youngster in Napa Valley. The Leonardini family of San Francisco purchased Whitehall Lane Winery from foreign investors in 1993 and brought in new equipment, a new barrel program, and plans for expanding production and acquiring vineyards. It now owns more than 100 acres of vineyards in Napa Valley and produces award-winning Sauvignon Blanc, Chardonnay, Merlot, and Cabernet Sauvignon. There's even an orange muscat dessert wine, Belmuscato. Located just north of the Ink House Bed &

The unique exterior of Whitehall Lane Winery is a standout along Highway 29 in Napa Valley. PHOTO: JEAN SAYLOR DOPPENBERG

Breakfast Inn, the tasting room is open from 11:00 A.M. to 6:00 P.M. daily. Barrel tasting tours are by appointment only.

Heitz Wine Cellar
436 St. Helena Hwy. South, St. Helena
(707) 963–3542

The winery you visit is not the current Heitz facility, but rather the original facility opened by Joe and Alice Heitz in 1961. They now do their winemaking at a 160-acre holding on Taplin Road, just east of St. Helena, aided by two of their children: David is the vice president and winemaker, Kathleen is chief operating officer. The winery built its reputation on Chardonnay, though now it is known more for its Cabernet Sauvignon. Three special Cabs are vineyard-designated: Martha's Vineyard (near Oakville), Bella Oaks Vineyard, and Trailside Vineyard (both near Rutherford). Heitz also makes Zinfandel and Napa Valley's only Grignolino, a light red. There is no charge for tasting. Heitz is open 11:00 A.M. to 4:30 P.M. daily.

Prager Winery & Port Works
1281 Lewelling Ln., St. Helena
(707) 963–PORT, (800) 969–PORT
www.PragerPort.com

Prager makes Chardonnay and Cabernet but is really known for its Port, which accounts for about 85 percent of production. One of the top sellers is the Royal Escort Port, produced from Petite Sirah grapes. Jim and Imogene Prager ditched a commercial insurance business in Orange County and founded the winery in 1980, and they have been joined by children John, Jeff, Peter, and Katie. Prager's facilities are inside an old carriage house, part of the John Thomann Winery and Distillery, constructed in 1865. The intimate tasting room is plastered with money donated by visitors—everything from Indonesian rupiah to Toys R Us Geoffrey dollars. There is a picnic table in front of the winery, and the $5.00 tasting fee can be applied to purchase. Prager is open daily from 10:30 A.M. to 4:30 P.M.

Sutter Home Winery
277 St. Helena Hwy. South, St. Helena
(707) 963–3104
www.sutterhome.com

What was once a small, family-run winery is now a gigantic family-run winery, the nation's fourth-largest (and the number-one table-wine brand name), thanks to unqualified marketing genius. The facilities date back to 1874, the name to 1906, when the new Swiss-American co-owner named it after her father, John A. Sutter (not to be confused with the California pioneer of the same name). Sutter Home has been owned by the Trincheros since 1947, and the family gets credit (or blame, depending on your outlook) for inventing white Zinfandel—which it originally called Oeil de Pedrix, "Eye of the Partridge"—in the 1970s. More recently, the winery introduced innovations such as 187-milliliter, "single-service" bottles and VinLoc seals, an aluminum alternative to traditional cork, and launched a fruit-flavored line of wines called Portico. Sutter Home has numerous vineyards in Napa and Lake counties but grows the bulk of its grapes in the Sacramento Valley, Sacramento Delta, and Sierra foothill regions. The company produces nine varieties of wine beyond the Zinfandel plus Fre, the best-selling nonalcoholic wines in America. They even make seven types of pasta sauce! There is no charge for tasting (the wine, that is). The facility is open daily, from 10:00 A.M. to 5:30 P.M. in the summer and 10:00 A.M. to 4:30 P.M. in the winter.

Louis M. Martini Winery
254 St. Helena Hwy. South, St. Helena
(707) 963–2736, (800) 321–WINE
www.louismartini.com

Louis M. was an Italian immigrant, born near Genoa, who founded the L. M. Martini Grape Products Co. in Kingsburg, California, in 1922. The "Grand Old Man" built his Napa Valley winery 11 years later, and it's still in the family, now headed by his grandchildren, Carolyn and Michael Martini. The company's vineyards are far-flung, stretching from Sonoma Valley to the Russian River Valley to Lake County to Chiles Valley to Pope

Valley (two areas in eastern Napa County). The winery makes a wide range of wines, from Cabernet Sauvignon to Barbera to Merlot. It also produces cream sherry and dry sherry. There are picnic grounds at the facility, which is open from 10:00 A.M. to 4:30 P.M. daily, and production tours are offered (call for the schedule). You can taste current releases for free, or pay $6.00 for library wines and get a souvenir glass.

Merryvale Vineyards
1000 Main St., St. Helena
(707) 963–7777, (800) 326–6069
www.merryvale.com

Merryvale is hard to miss, as it sits in Sunny St. Helena. That's not a reference to the town, but to the old winery that dates back to the 1930s. The stolid stone structure took new life when it was founded as Merryvale by four partners (the same four who started San Francisco's Pacific Union Realty) in 1983. And then Merryvale was purchased by the Swiss family Schlatter in 1996. The facility produces several varietals, including Chardonnay, Cabernet Sauvignon, Merlot, and a dessert wine called Antigua. The tasting charge is $3.00 for the standard choices, $5.00 for reserve wines, and $10.00 for a special "prestige" selection. There are no tours, but Merryvale does offer wine component tasting seminars every Saturday and Sunday at 10:30 A.M. Cost is $10.00, and reservations are recommended. The facility is open from 10:00 A.M. to 6:30 P.M. daily.

Beringer Vineyards
2000 Main St., St. Helena
(707) 963–7115
www.beringervineyards.com

Just as you pass through the "Row of Elms" that forms a canopy over Highway 29 just north of St. Helena, what you'll see to the west is Beringer Wine Estates, arguably the most majestic of all Napa Valley wineries. Beringer produces a half-dozen wines that vary from high-quality to high-volume. The tours, which run every half-hour and last about 45 minutes, are extremely popular. For a $5.00 fee, it

A Wine Tasting Primer

During your enological experience, remember that the pleasure of wine comes from several senses—sight, smell, taste, and touch. Here are a couple of suggestions to keep you from feeling completely lost during your first winery adventures. (Rest assured that you will learn much more as you travel from tasting room to tasting room).

Sight: Hold the glass to the light and enjoy the wine's color.

Smell: Swirl the wine gently in the glass to release its fragrances. Sniff sharply to carry the aroma to the nerve ends high in the nose.

Taste: Take a drink and roll it in your mouth to reach all the taste bud areas. Connoisseurs learn to draw in air over the wine still in their mouth. It looks silly, but it carries fumes to the nasal cavity, where most of the subtle olfactory differences emerge. Try to pick out tastes that are familiar to you, such as berry or pepper.

Touch: Chew the wine, just as if you were munching on some mashed potatoes. Note the amount of astringency present and get its "feel."

Aftertaste: Swallow the wine and note the taste sensations remaining, also known as "the length." The aftertaste should always be pleasant, though it's often quite different from your first impression upon sipping.

---

includes an excursion into the wine caves tunneled into the hillside, and a finale in the tasting room, where you receive mouthfuls of three or four different wines. You can also choose to pay for a tasting of reserves ($2.00 to $7.00) in the Founders Room. The winery's Rhine House, the impressive structure that grabs your attention from the highway, is a preserved historical landmark built by Jacob and Frederick Beringer in 1876. The tasting room, with its pine floors and slate roof, was Frederick's mansion. Beringer is open from 10:00 A.M. to 6:00 P.M. daily April through October, and from 10:00 A.M. to 5:00 P.M. November through March.

Charles Krug Winery
2800 Main St., St. Helena
(707) 967–2200

There is a lot of history working at this 19th-century structure. It was Napa Valley's first winery, founded in 1861 by the eponymous Prussian immigrant, political theorist, and editor of *Staats Zeitung*, the Pacific Coast's first German-language newspaper. Charles Krug, the winery, also shares the history of the Mondavi family,

that dynasty of California winemaking. Cesare Mondavi bought Krug in 1943; his wife, Rosa, took over upon Cesare's death in 1959, and their son, Peter, became general manager in 1966. Now Peter's sons, Marc and Peter Jr., oversee most of the winery's operations, including the winemaking, marketing, and sales. Charles Krug bottles at least 10 varieties of wine, including the full-bodied Vintage Selection Cabernet Sauvignon and Generations, a traditional Bordeaux blend. The facility is open daily from 10:30 A.M. to 5:30 P.M., and tours are at 11:30 A.M., 1:30 and 3:30 P.M. There is a $3.00 charge for tasting ($5.00 for reserves.)

Markham Vineyards
2812 St. Helena Hwy. North, St. Helena
(707) 963–5292
www.markhamvineyards.com

The fortress north of St. Helena, with its fountains and eucalyptus trees, has seen a lot of change in its 120-plus years. It was built of stone quarried from nearby Glass Mountain by Bordeaux immigrant and failed prospector Jean Laurent in 1874, but it was used for bulk wines until 1977, when the winery was purchased by Bruce Markham. He sold the business 11 years later to Mercian, Japan's largest wine company. And in 1993, the winery officially reopened after a multimillion-dollar renovation that included restoration of Markham's 6,000-square-foot stone cellar. The tasting is not in the old structure, but rather in a new addition on its north side. There is a $3.00 fee for four white wines, $5.00 for four reds. Markham's Merlot, Sauvignon Blanc, and Chardonnay all, at various times, have been rated number one in the state by *Wine Spectator*. Their less expensive Glass Mountain Quarry wines have also received accolades. Markham is open daily from 10:00 A.M. to 5:00 P.M.

St. Clement Vineyards
2867 St. Helena Hwy. North, St. Helena
(707) 967-3033, (800) 331-8266
www.stclement.com

The St. Clement winery is eye-catching anytime, but especially at night, when the pristine yellow Victorian is bathed by floodlights. The house dates to 1878, when it became Johannaburg winery, the eighth in Napa Valley. It was a private residence for most of the 20th century, until Dr. Bill Casey started St. Clement in 1975. The winery bottles five varietals and is best known for its Carneros Chardonnay and Cabernet Sauvignon. The $2.00 tasting charge applies to any purchase. St. Clement is open from 10:00 A.M. to 4:00 P.M. daily. They give daily tours at 10:00 A.M. and 2:00 P.M., but you must make reservations. If you are feeling flushed as you leave, use it as an excuse to sit on the porch swing on the veranda—you'll want to stay there all day.

Freemark Abbey Winery
3022 St. Helena Hwy. North, St. Helena
(707) 963-9694, (800) 963-9698
www.freemarkabbey.com

No, Freemark Abbey was never home to a group of wine-mad monks. The name comes from a triumvirate that purchased the winery in 1939: Charles Freeman, Markquand Foster, and Albert (Abbey) Ahern. Long before that (starting in 1886, to be exact), the winery was known as

Tychson Hill, named for California's first female vintner, Josephine Tychson. The current winemaker (and managing partner), Ted Edwards, concentrates on several varietals: Cabernet Sauvignon, Chardonnay, Merlot, Petite Sirah, Sangiovese, Viognier, and Johannesburg Riesling. Among those are three esteemed single-vineyard wines—Cabernet Bosche, Sycamore Vineyards Cabernet Sauvignon, and Carpy Ranch Chardonnay. You also should keep an eye out for the Edelwein Gold, a Sauterne-like dessert wine made only when conditions are right (10 times since 1973). The facility is open daily from 10:00 A.M. to 6:00 P.M. There are regular tours at 11:00 A.M. every day, and the $4.00 tasting fee includes the souvenir glass.

Folie à Deux Winery
3070 St. Helena Hwy. North, St. Helena
(707) 963-1160, (800) 473-4454
www.folieadeux.com

Give this one extra credit for a sense of humor. "Folie à deux" is a French term that means "shared madness of two." It's a psychiatric diagnosis that the original owners, two mental health professionals, found appropriate. They even requisitioned a logo that resembles a Rorschach inkblot. You don't have to be not-all-there to enjoy Folie à Deux's wines, however. Winemaker Scott Harvey is one of the best in the business, and his broad selection includes Sangiovese, Cabernet Sauvignon, and Muscat. He also makes a special Amador Zinfandel from the oldest Zin vines in California, those of the 1870s Grandpere Vineyard. There is no charge for a sampling of five basic wines or for a cave tour (Friday, Saturday, and Sunday, at 11:00 A.M. and 1:00 P.M.). You can sample reserve wines for $5.00. The tasting room, in a century-old farmhouse, recently had a facelift, and there are picnic grounds overlooking the vineyards. The winery is open from 10:00 A.M. to 5:00 P.M. daily.

Rombauer Vineyards
3522 Silverado Trail, St. Helena
(707) 963-5170

If the name rings a bell, think of food, not wine. Vintner Koerner Rombauer's great aunt, Irma Rombauer, has been in practically every kitchen in America. She's the author of *The Joy of Cooking*. Koerner makes six types of wine, including two—a Cabernet Franc and a Zinfandel—sold only from the tasting room. There is no charge for tasting. Rombauer is at the end of a long, steep driveway, and its views of the Napa Valley floor are hard to match—you should think about taking advantage of the picnic tables. It is open from 10:00 A.M. to 5:00 P.M. daily.

Wermuth Winery
3942 Silverado Trail, Calistoga
(707) 942–5924

When you consider great winemakers, you naturally think of, uh, Newfoundland. That's where Ralph Wermuth is from anyway, and his small upvalley winery has been making drinkable vintages since 1981. The wines are all dry, all crushed from Napa Valley grapes such as Colombard and Gamay, and all sold only on the premises. The $1.00 tasting fee is refundable with purchase, and you can get a quick tour of the facilities if you arrange it in advance. Wermuth is open daily from 11:00 A.M. to 5:00 P.M., though Ralph is forced to close shop for errand runs on occasion.

> ## Insiders' Tip
> Don't leave that case of Reserve Cabernet baking in the trunk of your rental car as you move from one tasting room to the next. If you bought it at Merryvale Vineyards in St. Helena, they will deliver it to your hotel (within Napa Valley) the same day—no charge.

Frank Family Cellars
1091 Larkmead Ln., Calistoga
(707) 942–0859

This one isn't as gargantuan as some of Napa's other champagneries, but it's a treat for visitors: a sublime spot on one of the valley's less-traveled crossroads, a charming picnic area behind the 1906 stone building, on the National Registry of Historic Places, and sparkling and still wines sold only on the premises. The winery was known as Larkmead Cellars back in the old days, when it produced still wines, then was operated as Hans Kornell Champagne Cellars. The champagne line includes Blanc de Blancs, Blanc de Noirs, Brut, and Rouge. There is no charge for tasting. The winery is open daily from 10:00 A.M. to 5:00 P.M.

Schramsberg Vineyards and Cellars
1400 Schramsberg Rd., Calistoga
(707) 942–4558
www.schramsberg.com

When Richard Nixon and Chinese Premier Chou En-Lai raised a glass of bubbly for their "Toast to Peace" in 1972, it was a 1969 Schramsberg Blanc de Blancs they sipped. That was only one of the historic milestones marked by a one-of-a-kind winery. German immigrant Jacob Schram founded the business on Diamond Mountain in 1862, planting the first hillside vineyards in Napa Valley. Schram developed a good reputation, but the operation had crumbled by the time Jack and Jamie Davies (and their investors) purchased the property in 1965.

Jack and Jamie set about restoring Schram's old house and gardens and, most importantly, devoting the winery to champagne production. They were the first Californians to use Chardonnay and Pinot Noir grapes, the traditional Champagne varietals, in their sparkling wines, and their place in Wine Country history is now cemented. Schramsberg makes six types of champagne, including the world-renowned J. Schram prestige cuvée. You must book a tour to taste—three releases for $7.50 or $15.00 per glass for library selections. To find Schramsberg, which is open daily from 9:30 A.M. to 4:30 P.M., turn onto Peterson Drive from Highway 29, about 3 miles south of Calistoga.

Dutch Henry
4300 Silverado Trail, Calistoga
(707) 942–5771, (888) 224–5879
www.dutchhenry.com

The two families that own Dutch Henry, Chafen and Phelps, run it like a mom-and-pop winery. (There is no relation to famous vintner Joseph Phelps—"unfortunately," says winemaker Scott Chafen.) They pour in the cellar, and a tour consists of looking in different directions while you get the lowdown. The winery, named for nearby Dutch Henry Canyon, produces only about 3,000 cases a year, and its line includes Chardonnay, Zinfandel, Merlot, Cabernet, Syrah, and Pinot Noir. Dutch Henry does no distribution away from the winery. There has never been a tasting charge, except for groups. The winery is open from 10:00 A.M. to 4:30 P.M. daily.

Stonegate Winery
1183 Dunaweal Ln., Calistoga
(707) 942–6500
www.stonegatewinery.com

Stonegate is less heralded and less imposing than its Dunaweal neighbors, Sterling and Clos Pegase (see next listings). Founded in 1973, it is now owned by California Wine Company, which also runs Bandiera Winery, near Cloverdale. Stonegate gets many of its grapes from the Calistoga area. It plucks Sauvignon Blanc from the vineyard around the winery, and Merlot and Cabernet Sauvignon from its plantings in Chiles Valley. Tasting is free. Stonegate provides tours and picnic tables and is open daily from 10:30 A.M. to 4:30 P.M.

Sterling Vineyards
1111 Dunaweal Ln., Calistoga
(707) 942–3345, (800) 726–6136
www.sterlingvineyards.com

The Napa uninitiated can be forgiven for unfailingly asking, "Is that a monastery up on the hill between St. Helena and Calistoga?" Not exactly. It's Sterling Vineyards, with its white stucco, Ionic-style architecture and knoll-top regality. Wine tasting here literally has been elevated to an event. A gondola takes you to the top of the hill, where you are free to sip samples, wander on a self-guided tour, and gaze upon antique wine-related artifacts and artwork by Picasso and Renoir. Wide-angle views of the valley are worth the trip up the hill. It's $6.00 for the whole experience ($4.00 for children 5 to 21, free for tots). Most of Sterling's production falls among four wines—Cabernet Sauvignon, Chardonnay, Sauvignon Blanc, and Merlot, including several vineyard-designated versions. It also bottles small lots of lesser-known wines that it sells only at the winery, such as Malvasia Bianca and Charbono. Sterling was founded by English paper broker Peter Newton in 1964, sold to Coca-Cola in 1977, then to Joseph E. Seagram and Sons in 1983. Newton left behind a Brit legacy—the old bells of St. Dunstan's Church, which chime on the half-hour. Sterling is open every day from 10:30 A.M. to 4:30 P.M.

Clos Pegase
1060 Dunaweal Ln., Calistoga
(707) 942–4981
www.clospegase.com

Jan Shrem's winery is named for the winged horse Pegasus, whose hooves are said to have unleashed the Spring of the Muses, bringing both wine and art to the masses. Shrem, who built his fortune publishing reference and technical books in Japan, is preoccupied with both wine and art. His collection of sculpture and painting is profiled in our Arts and Culture chapter, and his wines—Cabernet Sauvignon, Chardonnay, Merlot, and Petite Sirah Port—are some of the best in the valley. The winery itself, designed by renowned Princeton architect Michael Graves (who was commissioned to build a "temple to wine"), is a stark, modern landmark of earth tones, angles, and curves. Public tours depart at 11:00 A.M. and 2:00 P.M. daily and include the 20,000-square-foot aging caves. The tasting fee is $2.50 for two Chardonnays and a Merlot, or $5.00 for three different Cabernets. Clos Pegase is open from 10:30 A.M. to 5:00 P.M. daily.

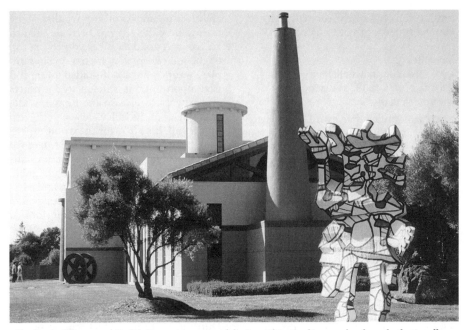

Clos Pegase Winery south of Calistoga is renowned for its striking architectural style and eclectic collection of modern sculpture. PHOTO: JEAN SAYLOR DOPPENBERG

Cuvaison Winery
4550 Silverado Trail, Calistoga
(707) 942–6266
www.cuvaison.com

When Silicon Valley engineers Thomas Cottrell and Thomas Parkhill started a small upvalley winery in 1969, they called it Cuvaison, a French term for the fermentation of wine on the grape skins. The name remains, though the winery is now owned by Thomas Schmidheiny, CEO of the world's largest cement company (Holderbank) and one of the richest men in Switzerland. John Thacher is the winemaker (and president), and he is particularly known for his Chardonnay. Cuvaison gets more than 90 percent of its grapes from its 400-acre vineyard in Carneros. Tours are at 10:30 A.M., and include a peek into newly completed aging caves. Tasting is $4.00 (or $5.00 for reserve wines), which includes a souvenir glass. The winery has a pleasant picnic area, shaded by 350-year-old oak trees, and is open from 10:00 A.M. to 5:00 P.M. daily.

Vincent Arroyo Winery
2361 Greenwood Ave., Calistoga
(707) 942–6995

Cozy? Not only is Vincent Arroyo a family operation, but Vincent is the only member of the family. He pretty much runs the show, with help from a few employees and a gregarious black Lab named Joy. There is nothing special about the tasting room—it's in a modern barn of a barrel house—but Arroyo has found a serenely perfect spot just north of Calistoga, tasting is free of charge, and the wines themselves are first-rate. (The standbys are Chardonnay, Cabernet Sauvignon, and Petite Sirah, and all are sold only at the winery.) Bring a picnic and watch the hawks circling overhead. The winery is open daily from 10:00 A.M. to 4:30 P.M.

Graeser Winery
255 Petrified Forest Rd., Calistoga
(707) 942–4437, (800) 898–4682
www.graeserwinery.com

Want to get a feeling for the Napa Valley wine industry circa 1890? Take a drive to

Graeser, about 2 miles northwest of Calistoga. The tasting room is in an 1886 home. If no one answers, ring the doorbell, a rope attached to the bell tower over the house. It's a bucolic setting once known as La Perlita del Monte ("The Little Pearl of the Mountain"), and Richard Graeser can genuinely claim a unique mountainside microclimate for his grapes, which are the traditional Burgundian varietals: Cabernet Sauvignon, Cabernet Franc, and Merlot. The winery is open daily from 10:00 A.M. to 5:00 P.M. There is no charge for tasting, and picnics should be mandatory. Richard will even autograph your bottle of wine, if you ask nicely. Ask about their Adopt-a-Vine program.

Chateau Montelena
1429 Tubbs Ln., Calistoga
(707) 942–5105
www.montelena.com

Montelena was one of the two Napa Valley wineries—Stag's Leap being the other—that rocked the French establishment at a famous blind tasting in Paris in 1976 (see the Close-up in this chapter). It was a Chardonnay that prevailed that day, and the winery still makes one of the valley's best, along with top-notch Cabernet Sauvignon and Johannisburg Riesling (the latter grown in northward Potter Valley and sold only in the retail room).

Chateau Montelena's name and origins go back much further than 1976. The winery was started by Alfred L. Tubbs in the late 1800s, but no wine had been produced for 50 years when new owner Jim Barrett filled the barrels again in 1972. The building, nothing short of a hilltop castle with walls 3 to 10 feet thick, dates back to Tubbs' day, and a subsequent owner, Yort Frank, added Jade Lake and its Chinese gardens. Montelena is open daily from 10:00 A.M. to 4:00 P.M. and gives daily tours at 11:00 A.M. and 2:00 P.M.; call to reserve. The $5.00 tasting charge applies to any purchase.

Sun-dappled mountain vineyards serve as a scenic backdrop to the down-home atmosphere of Graeser Winery, near Calistoga. PHOTO: JEAN SAYLOR DOPPENBERG

Variety Show

Don't know your Gamay from your Pinot Grigio? Who can blame you? The French have had thousands of years to learn the characteristics of various grapes. In typical American fashion, we have tried to catch up in a few decades, and we expect ourselves to incorporate Italian and German varietals as well. It can rapidly become perplexing.

On the other hand, too many wine drinkers, even some experienced ones, seem intent on limiting themselves to Chardonnay and Cabernet Sauvignon, with an occasional Merlot to lend a feeling of anarchy. They don't know what they're missing. There are a lot of delicious grapes out there, and some of them are obscure even in Wine Country. Don't be afraid to try any of them. And be fair to blends, which can make for some of the finest (and most coveted) bottles around. Remember, this is about personal taste—if you like it, it's a good wine.

The following list of varietals is neither complete nor guaranteed to apply to every wine you taste. It will, however, give you a general idea of what to expect when you sip a certain type. With a little practice (and practice was never this fun) you might even develop a pet grape or two.

Barbera: The grape variety has its origins in Italy, and Italian families in Sonoma and Napa make most of this varietal. It's a dry, full-flavored wine, often served with pasta or seafood stews in spicy tomato sauces.

Blanc de Blancs: The phrase means white wine made from white grapes, usually describing sparkling wines made to be light in style.

Blanc de Noirs: The phrase means white wine (usually sparkling wine) made from black grapes (usually Pinot Noir).

Cabernet Sauvignon: Currently this is the bedrock of California's dry red wines. Young wines tend to be more tannic (the quality that makes your cheeks pucker); the good ones become more velvety when aged.

Chardonnay: A dry white wine, it's enjoying the same prestige as red Cabernet Sauvignon. It's frequently called upon to complement the rich, buttery flavors of creamy sauces or lobster.

Fume Blanc: A white table wine, it is almost always dry. Some say it has a smoky flavor; you might consider that when you taste it. It's a great companion to well-seasoned poultry dishes.

Chenin Blanc: A white table wine, it is sweet enough to be considered a before-dinner wine, while still suitable for dinner. It's great with lunch or picnics.

Gamay Beaujolais: Light and fresh, it is the fruitiest of the red wines. It's usually served slightly chilled.

Gewurztraminer: Its spicy characteristic is so pronounced that many people prefer to drink it with appetizers rather than as a dinner wine.

Grey Riesling: This is a white that should be consumed when the wine is still young. It is spicy and sweet.

Johannisburg Riesling: A grape variety originated in the Mosel region of Germany, this white table wine is marked by a faint hint of sweetness. It is declared by many to be the perfect accompaniment to seafood.

Merlot: A currently trendy red table wine, Merlot is one of the traditional grapes of Bordeaux (along with Cabernet Sauvignon and Cabernet Franc).

Petite Sirah: Always dry, this red table wine is well suited to heavy meals centered around well-seasoned meats or pasta.

Pinot Noir: An infamously delicate grape, it is the principal representative of France's Burgundy reds. Pinot Noir thrives in relatively cool, moist areas with coastal breezes.

Sauvignon Blanc: This is a favored dry wine for table use, particularly with fish. Though it has acquired somewhat of a bad rap because of the many herbaceous $3.99 brands, Sauvignon Blanc can be happily complex.

Semillon: Often combined with Sauvignon Blanc, this is a fruity white wine.

Zinfandel: This red table wine comes from the most widely planted grape in the state (though the majority of it is picked for white Zinfandel). The grape, often grown in hot microclimates, produces a hardy, chewy red wine.

Sonoma County

Southern Sonoma

Bartholomew Park Winery
1000 Vineyard Ln., Sonoma
(707) 935–9511
www.bartholomewparkwinery.com

Formerly the Hacienda Winery, the winery and adjacent park have been renamed for Frank Bartholomew, former foreign correspondent with United Press International (later its president). The winery's picnic sites, set among native oaks, are unequalled, with tables overlooking vistas of vineyards. Frank's wife, Antonia—who lived to age 90—led the effort to recreate Agoston Haraszthy's Pompeian-style villa (see our History chapter), which stands sentinel over the vineyards he once cultivated. Within the winery there is a small museum celebrating the life of Haraszthy and the achievements of Frank Bartholomew in his days with United Press. The winery also sponsors a Punch Down Club. Members of this club get to "punch down" the relatively thick cap of skin that floats to the top of barrels during the fermentation process—the skin must be pushed down four or five times a day. Participants in this somewhat messy operation receive a bottle of "their" wine when it has aged. The winery offers complimentary tastings (except for large groups) and is open 10:30 A.M. to 4:30 P.M. daily.

Buena Vista Winery
18000 Old Winery Rd., Sonoma
(707) 938–1266, (800) 926–1266
www.buenavistawinery.com

Huge shade trees surround Buena Vista, the oldest premium winery in California, established in 1857 by Count Agoston Haraszthy (see the Close-up on Haraszthy, "The Father of California Viticulture," in our History chapter). The fountain courtyard, a lovely picnic spot, is home to a self-guided historic tour, but there's also a guided historic presentation daily at 2:00 P.M. (plus one at 11:00 A.M. during July, August, and September). Two of the winery's stone buildings are registered as state historic landmarks. Chinese laborers dug long tunnels into the hillside for wine aging, and Buena Vista's buildings are made from the salvaged rock. The Press House, built in 1862, houses a gift shop, displays a fine collection of art, and offers complimentary tastings. The Heritage Bar, on the second floor, features rare, intensely flavored vintage wines from the Carneros region. The 1997 season marked 140 years since the globe-trotting Count Haraszthy turned a shovel of sun-baked earth and proclaimed the birth of Buena Vista Winery. Today Buena Vista supplies wine to all 50 states and 30 countries around the world, an accomplishment that would not surprise the enterprising count. The winery is open 10:00 A.M. to

5:00 P.M.; tours are complimentary. Buena Vista has a second tasting room in downtown Sonoma, at the southeast corner of the plaza (494 First Street East) in Pinelli's Corner Store (once the historic Pinelli Mission Hardware Store). There is no charge for any tasting. Daily tasting hours are 11:00 A.M. to 5:30 P.M., and the phone number is (707) 939-0579. Both the winery and the downtown Sonoma tasting room feature wines by Buena Vista, Robert Stemmler, and Haywood.

Cline Cellars
24737 Hwy. 121, Sonoma
(707) 935-4310, (800) 546-2070
www.clinecellars.com

After spending his childhood learning farming and winemaking from his grandfather Avaleriano Jacuzzi (of spa fame), Fred Cline founded Cline Cellars in 1982 on the sandy soils of Contra Costa County. His brother Matt joined him in 1991 as winemaker, and they relocated to the Sonoma Valley. The tasting room is in an 1850s farmhouse with a large, old-fashioned porch. Picnic grounds surrounded by 1,100 rose bushes make for a very pleasant lunch stop, with sweeping views of the Sonoma Valley on a site that was once a Miwok village. Complimentary tastings feature Rhône-style red wines—Syrah, and Mouvedre—as well as several white wines. Facilities are available for special events and weddings. The winery is open 10:00 A.M. to 6:00 P.M. daily with tours at 11:00 A.M., 1:00 and 3:00 P.M.

Gloria Ferrer Champagne Caves
23555 Hwy. 121, Sonoma
(707) 996-7256
www.gloriaferrer.com

The vineyards stretch across the hills, and from the hillock above, the Spanish-style winery overlooks the estate vineyards and the rolling Carneros hills. This is one of seven wineries owned and operated by the Ferrer family of Barcelona, which has produced methode champenoise sparkling wine for 100 years. You can tour the facility with its state-of-the-art caves and learn the secrets of the class methode champenoise process. Others may choose to linger on the vista terrace, noshing gourmet appetizers and sipping sparkling wine. Picnic tables are available for those who buy a bottle of wine to go with the comestibles. There is often musical entertainment on weekends, and there's plenty of banquet and meeting space. Open 10:30 A.M. to 5:30 P.M. daily. Tours are on the hour, from 11:00 A.M. to 4:00 P.M.

Gundlach Bundschu Winery
2000 Denmark St., Sonoma
(707) 938-5277
www.gunbun.com

Jacob Gundlach and his brother-in-law, Charles Bundschu, established this winery in 1858 on land east of Sonoma that they called Rhinefarm. The enterprise gained international fame in the late 1800s and survived the 1906 earthquake. It suffered under Prohibition—its owners were reduced to selling grapes to other vintners. The resurrection of the winery began on Halloween 1970, when Jim Bundschu, great-great-grandson of the founder, decided to turn his winemaking hobby into a viable business. Operating on a shoestring budget, he and his brothers-in-law converted a dairy's milk tanks into fermentation vats and squeezed grapes with a muscle-wrenching, hand-operated basket press. Today Gundlach Bundschu produces 50,000 cases of premium, award-winning wines a year, specializing in Merlot, Pinot Noir, Chardonnay, Cabernet, and Zinfandel. Picnic tables are in a grove of oak trees overlooking a lake. Another attraction at Gundlach Bundschu is a 6-foot by 140-foot mural dedicated to the winery's farmworkers, completed in spring 1998.

Jim Bundschu's lighthearted humor is legendary, and local residents like to drive out to the tasting rooms occasionally just to see the wacky posters he creates as part of his marketing plan. In one, Bundschu's mother, behind the wheel of a 1947 Kaiser on the edge of the family vineyards, is exchanging words with a motorcycle cop who says, "If you can't say Gundlach Bundschu Gewurztraminer you shouldn't be driving." The room for complimentary tastings is open daily from 11:00 A.M. to 4:30 P.M., and self-guided tours are offered.

Ravenswood Winery
18701 Gehricke Rd., Sonoma
(707) 938–1960, (888) 669–4679
www.ravenswood-wine.com

The advertising copy says it all: "Ravenswood's hand-crafted releases possess a unique vintage and vineyard identity in addition to an intense, powerful ('gothic,' as one wine critic wrote) character with which the winery has come to be associated. These attributes arise from what can only be called stubborn and impractical Old World enological practices." Ravenswood produces some of the best Zinfandel in the world—and accounts for 70 percent of the winery's production. This winery also features picnic facilities and a barbecue in the vineyard every weekend from May through September. Open daily from 10:00 A.M. to 4:30 P.M., with tours (10:30 A.M., by reservation) and complimentary tastings of Zinfandel, Merlot, and Cabernet Sauvignon.

Roche Winery
28700 Arnold Dr., Sonoma
(707) 935–7115, (800) 825–8475
www.rochewinery.com

This small, family-operated winery is the first you see as you enter the Sonoma Valley from the south, just north of Sears Point Raceway. Owners Joseph and Genevieve Roche started with 10 acres in 1982, expanded to 25 acres in 1987, and plan to remain a small winery with carefully crafted estate wines. Housed in a modified barn at the top of a small hill, the setting commands a sweeping view of the valley, the bay, and the lights of the communities beyond. The tasting room features free sips of Chardonnay, Pinot Noir, Muscat, and Merlot, or $3.00 glasses of reserve wines. (Roche's Merlot is sold by lottery.) Lovely picnic facilities are available, and the winery is open daily from 10:00 A.M. to 6:00 P.M. in the summer and 10:00 A.M. to 5:00 P.M. in the winter.

Schug Carneros Estate Winery
602 Bonneau Rd., Sonoma
(707) 939–9363, (800) 966–9365
www.schugwinery.com

This lifelong dream of owner-winemaster Walter Schug spans four decades and two continents. A native of Germany's Rhine River valley and a graduate of a prestigious German wine institute, Walter left for California determined to find success with his Pinot Noir, which has since been proclaimed no less than world-class by critics in both the United States and Europe. The winery, built in 1990 of post-and-beam architecture, reflects the Schug family's German heritage. Schug still maintains close ties to Europe (one-third of Schug wines are sold there), and it's a likely possibility you'll meet European neighbors while you're in the tasting room to enjoy complimentary sips (or reserve wines at $5.00 per taste). Open daily from 10:00 A.M. to 5:00 P.M.

Sebastiani Vineyards
389 Fourth St. East, Sonoma
(707) 938–5532, (800) 888–5532
www.sebastiani.com

One of the few original family wineries still remaining, Sebastiani is extremely proud of its wines and its Italian heritage. Founder Samuele Sebastiani learned winemaking from the monks in Franetta,

Italy, before he came to America in 1894 at the age of 19 and went to work hauling cobblestones. In 1904 he bought the old Sonoma Mission vineyard, where the padres had been making altar wines for 80 years. He sold his first vino to local Italian stonecutters in demijohns the size of beach balls.

The winery is 3 blocks east of Sonoma Plaza, set amid the vineyards from which Sebastiani produces its special Sonoma Cask and Cherry Block Cabernet wines. A great convenience for visitors is the winery's trolley, which allows people to park at the winery and catch a shuttle back to the plaza. The visitor center underwent renovation in 2001. Tastings are also available at Sebastiani on the Square at 103 W. Napa Street in Sonoma (on the southwest corner of the plaza).

Viansa Winery and Italian Marketplace
25200 Arnold Dr., Sonoma
(707) 935–4700, (800) 995–4740
www.viansa.com
When Sam Sebastiani visited the homeland of his grandfather in Italy, he was astounded to see that Franetta, Italy, looked exactly like the Sonoma Valley. "It looked so much like Sonoma I damn near fell over," he said. The winery that Sam and his wife, Vicki (Viansa combines Sam and Vicki), established is about as Italian in aura as you will find this side of the Atlantic. Olive trees were imported from Italy, the architecture is Italian, and the garden paths that wind between levels of the winery are in Tuscan style.

The wine tasting room (sips are complimentary) is also a tasting room for some stunning gourmet foods—a manifestation of Vicki's longstanding interest in hospitality. (Her cookbook is on sale at the gift shop.) Visitors can wander about, picking up samples of olive-anchovy pesto, hot sweet mustards, blood-orange vinegar, and other aromatic foods. Vicki and her kitchen staff have also developed some unusual specialties that are available at the food counter, such as focaccia, sandwiches, and fine salads—all splendid foods for a picnic. Plenty of tables are available at various patio levels overlooking Sonoma Valley and Sam's award-winning

wildlife preserve. Sam Sebastiani adheres to his loyalty to Italian-style wines; his winery features Piccolo Toscano (a Chianti type of grape), Sothena (a Dolcetto grape), and Nebbiolo (the name of the grape and the wine) plus 40 other varieties. Wine and food tasting is offered from 10:00 A.M. to 5:00 P.M. daily. The winery also offers specialty wine and food tasting programs, such as Tuscan Wine and Food Pairing, a private guided tour with wine and gourmet food tasting.

Arrowood Vineyards & Winery
14347 Sonoma Hwy., Glen Ellen
(707) 938–5170, (800) 938–5170
www.arrowoodvineyards.com
It had been the philosophy of Richard Arrowood to make only reserve-quality Chardonnay and Cabernet Sauvignon. But he has been unable to resist experimenting with unusual varietals, so his portfolio has now expanded to include limited quantities of Merlot, Viognier, and Pinot Blanc. Hospitality and personal service are a top priority at Arrowood, whose tasting room is open daily from 10:00 A.M. to 4:30 P.M. Tastings are $5.00 to $10.00 per person. Visitors also can savor the spectacular view from the vineyard veranda.

Benziger Family Winery
1883 London Ranch Rd., Glen Ellen
(707) 935–3000, (800) 989–8890
www.benziger.com
You could easily spend an entire day at the Benziger Family Winery, perched on the side of Sonoma Mountain high above the Sonoma Valley floor and the town of Glen Ellen. Guests can picnic in the redwood grove, visit an experimental vineyard, enjoy complimentary wine tasting (or five reserve wines for $5.00), and take in a one-of-a-kind educational vineyard tour aboard a motorized tram. The Benzigers emigrated from White Plains, New York, to their mountain ranch next to Jack London State Park (see our Parks and Recreation chapter). They have since built a reputation for grape-growing innovation that produces award-winning wines in the Imagery series—Merlot, Chardonnay, and an unusual Bordeaux

varietal, Cabernet Franc. They also founded the Glen Ellen Winery (see subsequent listing) and later sold it. Wine tasting is available from 10:00 A.M. to 5:00 P.M. The winery also conducts six tram tours daily, with additional tours on weekends.

Chandelle of Sonoma
15499 Arnold Dr., Glen Ellen
(707) 938–5862, (800) 544–8890
www.chandellewinery.com

Flying is the theme of Chandelle Winery's colorful labels. They feature paintings of vintage aircraft—a salute, no doubt, to five-star Gen. "Hap" Arnold, who happens to be the grandfather of owner Robert Arnold. Robert and his wife, Mary Evelyn, opened a sales room for Chandelle wines in Jack London Village in Glen Ellen, the only place the wines are sold. Chardonnay and Cabernet wines are Chandelle's specialties. The winery is open daily for sales only (no tasting) from 10:00 A.M. to 4:00 P.M. Monday through Saturday and 11:00 A.M. to 4:00 P.M. on Sunday. Note that Chandelle is closed Sunday in winter.

Glen Ellen Tasting Room
14301 Arnold Dr., Glen Ellen
(707) 939–6277, (800) 684–5289
www.diageo.com

The winery opened a new tasting room and history center, the Chauvet Winery, in Jack London Village (next to Gen. Vallejo's 1850 grist mill). A fascinating display of historical photographs and other memorabilia delineates the colorful history of Glen Ellen and its renowned residents, including writer Jack London and his wife, Charmian (see our History and Attractions chapters for more on London). A special Train Room displays photos of trains that came through Sonoma Valley in bygone times. Once a month, the winery presents special events, which run the gamut from a ghost-story contest to a program of readings, food, and dance, inspired by the work of novelist and food writer M. F. K. Fisher. No wines are made here, but you can taste Glen Ellen and M. G. Vallejo wines as well as the winery's new line of premium vari-

etals: Expressions. The tasting room is open daily from 10:00 A.M. to 5:00 P.M.

Wellington Vineyards
11600 Dunbar Rd., Glen Ellen
(707) 939–0708, (800) 816–9463
www.wellingtonvineyards.com

Operating a small, family vineyard and winery producing just 6,000 cases a year, John and Peter Wellington nevertheless produce a wide range of wines, concentrating on reds like Zinfandel, Merlot, and Cabernet. They also produce a couple of unusual wines unique to the area, including a Rhône-style blend, Côtes de Sonoma. The winery and tasting room are surrounded by vines, some as old as 100 years. The tasting room is open daily for complimentary sips from 11:00 A.M. to 4:00 P.M.

Chateau St. Jean
8555 Sonoma Hwy., Kenwood
(707) 833–4134, (800) 543–7572
www.chateaustjean.com

Nestled against the tranquil slopes of Sugarloaf Ridge, Chateau St. Jean (named for former owner Ken Sheffield's sister and pronounced "gene") was founded in 1973. An elegant chateau on the grounds of this 250-acre estate was built in 1920

> ## Insiders' Tip
> In Wine Country, there are winery tours. And then there's the Ghost Winery Tour, a self-guided autumn romp of six winery sites—some in ruins, all picturesque. Call (707) 252-3270 for information and tickets.

and is now a showplace surrounded by beautiful gardens. It's a lovely spot for picnicking. Chateau St. Jean's Cabernet Sauvignon has been served at the White House, and Queen Elizabeth has sipped their Chardonnay. Open daily from 10:00 A.M. to 5:00 P.M.

Mayo Family Wineries
9200 Sonoma Hwy., Kenwood
(707) 833–5504
www.mayofamilywinery.com

It has been the lifetime dream of real estate broker Henry Mayo to own a home in the vineyards of Sonoma County and to raise his own grapes. Now he has achieved both goals. His first grapes were planted in 1989, harvested in 1993. At first he planned to simply raise and sell his grapes, since his location in Santa Rosa was not conducive to offering a tasting room. However, his son, Jeffrey, has now joined him, and they have developed an interesting plan to publicize their wines. Using the Mayo real estate offices on the main highway through Kenwood (now on the upper floor), they have turned the main floor into a tasting room and have rented tasting-room space to six other winery owners who join them in pouring their wines. Each winery owner takes one day to pour the wines of all, so there is always a knowledgeable owner on duty. The wineries represented, along with the Mayo family's, are Sable Ridge Vineyards, Nelson Estate Winery, Sunce Winery, Noel Winery, Meredith Winery, and Deerfield Ranch Winery. Tastings are complimentary, and the room is open daily from 11:00 A.M. to 6:00 P.M.

Kenwood Vineyards
9592 Sonoma Hwy., Kenwood
(707) 833–5891
www.kenwoodvineyards.com

When the Pagani brothers founded this winery in 1906, Jack London lived on the estate next door. Both estate owners are gone now, and the winery was bought by three college chums, all wine lovers, in 1970. The grapes they use are still grown on the London ranch, and the label on a special bottling shows a picture of Jack London's signature and a wolf, Jack's nickname. The tasting room is rustic, the sips are complimentary, and the atmosphere is charmingly informal. Kenwood is known for its Sauvignon Blanc, Zinfandels, and Cabernets. One of the charming features of this winery is the free food-and-wine pairings on weekends. Open daily 10:00 A.M. to 4:30 P.M.

Kunde Estate Winery & Vineyards
10155 Sonoma Hwy., Kenwood
(707) 833–5501
www.kunde.com

Louis Kunde arrived in California from Germany in 1884 and founded his ranch in 1904. Four generations of Kundes have worked the ranch, which stretches for 1.5 miles along Sonoma Highway and extends from the valley up into the mountains above. Today's tasting room is a replica of Louis Kunde's old barn, built on the site of the original. The Kunde family ages its wine in 30,000 square feet of caves dug into the hillside, providing an ideal environment for natural aging. Timbers from the old barn were used to handcraft tables and benches. Picnic grounds are surrounded by scenic vineyards. There's a nice gift shop inside, and tours are available Friday through Sunday. Chardonnay vineyards surround the tasting rooms, where samples are complimentary. Open daily from 11:00 A.M. to 5:00 P.M.

Landmark Vineyards
101 Adobe Canyon Rd., Kenwood
(707) 833–0053, (800) 452–6265
www.landmarkwine.com

Perhaps the most spectacular aspect of this Spanish Mission–style winery is its expansive interior courtyard, facing onto dramatic, hulking Sugarloaf Mountain. The hospitality center at Landmark is a magnificent facility, featuring a granite tasting bar, a warm fireplace for chilly days, and a full-wall mural by noted Sonoma County artist Claudia Wagar. The pond-side picnic area is a picturesque location for lunch or for just lounging and watching the clouds drift by. A tower conference room offers a 360-degree view that must be distracting to those attending the meetings held there. Landmark's production focuses on Chardonnay, and three labels have won awards: Overlook, from Sonoma County vineyards; Damaris Reserve, from Alexander Valley appellation; and Two Williams Vineyard, from southern Sonoma Valley. Tastings are complimentary, and the room is open daily from 10:00 A.M. to 4:30 P.M.

St. Francis Winery and Vineyards
100 Pythian Rd., Santa Rosa
(707) 833–4666, (800) 543–7713
www.stfranciswine.com

Joseph Martin, who left the corporate world in 1971 to become a vintner, named his winery after St. Francis of Assisi and San Francisco de Solano Mission in Sonoma. His first harvest came in 1979 with production of 4,000 cases. Today his benchmark varietals are Chardonnay and Merlot, rich with character and complexity, but the portfolio also includes Cabernet Sauvignon and Zinfandel. The new visitor center closer to Santa Rosa is a beauty. Open daily 10:00 A.M. to 5:00 P.M., it has terrific views and a huge gift shop and special reserve wine tasting bar. The regular tasting fee is $5.00; reserve wine tasting is $10.00.

Smothers Winery and Remick Ridge Vineyards
9575 Sonoma Hwy., Kenwood
(707) 833–6131, (800) 795–9463
www.smothersbrothers.com

The tasting room is filled with Smothers Brothers memorabilia, including gold records adorning the walls. Tommy Smothers (the goofy one in the act) bought 110 acres of vineyard land in 1972, and his brother, Dick (the straight man), bought a home and 30 acres of vineyard in the Santa Cruz mountains two years later. When Dick added Vine Hill Vineyard next to Tom's acreage, the Smothers Winery was born. The famous brothers had their first crush in 1977 and opened the tasting room in 1985. Dick has since sold out to his brother. Now Tommy grows the grapes, but the wine is made in Glen Ellen by Richard Arrowood. They produce Chardonnay, Cabernet, and

Insiders' Tip

Wine tasting is fun, but remember that you can be thrown in jail if you are drive with a blood alcohol level that exceeds 0.8 percent. Use a designated nondrinking driver or try the "sip and spit" method as an alternative to sipping and swallowing—many wineries provide an urnlike receptacle for this very purpose. Though spitting wine may sound uncouth, it's better than paying a hefty traffic fine, landing in jail, or, worst of all, hurting someone. For more information visit the California DUI Web site at www.dui.com.

a small amount of Merlot. This is also a tasting room for smaller production wineries such as Kaz, Moondance Cellars, Cale Cellars, and Adler Fels. There is a small picnic area, and the tasting room, fronting Sonoma Highway, is open daily from 11:00 A.M. to 4:00 P.M.

Ledson Winery & Vineyards
7335 Sonoma Hwy., Santa Rosa
(707) 833–2330
www.ledson.com

When this 16,000-square-foot French-Normandy structure was first erected, it seemed ideally suited to be a fancy haunted castle, set far back from the highway and with rocky mountains as a mysterious backdrop. But that all changed

The castle-like Ledson Winery in the Sonoma Valley features tasting of their award-winning wines as well as beautiful grounds and a fully stocked deli and gift shop. PHOTO: JEAN SAYLOR DOPPENBERG

when the winery opened and the warmth and beauty of the place became apparent. Owned by the Ledson family, long-time Sonoma Valley farmers, the winery has three tasting rooms, a clothing and gift boutique, and a terrific gourmet market. But what really sets it apart is the picnic grounds, where on any given weekend in summer there might be a jazz combo or an art show to add to your wining and dining experience.

Construction on the winery, which was originally intended as a private home, began in 1993. The Ledsons soon realized the emerging castle was getting too much attention for their liking, so they decided it would work better as a winery open to the public. Ledson wines are sold only at the winery and have garnered some great reviews in *Wine Spectator* while amassing a variety of awards. They are known for their Merlot and Chardonnay, but also produce Sauvignon Blanc, Johannisberg Riesling, and Orange Muscat. The winery is open daily from 10:00 A.M. to 5:00 P.M.

Matanzas Creek Winery
6097 Bennett Valley Rd., Santa Rosa
(707) 528–6464, (800) 590–6464
www.matanzascreek.com

On the face of it, Bill and Sandra MacIver were unlikely candidates to succeed in the wine business. He had a 20-year military career behind him; she had no experience but a vision of creating a perfect wine. In 1978 they came together as partners in marriage and business, and today Matanzas Creek Winery is recognized as one of the country's best.

Ensconced at the base of Bennett Mountain, the new, environmentally friendly winemaking facility boasts one of the most sophisticated research laboratories in California. There, Matanzas Creek's winemakers have conducted more than 100 experiments in progressive winemaking. In the early 1990s, Matanzas released a new wine, Journey, made in a radically progressive winemaking program. Although its $70 price raised some controversy, the first 1990 Chardonnay sold out on release and was hailed by critics as the finest Chardonnay ever produced in America. The tasting room is open from 10:00 A.M. to 4:30 P.M. every day. Tastings are $5.00, depending on what is poured. Picnic facilities are available as well as a self-guided garden tour that includes the largest planting of lavender in Northern California. Look for handmade lavender products in the gift shop.

Paradise Ridge Winery
4545 Thomas Lake Harris Dr., Santa Rosa
(707) 528–9463
www.paradiseridgewinery.com

Welcome to Paradise! For Walter and Marijki Byck, Paradise came to be on the day in 1994 when they opened the doors to their new winery, a California-style structure with breathtaking views from the decks. In fact, the view is so exciting the winery stays open late on Wednesday evenings just so visitors can catch the sunset. After purchasing a 156-acre ranch adjoining the old Fountain Grove Winery, the Bycks planted 18 acres of Sauvignon Blanc and Chardonnay grapes, determined to produce the finest wines possible. In addition to their award-winning wines, they also feature a historical exhibit and world-class sculpture garden. Tastings are complimentary. Open daily from 11:00 A.M. to 5:00 P.M. and until sunset on Wednesday.

De Loach Vineyards
1791 Olivet Rd., Santa Rosa
(707) 526–9111
www.deloachvineyards.com

Cecil and Christine De Loach have established a reputation as leading producers of premium wines and professional leaders in the industry ranks. He has served on the board of directors of the Wine Institute, and she is past president of the Sonoma County Wineries Association, both positions of prestige. Together, they cultivate 800 acres of vineyards in the Russian River Valley, producing Pinot Noir, Chardonnay, and Gewurztraminer as well as some remarkable Zinfandel from vines that were planted between the turn of the century. The winery also

makes Sauvignon Blanc, Merlot, and Cabernet Sauvignon plus a distinctive White Zinfandel. Picnic facilities are on the lawn in front of the winery, which is situated among the vines. Tours and tastings are complimentary. Open daily from 10:00 A.M. to 4:30 P.M., and tours are conducted at 11:00 A.M. and 2:00 P.M., by appointment only.

Northern Sonoma

Armida Winery
2201 Westside Rd., Healdsburg
(707) 433–2222
www.armida.com

Tastings here are charmingly casual (and complimentary), and the setting is spectacular. Built on the side of a hill, the winery looks out on the Dry Creek and Russian River valleys, with Alexander Valley, Geyser Peak, and Mount St. Helena to the east and south. High on the hillside, three geodesic domes house the winery, lab, and administrative offices. If you've been looking forward to a game of Italian bocce ball (or if you'd like to learn what it is), visit the bocce ball court near the picnic grounds. Vineyards are south of the winery, producing Amida's five varietals: Merlot, Gewurztraminer, Chardonnay, Pinot Noir, and the recently added Zinfandel. Tasting-room hours are 11:00 A.M. to 5:00 P.M. daily.

Belvedere Winery
4035 Westside Rd., Healdsburg
(707) 433–8236, (800) 433–8296

This winery, in the coastal foothills of the Russian River Valley, takes its name from the Italian word for "beautiful view." A trip to the winery reveals just that. Taste world-class wines while you enjoy a picnic on the sunny deck or under an oak tree in a beautiful garden setting. The picturesque vineyards of the Russian River Valley will spread out before you. Belvedere specialties are Zinfandel, Chardonnay, Merlot, and Cabernet Sauvignon from their premium vineyards in the Alexander, Dry Creek, and Russian River valleys. Tastings are complimentary from 10:00 A.M. to 4:30 P.M. daily.

Foppiano Vineyards
12707 Old Redwood Hwy., Healdsburg
(707) 433–7272
www.foppiano.com

This is the oldest family-owned winery in Sonoma County, whose history reaches back to 1896. Founded by John Foppiano, a disenchanted gold miner who decided to get back to his farming roots, the winery is now being run by fourth-generation Foppianos, producing 200,000 cases a year of Cabernet Sauvignon, Petite Sirah, Zinfandel, Merlot, Pinot Noir, Chardonnay, and Sauvignon Blanc. Some of the producing vines are 100 years old. Tastings are complimentary, and a self-guided vineyard tour is available. Winery hours are 10:00 A.M. to 4:30 P.M. daily.

Kendall-Jackson Winery
Wine Country Store
337 Healdsburg Ave., Healdsburg
(707) 433–7102, (800) 769–3649
www.kj.com

The hugely successful Kendall-Jackson operation encompasses 14 wineries. The largest of these is Kendall-Jackson itself. The company describes the 13 others—Cambria, Edmeades, Camelot, Cardinale, Stonestreet, Vina Calina (Chile), Calina (Chile), Mariposa (Argentina), La Crema, Robert Pepi, Lakewood, Hartford Court, and Kristone—as "Artisans and Estates."

To learn more about each winery and the wide span of varietals Kendall-Jackson produces, the Healdsburg store is the place to visit. The friendly folks at the K-J store will be happy to direct you to one of their other locations: Kendall-Jackson Wine Center, 5007 Fulton Road, Fulton, (707) 571–8100; and Cardinale Winery, 7600 St. Helena Highway, Oakville, (707) 945–1391. The Wine Center on Fulton Road features a viticulture exhibit, where students from Santa Rosa Junior College—and visitors—can become acquainted with 26 varietals and 19 trellising systems. The K-J Wine Country Store is open daily for tastings for a $2.00 fee from 10:00 A.M. to 4:30 P.M. The Wine Center is open daily from 10:00 A.M. to 5:00 P.M.

Martinelli Winery
3360 River Rd., Windsor
(707) 525–0570, (800) 346–1627

This family-run winery tends more than 350 acres of vines in the Russian River Valley, which it uses for its own wines and

The distinctive turrets of Martinelli Winery northwest of Santa Rosa were originally constructed as part of a hop kiln. PHOTO: JOHN NAGIECKI

sells to other vintners. The winery specializes in Zinfandel—the Jackass Hill variety from the vineyard of the same name is considered by experts to be extraordinarily complex. They also produce a fine Sauvignon Blanc, Gewurtzraminer, Chardonnay, and Pinot Noir. The winery is housed in an old hop kiln, just a short hop from U.S. 101 off the River Road exit. Open 10:00 A.M. to 5:00 P.M. daily for complimentary tastings.

Mill Creek Vineyards
1401 Westside Rd., Healdsburg
(707) 431–2121, (877) 349–2121
www.mcvonline.com

This beautifully landscaped winery is set on a rise above the vineyard, which has been operated since 1975 by the Kreck family. The tasting room, complete with working waterwheel and a mill pond, is in an air-conditioned two-story redwood building. The bar top, trusses, and beams are all made from one redwood tree from the Kreck ranch on Mill Creek Road. A 3,000-square-foot picnic deck overlooks the Dry Creek Valley, Fitch Mountain, and Mt. St. Helena. It is occasionally used for company picnics or seminars. Winery hours are 10:00 A.M. to 5:00 P.M. daily, and tastings are complimentary.

Rodney Strong Vineyards
11455 Old Redwood Hwy., Healdsburg
(707) 431–1533, (800) 678–4763
www.rodneystrong.com

In 1959, long before Sonoma County was "discovered" as a premium grape-growing region, Rodney Strong began an exhaustive search for the very best vineyards. Ultimately, he selected several vineyards in the Chalk Hill, Alexander Valley, and Russian River Valley appellations. The winery, a low-lying building with a roof spreading across it like the wings of a giant eagle, is situated among acres of prime vineyards. The winery's estate wines are named after the individual vineyards where the grapes grow—for example, the Charlotte's Home, a Sauvignon Blanc, and Alexander's Crown, a Cabernet. Picnic areas are available. For special occasions there's a garden area adjacent

to the vineyards (contact the vineyard for availability). Tours are conducted daily at 11:00 A.M. and 3:00 P.M. Free tastings are offered from 10:00 A.M. to 5:00 P.M. daily.

Windsor Vineyards Tasting Room
308-B Center St., Healdsburg
(707) 433-2822, (800) 204-9463
www.windsorvineyards.com

Windsor offers a wide variety of wines that have brought home several awards. In 1959, Windsor was one of the first wineries to stake a claim to Sonoma County. Vineyards were set out in three valleys—Alexander, Dry Creek, and Russian River.

All wines are sold direct to the consumer through one of the three tasting rooms (Healdsburg, Tiburon, and Marlboro, New York). The Healdsburg tasting room, where samples are complimentary, is open Monday through Friday from 10:00 A.M. to 5:00 P.M. and 10:00 A.M. to 6:00 P.M. Saturday and Sunday.

Dry Creek Vineyard
3770 Lambert Bridge Rd., Healdsburg
(707) 433–1000, (800) 864–9463
www.drycreekvineyard.com

Dry Creek Winery started in 1972 when ex-Bostonian David Stare began turning an old prune orchard into an award-winning winery. A trip he took to France in 1970 apparently inspired him to leave Boston and head for the University of California at Davis, where he studied viticulture and enology. Stare's was the first new winery in Sonoma County's Dry Creek Valley since the days of Prohibition, and it led to a dramatic wave of change in this long-neglected grape-growing region.

Stare now owns 135 acres of vineyards and also buys grapes from local growers to produce Fume Blanc, Chenin Blanc, Cabernet Sauvignon, and other wines, including his estate-bottled Meritage (a Bordeaux blend). The gray stone winery he built resembles a French country wine chateau. The tasting room, voted among the top 10 in Sonoma County by a local magazine, is casual and informal. When the weather turns cool in October, there's a warm fireplace. When the sun spreads harvest dessert wine called Eldorado Gold. Wine tastings cost $3.00 (refundable with the purchase of wine) and are offered daily from 10:00 A.M. to 5:00 P.M.

Lake Sonoma Winery
9990 Dry Creek Rd., Geyserville
(707) 431–1550, (800) 750–9463
www.lakesonomawinery.com

The newest member of the Korbel family (obtained in 1996), Lake Sonoma Winery is notable for its breathtaking view of Dry Creek Valley and Warm Springs Dam. Gourmet picnic fare is available in the deli and can be enjoyed on the wooded picnic grounds with a bottle of Chardonnay, Cabernet, Zinfandel, or Cinsault. The winery is adjacent to Lake Sonoma Recreation Area and is open daily from 10:00 A.M. to 5:00 P.M. in summer, 11:00 A.M. to 4:00 P.M. in winter. Tastings are complimentary.

Lambert Bridge Winery
4085 W. Dry Creek Rd., Healdsburg
(707) 431–9600, (800) 975–0555
www.lambertbridge.com

Established in 1975, the winery takes its name from a neighboring landmark bridge that spans Dry Creek. Many of the wines of this small, high-quality winery are available only in the charming tasting room, where the wine-stained tasting bar was made from oak casks. A crackling fireplace cheers frosty days, and on sunny days Lambert Bridge's picnic grounds may be the most elegant in Dry Valley. The tasting room also features gourmet mustards to complement the winery's wines, which include Fume Blanc, Pinot Noir, and Zinfandel. The winery, with complimentary samplings, is open daily from 10:30 A.M. to 4:30 P.M.

Pezzi King Vineyards
3805 Lambert Bridge Rd., Healdsburg
(707) 431–9388, (800) 411–4758
www.pezziking.com

Pezzi King Vineyards is family owned and operated. The name represents the blending of two important family names and honors the mothers of owners Jim and Jane Rowe. The Rowes use "balanced

warm yellow patches on the lawn, a picnic lunch in the gardens is a perfect idea.

The tasting room, where samples are complimentary, is open daily from 10:30 A.M. to 4:30 P.M. The first weekend of June marks Dry Creek's annual open house.

Ferrari-Carrano Vineyard & Winery
8761 Dry Creek Rd., Healdsburg
(707) 433–6700, (800) 831–0381
www.ferrari-carano.com

The Wine Shop at Villa Fiore (the name of the chateau that houses the Ferrari-Carrano operation) is one of California's friendliest and most enchanting wine country destinations. Visitors will discover magnificent gardens, critically acclaimed wines, and unique gifts. The spectacular underground barrel cellar where the wines of Don and Rhonda Carrano age are also a favorite. Among the wines poured at the wine shop are Fume Blanc, Chardonnay, Merlot, and a late and sustainable" viticulture techniques—which include vast additions of organically composted materials and the planting of nitrogen-fixing cover crops—to produce intensely flavorful varieties without sacrificing style, finesse, and balance. The James Rowe family released its first Zinfandel and Cabernet Sauvignon in March 1996, and they also produce a fine Chardonnay. Six picnic pavilions with redwood trees for shade offer panoramic views of Dry Creek Valley. The tasting room, where samples are complimentary, is open daily from 10:00 A.M. to 4:30 P.M.

Preston Vineyards
9282 W. Dry Creek Rd., Healdsburg
(707) 433-3372, (800) 305-9707
www.prestonvineyards.com

According to the folks at family-owned Preston Winery, "Having fun is no scandal." They take pride in being known as the alternative winery: the place to go when you want something different and delicious. Not only can you taste some unusual wines, but you can also enjoy some fresh bread baked in the forno and picnic among flowers, herbs, vegetable gardens, and olive trees. If that's not enough fun, you can play a game of bocce ball on the house courts.

Preston is slightly off the beaten path, but with so much going for it, the adventure is worth it. The 115 acres of grapes grow without insecticides and produce flavorful, eccentric wines such as Beaujolais, Viognier, Moscato Curioso, and Marsanne. You can sample them free in the tasting room, which is open (along with the bocce courts) from 11:00 A.M. to 4:30 P.M. daily.

Quivira Vineyards
4900 W. Dry Creek Rd., Healdsburg
(707) 431-8333, (800) 292-8339
www.quivirawine.com

For centuries, European explorers searched for the legendary New World land called Quivira. It was thought to be on the Pacific Coast in the region now known as Sonoma County. Three centuries ago European mapmakers placed it just about where the Quivira Winery is located now. Whatever else you find out here about the legends of Quivira, you will also encounter some excellent Sauvignon Blanc, Zinfandel, and a Rhône-style blend. The tasting room (samples are complimentary) is open daily from 11:00 A.M. to 5:00 P.M. Picnic grounds offer a splendid view of Dry Creek Valley.

Clos du Bois
19410 Geyserville Ave., Geyserville
(707) 857-3100, (800) 222-3189
www.closdubois.com

Clos du Bois got its start in Sonoma County as a vineyard operation in the early 1970s, with 590 acres of vineyards in the Alexander Valley. Today, it is one of Sonoma County's most honored wineries, located on a 40-acre site in the heart of the beautiful Alexander Valley, and with approximately 1,000 prime acres of vineyard in Alexander and Dry Creek valleys. The winery produces Sauvignon Blanc, Chardonnay, Gewurztraminer, Pinot Noir, Merlot, Zinfandel, and Cabernet Sauvignon. With such a roster, it's remarkable that they seem to do all of them well, some superbly. In addition, they produce an exceptional Winemaker's Reserve Cabernet Sauvignon, and their reserve Chardonnay from the Flintwood vineyard is impressive.

One aspect of the Clos du Bois tasting room that is appreciated by all is the extremely knowledgeable and friendly staff, who pour a wide variety of wines daily. If you're a neophyte, they will never blink an eye but patiently offer you their expertise. Tastings are complimentary from 10:00 A.M. to 4:30 P.M. daily.

Canyon Road Winery
19550 Geyserville Ave., Geyserville
(707) 857-3417, (800) 793-9463
www.canyonroadwinery.com

A warm and friendly tasting room serves Canyon Road's Cabernet Sauvignon, Sauvignon Blanc, Shiraz, Sangiovese, and Chardonnay, as well as wines of the Venezia and Nervo labels. A country deli and gift shop makes it easy to set down for a picnic with a shared bottle of Canyon Road wine.

Canyon Road's wine club, known as the Roadies Club, uses a newsletter to announce opportunities to join in the autumn crush and do a little grape stomping. Other benefits of Roadie membership include a seminar on wines in the spring, a chance to visit with the winemaker, and an opportunity to receive shipments of select wines at discount prices. Samples are complimentary, and the tasting room is open daily from 10:00 A.M. to 5:00 P.M.

Chateau Souverain
Independence Ln. at U.S. 101, Geyserville
(707) 433–8281, (888) 809–4637
www.chateausouverain.com

This architecturally striking winery is one of the few with a restaurant—the Cafe is open daily for lunch and Friday, Saturday, and Sunday for dinner (see our Restaurants chapter for more information). Chateau Souverain's "room with a view" tasting room features a host of award-winning wines, such as Cabernet Sauvignon, Merlot, Zinfandel, Pinot Noir, and Sauvignon Blanc made from selected vineyards within the Alexander Valley, Dry Creek, and Carneros appellations. Open daily from 10:00 A.M. to 5:00 P.M.; tasting is $3.00.

Insiders' Tip
Wine grapes rule around here: A small 70-acre, nine-hole golf course next door to Chimney Rock Winery in Napa Valley's Stags Leap appellation was plowed under in 2001 to make way for more Cabernet Sauvignon vineyards. The property owners implied that it didn't make sense to waste prime Stags Leap earth on golf links when it could be producing award-winning wine.

Field Stone Winery
10075 Hwy. 128, east of Healdsburg
(707) 433–7266, (800) 544–7273
www.fieldstonewinery.com

Eleven miles east of Healdsburg in the Alexander Valley, Field Stone Winery was built of large native cobblestones and is partially dug into an small knoll, creating a wine cellar in the European style. Beautiful picnic grounds under spreading oaks are the setting for summer events, including concerts, Shakespearean plays, and dinners. The estate-bottled wines include Cabernet Sauvignon, Merlot, and Petite Sirah, as well as three stylish whites—Sauvignon Blanc, Chardonnay, and Gewurztraminer. Picnic facilities are available, and complimentary tasting hours are 10:00 A.M. to 5:00 P.M. daily.

Geyser Peak Winery
22281 Chianti Rd., Geyserville
(707) 857–9400, (800) 255–9463
www.geyserpeakwinery.com

One of the fastest-growing wineries in Sonoma County, Geyser Peak now distributes wines throughout the United States, as well as Switzerland, Germany, and Hong Kong. Though particularly known for its Chardonnay, Geyser Peak produces a number of fine varieties, including Merlot, Cabernet Sauvignon, Zinfandel, Sauvignon Blanc, California Riesling, and Gewurztraminer.

You might want to consider joining the winery's Cellar Door Club for discount opportunities on select wines and a chance to attend special events. Samples are complimentary (unless you want to pop $5.00 for the reserve wines), and tasting room hours are 10:00 A.M. to 5:00 P.M. daily. A lovely picnic area overlooks the Alexander Valley, and the Panoramic Trail—winding up behind the winery—and the Margot Patterson Doss Trail—named for a well-known San Francisco walker and writer—will appeal to hikers.

Hanna Winery
9280 Hwy. 128, Healdsburg
(707) 431–4310, (888) 426–6288
www.hannawinery.com

Dr. Elias S. Hanna, a Marin County surgeon who was born and raised on a farm in Syria, founded Hanna Winery in 1985. His winery now produces about 34,000 cases of Sauvignon Blanc, Chardonnay, Cabernet Sauvignon, Merlot, and Pinot Noir annually. You can taste Hanna wines at two hospitality centers, one at 5353 Occidental Road in Santa Rosa and the other on Highway 128 in Alexander Valley. The patio of the visitor center in Healdsburg is a lovely place for a picnic, with sweeping views of the Alexander Valley and Hanna's magnificent hillside vineyard. It's also a grand setting for weddings or corporate events. The tasting room (samples are complimentary) is open daily from 10:00 A.M. to 4:00 P.M.

Johnson's Alexander Valley Wines
8333 Hwy. 128, Healdsburg
(707) 433–2319
www.johnsonwines.com

From time to time, the tasting room resonates with the mighty sound of a 1924 theater pipe organ. Tom Johnson makes the wine; Jay Johnson repairs old organs. This is a small, family winery producing seven varietals (Zinfandel and Cabernet are two) from family vineyards, all exclusively sold at the winery or on-line. Picnic tables are available, and you may enjoy an informal tour hosted by a member of the Johnson family. Open daily from 10:00 A.M. to 5:00 P.M. for complimentary tastings.

Pedroncelli Winery
1220 Canyon Rd., Geyserville
(707) 857–3531, (800) 836–3894
www.pedroncelli.com

John Pedroncelli, a native of Lombardy, Italy, bought the vineyard property that was to bear his name in 1927—the vines planted there had been yielding grapes for more than 20 years. During Prohibition, the winery sold grapes to home winemakers; after the repeal, it sold wine in bulk to other wineries. Today, Pedroncelli is run by John's sons, John and James, using grapes harvested from the Dry Creek Valley to produce excellent Cabernet, Zinfandel, and Pinot Noir wines. Tucked 2 miles up Canyon Road from U.S. 101, the charmingly rustic Pedroncelli Winery offers picnic tables for a pleasant lunch. Ask about getting on the winery's mailing list for its newsletter. The tasting room, where samples are free, is open daily from 10:00 A.M. to 4:30 P.M.

Simi Winery
16275 Healdsburg Ave., Healdsburg
(707) 433–6981, (800) 746–4880
www.simiwinery.com

In 1881 two Italian immigrant brothers, Guiseppe and Pietro Simi, bought a winery near the grain depot in Healdsburg for $2,250 in gold coins. They built a magnificent, hand-hewn stone winery, and their business soon doubled. Then, in the midst of success, both brothers died, and Guiseppe's teenage daughter Isabelle took over. Prohibition was a blow for her, but when it ended, she had one of the winery's enormous redwood tanks rolled outside and created a retail tasting room. Isabelle could be found there until her late 80s, still selling Simi wines.

Simi is now owned by the French company Moet-Hennessy, which has turned Simi's distinctive wines into part of a winemaking estate of worldwide recognition. There's a picnic area, and samples of the winery's complex, intensely flavored wines are available in the tasting room from 10:00 A.M. to 5:00 P.M. daily, where pouring is complimentary. Winery tours, conducted daily at 11:00 A.M., 1:00 and 3:00 P.M., will show you all the details from oak barrels to bottle lines.

Trentadue Winery
19170 Geyserville Ave., Geyserville
(707) 433–3104, (888) 332–3032
www.trentadue.com

Founded in 1969, family-owned and operated Trentadue has achieved an outstanding reputation not only for rare and unusual wines, but also for highly regarded, better-known varieties. Visitors are offered complimentary tastings of the many varieties (including Petite Sirah, Cabernet, and Sangiovese) and can spend time browsing through a fine collection of wine-related gifts, fine crystal, and china personally selected by Evelyn

Trentadue. A gourmet food shop supplies items to snack on in the picnic area. The tasting room is open daily, 11:00 A.M. to 4:30 P.M. Trentadue has a second retail outlet on the Healdsburg plaza at 320 Center Street, (707) 433-1082.

West County/Russian River

Davis Bynum Winery
8075 Westside Rd., Healdsburg
(707) 433–2611, (800) 826–1073
www.davisbynum.com

Believing that there is "something of a spiritual union between the organic farmer and his soil and his vines," Davis Bynum has cultivated 22 acres of vineyard in accordance with California organic farming standards. To increase the ecological diversity and health of his fields, Bynum has also mixed in 130 olive trees, 120 mandarin trees, caper berries, sea berries, lavender, plums, kiwis, pomegranates, avocados, guavas, and figs in with his vines. The cool, coastal Russian River Valley gives Bynum's wines an intense varietal character. They include Fume Blanc, Gewurztraminer, Zinfandel, Chardonnay, Pinot Noir, Merlot, and Cabernet Sauvignon. With the winery perched on a hillside, the picnic grounds offer a most pleasant view. The tasting room, where samples are complimentary, is open daily from 10:00 A.M. to 5:00 P.M.

Hop Kiln Winery
6050 Westside Rd, Healdsburg
(707) 433–6491
www.hopkilnwinery.com

Housed in an old stone building that was once a hop-drying kiln, the tasting room at Hop Kiln displays a fine collection of winemaking tools and a gallery of old photos showing the history of the hop industry, which bustled in Sonoma County during the early 1900s. The Hop Kiln was declared a state historic landmark in 1977 and has been the setting for several motion pictures, including *The Magic of Lassie* and the TV show *Homeward Bound*. The tasting room is cool, rustic, and pleasant and serves complimentary samplings of Zinfandel, Chardonnay, and two popular blends,

Marty Griffin's Big Red and Thousand Flowers. Owner and community activist Dr. Marty Griffin—a retired internist who founded the winery in the early 1970s—is less involved in Hop Kiln's winemaking these days and more intent on saving the nearby Russian River from run-off degradation and mining. Hop Kiln's grounds are a great place to have a picnic and reflect Griffin's love of nature. A picturesque pond inhabited by local wildfowl sparkles next to the tasting room, and trees provide plenty of shade around the outdoor tables. Winery hours are 10:00 A.M. to 5:00 P.M. daily.

Martini & Prati Wines
2191 Laguna Rd., Santa Rosa
(707) 823–2404
www.martiniprati.com

This is what wineries used to be! It's a unique experience—the only place in Sonoma County where you can fill a jug of Vino Rosso straight from the tank. It is said to be the oldest winery in continuous operation in the county, and it's still owned by the Martini family who opened it. If you have a picnic in mind, visit Elmo's Groceria and Italian Country Store, which is on-site. The Italian family tradition is reflected in the handcrafted style of wines produced—exceptional Sangiovese, Barbera, Vino Grigio, Muscato, and Port. To add to a lovely day, take a stroll through the landscaped grounds, which include an acre of lavender. The tasting room is open daily from 11:00 A.M. to 4:00 P.M. (pouring is complimentary), with tours offered at 11:00 A.M. or by appointment.

Mark West Vineyards & Winery
7010 Trenton-Healdsburg Rd., Forestville
(707) 836–9647, (800) 955–9585
www.markwestwinery.com

Named after British mariner and adventurer Marcus West, Mark West Vineyards stretches across 120 acres on a portion of the former San Miguel Rancho in the Russian River Valley appellation. The area is well-suited to growing Chardonnay, Gewurztraminer, Pinot Noir, and Merlot grapes. Along with the tasting room—where sips are complimentary—you'll find a tree-shaded picnic grounds, espresso bar, gift shop, and the largest private collection of insect-eating plants in the United States. The tasting room is open Thursday through Sunday from 11:00 A.M. to 5:00 P.M.

Topolos at Russian River Vineyards, Winery & Restaurant
5700 Gravenstein Hwy., Forestville
(707) 887–1575 (winery), (800) 867–6567 (orders), (707) 887–1562 (restaurant)
www.topolos.com

This small, family-owned winery, established in 1963, has won awards not only for its exceptional wines, but for its unique, environmentally sound agricultural methods. In 1999, Topolos was named "Environmental Business of the Year" by the Sonoma County Conservation Council. Prior to this distinction, owner Michael Topolos was named "biodynamic farmer of the year." Biodynamics is a method of farming based on the philosophy of Rudolf Steiner and follows a chemical-free, spiritual approach. Topolos's vineyard was the first in the nation certified as biodynamic—it is also certified according to California organic farm standards. Visitors can sample complimentary sips of Zinfandel, Chardonnay, Petite Sirah, and Alicante Bouschet and browse the gift shop. Greek cuisine is served at the adjoining restaurant, open for lunch and dinner (see our Restaurants chapter). The tasting room is open daily from 11:00 A.M. to 5:30 P.M.

Korbel Champagne Cellars
13250 River Rd., Guerneville
(707) 824–7000, (800) 656–7235
www.korbel.com

When the three Czech Korbel brothers emigrated from Bohemia, they settled in a redwood forest along the Russian River, tried several different enterprises—including cigar box manufacture—and finally resolved to become winemakers. They built their handsome, brick winery in 1886, including a quaint turreted tower at the south end. The story behind this tower is a fascinating one. Before leaving Prague, the youngest Korbel inadvertently

fired his pistola in the midst of the townfolk, who had gathered to hear the news called out by the town crier. He was jailed briefly, and upon his release the three brothers fled the country. The tower of the winery is a sentimental duplicate of the jail where young Joseph spent his last days in his home country.

Korbel has an excellent tour of both the champagne cellars and the antique rose garden that surrounds the old summer house. Korbel champagne is produced in the methode champenoise, the traditional French method in which the second fermentation takes place in the same bottle. Complimentary tastings are offered daily from 9:00 A.M. to 4:30 P.M., tours on the hour from 10:00 A.M. to 3:00 P.M.

Mendocino County

The wineries of Anderson Valley are clustered along a 6-mile stretch of Highway 128 near Philo. Morning fog off the Pacific, afternoon breezes, and sunny hillside vineyards make Anderson Valley a special place to grow cool-climate wine grapes, notably Pinot Noir, Chardonnay, and Gewurztraminer.

Farther north along U.S. 101, the Ukiah Valley is where the county's grape-growing began. Today it's where some of Mendocino's oldest and largest vintners make their home.

U.S. 101

Fetzer Vineyards
13601 East Side Rd., Hopland
(707) 744–7600, (800) 846–8637
www.fetzer.com

Bernard Fetzer, a lumber executive, purchased the winery's Redwood Valley Home Ranch in 1958 as a place to raise his large family and grow fine grapes for home winemakers. The family began making wine commercially in 1968. In 1981, Fetzer's 11 children took over and helped the winery grow into one of the leading varietal wine producers in the world. Fetzer wines have won critical praise and tons of gold medals, especially for their Chardonnay.

The tasting room and visitor center,

located 1 mile east of Hopland, features intimate vineyard and garden tours and offers tastings of new releases as well as older wines. A full-service deli with a spacious picnic area is also open to the public. The 50-acre Valley Oaks Ranch is home to vineyards, dozens of old barns, a dining pavilion overlooking Lake Fume, and the 5-acre 100 percent organic Bantera Garden, which includes countless varieties of fruits, vegetables, herbs, and flowers, both edible and decorative. All grapes and plants are grown organically, without use of pesticides or synthetic fertilizers. The winery also has implemented a variety of other environmentally friendly measures, which together earned it the U.S. EPA's Climate Wise Partnership Award two years in a row. Also on the property is a charming seven-room bed and breakfast inn (see our Bed and Breakfast Inns chapter). In 1982 Brown-Forman purchased the Fetzer label as well as the Hopland winery. The Fetzer family continues to grow grapes for Fetzer Vineyards under an exclusive contract. The tasting room offers complimentary tasting and is open from 10:00 A.M. to 6:00 P.M. daily.

Jepson Vineyards
10400 S. U.S. 101, Ukiah
(707) 468–8936, (800) 516–7342
www.jepsonwine.com

In addition to producing Chardonnay, Merlot, and Sauvignon Blanc, and some sparkling and dessert wines, Bob and Alice Jepson, along with winemaker Kurt Lorenzi, have created a special niche by producing Alambic Pot Still brandy, estate-grown and bottled. The winery's tasting room, where sips of a generous 8 to 10 wines are complimentary, is open every day from 10:00 A.M. to 5:00 P.M.

Milone Family Winery
14594 S. U.S. 101, Hopland
(707) 744–1396, (800) 564–2582
www.milonefamilywinery.com

In the early 1900s, Vincenzo Milone came to Mendocino County with his father, discovered some agriculturally rich land near Hopland, and planted grapes. They also built a hop kiln at the foot of Duncan's Peak, near their home. Today that hop kiln is the tasting room for Milone Winery. The kiln is one of the few left over from the days when the nearby village of Hopland was earning its name growing and curing hops. The tasting room is open from 10:00 A.M. to 5:00 P.M. daily. In January and February the tasting room is closed Tuesdays and Wednesdays.

Parducci Wine Cellars
501 Parducci Rd., Ukiah
(707) 462–9463, (888) 362–9463
www.parducci.com

Since 1932, Parducci Wine Cellars has made wine according to a simple philosophy: Wine is an honest, natural product that should never be overprocessed, never be masked by too much oak, and never have its essential flavor and aroma filtered away. Parducci is Mendocino's oldest operating winery, but it is dedicated to contemporary consumers, using modern winemaking techniques and evolving wine styles. Parducci's conviction is that whites should be fermented cold and bottled cold to retain the liveliness, crispness, and freshness of the varietals. Parducci white wines produce a slight spritz from carbon dioxide, a natural retainer of the varietal flavors for which Parducci wines are famous. The tasting room is open Monday through Saturday between 10:00 A.M. and 5:00 P.M., and Sunday 10:00 A.M. and 4:00 P.M., with complimentary tasting.

Redwood Valley Cellars
7051 N. State St., off U.S. 101,
Redwood Valley
(707) 485–0322
www.redwoodcellars.com

This is actually a tasting room for Barren-Pauli Winery in Petaluma. Redwood Valley Cellars also produces wine from grapes grown in Potter Valley. Located between Ukiah and Willits, at the West Road exit off U.S. 101, Redwood Valley Cellars offers complimentary tastings and picnicking daily from 10:30 A.M. to 5:00 P.M.

Highway 128

Greenwood Ridge Vineyards
5501 Hwy. 128, Philo
(707) 895–2002
www.greenwoodridge.com

Allan Green, a graphic artist turned wine-maker, has crafted a lovely Anderson Valley winery and tasting room with a wraparound deck and a view of the hilltop ridge where his vines grow. On one wall of the tasting room are the ribbons his wine received for its excellence—White Riesling, Late Harvest Riesling, Sauvignon Blanc, Chardonnay, Zinfandel, Pinot Noir, Merlot, and Cabernet Sauvignon. Three Greenwood wines have been included in the *Wine Spectator*'s annual list of the "Top 100 Wines of the World." In another corner of the tasting room (samples are complimentary, by the way), you'll see Green's collection of 5,000 wine corks, arranged innovatively into a sculpture. On a sunny day, it's pleasant to sit on the deck of the tasting room, which is open daily from 10:00 A.M. to 6:00 P.M. in summer and 10:00 A.M. to 5:00 P.M. in winter.

Handley Cellars
3151 Hwy. 128, Philo
(707) 895–3876, (800) 733–3151
www.handleycellars.com

Fermentation science is a natural interest for Milla Handley, the winemaker and owner who is also the great-great-granddaughter of brewing giant Henry Weinhard. After receiving her degree in enology and working six years in the wine industry, she and her husband, Rex, founded Handley Cellars in the basement of their home near Philo. Today's tasting room is a far cry from that basement winery. As visitors sip wine, they are surrounded by the Handley family's collection of folk art from around the world. Located 6 miles northwest of Philo, the tasting room offers complimentary samples of their unusual Pinot Menieur, as well as an excellent Pinot Noir. Complimentary hors d'oeuvres are presented along with the wines the first weekend of every month. The tasting room is open daily from 11:00 A.M. to 6:00 P.M. in summer and 11:00 A.M. to 5:00 P.M.

> ## Insiders' Tip
> "Liquid gold" brandy is being produced at Germain-Robin, a tiny distillery west of Ukiah in Mendocino County, said to be the finest brandy producer in America by cognac aficionados. The company's priciest nectar is Cask 4, an extremely limited production brandy (just 12 bottles were released in December 2001) that sells for $1,200 per bottle.

in winter. There is an inviting garden courtyard for picnics.

Husch Vineyards
4400 Hwy. 128, Philo
(707) 895–3216, (800) 554–8724
www.huschvineyards.com

Farming has been the occupation for three generations of the Oswald family, owners of Husch Vineyards. Theirs is the oldest winery in Anderson Valley and still contains some of its first varietal plantings. Originally planted in 1969 and bonded in 1971 by the Husches, it was purchased by the Oswalds in 1979. Currently, three members of the Oswald family are involved in the winery: Hugo, Miles, and Ken. All Husch wines are made from grapes grown only on the family-owned vineyards, including the original 21-acre block of Pinot Noir, Gewurztraminer, and Chardonnay. The tasting room is rustic, friendly, and open daily for complimentary samples from 10:00 A.M. to 6:00 P.M. in summer and 10:00 A.M. to 5:00 P.M. in winter.

Navarro Vineyards
5601 Hwy. 128, Philo
(707) 895–3686, (800) 537–9463
www.navarrowine.com

Ted Bennett has been making Anderson Valley Gewurztraminer since 1973, and over the years he has developed a successful formula for this grape, which requires a long growing season. His wife, Deborah, serves guests in the tasting rooms. "We're not a big corporate winery," she says. "We're the '70s homesteaders who happened to like wine." Navarro Vineyards seeks to make a fine wine but doesn't forget about "the guy in a camper van with three kids who just wants to enjoy a bottle," says winemaker Jim Klein, whose efforts produce 30,000 cases a year. The tasting room offers complimentary sips daily from 10:00 A.M. to 6:00 P.M. in summer, 10:00 A.M. to 5:00 P.M. in winter.

Roederer Estate
4501 Hwy. 128, Philo
(707) 895–2288
www.roederer-estate.com

The wines created by the European firm headed by Madame Orly-Roederer have been world-famous for 200 years. Now they are being produced in the Anderson Valley under the direction of her grandson, Jean-Claude Rouzard, who came here in 1981 in search of the perfect appellation. To create the perfect wine, Roederer uses only the first juice, pressed from the pulp with minimal skin contact. Subsequent pressings are not used, and even the first pressing is further critiqued, with 30 percent later discarded to be faithful to the Roederer style.

Roederer Estate winery is open every day from 11:00 A.M. to 5:00 P.M. A $3.00 sampling fee is charged but is deducted from each bottle of wine purchased.

Yorkville Vineyards & Cellars
Hwy. 128 at Mile Marker 40.4, Yorkville
(707) 894–9177
www.yorkville-cellars.com

The 30-acre vineyard owned by the Wallo family lies at 1,000 feet above sea level, where sun-filled days and cool nights combine to create premium-quality grapes. Since its establishment in 1982, the Yorkville Vineyards estate has been farmed organically. Instead of pesticides and herbicides, they count on seasonal cover to serve as an alternative for insects to attack instead of the vine. The cover also provides a host environment for beneficial insects that prey on unwelcome ones. Yorkville Vineyards has been certified organic by the state of California every year since 1986. Yorkville grows seven Bordeaux varietals and makes at least one unusual wine—Eleanor of Aquitaine, a half-and-half blend of Sauvignon Blanc and Semillon, aged in French oak barrels only. Picnics are encouraged, and complimentary tastings are offered from 11:00 A.M. to 6:00 P.M. daily in summer, 11:00 A.M. to 5:00 P.M. daily in winter (call in advance in winter).

Lake County

Guenoc and Langtry Estate Vineyards
21000 Butts Canyon Rd., Middletown
(707) 987–2385
www.guenoc.com

Whose charming countenance is that you see gracing bottles of Guenoc wine? It's Lillie Langtry—the "Jersey Lily," beloved stage actress of the late 19th century (see our History chapter). Langtry ran the business from 1888 to 1906, and her palatial home is still the centerpiece of the property. The vineyards sit on the border of Napa and Lake Counties in Guenoc Valley, the only federally approved appellation under single proprietorship. Grower Orville Magoon helps produce a wide range of wines, from Chardonnay and Cabernet Sauvignon to Petite Sirah, and even the occasional Port. There is no charge for tasting, though you can opt to pay $4.00 for a selection of reserve wines. Tours are by appointment, though you can take a self-guided tour of the grounds anytime. Hours are 11:30 A.M. to 5:00 P.M. daily.

Ployez Winery
11171 Highway 29, Lower Lake
(707) 994–2106

You probably thought the only thing French in Lake County was the fries at

Burger King, but along comes Gerald Ployez, a fourth-generation winemaker from Champagne whose east-of-the-Atlantic family still bottles under the Ployez-Jacquemari label. Gerald and his wife, Shirley, opened this winery in September, 1997. Gerald concentrates mostly on Chardonnay and Sauvignon Blanc, though he produces three types of red, too. He also makes Lake County's only sparkling wine, a Brut, and a Gamay Beaujolais. Over the next few years, the couple plans to plant about 23 acres around the winery in Chardonnay and Cabernet Sauvignon. Ployez is open daily from April through September, and Thursday through Sunday in the low season; the hours are 11:00 A.M. to 5:00 P.M., though you might find live music on Friday nights from 6:00 to 10:00 P.M. Tours are by appointment, and there is no charge for tasting.

Wildhurst Vineyards
3855 Main St., Kelseyville
(707) 279–4302, (800) 595–9463
www.wildhurst.com

When Myron and Marilyn Holdenried started this winery in 1991, it was really just a case of diversification: Myron is a fifth-generation Kelseyville farmer. In fact, he had already been growing grapes and pears for 25 years. Wildhurst started at the site of the old Steurmer Winery in Lower Lake, then moved to Kelseyville in 1996; a year later it unveiled its tasting room in a refurbished I.O.O.F. Hall. (The winery is 2 miles away, and not open to the public.) Wildhurst is primarily noted for its Merlot, but makes three other reds and a couple of whites, all under the Clear Lake appellation. Myron still sells grapes to Beringer, Kendall-Jackson, and Fetzer, but the top 25 percent of his crop is crushed for Wildhurst. The tasting room is open from 10:00 A.M. to 5:00 P.M. daily. There is no tasting fee.

Steele Wines
4350 Thomas Dr., Kelseyville
(707) 279–9475

Kendall-Jackson was the pride of Lake County until it "went Sonoma" a few

years ago. But Lake still can brag of its hold upon one of the men who nurtured that winery to prominence: Jed Steele. The former winemaker at K-J produced his first self-named vintage in 1991 and is going strong in the building formerly occupied by Konocti Winery. Jed dabbles in a number of varietals, but generally sticks to Chardonnay, Pinot Noir, and Zinfandel, with grapes from as far south as Santa Barbara County and as far north as Mendocino. Steele is open Monday through Saturday from 11:00 A.M. to 5:00 P.M., May through October; it's closed during the winter. There is a $1.00 charge for tasting, and you are encouraged to enjoy a picnic lunch among the lush gardens. You also might stumble upon a farmer's market if you arrive Saturday morning or the Harvest Festival (see our Festivals and Annual Events chapter) if you get there on the second weekend of October.

Wine Shops

As you would expect, they don't just make 'em, pour 'em, and sell 'em in the Wine Country—there is also a variety of stores dedicated to the display, presentation, storage, and properly outfitted enjoyment of wines. In addition, some shops offer amazing selections of wines from our four-county coverage area and beyond, along with all the decadent accouterments. So light up that fat, pricey cigar and take a look at a few of our favorite wine shops.

Napa County

J.V. Liquor Warehouse
426 First St., Napa
(707) 253–2624, (877) 4–MY–WINE
www.jvwarehouse.com

Great bargains in wine can be found here. Napa residents tend to shop at this store for their premium vino, and there is much to choose from. Most are at discount prices, and they will pack up assorted cases and ship them home for you, too. It's short on charm but it lives up to its reputation—and it's just across the river bridge from Copia.

The Vintage 1870 Wine Cellar
6525 Washington St., Yountville
(707) 944–9070, (800) WINE–4–US
www.vintagewinecellar.com

Ironic that the stables of the old Groezinger Winery would end up as the one piece of the property expressly devoted to wine. Unlike most wine shops, this one is licensed for tastings—they pour about a dozen selections, all day long. On the shelves you'll find everything from $5.00 bottles to an imperial of Mondavi 1978 Reserve Cabernet Sauvignon that goes for $1,000. The Cellar also sells a few cigars.

Insiders' Tip

If you have the time, try to visit local wine shops (listed in this chapter) before making major purchases at winery tasting rooms. Counterintuitive as it may be, you can often find better deals and a wider selection at the shops.

St. Helena Wine Merchants
699 St. Helena Hwy. South, St. Helena
(707) 963–7888, (800) 729–9463
www.shwinemerchants.com

Across the road from V. Sattui Winery is this unpretentious purveyor of wines. The Merchants aim to carry the sort of small-availability labels that out-of-state visitors read about, but can't find at home—Harlan, Dominus, and Maya come to mind as examples. Don't be surprised if you bump into a local winemaker or two during your visit.

Dean & DeLuca
607 St. Helena Hwy. South, St. Helena
(877) DEAN–WIN(E)
www.deandeluca.com

When those classy New Yorkers set up shop in Wine Country (see our Shopping chapter), it changed the face of retail wine sales in Napa Valley. D&D has the most extensive collection of California wines you could ever hope to see: 1,200 labels, and that's just 750-milliliter bottles. The wines are arranged alphabetically within varietal categories. Forget about trying to note every wine; by the time you make it to the last Zinfandel, they probably will have added a few more bottles. "We try for the newest, the latest, the hottest, the best," says John Hardisty, who manages the wine section. Rarely does Dean & DeLuca fall short of its goals.

Calistoga Wine Stop
1458 Lincoln Ave., No. 2, Calistoga
(707) 942–5556, (800) 648–4521

Before you even get to the wine, there's a lot of history worth noting here. The Wine Stop is in The Depot, that big yellow wood building that was what it claims to be. Built in 1868, it's the second-oldest train station left in California (though no trains have stopped here since 1963). The wine shop itself is jammed inside a 19th-century boxcar, which limits the elbow room but somehow doesn't impair the Napa-Sonoma–concentrated selection. (Owner Tom Pelter estimates that 75 percent of his stock is made in those two counties.) Pelter is a bundle of help, whether you're selecting or trying to get it home. He's also something of a Port aficionado, which explains the high density of Portugal's fortified wine in his store.

Enoteca Wine Shop
1345 Lincoln Ave., Calistoga
(707) 942–1117

Discreetly cached on the second floor of Calistoga's 111-year-old I.O.O.F. building is this classy wine shop. ("Enoteca" is an Italian word meaning "wine cellar" or "wine library.") Proprietor Margaux Singleton learned the trade while purchasing wine for such respected establishments as La Casa Sena Wine Shop in Santa Fe and All Seasons Cafe in Calistoga, and she has been accepted to enter the arduous Master of Wine program, headquartered in England. She and co-owner Frederick Schrader taste every wine before stocking it (no, they're not looking for assistants). They tend toward artisanal vintners who produce hundreds of cases rather than tens of thousands. And they draw from all over the world, as evidenced by their affection for the likes of Chateau Musar in Lebanon.

Sonoma County

The Wine Exchange of Sonoma
452 First St. East, Sonoma
(707) 938–1794, (800) 938–1794

Looking for a more efficient way to sample local wines than driving from one place to another? Interested in a place that carries hard-to-find wines and will even ship them anywhere allowed by law? The Wine Exchange is the place for you, with some 800 premium wines and 280 beers in stock. It's opposite the Sonoma Plaza, with a tasting bar that features 18 wines and six draft beers. The store is open from 10:00 A.M. to 6:00 P.M. Monday through Saturday, and 11:00 A.M. to 6:00 P.M. on Sunday.

Sonoma Wine Hardware
536 Broadway, Sonoma
(707) 939–1694, (866) 231–9463

Napa Valley Wine Hardware
659 Main St., St. Helena
(707) 967–5503, (866) 611–9463

You just scored your first case of great Cabernet Sauvignon—now, how can you store it properly back home? Your next stop should be at one of these shops. The stores do not sell wine (they leave that up to you); their main focus is wine storage systems. Under the same ownership, both stores have similar inventories, but the Sonoma store features a slightly larger showroom and a larger library of wine books. On display in both are a multitude of cabinets, racks, and other "hardware" for storing and enjoying wine, and lots of accessories, too.

Taylor & Norton Wine Merchants
19210 Sonoma Hwy., Sonoma
(707) 939–6611
www.taylorandnorton.com

You'll have no trouble finding every local and regional wine you've been looking for in this wine shop. More than that, Taylor & Norton carries wines from other U.S. areas (some not so easy to locate in this heavily promoted wine region), as well as wines from Europe and other foreign wine-producing regions. Ask owner Gregory Taylor anything—he's a knowledgeable expert. While shopping for wine, you might want to browse through a handsome selection of antique wine decanters and glasses, some from the Victorian era. They're pricey, but so beautiful you may not be able to resist taking home a souvenir. The store is open 10:00 A.M. to 6:00 P.M. Monday through Saturday.

The Wine Shop
331 Healdsburg Ave., Healdsburg
(707) 433–0433

It's all wine here; in fact, it's a wine bar, meaning it's licensed by the state to serve and charge for full glasses of wine, not tastings. But the selection is enormous: The shop specializes in hard to find, small production wines worldwide, with more than 600 wineries represented. They will ship your selections, too.

Attractions

So you've had a taste of wine tasting, feasted on some fabulous food, and now you're ready for something completely different. You've come to the right chapter. Sure, wineries, mud baths, and world-class restaurants are attractions in their own right, and all those selling points are detailed in other chapters. In this chapter, however, you'll find everything worth visiting that defies categorical lumping. That might be a culturally rich historical site (such as Fort Ross), a museum (such as the Triangle Tattoo Museum in Fort Bragg), a scenic jaunt (such as the Skunk Train), or even a good old-fashioned bit of fun (such as Sears Point Raceway). We also have included separate sections on balloon, plane, and glider rides and guided tours that range from quirky to luxurious.

Finally, let us point out the complete absence of anything approaching a major amusement park in the four-county area. Some may consider this a shortcoming, but most residents and our regular visitors would lay down their lives to keep out a Rollercoaster World or WinoDisney.

Price Code

The price code below reflects the admission price or fees for two adults in high season, not including gratuities, where appropriate.

$	Free or low cost
$$	$15 to $50
$$$	$51 to $150
$$$$	More than $151

Main Events

Napa County

Seguin Moreau Napa Cooperage $
151 Camino Dorado, Napa
(707) 252-3408
www.seguinmoreau.com

You've seen how the wine is blended, now take a good look at how the barrels get toasted. The only U.S. outpost of the famed French wine barrel makers, Tonnellerie Seguin Moreau Cooperage, is located in Napa. Watch the crew of skilled "coopers" bend, shave, and roast the oak staves over open flames in the floor, then hammer them together using steel hoops. It's a craft that has changed little in hundreds of years of winemaking. Admission is free.

Hakusan Sake Gardens $
1 Executive Way, Napa
(707) 258-6160
www.hakusan.com

The process begins with kernels of high-grade Sacramento Valley rice, milled at the company's private mill in Williams, California. Hakusan is one of only seven sake makers in the United States, and the only one in Wine Country. Sake, while comparable to wine in body and complexity, actually is brewed, like beer. It therefore is made to be refrigerated and consumed within a year, not aged. Hakusan, at the intersection of Highways 29 and 12, is open from 10:00 A.M. to 5:00 P.M. every day. There are self-guided tours, and for $1.00 you can sample about five varieties, both hot and cold. The brewery's offerings include cooking sake and sweet plum sake.

Copia: The American Center for Wine, Food and the Arts $$
500 First St., Napa
(707) 259-1600
www.copia.org

In addition to overseeing the winery empire that bears his name, Robert Mondavi has spent his golden years getting this mega-project off the ground (see the close-up in this chapter). At a cost of $50 million, the 80,000-square-foot cultural museum and educational center features lively programs, classes, exhibitions, and demonstrations to bring together world-renowned chefs and home cooks, winemakers and wine lovers, and artists—from experts to amateurs.

RMS Brandy Distillery $
1250 Cuttings Wharf Rd., Napa
(707) 253–9055
www.rmsbrandy.com

Step inside the Barrel House of the former Alambic Distillery, where hundreds of casks of brandy lie aging. But don't linger unless you're looking for a good buzz; the scent is enough to curl your nose hairs. The distillery, the largest one of its kind in North America, was started as a joint venture of Remy Martin and Schramsberg Vineyards in 1982 (Schramsberg is no longer involved). They offer 40-minute tours from 10:30 A.M. to 4:15 P.M., taking you into the Barrel House, the video and aroma room, and the Still House, where eight huge alambic stills, much like those used for centuries in Cognac, do their business. A variety of spirits may be purchased in the retail room. Cuttings Wharf Road leaves Highway 12/121 about 1.3 miles west of Highway 29.

> ## Insiders' Tip
> Don't get miffed at the proprietors if they fail to offer you tastes at RMS Brandy Distillery in Napa. Because of brandy's high alcohol content, tastings are prohibited by county law.

Napa Firefighters Museum $
1201 Main St., Napa
(707) 259–0609

This museum will give you a deeper appreciation of the folks who fight the flames. Inside you'll see a hand pumper and a steamer, hose carts, engines, ladder trucks, old fire equipment and uniforms, and photos from many eras of puttin' out fires. There is no admission fee, and the museum is open 11:00 A.M. to 4:00 P.M. Wednesday through Sunday.

Veterans Home of California $
California Dr., Yountville
(707) 944–4918

The museum in the old chapel of the Veterans Home features rotating displays of documents, photographs, models, uniforms, and weapons from various eras of U.S. military history. Unfortunately, it is open only on Friday and Saturday, noon to 2:00 P.M. However, just strolling around the manicured grounds of this Spanish Revival complex, much of which dates back to 1918, is a pleasure. The landscaping comprises a working horticultural exhibit, with dozens of trees and plants labeled. Look for the signs on Highway 29 just south of Domaine Chandon.

Napa Valley Museum $
55 Presidents Circle, Yountville
(707) 944–0500
www.napavalleymuseum.org

Looking like a Lexus in a parking lot full of Packards, the Napa Valley Museum opened to the public in 1998, on the site of the Veterans Home of California in Yountville. A major capital project that was years in the planning, the nonprofit museum celebrates the artistic, historical, and cultural heritage of the valley, with a permanent exhibit called "The Land and People of the Napa Valley." Its central, permanent exhibition is "California Wine: The Science of an Art." Using music, the spoken word, and the power of technology (including 26 videodisc players and nine microcomputers), it effectively presents the winemaking process in near entirety.

Temporary exhibitions have included Gold Rush photography and a collection of 19th-century prints by Andrew Jackson Grayson, a local bird artist of renown, as well as display of textiles of the Andes. The Napa Valley Museum is open Wednesday through Monday from 10:00 A.M. to 5:00 P.M. (until 8:00 P.M. on the first Thursday of the month). Admission is $4.50 for adults, $3.50 for students and seniors age 60 or older, and $2.50 for youth ages 7 to 17.

Silverado Museum $
1490 Library Ln., St. Helena
(707) 963–3757
www.napanet.net/vi/silverado

A California museum devoted to a Scottish novelist might seem a bit strange, but, hey, Robert Louis Stevenson did help immortalize the area with his *The Silverado Squatters.* He also penned classics such as *Treasure Island, Dr. Jekyll and Mr. Hyde,* and others you'll read all about at the museum. It has first editions, artifacts from the Stevenson home, personal letters and photographs, and a few original manuscripts (though most of those reside at Yale University). The museum is closed Monday but open every other day from noon to 4:00 P.M.

Bale Grist Mill State Historic Park $
3369 Hwy. 29, St. Helena
(707) 963–2236

The friendly miller, Keith, will tell you how this park is a working reminder of the days when "milling" involved more than driving to Safeway for a bag of all-purpose flour. Dr. Edward Bale built the wood-framed mill in 1846, and it has been painstakingly refurbished. The park is open 10:00 A.M. to 5:00 P.M. daily, but the best times to visit are weekend days at 11:30 A.M., 1:00, 2:30, and 3:30 P.M. That's when the park cranks up the wooden, 36-foot water wheel and gets those original quartz stones to grinding wheat or corn. Also displayed are artifacts such as 50-pound sacks of grist, worn millstones, and the whisks used to clean them. Admission is $1.00 for adults; children under 16 free. From here you can hike to adjacent Bothe-Napa Valley State Park (see our Parks and Recreation chapter).

The Sharpsteen Museum $
1311 Washington St., Calistoga
(707) 942–5911
www.napanet.net/vi/sharpsteen

If every small town in America had a museum as lively and authentic as the Sharpsteen, maybe we wouldn't be so ignorant of history. The museum was founded in the 1970s by Ben Sharpsteen, who produced such films as *Fantasia* and *Snow White* for Walt Disney. (Sharpsteen's Academy Award "Oscar" statuette from his days with Disney gleams inside a special display case.) The crowning piece of his legacy is a 32-foot, scale-model diorama that lays out the grounds of Sam Brannan's Calistoga spa, circa 1860 (see our History chapter for more on Brannan). One of the original cottages from that spa serves as a museum annex.

The Sharpsteen also has a restored Bill Spiers stagecoach that once ran from Calistoga to Middletown, an exhibit on the local Wappo tribe, an interactive display on geothermal activity, and a bunch more. The museum is open 10:00 A.M. to 4:00 P.M. daily from April through September and noon to 4:00 P.M. daily from October through March. There is no admission charge, thanks to the eager volunteer staff. They do, of course, accept donations.

Pedals Past Bicycle Museum $
1458 Lincoln Ave., Car 12, Calistoga
(707) 942–9469
www.pedalspast.com

Here's a museum that will make you feel like a kid again—a shrine to bicycles that resides within a restored railroad car. Run by a couple of Napa Valley natives who traveled the United States for four years to gather together this collection, they claim it is the only museum of its kind on the West Coast. There are more than 60 bikes on display, and the exhibit changes every few months. The bikes are mostly American-made balloon tire two-wheelers from the pneumatic tire era (1933 to 1970), with all the major brands of the period represented—Schwinn, Monark, Shelby, Colson, Columbia, even Sears Roebuck and Montgomery Ward machines. Because the museum survives

The Sharpsteen Museum in Calistoga is like no other small-town museum—it houses such diverse items as a genuine Academy Award Oscar statuette and a stagecoach. PHOTO: JEAN SAYLOR DOPPENBERG

solely on donations, there's an excellent assortment of memorabilia for sale and a large reference library. They will also escort you on a historical tour of Calistoga on one of their vintage machines, for $40 to $75, depending on the extras. Hours are generally 11:00 A.M. to 4:00 P.M. Wednesday through Saturday, or by appointment.

Old Faithful Geyser of California $
1299 Tubbs Ln., Calistoga
(707) 942–6463
www.oldfaithfulgeyser.com

About every 40 minutes on the yearly average (depending on how much water is in the aquifer), the earth gurgles, puffs, and blows a stream of boiling water (350 degrees hot!) about 60 feet into the air off Tubbs Lane. Welcome to Calistoga's geyser, one of only three in world that can call themselves "Old Faithful" without shame. Both the visitors building and the private home on the property are heated

entirely by thermal means. There is a working seismograph in the entryway (the geyser is said to predict earthquakes), and outside near the erupting pond, for some reason, is a pen of Tennessee Fainting goats, a rare breed suffering from myatonia, which causes them to lock up and topple when startled. The Old Faithful complex is open from 9:00 A.M. to 6:00 P.M. daily in the warm months, 9:00 A.M. to 5:00 P.M. in the winter. Admission is $6.00 for adults, $5.00 for seniors, and $2.00 for kids ages 6 through 12.

Villa Ca'Toga $$
Off Tubbs Ln., Calistoga
(707) 942–3900
www.catoga.com

Italian artist Carlo Marchiori is one of the eminent trompe l'oeil artists in the world, and Villa Ca'Toga—a mansion and work-in-progress on the outskirts of Calistoga—is his vision come to life. Faux pillars, staircases, and hanging plants are painted in three-dimensional realism on two-dimensional walls. Alcoves end abruptly at painted backdrops, and surprises lie around every corner (even for the initiated—Marchiori is constantly adding new sculptures). The house is open Saturdays from May and October for a one-hour tour that begins at 11:00 A.M. Reservations are necessary, and you pick up your tickets and a map to the property at the Ca'Toga Galleria D'Arte at 1206 Cedar Street in downtown Calistoga (see our Arts and Culture chapter). Tickets are $20 per person, and children over 12 are welcome. Following the tour you are free to roam the gardens at your leisure, but leave your camera in the car—no photography is allowed inside the Villa.

Sonoma County

Southern Sonoma

Depot Park Museum $
270 First St. West, Sonoma
(707) 938–1762
www.vom.com/~depot

This is more than a museum; it's an authentic piece of Sonoma city's history. Originally the depot was on the downtown plaza, much to the chagrin of Sonomans, who felt the plaza had been turned into a railroad yard, turntable and all. After some pressure, the depot was moved in 1890 to its present site, where Northwest Pacific operated until it went out of business, and the city bought the property. It was gradually sinking into oblivion when the Sonoma County Historical Society took over the depot in 1976. But while the society was setting about restoring it, the depot burned. By 1978 it had been rebuilt, and the museum now houses a terrific collection of historic memorabilia focusing on the 19th century. Several rooms are furnished in Victorian style, and a good deal of emphasis is placed on the life of General Mariano Vallejo (see our History chapter). Pioneer artifacts and exhibits of Native American culture are nicely displayed. Temporary exhibits shed light on specific historical periods, crafts, and events. The museum

is open Wednesday through Sunday from 1:00 to 4:30 P.M. There's no admission, but donations are welcome.

Train Town $
20264 Broadway, Sonoma
(707) 938–3912
www.traintown.com

Train Town is the most well-developed scale railroad in America—a joy for anyone of any age. It is just plain, clean fun for old and young. You climb into a miniature train, one-fourth the normal size, and chug your way through 10 acres of planned landscaped park filled with thousands of native trees, animals, bridges over lakes, tunnels, waterfalls, and replicas of historic buildings. Two miniature steam engines (on weekends; during the week it's likely to be diesel) and hand-crafted railroad cars take passengers on the 20-minute ride to Lakeville, a pint-sized, Western-flavored hamlet populated with geese and ducks. Along the way there's a stop to pet some llamas and goats. Trains operate daily in summer from 10:00 A.M. to 5:00 P.M. In winter they are on a shorter, weekend schedule. Train cars are protected overhead, but if showers start, passengers get to go around twice. The fare is $3.75 for adults and $3.25 for children 12 and younger and seniors. The expanded sidelights include a carousel, ferris wheel, and petting zoo.

Vintage Aircraft Co. $$$$
23982 Arnold Dr., Sonoma
(707) 938–2444
www.vintageaircraft.com

You step back into the 1940s when you step onto the tarmac and check out Christopher Prevost's fleet of authentic, 1940 Boeing-built Stearman biplanes. One of the planes is a North American-built, World War II Navy SNJ-4, designed to train pilot candidates for the Air Force and Navy. Meticulously restored and maintained, the planes tempt thrill seekers to take one of several rides offered by Prevost. A leisurely 20-minute ride over Sonoma Valley is $120 for one passenger, $170 for two. For the truly brave, Prevost offers a variety of aerobatic flights—the most intense is appropriately

Copia: The World's Only Wine, Food, Art (and Fun) Center

Robert Mondavi never does anything halfway, and his latest venture in Napa Valley is no different. In fact, it may be the crowning glory of his legacy.

Copia: The American Center for Wine, Food and the Arts is described as "a cultural institution, museum, and educational center dedicated to the character of wine and food in close association with the arts and humanities, and to celebrating these as unique expressions of American life, culture, and heritage." That's the official version of the Copia vision, but it's really a fun house for foodies and wine enthusiasts, with fabulous art and exhibits to round out the experience. You can bet it's the only place like it in the world.

After 10 years of visionary planning and more than 2 years of construction, Copia finally threw open its doors in November 2001 amid great fanfare. A parade along First Street in downtown Napa on opening day was led by Mondavi and cooking legend Julia Child, for whom the center's restaurant is named. Adding a bit of kitsch to the fun-filled parade were appearances by the Oscar Meyer Weinermobile and the Pillsbury Doughboy.

Built from private donations at a cost of about $55 million ($20 million from Mr. Mondavi alone), Copia is 80,000 square feet of stone, concrete, metal, and glass with gardens inspired by the 16th-century kitchen gardens at Villandry in France's Loire Valley. Rising along the banks of the Napa River, Copia, named for the goddess of abundance, is surrounded by three-and-a-half acres of organic culinary gardens ranging from olive to citrus orchards, to a collection of lavender shrubs from around the world, to groves of nut-bearing trees and beds of herbs and root vegetables.

Inside Copia are art exhibits and unique sculptures, an amphitheater for concerts and performances, an indoor theater for films and lectures, a rare books library, a demonstration kitchen, classrooms for learning about food and wine, a cafe featuring picnic-style fare, a gift shop, and gourmet dining and wine tasting.

A permanent exhibit, "Forks in the Road: Food, Wine and the American Table," takes a light-hearted look at the place of food and wine in American life today and features interactive exhibits that both kids and adults will find entertaining. There's more trivia than you can shake a ladle at: What sweet treat was named for a small Massachusetts town? The Fig Newton. What fizzy drink was originally called Lithiated Lemon? 7-Up! And where else will you see a display of food packets used by the astronauts or the war rations issued to soldiers (besides, possibly, the Smithsonian) or a collection of PEZ dispensers? You can leave behind a little piece of your life experience by recording your best tales of personal cooking disasters or favorite meals in a private kiosk for future visitors to watch and enjoy (remember to smile for the camera!). In a separate room of the exhibit, given the museum-quality environment they deserve, are ancient Greek and Roman wine urns and flasks—pieces of history worthy of the British Museum.

The center's inaugural art exhibit, "Active Ingredients," featured the work of seven world-renowned artists with a common theme: food procurement and consumption. Future art exhibits were being planned as this book went to press.

Julia's Kitchen, the center's 75-seat, full-service dining room with an open kitchen, is named for Julia Child, the legendary food maven and an advisor in Copia's development for more than five years. (As an honorary trustee of Copia, she also donated her personal collection of copper cookware, used for several decades in her own kitchen, to be put on display.) The restaurant's executive chef, Mark Dommen, has an impressive resume in America and abroad and describes his style of cooking as "California-French" (see our Restaurants chapter). The open kitchen allows visitors to watch distinguished American chefs and cooking teachers at work. For extra fun, ask for seats at the counter (there are only four), where you can watch the culinary action up close.

Copia is located at 500 First Street at the eastern edge of downtown Napa. Admission is $12.50 for adults, $10.00 for teens and seniors, and $7.50 for children. To learn more about this one-of-a-kind attraction, call (707) 259–1600 or visit www.copia.org.

named "Kamikaze." Weekday flights are by appointment. On weekends, Prevost does accept drop-ins, but appointments are recommended.

Sears Point Raceway $$
Hwys. 37 and 121, Sonoma
(707) 938–8448, (800) 870–7223
www.searspoint.com

You'll see some of the top names in the racing world compete here each year on the grueling road course, the rugged motocross dirt track, and the drag strip. Legends such as Mario Andretti, Al Unser (Sr. and Jr.), and Bobby Allison have all toured the track as well as Hollywood celebrities such as Paul Newman, Clint Eastwood, and James Garner. Annual events include NASCAR road races and sports car racing by the Sports Car Club of America with TRANS-AM, Formula Atlantic, and Pro Formula Ford entrants. Bike events include AMA motorcycle road races and several motocross races. Prices for events vary. (See our Spectator Sports chapter for more details.)

Historic Town of Sonoma $
Various sites

A national landmark and the largest square of its kind in California, the Sonoma Plaza evokes the feel of Old Europe. It is an ideal picnic spot, with numerous tables under nearly 200 trees, a playground, and a duck pond. A monument honors the raising of the Bear Flag here in 1846 (see our History chapter).

Surrounding the plaza are some of the buildings that marked the start of the village, then owned by Mexico and ruled by Gen. Mariano Vallejo. It makes a lovely walking tour, and one $2.00 ticket, available at any of the following sites, will give you access to the Mission, the Barracks, Vallejo's home, and the Petaluma Adobe.

Mission San Francisco Solano, founded in 1823 as the last of California's Franciscan missions, is diagonally opposite the plaza's northeast corner. Today's mission is a faithful re-creation of the original. Only the priests' quarters date from the founding. It's open daily from 10:00 A.M. to 5:00 P.M.

Sonoma Barracks, across from the mission, housed Vallejo's Mexican troops, sheltered the Bear Flag soldiers, and served as a U.S. military headquarters in the 1840s and 1850s. Today the Barracks are restored to their Mexican-era appearance, with exhibits inside and an attractive gift shop with California items. Grizzly bears once battled bulls in the enclosed courtyard behind the Barracks, while spectators gambled on the outcome. It's open 10:00 A.M. to 5:00 P.M. daily.

Toscano Hotel, a few doors down First

Street from the Barracks, served as an unpretentious hotel for Italian immigrants (hence the name Toscano, which means "man from Tuscany"). The two-story frame structure with kitchen has free docent tours on Friday, Saturday, and Sunday from 1:00 to 4:00 P.M.

Salvador Vallejo Adobe (Swiss Hotel) has a bar and restaurant that have long been favorites of residents and visitors alike. The locally famous drink, "Bear's Hair" sherry, is served in the saloon. Originally the adobe was built for Gen. Vallejo's brother, Salvador, in the 1840s. It has been known as the Swiss Hotel since the 1880s.

Salvador Vallejo Adobe (El Dorado Hotel), a Monterey Colonial adobe, has had a checkered history as a government office, college, winery, and hotel. Salvador Vallejo built it between 1836 and 1846. Subsequently it was occupied by the Bear Flag party members and U.S. Gen. John C. Frémont during the opening days of the Mexican-American War. Presbyterian settlers operated Cumberland College at the adobe from 1858 until 1864.

El Paseo de Sonoma (Pinelli Building) is one of several plaza structures built of native stone. The building survived a 1911 fire when Augustino Pinelli let firefighters douse flames with his barrels of wine. Today several shops and restaurants can be found on the passageway behind First Street East and Spain Street. Blue Wing Inn, on E. Spain Street across from the mission, was once a rowdy gold rush-era saloon visited by future President U.S. Grant, Lt. William Tecumseh Sherman, Kit Carson, and notorious bandit Joaquin Murietta. This wisteria-covered, two-story adobe now contains shops and residences.

Vasquez House, in the courtyard of El Paseo de Sonoma off Spain Street, was built by "Fighting Joe" Hooker, a U.S. Army officer and later a Civil War general, while he was stationed in Sonoma. The restored, frame dwelling houses a museum and serves as headquarters for the Sonoma League for Historic Preservation. It's open Wednesday through Sunday from 1:30 to 4:30 P.M. There is no charge,

and refreshments are available for purchase in the tea room.

General Vallejo's Home (Lachryma Montis) is not on the plaza but 3 blocks down W. Spain Street. Gen. Vallejo built this Gothic Revival home at a cost of $50,000 in 1851 and named it Lachryma Montis ("tears of the mountain") because of a spring on the property. Abandoning Spanish-style architecture, he built a grand Victorian and furnished it with European imports. He had redwood lumber hauled in from the port at Vallejo, while bricks and marble mantels were shipped from Hawaii. Landscaping, a glass pavilion (now gone), and every convenience of the time were included. The Vallejos' 15th and 16th children were born at Lachryma Montis.

Vallejo's once-great holdings eventually were reduced to only the acreage around this home. Many of the original furnishings are still in place. The kitchen located in a separate building kept the heat of cooking away from the rest of the house. A charming little guesthouse remains on the property, and a short walk up the hill leads to the room of one of the Vallejo children. Picnic tables are set around a stream that runs through the property. Now a state historic park, Lachryma Montis is open 10:00 A.M. to 5:00 P.M. daily.

Jack London State Historic Park $
2400 London Ranch Rd. off Arnold Dr.,
Glen Ellen
(707) 938–5216
www.parks.sonoma.net/JLPark.html

Jack London called it his "Beauty Ranch," but he wanted to achieve more than aesthetic satisfaction here. His goal was to achieve a scientifically operated ranch where new techniques could be developed. Many buildings remain from his experiment in ranching: stone stables where he kept his prize horses, remnants of a winery and distillery, the last vestiges of his famous scientific piggery, and the farmhouse where he lived for five years and wrote most of his stories. In the center of the 800 acres is the rubble of Wolf House, the lava-stone mansion he had hoped to live in, burned to the ground in 1913. The half-mile trail to the Wolf House ruins passes through a forest of oak, madrone, and buckeye trees. Nearby is London's grave, marked only by a stone from the ruins of the house.

At the top of the hill, as you enter the state park, is the House of Happy Walls, built by London's wife, Charmian, after his death. This fascinating museum provides a look at the life of a man who was first and foremost an adventurer. It contains memorabilia of his life as a war correspondent, his abortive trip around the world with Charmian in a ship he designed himself, and a load of information about his writing life. Displayed are some of the 600 rejection slips he received, the first from the *Saturday Evening Post*. Seven miles of hiking, mountain biking and equestrian trails are available. The museum is open daily except for major holidays from 10:00 A.M. to 5:00 P.M., and admission is $3.00 per car ($2.00 when seniors are riding).

Petaluma Historical Museum $
20 Fourth St., Petaluma
(707) 778–4398

A large, freestanding, stained-glass dome accents the beauty of this 1906 Carnegie Free Library—one of the hundreds that philanthropist Andrew Carnegie built

and donated in the early 20th century. You'll find a 19th-century, horse-drawn fire wagon here, along with Native American artifacts, pioneer relics, and displays describing Petaluma's dairy and poultry beginnings. An exhibit about the Petaluma River illustrates how the town became an important manufacturing and trading hub when Petaluma was one of California's largest cities.

By the way, this Victorian riverfront community has one of California's best-preserved downtowns. (It's on the National Register of Historic Places.) Petaluma's all-American appearance has not escaped the notice of Hollywood filmmakers, and movie sites can be found all over town. Some of the films shot here include *Peggy Sue Got Married*, *Basic Instinct*, and *Phenomenon*, starring John Travolta.

The museum offers brochures for self-guided walking tours of the city, featuring the famous Iron Front buildings and beautiful Victorian homes. In addition, docents costumed in Victorian attire lead guided tours of historic downtown on Saturday and Sunday at 10:30 A.M. May through October. It's free, but donations are accepted. Admission to the museum is also free, and hours are 10:00 A.M. to 4:00 P.M. Wednesday, Thursday, and Friday, 11:00 A.M. to 4:00 P.M. Saturday, and noon to 3:00 P.M. Sunday.

Petaluma Adobe State Historic Park $
3325 Adobe Rd. at Casa Grande Rd.,
Petaluma
(707) 762–4871
www.parks.sonoma.net/adobe.html

Once the headquarters of Gen. Mariano Vallejo's 100-square-mile Rancho Petaluma, this enormous two-story adobe overlooking Petaluma stands as a monument to California's early history. A self-guided tour of the structure offers views of the period-furnished kitchen, the living quarters where the Vallejo family stayed when they spent their summer holiday at the rancho, and the guest rooms. The rustic chairs and candle sconces are of Spanish motif. Outside you will find replicas of the beehive ovens where cooks baked bread for rancho residents. Occasionally the ranger in charge may put in a loaf or two, using the same recipe the Vallejo servants used. The ranch is open daily (except Thanksgiving, Christmas, and New Year's Day) from 10:00 A.M. to 5:00 P.M. The $3.00 admission fee, $2.00 for children ages 6 to 12, entitles you to visit any of the sites on historic Sonoma Plaza (see previous listing).

Luther Burbank Home and Gardens $
Santa Rosa and Sonoma Aves., Santa Rosa
(707) 524–5445
www.parks.sonoma.net/burbank.html

During his 53 years in Santa Rosa, horticulturist Luther Burbank changed the plant world, improving and hybridizing more than 800 varieties (see Close-up "Genius in the Garden").

This National Historical Landmark features Burbank's home, a carriage house, and the greenhouse where he performed his experiments. Outside you'll find a lovely garden filled with the plants Burbank introduced to the world. Docent-led house tours are offered on the half-hour Tuesday through Sunday from April through October. Tours, which are $3.00 for adults and free for children 12 and younger, run from 10:00 A.M. to 3:30 P.M. The gardens are open daily at no charge.

Jesse Peter Native American Art Museum $
Santa Rosa Junior College,
1501 Mendocino Ave., Santa Rosa
(707) 527–4479
www.santarosa.edu/museum

Dedicated to arts and crafts created by Native Americans from the 19th century up to the present day, this museum contains an extensive assortment of baskets, including the extraordinarily beautiful baskets of the Pomo tribe. Most items displayed represent the work of California tribes, although beadwork of the Plains and Plateau tribes is on hand as well as some Eskimo art. There are replicas of a Southwestern pueblo, a Pomo round-house, and a Klamath River xonta (a family shelter). The museum is open Monday through Friday (except for school holidays) from mid-August through May. Admission is free.

Sonoma County Museum $
425 Seventh St., Santa Rosa
(707) 579–1500
www.sonomacountymuseum.com

Housed in the old post office built after the 1906 earthquake, the museum was moved and restored as a part of local grassroots activities. The lower floor is devoted to an extensive collection of art exhibits, exhibits on the history and heritage of the county, and photographs of the local landscape and people. Included in the collection are Sonoma County landscapes by early California painters William Keith and Thomas Hill. The second floor is given over to exciting temporary exhibits. Past ones have included displays of cartoon art and a woodworking exhibit of bowls, boxes, and furniture. The Wild Oat Gift Shop has a particularly intriguing assortment of books and items on Sonoma County themes. The museum and gift shop are open Wednesday through Sunday year-round, from 11:00 A.M. to 4:00 P.M. A $2.00 donation is requested (students and seniors $1.00).

Redwood Empire Ice Arena $
1667 W. Steele Ln., Santa Rosa
(707) 546–7147
www.snoopyshomeice.com

Outside of Charlie Brown, who will always be universally loved, the Redwood Empire Ice Arena may be the most appreciated gift Charles Schulz (1922–2000) has given Sonoma County. His career started in Minnesota and ballooned to fame, with his work appearing in more than 1,800 newspapers in 65 countries worldwide. Schulz was a resident of Santa Rosa, where he created many of his cartoons.

The arena offers a full range of skating, and many world champions have glided across the ice here. Open daily, but hours vary, with mornings reserved for special programs and classes. The cost is $5.50 for adults and teens and $4.50 for children younger than 12. Aside from the arena, visitors will delight in the gift shop with hundreds of items from the lives of the Peanuts gang.

Charles M. Schulz Museum and Research Center $
One Snoopy Place, Santa Rosa
(707) 579–4452
www.charlesmschulzmuseum.org

Cartoonist Charles Schulz didn't live long enough to see this museum named in his honor come to life (he died early in 2000), but he would be proud of the result. Adjacent to Schulz's Redwood Empire Ice Arena (see previous listing), the $8 million museum was scheduled to open in June 2002. Within its 28,000 square feet are permanent and temporary displays of the cartoonist's 50-year body of work; a 100-seat auditorium; a research library and archives for students, cartoonists, and scholars; and classrooms. Admission fees were still being discussed at the time this book was updated, but $6.00 for adults and $4.00 for children is a pretty good bet.

Safari West $$$
3115 Porter Creek Rd., Santa Rosa
(707) 579–2551, (800) 616–2695
www.safariwest.com

This is a little different than those drive-through safari parks where tourists outnumber perplexed animals by about 100 to 1. Safari West is a private preserve and working ranch dedicated to conservation and propagation of endangered species—the 240 acres of Safari West are home to 400 exotic mammals and birds. You can gaze at herds of zebra or watch a giraffe crane its mammoth neck to eat out of your hand.

Guests spend an unparalleled two-and-a-half hours on a unique educational trek through the rolling hills of the preserve. Accompanied by a naturalist, groups get the rarest of opportunities to photograph herds of antelope, eland, gazelle, zebra, and many more types of animals. Because the critters live in vast acreage, they are comfortable with vehicles and can be seen up close. (One group was even treated to the birth of an antelope.) Wear comfortable clothing and bring sunscreen and a hat. Oh, and the proprietors can customize tours if you have a particular interest in, say, springboks. Cost of a basic tour is $48 for adults and $24 for children 16 and younger. Safari West now includes overnight accommodations. The South African–made "tents" include hardwood floors, bathrooms, and king-size beds. They go for $225 per night for two adults; a separate cottage is $300. Visits are by appointment only. Leave your pets at home.

Pacific Coast Air Museum $
2330 Airport Blvd., Santa Rosa
(707) 575–7900
www.pacificcoastairmuseum.org

Located next to Sonoma County's Charles M. Schulz Airport, the Pacific Coast Air Museum was formed by local aviators interested in restoring and preserving retired military aircraft. The collection ranges from a Korean War-era RF-86 Sabre and Huey helicopter—which saw combat in Vietnam—to an F-16 Viper flown by the commander of the Navy's Top Gun flight school and an F-14A Tomcat that saw duty on several U.S. carriers. Along with these and other aircraft, the museum features an extensive indoor display that reveals the inner workings of a jet turbine—via a cut-away exhibit—or a pilot's ejection seat and pressurized suit. The museum is open every Tuesday and Thursday from 10:00 A.M. to 2:00 P.M., and every Saturday and Sunday from 10:00 A.M. to 4:00 P.M. On the third weekend of each month, museum staff unlatch the canopy of a featured aircraft and let visi-

Zebras are among the wild animals you can almost reach out and touch at Safari West, located between Santa Rosa and Calistoga.

PHOTO: JAN BLANCHARD

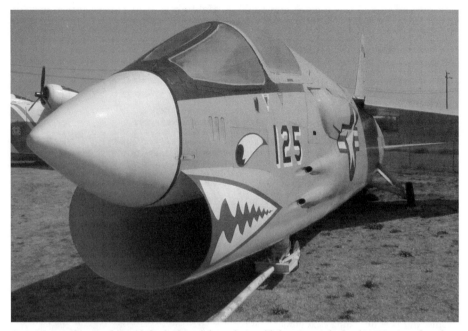

Peer into snarling intakes and climb aboard the cockpits of fighter jets and other historic aircraft at the Pacific Coast Air Museum in Santa Rosa. PHOTO: JOHN NAGIECKI

tors climb aboard to get a feel of what it's like behind the wheel of a war bird. The museum also sponsors a weekend air show—Wings Over Wine Country—each August (see our Festivals and Annual Events chapter).

Northern Sonoma

Windsor Waterworks and Slides $$
8225 Conde Ln., Windsor
(707) 838–7760
www.windsorwaterworks.com
This recreational park offers welcome relief from hot summer days. Among the attractions are an inner-tube slide, speed slide, body slide, splash fountain with squirt guns, swimming pool and wading pool, large picnic area with barbecue pits, and an arcade. Kids can also play table tennis, horseshoes, and volleyball. The park's newest attraction is an inflatable ship on which children can bounce. A snack bar is available. The park is open every day from May through September from 11:00 A.M. to 7:00 P.M. The entrance fee is $13.25 for those 13 and older and $12.25 for kids

ages 4 to 12. There's a special rate of $9.75 after 4:00 P.M. for the "afternoon splash." (See our Kidstuff chapter for more on this attraction.)

The Petrified Forest $
4100 Petrified Forest Rd., Calistoga
(707) 942–6667
www.petrifiedforest.org
It's not as spooky as it sounds, unless you think too hard about the advancing wall of muddy volcanic ash that leveled these trees about 3 million years ago, following massive eruptions to the northeast. The trees lay unmolested until 1870, when a gent later known as "Petrified Charlie" Evans happened upon a rock-hard stump while tending his cows. The rest is tourist-industry history. A short loop takes you past all the highlights, including The Monarch, a petrified, 105-foot redwood with a diameter of 6 feet. The museum and store—open 10:00 A.M. to 6:00 P.M.— are housed in the big red Ollie Bockee House. You'll want to sit on the porch. Admission is $5.00 for adults, $3.00 for

youngsters ages 12 through 17, and $2.00 for kids ages 6 to 11. Seniors 60 and over pay $3.00.

Healdsburg Museum $
221 Matheson St., Healdsburg
(707) 431-3325

This museum is in a refurbished Carnegie library building and features both permanent and changing exhibits. The county's history is depicted from prehistoric times to the present, and displays include antique firearms, 19th-century clothing, tools, and an outstanding collection of Pomo basketry and crafts. The archives contain more than 5,000 historical photographs and newspapers dating back to 1865. Healdsburg Museum is open Tuesday through Sunday from 11:00 A.M. to 4:00 P.M. Admission is free.

West County/Russian River

Luther Burbank Gold Ridge Experiment Farm
$
7781 Bodega Ave., Sebastopol
(707) 829-6711
www.wschs-grf.pon.net/bef.htm

On this 18-acre experimental farm, horticulturist Luther Burbank built a cottage and worked to perfect Gravenstein apples, plums, cherries, grapes, and lilies. Although he lived and worked in Santa Rosa, this is where he conducted his horticultural research between 1895 and 1926. Free guided tours, available by appointment from April through mid-October, explore Burbank's gardens and visit his restored cottage. The gardens are open for free self-guided tours year-round.

West County Museum $
261 S. Main St., Sebastopol
(707) 829-6711
www.wschs-grf.pon.net

A restored railroad depot houses the collections of the Western Sonoma County Historical Society. The Triggs Reference Room contains books, photographs, magazines, newspapers, audiotapes, and videotapes on local history. West County Museum is open Thursday through Sunday from 1:00 to 4:00 P.M. There is no admission fee, but donations are welcomed.

Fort Ross State Historic Park $
19005 Hwy. 1, Jenner
(707) 847-3286
www.parks.ca.gov

On a grassy, windswept bluff north of Bodega Bay stands a ruddy, wooden stockade, its main gate facing out over the Pacific Ocean. The 14-foot walls are made of weather-beaten redwood. Inside is a small chapel, dedicated to St. Nicholas and topped with an orthodox cross. In another building, seal and otter pelts hang on the walls above casks marked in Cyrillic characters.

Now part of a State Historic Park, Fort Ross provides a fascinating glimpse into the history of the settlement founded with the aim of providing food for the fledgling Russian colony in Alaska, where Russia's eastward push ended in the early 1800s (see our History chapter). The museum in the visitor center exhibits Russian and Native American artifacts, and the gift shop offers crafts made by the local Pomo tribe as well as goods imported from Russia.

Join more than 100 costumed participants for the annual Living History Day—held on the third or last Saturday of July—to get a taste of what life was like for the Russians nearly 200 years ago (see our Festivals and Annual Events chapter). The park is open daily from 10:00 A.M. to 4:30 P.M. There is no entrance fee for cyclists or hikers. Vehicles pay $2.00 for parking.

Berry's Saw Mill $
Hwy. 116 and Cazadero Hwy., Cazadero
(707) 865-2365

This authentic sawmill offers visitors an opportunity to see trees sawed, split, and planed into usable lumber. Visitors can explore the mill on an informal basis—guided tours are not offered. It's open at no charge Monday through Friday from 7:45 A.M. to 4:30 P.M.

Genius in the Garden

Luther Burbank (1849–1926) knew plants not just for what they were, but for what they could become. The nation's most renowned and prolific horticulturist, he dedicated his life to the propagation of new plant varieties, many of which are still valued today for their extraordinary beauty and utility.

Born in Lancaster, Massachusetts, Luther's career began at the age of 21, when he accidentally discovered a potato that had sprouted a seed ball on his farm. At the time, the European potato blight had recently spread to the United States and farmers were in danger of losing their crops. From the 23 seeds he found in the seed ball, Luther developed a hardy, high-yielding variety of potato, the "Burbank potato," which eventually became the predominant type grown in the United States—today's russet potato is a descendant of the Burbank variety.

But this was only the beginning for a man whose name would become associated with nearly a thousand other new plants. Perhaps sensing his destiny, Luther quickly sold the rights to his new potato for $150 to a local seed dealer and used the proceeds to finance a trip to Santa Rosa, where his brother had been living.

Inspired by his brother's letters describing a gardener's paradise, Luther had dreamt of California for years. When he finally set foot in Santa Rosa in 1875, he found it even beyond his expectations. Yet, like most people who believe they have

The Luther Burbank house and gardens in Santa Rosa stand as a testament to the nation's greatest horticulturalist. PHOTO: JOHN NAGIECKI

stumbled upon the Promised Land, Luther wanted to keep it a secret. Fearing that should the news leak out "all scuffs would come out here, get drunk, and curse the whole country," he warned his family back east to avoid speaking favorably about California.

It wasn't long before Luther acquired some land near "downtown" Santa Rosa—then a jumble of 726 houses, 6 hotels, 7 churches, and 22 saloons—and began his work. Though he had achieved some notoriety through early efforts, it wasn't until 1893, when he published his catalog "New Creations in Fruits and Flowers," that he achieved widespread fame. At the time, the propagation of new plant varieties was a slow, tedious process, and such a large offering—more than a hundred varieties—by a single individual was a surprise, if not downright shocking. Among individuals and groups who believed that God alone could "create" a new plant, Luther was considered an infidel.

But the results quickly trumped the skeptics. Gardeners from coast to coast and abroad bought Luther's plants, which were exceptionally hardy and high yielding. The catalog turned Luther into a popular hero, and his stature ranked with such greats as Thomas Edison and Henry Ford—Edison and Ford both personally admired Luther and visited him at his home in Santa Rosa.

Luther's plant varieties are legion, and it is difficult to do justice to the breadth and inventiveness of his creations. Varieties such as elephant garlic, plumcot (a cross between a plum and apricot), and the ubiquitous Shasta daisy are still popular today. Among Luther's more unusual creations was the spine-free cactus, which he intended for use in the desert as a cattle-friendly forage plant. Another extraordinary variety was the "paradox walnut." The "paradox" was that this walnut—a hardwood—grew as fast as most softwood varieties. Up until that time, all hardwood trees, valued for their fine grain, grew slowly.

Luther had a genius for detecting desirable qualities in young plants and nurturing them into new strains. Having had no formal training, he relied more on intuition than rigorous scientific methodology and employed his unique gifts on a large scale in thousands of simultaneous experiments. At the time of his death in 1926, he had more than 3,000 experiments underway and was growing more than 5,000 species.

Throughout his long career, Luther sought to produce high-quality plant varieties that would help increase the world's food supply. But, more importantly, his work was inspired by a deep love of beauty. "The urge to beauty," he wrote, "and the need for beautiful and gracious and lovely things in life is as vital as the need for bread."

The Burbank home and gardens—now a museum and park—in downtown Santa Rosa are open daily to the public. The gardens feature a wide assortment of Burbank plants, including many spectacular roses, a large paradox walnut dating from 1914, and an enormous cluster of spine-free cacti.

"I firmly believe, from what I have seen, that this is the chosen spot of all this earth as far as Nature is concerned." —Luther Burbank

A cannon salute during Living History Day at Fort Ross on the Sonoma Coast raises a cheer from costumed participants. PHOTO: JOHN NAGIECKI

Mendocino County

Real Goods Solar Living Center $
13771 U.S. 101, Hopland
(707) 744–2100
www.realgoods.com

This shop is a giant demonstration project for residential energy efficiency and alternative earth-friendly designs. The large main building at the center is built of straw bales, and it's powered entirely by solar panels and wind turbines. You can shop from a wide selection of environmentally conscious products such as solar panels, hemp goods, and water filtration systems and enjoy a tour of the 12 acres of beautiful, permaculture organic gardens and ponds. For the kids, there's a special area for playing and learning, including a unique solar calendar; they call it a 21st-century Stonehenge. The Solar Living Center is open daily from 10:00 A.M. to 6:00 P.M. Each August the center sponsors a solar festival that features environmental activists—Julia Butterfly and Ralph Nader spoke here in 2000—and music (see our Festivals and Annual Events chapter).

Grace Hudson Museum and Sun House $
431 S. Main St., Ukiah
(707) 467–2836
www.gracehudsonmuseum.org

Grace Hudson Museum is an art, history, and anthropology museum focusing on the life works of Grace Hudson, who painted more than 650 oils, primarily of the local Pomo people. She was already a talented painter when she married ethnologist Dr. John Hudson, and focused her art on Native American subjects. The museum displays Hudson's portraits of Pomos, exhibits of Native American arts and crafts, and changing shows by local artists. Sun House, which shares the site, is a charming Craftsman bungalow that served as the Hudson residence. The museum is open Wednesday through Saturday from 10:00 A.M. to 4:30 P.M. and noon to 4:30 P.M. on Sunday. Tours of the Sun House are offered on the hour, noon to 3:00 P.M.

Held-Poage Memorial Home and Library $
Mendocino County Historical Society,
603 W. Perkins St., Ukiah
(707) 462–6969

A treasure trove of historical information, the library holds 4,500 books on county, state, and national history. Along with 13,500 historical photographic negatives and microfilms pertaining to Northern California history, the library also offers documents, maps, scrapbooks, genealogies, and more. Researchers from all over the United States contact the society for assistance. All this information is housed in the historic Queen Anne-style Victorian home built in 1903 for William D. Held and Ethel Poage Held, who were dedicated to the collection of archival materials about California. The home is open every day but Sunday from 1:00 to 4:00 P.M. Closed holidays. Donations are welcome.

Pomo Cultural Center $
Marina Dr., Lake Mendocino, Ukiah
(707) 485–8285, (707) 485–8685 (gift shop)

This small museum was built by the Army Corps of Engineers and is operated by the local Coyote Tribal Council. The round shape of the center is modeled on the Pomo ceremonial dance house, where cultural knowledge was passed down through the generations. On display are examples of Pomo basketry, a demonstration of clam-shell money-making, and a hands-on exhibit of different animal skins. The Army Corps has staged its own exhibit—a large aquarium of various fish found in Lake Mendocino. A gift shop operated by the Tribal Council contains items made by local Native Americans. Admission is free. The museum is open 9:00 A.M. to 5:00 P.M. Wednesday through Sunday, June through October and is closed in winter.

Mendocino County Museum $
400 E. Commercial St., Willits
(707) 459–2736
www.co.mendocino.ca.us/museum

This large, modern museum displays artifacts and interpretations of the cultural history of the county, with a particular focus on local Pomo and Yuki tribes. A fascinating aspect is the collection of oral history interviews from Mendocino citizens. It's open Wednesday through Sunday from 10:00 A.M. to 4:30 P.M. Admission is free, but donations are gladly accepted.

Anderson Valley Historical Society Museum $
Hwy. 128, 1 mile north of Boonville
(707) 895–3207

In a century-old schoolhouse on the side of the road, this museum showcases Anderson Valley pioneer life. Displays include a sheepshearing shed, a blacksmith shop, Pomo Indian basketry and tools, and antique agricultural and lumber industry equipment. There is also an exhibit devoted to "Boontling," the valley's unique folk dialect. Open Friday through Sunday from 1:00 to 4:00 P.M. When the flag is flying, the museum is open.

Point Arena Lighthouse and Museum $
Lighthouse Rd., Point Arena
(707) 882–2777, (877) 725–4448
www.mcn.org/1/palight

The lighthouse, originally built in 1870 and rebuilt after the 1906 earthquake, still shines a warning to keep ships off the dangerous rocks and shoals. The light is now automated, and the old Coast Guard facilities have been turned into a maritime museum, with several guest cottages run by a local nonprofit organization. Visitors may climb the light tower and view the broad terraces that run down to the sea or admire the ancient Fresnel lens that remains in place in the light room at the top. Offshore, scuba divers enjoy the Arena Rock Underwater Preserve, an area of abundant marine flora and fauna, as well as the sunken wreck of a freighter. The lighthouse museum is open daily from 11:00 A.M. to 2:30 P.M. on weekdays and 10:00 A.M. to 3:30 P.M. on summer weekends and holidays. Admission is $4.00 for adults and teens and $1.00 for kids younger than 12.

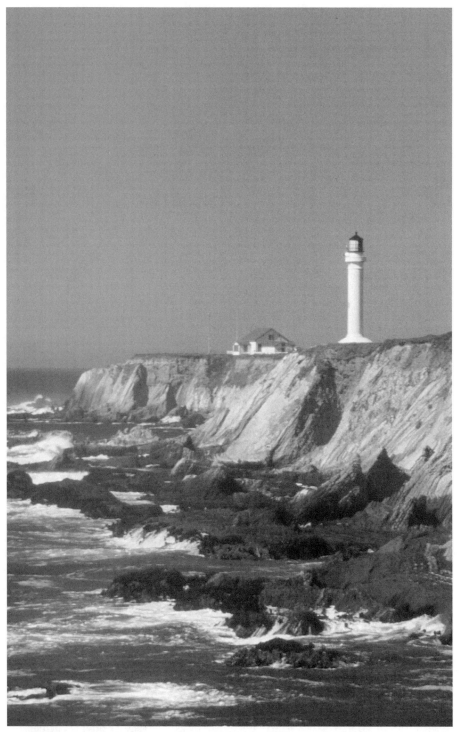

The Point Arena Lighthouse overlooks rocky bluffs and the wide sweep of Manchester State Beach along the Mendocino County coastline. PHOTO: JOHN NAGIECKI

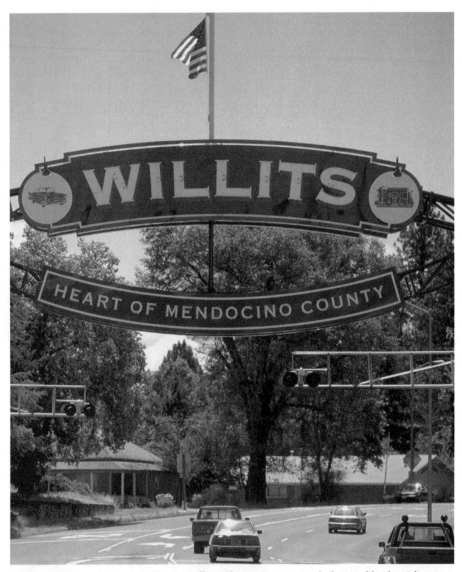

This sign welcomes visitors to Willits, a small Mendocino County town kick-started by the 19th-century lumber boom. PHOTO: BILL HOBAN

Greenwood State Park Visitors Center $
Hwy. 1, Elk
(707) 937–5804
www.mcn.org/1/mendoparks/greenwd.htm

This small history center tells the story of the tiny coastal town of Elk, from its founding by the Greenwood brothers in the late 1800s through its history as a logging and lumber town. Housed in the former L. E. White Lumber Company office—which was in operation from 1884 to 1916—the center includes a large mural depicting how lumber was transported down the steep cliffs to waiting ships. The center also contains historic photographs, artifacts, a story rail tracing the history of the local lumber industry, and archives. The visitor center is open on Saturdays and Sundays, March through October, from 11:00 A.M. to 1:00 P.M.

Passengers explore the historic area of Willits by horse-drawn carriage. PHOTO: BILL HOBAN

Ford House Museum $
735 Main St., Mendocino
(707) 937–5397

The Ford House, built in 1854, was origi-nally the residence of Mendocino lumber mill owner Jerome Bursley Ford. Today it serves as a museum and visitor center for Mendocino Headlands State Park. This is where to find out everything you need to know for your visit to the charming vil-lage of Mendocino and the wild shores off the Headlands. During the whale migra-tions from January through March, there are docent-led whale-watching walks on Saturday. At the height of the wildflower season in late spring, knowledgeable docents lead walks through a riot of color and tell about the flowers. The museum also posts displays on topics such as tide pools, whales, and sea vegetation. Ford House is open daily from 11:00 A.M. to 4:00 P.M. Admission is free, as are the docent walks, though small donations are encouraged.

Kelley House Museum $
45007 Albion St., Mendocino
(707) 937–5791
www.mendocino.org

The house looks like a home transplanted from a Maine coastal town, a reflection of the fact that many New Englanders did come to Mendocino in earlier times. Its walls display a collection of historic pho-tographs of days when redwood logs were loaded onto waiting ships via chutes and long piers. Displays tell the story of the logging and shipping industries that turned a wild, lonely coast into a thriving, driving city. The house is open Friday through Sunday from 1:00 to 4:00 P.M. during the months September–May. Dur-ing the summer months it is open daily 1:00 to 4:00 P.M. There is a $2.00 (sug-gested) admission fee.

Anchor Charters $$$
Noyo Harbor, North Harbor Dr., Fort Bragg
(707) 964–3854
www.anchorcharterboats.com

great abundance in this county), heathers, succulents, ivies, fuchsias, dwarf conifers, and other native species. Two creeks flow through the gardens, and more than 3 miles of trails provide easy access to the coast and opportunities for visitors to enjoy and learn about plants and nature.

A cliff house overlooks the ocean, where you can enjoy the drama of the sea—coastal bluffs are a vantage point for the gray whale migration. A favorite haunt of local painters, the grounds include picnic tables tucked in quiet spaces for those who have had the foresight to bring lunch. Two miles south of Fort Bragg, the gardens are open daily from 9:00 A.M. to 5:00 P.M. from March to October and 9:00 A.M. to 4:00 P.M. from November to February. Admission is $6.00 for adults, $5.00 for seniors, $3.00 for children 13 to 17, and $1.00 for kids 6 to 12.

Footlighters Little Theater $$
245 E. Laurel St., Fort Bragg
(707) 964-3806

A Gay Nineties night of family theater since 1943, Footlighter plays are written by the cast and performed by most of the same people year after year. There's a little light can-can, a chance to hiss the villain, and plenty of laughs. The audience sits around tables drinking coffee, beer, or soft drinks and munching on pretzels. The theater itself is a leftover from silent film days and has a white-painted fireplace decorated with a painting of a can-can dancer. The cast makes its own costumes, and nobody is paid. In fact, they pay dues to belong! Performances are every Wednesday and Saturday at 8:00 P.M., Memorial Day to Labor Day.

Once on the endangered species list, the gray whale has made a comeback and can be seen traveling between the Bering Sea and Baja California from late November through late April. Although whales can be seen from shore, it is exciting to board a charter boat and see them directly in the waters they inhabit. The really lucky watchers get so close they can reach out and pet one. Dress for any weather because it can change quickly from sunny and warm to cloudy and cool. Bring along a camera with a telephoto lens, a telescope (just like the old mariners), or a pair of binoculars. Other whale-watching excursions leave from Noyo Harbor as well (see our On the Water chapter). Anchor Charters cruises last approximately two hours and are $25 per person. They also offer fishing excursions for salmon, rock fish, and albacore tuna.

Mendocino Coast Botanical Gardens $
18220 N. Hwy. 1, Fort Bragg
(707) 964-4352
www.gardenbythesea.org

This 47-acre delight is one of only three botanical gardens in the United States situated oceanside. Founded in 1961, the gardens were purchased by grants from the California Coastal Conservancy and have been operated as a nonprofit public trust since 1992. The collections here are divided into garden "rooms" of perennials, rhododendrons (which grow wild in

Triangle Tattoo Museum $
356-B N. Main St., Fort Bragg
(707) 964-8814
www.triangletattoo.com

It's one of only a dozen places in the world dedicated to the documentation and preservation of tattoo history. The museum displays thousands of images of skin art, including those from several different countries and different periods in history. Several color prints of New Zealand's Maori people show both men

Disembarking from the Skunk Train, passengers head for the depot at Fort Bragg. PHOTO: BILL HOBAN

and women with the cultural markings called Moko. Other tattoo portraits highlight designs from Borneo, Samoa, Japan, India, Burma, Zaire, and Native American tribes. The tribal roots section includes an exhibit on the oldest documented finding of tattoos—on a 5,300-year-old Bronze Age iceman discovered in a glacier in 1983. The museum is open noon to 6:00 P.M. from Sunday through Thursday, noon to 8:00 P.M. on Friday and Saturday. Admission is free. Five tattoo artists are on hand, and international guests have been known to stop by.

Guest House Museum $
343 N. Main St., Fort Bragg
(707) 961–2840

Much of Fort Bragg's history is displayed here. Built entirely of redwood for the Fort Bragg Redwood Company in the 19th century, the building later became the guesthouse for friends and customers of C. R. Johnson, founder of Union Lumber Company. Along with a wonderful collection of photographs and artifacts the museum displays historic equipment such as steam donkeys, rigging blocks,

locomotives, and high wheels once used in log harvesting. The museum is open Friday from 1:00 to 4:00 P.M., and Wednesday, Thursday, Saturday, and Sunday from 10:00 A.M. to 4:00 P.M. during summer. Admission is $1.00.

California Western Railroad (Skunk Train)
$$$
Laurel Street Depot, Fort Bragg
(707) 964–6371
www.skunktrain.com

Named the Skunk Train by locals who did not enjoy the aroma emitted by the former gas locomotive engines, this pioneering logging railroad connects Fort Bragg on the coast with inland Willits. The 40 miles of serpentine track runs through scenic, dense redwood forests, across more than 30 bridges and trestles, and through two deep mountain tunnels. In 1885 the railroad was established to haul logs to the mill, and it still does today when it's not hauling passengers. Northspur, the halfway point, serves as a picnic stop, where you can relax under redwood trees and enjoy a snack from the outdoor grill. The fare for the full-day round trip is $35 for adults and $18 for children 3 to 17. The half-day trip is $27 for adults, $14 for children, though check on family packages. Reservations are recommended.

Lake County

Calpine Geothermal Plant Tour $
15500 Central Park Rd., Middletown
(707) 987–4270, (866) GEYSERS
www.calpine.com, www.geysers.com

Maybe you've already had a mud bath and a soak in a hot mineral pool. Can you stand just a little more hot water? Steam, to be exact, as it comes out of the ground to generate electricity at The Geysers. Technically, they aren't geysers, but "fumaroles," and they can usually be seen boiling up out of a distant hillside on the Sonoma County/Lake County line. It's steam from subterranean cauldrons and it's being corralled by Calpine Corporation to make electricity. There are 19 power units at the remote site, with a total net generating capacity of 850 megawatts, or enough to turn on the lights in 850,000 homes.

We don't know of another geothermal power plant tour anywhere in the world, and you can't beat the price: It's all free. Reservations are encouraged. Buses depart from the visitor center in Middletown at 10:00 A.M., noon, and 2:00 P.M., Thursdays through Mondays. Each tour from beginning to end takes approximately 75 to 90 minutes, and you'll learn all about the colorful history of the site. The visitor center has a gift shop and picnic area, along with interactive displays about geothermal energy.

Lower Lake Schoolhouse and Museum $
16435 Morgan Valley Rd., Lower Lake
(707) 995–3565

The 1,000 or so residents of Lower Lake went all out when they decided to build a community schoolhouse in 1877. The two-story brick building, with its mansard roof and Cobb Mountain lumber, stands today to remind us how plain and unimaginative most of our new educational facilities are. The Lower Lake Schoolhouse was more

than that, too. They held dances, traveling minstrel shows, films, even circus acts, and the building's preservation committee seeks to capture that atmosphere with art exhibits and performances in the second-floor auditorium. The museum features a period classroom plus exhibits on pioneer families and local mining history. It's all open Wednesday through Saturday from 11:00 A.M. to 4:00 P.M. There is no admission fee, but you might want to make a donation.

Anderson Marsh State Historic Park $
Hwy. 53 at Anderson Ranch Pkwy.,
Lower Lake
(707) 994–0688, (707) 279–2267

Eighty-four percent of the original marshland around Clear Lake has been destroyed, which makes Anderson Marsh that much more important to the wildlife that breeds in the ecosystem. There are 540 acres of wetlands or tule marsh plus oak and riparian woodland within the 1,067-acre park. The visitor center is in a farmhouse erected in the 1860s by farming brothers Achilles and John Melchisadeck Grigsby, with a prominent addition by John Still Anderson, a Scottish rancher whose family lived on the property for about 85 years. There are five short nature trails in the park, including the Cache Creek Trail, a 1.1-mile route with interpretive displays. Dogs and bicycles are not permitted on trails. The park is open from 10:00 A.M. to 5:00 P.M. Wednesday through Sunday, and parking is $3.00 per vehicle.

Clear Lake Queen $$$
Library Park, Lakeport
(707) 994–5432
www.paddlewheel.com

This attraction is made to feel old. It's a 110-foot, triple-deck, paddlewheel boat that would look more at home in the Mississippi Delta. (Sorry, the wheel is just for show—the *Queen* is powered by two massive diesel engines.) You can watch the shoreline activity—we don't know if the animals or the humans will be more intriguing—while you eat lunch or dinner. Prices run from $16 to $18 for sightseeing only to $28 for a two-hour lunch or brunch cruise to $35 for a three-hour dinner. (The dining floors are warm and enclosed.) The *Queen* runs Wednesday through Sunday during the summer, Friday and Saturday during the winter, and features music and dancing once a month. The price goes up those nights.

Lake County Museum $
255 N. Main St., Lakeport
(707) 263-4555
www.museum.lake.k12.ca.us

It has been said that the Pomo Indians who lived in the vicinity of Clear Lake were the most skillful basket weavers on the planet. Judge for yourself at this museum, where dozens of twined and coiled baskets are on display. Other Pomo artifacts include dance costumes and a small boat and hut. Lake County Museum also houses a research library and remnants of the early white settlers, including a firearm display. It's all inside a magnificent 1871 brick building that used to be the county courthouse—the first courthouse in California, in fact, to go on the National Register of Historic Places. It is open Thursday through Saturday from 9:00 A.M. to 4:00 P.M. in summer (noon to 4:00 P.M. in winter). A suggested donation is $2.00 for adults and $1.00 for children.

Balloons, Planes, and Gliders

It's hard to find a Wine Country brochure that doesn't include a photo of a multicolored hot-air balloon drifting over vine-scored hills. Somewhere along the way, ballooning became part of the everyday lexicon here. It is a natural fit. Hot-air balloons are splashy, even extravagant, but in a way that celebrates the physical environment rather than tramples it. Of course, the awe-evoking vistas have something to do with the popularity of our balloons and gliders too.

The flying machines are quite safe, and most pilots are FAA-certified; feel free to ask about their qualifications when you phone. It is true that balloon pilots have limited control over the direction of their rigs, except on a vertical scale. This means there is always a chance you'll make an unscheduled stop in an open field, but it will likely be a gentle one, and the company's chase team will be right on your heels. (Gliders are much easier to steer.)

As for capacity, the balloon gondolas accommodate anywhere from 4 to 16 passengers. Those of average size hold 6 to 8 people. Dress in layers when riding in a balloon—the shifts in altitude, the breezes, and the heat from the fire make it hard to predict what level of clothing will be comfortable. And if you are a tall person, be sure to bring a cap—radiant heat from the burner can be unpleasant after an hour or so.

Napa County

Balloons Above the Valley $$$$
5091 Solano Ave., Napa
(707) 253-2222, (800) GO-HOT-AI(R)
www.balloonrides.com

Launching from a variety of sites near Yountville, this company will take you on a drifting, one-hour flight and throw in a champagne brunch for $175 per person.

The Wine Plane $$$$
P.O. Box 4074, Napa 94558
(707) 747-5533, (888) 779-6600
www.wineplane.com

It had to happen eventually—first there was the Wine Train, now there's the Wine Plane, for the ultimate tour of the air over Wine Country. Jim and Kim Higgins gave up the corporate life in San Francisco to pursue their passions: flying and wine. There's a myriad of flights and prices, starting at $79 per person for a 35-minute tour, to the "Ultimate Sunset" ($199) that includes a prolonged buzz over the Golden Gate and a slow climb over the coast. Most tours include complimentary round-trip BMW livery service from your hotel or favorite winery. The FAA-certified and -inspected aircraft are a Cessna Centurion 210 and a Piper Navajo Chieftain. Jim flies the planes (he's FAA certified too), and Kim is the flight attendant, pouring vino while she acts as tour guide.

Adventures Aloft $$$$
Vintage 1870, Yountville
(707) 944–4408, (800) 944–4408
www.nvaloft.com

These experienced balloon pilots charge $185 for adults, $150 for youth ages 6 to 16. They will shuttle you to the launch site from anywhere in Napa Valley for no extra charge, with coffee and pastries served upon arrival and a sparkling wine breakfast afterward. You have the option of helping to blow up the balloons (no, your cheeks won't get tired) before your one-hour flight. Reservations are required.

Napa Valley Balloons, Inc. $$$$
P.O. Box 2860, Yountville 94599
(707) 944–0228, (800) 253–2224
www.napavalleyballoons.com

This is a scenic ride before you ever leave the ground. The company launches from Domaine Chandon at dawn, after a continental breakfast. Postflight, you get a champagne brunch at Napa Valley Grille and a color photo of the occasion. In between you'll spend an hour in the air (three to five hours for the entire experience). Meet the van at the southwest corner of Washington Square. It costs $175 per person. Reservations are required.

Bonaventura Balloon Company $$$$
Rancho Caymus Inn,
1145 Rutherford Cross Rd., Rutherford
(707) 944–2822, (800) FLY–NAPA
www.bonaventuraballoons.com

Bonaventura works "the heart of the valley," from Oakville to St. Helena. The balloons take off at sunrise and stay aloft for 60 to 90 minutes. The company never rushes a flight (only one per balloon each day) and never puts more than six people in the basket. The price, $165 to $195 per person, includes breakfast at either Rancho Caymus or Meadowood Resort.

Sonoma County

Aerostat Adventures $$$$
P.O. Box 2082, Healdsburg
(707) 433–3777, (800) 579–0183
www.aerostat-adventures.com

Aerostat enjoys an exclusive launch site out of the Rodney Strong vineyards near Healdsburg. The location affords spectacular views of the Dry Creek Valley, Alexander Valley, and Russian River wine regions. Upon touchdown, passengers can look forward to a big champagne brunch. Cost of the flight and brunch is $195.

Air Flambuoyant $$$$
250 Pleasant Ave., Santa Rosa
(707) 838–8700, (800) 456–4711
www.airflambuoyant.com

This is the largest and most experienced family-owned balloon company in North America, flying since 1974. Their specialty is small groups, though they also take large groups.

The flight lasts one hour, followed by a grand breakfast. Flights depart early to take advantage of favorable early-morning weather conditions. They leave from the Healdsburg area and fly over the wine valleys of Dry Creek and Russian River. Two or three times a year the captain, who has flown balloons all over the world, performs a wedding while aloft. (Yes, it's legal!) Flights are individually planned and start at $175 per person. Ask about group packages and special offers.

Lake County

Crazy Creek Soaring $$$$
18896 Grange Rd., Middletown
(707) 987–9112
www.crazycreekgliders.com

See the rolling range and forested hills of Lake County from 3,000 feet. Or better yet, put a parachute on your back and watch those shrubs get bigger and bigger. Glider rides range from $110 per person for 20 minutes to $140 for 30 minutes to $170 for 40 minutes.

True daredevils can sign up with an aerobatic pilot who will take you through a series of rolls and loop-the-loops for $150.

Tours

Napa County

Napa Valley Holidays $$$$
(707) 255-1050

Eli and Laura Glick's company customizes tours for parties of any size. Napa Valley Holidays' basic fee is $250 for two people, and that's an all-day commitment—perhaps four to six wineries, lunch, and an on-board docent brimming with behind-the-scenes information and anecdotes. The Glicks also are happy to help visitors with recommendations and reservations for dinner, spas, and the like.

Napa Valley Bike Tours $$$
4080 Byway East, Napa
(707) 255-3377, (800) 707-BIKE
www.napavalleybiketours.com

You feel the breeze, you burn the calories, but someone else wrestles with the logistics. Sound all right? These winery tours begin at 9:30 A.M., end about 3:00 P.M., and cost $95 per person. Along with a bicycle and helmet, you'll get a fully catered picnic, a friendly guide, and a support van to lug bottles of wine (and bodies of worn-out riders). Group size is limited to 10 to ensure safety and individual attention. You can also arrange half-day group tours of 10 to 40 cyclists for $65 per person. Napa Valley Bike Tours also rents cycles by the hour ($7.00) and day ($22.00)—tandems run $12.00 and $38.00.

Wine & Dine Tours $$$$
345 La Fata St., Ste. D, St. Helena
(707) 963-8930, (800) WINE-TOU(R)
www.wineanddinetour.com

A full-service company? Wine & Dine does everything but brush your teeth for you. In addition to guided tours, they handle restaurant reservations, accommodations, ground and air transportation, corporate meetings and event planning, balloon flights, spa treatments, and golf—for any number from 2 to 2,000. A typical day tour might include transportation, tours, and tastings at three wineries and an elegant lunch at one of the wineries. Rates vary, but figure on $400 total for a car (1 to 6 people) plus $45 per person for lunch.

Napa Valley Tours and Trail Hikes $$$
315 Clark Way, Angwin
(707) 965-2000, (800) 964-4142
www.napanet.net/tourism/tours/nvtth

These folks give you no shortage of options for getting outdoors and getting informed in Napa. They not only do winery tours but also offer an overlook hike with a gourmet picnic lunch and a Mount St. Helena hike. They now offer van service to the peak too. Small backpacks are provided, but it's up to you to wear sensible shoes. Tours range from $79 for a half-day winery circuit to $198 for an all-day, one-on-one trek.

Destination: Napa Valley Tours $$$
295 West Ln., Angwin
(707) 965-1808

If your tastes are more highbrow than hedonistic, this might be the package for you. Destination: Napa Valley Tours offers chauffeur-driven private tours of wineries, but goes far beyond that to incorporate local lore and wine industry history. Prices for a full-day experience range from $65 to $100 per person, depending upon location of pickup and return. (They'll go all the way to San Francisco to get you.)

Getaway Adventures & Bike Shop $$$$
1117 Lincoln Ave., Calistoga
(707) 942-0332, (800) 499-BIKE
www.getawayadventures.com

Getaway will rent you a bicycle anytime you drop in, but they can do a lot more than that upon request. They do winery tours: six varied wineries, a champagne cellar visit, and a shady picnic lunch for $89 (which includes basic tasting fees). They conduct an all-day Mount St. Helena extreme: a 4,000-foot, off-road descent for $89. And they even arrange kayak trips: Lake Berryessa, Lake Hennessy, or the Russian River for $109.

Sonoma County

Going Places Walking Tours for Women
$$$$
P.O. Box 2034, Sonoma
(707) 935–0595
www.goingplacestours.com

Founded by Karen Collins, former deputy director of California State Parks, Going Places provides an alternative high-quality, outdoor experience for women seeking to explore the Wine Country one step at a time—complete with the best in creature comforts. The five-day tour begins and ends in Sonoma and includes an exploration of the town's historic plaza, a walk through local vineyards, a visit to Jack London State Historic Park, a hike to Sonoma Mountain, and a van shuttle to the Napa Valley for more vineyard strolling and wine sampling. Tour guides transport luggage from inn to inn, so participants can wander the Wine Country without the burden of a heavy pack. The tour runs in April and May and is rated as easy/moderate. The cost, based on double occupancy, is $1,625.

Bikeman Bicycle Touring $$$$
18503 Sonoma Hwy., Sonoma
(707) 938–0453, (888) 525–0453
www.bikemantours.com

Bikeman offers daily guided Wine Country bicycle tours for beginning and intermediate cyclists, with stops at several outstanding wineries in the Sonoma and Kenwood areas. Every rider is supplied with a new 21-speed mountain bike and helmet, and a van shuttle is on hand to carry winery booty or to give weary cyclists a lift. Rates (including an elegant catered lunch) are $89 per person. Tours run from 10:30 A.M. to 3:30 P.M., Monday through Saturday.

Carriage Occasions $$$$
530 Irwin Ln., Santa Rosa
(707) 546–2568

Limousines and antique cars simply not ostentatious enough for you? How about a horse-drawn carriage? This company will meet you in Napa, Sonoma, or Alexander Valley and customize a two- to three-hour winery tour. Prices vary from town to town. You must book in advance.

Festivals and Annual Events

In Wine Country, every season brings its share of gala events. From January to December, there's always some kind of music, food, or farm celebration going on. In autumn, we have the "crush" and a slew of harvest fairs, and when spring blossoms begin to appear—whether apple, pear, or the venerated mustard blossom—we salute them in grand style.

Wineries play a major role in this celebratory milieu, sponsoring concerts and other major cultural events. Their lovely courtyards, grand estate lawns, and unique wine caves are some of the best places to listen to music, whether it's a symphony, chamber music, or jazz.

We couldn't possibly list all the festivals and events that occur throughout the year. We've selected some of our favorites to get you started. For more information, check with the local chambers of commerce listed in our Area Overview chapter.

January

Sonoma County

Sonoma Valley Olive Festival
Various locations, Sonoma
(707) 996–1090
www.sonomavalley.com

In case you didn't know, we grow lots of olives in Wine Country (see the Close-up in our Shopping chapter). So holding a shindig to salute the mighty olive seemed like a natural thing to do. The First Annual Sonoma Valley Olive Festival took place during winter 2001–2002, with a variety of oil tastings, special dinners, demonstrations of olives being turned into oil, a visual arts contest with olives as the theme, and more. The Feast of the Olive and Founders Dinner is the most expensive event, at $150 per person; the remaining festivities vary in price. The whole affair begins in early December and ends in late February.

Old-Time Fiddle Contest
Cloverdale Fairgrounds,
1 Citrus Fair Dr., Cloverdale
(707) 894–9550
www.cloverdale.net/visit/fiddleco.htm

Sixty or more contestants, novice to pro, gather at the fairgrounds on Citrus Fair Drive for an old-fashioned fiddling contest. But some of the best action is not on the stage; it's in a side room where curious visitors can look in on some wild, free-form jamming. This free event is sponsored by the Cloverdale Historic Society on the fourth Saturday of January. An area has been blocked off for a cafe, where the World Famous Hamburger Ranch & Pasta Farm serves its award-winning burgers. The indoor event usually draws a festive crowd of about 1,200. The 2001 contest was the 26th annual.

Mendocino County

Mendocino Crab & Wine Days
Various locations, Mendocino County
(800) 726–2780, (800) 466–3636
www.mendocinocoast.com,
www.gomendo.com

This is a 10-day festival in late January dedicated to our two favorite delicacies: premium wine and Dungeness crab. You can count on a series of winemaker dinners, cooking classes, and various crab-and-wine tastings up and down the Mendocino coastline. There's also Crab

Louie lunches, Dungeness crab specials nightly at most area restaurants, commercial crabbing demonstrations, and a crab-cake cook-off in the village of Mendocino. Bibs optional.

February

Napa County

Mustard Magic
The Culinary Institute of America
at Greystone, 2555 Main St., St. Helena
(707) 259–9020
www.mustardfestival.org

This grand fête officially launches the annual Napa Valley Mustard Festival on a Saturday in late January or early February. The focus is on the arts, including an exhibition and silent auction of entries in the Mustard Festival Fine Art Contest. Other pleasantries include hors d'oeuvres and desserts created by prominent local chefs, ultrapremium wine tastings, and music (live opera in 2000). Admission to Mustard Magic is $75 to $95 in advance, $125 at the door.

Blessing of the Balloons
Domaine Chandon,
1 California Dr., Yountville
(707) 944–8793

Only seven or eight balloons usually ascend to mark the first weekend of the Mustard Festival, but the Blessing draws anywhere from 200 to 400 people. You must convince yourself to leave your warm and cozy B&B pretty darn early to catch the action, which begins at 6:45 A.M., but it's worth it. Picture the blue light of dawn, a field of erupting mustard, and drifting planes of mist as Native American spokesman Rolando Solis offers traditional encouragement. There is no charge—except maybe a case of frostbite if you forget to dress warmly.

Chocolate Cabernet Fantasy
Sterling Vineyards, 1111 Dunaweal Ln.,
Calistoga
(707) 942–0680

Looking for a little decadence? Nero might have been attracted to this three-hour get-together off Dunaweal Lane, about 2 miles south of Calistoga. The Soroptimists fix the desserts (mostly chocolate), Sterling donates its renowned Cabs, and you take care of the rest. There is dance music too. The Fantasy is held on a Friday or Saturday night around Valentine's Day. Tickets are $20, with all proceeds going to charity.

Sonoma County

Japanese Cultural Festival
Rohnert Park Community Center,
Snider Ln. and Rohnert Park Expy.,
Rohnert Park
(707) 584–4851

Spend the first Saturday in February immersing yourself in the culture of the Japanese courtesy of the City of Rohnert Park. Practice the art of paper-folding known as origami, listen to taiko drummers, and observe the formal, elaborate, ancient art of the tea ceremony. It happens at the city community center, and it's all free except for food booths and trinket vendors, where you can spend some money.

Citrus Fair
Cloverdale Fairgrounds,
1 Citrus Fair Dr., Cloverdale
(707) 894–3992
www.cloverdale.net/citrusfa/citrusfa.htm

Here's how to brighten up winter. On the weekend nearest President's Day, the citizens of Cloverdale come together in a jolly event organized by the Citrus Fair Association. It starts off with a downtown parade then moves out to the fairgrounds, with square dancing, country-western dancing, line dancing, and regular dancing. There is a carnival for young people and beer tasting and wine tasting for grownups. Fifteen dollars will get you a glass that 60 to 70 participating wineries will fill. On Sunday you can attend a concert by a popular western music group such as Smokin' Armadillo. Admission is $6.00 for adults, $3.00 for seniors and kids ages 6 to 12.

Mendocino County

St. Mary's Mardi Gras
Redwood Empire Fairgrounds,
1055 State St., Ukiah
(707) 462-3888
www.redwoodempirefair.com

For Ukiah, it's the biggest money-raising event of the year, a two-day celebration on a weekend in mid-February that raises money for St. Mary's Elementary School. On Saturday night there's a dinner and dance held at Carl Purdy Hall at the fairgrounds, with live music by one of the local bands. But Sunday is given over to family fun, with carnival rides and game booths for children. For adults, a wine auction gives bidders a chance to vie for bottles of the vintners' best or for weekend getaways contributed by hotels or resorts. Entrance to the event is free; carnival tickets cost varying amounts.

March

Napa County

Mustard on the Silverado Trail
Various locations
(800) 686-6272
www.mustardfestival.org

The wine producers that line Napa Valley's "other" north-south artery, the Silverado Trail, demand overdue attention on a weekend in early March. About 15 wineries—including Mumm Napa Valley, Round Hill, Rutherford Hill, Sterling, and ZD (see our Wineries chapter)—go above and beyond the call of duty, offering special tours, wine-and-food pairings, entertainment, barrel tastings, and so forth. It's a great way to familiarize yourself with the "quiet side" of the valley, and it's free of charge. The two-day open house series is part of the Mustard Festival.

Napa Valley Classic Irish Festival
Kolbe Academy, 1600 F St., Napa
(707) 255-6412
www.kolbe.org

Nobody dyes the Napa River green for St. Patrick's Day, but the folks at Kolbe Acad-

Insiders' Tip

Napa Valley's annual Mustard Festival is launched the first weekend in February with a multitude of separate events. Each event has a separate admission charge (and a separate write-up in this chapter), but for $250 you can buy a patron's ticket that includes entry to Mustard Magic and the Photo Finish, admission for four to The Marketplace, and an official poster signed by the year's celebrated artist. All proceeds benefit Napa Valley nonprofit organizations. Call (707) 938-1133 for more information.

emy (see our Education chapter) do a fine job of celebrating from 2:00 to 5:00 P.M. on an afternoon near the holiday. Food, including wine and ales, is inside the school. The entertainment is in the yard (weather permitting), and includes bagpipes, singing, and traditional Irish dancing. Figure on $25 for adults, $15 for children ages 4 to 12. This is the academy's one major fundraiser each year.

The Awards
Various locations
(707) 259-9020
www.mustardfestival.org

Lest your springtime excursions begin to convince you that mustard is merely a treat for the eyes, here is an evening that pits Napa Valley's best chefs in a spread-off.

Guests get to taste the entries, along with food and wine. There is live music as well. The event, which moves each year and costs $75 in advance ($100 at the door), is held the night before The Marketplace (see next listing). It is coordinated by Barry Levenson of the Mount Horeb Mustard Museum in Wisconsin. The organizers of the competition remind you: When engaging in casual gastronomical activity, always use a condiment.

The Marketplace
Napa Valley Exposition,
575 Third St., Napa
(707) 259–9020
www.mustardfestival.org
This is the Mustard Festival's signature event. The Exposition's halls and open spaces come alive with cooking demonstrations by celebrity chefs, wine and mustard tastings, gourmet food products, microbrews, fine art, local crafts, horse-drawn carriage rides, eclectic musical offerings on three stages, historical displays, and barrel-making demonstrations. It's a two-day event (11:00 A.M. to 5:00 P.M. both days) on a weekend in mid-March. Admission is $7.00 for adults, $2.00 for children 12 or younger. Net proceeds benefit a wide range of nonprofit groups.

A Taste of Yountville
Washington St., Yountville
(707) 944–0904
www.mustardfestival.org
Come on down! Yountville likes to boast that it has "more gourmet restaurants and premium wineries than any other town of comparable size," and on the third weekend in March, the hamlet sets up a solid-mile gauntlet of food, olive oil, vinegar, mustard, wine, and beer for the sampling public. Local merchants get into the act with fashion shows, tours, furniture restoration displays, and even tips on table setting. Most demonstrations are free, and tasting tickets are reasonable (around $1.00). Even if you are beyond temptation, it might be worth your time to stroll the 6 blocks through downtown just to hear the live music and watch the entertainment. This is a Mustard Festival event.

The Photo Finish
Mumm Napa Valley, 8445 Silverado Trail,
Rutherford
(707) 259–9020
www.mustardfestival.org
With this grand finale, the Mustard Festival usually leaves 'em longing for more as it heads into hibernation for a year. Mumm's hallways and visitor center are filled with lovers of photography, food, wine, and music (doesn't leave many of us out, does it?) on the last Saturday in March or the first in April. The food is by Napa Valley chefs, the wine is primarily from Silverado Trail labels, and the camera work is by the contestants in the annual Napa Valley Mustard Festival Photography Contest. Awards are presented in the tasting room at about 9:00 P.M. Tickets to the Photo Finish cost $65 in advance or $75 at the door.

Sonoma County

Russian River Barrel Tasting
Alexander, Dry Creek, and
Russian River Valleys
(800) 723–6336
www.wineroad.com
This annual event sponsored by the Russian River Wine Road Association is a weekend festival of tasting, entertainment, and viticulture education. The tasting focuses on unreleased wines from wineries located in the Alexander, Dry Creek, and Russian River Valleys, offering participants the opportunity to taste wines straight from the barrel and to purchase "futures." And it's free.

Mendocino County

Whale Festivals
Mendocino and Fort Bragg
(707) 961–6300, (800) 726–2780
www.mendocinocoast.com
One of the best reasons to visit the Mendocino Coast in winter is to watch the gray whales cut through the choppy seas during their annual migration, a 12,000-mile round trip from the Arctic Circle to Baja California. It's a cause for celebration, and there are festivals in two cities—

in Mendocino the first weekend in March and in Fort Bragg on the third weekend—to welcome the migrating mammals. Whale-watching cruises set out from Noyo Harbor (various prices). There's music, marine art exhibits, discussions about whales at state parks, and samplings of wine, beer, and chowder all over the towns (pay as you taste) and more.

Lake County

Clear Lake Team Bass Tournament
Library Park, Lakeport
(707) 263–5092

This two-day tournament used to draw 200 to 225 boats. Lately, in the face of competing tourneys and a gradual decline in take at the lake, it has been more like 100. Still, that's enough to scare the resident largemouth, smallmouth, and spotted bass. There is a $100 entry fee per boat, and this is the only tournament in the area to offer a 100 percent payback (not to mention a Saturday night dinner). Boats enter the water at Library Park on a weekend in March, and weigh-ins are held at 3:00 P.M. Winners are determined by total combined weight for the two days.

April

Napa County

April in Carneros
Various locations
(707) 938–5906, (800) 825–9475
www.carneroswineries.org

The Carneros area, in the bay-cooled hills between Sonoma and Napa, is emerging as the Wine Country's next great appellation. You can judge for yourself over one weekend in mid-April, when 20 or more wineries open their doors and stage special events. About a quarter of the participating producers are normally open by appointment only, and others don't even have proper wineries there—guests are welcomed instead to production facilities. New vintages are released, accompanied by barrel tastings, food pairings, music, and even cigar-smoking demonstrations

Insiders' Tip

January through March brings a mass migration of crabs into the Wine Country. During those months, just about every church and civic group imaginable holds its annual fund-raising crab feed. If you're in the mood for crustacean, just check the events calendar in the local paper.

(inhaling optional). Maps are distributed at the open houses, and there is no charge for attending. The circuit tends to be less crowded on Sunday.

Kitchens in the Vineyards Tour
Various locations
(707) 578–5656, (707) 967–0835
www.napavalleymusic.com

The emphasis is on food during this all-day affair in late April or early May that gives you a peek into one-of-a-kind kitchens, dining rooms, and gardens from Yountville to St. Helena. The event benefits Music in the Vineyards' Chamber Music Festival held in August. Tickets are $35 in advance, $40 the day of the tour.

Sonoma County

Sheepshearing at the Adobe
Petaluma Adobe State Park,
3325 Adobe Rd., Petaluma
(707) 762–4871
www.petaluma.org

On a Saturday in mid-April, 4-H'ers and docents gather at the adobe building that was once the ranch home of General Vallejo (see our History chapter) to demonstrate the arts of wool cleaning, weaving, and sheep-shearing. It's all done to pay homage to an age-old craft. Looms are available for those who want to try their hand at the craft. Bring along a picnic and make a day of it. There's no charge for the event, but park admission is $3.00 per adult ($2.00 for ages 6 to 12).

Butter and Egg Days
Various locations, Petaluma
(707) 762–2785
www.petaluma.org

Petaluma celebrates its storied past through this popular event. Once known as the world's egg basket, Petaluma is now largely dairy country, thus the hometown Butter and Egg Days parade. This includes an egg toss in downtown and a parade of marching bands and (best of all) residents dressed as chickens and pats of butter. Viewers might also see giant papier mâché cows resembling Chinese dragons and floats designed to look like Victorian villages. The "Cutest Little Chick in Town" contest adds to the fun. It all happens the last complete weekend in April, and there are also food booths, other entertainment, and an antiques fair.

All sorts of interesting birds flock to the Butter and Egg Days parade in Petaluma. PHOTO: THE PETALUMA VISITORS PROGRAM

Apple Blossom Festival
Various locations, Sebastopol
(877) 828–4748
www.sebastopol.net

It's a weekend in April, and it's a salute to the apple and its snow-white blooms. Festivities include the crowning of the Apple Blossom Queen, a mile-long parade down Main Street, and two days of good time partying with plenty of blues, country, and gospel music. There's an art show, crafts made by local artisans, and plenty of products made from apples. A highlight of the festival is the self-guided, 30-mile auto tour through West County's scenic apple orchards (maps and road signage provided). The festival is sponsored by the local chamber of commerce, and events are held in Ives Park (282 High Street) and at the Veterans Memorial Building next door. Admission is $5.00 for adults, $2.00 for seniors and children ages 11 to 17.

Bodega Bay Fishermen's Festival
Westside Park, Bodega Bay
(707) 875–3422

This annual event takes place at Westside Park during a weekend in April. It features foot races, the Blessing of the Fleet, a boat parade, and a bathtub race that includes tubs crafted out of anything that floats—from Styrofoam to milk cartons. Directions to the park are well-posted. A $3.00 donation is requested.

Lake County

Pear Blossom Festival
Lake County Fairgrounds,
401 Martin St., Lakeport
(707) 263–6181

This popular event has little to do with pears or flowers and everything to do with square dancing. As many as 600 people—enough to fill three pavilions—join hands and promenade their partners at the fairgrounds. Prominent "callers" usually show up to fire off instructions to the dancers, while vendors outside sell down-home food and western outfits. You can join in, or you can just watch the choreography. There is no admission fee.

Napa County

MaiFest
Napa County Fairgrounds,
1435 N. Oak St., Calistoga
(707) 942–5356

Upvalley's wurst festival is one of its best. Watch traditional German folk dancing. Sway to the soothing oom-pah-pah of Ottmar Stubler and His Pretzel Benders. More to the point, eat and drink in the robust style of Bavaria. Spaten is the most-requested brew at this all-day Saturday event in late April or early May, though Napa Valley Brewing Company offers its competent lineup of microbrews along with three or four wineries. Tickets are $10 in advance, $12 at the gate. Food and beverages are extra (though reasonable), as are raffle tickets. First prize is two round-trip airline tickets from San Francisco to Munich. MaiFest bankrolls a scholarship fund for Calistoga High School.

Hidden Gardens Tour
Various locations
(707) 255–1836, (888) 255–1836

For the first Gardens Tour in 1996, the organizers at Napa County Landmarks were confronted with 106-degree temperatures, and a late-season drencher from El Niño washed out the 1997 edition. They were undaunted, and subsequent tours have been a big success. This is an organized, go-at-your-own-pace afternoon walking tour of pocket gardens and historic homes on a weekend in May or June. Explorers hit about 10 gardens, and then enjoy an outdoor reception. It costs $20.00 on tour day. If you buy tickets in advance, it's $8.00 for members of Napa County Landmarks and $15.00 for nonmembers. Landmarks also offers self-guided walking tours on 10 Saturdays between May and September. Call for details.

Merlot in May—International Merlot Conference
Sterling Vineyards,
1111 Dunaweal Ln., Calistoga
(707) 255–7667, (800) 709–7667
www.aboutwines.com

This conference featuring Merlot producers from around the world is now open to the public (over 21 only, please). If Merlot is your drink, you'll be in heaven. Sample a huge array of the red stuff from as many as 50 producers during a two-hour afternoon consumer tasting. Tickets are $15 and sold in advance only.

Picnic Day
Fuller Park, Napa
(707) 253–0376

On the Friday before Memorial Day, normally serene Fuller Park becomes a squirming, squealing square full of toddlers and preschoolers. Community Resources for Children sponsors this free event. There is ice cream and oodles of activities and games, from face-painting to bubble-blowing to lamb-petting. About 300 kids usually show up, at least 250 of whom wind up fighting over the same toy. To get to Fuller Park from Highway 29, take the Downtown Napa exit (Second Street), turn right at Jefferson Street, and proceed 2 blocks.

Sonoma County

Luther Burbank Rose Festival
Various locations, Santa Rosa
(707) 545–1414
www.lutherburbank.org

Find a spot along Santa Rosa's streets on a mid-May weekend to watch a parade that dates back to 1894 and now draws more than 20,000 people. Floats created with thousands of roses are the highlight of the parade, which begins in front of Burbank's home on Santa Rosa Avenue and winds its way through town to the Veterans Memorial Building. The event honors the world-famous horticulturist who improved 800 plant varieties, including the Santa Rosa rose, while living in Santa Rosa (see our Attractions chapter). Other festival events take place at various sites in the downtown area and include street fair exhibits, food booths, performances by singing groups, carnival rides, folk dancing, an antiques fair, a firefighter's competition, and displays of firefighting equipment. There's an awards ceremony to honor the best of the parade floats.

Sheepdog Trials
City Park, end of Second St., Cloverdale
(707) 894–5541
Anyone who has watched these clever little herding dogs at work can't help but be amazed at their skill and determination. They love their work and it shows. On the third Saturday in May, sheepdog trials are held at City Park (at the end of Second Street) starting at 9:30 A.M. At 11:30 A.M., there's a lamb barbecue followed by a ram auction. It's all free except the food. The event is sponsored by the Wool Growers' Association and largely attended by farmers.

Sonoma Country Fair
and Twilight Parade
Various locations, Healdsburg
(707) 431–7644
www.healdsburg.org
Scheduled for the last weekend in May, this is the longest-running event in Healdsburg and the only fair in California that's nonprofit. The Future Farmers of America sponsor this event, in which everything's free except the food. There's a parade on Thursday, a livestock show and auction on Friday, and kids' activities on Saturday. Food and game booths are run by local youth organizations.

Mendocino County

Willits Celtic Renaissance
Lenore St. South, Willits
(707) 459–7910
www.renaissance-faire.com
The Celtic Faire is a throwback to 16th-century Scotland. For two days on the third weekend in May, Recreation Grove is filled with guild booths, where vendors dressed in period costume sell jewelry, swords, and weaponry of a bygone era. Some booths represent the English (their brothers) as well as Germans, who are said to have fought as mercenaries for the Scots. The event draws some 1,500 people a day to live Scottish life as it was 400 years ago and to enjoy events where javelins are hurled and water balloons cat-

apulted. Jugglers juggle, and wenches walk about selling tidbits of food. The money collected goes for scholarships for local high school students on their way to college. Admission is $6.00 for adults, $3.00 for seniors and free for kids younger than 12.

Great Rubber Ducky Race
Wages Creek, Westport
(707) 964–2872
Westport is the northernmost town on the Mendocino Coast. It's isolated, and the residents like it that way. But the locals have a sense of humor, proven by their annual Great Rubber Ducky Race. It takes place on Mother's Day and is held on the wide, white sand beaches of Wages Creek just north of the town. Anyone who wants to enter can simply bring a rubber ducky from home (some people fancy them up a bit), launch it in the creek and wait to see how long it takes to float downstream to meet the ocean. Meanwhile, the barbecue coals are lighted (the menu is beef, not duck). Everyone is cool and laid back, watching the clouds float across the blue sky and keeping an eye on the fleet of ducks bobbing downstream.

The event is organized by the Westport Village Society to preserve the headlands as open space. Westport is a small town, but the ranks of rubber-ducky race entrants may reach 300, drawing heavily from nearby Mendocino, 9 miles south. Those who go there faithfully each year call it "a real hoot" and "a barrel of fun." The sunshine is free; race entry combined with the beef dinner is $10. It's a great day!

Lake County

Wild West Days
Upper Lake
(707) 275–9408
This community celebration on a Saturday in mid-May in Upper Lake along Main Street celebrates the wild and woolly days of Lake County's colorful history. Following a breakfast and parade in the morning, there's a street dance, chili cook-off, firefighters' competition, barbecue, and lots of entertainment.

Lake County Outdoor Passion Play
Hwy. 29, Lakeport
(707) 279-0349
www.lakecountypassionplay.org

We guarantee you will not find anything else like this in Wine Country. The extravagant dramatization of Jesus Christ's resurrection, staged the third weekend in May, features colorful costumes and an ecumenical cast of 150, not counting sheep, goats, or pigeons. It's said you can hear a pin drop when Pontius Pilate enters in a horse-drawn chariot. The play used to be one afternoon only, but with some 3,000 people attending, they had to carry it over for two days. (The show runs from 4:00 to 6:00 P.M.) Bring food and lawn chairs and settle next to Clear Lake. There is no charge, not even for parking, though donations are gladly accepted.

Memorial Day Parade
Main St., Lakeport
(707) 263-5092

Lakeport chooses the Saturday before Memorial Day for its biggest annual parade. The procession of civic floats and marching bands heads down Main Street as 500 to 600 people crowd the sidewalks. There are additional activities at Library Park before and after, including a pancake breakfast, music, crafts fair, and a barbecue. The only charge is for food.

June

Napa County

Napa Valley Wine Auction
at Meadowood Napa Valley
900 Meadowood Ln., St. Helena
(707) 942-9775, (800) 982-1371
www.napavintners.org

You can't say you've reached the upper echelon of Wine Country society until you've lifted your bidder's paddle at the Auction (see the Closeup in this chapter). Napa Valley's glitziest annual event, not to mention one of the nation's eminent charity auctions, takes place the first Thursday-through-Sunday block in June. Thursday features barrel tastings followed by gatherings organized by local vintners, such as intimate Thursday-night dinners or Friday luncheons. Saturday's live and silent auctions set world records, with astronomical bids for the most coveted of beverages (in 2000, a collector paid $500,000 for a single imperial of wine, a 1992 Screaming Eagle Cabernet Sauvignon). On Sunday, most Napa Valley wineries have open houses. All this, and you wouldn't believe how much more, for just $2,500 per couple.

Berryessa Lions Annual Lizard Races
Pleasure Cove, Lake Berryessa
(707) 966-2172

People can get pretty hot-blooded watching these cold-blooded creatures scamper across indoor-outdoor carpet on the first Saturday in June. Show up with a blue-bellied lizard and a feather and you, too, can enter the fray. (The feather is to be used only if your racer stalls.) There is no entrance fee, and the champions leave with nothing more than blue ribbons. Lizard "owners" are divided by age group, giving the adults a chance to win too. You reach Pleasure Cove via Highway 128—about 5 miles east of Highway 121, turn left on Wragg Canyon Road.

Vintage 1870 Father's Day Invitational
Auto Show
Vintage 1870, 6525 Washington St.,
Yountville
(707) 944-2451
www.vintage1870.com

When Dad begins to rebel against wide ties and cheap cologne, take him to a car show for Father's Day. The north parking lot of Vintage 1870 will be double-parked with 85 to 90 cars—from Vipers to DeSoto Coupes and from a 1939 Packard limousine to a boss old Woody. While you examine the cars, you can eat, drink (everything from Calistoga water to margaritas), and listen to music. The show runs from 11:00 A.M. to 4:00 P.M. and is free to the public, excluding food.

Wine Country Kennel Club
Napa Valley Exposition,
575 Third St., Napa
(707) 253-4900
www.infodog.com

The dog days of summer start a little early in Napa—on a weekend in late June, to be exact. That's when some 2,000 well-groomed pooches strut around the halls and grounds of the Exposition. There are separate shows on Saturday and Sunday, each from 8:00 A.M. until about 6:00 P.M. Saturday features an obedience competition; Sunday, a canine good-citizenship test. There are eight age-and-experience classes (including two puppy classes) and seven dog groups: sporting, hound-working, terrier, toy, nonsporting, herding, and miscellaneous breeds. The entry fee is generally $22 per dog, and no cash prizes are awarded. The animals vie for points, ribbons, trophies, and the ever-popular pat on the head. There is no charge to spectators. The Lions Club provides food, including a pancake breakfast.

Beringer Celebrity Golf Classic
Chardonnay Golf Club,
2555 Jamieson Canyon Rd., Napa
(707) 255-0950

Tired of being ignored as you scream at televised sporting events? The last Wednesday in June is your chance to bend the ear of a famous athlete or coach. Bay Area luminaries like Jim Plunkett, Bill Walsh, and Vida Blue have been spotted at recent Beringer Classics. The tournament had been staged at Silverado Country Club for years, but it moved to Chardonnay's Shakespeare course in 1997. Corporate groups pay a $1,500 entry fee; individuals pay $375 (just $300 if they don't feel the need to be paired with a big shot). It's expensive, yes, but the price includes a pregolf dinner at Beringer. More important, the event funds about half the annual athletic program at Justin-Siena High School, the only Catholic high school in Napa County.

Sonoma County

Ox Roast
Sonoma Plaza, Sonoma
(707) 938-4626
www.sonomavalley.com

For more than 30 years, the first Sunday in June has been marked by aromatic smoke rising from the town's central plaza. The annual Ox Roast is one giant picnic with barbecued beef, corn on the cob, and plenty of beer and wine. You'll pay $3.00 to $9.00 for the meal (beer and wine are extra, and there's also a vegetarian plate), and it all goes to benefit the local community center. The plaza is smack-dab in the center of town. You can't miss it.

Health and Harmony Music and Arts Festival
Sonoma County Fairgrounds, Santa Rosa
(707) 547-9355
www.harmonyfestival.com

For more than two decades, loyal throngs of locals have been buying hemp clothing, eyeing belly dancers, and pounding the drums of world-beat music at this Sonoma County institution. For some, the annual affair in mid-June is like returning to the hippie days of 1967—but the hippies all sport gray ponytails these days. There's always plenty of free music on several stages (Jefferson Starship one year, for example) and a huge number of vendors selling everything from holistic health products to Indian cottons. Be sure to check out the Eco Village, where everything is solar-powered. Women have their own place to hang out—the Goddess temple, featuring female performers and themes. Admission is $15 in advance, $20 at the door.

Cloverdale Heritage Days
124 S. Cloverdale Blvd., Cloverdale
(707) 894-4470
www.cloverdale.net

The citizens of Cloverdale close off the main boulevard of town once each year to celebrate the memory of days past. Events include wine tasting, cow-chip tossing (the local Boys & Girls Club collects the cow chips), a Gold Rush foot race, and a barbecue from 5:00 to 7:00 P.M. There's also country music and dancing outdoors on the plaza. It's all free except the food.

Stumptown Daze
Main St. and Rodeo Grounds, Guerneville
(877) 644-9001
www.russianriver.com

This is a great treat for Dad on Father's Day weekend. A parade, with school bands and preschool kids on bikes, starts at 11:00 A.M. Saturday and follows a route that's subject to local politics, so you might want to call in advance to find out where to park your folding chair. Those who arrive before the parade starts can enjoy a $5.00 cowboy breakfast ($3.50 for kids) served from 7:00 A.M. to noon by the Guerneville Rotary Club. After the parade everyone heads over to the town of Duncans Mills, about 6 miles west of Guerneville on Highway 116. At 2:00 P.M. the rodeo starts, with all those events you expect—calf roping, bull riding, and barrel racing. On Sunday there's another cowboy breakfast from 7:00 to 11:00 A.M., more free rodeo, and some horseback games. Where'd the name originate? Guerneville gained the moniker "Stumptown" in its early days when redwood trees were mercilessly chopped down, leaving only a forest of stumps.

Mendocino County

Spring Carnival
Redwood Empire Fairgrounds,
1055 N. State St., Ukiah
(707) 462-3884
www.redwoodempirefair.com

It's free to enter the gates to the spring fair, held the first weekend in June each year. Entrance to the carnival field is also free, with varying prices for individual thrill rides. Grandstand shows are held Friday and Saturday afternoons from 2:00 P.M. on and feature motor sports events such as stock car races. Admission to the grandstand is $10.00 to $12.00, and kids 10 and younger pay $8.00 to $10.00. The fair is sponsored by the Redwood Empire Fair Association.

Lake County

Middletown Days
Various locations, Middletown
(707) 987-0652
www.shop.middletown.ca.us

For more than 35 years, the southernmost burg in Lake County has taken the opportunity to say, "Welcome to Middletown," on the third weekend of June. The three days of activity include an old-fashioned hoedown at the arena in Central Park (noon to midnight on Friday); a parade that courses down Main Street on Saturday at 11:00 A.M.; lots of music, including a live band that performs at 9:00 P.M. on Saturday; and a gymkhana (Sunday, noon to dusk) that offers various tests of equine skill, concluded by the outrageous "hide ride," wherein competitors sit on a cowhide and get dragged around by a horse. The only costs are for entering events and for food, and those are quite reasonable.

July

Napa County

Napa County Fair
Napa County Fairgrounds,
1435 N. Oak St., Calistoga
(707) 942-5111

You could be forgiven for expecting to find 9-pound Chardonnay grapes or prize-winning Pinot pies at the eminent wine region's annual fair. But the five-day brouhaha (during the Fourth of July weekend) is more down-to-earth than that. Yes, there is plenty of wine to taste, but there are also the usual assortment of carnival rides, livestock exhibits, arts and crafts, and cavity-creating snacks. The fair also includes one or two nights of sprint car racing (see our Spectator Sports chapter) and two nights of concerts, with recent headliners such as country heavyweights LeAnn Rimes, Toby Keith, and Faith Hill. Admission is $5.00 for adults; $2.00 for kids ages 6 to 12. Two separate events—the Miss Napa County Fair Pageant and the Champagne Art Preview—are held on the eve of the fair. Expect about 35,000 people over the five days.

Fourth of July Celebrations
Napa (707) 257-9529
Calistoga (707) 942-6333

Veterans Park is the gathering place for a slew of activity in Napa, including food, carnival games, and wine tasting. Since

1995 the patriotism has expanded to include eight hours of music at the park by a lineup of five or six bands. When your ears are properly ringing, you can treat your eyes to a fireworks display.

Serving as interlude to the Napa County Fair is a sublime slice of Americana. People come from miles around for Calistoga's annual Silverado Parade, placing lawn chairs along the route hours in advance. Past parades have featured the sparkling rigs of the volunteer fire department, horsemen, bikers, clowns, a kazoo corps, floats ranging from sweet to absurd, and, for some reason, a large group of high-school martial-arts students from Kyoto, Japan. The procession starts at 11:00 A.M. You do not want to miss it.

Bastille Day
Domaine Chandon, 1 California Dr., Yountville
(707) 944–8844, (707) 944–2280
www.dchandon.com

More than 200 years after the fact, what does the revolutionary capture of Paris's most infamous prison mean to Napa Valley tourists? Party! French bands play folk songs or classic Parisian cafe music from 11:00 A.M. to 6:00 P.M., and the visitor center staff dresses up "French style." That phrase is interpreted liberally, so you have an equal chance of being greeted by a slinky French maid, Louis XIV, or a two-legged poodle. There is no admission fee, and you can "liberate" sparkling wine by the glass or bottle for the going rate.

Insiders' Tip

If you plan to watch Calistoga's Fourth of July Silverado Parade on Fair Way, near the end of the route, you had better dress for showers. The fire trucks have been known to hose down the crowd—strictly in retaliation, of course.

Napa Valley Shakespeare Festival
St. Helena Elementary School Theater,
1325 Adams St., St. Helena
(707) 251–WILL
www.napashakespeare.org

To be or not to be . . . the question is, "Which night shall we attend?" The Bard's most popular works (and the creations of other notable playwrights) are performed over four weekends, beginning the weekend after the Fourth of July, on Friday through Sunday nights at 7:00 P.M. In 2001, Tom Stoppard's *The Real Inspector Hound* was presented. Tickets run about $18 for adults and $14 for seniors, students, and children under 12.

Meadowood Croquet Classic
Meadowood Napa Valley,
900 Meadowood Ln.
(707) 963–3646, (800) 458–8080

This is no carefree backyard play day. Members of the U.S. Croquet Association flock to Meadowood in late July for a week of serious mallet-wielding. Guests at the resort may watch the preliminary competition for no charge during the week. On Saturday comes the finale: the championship round plus an auction (for charity) and an early-evening gourmet dinner. It's an elegant affair, with some 200 diners attired in natty whites and seated adjacent to the croquet courts. The finale package costs upward of $100 per person. During the rest of the year, Meadowood croquet pro Jerry Stark gives lessons in this rarefied sport of kings—ranging from $25 to $35 an hour.

Sonoma County

Old-Fashioned Fourth of July Celebration
Sonoma Plaza
(707) 938–4626
www.sonomavalley.com

You'd think someone rolled back the clock a few decades to see how Sonoma celebrates Independence Day. In fact, some Insiders say the Fourth of July is their favorite holiday here. Arrive early for a good place to watch the 10:00 A.M. parade that circles the Sonoma Plaza, and be sure to wear red, white, and blue like everyone else! Among the favorite annual entries is the Hometown Band, with its stirring Sousa marches. After the parade, townsfolk assemble in the plaza for more band music, the singing of the national anthem, a patriotic speech, and the presentation of awards for parade entrants. Locals laze around the rest of the day, then reassemble at nightfall for the big finale—a fireworks display put on by the city fire department (partially funded by an appreciative public) in a large field next to the Vallejo Home.

Salute to the Arts
Sonoma Plaza
(707) 938–1133
www.salutetothearts.com
On the third or fourth weekend in July, the entire Sonoma Plaza in the heart of town is transformed into an elegant, lively outdoor setting, featuring five stages filled with theater troupe performances and a variety of music and dance. Fine art by Sonoma Valley artists, children's activities, and the best in local cuisine, wine, and handcrafted beers are available. Admission to the festival is free. Tickets for food and wine may be purchased for $1.00 per taste, or you can employ various package prices that include a souvenir wine glass and plate.

Fort Ross Living History Days
Fort Ross State Park, Fort Ross
(707) 847–3286
www.parks.sonoma.net/fortross.html
On the last Saturday in July, some 100 volunteers and staff participants don period attire and reenact a typical day at Fort Ross in the mid-1800s, during the days of Russian settlement when the commandant and his wife lived elegantly in the wilderness surroundings (see our History chapter). Bring a picnic! Weather here is unpredictable, so also pack a sun hat and warm clothes. Admission is $3.00 per vehicle.

Sonoma County Fair
Sonoma County Fairgrounds,
1350 Bennett Valley Rd., Santa Rosa
(707) 545–4203
www.sonomacountyfair.com

This two-week event begins the last week in July and features carnival rides, a flower show, horse racing, livestock competitions, and a wide array of food and other vendors. This fair is a long-standing Sonoma County institution, and it is not to be missed. General admission is $5.00.

Mendocino County

Willits Frontier Days
Various locations, Willits
(707) 459–6330
www.willits.org
A three-day event during the Fourth of July weekend, it's claimed to be "the longest, continuous rodeo in California." Besides roping and steer riding, there is a Fourth of July parade, horseshoe pitching, dances, a carnival, cowboy breakfast, talent show, barbecue, and crafts show. Most of it happens in midtown or on the rodeo grounds.

Lake County

Clearlake International Worm Races
Redbud Park, Clearlake
(707) 994–3600, (800) 525–3743
Gentlemen and ladies, start your invertebrates. The Clearlake International Worm Races take place at Redbud Park on the Saturday closest to the Fourth, at the end of a parade route that begins at Austin Park. You'll also encounter food and craft vendors and after-dark fireworks. But let's face it, most people show up to see the slimy thoroughbreds. The event was started more than 30 years ago by C.C. Schoenberger, a direct descendant of Mark Twain. You can train your own nightcrawler or red worm, or you can rent one for 50 cents immediately prior to the starting gun. There is a $2.00 entry fee. Racers start in the bull's-eye of a 2-foot-diameter circle; the first to inch its way across the perimeter is the winner.

Lake County Roundup
Main St., Lakeport
(707) 279–4517
They ride into town from as far away as Los Angeles and Oregon on a weekend after

the Fourth, resting their steeds in the middle of Main Street. Palominos? No, but maybe Mustangs. The Roundup is an annual classic car show featuring food, music (highlighted by the Konocti Clickers, a group of cloggers), and close to 300 cherry street machines. There is no charge for viewing, but please don't kick the tires. The day before the show, there is a picnic and poker tournament at the county park plus a parade. All proceeds from food sales go to Hospice of Lake County.

Lake County Rodeo
Lake County Fairgrounds,
401 Martin St., Lakeport
(707) 995-3508
The Rodeo is staged at the same time as the Roundup (see previous listing). For two days in early July, the unsullied Lake County air is filled with dust, the thunderous beat of hooves, and, yes, possibly even the smell of manure. This is a full-menu rodeo with calf roping, steer wrestling, bronc riding, bull riding, etc. After the second day's competition, you can set the woods afire at the rodeo dance. The dance is included in the admission fee of $8.00 to $10.00.

August

Napa County

Napa Town and Country Fair
Napa Valley Exposition,
575 Third St., Napa
(707) 253-4900
www.napavalleyexpo.com
You can join the 65,000-odd people who come to the Exposition over five days in early to mid-August—just don't call it a county fair. Napa's one and only official county fair is in Calistoga in July (see previous listing), but this is a more-than-reasonable facsimile. There are homemade jams and oversized zucchini, 4-H livestock, crowd pleasers such as a lumberjack competition, a high-diving exhibition, wine tasting, and a kiddie carnival. Headliners at this event have spanned the range from Chubby Checker to Chinese acrobats.

Admission is $7.00 for adults and teens and $4.00 for seniors and children ages 6 to 12. There is an additional charge for events in the grandstand, specifically a rodeo and a demolition derby.

Mostly Mozart
Various locations
(707) 252-8671
On a Sunday afternoon in August, the Napa Valley Music Associates occupy a local winery or landmark to offer tribute to that impish Austrian composer. This musical event usually begins with a "legacy," a series of dramatic vignettes and musical samplers from the life of Wolfgang Amadeus M., and possibly Schubert or some other classical giant. Then featured visiting artists usually play chamber music. Tickets are about $30, and they include the legacy, the concert, a reception, and often a tour of the venue. All proceeds benefit NVMA's ongoing music programs.

Day for the Queen at Silverado
Silverado Country Club & Resort,
1600 Atlas Peak Rd., Napa
(707) 257-4044
www.qvhf.org
For one day in August, Silverado Country Club becomes a large, lush hat passed for Queen of the Valley Hospital (see our Healthcare chapter). The full bill includes a fashion show, tennis tournament and golf tournament, lunch, an evening barbecue, dancing, and a silent auction. The cost depends on how many events you mix and match. The fashion show and lunch are $45; golf and lunch are $130; golf, tennis, and the barbecue are $255; you get the idea. The 1999 event raised $90,000 toward a new CT scanner.

Sonoma County

Wings Over Wine Country
Charles M. Schulz Sonoma County Airport,
2330 Airport Blvd., Santa Rosa
(707) 575-7900
www.pacificcoastairmuseum.org
This two-day air show sponsored by the Pacific Coast Air Museum (see our Attrac-

tions chapter) showcases a variety of daredevil performances that will have you craning and squinting in disbelief. In addition to the aerial demonstrations by a variety of WW II aircraft and other vintage fighters, the event features an outstanding demonstration of an F-16 fighter jet in action, courtesy of the Air Force demo team. Bring your earplugs. Admission is $10.00 per day—children 12 and under are free and seniors are $5.00.

Sonoma County Folk Festival
Cinnabar Performing Arts Theater,
3333 Petaluma Blvd. North, Petaluma
(707)838-4857
www.socofoso.org

Renowned throughout the United States since 1986, this is a wonderful indoor music festival. It's a one-day event held in August, with a varied lineup of musicians. You'll hear everything from traditional and original acoustic music to blues, Caribbean grooves, country and '40s music. Instrumental workshops offer a chance to learn to play a variety of folk instruments from dulcimer to banjo, and there is a kids-for-kids concert.

Dixie Jazz Festival
Doubletree Hotel, 1 Doubletree Dr.,
Rohnert Park
(707) 539-3494

A late August weekend of solid jazz brings traditional purveyors of the genre from across the country. They play Dixieland and ragtime from 2:00 P.M. to midnight on Friday, 10:00 A.M. to midnight Saturday and 9:00 A.M. to 6:00 P.M. Sunday. Don't miss the gospel services Sunday morning. There are five venues at the Doubletree Hotel at 1 Doubletree Drive in Rohnert Park. For admission prices, which come in a variety of packages, call the above number.

Cotati Accordion Festival
La Plaza Park, W. Silva Ave. and
Redwood Hwy., Cotati
(707) 664-0444
www.cotatifest.com

On the weekend before Labor Day, accordion players from around the world descend on La Plaza Park. For them, this is a world classic—a two-day extravaganza with professionals playing tangos, Irish clogging music, and all else in between. Two stages are set up side by side for non-stop entertainment, while a jam tent gives visitors a chance to bring their own instruments and squeeze with the pros. The event's appeal is largely to a mature crowd, but on the morning of the second day, kid players show what they can do. Admission is $10 for one day, $18 for both. Kids 15 and under are admitted free.

Old Adobe Fiesta
Petaluma Adobe State Park,
3325 Adobe Rd., Petaluma
(707) 762-4871
www.petaluma.org

Costumed volunteers display craft demonstrations, food preparation, blacksmithing, and other period activities from 10:00 A.M. to 4:00 P.M. on this historic rancho (see our History chapter). There is also Hispanic music, Native American dancing, and a whisker contest. Enjoy food, kid games, farm animals and more. Park admission is $3.00 for adults, $2.00 for kids 6 to 12.

Gravenstein Apple Fair
Ragle Rd., 1 mile north of Bodega Hwy.,
Sebastopol
(707) 571-8288
www.farmtrails.org/gravfair.htm

Traditionally scheduled for a mid-August weekend at Ragle Park in Sebastopol, the Apple Fair features local cuisine and food demonstrations, an animal petting zoo, arts and crafts, and, of course, lots of Gravenstein apples and plenty of pie. Music and kids' activities fill the day. Admission is $6.00 for adults, $4.00 for seniors and kids ages 6 to 16, and $1.00 for kids younger than 5. Pets not allowed.

Mendocino County

SolFest
Real Goods Solar Living Center,
13771 U.S. 101, Hopland
(707) 744-2100
www.realgoods.com

Real Goods, a renewable energy retail store, hosts this annual environmental gala, where you can take a ride in an electric car, tour solar energy exhibits, attend an alternative energy workshop, or simply nosh and enjoy the music. The 2000 event featured speakers Ralph Nader and activist Julia Butterfly Hill. Cost for adults is $6.00 per day or $10.00 for both days.

Redwood Empire Fair
Redwood Empire Fairgrounds,
1055 N. State St., Ukiah
(707) 462–3884
www.redwoodempirefair.com
Held the second weekend in August at the fairgrounds on N. State Street, it's a bang-up event (literally, if you consider the Destruction Derby) with a big carnival, country-western concerts, lots of live-stock events, and plenty of family fun. Admission is $6.00 for adults and teens, $3.00 for kids 6 to 12, and free for those under 5.

Art in the Redwoods
Various locations, Gualala
(707) 884–1138
www.mcn.org/1/ga/
Held the third weekend in August, Art in the Redwoods includes fine art, crafts, food and beverage booths, games for children, and day-long musical and theatrical entertainment. The event is sponsored by Gualala Art Center, and the fun takes place at the center and Bower Park. There is a $5.00 admission charge.

Lake County

Blackberry Festival
Anderson Marsh State Historic Park,
Hwy. 53, Lower Lake
(707) 994–BERY

Anderson Marsh is worth a visit any time of year (see our Attractions chapter), but it's especially alluring the second Saturday in August, when the rangers (with help from the Rotary Club and the park's Interpretive Association) set back the clock to the beginning of the 20th century. The circular white picket fence serves as a time machine. Outside the

fence, there is thoroughly modern live music, food, and crafts; inside it, you'll see throwbacks such as butter churning, flint napping, and Victorian melodramas—all of which is mere pretense for eating blackberry pie and ice cream on a long summer day. That combination is likely to draw 4,000 to 6,000 people. Cost is $3.00 for adults, $2.00 for kids.

Summerfest
Konocti Harbor Resort & Spa,
8727 Soda Bay Rd., Kelseyville
(707) 279–4281, (800) 660–LAKE
www.konoctiharbor.com
Konocti Harbor has no qualms about long goodbyes. Lake County's premier resort takes 10 days to say "so long" to summer, ending with a fireworks show the night before Labor Day. Summerfest is actually a bundle of smaller outdoor events, each of which charges a separate admission fee of $30 to $50. The 1999 event also included a Celebrity Quarterback Shootout that drew a number of retired NFL slingers; that one cost $500 a head, though it included tickets to the other events. Meanwhile, standing for all 10 days is Festival Row, a carnival that includes laser tag, water slides, a karaoke bar, and lots of evening entertainment. Summer is so impressed it returns to Lake County every year.

September

Napa County

Symphony on the River
Third St. Bridge, Napa
(707) 254–8520
The Napa Valley Symphony brings its music to the masses for one night a year—the Sunday before Labor Day. The action centers around the Third Street Bridge in downtown Napa, where the symphony performs between 7:00 and about 9:15 P.M. Main Street is blocked off between Second and Third Streets, and many people also watch from China Point near the First Street Bridge. The show is followed by fireworks and preceded by a mixer at

Veterans Park, where vendors sell food, wine, and crafts starting at about 3:00 P.M. It's all organized by Friends of the Napa River.

Music Festival for Mental Health
Staglin Family Vineyard,
1570 Bella Oaks Ln., Rutherford,
(707) 944–0477
www.staglinfamily.com

Granted, it's not a very sexy title, but the event itself, staged in a big, open-sided tent overlooking the winery and Napa Valley, is rather divine. On a Saturday or Sunday in mid-September, 400 guests arrive for a reception with wine and hors d'oeuvres. At 3:30, there is a classical concert directed by a celebrity guest conductor (Benjamin Zander of the Boston Philharmonic performed at the 2001 event). Half the attendees (those smiling broadly) then stay for a lavish dinner prepared by a renowned chef such as Wayne Nish, Charlie Trotter, or Traci des Jardins. Some 40 to 50 small, ultrapremium Napa Valley wineries pour their goods throughout. The base price is $250 per person for the reception, $1,000 if you stay for dinner, and the best tables are reserved for $10,000 to $50,000. Every penny funds much-needed research into mental illness, primarily through the National Alliance for Research on Schizophrenia and Depression. The 2000 festival alone raised nearly $3.5 million.

Sonoma County

Women's Weekend
Various locations, Guerneville
(877) 644–9001
www.womensweekend.com

This annual event is a big party that features a golf tournament, author readings, a great pool party, exotic and unusual crafts and other wares, and music and entertainment. There's also a serious side too, with proceeds from various events donated to West County health centers to fight breast cancer.

Exotic and unusual crafts are among the highlights of the annual Women's Weekend in Guerneville.
PHOTO: JOHN NAGIECKI

Sonoma Valley Harvest Wine Auction
Various locations, Sonoma
(707) 935-0803
www.sonomavalleywine.com

Events during the Labor Day weekend occur at various wineries and vineyards and include a wine auction and dinner dance, celebrity-chef dinners, barbecue picnics, entertainment, and wine tasting panels. It's three days of irreverent fun and frivolity to raise money for various charities, while avoiding the pretentiousness of other wine auctions. (Tuxes may be worn, but only when accompanied by a "Kick me" sign.) Sunday's auctions culminate with an extravagant dinner buffet and live dance band. (See the Close-up in this chapter.)

Prices and package deals vary widely year to year as do the charities that benefit. Get information on tickets from Sonoma Vintners and Growers Alliance at the listed number.

Heirloom Tomato Festival
Kendall-Jackson Wine Center,
5007 Fulton Rd., Santa Rosa
(800) 544-4413
www.kj.com

The lowly tomato is elevated to superstar status at this festival dedicated to the enjoyment of the juicy fruit that comes in all shapes and colors. In early September, at the height of the tomato harvest in local backyards, as many as 150 different varieties can be sampled in some fashion. For five hours, nearly 40 restaurants and purveyors of gourmet food offer tomato-inspired goodies in bite-size portions, along with cooking demonstrations, wine tasting, food and wine seminars, and even an art show. Amateur gardeners can enter their own tomato crop in a contest with categories such as Ugliest Tomato. Tickets are sold in advance only for $30 per person.

Russian River Jazz Festival
Johnson's Beach, Guerneville
(707) 869-3940
www.sonic.net/rrjazz

At least eight internationally recognized jazz artists get together the first week in September for two all-day concerts on the Russian River. Food and drinks are available. Prices for jazz under the redwoods range from $33 to $75 for two days. This festival was planning to change its long-time location on the river effective with the 2002 event. Call to learn the latest.

Valley of the Moon Vintage Festival
Sonoma Plaza
(707) 996-2109
www.sonomavalley.com

The 100-year-old Valley of the Moon Vintage Festival, held annually on the last weekend in September on the plaza in Sonoma, is among the oldest wine harvest celebrations in the country. It features a traditional Friday evening wine tasting party and a full weekend of historical pageants, the blessing of the grapes, parades, concerts, and wine and food tastings. The festival is easy to find—just drive to Sonoma, and it'll be smack in the center of town. If you want to attend the Friday night wine tasting event, however, you'll need to order tickets at least a month in advance—it's a sellout every year.

Mendocino County

Roots of Motive Power Festival
Mendocino County Museum,
400 E. Commercial St., Willits
(707) 459-9036, (707) 459-7910
www.rootsofmotivepower.com

This is a way to relive the excitement and dangers of everyday lumberjack work in the redwoods. In mid-September the Mendocino County Museum brings out some of the tools of the trade—antique locomotives and yarders and old steam donkeys (a steam-powered machine that replaced the donkey for pulling large logs). What really draws a crowd is the two-day lumberjack handcar race event, held in front of the Skunk Train railroad depot (see our Attractions chapter). Two handcars, with four people aboard each, engage in a drag race, pumping for 100 feet or so. Want to see how well you'd do as a lumberjack? It costs $5.00 to enter the races. It's a popular contest, and during the two days some 40 teams head down the track, pumping away. Other than the race entry fee, the entire event is free.

Fiesta Patrias
Redwood Empire Fairgrounds,
1055 N. State St., Ukiah
(707) 463–8181
www.redwoodempirefair.com

To celebrate Mexican Independence Day on September 16, the Latino Club of Ukiah stages a Fiesta Patrias event to select a Latina queen. Actually the object is not so much a beauty contest as a way to raise money for a scholarship fund. The contenders spend a lot of time and energy before the event in soliciting money from merchants, selling tamales and tickets, and other fund-raising endeavors. One queen is selected for her beauty, but the real winner is the girl who collects the most money. Each year some $10,000 is made available to help local students of Latin descent go to college. The festivities include fireworks and folk dancing.

Mendocino County Fair and Apple Show
14400 Hwy. 128, Boonville
(707) 895–3011
www.mendocountyfair.com

This is a traditional three-day family event held on a mid-September weekend and highlighted by a rodeo, sheepdog trials, rides for kids of all ages, and country-western dancing in the town of Boonville, located in the Anderson Valley. Admission is $6.00 for adults and $3.00 for children younger than 12.

Paul Bunyan Days
Various locations, Fort Bragg
(707) 964–8687
www.paulbunyandays.com

Held each year on Labor Day weekend, this community celebration is a tribute to Paul Bunyan, the legendary giant lumberjack and folk hero who seems to show up everywhere there's lumber, from the north woods of Minnesota to the forests around Seattle. Numerous events keep things hopping for four days. A Sunday logging show gives visitors a look at what

The annual *Blessing of the Grapes*, part of the Valley of the Moon Vintage Festival, takes place at Mission San Francisco de Solano in Sonoma.
PHOTO: SONOMA INDEX-TRIBUNE

professional loggers do in the way of very strenuous activity. Watching the loggers costs $6.00, but other events like the parade, the 19th-century dress revue, the fiddlers' contest, and the fire department water fight are free. The location changes, so call for the current site.

Winesong
Mendocino Coast Botanical Gardens
18220 Hwy. 1, Mendocino
(707)961–4688
www.winesong.org

More than 60 wineries and 50 restaurants participate in this wine tasting and auction, held at the delightful 47-acre botanical gardens in mid-September (also see our Attractions chapter). Winesong benefits the Mendocino Coast Hospital Foundation. The site is filled with native

Wine Auctions for Charity:
From Ultrachic to Down-home

Napa Valley and Sonoma Valley are only a few miles apart, yet the two regions are worlds apart when comparing their annual wine auctions for charity. The Napa Valley Wine Auction is the big kahuna of charity wine auctions, the largest of its kind in the world. On the quieter side of the Mayacmas range, the smaller Sonoma Valley Harvest Wine Auction shares the same noble goal as its neighbor: to raise gobs of money for local charities.

In general, both auctions are three-day events in summer, with two days set aside for a whirlwind romp of winery dinners, open houses, and special wine and food tastings. Both weekends are capped off with their main attraction, the live auction, set on the grounds of their respective destination resorts: Meadowood in Napa Valley and the Sonoma Mission Inn & Spa in Sonoma.

The number of lots (or packages) up for bid at auction reach about 150 at the Napa event and about 80 in Sonoma. The lots vary significantly; some are wine only, from one bottle to many, perhaps in custom-designed boxes. Or a single lot may be wine combined with a special event or culinary experience—say, 13 bottles of several varieties of Cosentino wines in big-bottle formats, plus dinner for six at the winery, and a specially handcrafted pendant from the collections of Carrera y Carrera in Madrid (winning bid at the Napa Valley event in 2001: $28,000). Bids like these (and the $650,000 paid for eight double magnums—that's 24 liters—of Screaming Eagle Cabernet Sauvignon) really add up: The 2001 Napa Valley auction raised close to $7.6 million, down a couple of million from the 2000 event.

At the Napa auction, 2,000-some attendees mill about and schmooze while sampling finger foods served by restaurants such as The French Laundry and Bistro Jeanty. The bright white tent where the bidding takes place seems large enough to conceal a 747, with closed-circuit TVs to help all those with bidding paddles stay connected to the action. Dress is "Wine Country casual" but there are plenty of colorful silk sundresses, summery hats, and designer duds, too.

You're likely to spot a show business celebrity here and there in the crowd, as well as celebrities from the world of wine. One year, Robin Williams took a turn at the podium, performing a frenzied 10-minute parody of the haughty and hefty auction catalog. In 2001 Robert Mondavi got up on stage dressed a la Vanna White to "spin the bottle." In sleeveless long gown, pearls, and flowing blond wig, the 88-year-old wine baron was a sight to behold.

Food also figures prominently throughout the weekend. The evening before the live auction the big tent is filled to capacity for a black-tie gala and fabulous feast. (The 2001 dinner was created and overseen by Wolfgang Puck, with entertainment by Broadway star Joel Grey.) The next day, when the last gavel falls after the auction, the crowd moves out of the tent and across the meadow to row upon row of white linen-topped tables for a "picnic" dinner and dancing. It's safe to say it's one of the most elegant and largest picnics you will ever experience.

The Sonoma Valley is no less refined when it comes to wine affairs and winemaking talent, but the Sonoma vintners long ago decided that their auction wouldn't be as big or as high falutin' as Napa's. Each year they set out to raise a serious pile of cash, just like Napa, but they have a lot of laughs doing it.

For instance, in 2001, the Napans dubbed their auction—its 20th year—the puffed-up "Ode to Napa Valley." The Sonomans, in their characteristic down-to-earth approach, chose "An Oasis of Irreverence" as their theme, and the vintners posed for their popular annual poster as island castaways gathered around a case of wine that's washed ashore. The caption? "Now all we need is a corkscrew."

The tranquil grounds of Meadowood are transformed for the world-class Napa Valley Wine Auction. PHOTO: FAITH ECHTERMEYER

Scaled down in size from its neighbor's event, the Sonoma live auction is also less stuffy, and the vintners provide the goofy entertainment and the stand-up comedy. Tommy Smothers, owner of Remick Ridge Winery in Sonoma Valley and half of the legendary Smothers Brothers, takes the stage frequently during the bidding to energize the audience and keep the fun and games moving along. As in Napa, dress is "Wine Country casual," but in Sonoma that means just about anything goes, from Hawaiian shirts and shorts for the men to sundresses for the ladies. And at the podium in 2001, there were plenty of coconut bras and grass skirts (on both sexes) to add to the hilarity. The result was effective: Nearly $600,000 was raised at the 2001 affair, beating the previous year's tally by more than $80,000.

Yes, the big bucks really do go to local charities. The beneficiaries in Napa Valley include 27 healthcare, youth, and housing nonprofit agencies. In Sonoma Valley, the good causes range from community health centers to vineyard workers' services to the regional Boys and Girls Club.

So how much will a bidding paddle at one of these auctions set you back? Napa's three-day event is $2,500 per couple; Sonoma's about half that, at $600 per person. These prices are generally all-inclusive of the special dinners and tastings leading up to the auctions, but do not include accommodations or transportation. Anyone is welcome to request an invitation to attend these auctions, but it really helps if your credit rating is solid, you possess at least one platinum card, and you have spousal support to spend with abandon. You will walk away not only with some killer wine but also with the knowledge that you contributed significantly to improving the quality of life for the less fortunate, and you had a good time doing it.

You can learn more about these auctions—and request an invitation—by visiting their respective Web sites: www.napavintners.org and www.sonomavalleywine.com.

plants—rhododendrons, heather, fuchsia, and dwarf conifers. Two creeks flow through the gardens, and more than 3 miles of trails allow visitors to find their way to the cliff house overlooking the dramatic seascape. It's a perfect site to sample Mendocino's famous wines. There's no entrance fee, but there is a charge for the wine.

Lake County

Lake County Fair
Lake County Fairgrounds,
401 Martin St., Lakeport
(707) 263–6181

The wine tasting tables are the only reminders that this isn't Missouri or Iowa. Lake County throws an old-fashioned fair every Labor Day weekend, with a carnival, livestock exhibits, draft-horse wagon rides, and four days of goings-on. There are musical acts, a horse show, a demolition derby, and a mini-rodeo (bull riding only). The sun can still get a bit aggressive here in early September, but there is plenty of shade at the fairgrounds. The cost is $6.00 for adults, $3.00 for children.

West Coast Seaplane Splash-In
Clear Lake, Lakeport
(415) 472–0227

Lake County's annual D-Day comes on the Friday before the last weekend in September, when 35 to 40 seaplanes descend upon tranquil Clear Lake. They range from straight float planes to amphibians, from prewar to contemporary. It's a loosely organized event that includes a safety seminar and a Friday or Saturday night dinner. There is no fee for watching the invasion, and you can bet on good weather: The event's had only 2 bad years in nearly 20.

Kelseyville Pear Festival
Various locations, Kelseyville
(707) 279–9022

The citizens of Kelseyville have figured out a constructive use for those late-season Bartletts. On the last Saturday of September, they stuff the succulent fruits into pie crusts, cookie batter, jam jars, ice cream, and anything else they can think of, and they build a whole weekend around them. There's even a pear-packing competition among the local packing houses. You'll also enjoy a parade down Main Street (led by antique tractors), followed by a petting zoo, craft vendors, and a dance performance, and it's all free. In conjunction with the Pear Festival is the Kelseyville Quilt Show, a two-day event featuring at least 100 fine bedspreads—some old, some new, some for sale, some just to admire. The Quilt Show is at the Kelseyville Presbyterian Church at Third and Church Streets, and admission is $3.00. Also part of the festival is a fine art show at the Bank of Lake County, 4280 Main Street.

Pedal the Puddle
Library Park, Lakeport
(707) 263–1845, (707) 263–6311

A major cyclist alert goes out to Clear Lake residents on a Sunday in late September or early October. About 250 pedalers start at Library Park (which hugs the lake between First and Third Streets in Lakeport) and embark on one of three rides: a 30-miler, a 60-miler, or a 100-miler, the last of which pretty much circumnavigates the elongated "puddle." Any type of bike is welcome as long as you have the entry fee ($25 to $35). The Pedal is organized by the Lakeport Rotary Club.

October

Napa County

Southwest Art in the Wine Country
Lee Youngman Galleries,
1316 Lincoln Ave., Calistoga
(707) 942–0585

If your idea of art is Native American spirit guides, dusty cowboys, fiery desert sunsets, and howling coyotes, don't miss this annual show at an upvalley winery. About 35 artists usually display varied works in late September or early October. Saturday is by RSVP only; Sunday is open to the general public, at no charge. A silent auction benefits the Boy Scouts of America.

Calistoga Beer and Sausage Festival
Napa County Fairgrounds,
1435 N. Oak St., Calistoga
(707) 942–6333

You might think you have to speak in hushed tones when you discuss beer in the Wine Country, but this festival is well-regarded. (The 2001 event, the 18th annual, had its largest turnout ever.) The sudsfest features a chili cook-off, music, and samples from about 30 microbreweries (see the Close-Up in our Wineries chapter), not to mention sausage companies, mustard makers and, quite possibly, pretzels from Snyders of Hanover. Twenty dollars gets you in the door and entitles you to a bottomless souvenir cup and borderless plate. It's a one-day affair in late September or early October.

Ghost Wineries Tour
(707) 252–3270
www.napalandtrust.org

Just as September in Wine Country brings on the crush, October hustles in the annual one-day Ghost Wineries Tour. Typically, five or six "ghost" wineries (some of the oldest forced to close during Prohibition) are revisited on a self-guided tour. Additional staff are on hand to greet visitors, and picnics are encouraged. Participants drive their own vehicles between the wineries at their own leisure.

Old Mill Days
Bale Grist Mill State Historic Park,
3369 N. St. Helena Hwy., St. Helena
(707) 942–4575

The folks at the Grist Mill celebrate the end of harvest by partying like it's 1869. Coopers, weavers, storytellers, and old-time fiddlers don period costumes to lend a touch of authenticity to the 19th-century goings-on. The kids can make cornhusk dolls or dye wheat. And the park rangers offer nonstop tours of the mill, which will be busy grinding whole-wheat flour and cornmeal. It's a two-day event in mid-October. The cost is $4.00 for adults and $2.00 for children.

Napa Valley Open Studios Tour
Various locations
(707) 257–2117
www.artscouncilnapavalley.org

Come see real, live artists in their natural habitats! On successive weekends in mid- to late October, Napa Valley creative types throw open the doors to their studios and welcome the self-guided with refreshments. The format tends to be upvalley one weekend and downvalley the next. The Napa Valley Arts Council distributes maps prior to the free event; all you do is drive and gawk. At least 80 artists usually participate, including big names such as Earl Thollander, Catherine Anderson, Davis DeSelle, and Ann Hunter Hamilton. The settings run from valley tip to valley bottom, and the media run from photography to metal sculpture to oil painting. If nothing else, the tour shows that all artists do not live in cramped, unkempt studio apartments. That's just writers.

Hometown Harvest Festival
Adams St., St. Helena
(707) 963–5706

For decades, St. Helena marked the end of the grape harvest with a municipal celebration. Sometime in the 1960s, the city fathers decided to adopt a more refined image, and the harvest bash was abolished. It made a welcome comeback in 1987. The festival, a one-day event on a Saturday in October, includes arts and crafts, a fun run, a carnival, wine tasting, and a canine Frisbee-catching contest. The highlight is the pet parade, an advancing column of dogs, cats, horses, llamas, roosters, and lizards. (One recent costume award went to a hamster.) Most of the action swirls around St. Helena Elementary School, on Adams Street between Oak and Stockton Streets. There is no admission fee, and most of the proceeds from vendor sales go toward building St. Helena a new community center.

Sonoma County

Sonoma County Harvest Fair
Sonoma County Fairgrounds,
1350 Bennett Valley Rd., Santa Rosa
(707) 545–4203
www.harvestfair.org

This harvest festival on the first full weekend in October features a world-championship grape stomp, wine tasting, produce exhibits, food, arts, crafts, amateur beer and wine booths, music, and kids' exhibits. This bustling fair brings in droves of wine lovers from San Francisco. Wine and food tasting tickets are extra, but you get a souvenir glass, and you will sip the top award winners in their specific categories—perhaps the only chance you'll get, because the wines are sometimes very limited production vintages. General admission is $5.00, but it's $2.00 for seniors on Friday and $2.00 for kids ages 7 to 12.

Mendocino County

Chainsaw Sculpture Championship
Fort Bragg
(707) 964–4251
www.fortbragg.com

Where else can manly men bearing chainsaws demonstrate their sensitive side? Leatherface would blend right in, as long as he can sculpt. Professional and novice chainsaw sculptors from around the nation gather every year in October to reduce a block of redwood or pine into a thing of beauty, based on certain themes (in 2001, it was nautical, wine, and timber). In the process, they generate truckloads of sawdust over four days to complete their mission. Three winners are chosen from the pro, intermediate, and novice categories, and cash prizes are awarded. Later, the stately sculptures are auctioned off to benefit the Fort Bragg-Mendocino Coast Historical Society.

Lake County

Harvest Festival
Steele Winery, 4350 Thomas Dr., Kelseyville
(707) 279–1420, (707) 279–9475

The only thing better than watching people peel off their shoes and stomp the juice out of ripe grapes is hopping into the tub yourself. Well, here's your chance. When Steele bought Konocti in 1995, it continued the old winery's traditional harvest bash, with crafts, barbecue, music, wine tasting, and the oldest form of crushing. It's a two-day event on the second weekend of October, with a Lakeport Chamber of Commerce-sponsored vineyard run on one of the days.

Wine Auction Gala
Buckingham Golf and Country Club
Kelseyville
(800) 595–WINE

Napa and Sonoma Counties have their big benefit auctions, and this is one of Lake County's newer events. Food, music, and silent and live auctions take place for one evening. It's a black-tie affair, with proceeds going to various Lake County community services. Tickets will set you back $75 per person.

November

Napa County

Napa Valley Wine Festival
Napa Valley Exposition,
575 Third St., Napa
(707) 253–3563

Encouraging kids to drink is not good, but encouraging kids through a drinking festival is another matter altogether. This gig on the first Saturday in November raises about $50,000 a year for the Napa Valley Unified School District. The fun includes a live auction, with about 50 valley wineries pouring and 1,000 guests sipping, student-provided music as a backdrop, and a pasta dinner for sustenance. Tickets are $30 in advance, $35 at the door.

Festival of Lights
Vintage 1870, 6525 Washington St.,
Yountville
(707) 944–2451

This isn't so much the lighting of a tree as the lighting of a town. At about 6:00 P.M. the day after Thanksgiving, all of Yountville flicks its switches and is bathed in fairy lights. Christmas is beckoned with singers, street performers, hayrides, and roasted chestnuts from 2:00 to 9:00 P.M. There is no admission fee, though you must buy tickets for food and wine. The extravaganza sets off a month of special dinners, musical performances, and the like around Yountville.

Sonoma County

Santa's Arrival
Petaluma Riverfront, Petaluma
(707) 769-0429
www.petaluma.org

On the last Saturday in November, Santa makes his way into Petaluma by boat. While awaiting his arrival, the children stay busy with a variety of entertainment options. As might be expected, Santa's first move is to start handing out candy canes. Then he steps into an antique wagon chosen from the collection at the county museum (considered the largest collection in North America) and leads a parade of beautiful wagons in a circular route around town. It ends in historic Petaluma, where merchants hold a "Share the Spirit" event with an array of treats for all.

Mendocino County

Thanksgiving Festival
Mendocino Art Center,
45200 Little Lake Rd., Mendocino
(707) 937-5818
www.mendocinoartcenter.org

A jolly festival at the Mendocino Art Center to survey the newest in professional arts and crafts occurs the weekend after Thanksgiving. Every inch of the center (and outside it, if the weather is cooperative) is filled with booths displaying crafters' works, from tie-dye to watercolors. A separate room has been reserved for kids to play, and there is always a visit from Santa.

December

Napa County

Carols in the Caves
Various Napa and Sonoma wineries
(707) 224-4222
www.cavemusic.net

Local musician David Auerbach is a multi-instrumentalist. That term is defined at his performances, where he is likely to play two dozen musical devices including dulcimers, pan pipes, and psalteries. As you might guess, he specializes in unusual folk instruments, and he brings out the best of each in the flawless acoustic environment of wine caves. The Carols series consists of a minimum of eight simple, informal concerts, two or three per weekend between Thanksgiving and Christmas—and sometimes running into January for a Twelfth Night celebration. Locations vary from year to year and week to week. Cost for each show is about $30 per person, unless it includes dinner, in which case you'll pay at least $125. It is customary for the host to pour complimentary wine during the intermission (or dinner).

Holiday Candlelight Tour
Various locations, Napa
(707) 255-1836

On the second Saturday in December, Napa County Landmarks (a local preservation society) organizes a 3:00 to 8:00 P.M. walking tour in a selected historic neighborhood. The stroll and open houses are usually in Napa but can turn up anywhere in the county. Many of the hosts put out cookies or cider, and there is a sweets-and-wine reception from 4:00 to 10:00 P.M. at a particularly fabulous building. Expect eight or nine stops, with strolling carolers and glowing luminaries along the way. The cost is $15 for Napa County Landmarks members, $18 for everyone else signing up in advance. It's $25 if you pay at the door.

Pioneer Christmas
Bale Grist Mill State Historic Park,
3369 N. St. Helena Hwy., St. Helena
(707) 942-4575

Ever wonder how Americans celebrated Christmas in the 1850s? Well, don't expect any Tickle Me Elmos or Muzak renditions of "Silver Bells" if you visit the Bale Grist Mill on a weekend day in mid-December. What you can expect are Christmas carols sung to the accompaniment of mandolin and fiddle. You can string popcorn and cranberries, drink apple cider, and, for a nominal charge, decorate gingerbread cookies. Longtime miller George Stratton probably will be there giving tours and he may be grinding out fresh flour and cornmeal too. Adults pay $4.00; it's $2.00 for the kids.

Sonoma County

Sonoma Valley Olive Festival
Various locations, Sonoma
(707) 996-1090
www.sonomavalley.com

December is the official kickoff month for this several-weeks-long annual event (see more details under the January listing).

Russian River Christmas Extravaganza
Various locations, Guerneville
(707) 869-9000
www.russianriver.com

Guerneville celebrates the holidays with a series of events guaranteed to raise everyone's spirits. The first is an evening open house with hors d'oeuvres and refreshments available free at many downtown businesses. The highlight of the evening is the lighting of the Christmas tree in Guerneville Plaza along with carolers and carriage rides throughout downtown. Next is the World Dance Celebration held at the Veterans Hall. This cultural music and dance exhibition features African, Irish, Scottish, Mexican, Caribbean, and other

ethnic dance. The crowning event is the parade of lights, featuring trucks, horses, marching bands, antique cars, floats, and more, all decorated with Christmas lights. Check the Web site or phone number for exact dates and times.

Holiday Crafts Fair and Open House
Various locations, Cloverdale
(707) 894-4470
www.cloverdale.net

The first Saturday in December, Cloverdale shop owners host an open house with hors d'oeuvres and refreshment. The afternoon features the Parkside Chapel Singers performing in the downtown plaza. And there's Christmas cheer to be had at the Wine and Visitor Center.

Mendocino County

A Smalltown Christmas
Various locations, Ukiah
(707) 462-4705
www.ukiahchamber.com

Santa flies into the local airport, and from there he rides a fire truck around town to visit all the shopping centers. A music program is held in the downtown area and is followed by the "Truckers Light Parade." Kick off the Christmas spirit with this event, the first weekend in December.

Lake County

Christmas Open House
Anderson Marsh State Historic Park,
Hwy. 53, Lower Lake
(707) 994-0688

This is sort of a wintry version of the Blackberry Festival (see August), held on a Saturday (usually) in early December. The historic house is spruced up with handmade 19th-century holiday decorations. Come inside for Christmas carols, cider, and cookies. There is no admission charge.

Shopping

Malls
Unique Shops
Antiques
Bookstores

Like our award-winning nectar of the gods and the mouth-watering cuisine, the shopping possibilities in Wine Country are varied and fanciful. We are not overrun with mega-malls or endless discount outlet store complexes, though those that we have come in handy when you need to buy toothpaste or film or you require a huge assortment of apparel options.

Instead, what we spotlight in this chapter are the one-of-a-kind shops selling one-of-a-kind items in towns that are tucked amid sprawling vineyards or washed by the wild Pacific. But don't be fooled—these are not the quaint country villages of TV's Cabot Cove or Mayberry USA. These are cosmopolitan communities—meccas for lovers of fine wines, fine foods, and all things unique and excellent.

Wine Country shopkeepers are savvy and world-wise in their selection of merchandise, and you will fall under the spell cast by the picturesque streets of Healdsburg, St. Helena, and Calistoga. You may find yourself popping in and out of the shops and galleries clinging to the four sides of Sonoma's historic plaza. And a stroll among Mendocino's dozens of specialty shops is certain to bring the credit cards out of your jeans pocket.

Wineries add to the galaxy of possibilities here. Drop in at one of the winery gift shops, and you'll see lots of things to bring home to friends. And if you're into antiques, you've come to the right place. Santa Rosa has devoted most of a city block to the sale of antiques. Tiny Sebastopol (population 7,700) has about 15 antiques shops, including one collective with more than 100 dealers. And those are just the big ones.

As for those malls and outlets, try the Napa Factory Stores (a maze of classic-label clothing emporiums) or the Petaluma Village Factory Outlet, where the dazzling possibilities may keep you rooted to the place for days. Almost every town in Wine Country has some sort of mall or shopping strip—generally anchored by a food market and a drug store, with various other shops between. We have listed those that are larger, especially those with nationally recognized stores or with particularly intriguing specialty shops. You'll find these in our first section of listings.

Next, we detail the various specialty shops scattered throughout Wine Country that are unique to our area, and we follow that up with a breakdown of antiques stores and bookstores throughout the four-

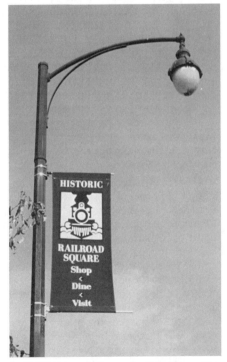

Railroad Square in downtown Santa Rosa offers interesting boutiques, antiques stores, and an assortment of fine dining options. PHOTO: JEAN SAYLOR DOPPENBERG county region. Expect these stores to keep reasonably regular hours—if operating times are particularly unusual, we'll let you know in the listings. It's always a good idea to make a call if you're not sure when a place is open.

Malls

Napa County

Napa Premium Outlets
Hwy. 29 at First St. exit, Napa
(707) 226–9876

The factory stores have done the improbable in Napa Valley—in the middle of Wine Country, they've become a big tourist draw in and of themselves. The immense Napa facility features more than 45 premium designers and brand-name outlets, including heavy hitters such as Calvin Klein, Nautica, Ellen Tracy, Ann Taylor Loft, BCBG, Max Studio, J. Crew, Timberland, Tommy Hilfiger, Jones New York, and Dansk. You can expect savings of 25 percent to 65 percent off normal retail price tags. Napa Premium Outlets also has the Courtyard Cafes with a choice of quickie cuisines, plus the table-service Fujiya Restaurant. The stores are open Monday through Thursday from 10:00 A.M. to 8:00 P.M., Friday and Saturday from 10:00 A.M. to 9:00 P.M., and Sunday from 10:00 A.M. to 6:00 P.M.

Napa Town Center
First St., between Coombs and
Franklin Sts., Napa
(707) 253–9282

Roughly bordered by First, Franklin, Pearl, and Coombs Streets, Napa Town Center is the pulsing heart of the city's downtown shopping. The courtyard mall has winding pathways through cobblestone paseos and at least 20 shops, including McCaulou's Department Store, Waldenbooks, and Miller's Outpost. It also houses the Napa Valley Conference and Visitors Bureau, the stationary welcome wagon for a high percentage of Wine Country tourists. Napa Town Center is bordered by a half-dozen or more restaurants and snack shops. The Center presents two Bridal Fairs each year and holiday events at Christmas, plus regular Popcorn Pete's Kid Club Shows. And every Friday from May through September it hosts the Chefs Market, with produce, baked goods, crafts, and more.

Vintage 1870
6525 Washington St., Yountville
(707) 944–2451
www.vintage1870.com

You can't miss Vintage 1870 any more than you could have missed the building when it dominated the landscape as the Groezinger Winery. Built (as you might guess) in 1870 by Gottlieb Groezinger, the massive red-brick winery now contains a warren of specialty shops featuring fine art, foodstuffs, T-shirts, antiques, home and garden accessories, clothing, linens—more than 40 shops and galleries on two levels. Vintage 1870 has several cafes, snack shops, and restaurants for the hungry purchaser, as well as a trellis-shaded picnic garden. It also has an excellent wine cellar—see our Wineries chapter for more details. Get there early enough and you can watch the hot-air balloon departures.

St. Helena Premium Outlets
Hwy. 29, 2 miles north of St. Helena
(707) 963–7282

The St. Helena collection of factory stores is much smaller than its relatives in Napa and Petaluma, but a poor cousin it isn't. The tucked-away line of shops on the west side of the highway includes Brooks Brothers, Donna Karan, Joan & David, Movado, Coach, London Fog. Traditional retail establishments would have a hard time matching the prices here (25 to 65 percent less at the outlets), and even more trouble matching the parklike setting, which includes picnic tables. There is also a Spirits in Stone gallery on the premises (see Sonoma listings). The stores are open daily from 10:00 A.M. to 6:00 P.M.

Sonoma County

The plaza areas in the cities of Sonoma and Healdsburg could easily be considered shopping centers. But with so many wonderful stores meriting individual listings, we have placed the write-ups for those shops under the subsequent "Unique Shops" heading. What follows is information on the more traditional mall-type alternatives in Sonoma County.

Petaluma Village Premium Outlets
2200 N. Petaluma Blvd., Petaluma
(707) 778–9300
www.premiumoutlets.com

It's outside the mainstream shopping area of Petaluma, but it's an irresistible magnet for shoppers looking for bargains on the finest designer fashions and name-brand merchandise. The maze of stores includes Brooks Brothers, Gap, DKNY, Mikasa, Reebok, Saks Fifth Avenue—and that's just a start. If you're tired of boutique shopping, this is your place. You'll find about 50 shops to get lost in, every day of the week. Hours are 10:00 A.M. to 8:00 P.M. Monday through Saturday and 10:00 A.M. to 6:00 P.M. on Sunday.

Raley's Towne Center
6547 State Farm Dr., Rohnert Park
(707) 545–3844

It's new, and it's a cool, wonderful place to spend a summer day or escape a rainy, wintry one. Find dress bargains at Ross Dress for Less, or sink into a slice of pizza at Little Caesars. There is also a Radio Shack, Kragen Auto Parts, Beauty Store & More, and Precision Hairstyling in this center. Hours of individual stores will vary.

Coddingtown Mall
U.S. 101 and Steele Ln., Santa Rosa
(707) 527–5377

This is the old standby shopping mall for locals. Some Wine Country patrons come just to spend a few Sunday hours sitting on the comfy benches and sipping soda or a latte while people-watching. Anchor stores are Macy's Department Store, Gottschalks, and JCPenney, with lots of likely favorites filling the spaces between, such as Miller's Outpost, Cobbie Shoe Shop, and Clothes Time. One of the most charming shops here or anywhere is The Classic Duck,

crammed with exquisite gift and home accessories that will keep you spellbound while time passes and spouses wait.

Montgomery Village
Montgomery Dr. and Farmers Ln.,
Santa Rosa
(707) 545–3844

This is an architecturally appealing shopping center, dripping with ivy and landscaped with exotic shrubs and plants. Montgomery Village was built using the ranch-style Town and Country architecture so popular in the 1950s. The shops are tidy and specialized. You can find kid stuff at Gingerbread Storybooks and Whimsy, perk up your home decor with finds from Home Sweet Home, be dazzled by gorgeous tabletop settings at Company's Comin', pick up some stylish leisure clothes at Barbara Friday Weekend Wear, or indulge in awe-inspiring baked goods at Michelle Marie's Patisserie. In all, Montgomery Village includes 50 shops and a few restaurants. Shops are open seven days a week from 10:00 A.M. to 9:00 P.M.

Santa Rosa Plaza
Downtown exit off U.S. 101,
Santa Rosa
(707) 544–7467

This shopping mall is downtown, poised at the end of Fourth Street, which itself is a five-block shopping mall in its own right. The anchor stores of Santa Rosa Plaza are Macy's, Mervyn's, and Sears. More than 110 additional specialty shops, eateries, and special services are lined up on two levels, with lots of apparel shops (Eddie Bauer, Gap, Victoria's Secret) and places to buy cards, music, jewelry, sporting goods, and more. Shops are open seven days a week.

Mendocino County

Depot Marketplace & Museum
401 N. Main St., Fort Bragg
(707) 964–6261

For most of this century, the California Western "Skunk" train depot has been the busiest place in town (see our Attractions chapter for more on the train). Today, the depot at the end of Laurel Avenue attracts crowds for another reason. Several years ago an old Ford dealership was turned into a shopping mall and railroad museum. Some unusual little shops are clustered around immense hunks of equipment and a steam engine that occupies center stage as you enter.

Boutique Mystique displays gorgeous quilts. They're a little pricey (around $900), but they're real works of art.

Fuchsiarama also has gorgeous quilts glorifying its walls. (The name comes from a lovely spot 2 miles north of Fort Bragg that is smothered in fuchsia blossoms. It's a great place for a picnic.)

Tylart Shop is for you if you've got any Scandinavian blood. You'll recognize the trolls there when you see them—those ugly elves whose very name has terrified school children for centuries. This shop has them by the hundreds, and they're hardly scary at all. Depot Marketplace shops are open from 10:00 A.M. to 6:00 P.M. in summer, and until 5:00 P.M. in winter.

Unique Shops

Napa County

Shackford's
1350 Main St., Napa
(707) 226–2132

World-class restaurants necessitate a lot of chefs, and most Napa Valley kitchen whizzes do their shopping at Shackford's. So do the common cooks, and one step into the store will show you why. This is the nirvana of pots and pans. You'll find whole aisles of knives (Wusthof Trident, Sebatier, Forschner, and many more), pans (Calphalon, All-Clad, Look, etc., etc.) and cutting boards (wood, acrylic, poly, yada-yada-yada). The Kitchen Aid mixers are lined up like a Panzer division, and the pot racks hang like chandeliers. What else? Dozens of cookie cutters and candy forms, canning supplies, every possible component of cake decoration, and gadgets too numerous to look at, let alone mention. It's all priced competitively.

The Beaded Nomad
1238 First St., Napa
(707) 258–8004

There aren't many stores where prices start at three cents. The Nomad stocks more types of beads than you thought existed on the seven continents of this world—beads of metal, thread, plastic, glass, wood, fimo (a polymer clay), ceramic, and even hemp. The bins in which they nest become a three-dimensional quilt of colors, shapes, and designs. You can assemble your beads right there in the store (mixing is encouraged), and they'll provide design assistance and repair. The shop even offers classes in basic and advanced stringing. It also carries masks and jewelry from various exotic locales.

JHM Stamps & Collectibles
The Book Merchant and Sirius Bindery
1330 Second St., Napa
(707) 226–7511 (JHM),
(707) 259–1326 (Book Merchant)

Double your high-brow pleasure at one address housing two business. JHM, the only stamp shop within a 40-mile radius, has been on Second Street for more than 20 years. They have stamps from all over the world and a wide range of philatelic supplies—albums, refill pages, catalogs, and more. JHM also has boxes of blank postcards from every state in the union. The Book Merchant deals in antique and collectible books, especially those concerning local history. You might find a five-part library of Freemasonry, old pulp paperbacks, a 24-volume Dumas collection, signed first editions, or the complete work of Dickens in 20 volumes. The prices range from $5.00 to $1,000.00. The bindery is especially popular with people trying to preserve family relics.

Inti
1139 First St., Napa
(707) 258–8034

That this store was named for the Incan sun god tells you all you need to know about the business. It's a hodgepodge of imported multi-ethnic crafts popular with hippie kids—and anyone else looking for interesting decorations that won't devastate their checkbooks. Inti has jewelry, wood carvings, furniture, musical instruments, purses, candles, incense, batiks from Bali, and rugs from Peru. Oversized tapestries hang on the walls, and clothing from India and Indonesia hangs on racks. Look for the arpilleras—long Peruvian quilts that tell stories through applique.

Napa Valley Keyboards
1141 First St., Napa
(707) 224-5397

When a local winery or resort needs a grand piano for a one-night fête, it goes to Napa Valley Keyboards. That's partly because this is the only piano store in Napa County, but also because of the shop's sterling reputation. They have both new and old pianos of varying sizes and new electronic keyboards too. All pianos are tuned twice—once in the store and again after delivery. One drawback: Few of them fit in the trunk of a rental car.

Paint Your World
1349 Napa Town Center, Napa
(707) 226-7484

Looking for a completely original gift? Hire yourself as the artisan. At Paint Your World, you buy a plain ceramic piece (anything from a plate or cup and saucer to a serving bowl or switch plate) for the going rate and decorate it yourself. The materials charge is $6.00 for the first hour or $9.00 for the livelong day, and most customers finish in about an hour. The store provides a spectrum of paints, a work station, and an apron. They glaze and fire your pieces, and you return to pick up the finished product. All the materials are nontoxic and dishwasher-safe. Paint Your World also hosts kids' parties at $16 to $20 per child, and they toss in cake, juice, balloons, and the ceramic article of choice.

Overland Sheepskin Company
6505 Washington St., Yountville
(707) 944-0778
www.overland.com

If it once bleated, you'll find it here. Overland's Jim Leahy began making sheepskin coats by hand in Taos, New Mexico, in 1973. Now the family-owned company sells its woolly wear at 11 locations around the nation, including this locale in Yountville. Try on the sheepskin slippers, or sit on a stack of amazingly plush rugs. Almost everything is 100 percent sheepskin, from the car seat covers to the coats (even the lining). Overland sells leather goods made by other manufacturers, including Australian outback dusters, hats, footwear, and water buffalo bags from India.

Mosswood
6550 Washington St., Yountville
(707) 944-8151

When you have fully decorated your house and it's time to turn to the garden, Mosswood is here for you. This place has fountains, bird feeders, statuary, weather vanes, wind chimes, and more. The line of birdhouses is particularly impressive, with copper-domed, thatched-roof, and pebbled models. Mosswood also carries decorative interior accessories, including the Gracey Knight collection of bright, handpainted furniture, featuring dozens of different knobs and pulls.

Napa Valley Grapevine Wreath Company
8901 Conn Creek Rd. (Rutherford Cross Road), Rutherford
(707) 963-8893

While most grape-growers are pruning, stacking, and burning vines in the winter, this company is building its inventory. The Wood family (a partner in the original Freemark Abbey investment group) trims its 80 acres of Cabernet Sauvignon plants, strips the leaves, and fashions the vines into decorative wreaths—and a whole lot more. They make dozens of styles of baskets, plus cornucopias, hearts, crosses, stars, wine carriers, even reindeer and magic wands. All of it is handmade, distinct, and highly durable.

Dean & DeLuca
607 St. Helena Hwy. South, St. Helena
(707) 967-9980
www.deandeluca.com

Twenty years after the first Dean & DeLuca opened in SoHo in 1977, the ultrapremium food purveyors brought their act to Napa Valley. And while the massive wine section (see our Wineries chapter) is what sets this one apart from the other four branches, there is plenty more to woo your senses. Such as jam and marmalade jars by the dozen and an ocean of olive oil compartmentalized into 16-ounce bottles. You can find dried beans and rice, dried fruit, tins of dried herbs, teas and coffees, cigars, chocolates, and sweetly packaged edibles you never knew existed. And you can complete the experience with a high-quality cooking utensil, a cookbook, or a basket. Dean & DeLuca has a sandwich-and-salad bar called Market Cafe, an espresso bar and bakery, fresh produce, and a central deli with no end of meats, cheeses, and olives. But most of all it has its reputation for service, a commodity delivered by a squadron of friendly attendants in white chef's coats. This is a great place for assembling a delicious feast to enjoy at your favorite winery's picnic area.

St. Helena Olive Oil Co.
Hwys. 29 and 128, Rutherford
(707) 967–1003
www.sholiveoil.com

Olive oil is as ancient a pursuit as wine, and it gets the same reverent treatment at St. Helena Olive Oil Co. This is one place where you can sample some of the best. Most of the fruit comes from the Central Valley, but the company recently contracted with a Napa Valley olive grower to produce the high-end Cask 85 line. St. Helena Olive Oil also imports balsamic vinegar from Italy and makes a few types of its own, including five flavored balsamics (with fresh berries) and a Cabernet

vinegar. Everything is natural—no sugars or preservatives—and available in 60-ml., and 250-ml., or 375-ml. vessels.

Napa Valley Olive Oil Co.
835 Charter Oak Ave., St. Helena
(707) 963–4173

For more than 50 years, this white clapboard barn has been distributing premier olive oil to Napa Valley and the world. The old mill and hydraulic presses are still here, but the olives are pressed in the Sacramento Valley now. Still, the Particelli family bottles and packages all of its oils in St. Helena (except for the extra virgin). That's a lot of bottling—about 100,000 cases per year. The oil is available in sizes ranging from pints to gallons.

Napa Style
801 Main St., St. Helena
(707) 967–0405, (866) 776–6272
www.napastyle.com

Here are two words you'll be hearing a lot more of in the future: gray salt. It's the best type of salt for cooking, so says Michael Chiarello, and he should know. He founded Tra Vigne in St. Helena, among other achievements in the food world. Add this new business venture into the mix and he's a bit like the Martha Stewart of the West Coast (he has a TV show too). His retail store in St. Helena and mail order catalog are devoted to entertaining with style—*Napa style*—and both feature glassware, table linens, and small appliances, along with staples such as gray salt (harvested from France's Normandy coast), olive oils and vinegars, pasta, and preserves. The store is at the corner of Charter Oak Avenue and Main Street.

Flying Carpets
1152 Main St., St. Helena
(707) 967–9192

If you don't have the cash for a six-month trip to the Middle East and Asia, you might settle for a half-hour in this store. Flying Carpets has rugs from 14 countries. Some are old (more than a century in a few cases), some are new, all are handmade. There are about 1,000 in the store at any given time (give or take a couple hundred)—rugs on the floor, on the walls, and rolled up and posted like dandy soldiers. Ray Tokareff, who co-owns the business with his wife, Marsha, teaches "rug appreciation" at Napa Valley College. The shop also does washing, repair, and appraisals.

Holly Golightly Goes to Italy
1269 Main St., St. Helena
(707) 967–8881

When you enter this store, you're sure to utter "bellissimo!" It's the best word to describe the exquisite collection of Italian imports, from fabrics of all types, to bedspreads and lamp shades, to richly draped curtains and yards and yards of ribbon. Sprinkled throughout the store are delightful objects perfect for jazzing up your villa—chandeliers, ceramics, teapots, and old furniture. This is the type of boutique you might expect to see on *Lifestyles of the Rich and Famous,* though the prices and the proprietors are much friendlier. Named for owner Holly Wilkey (who runs the establishment with her partner Giondomenico Busato), it is one of only two Holly Golightly stores on the planet—the other is in Filasi del Lago, Italy.

Vanderbilt and Company
1429 Main St., St. Helena
(707) 963–1010

"Barn" would be too pedestrian a word for this up-market emporium of home furnishings. But the effect created by the room's high open beams and skylights is not far removed. Inside are semi-enclosed alcoves devoted to, say, boldly painted Vietri tableware or the ornately muraled Wright Collection of furniture. Vanderbilt has glassware from Salas and Schott, a brimming Crabtree & Evelyn cupboard, linens and tablecloths, pillows and pillowcases, candles, baskets, and woven or twisted wine racks.

Calla Lily Fine Linens
1222 Main St., St. Helena
(707) 963–8188

None of this "we sell a little bit of everything" here. Calla Lily inhabits a well-defined realm of linens, towels, rugs, and bathrobes, and only the best of each. The colors tend to be soft and muted, the prices steep, but the owners explain that some of the linens will last decades. Calla Lily also handles custom orders and offers select personal care products for the discriminating visitor.

R. S. Basso Home
1219 Main St., St. Helena
(707) 963-0391
186 N. Main St., Sebastopol
(707) 829–1426
115 Plaza St., Healdsburg
(707) 431–1925

Ron and Mary Basso began making custom sofas and chairs in the early 1980s in Sebastopol, and their presence has spread to two additional Wine Country locations, plus others in Palo Alto and Danville. They also operate a fabric store. The Bassos still manufacture the frames to specification in Sebastopol, and you can choose from thousands of fabrics to cover yours. They ship all over the nation, or farther—Ecuador on at least one occasion. The St. Helena store is packed with a lot more than couches. R.S. Basso has fine art, floor and table lamps, figurines, wrought-iron chandeliers, and framed sketches and photos from eras past. And check out the magnificent mirrors, framed by embossed tin, inlaid stone tiger stripes, or handpainted Devonshire roses.

Tantau
1220 Adams St., St. Helena
(707) 963–3115

Owner Sally Tantau has been an interior designer in Napa Valley for more than 25 years, which helps to explain the inviting layout of this store. Tantau features the functional artwork of many valley locals, including drapery rods shaped like olive branches, colorful tissue boxes, and handpainted tables. You'll also find jewelry, festive bowls, cups and plates, upholstered furniture by Lee and Shabby Chic, wall art and candles, plus enough picture frames to surround every head in Wine Country.

Tapioca Tiger
1234 Adams St., St. Helena
(707) 967–0608

Not all kid stores are alike, as this one adeptly proves. Tapioca Tiger finds some items made just down the road and others manufactured overseas. The shop specializes in clothing (boys and girls, newborn to size 7) and toys. The clothes are highly original designs, everything from sweetly sophisticated European items to funky domestic lines. Many of the toys are handmade by small producers—items like wooden dinosaurs and dressable plush cats. Tapioca Tiger also features children's bedding and furniture.

Fideaux
1312 Main St., St. Helena
(707) 967–9935

Greeting customers on a recent visit to this shop was a shirt that read, "I Kiss My Dog on the Lips." If that sentiment warms your heart rather than turns your stomach, this is the store for you. Dogs and cats are shaggy royalty here. Fideaux offers numerous squeeze-and-squeak toys, a wide selection of pet collars, collapsible dog dishes for hiking, pet futon beds (made for the Fideaux label), and even wine-barrel doghouses. They also stock the basics: shampoo, food, kitty litter, etc. Feel free to bring Ranger or Lucky with you, if he or she is on a leash.

WilkesSport
1219 Main St., St. Helena
(707) 963–4323
10466 Lansing St., Mendocino
(707) 937–1357

The well-heeled crowd that buys its tailored suits from the Wilkes Bashford Company of San Francisco probably looks here for its weekend activewear. The shop has a small but flawless selection of pants, sport coats, shirts, shoes, and accessories, featuring fine Italian fabrics. Examples of the manufacturers are Zegna for men and Piazza and Sempione for women.

Amelia Claire
1230 Main St., St. Helena
(707) 963–8502

Lady, if you really want to go local, drop into Amelia Claire and emerge with a new ensemble. Rene Sculatti's boutique specializes in sun hats, shoes, and accessories for those see-and-be-seen summer months. Name a color and a decorative twist for your head, and you'll probably find both here—and you may even find it at impulse-buying prices.

Bale Mill Classic Country Furniture
3431 St. Helena Hwy. North, St. Helena
(707) 963–4595

The old sign out front says "Pine Furniture," but Bale Mill has gone way beyond that. The company now stocks both the in-demand and the unexpected: huge iron canopy beds and pillars, wicker chairs, marble tables, stone fountains, copper lamps, and even a few antiques like typewriters and clocks. Some of the wood is painted or varnished, but some of it is left rough. It's all contained in an old white house perched on Highway 29 north of St. Helena. Don't forget to investigate the rooms upstairs.

Hurd Beeswax Candle Factory
3020 St. Helena Hwy. North, St. Helena
(707) 963–7211

Located in the Freemark Abbey Winery complex, this candle store goes above and beyond most. Wax workers produce the merchandise right in the shop, and the possibilities in designs and sizes are endless. There is also a display of bees busy at work, making some of the raw material from which the two-legged artisans create their masterpieces.

Calistoga Pottery
1001 Foothill Blvd., Calistoga
(707) 942–0216
www.calistogapottery.com

Sally and Jeff Manfredi run this pottery studio from the back of their home, and, while popularity has surged, in some ways it's all very similar to how it was in 1980. Everything is fired on-site. And they have remained loyal to a handful of rugged-looking glazes because their customers, in turn, have remained loyal to Calistoga Pottery. The company aims for utilitarian stoneware—platters, plates, pitchers, bowls, mugs, kettles, etc.—that complements food. (Sally used to be a painter,

Jeff a chef.) Much of the work is made to order, but you can always find some pots for sale on the shelves. The Manfredis will hand-letter messages at no charge.

Wexford & Woods
1347 Lincoln Ave., Calistoga
(707) 942–9729, (800) 919–9729

If your mud bath is over, but you just can't stand the thought of ending your spa experience, rinse off and stroll into Wexford & Woods. Close your eyes, breathe in the mingled scents of innumerable skin- and hair-care products, then start exploring. You'll find triple-milled soaps from France, organic cleansers from Australia, and Dead Sea bath salts from Israel, not to mention soap bars of every possible size, color, fragrance, and ingredient—but all of one lofty quality. Nearly every line can be sampled, and most of it is 100 percent natural. Wexford & Woods also has a wide selection of baskets they will custom pack and gift wrap for you.

The Artful Eye
1333-A Lincoln Ave., Calistoga
(707) 942–4743

Several media are represented at this shop—ceramics, oil painting, iron—but what stands out immediately is the collection of colored glass, most of it mouth-blown (often referred to as handblown). The vases, oversized wineglasses, and decorative flowers seem to writhe in the light as you look around the room. The Artful Eye also offers wearable art-like jewelry (from paper to gold) and clothing.

The Candy Cellar
1367 Lincoln Ave., Calistoga
(707) 942–6990

If you have not just one sweet tooth but a whole mouthful of them, abandon all hope when you enter this place. You'll see barrels filled with saltwater taffy, jawbreakers, swirls, crunches, bubble gum, lollipops, and all the Jelly Bellies of the rainbow. Most of it is sold by weight, so you can mix and match. Anyway, you'll probably head straight for the award-winning fudge—10 to 15 flavors mixed right on the spot, including the likes of chewy praline, maple nut, rocky road, and caffe latte. And remember: Pretend you're shopping for your nephew, and no one will shoot you any reprimanding glances. The Candy Cellar also sells stuffed animals and puzzles.

Sonoma County

Southern Sonoma

Along the dozens of buildings from yesteryear that rim the plaza in the town of Sonoma, visitors come to search out galleries, specialty shops, and fine boutiques to find the unusual, the elegant, the unexpected. Beyond the main streets are more shops tucked into El Paseo de Sonoma, a charming enclave behind the corner of East Spain and First Streets. The path down the Mercato leads to more wonderful shopping. The plaza is Sonoma's main shopping scene. Here are just some of the many retail establishments you can explore. Unless otherwise noted, they are all open seven days a week.

Spirits in Stone
452 First St. East, Sonoma
(707) 938–2200
www.spiritsinstone.com

Laura and Tony Ponter are on a mission: to import the best in elegant, simple sculpture from the Shona ("people of the

Small specialty stores and restaurants beckon visitors into El Paseo de Sonoma, a quiet courtyard off Sonoma's Plaza. PHOTO: JEAN SAYLOR DOPPENBERG

How about a nice courtyard where you can sit among fruit trees or admire garden art while your companion shops? Viva Sonoma has taken up residence in Sonoma's second-oldest wood house (built in 1865 and located just a block east of the Plaza) and beautifully filled it with imported folk art, ceramics, linens, and more. If you've wondered how the local women put together that "Sonoma look," this is a great place to shop for some of its essentials, including dresses and skirts of natural fibers.

Sign of the Bear
435 First St. West, Sonoma
(707) 996–3722

Here's a great place to pick up handmade kitchen utensils, paella pans, cookie molds, madeleine pans, wooden bowls, immense Italian platters, and spaghetti drainers—all those things you need to feel like a professional chef or to make a friend who actually is one very happy.

The Flag Store
20089 Broadway, Sonoma
(707) 996–8140

How often do you run into a store totally devoted to flags of the world? You'll find every flag here, including some in the category of "discontinued country." Owner Dallas Dutson is a leading authority on flags and serves as a consultant to the White House on the subject. The flags come in every size and every price. Maybe you'll find one for your alma mater or favorite historic event.

Bear Moon Clothing
117 E. Napa St., Sonoma
(707) 935–3392

This is the place to go to find products that keep the environment in mind. Brand names include S.F. City Lights, Royal Robbins, Mishi, and Woolrich Outdoor Wear. You'll find clothing and soft linens, cottons, tencel, and down-to-earth blends for life's simple pleasures. It's all natural. The store's motto, "quality clothing in natural fabrics with fashion and the environment in mind," pretty much sums up what Bear Moon is all about.

mist") tribe in Zimbabwe and to demonstrate that "the spirit in stone" has much to teach us all about dignity, compassion, and peace. There is something almost magnetic about these profound sculptures—a feeling that you must reach out and touch them, and you are encouraged to do so. Large pieces are pricey, but the smaller sculptures are affordable and tempting for any lover of fine things. (See the gallery listings in our Arts and Culture chapter for more information.)

Viva Sonoma
180 E. Napa St., Sonoma
(707) 939–1904

Sonoma Cheese Factory
2 W. Spain St., Sonoma
(707) 996-1931
www.sonomajack.com

This may be the most popular shop on the plaza. People see cheese makers produce this extraordinary local cheese and sample or buy one of the dozens of varieties of Jack or Cheddar cheese. There's an array of gourmet items to go with the cheese. You can take it all home or turn it into a picnic on the green plaza lawn. If you like, they'll make you a sandwich to eat at the sidewalk tables.

Vella Cheese Company
315 Second St. East, Sonoma
(707) 938-3232, (800) 848-0505
www.vellacheese.com

Some of the best cheese in the world is made on East Second Street, around the corner from the main drag, by Thomas Vella and his son, Ignazio. The family has operated out of the same 1905 rough-cut stone building since 1931; it's an architectural wonder in shaky, earthquakey California. The shop doesn't have the same exposure as the main street shops, but Vella Dry Jack has won international prizes, and the Cheddar is so sharp it makes your mouth pucker.

Milagros
414 First St. East, Sonoma
(707) 939-0834
www.milagrosgallery.com

Following the covered passageway called El Paseo, which winds between East Spain and East First Streets, you'll suddenly believe you've wandered into another country and another time. There before you is Milagros, a fabulous store of affordable fine Mexican folk art, featuring whimsical Oaxacan wood carvings, Spanish Colonial sconces, handcrafted jewelry from all over Latin America, Talavera bowls, and wonderful masks. This shop also displays a rare collection of religious Mexican folk art. Milagros, which means "miracles" in Spanish, is named after the figures sold in front of churches in Mexico.

Sonoma Rock & Mineral
414 First St. East, Sonoma
(707) 996-7200

El Paseo courtyard has another shop worthy of a visit, particularly if you're interested in things lapidary. It's hard to believe the earth holds such wondrous rocks and stones. The display is professionally arranged in a spacious setting, with beautiful polished stones to buy.

The Legacy Gift Shop
452 First St. East, Sonoma
(707) 935-9447

If you love decorating your home, you'll go crazy here. Tableware and vases, chairs and umbrella stands, and candle holders in 100 shapes—they're all exquisite additions to the stylish home. The Legacy is also a great spot to find a memorable gift for a new bride. The shop is along the Mercato, the shop-filled promenade off First Street East.

La Villeta de Sonoma
27 Fremont Dr., Sonoma
(707) 939-9392

The beautiful handcrafted terra-cotta designer accessories in this unusual shop were all created by some of Mexico's best creative sculptors and ceramic artists. But what you see here won't remind you of Mexico; it will remind you of Portugal or Italy, Greece or Spain, even North Africa. The shop opened in mid-1997, and is a branch of a larger store in Guadalajara, where artisans respected in their fields turn out urns and plates, paintings, and furniture that are styled from the beautiful museum pieces of the Mediterranean. There's always something new because the owner, Mardo, travels back to Guadalajara and other Mexican cities about every six weeks. Prices? Anywhere from $4.00 to about $10,000.00. The shop is at the junction of Highway 116 and Highway 121.

Other Southern Sonoma Shops
The Olive Press
14301 Arnold Dr., Glen Ellen
(707) 939-8900, (800) 965-4839
www.theolivepress.com

Wine Country's Fabulous Farm Trails

Wandering from one winery to another, Wine Country visitors are likely to come across green and white signs posted in some farmyards announcing "Farm Trails." Wine isn't the only thing this countryside turns out. Produce is our other forte.

Agriculture is as important to Wine Country as moviemaking is to Hollywood. And just leave it to California farmers to turn our agricultural Eden into an attraction for the family.

Farm Trails was organized in 1973 by a group of farmers dedicated to the promotion and preservation of the agricultural heritage of the region. During the ensuing 25 years it has guided consumers through the spectacular countryside to "experience a farm," sample local fresh foods and wines, or select a rare plant from a specialty nursery. Maps and a guide have been printed to lead you to 100 farms open to the public, all eager to sell their goods directly to drop-in consumers. You can pick one up at the California Welcome Center in Rohnert Park or at a number of Wine Country visitor bureaus, hotels, fruit stands, and grocery stores.

The maps outline in fine detail the tranquil backroads and old-time farms that lie slumbering off the main thoroughfares. You'll never forget your first tangy bite of a Gravenstein apple picked right off the tree or the juicy you-pick-it strawberry you pop in your mouth. This is where tomatoes come in multiple hues—yellow, orange, and red. Fresh salad greens are sprinkled with pansy, nasturtium, and rose petals. Take home jams, jellies, and chutneys made from local berries and apples, and don't forget to sample speckled butter lettuce, red orach spinach, dragon tongue beans, melons, raspberries, cherries, walnuts, and, for the home winemaker, grapes for crushing. The product index includes other intriguing headings—hayrides, goats (pygmy), llamas and emus and pigs (Vietnamese), quails (and quail eggs), bees, wax, and pollen.

Locals always stick their necks out for visitors along the Farm Trails. PHOTO: JOHN NAGIECKI

While Sonoma County may seem rural, Napa County produces specialty foods that have become world-famous—olive oils in various degrees of virginity, flavored vinegars, microbrewed beers, award-winning mustards, salsas, cider, candies, baked goods, and wines that have won awards but won't appear on your grocer's shelves. There's even a farm where weavers can buy angora wool and mohair for home spinning.

Does all this remind you of Provence in France or Tuscany in Italy? Perhaps we have grown so accustomed to this fresh food and produce we are only now discovering that such comparisons are valid on many levels. Like those cherished European regions, we have rural landscapes with flowing hillsides grazed by sheep and cows, vineyards thick with choice grapes, and a striking seashore where fishermen pull in catches of crab and harvest succulent oysters. The area offers a chance to find out what goes on behind the scenes beyond the level of supermarket shopping.

The produce of the Farm Trails group is as diverse as California's terrain and climate. From the fog-chilled valleys near the coast to the sunbaked fields inland, you'll find everything from smoked salmon to cacti and, best of all, have a chance to chat with the people who make their living from agriculture. Here you can learn the pleasures and pitfalls of an industry that's seldom showcased.

One of the first farms to join the Farm Trails organization was Kozlowski Farms, which also was one of the first Sonoma County farms to go organic. The farm started as a raspberry ranch in 1947 and turned into a roadside sales stand when Carmen Kozlowski decided to cook up some raspberry jam and sell it to passersby. Now that same kitchen is turning out 65 different products, all from the fields of organic fruits where it all started. Besides raspberry jam, you can buy fresh berries and organic apples in season, mustards, salad dressings, cider, fresh pies, tarts, and cookies. And Carmen, who has retired, no longer has to worry every time a big car drives up that it might be the county authorities asking for a kitchen permit.

There's really no limit to what you might run into as you toodle along the Farm Trails. In Napa County, along with the olive oils mentioned, pick up some dried fruit, lively vinegar, or, if you can manage it, some naturally raised lambs, goats, or suckling pigs. Wreaths made of grapevines might be easier to pack out—they are charming and lasting. You also might find yourself in a wooden drying shed where the walls, ceiling, and floor are dense, bright cushions of dried flowers—calendulas, Johnny jump-ups, bachelor buttons, and sunflowers—it's summer's bounty preserved for winter's enjoyment.

Admittedly, this is not supermarket shopping. Sometimes you'll be drawn down narrow farm roads and into rough-hewn barns to buy your goods. That's the adventure part of the journey. What makes it worthwhile is the intimacy of these visits to farmers' homesteads. Some trails meander through countryside so beautiful it's hard to leave it at day's end. That in itself is a reward! The trail guides and maps issued by each county are your passport.

You'll discover products you didn't know existed, and you'll find new ways to use the ones you're used to seeing. Lace a spinach salad with strips of smoked duck, sun-dried tomatoes, and goat cheese. Bake a persimmon pie. Liven up potato salad with some zippy new mustard. Use quail eggs next time you make deviled eggs and garnish them with fresh herbs. You also might want to plan your trip to coincide with a number of fairs, festivals, and other agricultural events taking place. Your Farm Trails map and guide will reveal what's happening and where.

Inspired by the cooperatives of northern Italy, the Olive Press was created by a group of olive aficionados. Its purpose? To press olives for commercial producers, small-harvest growers, and hobbyists eager to make oil from homegrown olives. Visitors can sample a premium selection of olive oils, and during harvest season (October through March) they can view the pressing process. A bounty of olive-related specialty foods and gifts is available for purchase.

Snoopy's Gallery and Gift Shop
1666 W. Steele Ln., Santa Rosa
(707) 546-3385
www.snoopygift.com

Snoopy's Gallery features a museum containing awards, drawings, and personal memorabilia from Peanuts creator Charles M. Schulz. The gift shop has the largest selection of Snoopy products in the world. The Redwood Empire Ice Arena is one block away on the right (see our Attractions chapter).

Sonoma Outfitters
145 Third St., Santa Rosa
(707) 528-1920, (800) 290-1920
www.sonomaoutfitters.com

For sports enthusiasts, this is the place to go. It's immense (more than 11,000 square feet), and the inventory is sure to cover everything you need for just about any sport. There's an enormous amount of boating and camping equipment—tents and sleeping bags, hiking boots and climbing shoes, canoes, rubber and plastic kayaks, ski clothing, in-line skates, you name it. It's sports equipment from wall to wall. The knowledgeable staff can help outfit you and your family for almost any outdoor recreation.

Northern Sonoma

The pretty plaza that makes Healdsburg so charming was built in 1852 by Harmon Heald, who sold lots for $15. Today, $15 will barely cover lunch, and the stores that sold harnesses and hardware in Heald's day are now occupied by charming shops

The Rodney Strong Winery tasting room, like many winery tasting rooms, offers shoppers a wide selection of gifts. PHOTO: M. J. WICKHAM

filled with jewelry, books, fine art, clothing, and home furnishings. These shops are open every day.

The Irish Cottage
112 Matheson St., Healdsburg
(707) 433–4850

If your passion is country decor, you'll want to dawdle here. The owner returns to her homeland in Ireland from time to time to find genteel Old Country pieces to add to her collection of distinctive pine tables, antique furniture, primitives, collectibles, and decorative accessories. But it's not all Irish, and it's not all antique. The cottage is cozy and cluttered, with plenty of linens, pillows, rugs, and textiles to warm up your home with country coziness.

Robinson & Co.
108 Matheson St., Healdsburg
(707) 433–7116

Billed as "purveyors of fine coffees and cookwares," the store lives up to the claim. You encounter the aroma of coffee beans when you walk in, and there is a varied inventory of kitchenware. The shop is contemporary and glossy, filled with all the accoutrements you need to become a world-class chef, including the cookbooks that tell you how to go about it. David Robinson, the store's personable and welcoming owner, will be happy to acquaint you with a wide range of other products, including Italian porcelain, European and Australian pottery, French hand soaps, spices, and Williamsburg candles.

Oakville Grocery Co.
124 Matheson St., Healdsburg
(707) 433–3200
7856 St. Helena Hwy., Oakville
(707) 944–8802, (800) 736–6602
www.oakvillegrocery.com

This is a branch of the same wonderful gourmet grocery store whose jam-packed shelves in the Napa Valley have attracted passersby for decades. At this location it has metamorphosed into a gentrified, glossy emporium of most everything gourmet and delicious. Here you can stock your kitchen pantry with exotic mustards, duck pâté, caviar, Greek olives,

On the outside, Oakville Grocery in Napa Valley's Oakville reminds you of grandmother's old general store. Inside, it's packed to the rafters with gourmet food and wine. PHOTO: JEAN SAYLOR DOPPENBERG

and more. The vegetable section has a display of onions, carrots, and other good things that are so fresh and perfectly formed you may think they're made of porcelain. You can eat lunch here too, selecting salads, sandwiches, and yummy desserts to be eaten under umbrellas on the sun-drenched patio. Be sure to pick up a copy of their latest catalog—your mouth will water—that features custom gift packages for ordering by mail for yourself and others.

Art and All That Jazz
119 Plaza St., Healdsburg
(707) 433–7900
www.artandjazz.aol.com

Jessica Felix, whose works have been shown at the Smithsonian Museum as well as prominent galleries across the country, has been designing spirited jewelry since 1970. Her shop serves as a gallery that includes the work of others in art glass, ceramics, photography, collage, and an eclectic selection of jazz and Brazilian music. But her works take center stage in this shop. Jessica demonstrates an uncanny ability to take simple ideas and transform them into powerful images that incorporate the spirit worlds of Alaska, the Canadian northwest, and Africa. She's also proud of the store's new wine design jewelry.

West County/Russian River

Incredible Records & CDs
112 N. Main St., Sebastopol
(707) 824-8099

Forget the Rock & Roll Hall of Fame in Cleveland. Sonoma County has its own "museum" masquerading as a record/CD store in Sebastopol. If not for the racks upon racks of new compact discs, you'd swear you'd entered a time warp back to those heady days of sex, drugs, and rock-and-roll. Owner Jonathon Lipsin had a similar store in Toronto for many years, with much of the same priceless rock memorabilia on display. It's not exhibited in fancy museum-style; it's mostly a jumble of taped and push-pinned treasures, creating a mosaic of the weird and the wonderful, with no wall space left unused. There are vintage rock posters aplenty; a rare collection of early Beatles photos (including the proof sheets) taken by photographer Dezo Hoffmann, who accompanied the moptops around the world; The Who's contract to perform at Woodstock in 1969 (they earned $12,500, by the way); a fringed vest worn by Steve Miller in the '60s; a guitar used by Randy Bachman in the '70s; and an assortment of odd pencil drawings made by Jim Morrison at the tender age of 14, which foretold his future legacy as the Lizard King. And that's just for starters.

Lipsin also stages live performances in the store of many types of music (Ramblin' Jack Elliot, for instance). Oh, and he sells vinyl too—about 10,000 popular and obscure titles in all categories of music. Don't be surprised to find Carlos Santana or Tom Waits standing next to you at the racks—they pop in from time to time to do their record shopping.

California Carnivores
7020 Trenton-Healdsburg Rd., Forestville
(707) 838-1630
www.californiacarnivores.com

It's been called "Little Shop of Horrors," but it's one of the most fascinating spots you'll see in a month of Sundays. About 550 carnivorous plants grow here, with about 120 varieties for sale. These are the meat-eaters of the plant world and are endless fun to watch. An unsuspecting fly circles above the Venus's flytrap and makes what will be its final landing. In two seconds it triggers a hairlike finger, the plant snaps tight with a crushing device more terrifying than anything in a James Bond movie, and it sucks the life out of the fly. Other plants, like the pitcher plant or the bladderwort, are even more unkind to insects. The plants are easy to care for and inexpensive—you could get a dandy one for between $4.00 and $10.00 and perhaps be fly-free forever. If you'd like to send one to a friend, a mail-order service is provided.

Hand Goods
3627 Main Street, Occidental
(707) 874-2161
www.handgoods.com

Proclaiming a "distinctive mall-free experience," Hand Goods is located in the tiny hillside hamlet of Occidental. Since 1971, the shop has offered a wide variety of fine, locally made handcrafts, featuring the work of over 100 artists. The ceramics encompass everything from functional tableware to ornamental sculpture, from painted oil lamps to Ikebana vases. You'll also find Shaker boxes and fine furniture, embroidered Thai jackets, and batik baby clothing. If it's jewelry you're looking for, Hand Goods offers a wide selection of local and imported earrings, necklaces, pins, and bracelets in every price range. Hand-woven Zapotec rugs from Oaxaca are a perennial favorite and come in all sizes and colors. The store also has a small but eclectic book selection, encompassing everything from current paperbacks to a variety of metaphysical titles. To get there, take Highway 12 from Santa Rosa to Sebastopol and continue to Freestone. Turn right onto the Bohemian Highway and follow it to Occidental.

Mendocino County

U.S. 101

Real Goods Store
13771 S. U.S. 101, Hopland
(707) 744-2100, (800) 994-4243
www.realgoods.com

Built as part of the Solar Living Center (see our Attractions chapter), Real Goods is both a retail store and educational center. A thousand items are available including a vast number of high-tech devices—from a laptop briefcase that doubles as a solar collector (yes, it will power your PC wherever you go) to a better mouse trap (it does not crush or kill its victims). Stop in (or order a catalog), buy some hemp socks or a solar-powered fountain, and learn to spurn bugs without noxious repellents. The array of innovative products they offer is mind-boggling, and makes you wonder why we keep burning fossil fuels. They also offer courses and private consulting about alternative energy strategies and products.

Hoyman-Browe Studio
323 N. Main St., Ukiah
(707) 468-8835
www.earthenware.com

Trained in the European school of pottery making, Douglas Browe and his wife, Jan Hoyman, have established a studio in the traditional, old-time format—training apprentices and displaying their work. Much of the output from the studio is sold to restaurants across the country, but the showroom at the studio doesn't just have pots. There are tea sets, huge presentation platters, jardinieres, and 10-gallon flower pots, as well as tableware with bright designs of fruits, flowers, and vegetables. More good news: These pieces are available as seconds with tiny, imperceptible flaws.

Mendocino Bounty
200 S. School St., Ukiah
(707) 463-6711

This small shop is filled with food and wine made in Mendocino County and stuff for the kitchen. You'll find colorful bowls, linens, and gift baskets filled with products. If you wish, the basket can be custom-designed—let's say a pasta basket filled with grapeseed oil, organic herbs, and unusual pastas that are hard to find anywhere else. There's a breakfast basket with honey, local syrup, breakfast cakes, and a special waffle mix prepared by Mendocino's famous Cafe Beaujolais (see our Restaurants chapter). If you'd like a snack while you shop, there's a small copper bar with stools where you can sample lasagna made at Boonville Farms and various other treats. Closed Sundays.

Grace Hudson Museum
431 S. Main St., Ukiah
(707) 467-2836
www.gracehudsonmuseum.org

Grace Hudson's portraiture of Native Americans—particularly the Pomo tribe—brought her national recognition. The museum's gift shop collection of Native American crafts, books, and jewelry reflects that same fascination. A fine sampling of books explores all facets of Native American culture, and there's a nice selection of items for children. The gift shop is open Wednesday through Sunday. A jaunt through the museum is free, but donations are appreciated (see our Attractions chapter).

Mendocino Coast

Velvet Rabbit
38140 Hwy. 1, Gualala
(707) 884-1501

Shop to operatic music while you browse through the works of selected artisans in a variety of fields, from stained glass, bronze sculptures, carved stone, and wooden boxes from England, to china, crystal, hand-blown glass, and shells from all over the world.

The Courtyard
Kasten and Main Sts., Mendocino
(707) 937-0917

Here you'll discover all those kitchen gadgets that will make you wonder how you ever got along without them. How about a new garlic press? Or a potato peeler made in Switzerland? The display of imported English teapots is large instruments you've probably never seen before. You can spend from $1.00 to $4,000.00. If you want something small for the kids, you'll find that there too—bongo drums, harmonicas, or Irish tin whistles. Ask to get on the catalog list.

The Golden Goose
45094 Main St., Mendocino
(707) 937-4655

Don't even think of saving this shop for the end of your shopping tour. They've got beds covered with down quilts and down pillows so fluffy you'll be overcome by the need to plop into bed and forget the rest of your stops. If you'd like to take home a bed full of luxurious sheets and down, it will probably run up a bill of about $1,500. To go with it, you can pick up a flannel nightshirt made in England that looks like sheep's wool. This is sheer luxury.

Panache
Kasten and Albion Sts., Mendocino
(707) 937-1234
www.panachegallery.com

You'll find art galleries all over town because Mendocino is artists' heaven. But it's worth stopping in here to see the metal sculpture of Don Quixote that's on exhibit front and center. It's like none other. Panache is also the place to buy the fruit and vegetable paintings of Gerald Stinski, who moved to Mendocino in 1991 to pursue his art dreams. Now his paintings sell as fast as he turns them out, all with four-figure price tags.

The Irish Shop
45050 Main St., Mendocino
(707) 937-3133

Did you forget to pick up that fisherman's sweater last time you were in Killarney? You'll find it here, along with anything you might need from Scotland or Wales. The shop also carries high-quality food products such as the award-winning Christine and Rob's Old Fashioned Oatmeal, as well as Norwegian sweaters, Geiger jackets from Austria, men's caps, dolls, mohair afghans, and handmade Teddy bears.

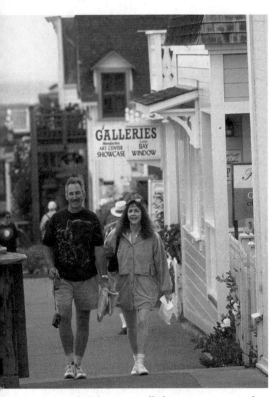

Satisfied shoppers stroll along Main Street in the historic oceanside village of Mendocino. PHOTO: BILL HOBAN

enough to convince you you're back in Sussex. Maybe you'll go home with a matching set of table linens and crockery. If you don't know how to cook, the shop will take care of that too—there is a large library of cookbooks.

Lark in the Morning Musique
10460 Kasten St., Mendocino
(707) 937-5275
www.larkinam.com

If you have a passion for musical instruments, you shouldn't pass this one up. From alpenhorns to zithers, they fill every corner and hang from the ceiling—dulcimers, mandolins, banjos (with four or five strings), hurdy-gurdies, ukuleles, concertinas and accordions, harps, bagpipes, and drums of every size. There's barely enough room to turn around inside, but it's chockfull of fascinating

Deja-Vu Hat Co.
10470 Lansing St., Mendocino
(707) 937–4120, (800) 489–8125
www.dejavuhats.com

Who wouldn't want to see the largest selection of hats in Northern California? There's something for everyone who owns a head—felts, fine fur, straws, Stetsons, Akubras, Borsalinos, Panamas, and Deja-Vu's own dress hats.

Mendocino Coast Botanical Gardens
18220 N. Hwy. 1, Fort Bragg
(707) 964–4352
www.gardenbythesea.org

This 47-acre showcase garden displays wondrous collections of rhododendrons, azaleas, heathers, and succulents. Some of these species can be purchased in the retail nursery that helps support the non-profit effort. Travelers might consider one of the sempervivum ("live forever") succulents, as a memento Northern California. They're inexpensive (about $4.00), and they travel well. There's also a gift shop with cards, vases, and so forth, as well as a shop for outdoor garden supplies (including some irresistible ceramic frogs). Admission prices are $6.00 general, $5.00 for seniors, $3.00 for juniors 13 to 17 and $1.00 for kids 6 to 12. (For more on the Mendocino Coast Botanical Gardens, see our Attractions chapter.)

Harvest Market
171 Boatyard Dr., Fort Bragg
(707) 964–7000

Well, yes, it's a grocery store. But this is the one you wish was just around the corner from your kitchen. Homegrown produce, fresh local seafood, and fresh-baked bread are imaginatively displayed. The folks at Harvest Market will make you a picnic basket to go or fill your ice chest with the best foods in town.

Hot Pepper Jelly Company
330 N. Main St., Fort Bragg
(707) 961–1422, (800) 892–4823
www.hotpepperjelly.com

With 30 varieties of jelly to sample, you'll be licking your lips and fingers for hours. Don't neglect the old-time favorites, ginger pepper, Chardonnay conserve, or very cherry marmalade. For kicks, try the jalapeno pepper jam. All of Carol Hall jellies are handmade in small batches. They're sold nationwide, and the lineup also includes chutneys, dessert toppings, fruit syrups, mustards, vinegars, and salsa. The peach cobbler jam won an Oscar at the New York Fancy Foods Show. Ask for a free catalog.

For the Shell of It
344 N. Main St., Fort Bragg
(707) 961–0461

Here you'll find pieces of the ocean, without the water. Long aisles hold everything from scallop shells for serving seafood to tiny shells made into earrings. But these are not local shells—remember that the state parks system discourages you from carrying any part of the beach away.

Fiddles & Cameras
400 N. Main St., Fort Bragg
(707) 964–7370

As befits a small community, sometimes retailers double up on their specialties. Fiddles and cameras are precisely what you can buy at this store. The stock runs to mostly stringed instruments of all types, instructional tapes, and sheet music and music books. But there's also a huge selection of cameras, and you can pick up binoculars for spotting whales, too.

> ## Insiders' Tip
> If your timing is on, you can let the Farm Trails come to you. Wine Country features some two dozen farmers' markets, with growers setting up stalls to offer fresh produce. The markets are usually held once a week during summer and fall, but the day varies, so inquire locally.

Lake County

Bright Lights Candle Company
16275-A Main St., Lower Lake
(707) 994–0333

When this company was launched in 1993, it was a small operation that exclusively made candles designed by German maker Volker Wagner. Since then it has grown into a business that supplies about 3,000 gift shops in the United States, plus a few hundred more in Canada. The designs now include tapers, pyramids, balls, pillars, teardrops, flames, and persimmons, plus a small number of wax statuettes created by local artists, all available in a variety of color combinations. Peek through the glass of the retail room, and you'll see hot candles being hung on the taper rack.

Antiques

Napa County

Irish Pedlar Antiques
1988 Wise Dr., Napa
(707) 253–9091

In the 1800s the Irish used pine exclusively in their furniture construction. Much of it was done in the home, in a primitive style. (No two pieces seem to be exactly the same dimension.) The Irish Pedlar specializes in the sale of such items, the bulk of it made between 1880 and 1890. They do sell some American pine, as well as ceramics and old American linens. All of it is authentically old, and nothing is broken or ripped. The shop is on the north side of the John Muir Inn.

The Neighborhood
1400 First St., Napa
(707) 259–1900

Yes, it is almost big enough to be its own neighborhood. This showroom takes up half a block in downtown Napa, and inside it displays on two levels. Poke around and find everything from mission benches to barber chairs, framed photos of American Indians to ice sleds, and rough willow chairs to green bottles from the old Vichy Hot Springs in Sonoma.

Red Hen Antiques
5091 St. Helena Hwy., Napa
(707) 257–0822

This is something of a local landmark about halfway between Napa and Yountville. It has been Red Hen since 1983, and it was the Napa Valley Garden Shop for many years before that. Look for the big chicken facing the highway. Inside you'll find a collective of 80 dealers peddling a wide range of goods.

Antique Fair
6512 Washington St., Yountville
(707) 944–8440
www.antiquefair.com

This shop has been around for a long time (since 1971), but not as long as its merchandise. Antique Fair specializes in high-quality French antiquities from about 1890, la crème of Lyon and Paris estates. They have jewelry, statuettes, silverware, armoires, and bookcases. And if they're known for one thing, it's probably old beds they have converted to queen size.

Erika Hills Antiques
115 Main St., St. Helena
(707) 963–0919

Just south of St. Helena you will spy a line of statuary along Highway 29, and behind it, a former church that has been painted ocher and converted into an antiques store. This is Erika Hills, the namesake house of ancient delights. Inside you will find Limoges plates, Venetian glass, brightly accented Mexican chairs, baroque angels from Austria, and sturdy oak chairs salvaged right off the farm. Most, but not all, of the furniture is painted, and everything leans toward the high end.

St. Helena St. Helena Antiques
1231 Main St., St. Helena
(707) 963–5878

This ultrahigh-end locale feels like a turn-of-the-century shop in London or New England. Customers are met at the door by two life-size, cartoonish "greeters"—a chef and a winemaker—carved from single trunks. (They're menu boards from the 1860s.) Inside is everything from

Provençal ceramics to 19th-century baskets to vintage pond boats.

If there is a specialty, it's wine-related items: corkscrews, bottles, racks, and practically anything that might have been salvaged from an old winery.

Lone Dog Fine Art & Antiques
1345 Lincoln Ave., Ste. A, Calistoga
(707) 942–1115

The shop is a relative newcomer, but proprietor Frederick Schrader has a wealth of experience in gathering artifacts. Lone Dog shares space with Enoteca Wine Shop (see our Wineries chapter) in the wonderfully restored I.O.O.F. building (also known as the Oddfellows building). It's the perfect setting for Schrader's collection, which includes framed lithographs of 19th-century local scenes, and wine-related tools and paraphernalia.

Sonoma County

Southern Sonoma
Country Pine Antiques
23999 Arnold Dr., Sonoma
(707) 938–8315
www.countrypineantiques.com

Looking for English and Victorian or Georgian pine designs and furnishings from the period 1820 to 1900? Country Pine Sonoma either has it or can obtain it for you. This is a one-of-a-kind showplace of unique pine antiques that would fit perfectly in the modern home.

Margaret's Antiques of Sonoma
472 W. Second St., Sonoma
(707) 938–8036

Tucked away in a cozy white cottage that dates to the 1870s and is now an historic landmark, Margaret's Antiques replaced the family that lived in the house for 100 years. The shop's specialties are art glass, china, furniture, dolls, pottery, and linens from the 1800s, although they do have a few collectibles that are more recent.

Cat & The Fiddle
153 W. Napa St., Sonoma
(707) 996–5651

Insiders' Tip

If you're really on the hunt for bargains, you can bypass the up-market antiques stores and head to the Salvation Army's distribution center for North Bay counties. It's at 200 Lytton Springs Road, just north of Healdsburg. The bargains galore are housed in a big complex of 1870s Mission-style buildings. Originally built as a plush resort hotel, the property became a military academy for boys before the Salvation Army bought it in 1905.

With a storefront shop in the main plaza shopping area, this place gets a lot of exposure. The specialty here is French tables, armoires, and buffets, with some English and American antique pieces and gifts. New things that complement antique furnishings are also sold here.

Chelsea Antiques
148 Petaluma Blvd. North, Petaluma
(707) 763–7686

This is a collective that features a wonderful selection of decorative antiques, collectibles, and architectural and garden items in three buildings. Chelsea represents just about every field of antiques collecting.

Vintage Bank Antiques
101 Petaluma Blvd. North, Petaluma
(707) 769–3097

It's one of those wonderful old banks that has ceilings two stories high and a small window on the second level overlooking

Our Other Nectar

Color, bouquet, and taste—the words traditionally associated with wine tasting. But there's another nectar grown and bottled in Wine Country that is judged by foodies in much the same way: olive oil.

Color refers to the tinged green from the chlorophyll found in green olives or the yellow of mature olives. As the oil becomes oxidized, a red tint may appear.

Bouquet is determined by the volatile compounds in the oil, such as alcohols, ketones, and esters.

Taste involves the bouquet in combination with the four gustatory senses: salty, acid, bitter, and sweet.

Today's emphasis on improved health and better eating has brought a new appreciation for olive oil—not only the one- and three-liter bulk offerings found in most supermarkets but the hand-harvested, finely milled, flavorful, creatively bottled, and limited-availability artisan varieties found in places such as Wine Country.

As new labels come on the market, Wine Country–grown olive oil is increasingly competing for space alongside wine on the shelves of the area's chic groceries and shops—and in the pantries of gourmets everywhere.

Indeed, countless wineries now bottle their own brands and feature them prominently in their gift shops. The oils may be infused with many flavors, ranging from lemon to hot chili. Other creative combinations may blend orange and thyme, basil and chili, and mixed herbs and sun-dried tomato. And a meaty porcini mushroom-flavored oil is reputedly an aphrodisiac.

Olive oil production is not new to California. In fact, we've been at it since the late 1800s. But when lower-cost imports from Italy and Spain began eroding the market in the mid-1900s, olive orchards were abandoned for more profitable crops. Today, however, California accounts for approximately 99 percent of all the olive oil produced in the United States, amounting to about 325,000 gallons in 1998. Only a fraction of this output is gourmet-class extra-virgin, which sells for $10 to $40 per liter.

The olive varieties that produce the finest oils in the world, mostly from Tuscany, are Frantoio, Leccino, Pendolio, Maurino, Moraiolo, and Taggiasca. While some of these varieties are grown in California, the most common trees in Wine Country bear the Mission, Marzanillo, and Sevillano fruits. The latter two are large-fruited table olives that may yield only 12 to 15 gallons of oil per ton of fruit, while the Mission and Italian varieties may produce 40 to 50 gallons per ton. To meet production demands, many Wine Country labels are augmented with oils from olives grown in California's Central Valley, creating a sort of "meritage" of oil.

Olive trees are grown for oil production in all four Wine Country counties, and the olives are generally harvested concurrently with the autumn grape crush.

Harvesting is one of the most expensive operations in an olive orchard—accounting for about 45 percent to 65 percent of total production costs—because the best quality oils come from hand-harvested fruit.

Transforming olives into oil is not complicated. High-quality fruit is crushed in either stone grinders or metal hammer mills. The paste is then mixed until oil droplets begin to form, and then pressed in either single batch hydraulic presses or continuous flow spinning presses. The olive juice—containing both water and oil—is then separated in centrifuge separators similar to those used to separate cream from milk. From that, the "liquid gold" is revealed.

Newly pressed olive oils, which have the strongest flavors, are sometimes known as one- or two-cough oils. When the oil hits the back of your throat, the bitterness may produce an involuntary cough . . . or two—much like gulping down a shot of whiskey. But with olive oil, bitter is often considered a desirable trait.

Several Wine Country companies offer a peek into the production of their olive oil. In Sonoma County, the

There is no shortage of oil in Wine Country—distinctive home-grown olive oils dominate the shelves in most upscale groceries. PHOTO: LOREN DOPPENBERG

Olive Press in Glen Ellen (707–939–8900; www.theolivepress.com) operates as a co-op for a handful of small-harvest producers to press at a common facility. Learn about the hammermill pressing technique and purchase an olive cutting to take home. The store is located at 14301 Arnold Drive. McEvoy Ranch near Petaluma (707–778–2307; www.mcevoyranch.com) runs a picturesque 70-acre orchard with approximately 11,000 organically-grown olive trees of the Tuscan varieties, and does custom crushing for other olive growers. It also propagates olive trees for sale to the public. Visits are by appointment only.

In Napa Valley, St. Helena Olive Oil Company (800–939–9880; www.sholiveoil. com), located at the Rutherford Crossroads (the corner of Hwys. 29 and 128) has a retail showroom selling oodles of olive oil labels, wine vinegars, and other goodies. The store also features a demonstration press. Napa Valley Olive Oil Company (707–963–4173) now bottles its oils elsewhere but keeps the original press on display for visitors. The store is located at 835 Charter Oak Avenue, east of Tra Vigne restaurant, in St. Helena—look for the big white barn. For tastings only, try Tra Vigne's Cantinetta, where you can sample oils without an appointment. It's at Tra Vigne, on the corner of Highway 29 and Charter Oak Avenue in St. Helena.

Trade shows and other events focused on olive oil proliferate around California, but one of the newest is the annual Festival of Olives. Until now held at various sites around Napa and Sonoma counties, the most recent Festival took place at Copia, the American Center for Wine, Food and the Arts in Napa (see our Attractions chapter). Sonoma Valley also hosts an annual festival dedicated to the appreciation of the little orb (see our Festivals and Annual Events chapter).

With the olive oil market firmly established in California, an upstart industry will soon make its presence known in a big way on a gourmet grocer's shelf near you: grapeseed oil. Though not a new phenomenon, grapeseed oil is quickly building a reputation as a superior cooking oil—and a terrific moisturizer oozing with Vitamin E. A handful of Wine Country entrepreneurs is already hard at work marketing the benefits of grapeseed oil for better health inside the body and out. And it just so happens we are flush with grapeseeds 'round here.

the bank floor—so the manager could monitor his tellers and cashiers. Today it's a collective for 48 dealers, giving you three floors to explore. Even the bank vault is within the dealers' domain. What you'll find here is lots of jewelry, furniture, vintage clothing, porcelain, gentlemen's collectibles, dinnerware, and lots more.

Antique Marketplace & Annex
248 Petaluma Blvd. North, Petaluma
(707) 765-1155

It claims to have the finest and largest selection of antique furniture in Petaluma. Included is a large selection of pine and country furniture.

Kentucky Street Antiques
127 Kentucky St., Petaluma
(707) 765-1698

Nine dealers display their collections here, showing everything from country to classic—furniture, china, glassware, toys, tools, old advertising, paper, and jewelry.

Whistle Stop Antiques
130 Fourth St., Santa Rosa
(707) 542-9474

This is where it all began—Sonoma County's original collective, now 25 years old. With 10,000 square feet of space and more than 35 dealers, it's a collector's paradise with thousands of items from dishes to doorknobs. You'll also find clock repair, refinishing supplies, antique books, and a wonderful assortment of glassware, jewelry, furniture, and collectibles.

Railroad Square Basement Antiques
100 Fourth St., Santa Rosa
(707) 569-9646

You enter this shop on Wilson Street. It features a fine collection of vintage furniture, glassware, pottery, kitchenware, china, and cookbooks. Closed Tuesdays.

Northern Sonoma

Mill Street Antiques
44 Mill St., Healdsburg
(707) 433-8409

Look for the Big Blue Building, where more than 40 dealers showcase their wares

in 20,000 square feet of space. You'll find furniture—classic to country-glass, china, silver, fine oil paintings by listed artists, plus some eccentric goodies that need a home—gas station collectibles, metal signs, and 1950s memorabilia.

Healdsburg Classics
226 Healdsburg Ave., Healdsburg
(707) 433-4315

This is an enormous warehouse with a roster of some 20 dealers. It would be difficult to name something that isn't here, rather than what is. However, anyone looking for indoor-outdoor furniture or yard pieces will certainly not be disappointed.

Antique Harvest
225 Healdsburg Ave., Healdsburg
(707) 433-0223

Items range from country pine to Victorian, with lamps, brass, Art Deco furnishings, and Maxfield Parrish prints to boot. Meander through and check out the wares of more than 12 dealers.

Jimtown Store
6706 Hwy. 128, Healdsburg
(707) 433-1212
www.jimtown.com

Not only can you find American antiques, folk art, and primitives here, you can also have some "real food" (as they advertise) and a truly good cup of coffee.

Sonoma Coast

Wooden Duck Antique Shop
132 Bodega Ln., Bodega
(707) 876-3176

You'll spot the big yellow house (once a Druids hall) from the highway as you head toward the ocean. The store is open only Saturday and Sunday, but you'll find some fine 18th- and 19th-century furniture, plus a lot of Americana—pewter, glass, silver, whale oil lamps, plus some English Staffordshire china. There's also a fine collection of antique guns.

West County/Russian River

Llano House Antiques
4353 Gravenstein Hwy. South, Sebastopol
(707) 829-9322

Housed in the oldest wooden building in Sonoma County, Llano House Antiques deals mainly in American oak furniture, Depression glass, and kitchen collectibles.

Antique Society
2661 Gravenstein Hwy. South, Sebastopol
(707) 829–1733
www.antiquesociety.com

Antique Society is right when they claim "there's no place quite like" their collective. With more than 100 dealers, it is simply immense. You'll find just about anything you're looking for here, and they claim to have "country prices."

School Bell Antiques
3555 Gravenstein Hwy. South, Sebastopol
(707) 823–2878

Housed in a charming old schoolhouse is a 24-dealer collective. The schoolhouse alone is worth the visit.

Sebastopol Antique Mall
755 Petaluma Ave., Sebastopol
(707) 823–1936
www.sebastopolantiquemall.com

Want to take home a star? You'll find fabulous studio portraits and scene stills of yesterday's film stars—say, John Wayne, or Elvis—with autographs guaranteed authentic, all from the private collection of Laurel Proeme. A signed photo might be had for $75, with Elvis going for a little more. If you'd like to take Marilyn Monroe home with you, dig deep—you'll need at least $1,000. You'll find a lot more, and since this is a mall you can also stop for coffee, wine, or lunch at a gourmet cafe.

Mendocino County

Hopland Antiques
13456 U.S. 101, Hopland
(707) 744–1023

Lots of the merchandise in this large building came from buying complete estates, so you'll find a lot of furniture, home accessories, and some excellent estate jewelry.

Li'l Stinker Antiques
20029 N. U.S. 101, Willits
(707) 459–2486

It's all furniture here—no small stuff. Some of it dates back to the 1830s. The store has been in business under the same owner since 1967.

Whistlestop Antiques
350 N. Franklin St., Fort Bragg
(707) 961–0902

Here they call about half the stock "temporary collectibles" and the other half antiques, on the assumption half the collecting community are "only temporary custodians." The extensive selection of elegant glassware includes Fostoria, Heisey, Cambridge, and many others, as well as Depression glass and Carnival glass. They also carry a fine line of American furniture. To give a nice touch of nostalgia, a model train runs through the store from time to time.

Lake County

Decker's
14915 Olympic Dr., Bldg. G & H, Clearlake
(707) 994–0952

Joyce Decker invites you to "come dicker with Decker." She buys 90 percent of her wares locally, so the shop will give you a glimpse into the Lake County of the past.

Expect a big assortment of toys, art, primitives, pottery, rugs, furniture, cast-iron and kitchen gadgets, jewelry, and much more.

Ussery's Antiques
14913 Lakeshore Dr., Ste. C, Clearlake
(707) 995–2733

The emphasis is on glassware and crystal, as this store is an authorized Fenton Art Glass dealer. There's also a good selection of furniture, dolls, jewelry, and crafts. Closed Sundays and Mondays.

One Man's Junk, Another Man's Gold
3780-B Main St., Kelseyville
(707) 279–9744
www.kelseyvilleantiques.com

At First and Main Streets, One Man's Junk is truly in the heart of old Kelseyville. The shop offers neon signs, glassware, and lots of kitchenware, plus an interesting concentration of petroleum memorabilia—restored gas pumps, oil cans, road maps, and the like. If nothing else, you'll hear some good, lowdown blues on the speakers.

Bookstores

Napa County

Bookends Book Store
1014 Coombs St., Napa
(707) 254–7323

Bookends counts a couple of big-chain book stores as neighbors in downtown Napa but manages to hold its own. How? With substantial sections on subjects such as computers, business, biography, self-help, crafts, children's books, and family (things like birth, child rearing, and weddings).

Bookends has plenty of magazines and fiction and a large collection of travel guides and maps, including a comprehensive set of Wine Country maps.

Copperfield's Books
1303 First St., Napa
(707) 252–8002
www.copperfld.com

Wine Country literati have been relying on Copperfield's for years. The Napa edition, like its brethren in Sonoma County, is both well stocked and well staffed. This one sells new, used, and rare books.

Open Door Book Store
1030 Clinton St., Napa
(707) 252–4848

Has your third eye been a little bloodshot lately? The Open Door specializes in that arching umbrella known as the metaphysical: spiritual quests, Zen meditation, Buddhism, plus more down-to-earth fare such as *The Arthritis Cure Book*. They stock no fiction and no occult. They do have lots of cards and jewelry.

The bookstore is affiliated with the Napa Valley Center for Spiritual Living, a religious science community. The Center organizes ongoing classes, poetry readings, and book review groups.

Waldenbooks
1370 Napa Town Center, Napa
(707) 252–7326

If you are familiar with the printed word, you know about Waldenbooks. It's a national chain renowned for its hard-to-beat prices, whether you're hunting for fiction, coffee-table art books, or travel guides like this one. The store has a brimming periodicals rack, too.

Main Street Books
1315 Main St., St. Helena
(707) 963–1338

This business has been around since 1983, but recently reinvented itself. Main Street Books is now an extremely small shop that emphasizes used items. (It's the only upvalley used-book store.) The cramped quarters and carefully selected titles are bound to remind you of a classic London book stall.

The Calistoga Bookstore
1343 Lincoln Ave., Calistoga
(707) 942–4123

This bookstore, nicely set in the 19th-century Oddfellows Building, knows its audience. Catering largely to tourists, it has a large collection of oversized coffee-table books and Northern California travel guides. And because this is a spa town, Calistoga Bookstore gets into the act with material on massage, Reiki, reflexology, nutrition, yoga, and other healthful pursuits. It even goes one step further—into Celtic and Arthurian, New Age and Eastern religion, feng shui, and sexuality.

Sonoma County

Southern Sonoma

Sonoma Bookends Bookstore
201 W. Napa St., No. 15, Sonoma
(707) 938-5926
www.sonomabookends.com

It's a general interest bookstore with an eye toward tourists in the wide selection of Wine Country books. The store's travel section focuses on California, but there's also a fine selection of U.S. Geological Survey maps.

Readers' Books
127 E. Napa St., Sonoma
(707) 939-1779
www.readersbook.com

Described by *Travel & Leisure* as a "honey pot" ("You can't help but get stuck there"), Readers' is a bookstore with many rooms, one of which is strictly for children's books and serves as a gathering room for youngsters. The store has gained some fame for its authors' readings.

Adobe Drug
303 W. Napa St., Sonoma
(707) 938-1144

It's a lot more than a pharmacy, with a fine gift section, a great collection of books by local authors, and plenty of good, old-fashioned friendliness. Closed Sundays.

Jack London Bookstore
14300 Arnold Dr., Glen Ellen
(707) 996-2888

Used and new books are sold here, with a special concentration of books dealing with the life of author Jack London. Closed Tuesdays.

Book Warehouse
2200 Petaluma Blvd. North, Petaluma
(707) 778-6981

This is a clearance bookstore tucked in the southwest corner of the Petaluma Village Premium Outlet. It sells the same range of books as any general bookstore, but all have been purchased from stock that has not been sold in other stores.

Copperfield's Books
www.copperfld.com
140 Kentucky St., Petaluma
(707) 762-0563
2316 Montgomery Dr., Santa Rosa
(707) 578-8938
650 Fourth St., Santa Rosa
(707) 545-5326
138 N. Main St., Sebastopol
(707) 823-2618

Copperfield's has built its business on customer service and is highly respected in Sonoma County. The shelves are filled with general interest publications, and there's a great children's section with occasional special events for children (see

Insiders' Tip

The historic *Sonoma Index-Tribune* newspaper, established in 1879 in Sonoma Valley, published the first in-depth history of the valley in 1997. The 329-page hardcover goes for $29.95 and will look great on your coffee table back home. It'll let everyone know where you spent your vacation. The book is available at the newspaper's offices at 117 W. Napa Street in Sonoma and other selected outlets.

our Kidstuff chapter). The Fourth Street store in Santa Rosa and the Petaluma store both deal in new and used books.

Barnes & Noble
700 Fourth St., Santa Rosa
(707) 576–7494

Having established the largest bookstore in all of Wine Country, Barnes & Noble has become a place for customers to relax in comfortable cushioned chairs (with a cup of coffee from the adjoining Starbucks) while deciding on book purchases. Barnes & Noble purchased a defunct furniture store for its shop and helped revitalize the Fourth Street shopping district. This is a very large bookstore, and it's just across the street from Copperfields.

Lakeside Village Bookstore
4275 Montgomery Dr., Santa Rosa
(707) 538–0579

Both new and used books are sold here, and they buy and trade too.

Insiders' Tip

Visitors to Wine Country farmers' markets may occasionally find a surprise nestled between the cukes and the arugula: a world-renowned chef signing copies of his latest cookbook. The French Laundry's Thomas Keller popped in at the weekly farmers market in Yountville one day and autographed 58 books in just one hour. The first in line to get Keller's John Hancock was the mayor of Yountville.

Waldenbooks
583 Coddingtown Mall, Santa Rosa
(707) 542–7065

Its location in a busy shopping mall makes this a very popular stop. It's a particularly tidy store with easy to locate sections, and there are large, enticing bargain bins at the front entrance filled with best sellers. The staff here is pleasant and helpful with special orders.

Northern Sonoma
Toyon Books
104 Matheson St., Healdsburg
(707) 433–9270
www.toyonbooks.com

Travelers looking for more information about Sonoma County's wineries will find a fine selection of wine-related books at the front of the store. The selection at Toyon Books is geared toward general reading, but a group of books specializes in spiritual and self-awareness subjects.

Levin & Company
306 Center St., Healdsburg
(707) 433–1118

It would be hard to find a more appealing bookstore—a large, airy room displays books on three large islands in the center of the store. Beyond that there's a cozy room with a comfortable couch in the mystery novel section, and then another cozy room with books on women's studies. A WPA-style mural spans one wall. There's also a children's room.

Levin & Company offers primarily new books—quality fiction, interior design, and garden titles. Upstairs in the loft, you'll find an art gallery displaying the works of some 15 local artists.

Sonoma Coast
Fort Ross Book & Gift Shop
19005 Hwy. 1, Jenner
(707) 847–3437

Located 11 miles north of the town of Jenner, the state park has a unique selection of books highlighting the Russian settlers and Native Americans, plus the natural history of the Fort Ross area (see our History chapter).

Mendocino County

U.S. 101

The Bookworm
202 S. State St., Ukiah
(707) 463–1901
With some 60,000 titles, the Bookworm sells both new and used books.

The Mendocino Book Company
102 S. School St., Ukiah
(707) 468–5940
It's billed as the largest bookstore between Santa Rosa and Portland, with special orders and mail orders welcome. It's a true family bookstore, featuring a special young readers room. In addition to books, there's an excellent selection of magazines and newspapers.

Leaves of Grass Bookstore
630 S. Main St., Willits
(707) 459–3744
Besides the books, this store has an excellent selection of U.S. Geological Survey topographical maps. Also available are educational games and toys for kids, plus books on tape for travelers.

Mendocino Coast

Gallery Bookshop & Bookwinkle's Children's Books
Main and Kasten Sts., Mendocino
(707) 937–2665
www.gallerybooks.com
Here's a world-class bookstore stocking more than 25,000 titles, plus cards, magazines, and newspapers. The section on local history is comprehensive, and Bookwinkle's is a perfect place to shop for children's books.

Ford House Visitor Center
735 Main St., Mendocino
(707) 937–5397
This is one of Mendocino's earliest residences as well as the headquarters of the State Historic Park. Here you can find out about beach walks and whale watches. The selection of books covers everything that ever happened to Mendocino and the people who have lived here. There are even books about the movies that have been filmed in Mendocino. (See our Attractions chapter.)

Cheshire Bookshop
363 N. Franklin St., Fort Bragg
(707) 964–5918
This full-service bookstore has been run by the same owner in Fort Bragg since 1973. The shop is spacious, uncrowded, and well organized.

Lake County

The Book Stop
305 N. Main St., Lakeport
(707) 263–5787
Hiding in Lakeport is the type of bookstore you'd expect to find in San Francisco (which explains why it has become a regular stop for city vacationers). The Book Stop is divided into five rooms: the main room, with more than 80,000 new and used tomes; the antiquarian book room, with both paperback and hardcover editions; the mystery room; the literature and nonfiction room; and the Nature and Discovery Shop, as profiled in our Kidstuff chapter. The store also has a religious section, a large supply of easy listening CDs, gardening tools, and even a collection of minerals and fossils.

Catfish Books
1013 11th St., Lakeport
(707) 263–4454
No, it doesn't deal primarily in fishing manuals. The name is simply a playful nod to nearby Clear Lake. Catfish has new and used material for all ages. Special orders are the house specialty.

Agape Christian Book Store
1859 N. High St., Lakeport
(707) 263–3120
This Christian bookstore (pronounced uh-GAH-pay) has been in Lakeport for more than 20 years. It stocks Christian books, gifts, jewelry, and Bibles—primarily geared to Protestant readers—by the dozen.

Arts and Culture

Writer Jack London loved the Wine Country. He arrived in the early 1900s to live on a ranch above the Sonoma Valley—which he called the "Valley of the Moon." London found a powerful muse here, writing most of the works that comprise his oeuvre, including *The Call of the Wild*. Though he achieved lasting renown as one of America's most prolific writers, London was not the first—nor the last—to be inspired by this land. Robert Louis Stevenson was perhaps the earliest to arrive, making St. Helena his temporary home in the 1880s. Other writers that followed include Ambrose Bierce, James Conaway, M. F. K. Fisher, Ursula LeGuin, David Bromige, and Paul Erdman.

The natural tranquility and abundant beauty of the place has stirred the soul and inspired the imagination of numerous other artists and art lovers. Today's small Wine Country towns are little bohemias, featuring elegant galleries and charming craft shops brimming with both local creations and works of art from around the world (see our Shopping chapter). Though writers and visual artists—from photographers to ceramic designers—have been particularly smitten by the landscape, an assortment of musicians and other performers also call this home. Don't be surprised to bump into pop rock artist Boz Scaggs while visiting Oakville, the gravely voiced Tom Waits while shopping in Sebastopol, Tommy Smothers while dining in the Valley of the Moon, or former Grateful Dead percussionist Mickey Hart while strolling through Occidental—all are local residents. And for the haute monde set, the Wine Country offers a fine array of opera and theater choices. Performers formerly part of the mainstream opera world have migrated here to find the freedom to conduct productions in a less formal style and atmosphere—others, like ballerina Natalia Makarova, have simply made this their second home. Says Doug Hundley, director of Ukiah Playhouse in Mendocino County, "I am daily amazed at the level of talent in this small town."

But while the performances themselves are often world class, don't expect the venues to necessarily resemble the upscale palaces of New York or Paris. The ambiance is generally more down-home, particularly in the smaller communities. No one likes to waste a good building, so abandoned grammar schools are becoming performing arts centers, churches have become theaters, and former libraries have become museums.

But the greatest of innovations may be in the use of the wineries themselves. Tasting rooms frequently double as art galleries and the winery courtyards and surrounding grounds often serve as theaters and concert halls. One example is Sonoma's Buena Vista Winery, whose artist-in-residence program features a selected Bay Area artist each month—the winery's tasting room becomes not only a gallery showcasing the artist's work but a working studio where patrons can observe works in progress. Another example is the Robert Mondavi Summer Music Festival, held each year at the Mondavi Winery in the Napa Valley. A 30-year tradition, the festival has featured such greats as Ella Fitzgerald, Harry Belafonte, Sarah Vaughan, and Robert Cray, with concert proceeds benefiting the Napa Valley Symphony.

That's just a small sampling of what's available. In this chapter, we offer you a rundown of some of the Wine Country's best arts and culture, presenting them in three categories: theater, music and dance, and visual arts. Relax and enjoy!

The wine-aging caves of Clos Pegase are filled with an extensive collection of glass, stone, ceramic, wood, and terra-cotta representations of Bacchus and his attendants, many of which are 18th- and 19th-century Italian and French originals. PHOTO: CLOS PEGASE WINERY

This bejeweled bovine is one of the many art-works on display at Copia: The American Center for Wine, Food and the Arts in Napa. PHOTO: JEAN SAYLOR DOPPENBERG

Theater Companies and Venues

Napa County

Dreamweavers Theater
1637 Imola Ave., Napa
(707) 555-5483
www.dreamweavers.napanet.net

This is Napa's only nonprofit live theater, supported by memberships, donations, and ticket sales—and completely staffed by volunteers. The troupe incorporated in 1987 and in 2000 renovated a former night-club in the River Park Shopping Center. There is a main theater for big productions and a "black box" area for smaller shows.

Dreamweavers has traditionally staged five shows a year for four weekends each, with smaller projects filling the gaps. Tickets typically run $12 to $15. Dreamweavers also sponsors a young actors' theater, with performances by the kids.

Napa Valley College Theater
2277 Napa-Vallejo Hwy., Napa
(707) 253-3200
www.nvc.cc.ca.us

The drama students of Napa Valley College stage several events at their campus theater during the academic year, August through May. Some examples of recent undertakings are *Amadeus, The Snow Queen, Oklahoma, De Donde, Noises Off,* and *The Servant of Two Masters.*

Prices range from $5.00 to $12.00; ask about student and senior discounts. See the Music and Dance section for more NVC productions.

Tucker Farm Center
1201 Tucker Rd., Calistoga
(707) 942-9695

Nobody is trying to be facetious here. It really is a theater, but for most of its existence it has served as a working support center for local farmers. The stage company, mostly Calistogans, performs original works in the summer, fun musicals and comedies in the spring and fall. The theater building, which doubles as a meeting hall or whatever else the growers need it for, holds about 120 patrons for most performances. Admission is $10 to $20. The center is off Highway 29, just north of Bothe-Napa Valley State Park.

Sonoma County

Andrews Hall
276 E. Napa St., Sonoma
(707) 938-4626

A classic brick structure, Andrews Hall is a leftover from 1916, when it was the Sonoma Grammar School. More recently it achieved modest national exposure when it was selected as one of the settings for the hit movie *Scream.* It's a small the-ater that's now part of the Sonoma Community Center and will seat up to 299—it takes on no airs for being grand. There's a friendly hometown atmosphere about it, and it offers a surprisingly diverse assortment of talent, with five major performances staged each winter season using mainly local actors.

The stage is small, so plays generally run to those requiring few actors and uncomplicated sets such as *Mame, A Child's Christmas in Wales,* and murder mysteries. December usually brings a Christmas-themed production; in 2000 Andrews Hall staged *Inspecting Carol,* a comedy about a theater company putting on a Christmas production. Occasional musical evenings bring the internationally recognized Brass Works of San Francisco or a performance by the Baguette Quartet. The intimate, 50-seat Black Box Theater behind Andrews Hall stages one-act plays, sometimes written by local authors. Admission is set at $10 to $12 per event at Andrews Hall, or a season of five performances is $60.

The venue also puts on regular guest artist lectures, in conjunction with the ceramics and art department. Workshops in disciplines such as writing and painting also enrich Andrews Hall's calendar.

Avalon Players
Buena Vista Winery,
18000 Old Winery Rd., Sonoma
(707) 938–1266, (800) 926–1266

This group has been performing Shakespeare's plays at Buena Vista Winery since 1980 and has become something of a tradition among theater lovers. A lighthearted spirit of fun prevails, and people come from Los Angeles and San Francisco—there are even some regulars from as far away as Texas—to watch the Avalon group perform. One group of 30 friends has come every season for the past several years. Whole families attend, kids and grandparents included. This is "Shakespeare with a twist"—the audience can expect an occasional actor to leave the stage and carry on his performance amidst the viewers. In 2000, the theater put on *Taming of the Shrew.* Children are a part of the cast because the director, Kate Kennedy, also teaches acting to kids. The kids play demanding roles and often put in star performances.

Seating is at picnic tables and is on a first-come, first-served basis. It has become the custom among those who come often to bring some fanciful picnic fare and elaborate table settings. Buena Vista wine is available, of course. Tickets are priced at $18 for adults, $10 for kids. Buena Vista Winery is at the eastern edge of Sonoma. Once on E. Spain Street, follow the directional signs.

Sonoma State University
1801 E. Cotati, Rohnert Park
(707) 644–2353
www.sonoma.edu/Depts/PerformingArts/

This university is one of 20 campuses in the California state university system (see our Education and Child Care chapter). Performing arts get top billing at Sonoma State, with works from the pens of local playwrights and international favorites performed year-round, along with dance recitals and musical concerts. The school's Everett B. Person Theatre seats 475, and it has featured such Broadway plays as *You're a Good Man Charlie Brown* and *Scapino.* A smaller theater seating 175 presents plays in the round, mostly student productions suitable for the more

> ## Insiders' Tip
> The Uptown Theater in Napa is being restored to its former glory. (It first opened in 1937 but fell into disrepair over the years and later closed.) Co-owner Francis Ford Coppola brought in technicians from New York to work on the stage and sound systems, and the theater's new seats were custom-created by a French chair maker. A fall 2002 reopening is planned.

intimate stage. *Waiting for Godot* is a good example. There is also Warren Auditorium, which is devoted to music events throughout the year, from jazz to chamber music. Prices of tickets vary but generally run in the range of $5.00 to $25.00.

Spreckels Performing Arts Center
5409 Snyder Ln., Rohnert Park
(707) 588–3400
www.spreckelsonline.com

This is one Sonoma County building designed specifically for the arts. When the City of Rohnert Park was developed in the late 1970s, an $8-million performing arts complex of 35,000 square feet was included in the master plan. It is the home of the Pacific Alliance Stage Company, founded by Spreckels director Michael Grice, Smuin Ballet/SF, and Orchestra Sonoma. The Spreckels Center also serves as a home away from home for top touring performers.

The center houses two theaters designed and built exclusively for dance, music, and theatrical performances. The Nellie W. Codding Theatre seats 511 patrons and offers a variety of performances from nationally known arts groups. The innovative Bette Condiotti Experimental Theatre seats 175 and presents more unusual and creative programming as well as special productions by local arts groups, schools, and civic organizations. Both theaters are attractive, but the Codding Theatre is stunning with its red carpeting, luxurious fabric theater seats, and midnight blue catwalks and ceiling. Codding productions include Broadway hits, an extraordinary ballet program featuring 12 of the Bay Area's most charismatic soloists, a performance of *The Nutcracker* at Christmas, and symphony performances. Main Stage ticket prices usually run $11 to $22.

The Santa Rosa Players
Santa Rosa
(707) 544–7827, (707) 579–8618

Santa Rosa's oldest theater group, so they say, stages musicals, tragedies, and comedies. Their venue is the Merlot Theater at Luther Burbank Center for the Arts. The 2002 season was expected to include performances of *Damn Yankees, Hello Dolly,* and *Once Upon a Mattress.*

Luther Burbank Center for the Arts
50 Mark West Springs Rd., Santa Rosa
(707) 546–3600
www.lbc.net

This elegant center became a reality in 1981 when the Christian Life Center, a religious organization, was forced to sell the property as part of its bankruptcy proceedings. The Luther Burbank Foundation moved in and reopened it as a regional arts hub. It's still going strong, with concerts and cultural events of all kinds. It serves as host to many groups, including the Actors' Theatre, the Redwood Empire Lyric Theatre, the Redwood Empire Ballet, Ballet California, the California Museum of the Arts, and the Santa Rosa Symphony (see the symphony's listing in "Music and Dance" later in this chapter).

Multilayered chandeliers light up the expansive 6,000-square-foot lobby, which is matched by the huge 1,500 seat main theater. Expect the finest in ballets, choral performances, symphonies, films, operas, and concerts of all kinds in this inviting setting. Engelbert Humperdinck, Ballet Folklorico de Mexico, Ani DeFranco, Yo Yo Ma, Nanci Griffith, Buddy Guy, Jethro Tull, and the New Pickle Circus—to name just a few—have all stood on the center's stage at one time or another. Tickets run from $15 to $50, depending on the event.

Other rooms at the Burbank Center include the East Auditorium, which seats 425—it's ideal for school plays and recitals, giving them a professional touch with theatrical lighting, a sound booth, and audiovisual equipment. The Chamber Chapel seats 325 and has a spectacular, high-vaulted ceiling and stained-glass windows. The Exhibit Hall, a 9,000-square-foot venue, hosts trade shows, art exhibits, and wine tastings.

Santa Rosa Junior College Summer Repertory Theater
11501 Mendocino Ave., Santa Rosa
(707) 527–4343
www.santarosa.edu/srt

With nearly 30 seasons under its belt, the SRT is a long-time local favorite. Running from mid-June into early August, plays rotate throughout the season and include musicals, dramas, and comedies. The 2000 lineup included *The Wizard of Oz*, *H.R. Gurney's Tale of Sylvia*, *Romeo and Juliet*, and *Victor/Victoria*. Performances are held variously at the college, Luther Burbank Center for the Arts (see previous listing), or local high schools. This is a professional training program geared to actors in graduate school, all of whom come on scholarships for summer work. Paid directors are well known and usually work on a rotating basis—six work each season. Tickets range from $8.00 to $14.00.

Sonoma County Repertory Theatre
415 Humboldt St., Santa Rosa and
104 N. Main St., Sebastopol
(707) 544-7278, (707) 823-0177
www.sonoma-county-rep.com

Voted Sonoma County's "Best Theatre Troupe for 1996," Main Street Theatre was formed in 1991 and in 1996 added a sister company in downtown Santa Rosa, the Sonoma County Repertory Theatre. Now working together as the Sonoma County Repertory Theatre, the group offers an intriguing selection of fare. The 2001 season included *Picasso at the Lapin Agile* and *Women in Mind*.

In addition, the two theaters will continue to offer year-round, multidisciplinary training for both children and adults, plus children's theater and a summer Shakespeare festival. Admission prices at both theaters are generally $15 or $12 for students and seniors.

Mendocino County

Ukiah Playhouse
1041 Low Gap Road, Ukiah
(707) 462-9226

Offering an eclectic mix, Ukiah Playhouse stages five plays each season (October to June). In addition, the Playhouse offers readings for original, unproduced scripts, one of them eventually selected for production. These can be tricky presenta-

tions, as the audience must become accustomed to the fact that there is no action on stage.

Ukiah Playhouse has been producing plays since 1977, sometimes performing in rented spaces such as an abandoned 7-Eleven. It was reborn and revitalized in the mid-1980s when members of the company set out to build their own theater. The whole community came together, with everyone donating materials to the cause, landscaping included. The present structure seats 138 but will be enlarged to seat 198. Tickets for play productions are priced at $10 to $12—season passes are $50. The staged readings are $4.00 or $5.00.

Mendocino Theater Company
45200 Little Lake St., Mendocino
(707) 937-4477
www.mcn.org/1/mtc

The Mendocino Theatre Company has been offering high quality theatre productions for nearly 25 years. The cozy 83-seat Helen Schoeni Theatre offers an intimate setting for a mix of comedies (*Picasso at the Lapin Agile*), drama (Eugene O'Neill's *A Moon for the Misbegotten*), and mainstream presentations. The theater adjoins the historic Mendocino Art Center (see listing under "Visual Art Venues and Organizations" in this chapter and our History chapter). The company produces six plays a year with shows Thursday through Sunday nights. The 2001 season included *Of Mice and Men*, *Private Eyes*, *The Complete History of America*, and others. Tickets are $10 to $15.

Gloriana Opera Company
721 N. Franklin St., Fort Bragg
(707) 964-7469
www.mcn.org/d/gloriana

Here's musical theater in grand style, featuring a full cast with lavish costumes, sets, and choreography. This group has been creating melodious magic since 1977, performing musical theater from *The Mikado* to *Fiddler On the Roof*. The company's new theater seats 150. The season is year-round, with performances Thursday through Sunday at 8:00 P.M. Tickets are priced at $10.00 and $8.00, with discounts available for series of shows.

Looking at theater from a different angle, Gloriana also has experimented with a series called Showcase Performances, designed to combine the highest values of musical theater with an elegant simplicity of production style, minimal sets, and simple costuming. Children's programs and workshops offer kids opportunities to express themselves in a creative environment through the skills and techniques of musical theater. For kids fourth grade and up, there are workshops in acting, singing, dancing, and makeup.

Another offbeat sideline is the Rent-A-Singer and Rent-A-Costume program. For weddings, parties, or other special events, Gloriana will send out a fully equipped theater company, a group of carolers, an a capella ensemble, or their children's chorus.

Lake County

Lake County Repertory Theater
(707) 262–0525, (707) 274–2281

The theater group was formed in 1981 but was inactive for several years as it searched for a home. They found it in 1994, at the Lake County Museum in Lower Lake (seating capacity 120). The theater stages two plays a year—one in spring and one in fall. Recent productions have included *Steel Magnolias* and *Dracula*. They prefer to keep things light. Admission is $6.00 to $7.00.

Lakeport Community Players
(707) 262–0525, (707) 274–2281

When the Lakeport campus of Mendocino College dropped its drama department for budgetary reasons in 1991, those staff members eventually reorganized as the Lakeport Community Players, an auxiliary of the Lake County Arts Council. They do splashy musicals, Woody Allen farces, mysteries, and dramas. Recent examples: *Guys and Dolls* and *Harvey*. They are in the process of raising funds to renovate the Soper-Reese Theater (at Main and Martin Streets), which

they hope to make their permanent home. They also do melodramas at the Blackberry Festival and the Lake County Fair (see our Festivals and Annual Events chapter).

Music and Dance Organizations and Venues

Napa County

Jarvis Conservatory
1711 Main St., Napa
(707) 255–5445

The Jarvis Conservatory was founded in 1973 as a nonprofit generator of scholarships for students of the performing arts. The corporation took a great leap in 1994 when it acquired its own educational facilities. And what facilities they are, centered around the Lisbon Winery, a registered historic landmark built in 1882. Performances are in a 221-seat theater in the acoustically superb, expensively equipped, stone winery building. The Conservatory's offerings feature a mix of students and visiting professionals. Recent artists have included the Jose Limon West Dance Troupe and pianist/conductor Donald Runnicles. The premiere Saturday of each month is opera night, and the specialty of the house is zarzuela, a splendidly costumed, melodramatic form of Spanish opera. Admission for all shows can range from $10 and $30.

Napa Valley Symphony
2407 California Blvd., Napa
(707) 22–MUSIC

The symphony, conducted by Asher Raboy, plays with an assurance and aptitude you might not expect to find in a city of 72,500. Its primary venue is the Lincoln Theater at the Veterans Home of California (see our Attractions chapter) in Yountville. The Napa Valley Symphony has tackled Beethoven, Tchaikovsky, and Mahler; Baroque chamber music; and jazzy compositions by Artie Shaw. It has welcomed guests such as pianist Ursula

Oppens, clarinetist Todd Palmer, and violinist Amy Oshiro. And on occasion it leaves the Lincoln for special performances at Robert Mondavi Winery or St. John's Catholic Church in Napa. Single tickets in section A are $32 for adults, $16 for students and children younger than 16; in section B, prices are $26 and $13. You also can subscribe to a series of five Tuesday evening or Sunday matinee concerts. Adult series prices range from $85 to $150.

Napa Valley College Theater
2277 Napa-Vallejo Hwy., Napa
(707) 253-3200
www.nvc.cc.ca.us

The college's esteemed music program puts on a variety of performances, such as orchestra and vocal recitals, even cabaret nights, during the August-through-May academic year. The theater also has lured independent groups like the North Bay Philharmonic Orchestra, the North Bay Wind Ensemble, and the Billy Browning Jazz Orchestra. Occasionally events are staged off campus, usually at wineries. Prices range from $5.00 to $10.00. Ask about senior and student discounts.

Chamber Music in Napa Valley
809 Coombs St., Napa
(707) 252-7126

This group brings the soothing sounds of chamber music to the Wine Country. Recent guests include Isaac Stern, the Prazak Quartet (a renowned group from Prague), and tenor James Morris. Most performances are at the First United Methodist Church in Napa, though the chamber music sometimes drifts to the wine caves of S. Anderson or Clos Pegase. The church performances are generally $15, while winery shows are $25 and include wine tasting.

Robert Mondavi Winery
7801 St. Helena Hwy., Oakville
(707) 226-1395 ext. 4392
www.robertmondaviwinery.com

While Robert serves as unofficial wine ambassador to the world, his wife, Margrit Biever, does her part to make the

Insiders' Tip
In Napa Valley, you're never too young to begin an appreciation for classical music. Every year, the Napa Valley Symphony performs "Fifth Grade Concerts," serving the entire fifth-grade population of Napa County, free of charge to the schools.

winery a center of culture in the Wine Country. It seems as though there is always a note of music in the air here, whether it's the Preservation Hall Jazz Band kicking off the outdoor Summer Concert Series or Italian opera to benefit renovation of the Napa Valley Opera House. Mezzo-soprano Marilyn Horne gave a performance here in 2001. Call the winery for a schedule and admission fees.

Paulin Hall Auditorium
Pacific Union College, Angwin
(707) 965-7362
www.puc.edu

The forested heights of Howell Mountain might be an unlikely spot for the sweet melodies of classical music, but Pacific Union College (PUC) is able to attract frontline talent to Paulin Hall. Recent performers have included soprano Marnie Breckenridge, Romanian-born pianist Eduard Stan, and Troika Balalaikas, an American trio that dresses in traditional costume and plays the folk songs of Czarist Russia. The Fine Arts series usually runs from October to April. The cost is $5.00 for adults and $3.00 for children per show, or pay $20.00 and $9.00, respectively, for five programs. There are numerous other events at Paulin that are not part of the Fine Arts series. Any shows requiring an organ take place in PUC's church sanctuary, home of the state's largest tracker pipe organ.

Sonoma County

Sonoma Valley Chorale
Veterans Memorial Building,
126 First St. West, Sonoma
(707) 935–1576
www.sonomavalleychorale.org

This professional-level, 140-member chorus, under the direction of Jim Griewe, has been singing together since the early '70s. Its annual concert series brings audiences to their feet with music that might be classical, sacred, or Broadway. The chorale has sung with the Napa Valley and Santa Rosa symphonies (see listings in this section) and even for the opening ceremony at a Giants baseball game. They've made two European tours, singing their way through France, Italy, and Great Britain—they toured Germany in 2001. Their regular venue is the Veterans Memorial Building auditorium, which has tiered, theater seating for 400. Tickets are $12 for adults and $10 for seniors and children.

Cinnabar Performing Arts Theater
3333 Petaluma Blvd. North, Petaluma
(707) 763–8920
www.cinnabartheater.com

In the summer of 1970, Marvin Klebe abandoned his career singing baritone with the San Francisco Opera Company, bought a 60-year-old, two-room schoolhouse on the outskirts of Petaluma surrounded by dairy cows and chickens, and began transforming the structure into a theater. Disenchanted with the usual regimentation of grand opera, Marvin's goal was to provide a stage for experimental works that would involve the local community.

Today Cinnabar Theater features an outstanding array of entertainers, performing everything from Bach to rock. Candlelight concerts give a rare and romantic opportunity to hear chamber music the way some of our ancestors did. Concerts are held not only at Cinnabar Theater, but also in some of Petaluma's loveliest gardens and mansions, intimate art galleries, and in the downtown Polly Klaas Theater (a school for young acting hopefuls). The Summer Music Festival presents the best in classical music, ethnic music, musical comedy, opera, and children's music.

In 1983 Marvin and his wife, Jan, created Cinnabar Children's Theater workshop. In the first year, the children mounted a musical production of *The Hobbit* that they wrote and publicized themselves. Children's programming and training play a role of growing importance at Cinnabar. Classes are packed. A free brochure outlining Klebe's many ventures is available. Performance tickets are $9.00 to $22.00.

Santa Rosa Symphony
50 Mark West Springs Rd., No. 305,
Santa Rosa
(707) 546–8742
www.santarosasymphony.com

The Santa Rosa Symphony was founded by George Trombley in 1927. Thirty-two eager (and some talented) amateur musicians played for the first time at the local Elks Club. It is said that Mr. T (as his players called him) was fond of spirited selections. Under his direction the orchestra played Dvorak's *Slavonic Dance* at most concerts. These performances were enlivened by the gusto of Mr. T, who stomped his foot on the podium until the dust flew. Trombley's tenure lasted 30 years, when Maestro Corrick Brown took over the baton and held it for another 37 years.

The orchestra has long since left the Elks Club and now makes its home at the Luther Burbank Center for the Arts (see listing under "Theater Companies and Venues" in this chapter). Its conductor is Jeffrey Kahane, the world-renowned pianist, who assumed the podium in 1995. It is the only orchestra of its size and quality (there are 80-plus musicians) between Sonoma County and Eugene, Oregon. The concert season consists of seven three-day events plus a pops concert and picnic in June (table seating and lawn seating are available), a Redwoods Music Festival in August, and other special events in August and September. Kahane is particularly eager to work with young people and has established a Symphony Youth Orchestra, providing two free concerts for children (particularly popular with kindergarten through third-grade students). Adult ticket prices range between $17 and $30.

Mendocino County

Mendocino Ballet
209 South State St., Ukiah
307 E. Redwood Ave., Fort Bragg
(707) 463–2290, (877) 354–5172
www.wildirisdesign.com/ballet

This regional dance company offers students the opportunity to demonstrate their talents in local dance productions. The ballet has been offering classical and contemporary works by local and guest choreographers, and it features regular performances of *Peter and the Wolf, The Dream of Sleeping Beauty, Sweet Coppelia,* and the *Nutcracker.* Founder Mary Knight operates a dance school to train the ballet company's performers. She instructs young children in ballet fundamentals and offers teenage students advanced training in a variety of choreography styles. The company also presents lecture demonstrations in schools throughout Lake and Mendocino Counties, offering an educational arts experience to thousands of children.

Lake County

Lake County Community Chorus
P.O. Box 1216, Lakeport
(707) 263–5526

The chorus, an auxiliary of the Lake County Arts Council, gets together a few times a year to belt out everything from Mozart to Christmas carols to Broadway standards. Admission is along the lines of $5.00. The chorus' venues include the Lower Lake Schoolhouse and Museum, and the Soper-Reese Theater.

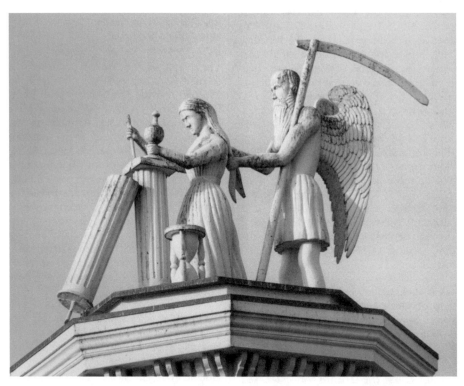

Father Time and the Maiden, *a 19th-century statuary carved from a single block of redwood by mill worker Erick Albertson, sits atop the Masonic Lodge Building in Mendocino.* PHOTO: JOHN NAGIECKI

Visual Arts Organizations, Venues and Galleries

To make it easier for you to skip from one gallery to the next one you will encounter, listings in this section are presented in the intra-county geographical sequence outlined in How to Use This Book.

Napa County

di Rosa Preserve
5200 Hwy. 121/12, Napa
(707) 226–5991
www.dirosapreserve.org

The subtitle of this collection is Art & Nature, and, indeed, many of the pieces are blended into the scenery of Carneros, that cool-climate grape-growing region on the north side of San Pablo Bay (see our Wineries chapter). Rene and Veronica di Rosa have been gathering artwork for more than 30 years, and their current display tends to the whimsical, even outrageous. All of it was produced in the Bay Area in the latter part of the 20th century. The indoor space includes a circa-1886 winery the di Rosas converted into their home, plus some contemporary galleries full of works of various media. Rene originally moved to Carneros to grow grapes, which he did as Winery Lake Vineyards until he sold the planted land to Seagram, the corporate beverage giant, in 1986. Admission is $10 and by guided tour only. The Preserve offers two tours a day—9:25 A.M. and 12:55 P.M.—Tuesday through Friday from October through May, and Monday through Thursday from June through September. There are also Saturday morning tours at 9:25 A.M. and 10:25 A.M.

Jessel Miller Gallery
1019 Atlas Peak Rd., Napa
(707) 257–2350
www.jesselgallery.com

On the road to Silverado Country Club, in a stately, vine-covered, white-brick building, is the studio of esteemed watercolorist Jessel Miller. The gallery shows the work of both emerging and established artists, in media from oil to collage to jewelry. It also offers public tours, lectures, and demonstrations. The gallery is open 10:00 A.M. to 5:00 P.M. daily.

Henry Joseph Gallery
2475 Solano Ave., Napa
(707) 224–4356

This gallery is devoted to the California style—that spontaneous, impressionistic form spawned by a group of Californians in the 1930s. Painters such as Charles Surrendorf, Jade Fon, and Justin Faivre made the California style easily distinguishable from traditional English watercolor. The gallery also represents prominent Napa Valley artists like Roger Blum, Bill King, and Jay Golik. If you pop for an original, you can have it framed at the affiliated Napa Frame Studio. Hours of operation are 10:00 A.M. to 5:30 P.M. Tuesday through Friday and 10:00 A.M. to 3:00 P.M. Saturday.

Napa Valley Art Association
1520 Behrens St., Napa
(707) 255–9616

The Napa Valley Art Association was formed as a nonprofit corporation in 1953 to provide local artists with satisfactory facilities. At the association's once-a-month meetings (usually on the fourth Monday), guest artists demonstrate their skills and ideas. Those demonstrations are often videotaped for future observation. You can pay a $24.00 annual fee for membership or surrender a nominal $2.00 charge to attend a single meeting. The association hosts occasional shows of its members' work—everything from still lifes to portraits and landscapes to abstracts, in all sorts of media. Call the association for more information.

The Hess Collection Winery
4411 Redwood Rd., Napa
(707) 255–1144
www.hesscollection.com

Donald Hess, the Swiss businessman who made his millions bottling water before he turned to wine, is a passionate art collector, and some of the best of his collection is here in Napa Valley. His three-story, 13,000-square-foot gallery is part of the winery and just as much of a draw to visitors. Hess collects only works by living artists, and the list is impressive: Francis Bacon, Frank Stella, Henri Machaux, and Theodoros Stamos, just to name a few. Some of the outstanding conceptual pieces include a group of oversized, headless figures fashioned by Polish artist Magdalena Abakanowicz and a vintage Underwood typewriter going up in flames, a work by Argentinian Leopoldo Maler. There is no charge to enter the museum, which is open 10:00 A.M. to 4:00 P.M. daily.

Images Fine Art
North: 6540 Washington St., Yountville
(707) 944-0404
South: 6505 Washington St., Yountville
(707) 944-0606

North and south have never been closer than at these twin galleries in downtown Yountville. The northern room came first; the southern was added in 1996. Neither has a specialty, just best-selling artists represented in a dramatic, two-story space with vaulted ceilings. Contributors include David Dodsworth, Guy Buffet, Roy Fairchild, and Pradzynski. Both galleries are open daily from 10:00 A.M. to 5:00 P.M.

RAKU Ceramics Collection
Beard Plaza, 6540 Washington St., Yountville
(707) 944-9424

Raku, the process originally used to make bowls for tea ceremony in medieval Japan, involves using tongs to remove red-hot pots from the kiln, then cooling the ceramics quickly in the air or in water. Most of what you see here gets an additional copper-flashing technique. The pots, sprayed with copper, are covered with a pail after firing. When the pot is removed, the copper oxidizes and flashes in a rainbow of colors. RAKU has work by more than 75 ceramists, including Greg Milne, Ed Risak, and Tom and Nancy Giusti. Open daily from 10:00 A.M. to 5:00 P.M.

Did you know that Napa was the birthplace of the loudspeaker and the Magnavox Corporation? The first speaker was invented by Peter Jensen and Edwin Pridham at 1601 First Street in 1915. This statue, by Franco Vianello, was dedicated in 1985. PHOTO: TINA LUSTER-HOBAN

Mumm Napa Valley
8445 Silverado Trail, Rutherford
(707) 942-3434
www.mummnapavalley.com

Mumm's corporate owners, Joseph E. Seagram & Sons, have been appreciative of photographers, making the winery perhaps Napa Valley's premier venue for that industrial art. Luminaries such as Imogen Cunningham, Galen Rowell, Sebastio Salgado, and William Neill have been represented on the walls. But the rotating exhibitions have a hard time diverting attention from the winery's one permanent collection: "The Story of a Winery" by Ansel Adams. The legendary Californian was hired in 1959 to document construction of new wine cellars, care of the vineyards, and the process of winemaking from vine to bottle. The Smithsonian

Institution circulated the best of the photos for three years, and now Mumm has dozens of gelatin silver prints. There is no admission charge to the galleries, which are open from 10:00 A.M. to 5:00 P.M. daily.

I. Wolk Gallery
1354 Main St., St. Helena
(707) 963–8800
www.iwolkgallery.com

Ira Wolk's second-floor gallery is a definitive St. Helena establishment—tasteful art in a lovely, immaculate space. The gallery features everything from paintings and works on paper to photography and sculpture. It is open Wednesday through Monday from 10:00 A.M. to 5:30 P.M.

Art on Main
1359 Main St., St. Helena
(707) 963–3350

One of St. Helena's most prominent and centrally located spaces, Art on Main focuses on, but is not limited to, images of vineyards and wine. It's primarily a venue for Northern California artists and traditional styles. An example is Gail Packer's extensive series of multiplate etchings, with frames designed by artist Hildy Henry. Other contributors include Garberville's Josh Adam and Hopland's Ray Voisard. Open daily from 10:00 A.M. to 5:00 P.M.

Rasmussen Art Gallery
Pacific Union College, Angwin
(707) 965–7362
www.puc.edu

Pacific Union College's stylish art gallery is largely a showplace for its own students, faculty, and alumni. It isn't limited to these groups, though. Other recent exhibitions have included the drawings of Samuel Fleming Lewis and the experimental photography of Cliff Rusch. Admission is free, and the gallery is open from 1:00 to 5:00 P.M. on Tuesday, Thursday, Saturday, and Sunday.

Clos Pegase Winery
1060 Dunaweal Ln., Calistoga
(707) 942–4981
www.clospegase.com

Art is everywhere at Clos Pegase, from the winery itself—something of a huge modern sculpture—to French and Italian carvings of Bacchus tucked into the wine caves. The variety is impressive, too, from granite sculptures to watercolors and collages. Clos Pegase offers a self-guided walking tour of the premises, as well as guided tours of the facility and wine caves at 11:00 A.M. and 2:00 P.M. (no reservation required). Among the pieces are a giant bronze thumb by Cesar Baldachini (designer of the "Cesar," the French equivalent of the Oscar); Michael Scranton's *Wrecking Ball*, an enervating installation in the Reserve Room; and a Henry Moore sculpture (*Mother Earth*) in the portico. In addition, a wine-in-art slide presentation, created by proprietor Jan Shrem, is given inside the caves at 2:00 P.M. on the third Saturday of each month (December and January excluded). The show is free.

Ca'Toga Galleria D'Arte
1206 Cedar St., Calistoga
(707) 942–3900
www.catoga.com

Escape into a world of Renaissance, Baroque, and neoclassic styles of painting in Carlo Marchiori's fabulous gallery off Lincoln Avenue. You may recognize his work—he has been commissioned to produce murals found in the world's finest hotels and attractions, including San Francisco's Westin St. Francis and Tokyo's DisneySea. He also lives in Calistoga, and his Villa Ca'Toga outside of town is open for weekly tours in summer (see our Attractions chapter). The gallery is open 11:00 A.M. to 6:00 P.M. daily; closed Tuesday and Wednesday.

Lee Youngman Galleries
1316 Lincoln Ave., Calistoga
(707) 942–0585, (800) 551–0585
www.leeyoungmangalleries.com

Owner Lee Love Youngman has long been surrounded by creative men. Her father, Ralph Love, was a painter from the Early California school who has work hung in major museums. And her husband, Paul Youngman, is noted for his contemporary landscapes, architectural renderings, and

The world's largest thumb? Possibly. Cesar Bal-dachini, who designed the "Cesar," the French equivalent of the Oscar, also designed this giant bronze thumb that rises from the ground at Clos Pegase Winery. PHOTO: CLOS PEGASE WINERY

marines. Lee's gallery has a decidedly Southwest bent. It represents more than 60 full-time artists, including big shots such as Neil Boyle and Mark Geller. The gallery is open 10:00 A.M. to 5:00 P.M. Monday through Saturday and 11:00 A.M. to 4:00 P.M. Sunday.

Sonoma County

Spirits In Stone
452 First St. East, Sonoma
(707) 938–2200
www.spiritsinstone.com

"Must touch to appreciate" is the byword when visiting this collection of Zimbabwe Shona sculpture. The form's sleek surface is beyond description. *Newsweek* has called Shona sculpture "the most impor-

tant new art form to emerge from Africa this century." You can also find African photographs, paintings, and music at this museum-quality gallery, which is open daily from 10:00 A.M. to 6:00 P.M. (See our Shopping chapter for more on Spirits In Stone.)

Sonoma State University Art Gallery
1801 E. Cotati Ave., Rohnert Park
(707) 664–2295
www.sonoma.edu/ArtGallery

Changing exhibits of contemporary art are combined with works by artists known regionally, nationally, and internationally. The gallery is open Tuesday through Friday from 11:00 A.M. to 4:00 P.M. and noon to 4:00 P.M. on weekends. Admission is free.

Cultural Arts Council of Sonoma County
602 Wilson St., Santa Rosa
(707) 579–2787
www.pressdemo.com/community/cacsc

Curating new exhibits every eight weeks, the council serves as a resource center for artists and provides a gallery for their work. A typical art competition commissioned by the Sonoma Land Trust challenged artists to portray imagery inspired by Sonoma County's agricultural environment. It's not just two-dimensional art. For five years the council has sponsored a gospel music concert, sharing a unique American art form in performances at Santa Rosa High School. The council also sponsors events such as First Night Santa Rosa, a New Year's Eve celebration of the arts in downtown Santa Rosa featuring jazz, rock, big band, mime, comedy, theater, and dance.

Sonoma Museum of Visual Art
Luther Burbank Center for the Arts,
50 Mark West Springs Rd., Santa Rosa
(707) 527–0297
www.lbc.net/museummain.html

The only fine arts museum serving the Northern California coast and northern San Francisco Bay Area, the Sonoma Museum of Visual Art (MOVA) features local artists whose work transcends conventional painting, sculpture, photography,

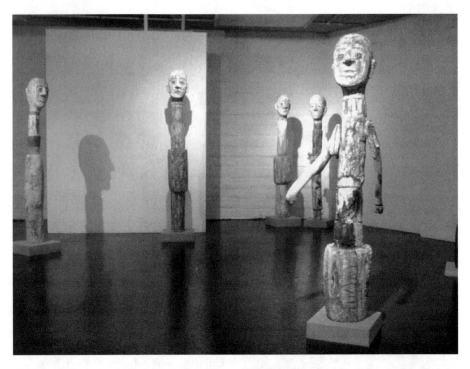

The Sonoma Museum of Visual Art showcases contemporary work, such as the sculpture of Carol Setterlund, pictured above. PHOTO: THE SONOMA MUSEUM OF VISUAL ART

and architecture. An interactive salon is held at Sonoma MOVA on occasional Friday evenings throughout the year. These feature guest speakers from all walks of the artistic community. In the summer months, visitors can enjoy the outdoor Film Cafe, which pairs short experimental films with excellent local food and wine. Museum hours are Monday through Friday from 10:00 A.M. to 4:00 P.M. (later on Thursday, to 8:00 P.M.), and Saturday and Sunday from 11:00 A.M. to 4:00 P.M.

The Ren Brown Collection
1781 Hwy. 1, Bodega Bay
(707) 875–2922, (800) 585–2921
www.renbrown.com

Housed in a building with shoji screens and a small Japanese garden, this gallery is dedicated to showing contemporary art from both sides of the Pacific. The major focus is on modern Japanese prints by artists such as Shigeki Kuroda, Toko Shinoda, and Ryohei Tanaka, whose works

often appear in prominent museums. The items shown at Ren Brown represent the largest selections of contemporary Japanese prints in California. Also featured are the works of several regional California artists. You'll see watercolor, sculpture in stone and bronze; acrylic paintings; as well as woodcut, silkscreen, mezzotint, and lithograph art. All in all, some 75 artists are represented on two floors of the gallery, which is open every day except Tuesday from 10:00 A.M. to 5:00 P.M.

Christopher Queen Galleries
John Orr's Garden, No. 4, Duncans Mills
(707) 865–1318
www.duncansmillscamp.com/christopher.htm

On Highway 116 in historic Duncans Mills, this gallery features nationally known wildlife artists, including Thomas Brenders, John Bateman, and Thomas Quinn. Serigraphs by John Powell and Don Hatfield also are on display. The

Upstairs Salon features an extensive display of important early California artists. The galleries are open every day but Tuesday from 11:00 A.M. to 5:00 P.M., and by appointment.

Sea Ranch Lodge
Hwy. 1, North, Sea Ranch
(707) 785-2371

Various artists and photographers display their work in the Sea Ranch Lodge's Fireside Room overlooking the ocean (for more on Sea Ranch, see our Real Estate chapter). New exhibits are posted each month, introduced with a reception of wine and hors d'oeuvres. Call for a list of upcoming exhibits.

Mendocino County

Gualala Arts Center
46501 Old State Hwy., Gualala
(707) 884-1138
www.gualalaarts.com

In the early 1900s, Gualala was a lumber mill center, abandoned when sawmills closed down. But in the 1960s, the beauty of the area attracted artists and other creative people. They painted, photographed, wrote, acted, and watched whales. They attracted other talented people, and during the last three decades Gualala has become recognized as a center for the arts, drawing people from miles around to soak up the cultural atmosphere.

The focal point of all this art activity is a 15,000-square-foot arts center, established in 1997 and set in the forest. The scope of the center's activities is somewhat overwhelming. You'll find popular and classical music concerts, lectures, exhibits, youth and adult art classes, theater productions, and meeting space for artists, photographers, quilters, poets, weavers, and book groups. They do all this with one salaried secretary, a professional executive director, and a lot of volunteers.

The first Sunday of every month is given over to chamber music concerts (tickets are $15), but it's likely you will run into some kind of music event any time you happen to be in town. A wide variety of events—from theater presentations to lecture series—is held in the multipurpose room (seating capacity, 350). The mid-August Art in the Redwoods extravaganza (see our Festivals and Annual Events chapter) attracts more than 350 artistic entries

This jungle mural greets shoppers and walkers in downtown Santa Rosa. PHOTO: TINA LUSTER-HOBAN

and approximately 5,000 people attend each year.

Alinder Gallery
39165 Hwy. 1, South, Gualala
(707) 884–4884
www.alindergallery.com

Internationally respected authorities Mary and Jim Alinder manage this gallery. While specializing in original Ansel Adams images, the gallery maintains an excellent inventory of work by many other great photographers. Alinder Gallery is open Tuesday through Sunday from 10:00 A.M. to 6:00 P.M.

Mendocino Art Center
45200 Little Lake St., Mendocino
(707) 937–5818, (800) 653–3328
www.mendocinoartcenter.org

This is an educational organization that features classes in everything from furniture making to bead artistry. Year-round courses in fine arts, ceramics, and children's art, conducted by paid artists-in-residence, draw students from around the country. A spacious gallery at the center features the work of established and emerging artists of local, regional, and national reputation. An additional showcase gallery is at 560 Main Street, open every day from 10:00 A.M. to 5:00 P.M. in spring and summer, 10:00 A.M. to 4:00 P.M. in winter.

Northcoast Artists Gallery
362 N. Main St., Fort Bragg
(707) 964–8266

This is a cooperative gallery with 22 artists showing their work. Started in 1986 with nine artists, it's now like a family, with four members of the original group still involved. Others come and go. Artists in oil paintings, ceramics, woodwork, and producers of silk-screens and fine paper products are featured. The gallery is open daily from 10:00 A.M. to 6:00 P.M.

Lake County

Nordhammer
3566 Big Valley Rd., Kelseyville
(707) 279–9116
www.nordhammer.com

Rolf Nord Kriken is a sculptor famed for his oversized bronze renderings. His works include the California Vietnam Veterans Memorial in Sacramento; the All Veterans Memorial in Cleveland; and the Danville Memorial in Danville, California. He does fine-art castings, too. Call between 9:00 A.M. and 4:30 P.M. for an appointment.

Lake County ARTS Council and Main Street Gallery
325 N. Main St., Lakeport
(707) 263–6658
www.lakecountyartscouncil.com

What would the Lake County arts scene be without this umbrella organization? Let's hope we never find out. The ARTS council has its fingers in a lot of pots. It owns and operates Main Street Gallery at the above address, giving local artists a place to show and sell their work; it hosts open-mike nights for musicians, poets, and storytellers on the first and third Thursdays of each month; it administers the Art in Public Places program, beautifying the county while giving artists a year-round forum; it showcases student artwork in vacant buildings (called Phantom Galleries) around the lake; and it compiles a Cultural Events Calendar published by the *Lake County Record-Bee* on the first Wednesday of each month. It does a lot more, too, but that should give you the basic idea.

D. Gutierrez Gallery
9445 Main St., Upper Lake
(707) 275–2005

Dick Gutierrez is an award-winning artist known for realistic renderings of pastoral scenes and still lifes. Both framed and unframed prints of his work are available here. The venue is open 10:00 A.M. to 4:00 P.M. Friday through Monday.

Parks and Recreation

Ah, the great outdoors. We have it in spades in Wine Country, from majestic inland mountains to the crashing waves of an unspoiled and awe-inspiring coastline. If you're itching to hike, bike, or otherwise become one with nature, this chapter will point you in the right direction.

First we present the primary parks and recreation areas in the four-county region, followed by separate sections on golf, bicycling, bowling, horseback riding, hunting, swimming, and tennis. There is no individual section on hiking, as almost all of the parks offer trails. While campgrounds and primitive camping sites are mentioned in these listings, more specific information may be found in our Camping chapter. If you break out in a rash at the sight of Winnebagos, or you're wanted by the California Park Service for absconding with a Chumash arrowhead in 1973, don't fret. There is plenty of recreational activity that goes beyond hiking and camping in the parks. If you still run out of things to do, turn to our On the Water chapter and read about a whole different order of activities.

Parks

Like the statewide system as a whole, the California state parks within the Wine Country offer an almost inconceivable diversity of ecosystems. While visitors to Mackerricher State Park are turning up their collars and waiting for the dense coastal fog to lift on a summer morning, folks are already in the water at Clear Lake State Park. See the grasslands of Austin Creek one day and the redwood canopy of Admiral William Standley the next, and try to convince yourself you're on the same planet. And that doesn't even address the historic parks, which are listed in the Attractions chapter.

Good news came for state park visitors in 2000: across-the-board fee reductions. Stating that he wished to make our state park system more accessible to all Californians—and out-of-state visitors, too—Gov. Gray Davis dropped day-use fees at all state parks. Camping fees were also trimmed in early 2001.

Included in this section, along with the state lands, are major regional parks and recreation areas that offer more than a lawn and a playground. You're never far from one of them. (You're probably even closer to a municipal park—consult a local map or ask around.) Deciding where to go might depend on when you'll be there. Only the inland, northern entries, such as Mendocino National Forest, are likely to be affected by winter snow. But all the

This gazebo at the park at Lakeport, overlooking Clear Lake, offers shade and a break from the beach. PHOTO: TINA LUSTER-HOBAN

When It's Time to Park It

Here are some helpful numbers and Web sites to keep in mind when considering a visit to one of the state parks.

California State Park Information
(916) 653–6995
www.cal-parks.ca.gov

ReserveAmerica Camping Reservations
(800) 444–7275
www.reserveamerica.com

ReserveAmerica Customer Service/
Cancellations
(800) 695–2269

Special Services for the Handicapped
(916) 653–8148

Caltrans Road/Weather Information
(800) 427–7623

---

parks have a chance of being wet and dreary between November and February, while spring and autumn are always safe bets. Summer takes more thought. The coastal parks and state beaches are wonderful retreats from the heat, but some of the valley parks will put you right into the oven.

Unless otherwise stated, parks are open year-round and 24 hours a day. Most regional parks have no admission charge. Pets are welcome in campgrounds and picnic areas but usually not on trails or beaches.

With millions of jittery city folks visiting California's parks each year, the campgrounds are often filled to the brim, especially between Memorial Day and Labor Day. You can make reservations up to seven months in advance by phoning ReserveAmerica (see the number subsequently listed). All major credit cards are accepted.

In Sonoma County, several regional parks with camping facilities now take reservations. Because the nearly 200 campsites at the county's four coastal campgrounds are occupied by more than 100,000 people each year, this new reservation system is a welcome change. You can call (707) 565-CAMP (2267) to reserve a camping spot at these Sonoma County regional parks: Gualala Point, Stillwater Cove, Doran, Westside, and Spring Lake. (All are profiled in this chapter and in our Camping chapter.)

Napa County

Bothe-Napa Valley State Park
Hwy. 29, 4 miles south of Calistoga
(707) 942–4575

A trail of cars crawls along Highway 29, but you can leave it behind by exploring this 1,900-acre retreat. Follow shady Ritchey Creek with its redwoods and maples, then venture deeper into terrain covered by oak, hazel, laurel, and madrone. From Coyote Peak you can gaze east into a rugged canyon—not a vineyard in sight. And in summer you can enjoy the cool, spring-fed swimming pool in the picnic area. There is a campground (see our Camping chapter) and a horse concession with guided rides. Bothe is just off Highway 29, between Calistoga and St. Helena. Parallel to the Highway runs a 1.02-mile trail that connects Bothe with the Bale Grist Mill Historic Park (see our Attractions chapter).

Robert Louis Stevenson State Park
Hwy. 29 between Calistoga and Middletown
(707) 942–4575

Between Calistoga and Middletown, at the crest of Highway 29, is Stevenson State Park. Less than a mile from the trailhead rests a memorial to the noted author, who in 1880 spent his honeymoon squatting here and weathering a long illness. (His experience wound up as the basis for *The Silverado Squatters;* see our

History chapter.) A steep 100 yards from the memorial, you will encounter a fire road/trail that winds 5 miles to the top of Mount St. Helena, offering brilliant views throughout. If you spin in a circle at the 4,343-foot summit, you'll probably be able to see the snow-capped Sierra Nevada Mountains to the east, the shining Pacific to the west, Mount Diablo to the south and, on good days, Mount Shasta, 192 miles to the north. The trail is highly exposed, so bring plenty of water and sunblock. The picnic area near the highway is lovely, although a bit noisy. Be advised there are no restrooms and parking is limited, but the vistas at the top are usually worth the trouble.

Sonoma County

Southern Sonoma

Sonoma Valley Regional Park
13630 Hwy. 12, Glen Ellen
(707) 565–2041
www.sonoma-county.org

A 162-acre spread just outside Glen Ellen, Sonoma Valley has a paved, 2-mile bicycle trail and about 5 miles of hiking trails through meadows and oak-dense terrain, plus a picnic area. Just across the Highway is Bouverie Wildflower Preserve. Open daily from sunup to sundown. Dogs must be leashed. Parking is $3.00.

Sugarloaf Ridge State Park
Adobe Canyon Rd.,
11 miles north of Sonoma on Hwy. 12
(707) 833–5712
www.parks.sonoma.net/sugarlf.html

Standing at the summit of Bald Mountain, you don't have to choose between Sonoma and Napa valleys—you can see them both at the same time. It's a startling view that is aided by identifying signs. And speaking of distant vistas, Sugarloaf recently added an observatory with the most powerful publicly accessible telescope in the state. The park as a whole is rugged and steep, an adventurous contrast to the gentle valleys below. Look for deer, gray fox, and even bobcat and mountain lion. The chaparral can get hot in the summer, but you'll be shaded (sometimes

> ## Insiders' Tip
>
> Robert Louis Stevenson State Park is a potentially dangerous place. Mountain lions and rockslides? They're nothing compared to crossing Highway 29 from the parking lot. The lot is just north of the road's crest, and vehicles tend to barrel down obliviously. Sorry, we have no secret passageways to divulge, just a piece of advice: Look both ways before crossing.

by redwoods) if you stay next to Sonoma Creek.

Because day parking is limited, the road entering Sugarloaf Ridge tends to congest with spillover traffic, so try to arrive early on weekends. The 7-mile Bald Mountain loop is the highlight of the park's numerous and well-marked trails. The park is on Adobe Canyon Road, 9 miles east of Santa Rosa or 11 miles north of Sonoma on Highway 12. (See our Camping chapter for more information.)

Helen Putnam Regional Park
411 Chileno Valley Rd.,
1 mile southwest of Petaluma
(707) 565–2041
www.sonoma-county.org

Just outside downtown Petaluma, 216-acre Helen Putnam Park has hiking, biking, and horse trails that lead to exceptional views of town and farmland. There is a playground and a picnic area with a gazebo. The park is open sunrise to sunset. From Petaluma Boulevard, go west on Western Avenue and turn left on Chileno Valley Road. Parking is $3.00. Dogs must be leashed.

Fairfield Osborn Preserve
6543 Lichau Rd., east of Cotati
(707) 795-5069
www.sonoma.edu/Org/preserve

Formerly operated by The Nature Conservancy and now owned and managed by Sonoma State University, Fairfield Osborn is a jewel of a preserve that butts up against the western slope of 2,465-foot Sonoma Mountain, east of Cotati. The 210-acre holding has 6 miles of trails through oak woodlands, meadows, and riparian forest. The preserve is not open to the public on a daily basis. However, on Saturdays and Sundays in the fall and spring, naturalists lead hikes at 10:00 A.M. and 1:00 P.M. No reservations are required.

The cost is $3.00 for adults; children 12 and under are free. Please call for directions and exact dates.

Crane Creek Regional Park
6107 Pressley Rd., east of Rohnert Park
(707) 565-2041
www.sonoma-county.org

No, Rohnert Park isn't made up entirely of Home Depots and Targets. This pleasant, 128-acre park is just east of Sonoma State University, in the foothills of the Sonoma Mountains. It has a picnic area and 3 miles of trails open to people on foot, bicycles, and horses. Follow the creek past buckeye, oak, and maple. Crane Creek is on Pressley Road; take Roberts Road east from Petaluma Hill Road. The park is open sunrise to sunset. Parking is $3.00. Dogs must be leashed. Drinking water is not available in the park.

Annadel State Park
Channel Dr., southeast of Santa Rosa
(707) 539-3911
www.parks.sonoma.net/Annadel.html

One minute you're in Santa Rosa—largest city in the Wine Country—and the next you're hiking in the solitude of a 5,000-acre parcel of undulating meadow and oak woodland. Within Annadel, you'll find one large natural marsh and one man-made lake, Ilsanjo, stocked with black bass and bluegill. One of the best hikes is the Warren Richardson-Ledson Marsh Loop, a 7.5-mile outing that takes you to Ledson with its bulrushes, cattails, and bird life. Primary trail junctions are marked, but you should think about carrying a park map to help you sort out the details. There are several picnic sites in the park, which is open 9:00 A.M. to sunset daily. Get there by taking Montgomery Drive to Channel Drive on the east side of Santa Rosa.

Spring Lake Regional Park
Summerfield Rd., Santa Rosa
(707) 539-8092
www.sonoma-county.org

Most of this 320-acre park is consumed by the central lake, popular with boaters and swimmers in the summer. Around the lake are a 2-mile bike path and a parcourse plus about 15 miles of hiking and equestrian trails. Spring Lake also has a developed campground, scads of picnic tables, and a visitor center that's open on weekends. The park is attached to the north end of Annadel State Park. The west entrance is on Newanga Avenue, off Summerfield Road in Santa Rosa; the east entrance is on Violetti Drive, off Montgomery Road.

Northern Sonoma

Lake Sonoma
Stewarts Point-Skaggs Spring Rd.,
off Dry Creek Rd.
(707) 433-9483
www.parks.sonoma.net/laktrls.html

Lake Sonoma's primary recreational offerings are detailed in our On the Water chapter. However, the 18,000-acre park that surrounds the lake is filled with possibilities of its own, including more than 40 miles of trails with views of the lake. The visitor center has Pomo Indian artifacts, and the California Department of Fish & Game operates a nearby fish hatchery (see our Kidstuff chapter). A self-guided nature trail begins at the center. Lake Sonoma also has a large developed campground and 15 primitive campgrounds around the lake (see our Camping chapter). From Geyserville, go west on Canyon Road, turn right on Dry Creek Road and, after about 3 miles, bend left onto Stewarts Point-Skaggs Spring Road.

Sonoma Coast

Doran Regional Park
Westside Regional Park
Off Hwy. 1
(707) 875-3540
www.sonoma-county.org

These two recreation areas are on the south and northwest sides, respectively, of ultraprotected Bodega Bay. The bay's water-based attractions are profiled in our On the Water chapter. But the parks also feature wavy sand dunes and, at Doran, a 2-mile stretch of beach. Each park has a campground, with 47 sites at Westside and 128 at Doran (see our Camping chapter). Each is reached from Highway 1. For Doran Park, turn west at Doran Park Road; for Westside Park, turn west at Bay Flat Road. Parking is $3.00 for day use. Dogs must be leashed.

Sonoma Coast State Beach
off Hwy. 1
(707) 875-3483
www.parks.sonoma.net/coast.html

The 100-foot bluffs, the ruinous offshore rocks and arches, the coastal scrub plateaus, the black-sand coves—it all adds up to a dramatic oceanside landscape. The park stretches 16.6 miles along the jagged coastline and offers three trails. The main attraction is Goat Rock, a large, wave-battered massif near the main parking lot. In spring, the bluffs are decorated with lupine, sea pinks, and Indian paintbrush. There is whale watching from Bodega Head and a seal colony at the mouth of the Russian River. Numerous marked and unmarked roads provide access to the beaches, some of them ending in parking lots, some not. All are found off Highway 1 between Bodega Bay and the high bluffs 4.8 miles north of Jenner—the town with the visitor center. There are two campgrounds, at Bodega Dunes and Wrights Beach. There also are two environmental camps; ask for a map at the visitor center. A final word: To get in this water, you'd have to be a lunatic, a harbor seal, or a surfer.

Stillwater Cove Regional Park
Hwy. 1, between Fort Ross and Salt Point
(707) 847-3245
www.sonoma-county.org

Even if you're not an abalone diver or a surf fisher, Stillwater Cove is a worthwhile

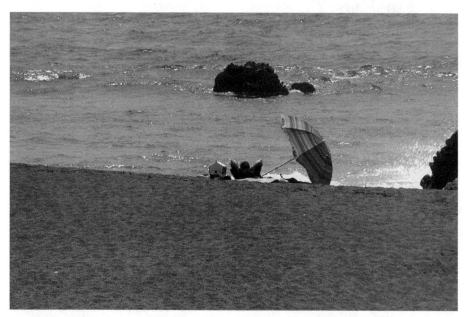

A sunbather soaks up some rays along the coast north of Portuguese Beach, part of the Sonoma Coast State Beach area. PHOTO: TINA LUSTER-HOBAN

stop. It has a picnic area and 5 miles of hiking trails amid the redwoods. It also has one developed campground with showers and flush toilets. In the park is a preserved, one-room schoolhouse from the 19th century. Day use parking is $3.00. Dogs must be leashed.

Salt Point State Park
Off Hwy. 1
(707) 847–3221
www.parks.sonoma.net/coast.html

Salt Point and neighboring Kruse Rhododendron State Reserve (see the following listing) have a little bit of something for everyone. Salt Point has about 10 miles of rocky coastline featuring sea stacks, arches, and tafoni—those eerily sculpted knobs, ribs, and honeycombs that look like they were crafted for horror movies. The inland portion of the 6,000-acre park has hiking trails through coastal brush, Bishop pine, and Douglas fir, not to mention a ridge-top pygmy forest with half-pint cypress, pine, and redwood. Salt

Insiders' Tip
A few rules to remember when encountering the California State Park system: (1) Do not disturb flowers, rocks, plants, animals, or artifacts—and, yes, putting something in your pocket is considered a disturbance; (2) Do not gather firewood; and (3) Hunting or possession of firearms (loaded or unloaded) is probably prohibited, so check with the individual park beforehand.

Point also boasts one of California's first underwater parks, Gerstle Cove Marine Reserve, a favorite for scuba divers (and for fish, which are fully protected there). The park has two campgrounds plus walk-in campsites; see our Camping chapter for more on that. It straddles Highway 1, about 16 miles north of Jenner or 18 miles south of Gualala.

Kruse Rhododendron State Reserve
Off Hwy. 1 on Kruse Ranch Rd.
(707) 847–3221
www.parks.sonoma.net/coast.html

This 317-acre reserve near Salt Point State Park was donated in 1933 by Edward P. E. Kruse, whose family raised sheep, logged, and harvested tanbark there. From April through June, the pink and violet rhododendron blossoms brighten the shady forest of fir and second-growth redwood. Five miles of hiking trails offer great opportunities to view the blooms. The reserve is off Highway 1, toward the north end of Salt Point, and is open sunup to sunset

Gualala Point Regional Park
Off Hwy. 1, 1 mile south of Gualala
(707) 785–2377
www.sonoma-county.org

Located just south of the town of Gualala, the park offers both seaside and riverside environments. Anglers show up for saltwater and freshwater fishing. Hikers enjoy 6 miles of trails. Picnickers have several site options, some with barbecue pits. And campers are greeted by a developed area in the redwoods. The visitor center is open 10:30 A.M. to 3:00 P.M. Friday through Monday. Day use parking is $3.00. Dogs must be leashed and have proof of rabies vaccination.

West County/Russian River
Ragle Ranch Regional Park
500 Ragle Rd., 1 mile north of Bodega Hwy., Sebastopol
(707) 565–2041, (707) 823–7262
www.sonoma-county.org

This 157-acre park offers the usual family-oriented facilities—baseball diamonds, playgrounds, a soccer field, a volleyball court, and picnic sites—but also claims hiking and equestrian trails through rugged oak woodlands and marshes. There is a parcourse too. Each August the park hosts the annual Gravenstein Apple Fair (see our Festivals and Annual Events chapter).The park is off Ragle Road, 1 mile north of Bodega Highway on the western perimeter of Sebastopol, and is open sunup to sunset.

Armstrong Redwoods State Reserve
Armstrong Woods Rd., near Guerneville
(707) 869–2015
www.parks.sonoma.net/Armstrng.html

In the 1870s, lumberman Col. James Armstrong saw the errors of his clear-cutting ways and preserved a large chunk of old-growth redwood forest for posterity. Today it forms the core of 805-acre Armstrong Redwoods Reserve. Don't forget to say hello to two of the most impressive specimens in the park: the 1,400-year-old Colonel Armstrong Tree and the tallest tree in the area, the 310-foot Parson Jones Tree, (named for the Colonel's son-in-law). Next to the Jones Tree is a gigantic log cross section, whose growth rings chart the course of history back to the first millennium— unfortunately, the tree had been cut by vandals in the 1970s. To get to Armstrong from Guerneville, turn north off River Road onto Armstrong Woods Road and proceed 2.2 miles. The reserve is open daily from 8:00 A.M. to one hour after sunset.

Austin Creek State Recreation Area
Armstrong Woods Rd., near Guerneville
(707) 869–2015
www.parks.sonoma.net/austin.html

Directly adjacent to Armstrong Redwoods Reserve is 5,683-acre Austin Creek State Recreation Area. Austin Creek has miles of trails that hikers have to share with horses, which often come in large groups. (Mountain bikes are allowed only on paved roads and on a 5-mile dirt road called the East Austin Creek Trail.) Keep an eye open for deer, wild turkeys, raccoons, and possibly even world-famous ceramic artists. One of the latter, Marguerite Wildenhain, lived here, and her home and workshop—Pond Farm—are within the park, though off-limits since Wildenhain's death. There is a drive-in campground and four backcountry campsites within the recreation area. To get to Austin Creek, follow the directions for Armstrong Woods and, after reaching the entrance, continue another 3.6 miles to Bullfrog Pond Campground.

Mendocino County

U.S. 101

Lake Mendocino Recreation Area
Lake Mendocino Dr., off U.S. 101
(707) 462–7581
www.spn.usace.army.mil/mendocino.html

About as pretty as man-made lakes come, Lake Mendocino is surrounded by 1,800 acres of hills, vineyards, and pear orchards. There are 18 miles of riding trails and nearly as many of hiking trails. You can also take advantage of five day-use picnic areas and three developed campgrounds. (You can reach another 20 primitive campsites with a boat.) To get there, head east on Lake Mendocino Drive from U.S. 101, just north of Ukiah, or go south on Marina Drive from Highway 20 near Calpella. (See our On the Water chapter for more details.)

Montgomery Woods State Reserve
Orr Springs Rd., north of Ukiah
(707) 937–5804
www.cal-parks.ca.gov/north/russian

Here you can find all your major appliances, from microwaves to washers and dryers. Oh, wait, that's Montgomery Ward. Montgomery Woods is an isolated sanctuary northwest of Ukiah. The 2-mile nature trail not only guides you alongside giant trees, but also takes you right through them, with steps and passageways carved into toppled specimens. You'll visit five redwood groves along Montgomery Creek, including the splendid Grubbs' Memorial Grove. You can pick up a printed guide at the beginning of the trail. Montgomery Woods has one creekside picnic site and no water. It is open sunrise to sunset. From downtown Ukiah, take Orr Springs Road northwest for about 12 miles.

Grizzly Encounters of the Wine Country Kind

As many as 10,000 grizzly bears once roamed the hills and valleys of California. Until about 1880, they lumbered about Wine Country, feeding on salmon from rivers and snatching whatever grub (grapes and grape growers included) they could get their paws on.

Though now extinct in California, the bear is not forgotten, and stories of local encounters with these powerful bruins remain among the more colorful episodes in the annals of Wine Country's pioneer past. One particularly dramatic and somewhat farcical story involved a millman named Andy Stump and a rather protective mother bear.

The encounter—as described in *History of Sonoma County* by Ernest Latimer Finley—took place in the fall of 1852 in the vicinity of the coastal town of Bodega. A local sawmill employee named West was believed to have murdered a coworker for his gold, but no one could prove it with certainty. One day an argument broke out between West and Andy Stump, and in the heat of their exchange Andy accused West of the murder and threatened to avenge the crime right there. Rather than denying the charge, West turned pale, panicked, and ran.

Andy and the other mill workers ran after West, believing the man had incriminated himself by choosing to flee. Andy stayed hard on West's heels, chasing him through the mill yard, into the woods, and down a steep embankment thick with heavy underbrush. West did not see the small grizzly cub hiding among the thickets and accidentally kicked it as he passed, causing it to let out a painful yelp. Andy, in the meantime, had fallen and was tumbling down the ravine. He did not see the mother bear that lay in his path until he landed right on top of it, at the precise moment the bear started to charge West in defense of her cub.

What happened next is almost too incredible to be true. Her paternal instincts fully engaged, the bear lunged at West as if Andy—who was still recovering from his tumble and further shocked by where he had landed—wasn't there. The latter held on tight, fearing, as Finley describes, that "his brains would be dashed out against trees or rocks if he let go."

As the story goes, West was able to avoid capture for several hundred yards, as the weight of a rider slowed the bear some. Though it did not last more than a few minutes, the pursuit was certainly extraordinary. Finley describes it as, "such a chase as perhaps has never been duplicated in history—a man . . . fleeing for life from an angry she-bear, to the hair of whose back clung another man . . . with garments ripped in shreds and face and limbs cut and scratched by twigs and brambles."

As the bear raced by a section of stream, Andy saw his chance, leaping off the animal and into a deep pool almost 20 feet below. He stayed in the stream until he was sure that the bear had continued on and had not decided to come back looking for him. Eventually, he crawled up the bank and limped back to the mill.

A search party later found West's mangled body not far from where Andy had made his exit. Another body was found near the bear's den; it was the coworker that West was believed to have murdered. As it turned out, the bear had also been feasting on the coworker's flesh. However, the man's neck had also been cut by a razor. This led everyone to conclude that West had indeed robbed and killed the man first, leaving his body for the bear to consume.

Admiral William Standley State Recreation Area
Branscomb Rd., off U.S. 101,
14 miles west of Laytonville
(707) 247-3318
www.cal-parks.ca.gov/north/ncrd/
awssra.htm
Admiral Standley's namesake is small (45 acres), hard to get to, and rarely crowded. It's a beautiful piece of forest, with virgin redwoods interspersed among Douglas firs, madrone, rhododendron, and mushrooms. It is also a popular salmon and steelhead fishing spot. However, there are no trails so don't wander far from the parking area. From U.S. 101 in Laytonville, turn left on Branscomb Road, and drive 12 miles. The recreation area is set on either side of the road, and signs can be difficult to spot. It is open sunup to sundown.

Standish-Hickey State Recreation Area
U.S. 101, 1 mile north of Leggett
(707) 925-6482
www.cal-parks.ca.gov/north/ncrd/
shsra.html

This sizable park presents your basic gigantic redwoods plus access to the south fork of the Eel River. The Big Tree Loop starts at Redwood campground and ends near Miles Standish Tree, a 225-foot, 1,200-year-old giant that towers over its second-growth neighbors. Still visible on its side are the ax marks delivered—as the legend goes—by a 1930s evangelist who vowed to chop down the biggest tree he could find. Miles Standish lives on, while the evangelist has gone to that great lumber mill in the sky. In summer it's swimming that lures most visitors. The Eel is punctuated with deep pools formed by rock outcrops. The best is at the tail end of a wide bend, where the Big Tree Loop crosses the river. The pool is nearly 20 feet deep, with a sandy floor. There is no shade, so bring sunscreen and a hat. Standish-Hickey has three campgrounds and a picnic area.

Smith Redwoods State Reserve
U.S. 101, 4 miles north of Leggett
(707) 247-3318
www.cal-parks.ca.gov/north/ncrd/srsr.htm
Little more than a roadside attraction, this 665-acre park has no trails or picnic facili-

ties. It does, however, give you an up-close encounter with some of the largest trees in the world. Don't be shy, big fella, give that tree a hug. You can walk through two stumps. And if you're in need of a dunk, both a 60-foot waterfall (across the Highway) and the South Fork of the Eel River are close at hand. It is open sunup to sundown.

Highway 128
Mailliard Redwoods State Reserve
Fish Rock Rd., off Hwy. 128
(707) 937-5804
www.mcn.org/1/mendoparks/maill.htm
There isn't much here for hikers or bikers, but if you're in the area, your eyes will appreciate the detour. Mailliard has 242 acres of virgin and second-growth redwoods along the headwaters of Garcia River. You can reach the park from Highway 128, 7.3 miles east of Boonville. Turn south on Fish Rock Road and proceed about 3 miles. There is one picnic area nearly a mile into the park. Open sunrise to sunset.

Hendy Woods State Park
Philo-Greenwood Rd., off Hwy. 128
(707) 895-3141
www.cal-parks.ca.gov/north/russian/
mendo/hwsp148.htm
There are campsites (see our Camping chapter), a picnic area, and trails for hikers, mountain bikers, and equestrians. The Gentle Giants All-Access Trail is a surfaced path that accesses Big Hendy, Anderson Valley's last extensive grove of old-growth coastal redwoods. Another short trail leads to the hermit hut, a partially collapsed, thatched-roof lean-to that the Boonville Hermit used as his abode from the end of World War II (when he jumped his Russian ship) until he died in 1981. To get to Hendy Woods, take Highway 128 2.8 miles west of Philo and turn south on Philo-Greenwood Road.

Navarro River Redwoods
Hwy. 128, between Navarro and Hwy. 1
(707) 937-5804
www.cal-parks.ca.gov/north/russian/
mendo/nrrsp144.htm

Because this is America, you get to enjoy the beauty of Navarro River without leaving your rental car. The park straddles Highway 128 between Navarro and the coast, and the highway basically shadows the river. It's a shady corridor of second-growth redwoods, alders, and tan oak. There are plenty of turnouts if you want a breath of fresh air or a short stroll. In the fall, you'll likely see people fishing for steelhead. The river also has one overnight campground (see our Camping chapter).

Mendocino Coast

Schooner Gulch
Off Hwy. 1, 3.5 miles south of Point Arena
(707) 937–5804
www.cal-parks.ca.gov/north/russian/ mendo/sgsb164.htm

This park contains two beaches, separated by a bulging headland. The north lobe is Bowling Ball Beach, named for the perfectly spherical boulders revealed at low tide. (It might be worth it to consult a tide chart before visiting.) The cliffs abutting this mile-long strand of hard-packed sand are misshapen and interesting. The south lobe is Schooner Gulch, which is rockier and preferred by fishermen. The actual gulch feeds into the sea amidst a jumble of logs. There is no water in the park, so bring your own. It's open sunrise to sunset.

Manchester State Beach
Kinney Rd., off Hwy. 1
(707) 937–5804
www.cal-parks.ca.gov/north/russian/ mendo/msp147.htm

Manchester's diverse topography encompasses rocky shore, dunes (both grassy and bald), marshes, a lagoon, and a coastal plain. It's a place where anglers, bird-watchers, and rowdy kids can find common ground. The avian wealth includes northern harriers, tundra swans, ducks, herons, and pelicans. The drift-log shelters along the 5 miles of beach attest to the relentless winds that buffet the area. There is a primitive campground (see our Camping chapter) and hiking trails, including the 5-mile Beach-Inland Loop. To reach Manchester from Highway 1, turn west onto Kinney Road and drive a little more than a half-mile.

Greenwood Creek State Beach
Hwy. 1, near Elk
(707) 937–5804
www.mcn.org/1/mendoparks/greenwd.htm

This park is quite small on the horizontal scale, but impressive on the vertical—it encompasses both the gravelly beach and the overlooking bluff, some 150 feet above. Most of the picnic sites are up top. From the shore you can see the three rock islands that punctuate the cove and watch for the bobbing heads of harbor seals. Greenwood Creek is west of Highway 1, adjacent to the town of Elk. The visitor center is Elk's original mill office (see our Attractions chapter). Greenwood Creek State Beach is open sunrise to sunset.

Van Damme State Park
Hwy. 1, 2.5 miles south of Mendocino
(707) 937–5804
www.cal-parks.ca.gov/north/russian/ mendo/vdsp142.htm

Don't worry, you aren't likely to be bothered by aggressive action-adventure heroes in this fascinating park. What you will get is a smorgasbord of redwoods,

> ## Insiders' Tip
> Beware the western black-legged tick: Though the odds are slim of catching Lyme disease in Northern California, it has been known to happen. *Ixodes pacificus* is the bearer of the disease in this neck of the woods, so check yourself for ticks after hiking through grass or forests.

beach, underwater bounty, swamp, and pygmy trees. The Fern Canyon Trail is a 4.9-mile meander through a dark, cool fern forest. Separate mini-trails take you to the pygmy forest, with its 4-foot pines and cypresses, and a bog. Hikers and bikers share some trails, but not all. If you get claustrophobic in the woods, take a kayak tour of the small cove accessible at the Van Damme beach parking lot.

Van Damme has both developed campgrounds and hike-in tent sites, as discussed in our Camping chapter. It has a picnic area on the beach and an undersea preserve. And don't miss the re-created surge channel at the visitor center. The park is 2.5 miles south of Mendocino on Highway 1—turn east for the main park, west for the beach.

Mendocino Headlands State Park
Main St., Mendocino
(707) 937-5804
www.cal-parks.ca.gov/north/russian/
mendo/mhsp158.htm

This is the town of Mendocino's wraparound park on the bluffs, offering spectacular views of the sea on all sides. Spring brings wildflowers, winter ushers migrating gray whales, and summer draws sunbathers and hardy swimmers to Big River Beach, just south of the headlands. The miles of blowholes, arches, and craggy stacks are there year-round. There is a picnic area along Heeser Drive at the north end of town; in town is the Ford House Visitor Center with its fine historical displays. The Headlands Trail, 6 miles round-trip, skirts the edges of the bluffs. The park is open sunrise to sunset.

Russian Gulch State Park
Off Hwy. 1, 2 miles north of Mendocino
(707) 937-5804
www.cal-parks.ca.gov/north/russian/
mendo/rgsp141.htm

Here you have the option of walking along the coast, where waves crash like giant cymbals, or wandering through the serenity of the forest. The Headland Trail offers two sideshow oddities: a blowhole fed by a sea cave and an inland punchbowl, connected to the sea by another hid-

den cave. The Fern Canyon Trail, meanwhile, takes you alongside Russian Gulch to a delicate, 36-foot waterfall. It's a 6-mile round-trip stroll through alder, California laurel, redwood and, of course, ferns. The park has campsites (see our Camping chapter) and a picnic area.

Caspar Headlands State Beach and Reserve
Point Cabrillo Dr., off Hwy. 1, Caspar
(707) 937-5804
www.cal-parks.ca.gov/north/russian/
mendo/chsb161.htm

These twin holdings are small (less than 5 acres between them) and highly regulated. You can visit the bluff-top reserve, with its far-reaching views—only with a permit, obtainable at the Mendocino District Office, 2 miles north of Mendocino. Get a

A stoic face carved into a stump looks out to sea from Mendocino Headlands State Park. PHOTO: JOHN NAGIECKI

map there, too, as the reserve interlocks with a private housing development, and it's easy to trespass. The beach, about a quarter-mile long, opens onto a square bay. It's popular with swimmers, divers, and anglers. This is no place for the meek. Caspar Headlands has no toilets, no picnic tables, and no water. Undeterred? From Highway 1 in Caspar, turn west on Point Cabrillo Drive. The park is open sunrise to sunset.

Jug Handle State Reserve
Off Hwy. 1, just north of Caspar
(707) 937–5804
www.cal-parks.ca.gov/north/russian/
mendo/jhsr154.htm

This is another coastal park that gives you surf-and-turf options. One trail roams the soaring headlands, with views of Jug Handle Bay to the north and a similar inlet to the south. Look for sea stacks and an arch. The Ecological Staircase Trail is a 5-mile, round-trip tour of three marine terraces—a geologic showcase that displays about 250,000 years of elemental activity. The first terrace is meadow-transition habitat, the second is a mixed conifer forest, and the third is redwood-Douglas fir complex. At the end of the line, for no extra charge, is a pygmy forest. The trails are for hikers only, and visitors should bring their own water. Jug Handle is open sunup to sundown.

Jackson State Forest
State Department of Forestry,
802 N. Main St., Fort Bragg
(707) 964–5674

Sprawling between Willits and the coast in the vicinity of Highway 20, this state holding has 50,000 acres of oak, pine, and redwood, not to mention a pygmy forest. There are 25 miles of fire road and two other trails suitable as footpaths. It's a mixed bag—as state forests often are—with some pristine areas and others that have been logged or mined. Jackson has campgrounds in two areas. One is near the hamlet of Dunlap, about halfway between Willits and the coast. The other, highlighted in our Camping chapter, is about 6 miles east of Highway 1.

Mackerricher State Park
West of Hwy. 1,
3 miles north of Fort Bragg
(707) 937–5804
www.mcn.org/1/mendoparks/macker.htm

Mackerricher is a prime slice of Northern California coast, with 8 miles of beach, large dunes, grassy headlands, and even freshwater Lake Cleone. Gray whales migrate offshore between December and March, and humans migrate to the headlands to watch them. If you're into cetacean anatomy, a 30-foot gray whale skeleton lies near the ranger station, just beyond the main entrance. The footpaths are varied. The Laguna Trail circles the lake and its marshy border. The Seal Point Trail leads to a (harbor) Seal Watching Station. And the Haul Road Bicycle Route is a one-time logging road that runs the length of the park, about 7 miles. It's closed to motorized vehicles and so is popular with cyclists and runners. Of course, you can simply walk down the beach for miles if you prefer. Mackerricher has two campgrounds (see our Camping chapter) and several picnic areas. The main entrance is 3 miles north of Fort Bragg, just west of Highway 1. The Pudding Creek Day Area is only a half-mile north of Fort Bragg.

Westport-Union Landing State Beach
Off Hwy. 1, just north of Westport
(707) 937–5804
www.cal-parks.ca.gov/north/russian/
mendo/wulsb150.htm

North of the town of Westport is a series of four oceanside bluffs, separated by creek canyons and interspersed with beaches. Together they form this skinny park, with its 50-foot cliffs and craggy shoreline. It's a favorite haunt for storm-watchers, who can practically feel the spray from the angry waves. Anglers come for spawning surf smelt in spring and summer. Pete's Beach and the sand below Abalone Point are fun to explore, but they don't offer much wiggle room, so watch out for sleeper waves—large, forceful waves that appear without warning. Westport-Union Landing has several access points off Highway 1, between a quarter-mile and 4 miles north of Westport. It offers open, grassy campsites but no water.

Sinkyone Wilderness State Park
County Rd. 431, west of Leggett
(707) 986-7711
www.cal-parks.ca.gov/north/ncrd/
swsp.htm

Wonder what the Mendocino Coast looked like before a certain bipedal mammal clogged up the scenery? Here's your answer. The Sinkyone Wilderness is part of the Lost Coast, a once-busy stretch of shoreline that has been isolated by its lack of contact with major roads. There are two entrances to the park, one at the south end and another at the north. Between them lies a long expanse of unadulterated nature: forested ridges, rugged coast, black-sand beaches, and riparian ecosystem. The Needle Rock Visitor Center is in a restored, turn-of-the-century ranch house; nearby is a short trail to Needle Rock Beach. There is a drive-in campground at Usal Creek (the south entrance) and walk-in sites near Bear Harbor in the north. To get to Usal Creek, follow Highway 1 west from Leggett and, 14 miles later, turn right on County Road 431 and proceed 5.5 miles. To get to Needle Rock, make your way to Redway, 2.5 miles west of Garberville and U.S. 101. Turn south on Briceland Road and continue past Whitethorn; the road turns to gravel after 17 miles. Then, it's 7.2 miles to the visitor center.

Lake County

Boggs Mountain Demonstration
State Forest
Off Hwy. 175,
1 mile north of Cobb
(707) 928–4378

Here's what pine trees do: They sway gently in the breeze and drop needles on your head. There, now you don't need a demonstration. You might want to visit anyway, to get a sample of the 3,493 acres of oak, Douglas fir, and ponderosa pine—it's 97 percent forest. There are 14 miles of trails for two legs, four legs, or two wheels,

and one developed campground. The main entrance is at the California Forest Service heliport.

Clear Lake State Park
Soda Bay Rd., near Kelseyville
(707) 279–4293

It seems that the entire 100 miles of Clear Lake shoreline are devoted to leisure and recreation, and this 565-acre park is no exception. The visitor center, alongside Kelsey Creek Diversion, is a good place to start, with its broad porches and aquarium full of Clear Lake citizens. There is a boat launch and four campgrounds; some of the sites are shaded or next to the water (see our Camping chapter). There is a pleasant, gravel-beach swimming area facing Dorn Cove. When you've had enough splashing, take the Indian Nature Trail, featuring 20 interpretive stations, or the Dorn Trail, a 1.5-mile loop that offers some nice views of the water. Clear Lake State Park is on the southwest shore of the lake. Turn north off Highway 29 in Kelseyville and follow the signs for the park. Three miles thereafter, you'll turn right on Soda Bay Road.

Cow Mountain Recreation Area
Scott Creek Rd.,
off Hwy. 29 in Lakeport
(707) 468–4000

This sprawling domain, administered by the federal Bureau of Land Management (BLM), has one leg in Mendocino County and another in Lake County, with the bulk of its 50,000 acres in Lake. It features about 40 miles of hiking, biking, and equestrian trails that weave in and out of chaparral, oak scrubland, and pine forest. It also has five small, primitive campgrounds. As in most BLM holdings, seasonal hunting is permitted, so don't wear that cap with the foam antlers. There is even a shooting range in the area, near Willow Creek Recreation Site. Nearly half of Cow Mountain's southern portion is accessible to off-highway vehicles. There are two main entryways into the park: From U.S. 101 in Ukiah, take Mill Creek Road east; or from Highway 29 in Lakeport, take Scott Creek Road west.

Mendocino National Forest
(707) 983–6118

If we tried to present a detailed account of the options here, the book would be called "Insiders' Guide to Mendocino National Forest." This is an immense, million-acre tract of terrain in the North Coast Mountain Range that encompasses almost all of the upper half of Lake County and the northeast tip of Mendocino County, not to mention parts of Glenn, Tehama, and Trinity Counties. The forest boasts two wilderness areas (closed to motorized vehicles), 2,000-acre Lake Pillsbury, several smaller lakes, and various tributaries of the Eel River. Trails? Yes, more than 160 miles, including off-highway vehicle paths near Upper Lake and Stoneyford. Campgrounds? Ten developed sites (see our Camping chapter) and numerous primitive camps. There are many routes into the forest. Perhaps the most prominent is Elk Mountain Road, which heads north from the town of Upper Lake. About a mile north of Upper Lake is a ranger station dispensing maps and advice. Another station is on Highway 162, where the route name changes from Covelo Road to Mendocino

Golf

The Wine Country isn't a hacker's mecca in the way of a Scottsdale or a Myrtle Beach. On the other hand, the mild climate and the stunning terrain do lend themselves to the links, especially for those who consider walking from fairway to green a form of exercise.

The facilities in our coverage area range from nine-hole pitch-and-putts to manicured, PGA-caliber courses. All of them have some sort of refreshment option—either a snack bar or a full-service restaurant. And practically all of them have pro shops where you can stock anything you forgot to pack. Following are some basic descriptions of the public courses; private clubs (with one major exception that does facilitate play by nonmembers) are not included. Like airfares, greens fees are always fluctuating, but we give you some general figures in the listings.

Napa County

Silverado Country Club & Resort
1600 Atlas Peak Rd., Napa
(707) 257–0200, (800) 362–4727
www.silveradoresort.com

Although part of a private club, the two 18-hole championship courses at beautiful Silverado—designed by Robert Trent Jones Jr. and opened in 1965—can be accessed by Wine Country visitors. Guests at the Silverado resort (see our Spas and Resorts chapter) receive extended golfing privileges, and reciprocal arrangements with selected clubs around the country are also honored. Some allowances are made for nonguests who make arrangements two days in advance. (In-house guests play for $140.) Call to find out more, and ask about special room-and-golf packages too.

The club hosts the annual Beringer (formerly Transamerica) Senior Golf Tournament, where you might find a celebrity or two asking if they can play through. For instance, former PGA Player of the Year and NBC golf analyst Johnny Miller used to be the touring pro at Silverado and still plays the courses often. The north course is 6700 yards; the south course is 6500 yards.

Napa Golf Course at Kennedy Park
2295 Streblow Dr., Napa
(707) 255-4333
www.playnapa.com

With John F. Kennedy Memorial Regional Park and the Napa River to the west and the open spaces of Napa Valley College to the north, this is a nicely placed 18-hole, par 72 course that runs about 6730 yards. The cost is $30 during the week, $40 on weekends for nonresidents; $17 on weekdays and $24 on weekends for locals. A cart is an additional $23. Ask about the reduced senior rates. Napa Golf Club is easy to walk but quite difficult to shoot. This is a challenging course.

Chardonnay Golf Club
2555 Jamieson Canyon Rd., Napa
(707) 257-1900, (800) 788-0136
www.chardonnaygolfclub.com

Southeast of Napa, where the cool breezes of San Pablo Bay keep the terrain lush and green, Chardonnay offers a public 18-hole, par 72, 6816-yard course called The Vineyards. The club also has a private course called The Club Shakespeare, a qualifying site for the 1998 U.S. Open. Rates for The Vineyards range from $60 to $90, depending on the season, and that includes a cart. There is a grass driving range, a bar and grill (Sandtrap), and tournament and banquet facilities. And only in Napa Valley would you have to abide by the rule, "Vineyards are out of bounds." Jamieson Canyon Road is another name for Highway 12 between Highway 29 and I-80. Proper golf attire is required.

Vintners Golf Club
7901 Solano Ave., Yountville
(707) 944-1992
www.vintnersgolfclub.com

Napa County's newest golfing attraction is a nine-hole course with true, fast greens

and a backdrop of the historic Veterans Home of California buildings. Total yardage is 2700; par is 34. Vintners is full of amenities, including a clubhouse that serves breakfast, lunch, and appetizers (including alcohol), and a full pro shop. A lighted, covered, 36-stall driving range has been joined by a smaller grass range. Here are your greens fees: $18 for 9 holes and $24 for 18 holes during the week; $28 for 9 holes and $36 for 18 holes on Saturday and Sunday. Rent an electric cart for 9 holes ($16) or 18 ($24).

Mount St. Helena Golf Course
Napa County Fairgrounds,
1435 N. Oak St., Calistoga
(707) 942-9966

The course itself is modest—nothing special, one might go so far as to say—but Calistoga's scenic situation, within a horseshoe toss of rugged hills, makes this a fine place to spend a few hours. Play all day for $12 during the week, $18 on weekends. After 4:00 P.M. the price dips to $7.00 during the week and $10.00 on weekends. The nine-hole course is 2748 yards and par 34 for men, 2647 yards and par 35 for "ladies," as they say in the golf world.

Aetna Springs Golf Course
1600 Aetna Springs Rd., Pope Valley
(707) 965-2115, (800) 675-2115
www.aetnasprings.com

Depending on your definition of a golf course, this might be the oldest west of the Mississippi. Evidence indicates they were aiming for four holes at Aetna Springs as early as 1891. Today, it's a modest nine-hole course (par 35, 2690 yards) far off the beaten track on 672 acres, but it's worth every minute of drive time. Ancient oak trees and rocky streams add not only to the scenery, but also to the challenges of the course. And then there is all that history. Aetna Springs Resort was once a retreat for the mighty, and it later was purchased by the Unification Church. Fees are only $16 for 18 holes during the week ($10 for students and seniors) and $22 on weekends. Carts are $18. From Angwin, go north on Howell Mountain Road, then turn left on

Pope Valley Road. Proceed about 4 miles to the Aetna Springs sign.

Sonoma County

Sonoma Mission Inn Golf Club
17700 Arnold Dr., Sonoma
(707) 996–0300
www.sonomagolfclub.com

Part of the Sonoma Mission Inn, the clubhouse is strictly modern, but Sonoma Golf Club dates back to 1926. It was designed by Sam Whiting and Willie Watson, the same duo that laid out the lake course at the Olympic Club in San Francisco, and it is beautiful. The facility has 83 sand bunkers, three lakes, and surrounding views of the Mayacmas Mountains. The course plays 6583 yards from the regular tees. Soft spikes are mandatory, as are collared shirts and slacks. The tab is $60 to $80 during the week, $70 to $100 on Friday and on weekends. That price does not include a cart.

Los Arroyos Golf Course
5000 Stage Gulch Rd., Sonoma
(707) 938–8835

This nine-hole course is just southwest of Sonoma, adjacent to Highway 116. Weekend greens fees are $12 for 9 holes and $17 for 18. Play during the week for $10 or $15. Pull-carts are $2.00 and Los Arroyos has a snack bar.

Adobe Creek Golf & Country Club
1901 Frates Rd., Petaluma
(707) 765–3000
www.webfairway.com/adobecreek

Adobe Creek, designed by Robert Trent Jones Jr., is an 18-hole, par 72, 6986-yard course on the southeast edge of Petaluma (just south of Petaluma Adobe State Historic Park). It has a grass driving range, and greens fees range from $22 to $57 depending on time of the week and day. Carts are $13 to $26. Collared shirts and soft spikes are mandatory.

Rooster Run Golf Club
2301 E. Washington St., Petaluma
(707) 778–1211
www.roosterrun.com

Rooster Run opened in the spring of 1998 and has since become the Wine Country's supreme public-golf bargain. Situated across the street from Petaluma Airport, the course is subject to the same afternoon winds that bedevil its neighbor, Adobe Creek Golf Course. The front nine includes an island green on the par-3 number 6. You'll need an oasis after number 5—rated the course's most difficult. Rooster Run management likes to boast that the course includes "the toughest four finishing holes in Northern California golf." Believe it. Regular rates are $28 Monday through Thursday, $34 Friday and $45 on weekends; the corresponding rates for certified Petaluma residents are $22, $25, and $36. Seniors play for $15 Monday through Wednesday. Juniors pay $10 after 2:30 P.M. Monday through Thursday.

Mountain Shadows Golf Resort
100 Golf Course Dr., Rohnert Park
(707) 584–7766
www.webfairway.com/mountainshadows

Mountain Shadows, just off U.S. 101 in Rohnert Park, has two championship courses and a spacious practice range. The 6675-yard North Course is scenic and friendly; the 6720-yard South Course is more challenging, with plenty of trees to foil your plans. This course is undergoing major renovation, with the South course scheduled to reopen in spring 2002 and the North course in 2003. Both are par 72. The fee ranges from $25 to $35, depending on tee time and course.

Sonoma Fairgrounds Golf Center
1350 Bennett Valley Rd., Santa Rosa
(707) 577–0755
www.empiregolf.com

This user-friendly facility sits inside the racetrack at the Sonoma County Fairgrounds. It's right off Highway 12, just east of U.S. 101, and it offers practice greens and a lighted driving range in case you feel like swinging after sundown. The nine-hole, par 30 executive course costs between $9.00 and $12.00, depending on tee time.

Bennett Valley Golf Course
3330 Yulupa Ave., Santa Rosa
(707) 528-3673

Bennett Valley is the perfect place for a golf course, with the peaks of Annadel State Park forming a backdrop to the east. It's an 18-hole, par 72 course that runs 6600 yards. You'll pay $25 on weekends, $18 during the week if you're an out-of-towner; residents pay $18 and $14. A cart costs an additional $22. Bennett Valley has a snack bar/restaurant.

The Oakmont Golf Club
7025 Oakmont Dr., Santa Rosa
(707) 539-0415 (West Course),
(707) 538-2454 (East Course)

This is one of the Santa Rosa area's premier facilities, with two 18-hole courses: the championship, par 72 West Course and the executive, par 63 East Course. Oakmont is just southeast of town, off Highway 12 where it starts to bend down toward the Valley of the Moon. Prices range from $30 to $45. Carts are $26 each. You can choose between a snack bar and a sit-down restaurant. PGA director of golf Jeff Pace is the resident expert.

Wikiup Golf Course
5001 Carriage Ln., Wikiup
(707) 546-8787
www.mygolf.com/golf/courses/1827#GI

Wikiup is a cul-de-sac neighborhood just north of Santa Rosa, and the community pretty much revolves around the nine-hole, par 29 executive golf course. Weekday green fees are $11 for 9 holes, $16 for 18; on Saturday and Sunday it's $14 for 9 and $21 for 18.

Windsor Golf Club
6555 Skylane Blvd., Windsor
(707) 838-7888
www.windsorgolf.com

This is a challenging and well-maintained facility—a par 72, 6169-yard championship course—that has hosted the Nike Tour on several occasions. Nontournament greens fees are $30 to $49. Twilight (after 2:00 p.m.) rates are several bucks less. A full cart will cost you $22 or $16 after 2:00 P.M. Windsor has a restaurant and a snack bar,

and golf lessons are available. Because of the frequency of tournaments, call in advance for reservations.

Healdsburg Tayman Park Golf Course
927 S. Fitch Mtn. Rd., Healdsburg
(707) 433-4275
www.taymanparkgolf.com

At the east edge of central Healdsburg, about a quarter-mile from one stretch of the Russian River and a half-mile from another, this course is a par 70 nine-holer. It costs $11 for 9 holes, $19 for 18 holes. Carts are $5.00 each per person, per nine holes. It's also known as Tayman Park Golf Course. This property recently underwent some upgrading.

Bodega Harbour Golf Links
21301 Heron Dr., Bodega Bay
(707) 875-3538
www.bodegaharbourgolf.com

This seaside course offers wonderful salty breezes and ocean sparkle. Designed by Robert Trent Jones Jr., Bodega Harbour has rolling fairways, cavernous pot bunkers, native coastal rough, and marshlands. (Remember, players are prohibited from entering the marsh on holes 16, 17, and 18.) The 18th has been voted the best finishing hole in Northern California. The par is 70, and the yardage measures 5685 from the white tees. Greens fees are $60 Monday through Thursday, $70 on Friday, and $90 on Saturday and Sunday (all rates include cart rental). The clubhouse restaurant serves lunch daily, dinner on Friday and Saturday nights, and breakfast on weekend mornings. Bodega Harbour Golf Links has golf-and-lodging packages in conjunction with several hotels in Bodega Bay and with vacation rental agencies that offer private homes bordering the course. Contact Bodega Harbour for more information.

Sebastopol Golf Course
2881 Scott's Right-of-Way, Sebastopol
(707) 823-9852

This is your one and only option in Sebastopol. It's a 9-hole, par 66 for 18 holes course. Weekdays you'll pay $10 for 9 holes, $18 for 18 holes. Carts are $10 for 9 holes; $15 for 18.

Northwood Golf Course
19400 Hwy. 116, Monte Rio
(707) 865–1116
www.northwoodgolf.com

Set in an elbow of the Russian River and surrounded by redwood trees, this is one of the more beautiful Wine Country courses. The wind is almost always gentle and the temperatures are moderated by the tall trees. Northwood is a par 36, nine-hole course. During the week it is $24 for 18 holes, $16 for 9; on weekends it's $37 for 18 holes, $20 for 9. Twilight rates ($15 on Saturday and Sunday, $12 on weekdays) are in effect after 3:00 P.M.

Mendocino County

Ukiah Municipal Golf Course
599 Park Blvd., Ukiah
(707) 467–2832

Mendocino County's biggest city has its only 18-hole golf course, par 70 Ukiah Municipal. The 5850-yard course is known to be fairly forgiving. Greens fees vary, but generally work out to $18 on weekdays, $21 on weekends. Add $20 if you want a cart. Ukiah Municipal has a snack bar.

Little River Inn
7751 Hwy. 1, Little River
(707) 937–5667
www.littleriverinn.com/amenitys.html#golf

The Inn, a popular vacation retreat (see our Spas and Resorts chapter), also has a nine-hole, par 35 golf course. Actually, it has an 11-hole course, so if you play 18 holes (par 71, 5458 yards) you can experience two new greens. There is a driving range (off mats, not grass) and a putting green. The rates for nine holes are $20 on weekdays, $30 on weekends. For 18 holes you pay $30 during the week, $35 on weekends. Carts are $16 for 9 holes, $24 for 18 holes.

Lake County

Cobb Meadows Golf Course
16451 Golf Rd., Cobb
(707) 928–5276

In the heart of the Boggs Mountain State Forest is this rarefied nine-hole, 2250-yard course with all par 3 and 4 holes. The layout is relatively level, despite the surrounding peaks. The fees are $12 for 9 holes, $17 for 18 during the week, and $14 and $20, respectively, on weekends. Renting a cart for 9 holes will cost you $12, while the fee for 18 holes is $20. The restaurant generally is open for dinner Thursday through Sunday.

Adams Springs Golf Course
14347 Snead Ct., Loch Lomond
(707) 928–9992

Adams Springs is just north of Boggs Mountain State Forest. It's a challenging par 34, nine-hole course set among whispering pines (as if there were any other kind of pine), but the wide fairways are forgiving. You'll pay $10 for 9 holes, $16 for 18 during the week, and $14 and $20, respectively, on weekends. Total yardage for Adams Springs is 2640. There is a snack bar, and carts rent for $20 for 18 holes.

Clear Lake Riviera Golf Course
10200 Fairway Dr., Clear Lake Riviera
(707) 277–7129

Not even whizzing golf balls can foul the view at Clear Lake Riviera. To the west is 4,200-foot Mount Konocti, to the north a broad vista of the lake. It's a hilly, par 36, nine-hole course with two sets of tees and fine views, complemented by a putting green and an above-average dining room. The cost: $19 for 9 holes, $25 for 18 during the week, and $24 and $33, respectively, on weekends. Those prices included cart rental.

Buckingham Golf and Country Club
2855 E. Lake Dr., Kelseyville
(707) 279–4863

On a thumb that pokes into Clear Lake, with four fairways encircling the much smaller body of Little Borax Lake, is Buckingham Golf Course, a nine-hole, par 36 facility with tight fairways and plenty of shade. The weekday fees for the 3159-yard course are $15 for 9 holes or $22 for 18; it's $18 or $26 on weekends. Cart rental is $9.00 per person for 9 holes, $14.00 for 18. There is a snack bar on the course and a restaurant in the clubhouse (look for the Tee Room in our Restaurants chapter).

Hidden Valley Lake Golf Club
19210 Hartman Rd., Hidden Valley Lake
(707) 987–3035
www.hiddenvalleylakegc.com
This is Lake County's only 18-hole golf course, a par 72 with a relatively flat and open front 9 and a back 9 that winds through the hills and nuzzles the hefty homes of the Hidden Valley subdivision. There is a driving range and a putting green. Greens fees are $35 during the week and $45 on weekends, including a cart. Knock off a few bucks for twilight play after 2:00 P.M. The scene includes a sit-down restaurant and golf lessons.

Bicycle Rentals

Napa County

Bicycle Trax
796 Soscol Ave., Napa
(707) 258–TRAX

Napa Valley Bike Tours & Rentals
4080 Byway East, Napa
(707) 255–3377

St. Helena Cyclery
1156 Main St., St. Helena
(707) 963–7736

Palisades Mountain Sport
1330B Gerard St., Calistoga
(707) 942–9687

Getaway Bike Shop
1117 Lincoln Ave., Calistoga
(707) 942–0332, (800) 499–BIKE

Sonoma County

Sonoma Valley Cyclery
20093 Broadway, Sonoma
(707) 935–3377

The Goodtime Bicycle Company
18503 Hwy. 12, Sonoma
(707) 938–0453

The Bicycle Factory
110 Kentucky St., Petaluma
(707) 763–7515;
195 N. Main St., Sebastopol,
(707) 829–1880

Rincon Cyclery
4927 Sonoma Hwy., Ste. H, Santa Rosa
(707) 538–0868, (800) 965–BIKE

Spoke Folk Cyclery
201 Center St., Healdsburg
(707) 433–7171

Mendocino County

Catch a Canoe & Bicycles Too
Hwy. 1 and Comptche-Ukiah Rd.,
Mendocino
(707) 937–0273, (800) 320–BIKE

Fort Bragg Cyclery
579 S. Franklin St., Fort Bragg
(707) 964–3509

Lake County

The Bicycle Rack
302 N. Main St., Lakeport
(707) 263–1200

Bowling

Lest we be accused of catering to elitist ideals of recreation, herein is a quick look at bowling, a game even Ralph Kramden could appreciate. Most of the following lanes include cocktail lounges, video games, and other stalwarts of the genre. Call to make sure you won't get edged out by league play. And here's hoping your memories of the Wine Country won't include any 7–10 splits.

Napa County

Napa Bowl
494 Soscol Ave., Napa
(707) 224–8331

Bicycling

Though some visitors go about wine tasting as if it were a road rally—trying to visit the most wineries in the shortest time possible—that's not an approach we recommend. Take your time and savor not only the wine but the countryside in between. The best way to ensure a casual pace is to tour by bicycle. Wine Country roads are generally conducive to biking, with ample shoulders and side roads where traffic is often light. Still, you need to be mindful of other vehicles and always, always ride single file—cyclists who ride two abreast are simply asking for trouble.

Rentals are easy to find, and many of the establishments offer maps and sound advice. Not surprisingly, spring and fall are the ideal times to hop aboard. If you make a summer excursion, start early and take plenty of water. We have included a few popular off-the-beaten-path cycling areas and routes—this is but a scratch on the surface, meant to get you interested enough to dig deeper. After that we list shops that rent bikes. (Companies that offer special bicycle tours are listed in our Attractions chapter.) Call first to make sure the shop has what you want, i.e., a mountain bike or a road bike (some have tandems too). Expect to pay $10 to $15 per hour or $30 to $40 per day. Most shops throw in a helmet, plastic water bottle, and saddle bag, and some will even deliver your wheels to your hotel.

Promise us you won't be careless enough to leave the driveway or parking area without a helmet.

Las Posadas State Forest

This is one of Napa County's most popular mountain-biking areas, located in the hills near Angwin. Miles of trails—from single-track to fire road—crisscross the dusty, pine-covered landscape. You can stumble upon some nice views of Chiles Valley to the east. From Howell Mountain Road just south of Pacific Union College, turn east on Las Posadas Road and go nearly to the end of the road. (Look for the "Beware of Mountain Lions" sign, an ominous entry point.)

Highland Springs Loop

Here is an intermediate, 34-mile ride for mountain or hybrid bikes. It starts near Kelseyville, on the south shore of Clear Lake, and follows the Old Toll Road, long ago replaced by Highway 175 as a major motor vehicle route. The ride takes you through rustic Donovan Valley and over the mountains to Hopland. You can either return on Highway 175 or retrace your tracks.

Annadel State Park

Annadel's miles of dirt and gravel roads let you customize your own combination of trails. A good one to start with is a double loop around Lake Ilsanjo and Ledson Marsh. Start from the parking area at the end of Channel Drive and take the Warren Richardson Trail up to the lake.

Skirt the lake counter-clockwise and turn left on the Rough Go Trail. Cross the dam and aim right at the next intersection, riding onto the Canyon Trail. Make a left at the Marsh Trail for a climb to Buick Meadows, then a descent to the marsh. Stay on the trail as it loops around the marsh, then make a right onto the Burma Trail, which will return you to the Warren Richardson Trail. It sounds complicated, but all intersections are well posted. The whole ride is about 12 miles. To get to Annadel from Highway 12 east of Santa Rosa, turn south on Los Alamos Road, make a right onto Melita Road, and merge onto Montgomery Drive. After 0.7 mile, turn left on Channel Drive and proceed into the park.

Cyclists take a break among the vineyards in Dry Creek Valley in Sonoma County. PHOTO: DESTINATION SONOMA COUNTY

Van Damme State Park

If you are visiting Mendocino, you can ride south about 3 miles on Highway 1, an exhilarating romp with views of the spectacular coastline. After a nice downhill stretch to the park, turn left and follow signs to the Pygmy Forest. You'll be in Fern Canyon, on an old skid road used by ox teams to haul logs down to the mouth of Little River, site of a former lumber mill. After your only steep climb, on the Logging Road Trail, you'll reach the entrance to the Pygmy Forest. Dismount and do the nature trail on foot.

From here you can continue on to the Little River-Airport Road. Make a right and head back to the coast Highway.

Pacific Coast Highway

Cyclists from around the world come to ride the two-laned Pacific Coast Highway, otherwise known as Highway 1. During the summer months you are likely to see long-distance riders on the route, some having pedaled all the way from Anchorage, Alaska—look for the especially lean-looking cyclists on bikes draped heavy with overstuffed panniers. If riding to Alaska sounds too gung ho, you can whittle it down to say 160 miles—the distance of the Mendocino-Sonoma coast.

A popular tour loop among Santa Rosa cyclists begins with a short Greyhound bus ride to Willits, followed by a half-day ride aboard the Skunk Train to Fort Bragg (see our Attractions chapter). They then ride the coast from Fort Bragg to Jenner, and turn inland at the Russian River, following it most of the way back to Santa Rosa. The round-trip tour (about 140 miles on the bike) can be comfortably done in a week, and fit riders can complete it in a few days. If you're thinking that maybe you'd like to try the trip in reverse, riding from Jenner to Fort Bragg, think again. The winds blow north to south along the coast, and cyclists headed north will be buffeted back by the gusty wind—those going south get an added boost.

One drawback to this route, no matter which way you go, is the preponderance of logging trucks and sightseeing RVs. These can become hazardous on curvy, shoulderless roads, which the road frequently is. Signs along Highway 1 frequently warn vehicles to beware of heavy bicycle traffic; nevertheless, not all drivers are wise or courteous enough to heed the warning.

Sonoma County

AMF Boulevard Lanes
1100 Petaluma Blvd. South, Petaluma
(707) 762-4581

Double Decker Lanes
300 Golf Course Dr., Rohnert Park
(707) 585-0226

Continental Lanes
765 Sebastopol Rd., Santa Rosa
(707) 523-2695

Windsor Bowl
8801 Conde Ln., Windsor
(707) 837-9889

Mendocino County

Yokayo Bowl
1401 N. State St., Ukiah
(707) 462-8686

Noyo Bowl
900 N. Main St., Fort Bragg
(707) 964-4051

Lake County

Clearlake Bowl
14060 Lakeshore Dr., Clearlake
(707) 994-6627

Sports Bowl
872 Lakeport Blvd., Lakeport
(707) 263-4828

Horseback Riding

Many of the trails in the state parks, state forests, and recreation areas of the Wine Country are open to horses. You did bring yours, didn't you? If it wouldn't fit in your overnight bag, there are a few outfits that will rent you a steed. You provide the cowboy hat and the harmonica.

Sonoma Cattle Co. & Napa Valley Trail Rides
P.O. Box 877, Glen Ellen 95442
(707) 996-8566
www.napasonomatrailrides.com

This is a private concessionaire that for 15 years has been leading groups into three Wine Country State Parks: Bothe-Napa Valley, Jack London, and Sugarloaf Ridge (see previous listings in this chapter). The Jack London rides—offered April through November—skirt vineyards owned by the author's descendants. The Bothe ride also is available for reservation April through November, offering the shade of Ritchey Creek and the peace of the Mayacmas Mountains. The company operates year-round in Sugarloaf Ridge, weather and trails permitting, and the views from the saddle are fabulous.

You can choose from a variety of forays, from a two-hour Sonoma Valley ride ($55 per person, $125 with winery stop and lunch) to a 90-minute Napa Valley trot ($57) to a half-day ride in Annadel State Park ($125 to $250). Reservations are a must. Riders must be at least eight years old. Open-toed shoes are not permitted, and the weight limit is 240 pounds.

Chanslor Guest Ranch and Stables
2660 Hwy. 1, Bodega Bay
(707) 875-3333
www.chanslorranch.com

You can lead a horse to the water, but you can't make him surf. Chanslor offers $50 beach rides from their inland property—over the dunes to Bodega Bay and back. There are other options, too: the one-and-a-half-hour Salmon Creek Trail ($50), which winds into a canyon and around much of the company's 730 acres; the one-hour Eagle View ride ($30), where you are likely to spot a couple of resident bald eagles; and a half-hour, $25 trek through the Wetlands Preservation Habitat.

Hunting

While some are out hunting for the perfect Zinfandel, others are combing the hills, rifle in hand, looking to bag something to complement their wine. The huge tracts of forested land within the Wine Country present numerous options for hunters. Below we offer an introduction to those options, highlighting the most popular areas and targets.

We stick primarily to public lands administered by the U.S. Forest Service, the Bureau of Land Management, the California Department of Fish & Game (DFG), and similar organizations. If you want to hunt on private land, be sure to obtain written permission from the landowner. And whether you're on public or private property, please don't leave any litter behind. It's the kind of behavior that gives hunters a bad name.

California's hunting license year runs from July 1 through June 30. You can pick up resident licenses and regulation booklets at most sporting goods stores or at the Region 3 DFG Headquarters at 7329 Silverado Trail, near Yountville in Napa County. Each resident license costs $29.95 if purchased directly from the DFG, slightly more from an agent (upland game bird and waterfowl stamps are additional). If you're visiting the area and just happen to have brought your rifle along, you can request a two-day, nonresident hunting license ($29.15) from the DFG. Call (916) 227-2271 for details.

Napa-Sonoma Marshes
Wildlife Area
Department of Fish and Game
(707) 944-5500

On the west bank of the lower Napa River, where it widens out before dumping into Carquinez Strait, are 2,000 acres of public lands divided into six units. The hunting areas are accessible by boat via Mud Slough, Hudeman Slough, and Tolay Creek. Besides the abundance of waterfowl, you might scare up a pheasant or dove.

Cedar Roughs
Bureau of Land Management
(707) 468-4000

This little-known, 7,000-acre pocket west of Lake Berryessa is run by the BLM. The only public access to Cedar Roughs is a 1-mile foot trail that begins on Pope Canyon Road, 3 miles north of the Pope Creek Bridge, which is at the lake. The trail rises steeply to a broad plateau of glades and forests that harbor deer, bobcat, bear, coyote, gray squirrel, rabbit, quail, dove, and pigeon.

Petaluma Marsh Wildlife Area
Department of Fish and Game
(707) 944-5500

This 1,900-acre tidal salt marsh along the Petaluma River, north of its confluence with San Antonio Creek is accessible only by boat. (There are several public ramps along the river.) The marsh is a mecca for ducks, geese, and other waterfowl.

Lake Sonoma Wildlife Area
Department of Fish and Game
(707) 944-5500

The area around Lake Sonoma is leased by the California Department of Fish and Game from the U.S. Army Corps of Engi-

When's Wabbit Season?

Here are the parameters of the hunting seasons for some common game animals in the Wine Country:

Deer: generally opens in mid-September, closes the end of October.

Bear (northeast of Highway 128 only): opens the second Saturday in August, closes on December 31 (or when the statewide quota of 1,500 bears is reached).

Wild pig: open all year.

Cottontail rabbit, snowshoe hare: opens July 1, closes the last Sunday in January.

Jack rabbit, black-tailed and white-tailed rabbit: open all year.

Tree squirrel: opens the second Saturday in September, closes the last Sunday in January.

Raccoon: opens November 16, closes March 31.

neers. It is managed with the idea of providing special hunts for deer, wild pig, and turkey, especially for junior hunters. The hunts are by permit only. Call the DFG for specific information and dates.

Jackson State Forest
State Forest Headquarters
(707) 964–5674

Sizable Jackson State Forest, east of Fort Bragg in Mendocino County, is home to game animals such as deer, black bear, gray squirrel, rabbit, mountain and valley quail, and band-tailed pigeon. Check for possible road closures and firearms bans within the forest.

Knoxville
Bureau of Land Management
(707) 468–4000

Along the Napa-Lake county line, southeast of the town of Lower Lake, are 17,700 acres of public land in the Knoxville area. The rugged, isolated landscape tends to be hot in the summer and wet in the winter, but when did that ever discourage hunters? From Knoxville Berryessa Road south of the Homestake Mining Company, you'll see a signed access point. Follow the road and gun for deer, bobcat, gray squirrel, rabbit, quail, dove, or pigeon.

Boggs Mountain
State Forest Headquarters
(707) 928–4378

The State of California bought 3,460 acres on Boggs Mountain from the Calso Company in 1949 and turned them over to the state's Forest Service. If you hunt here, use extreme caution, as the area is popular with hikers and bikers in addition to deer, wild turkey, mountain quail, wild pig, and gray squirrel.

Cache Creek
Bureau of Land Management
(707) 468–4000

The Cache Creek drainage flows from Clear Lake south to Capay Valley in western Yolo County. Public access to the 45,000 acres of public land—divided among several state and federal entities—is via the Cache Creek Wildlife Area parking lot, 8 miles east of Clearlake Oaks on Highway 20. With no public roads, the area is limited to walkers and horses, and certain areas are closed in the spring to let the elks calve. Resident game includes deer, rabbit, dove, quail, and wild turkey.

Cow Mountain
Bureau of Land Management
(707) 468–4000

The Cow Mountain Recreation Area (see the Parks section of this chapter) consists of about 54,000 acres of mountainous terrain. You're likely to find deer, rabbit, gray squirrel, bobcat, coyote, dove, and quail. Public access is from Ukiah on Mill Creek Road, from Lakeport on Scotts Creek Road, or from Kelseyville on Highland Springs Road/Old Toll Road.

Mendocino National Forest
National Forest Headquarters
(707) 983–6118

As profiled earlier in the chapter, this sprawling territory covers about 1,700 square miles of the Coast Range mountains. With the exception of a state game refuge that lies outside the Wine Country, practically all public land in the forest is open to hunting. In addition to the forest headquarters in Willows, you can obtain district maps from the Forest Service office in Upper Lake (707-275-2361) or Covelo (707-983-6118). Common game includes deer, valley and mountain quail, band-tailed pigeon, wild turkey, rabbit, gray squirrel, black bear, blue grouse, dove, bobcat, and coyote.

Swimming

If you are not fortunate enough to be staying (or living) next to any of the Wine Country's lakes during those summer hot spells, you might feel the need to jump into a different body of water—specifically, the rectangular, chlorinated kind. Here is a partial list of public swimming facilities. All of them are open from Memorial Day weekend through Labor Day weekend; some are accessible for longer periods of time. Call for more information on lessons, admission fees, and no-kids or kids-only periods.

Napa County

St. Helena Community Pool
1401 Grayson Ave., St. Helena
(707) 963–7946

Sonoma County

Petaluma Swim Center
900 E. Washington St., Petaluma
(707) 778–4410

Alicia Pool
300 Arlen Dr., Rohnert Park
(707) 795–7265

Benicia Pool
7469 Bernice Ave., Rohnert Park
(707) 795–7582

Ladybug Pool
8517 Liman Way, Rohnert Park
(707) 664–1070

Honeybee Pool
1170 Golf Course Dr., Rohnert Park
(707) 586–1413

Finley Aquatic Complex
2060 W. College Ave., Santa Rosa
(707) 543–3760

Ridgeway Swim Center
455 Ridgeway Ave., Santa Rosa
(707) 543–3421

Healdsburg Municipal Swimming Pool
360 Monte Vista Ave., Healdsburg
(707) 433–1109

Cloverdale Memorial Pool
105 W. First St., Cloverdale
(707) 894–3236

Ives Pool
7400 Willow St., Sebastopol
(707) 823–8693

Mendocino County

Ukiah Municipal Swimming Pool
511 Park Blvd., Ukiah
(707) 467–2831

Willits Municipal Swimming Pool
429 N. Main St., Willits
(707) 459–5778

Lake County

Middletown County Park Community Pool
20962 Big Canyon Rd., Middletown
(707) 262–1618

Westshore County Park Swimming Pool
250 Lange St., Lakeport
(707) 263–3077

Insiders' Tip

Stocking up on firewood for a camping trip? See if you can track down some Pacific madrone (a tree named by Father Crespi of the Portola expedition in 1769). The madrone makes a delightfully smoke-free fire.

In addition, many high schools open their pools to the public during summer vacation. To find out if such options exist in your area, call the municipal recreation numbers listed below in the Tennis section.

Lastly, some spas permit walk-in (dive-in?) swimmers who pay for day use of their mineral pools. Search our Spas and Resorts chapter for relevant information.

Tennis

If you think tennis is just the sort of vigorous-yet-natty sport that would flourish in the Wine Country, you're right on target. Because of the geographic enormity of the area, however, a complete list of available courts would be harder to handle than an Anna Kournikova first serve. Instead we provide a list of city recreation departments throughout the four-county region. The folks on the other end of the line will tell you where the courts are—many of them are after-hours high school facilities—whether you need reservations, what it costs to play there, and whether the courts are lighted.

Napa County

City of American Canyon Recreation
(707) 647–4566

City of Napa Parks and Recreation
(707) 257–9529

Town of Yountville Recreation
(707) 944–8712

City of St. Helena Recreation Department
(707) 963–5706

City of Calistoga Parks and Recreation
(707) 942–2838

Sonoma County

Sonoma City Hall
(707) 938–3681

City of Petaluma Parks & Recreation
(707) 778–4380

City of Cotati
(707) 792–4600

City of Rohnert Park Recreation Department
(707) 588–3456

City of Santa Rosa Recreation & Parks Offices
(707) 543–3282

Town of Windsor Parks and Recreation
(707) 838–1260

City of Healdsburg
(707) 431–3300

City of Cloverdale
(707) 894–2521

City of Sebastopol Recreation Information
(707) 823–1511

Mendocino County

City of Ukiah Recreation
(707) 463–6237

City of Willits
(707) 459–4601

City of Point Arena
(707) 882–2122

Fort Bragg Recreation Center
(707) 964–2231

Lake County

City of Clearlake
707) 994–8201

City of Lakeport Parks and Recreation
(707) 263–5615

On the Water

Great rivers, fine lakes, and a spectacular ocean—take your pick. We've got them all, along with a full range of equipment rentals and charter services to keep you swashing and splashing till the salmon swim home. From all-day deep-sea fishing excursions to an afternoon swim in a lake, the variety of aqua activities and adventures available in the Wine Country will surprise and excite you.

The best place to begin is along the 150 miles or so of coastline that borders the Pacific in Sonoma and Mendocino Counties. If you're thinking palm-studded sandy beaches, you'll be surprised by what you find here. This section of the state's coast bears little resemblance to its southern counterpart—that relatively mild stretch of oceanfront lined with sunbathers from Santa Barbara to San Diego. North of San Francisco the continent drops precipitously to the sea, with narrow crescents of beach occasionally flanking the rocky bluffs—you will not see a single high-rise hotel along this coast. And the ocean is rarely even-tempered here, alternating between violent fits of rage and quiet moods of calm. Its best times are during the summer months, when the sun burns through the morning fog and the wind is low.

Our rivers generally flow lazily through forests, meadows, and marshes, rarely achieving enough momentum to produce whitewater. A short section of the Russian River above Cloverdale and the portion of the Eel River in Mendocino County are two exceptions. When water volume is high, these stretches can get quite rough, reaching Class IV and V whitewater status. And of course, during the rainy winter months many Wine Country creeks—which are dry in summer—flow with gusto, some serving as spawning grounds for salmon and steelhead.

As for the lake situation, well, generally speaking, this is no Minnesota. In fact, we've had to build dams to impound water, flooding farmlands and, in one case, an entire city. Only in Lake County will you find natural lakes in Wine Country. There are a handful there, including Clear Lake and the Blue Lakes. All are teeming with fish and great for swimming and watersports.

So here's a rundown of things you can do to take advantage of our waters.

The Pacific

Sonoma County

Sonoma Coast

The Sonoma coast feels wild and remote. It is hilly, almost mountainous at times, with coastal ranches stretching for miles along the bluffs. Bodega Bay, the county's largest coastal town, is home to approximately 300 commercial fishing boats. Its protected harbor is also an attractive spot for sporting activities. The shoreline on the west side of the harbor is great for windsurfing or launching a kayak. There's hardly a day when you don't see the fluorescent sails of a windsurfer darting about or the rhythmic movements of a kayaker plying the waters.

Surfers looking for the perfect wave will not be disappointed. Two of the most popular spots are Salmon Creek, just north of Bodega Bay, and Goat Rock State Beach, farther up the coast near Jenner. But it's always a good idea to contact a local surf shop for advice—it's a long coastline, and you can spend a lot of time looking.

Sportfishing is big at Bodega Bay. Charter boats sail every day, and, depending on the season, come back with a mix of rock cod, lingcod, halibut, salmon, alba-core tuna, and crab. Lots of families also find it fun to drop a line right off the wharf behind the Inn at the Tides Restaurant or on the pier on the west side of the bay.

North from Bodega Bay is a series of state beaches accessible from clearly marked parking areas. These are a part of the Sonoma Coast State Beach, and they are ideal spots for fishing, beachcombing, picnicking, and beach parties—unfortunately, the chilly waters are unsafe for swimming and there are no lifeguards. A ranger station, just north of Bodega Bay at Salmon Creek, is where you can get maps and information. Park rangers also offer whale-watching walks.

See our Parks and Recreation and Attractions chapters for more information on the Sonoma Coast State Beach and other coastal-area recreation sites, including Doran and Westside regional parks, Stillwater Cove Regional Park, Fort Ross State Park, Salt Point State Park, Kruse Rhododendron State Reserve, and Gualala Point Regional Park.

Mendocino County

Mendocino Coast

For sheer drama, nothing compares with the splendor of the view from the town of Mendocino, built on a rocky peninsula, where the sound of waves crashing against the cliffs is always in the air. The shoreline here is a labyrinth of rugged offshore spires and sea stacks, churning coves, and wave-sculpted arches and sea tunnels. This is one of the most soul-stirring settings in the state, with ocean views often mesmerizing visitors for hours. A popular activity here—aside from shopping—is to find a comfortable spot on the bluffs and simply watch wave after wave roll in.

Another favorite attraction along this scenic seashore is at Russian Gulch State Park, where a unique "punch bowl" was formed when a large sea cave collapsed. Waves enter through a tunnel in one side and crash around the interior of the bowl, letting go a distinctive array of throaty echoes. Russian Gulch State Park is just 2 miles north of Mendocino (see our Parks and Recreation chapter).

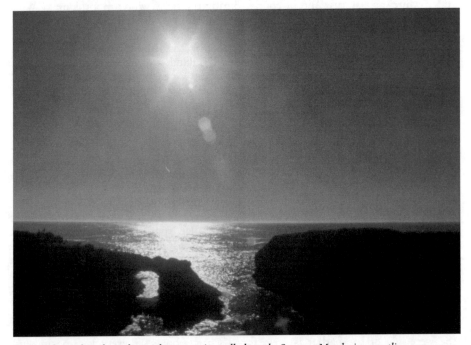

Spectacular rock arches enhance the ocean views all along the Sonoma-Mendocino coastline. PHOTO: JOHN NAGIECKI

Fishing is a popular sport along the Mendocino Coast. Greenwood Creek State Beach, a new day-use state beach near the town of Elk (at the intersection of Highway 1 and Highway 128), is popular with picnickers and ocean anglers who want easy access to the beaches. Additional angling spots along the Mendocino Coast include Schooner Gulch State Park and Manchester State Beach, on Kinney Road off Highway 1, where there's a bonus of two creeks that run with salmon and steelhead during winter. (See our Parks and Recreation chapter for more on Manchester State Beach and Schooner Gulch.)

Abalone diving is a popular sport around these parts for the adventuresome, experienced diver. The abalone is a giant marine snail with a powerful foot that can lock a strong grip on rock surfaces. One of these mollusks can yield more than a pound of delicious white meat. Unfortunately, abalone is becoming an endangered species. Rules for abalone diving (including size limits) are strict. The mollusks can be harvested from April to December, excluding July, but check with the state Department of Parks and Recreation at any state beach for regulations—all abalone divers must have a valid fishing license bearing an abalone stamp. And above all, consult with park rangers and locals about the dangers of abalone diving. Every year brings its share of drownings—even among veteran divers—along this shoreline.

For more information on other popular recreational spots on or near the Mendocino Coast—including Van Damme State Park, Mendocino Headlands State Park, Jug Handle State Reserve, Jackson State Forest, Mackerricher State Park, Westport-Union Landing State Beach, and Sinkyone Wilderness State Park—see our Parks and Recreation chapter.

The Rivers

Napa County

Napa River

Though most of the Napa River's length snakes from Mount St. Helena to the town

> **Insiders' Tip**
>
> The ocean along the Northern California coast is unsafe for swimming. It's cold, about 50 degrees, and the strong currents will whisk you off toward Japan before you can say sayonara. On top of that, large and powerful waves—called sleeper waves—also occur without warning, occasionally sweeping beachcombers off coastal rocks and sand shores. Take our advice, enjoy the view, build sandcastles that are high and dry, and stay clear of the breakers.

of Napa, the big-time angling is mostly confined to extreme points south, especially as the river broadens between the Butler Bridge (the airborne stretch of Highway 12/29) and Carquinez Strait. Summer fishing isn't great in these tidal waters, but autumn brings hungry striped bass and sturgeon. Try live bait, such as mudsuckers or bullheads for the stripers, live bass shrimp or mud shrimp for the sturgeon.

The many sloughs that feed into Napa River in this marshy area are also good bets for striped bass. If you're looking for a full-service resort, try the Napa Valley Marina, (707) 252-8011, or Napa Sea Ranch, (707) 252-2799, both on or near Cuttings Wharf Road.

Sonoma County

Russian River

Called Slavyanka (Slavic girl) by Russian settlers in the 19th century, the Russian

A fisherman tries his luck in search of the elusive steelhead in the still waters of the Russian River. PHOTO: JOHN NAGIECKI

River begins in Mendocino County just above Ukiah. The East Branch of the Russian receives water diverted from the Eel River, which flows through am aqueduct cut through a hill. The diversion, which has been going on since 1908, has recently become controversial because of its impact on the Eel River's fisheries. Water from the Eel is used to feed the PG&E Potter Valley hydroelectric plant; it also helps to keep the Russian from being reduced to a trickle through the dry summer months.

Below Hopland, the Russian falls precipitously through a narrow canyon—alongside U.S. 101—and then slows to a more languid pace for the rest of the trip through Sonoma County. It rolls past small wineries, campgrounds, and several towns before reaching the sea at Jenner. During the summer months, canoeists, kayakers, rafters, and inner-tubists converge on the river. The more ambitious paddle the entire 70-mile stretch of relatively flat water below Cloverdale to Jenner, while most visitors opt for a one-day trip of about 10 miles—often between Forestville and Guerneville. April through

September is the best time to canoe the Russian. It's a beautiful run through quiet waters among redwoods, past summer resorts, quaint old homes, and the occasional nude beach. (See our Provisioners listings in this chapter for information on area river outfitters.)

For more on Russian River area wineries, see our Wineries chapter. To find out about camping options, see our Camping chapter.

Mendocino County

Eel River

This river is a sight to behold, sparkling in emerald greens, turquoise blues, and foamy white as it tumbles over boulders, through narrow gorges, and past tall redwood and fir forests. The Eel begins in a cauldron formed by an ancient volcano in Mendocino National Forest, and then winds north for nearly 150 miles before spilling into the Pacific near Ferndale in Humboldt County. The third-largest river in the state (following the Sacramento and the Klamath), the Eel and its tributaries are home to chinook and coho salmon and steelhead, which migrate from the ocean to the river's spawning grounds each year. Though several dams, a hydroelectric plant, and the massive Russian River diversion—about 52 billion gallons annually—have all had an impact on the fish population, the river still boasts one of the most abundant fisheries in the state and has a reputation for producing large, hard-fighting lunkers.

The Russian River water diversion has kept the Eel in near drought condition every summer and fall for almost 100 years. While it is hardly a boatable river during these times, it is great for swimming, particularly in the deeper holes. At other times of year, however, this is not a swimmer's river. During high water flows, the Eel becomes a roaring torrent, running hell-for-leather to the sea. The Mendocino County section offers some of the best whitewater in the state. It's a heart-thumping ride, featuring mile after mile of Class III and IV rapids. A word of advice and caution: This is a difficult whitewater river navigable by expert guides or highly experienced kayakers only—anyone else will certainly be ground to a fine pulp by the sharp rocks and churning waters. Inner-tubists, neophyte river rafters, or any other novice boater should head for the more placid waters of the Russian River. (See our Provisioners listings in this chapter for information on area river outfitters.)

Gualala River

Although the portion of the Gualala River most people see is the wide swath that spreads out where the river joins the Pacific (and where kayakers set out to sea), the Gualala does wind far into the interior of the county, through forests of redwoods and groves of ferns. In a good wet year, when winter rains have drenched the land and the river is full, it is possible to kayak almost 10 miles inland. That would be a rare year, but even paddling only a mile or so upriver is rewarding, giving a different view of the natural splendors of Northern California. With some luck, you'll witness soaring ospreys, great blue

herons, and brown pelicans; catch a glimpse of the playful river otters; and watch the variety of birds that call the forest home.

Motorboats are not permitted on the river, but anglers in rowboats sometimes make their way upstream to cast a line in search of trout. During the winter rainy season, the river swells and roars out to sea, washing out beach sands that had accumulated near its mouth during the summer.

Navarro River

Motoring along the rolling hills of Highway 128 and into Anderson Valley, drivers suddenly encounter "a redwood tunnel to the sea" and their first look at the Navarro River. For first-time visitors and longtime residents alike, the redwoods along the Navarro River are a magnificent sight to behold. Second-growth redwood groves stretch along the river, making a home for riverbank denizens such as the belted kingfisher, along with families of raccoons and black-tailed deer. This is a great river for kayaking, and some of the kayak companies operating out of Sonoma County bring groups here (see Provisioners, listed subsequently, for more information).

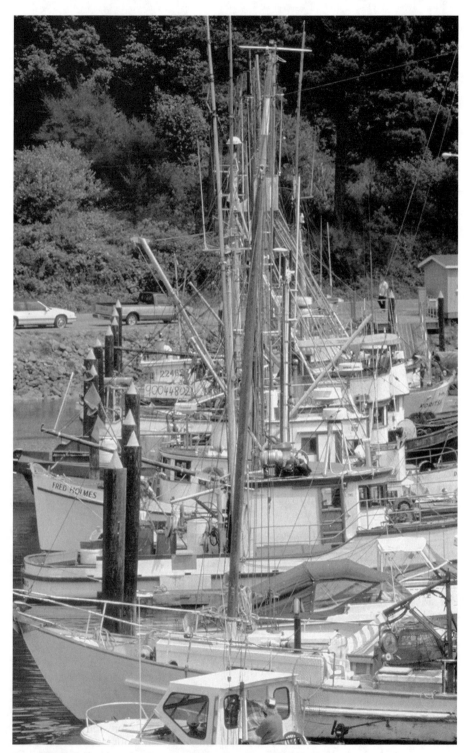

Boats line the docks where the Noyo River enters Fort Bragg Harbor. PHOTO: BILL HOBAN

The Lakes

Napa County

Lake Hennessey

About 5 miles east of St. Helena is an 850-acre reservoir owned by the city of Napa and surrounded by rolling hills covered with grass and dappled with oak trees. Lake Hennessey was formed by the construction of Conn Dam. The Department of Fish and Game stocks Lake Hennessey with trout in the fall, winter, and spring, and you'll find a few bass, bluegill, and catfish as well. Motorized boats are allowed on the water if they don't exceed 14 feet and 10 horsepower; sailboats are permitted if they are 16 feet or shorter. Swimming and kayaking are prohibited. There is a $4.00 access fee for visiting the lake, and an additional $1.00 special fishing permit is also required. There is no particular place to pay for the fishing permit, so just be ready to fork over the buck if you see the Lake Hennessey caretaker.

Lake Berryessa

It was 40 years ago that Putah Creek was dammed, creating Lake Berryessa between two legs of California's Coast Ranges (and drowning the town of Monticello). The ragged perimeter gives Berryessa 165 miles of shoreline, more than surrounds massive Lake Tahoe. The north end of the lake is shallow, with gentle, grassy hills sloping down to the water. Contrast that with the south end and its steep, rocky terrain dotted with manzanita and oak. The eastern shore of the lake, meanwhile, is off-limits to the public.

The Bureau of Reclamation maintains three day-use facilities and a launch ramp at Capell Cove, plus picnic sites at Smittle Creek and Oak Shores. The trout and salmon fishing are great here in the spring; in the fall, the trout feed on shad near the surface early in the day. Cast between the dam and The Narrows, or troll in Markley Cove or Skiers Cove. Look for largemouth bass in the coves, smallmouth and spotted bass on the big island in the middle of the lake or at steep, jagged points in up to 40 feet of water. Bluegill usually hang out in the backs of shallow coves all around the lake, and catfish are plentiful at Capell Cove, Pope Creek, and Putah Creek.

There are several marinas along Knoxville Road and Highway 128. Keep in mind that this lake is heavily trafficked, especially in the summer. Berryessa welcomes more than 1.5 million visitors each year.

Sonoma County

Lake Sonoma

Designed to control Russian River flooding, the Warm Springs Dam has created some 3,600 surface acres of scenic recreational waters. Located 11 miles north of Healdsburg on Dry Creek Road, this is primarily a boating lake, although waterskiers and Jet Skiers are allowed in designated areas. Skiing is not always considered desirable because of the many large trees that have been partially submerged. Kayakers, however, have no trouble paddling their way through the treetops.

Fishing is the main recreational sport. Generally speaking, boat fishing is more successful than shore fishing, and the upper reaches of the lake usually produce the best results. Fish include smallmouth bass, red ear sunfish, green sunfish, and rainbow trout. A public boat ramp is available, as well as the full-service Lake Sonoma Marina. The fish hatchery is always great fun (see our Kidstuff chapter), and there's an interesting visitor center. Swimming is a possibility, but much of the shoreline is rocky.

Mendocino County

Lake Mendocino

Ten miles north of Ukiah off Highway 20, Lake Mendocino offers a variety of activities, including water-skiing, pleasure boating, sailing, windsurfing, and swimming. It's an aesthetically pleasing body of water and is popular in the Ukiah Valley, where summer temperatures can be sweltering.

Everything you could want for fun in the water can be rented here—Sea-Doos, Jet Skis, fishing boats, and pontoon boats.

All you need is a swimsuit. The visitor center offers information about the lake, Pomo Indian culture, and the Coyote Valley. The Interpretive Cultural Center has exhibits of Pomo Indian crafts, pottery, jewelry, and decorative arts. This area is a great place for a summer picnic.

Lake County

Clear Lake

They don't call this Lake County for nothing. It has several significant wet spots, but really it has Clear Lake. Three things about Clear Lake are, uh, clear: It is big, it is shallow, and it is old. With 43,785 acres of surface area, this is the largest natural freshwater lake within California. And yet the volume of water contained herein is not staggering. That's because the average depth of the lake is less than 30 feet.

Scientists are convinced that lakes of some sort have existed at this site for some 2.5 million years, possibly making Clear Lake the oldest lake in North America. They figure the upper arm, between Lakeport and Lucerne, has been under water continuously for 450,000 years.

In terms of its importance to the identity of the county, Clear Lake is the undeniable hub. Almost all the towns in Lake County are clustered around the shoreline, and access for all is faithfully preserved. There are 11 public ramps around the lake, providing an array of launch points. Remember that permission is required for use of beaches and ramps not posted "public." (While you're at it, remember to reduce your boat speed to 5 mph within 500 feet of shore.)

Clear Lake is known as the Bass Capital of the West. Two-thirds of the fish caught here are largemouth bass. Spring is the time to get them, especially from docks or in pockets formed in the beds of tule reeds. Two specific hot spots are the north end of the lake from Lakeport to Rocky Point and the shoreline from Clear Lake State Park to Corinthian Bay. Bass might be the most plentiful, but they aren't the biggest fish to fry here. The Clear Lake record for a largemouth bass is 17.5 pounds; the record for a catfish is nearly twice that. Channel catfish are nearly everywhere on the lake, but seem to be particularly active at Rattlesnake Island, Rodman Slough, and Horseshoe Bend. The bluegill and crappie fishing is considered fair at Clear Lake.

Sometimes the action on Clear Lake is overhead: A contingent of seaplane owners and pilots converges annually for a "Splash In" event (see our Festivals and Annual Events chapter), and model seaplane hobbyists often hold meets around the lake.

Indian Valley Reservoir

Northeast of Clear Lake, in isolated terrain at 1,475 feet near the Colusa County line, is this 3,700-acre reservoir created by construction of the Indian Valley Dam. The 6-mile-long lake with approximately 39 miles of shoreline is open to all boating, though a 10-mph speed limit is imposed. Two public launch ramps are available. If you're not swimming in the reservoir or hunting around it, you can fish for rainbow trout, largemouth and smallmouth bass, catfish, or red ear perch.

Blue Lakes

Upper Blue Lake and Lower Blue Lake are two small, slender fingers alongside Highway 20, just northwest of Clear Lake. Their

> ### Insiders' Tip
> So you caught a big fish in Clear Lake. Now what? We recommend throwing it gently back into the lake, not into a frying pan. That's because the fish in Clear Lake harbor high levels of natural mercury contamination. Check the regulations at the time of your visit, but plan on fishing for sport, not for food.

scale is almost insignificant from a county-wide perspective, but they are consistently popular because of their natural beauty, with pine trees creeping practically to the water's edge. The lakes attract canoers (because motor boats are relegated to 5 mph) and windsurfers (because of the steady breezes that flow from the canyons). Blue Lakes is a fairly hot spot for anglers, too, with varying supplies of trout, catfish, bluegill, and largemouth bass.

Lake Pillsbury

Two-thousand-acre Lake Pillsbury is tucked away in the mountains of Mendocino National Forest—you must negotiate 15 miles of dirt road to get there—but it, too, is man-made. It's scenic nonetheless, as evidenced by the number of campsites constructed along its edge (see our Camping chapter for a sampling). It's warm, too—more than 70 degrees in the summer despite resting at 1,800 feet. The lake is open to all boating, with most of the rod-and-reel action devoted to black bass, rainbow and brown trout, and bluegill. Lake Pillsbury's 65 miles of shoreline and environs are laced with USDA Forest Service hiking and biking trails.

Provisioners: Charters, Watercraft, Lessons

Here's a sampling of Wine Country businesses that cater to the aqua-nut. You'll find information on renting everything from a Jet Ski to kayaks, and lots of these folks will either guide you along or teach you what you need to know to have a safe and enjoyable experience.

If you're planning an inland fishing trip, there are many top-notch places to pick up bait and tackle (also see King's Sport and Tackle listing, below). In Napa County, these include A&M Market, 2877 Solano Avenue, Napa, (707) 255-0400; and Sweeney's Sports, 1537 Imola Avenue, Napa, (707) 255-5544.

In Lake County, stop in at Don's Bait & Tackle, 14531 Lakeshore Drive, Clearlake, (707) 995-9668; Ed's Market, 3657 E. Highway 20, Nice, (707) 274-8029; Gar-

> ### Insiders' Tip
> The California Department of Fish and Game declares two Saturdays each year as free fishing days. This means that residents and nonresidents alike can reel 'em in without a fishing license—all other fishing regulations, such as bag and size limits, gear restrictions, fishing hours, and stream closures remain in effect. For dates and details contact the department at 7329 Silverado Trail, Napa, (707) 944-5500, or through their Web site at www.dfg.ca.gov.

ner's Resort, 6035 Old Highway 53, Clearlake, (707) 994-6267; Kits Corner Store & Gas, 7990 Highway 29, Kelseyville, (707) 279-8954; or Lakeport Tackle, 1050 N. Main Street, Lakeport, (707) 263-8862.

Napa County

A Wet Pleasure Jet Ski & Boat Rentals
5800 Knoxville Rd., Lake Berryessa
(707) 966-4204

A Wet Pleasure has a full lineup of aluminum fishing boats (14- or 16-footers), ski boats, pedal boats, 24-foot patio boats, and Yamaha Jet Skis. Boat rentals cost $60 for eight hours.

Sonoma County

W.C. "Bob" Trowbridge Canoe Trips
13840 Old Redwood Hwy., Healdsburg
(707) 433-7247, (800) 640-1386 (information and reservation line)
www.trowbridgecanoe.com

The company, named for the man who started it in 1953 (and whose granddaughter still helps run the shop), offers a wide range of canoe and kayak outings on the Russian River from April to October. You can choose from afternoon, half-day paddles for two to three hours; full days from four to six hours; or even a five-day canoe excursion.

Burke's Russian River Canoe Trips
8600 River Road., Forestville
(707) 887–1222
www.burkescanoetrips.com

Burke's provides your canoe, paddles, and life jackets for the day for a total of just $35 per canoe. Your trip begins at Burke's base near Forestville and ends 10 miles downstream at Guerneville. Burke's then shuttles you back to your car at Forestville. It's a leisurely four- to five-hour downstream paddle, with the opportunity for many stops on warm sunny beaches.

Bodega Bay Sportfishing Center
1500 Bay Flat Rd., Bodega Bay
(707) 875–3344
www.usa.fishing.com/bodegabaysport fishing.html

These folks operate three charter boats out of Bodega Bay for either full-day or half-day fishing trips for bay or ocean fishing. You'll be going after rock cod, lingcod, salmon (April through November), halibut, and Dungeness crab. Fishing tackle is available. Whale-watching trips run from November to February. The center also specializes in evening cruises.

The cost of excursions ranges from $50 to $60 if you're going for the fish listed above, and you can fish for them in combinations. Going out 60 to 80 miles for salmon or halibut would require a negotiated cost. At the high end of the scale there's albacore tuna, and those trips will run you from $125 to $150.

The company also operates from another location, a boathouse called Fish and Chips and Fishing Trips, at 1445 Hwy. 1. It's the culinary extension of the business, with a sit-down restaurant that serves fish and chips, calamari, scallops, prawns, oysters, hot dogs, burgers, beer, and wine. Food is also available for takeout, and box lunches may be ordered.

Bodega Bay Surf Shack
1400 Hwy. 1, Pelican Plaza, Bodega Bay
(707) 875–3944
www.bodegabaysurf.com
Bodega Bay Kayak
1580 East Shore Drive,
Blue Whale Shopping Center, Bodega Bay
(707) 875–8899
www.bodegabaykayak.com

These two shops are a must-stop for any visitor eager to glean the optimum amount of local surfing or kayaking knowledge. Bob Miller, the Surf Shack's friendly and welcoming owner, has been surfing nearby Salmon Creek Beach and other primo wave spots since 1984. His shop offers surfboards, wetsuit rentals, and surfing lessons. Bike rentals also are available, along with a great selection of men's and women's beachwear and casual clothing. The nearby kayak shop offers single and tandem kayaks for half-day and all-day rental on sheltered Bodega Bay. More adventurous paddlers may want to consider signing up for the shop's guided tour of the coast.

High Tide Surf Shop
9 Fourth St., Petaluma
(707) 763–3860
www.waveslave.com

Located in the McNear Building, part of Petaluma's historic downtown, High Tide is a relative newcomer, having arrived in 1992. If you should pass through "the crossroads to the beach," as proprietor Len Crain likes to call the neighborhood, don't expect his shop to be open before noon. Then again, you might want to avail yourself of a High Tide public service, a continuous broadcast of the coastal weather report and surf conditions emanating from a not-so-loud speaker above the recessed doorway.

High Tide stocks a complete line of custom surfboards, body boards, skim boards, and accessories, plus a large selection of wetsuits for men, women, and children of all sizes and shapes. Even if the

An old fishing boat lists lazily in the shallows of Bodega Bay. PHOTO: JOHN NAGIECKI

surf isn't calling your name, there's a rack full of Hawaiian shirts and a good selection of swimwear.

Windwalker Board Sports and School of Windsurfing
4347 Harrison Grade Rd., Occidental
(707) 874-2331
www.wind-walker.com
Windwalker offers windsurfing lessons in Bodega Bay, where conditions are particularly favorable for learning the sport—a mile of 3-foot-deep water with consistent winds. The shop also rents wetsuits, boards, and sails.

Windwalker is unique in another respect: It offers bed and breakfast packages in a variety of accommodations and a wide price range.

King's Sport and Tackle Shop
16258 Main St., Guerneville
(707) 869-2156
You can buy just about anything you need for the outdoor life here. Whether you're a camping, fishing, or archery enthusiast, or you don't know a striped bass from a catfish, Steve Jackson, King's friendly and knowledgeable owner, can provide you with sportswear, footwear, camping gear and accessories, fresh and saltwater bait and tackle, and guns and ammo. He's also got custom, hand-tied flies, dry bags for river activities, and equipment for abalone diving.

King's also provides guide service for fishing on the Russian River during steelhead, salmon, and bass season. A local hunting guide is available to help you stalk wild boar, deer, and turkey. King's rents kayaks ($25 a day for one-person kayaks, $40 for two) and gives guided river tours at any time of year, weather permitting.

Mendocino County

All Aboard Adventures
Noyo Harbor, Fort Bragg
(707) 964-2079, (707) 964-1881
www.allaboardadventures.com

Hop aboard Captain Tim's *Sea Hawk* for salmon, rock cod, and lingcod fishing. Tim has been working charter boats for 22 years out of Fort Bragg, and the *Sea Hawk* is his newest purchase. Trips are at 7:00 A.M. and 1:00 P.M. daily. Deep-sea fishing trips are between $45 and $55 (tackle kits are extra, rod and bait are included). During January through April, All Aboard features two-hour whale-watching excursions for $25.

Rubicon Adventures
9743 Hwy. 116, Forestville
(707) 887-2452

Owner Bill Mashek has been leading whitewater tours since 1971. He offers a one-day whitewater excursion on the Eel River for $45 per person during the months of April and May (wetsuits not provided). Bill brings the boats—deluxe seven-person whitewater rafts—rafting guides, and lunch and takes care of the

Tributary Whitewater Tours
20480 Woodbury Dr., Grass Valley
(800) 672-3846
www.whitewatertours.com

Tributary has been guiding whitewater tours on all the major California rivers for more than two decades. Its two-day Eel River trip in Mendocino County runs during the months of April and May, and costs approximately $200 per person (wetsuits and camping gear are extra). The company provides the boats—deluxe seven-person whitewater rafts—guides, and all meals. Though their headquarters is located near the Sierra Nevada Mountains, Tributary will rendezvous with clients for the Eel River trip at the take-out point at Dos Rios off Highway 162.

Lake County

Disney's Water Sports
401 S. Main St., Lakeport
(707) 263-0969
www.disneywatersports.com

No magic kingdom or amusement park rides here, just Jet Skis, aluminum fishing boats, patio boats, kayaks, ski boats, parasail rides, pedal boats, Ski Doos, and water ski lessons.

On the Waterfront
60 Third St., Lakeport
(707) 263-6789

Here you can rent 18-foot Bowrider ski boats, fishing boats, patio boats (with AM/FM stereo cassette!), pedal boats, a variety of personal watercraft (including stand-up and three-seat Jet Skis), and accessories such as skis and kneeboards.

Spectator Sports

The Wine Country approach to spectator sports varies from the occasional upscale PGA golf event to the more populist sprint-car racing. And professional-level happenings are always available in the Bay Area and Sacramento. No fewer than eight pro sports franchises take the field (or diamond, or court, or rink) within two hours of the Wine Country—each is covered in this chapter. Though the list goes on and on, we had to draw the line somewhere. Other Bay Area sporting events—from boxing matches to major golf and tennis tournaments—are not listed here.

Also note that some sports outings seemed more appropriately included in our Festivals and Annual Events chapter—the annual rodeo at the Sonoma County Fair is an example. And if the activity is more participatory than vicarious in nature, look for it in the Parks and Recreation or our On the Water chapters.

The radio stations listed below every franchise name are the teams' English-language flagship stations, and the phone numbers are ticket sources. For major events you also can try TicketMaster at (800) 523–1515. Now go buy a bucket of popcorn and an official program, and root, root, root for the home team.

Baseball

San Francisco Giants
Pacific Bell Park, China Basin
(415) 468–3700, (800) 5–GIANTS
www.giants.mlb.com
KNBR 680 AM

One of two franchises—the Los Angeles Dodgers being the other—to open major league baseball to westward expansion in 1958, the Giants have been a team of individual standouts but little collective success (notwithstanding a division title in '97 and a near miss for the National League wild card berth in '98). The team has won four National League West championships and two pennants in its 40-or-so years in San Francisco, losing the World Series to the Yankees in 1962 and to the Oakland A's in 1989.

Yet in this city, style points are almost as valuable as titles, and the Giants have had plenty of style. The 1960s squads had big clout from legendary center fielder Willie Mays, first basemen Willie McCovey and Orlando Cepeda, and the brilliant pitcher Juan Marichal. The Giants didn't have a losing season in San Francisco until 1972, but they suffered several close eliminations. In each season from 1964 to 1966, for example, the team was in contention up to the final few games of the year.

The Giants of the 1970s and early '80s played hard but fell short of victory. Finally a slugging lineup that included Will Clark, Kevin Mitchell, and Matt Williams took the team to division titles in 1987 and 1989. Those three players are gone now; however, Barry Bonds continues to be a one-man draw. In 2001, Bonds went down in the history books for hitting 73 home runs during regular season play. He also set records for slugging percentage (.863) and walks (177). He continued to make headlines after the season was over when he re-signed with the Giants in a lucrative, five-year deal worth $90 million.

When the moody Bonds is focused on business, he is arguably one of the five best all-around players in major-league history.

Candlestick Park, at the south end of San Francisco off U.S. 101, was considered a jewel when it opened in 1960. But after years of frigid ninth innings and wind-tormented pop flies, Giants president Peter Magowan announced that the team would be moving to a new, privately financed stadium in the China Basin area of San Francisco. That stadium, Pacific Bell Park, hosted the home opener in the year 2000. Designed by the renowned architectural group of HOK Sports Facilities, it's a nostalgic wonder along the lines of Baltimore's Oriole Park at Camden Yards and Cleveland's Jacobs Field. Pac Bell Park hugs San Francisco Bay—so close, in fact, that prodigious drives to right field end up in salt water, retrieved by a canine employee. The stadium includes a brew pub, a bayside promenade that allows fans to peek through the fence for no charge, and, unlike 3Com Park, ample public transportation options. Current Giants ticket prices range from $9.00 to $45.00.

Oakland Athletics
Network Associates Coliseum,
off I–880, about 5 miles south of I–980
(510) 568–5600
www.athletics.mlb.com
KFRC 610 AM/KVON 1440 AM

The Athletics' history in Oakland has been the steepest of roller-coaster rides. The A's had been unqualifiedly dreadful in Kansas City, but they immediately posted their first winning record in 16 years after moving to the Bay Area in 1968. The A's improved steadily and soon captured three consecutive World Series (1972–74), a feat that no team has duplicated since. Those Athletics—known as the rollicking Mustache Gang—were put together by maverick owner Charles O. Finley. Reggie Jackson hit the home runs and made the headlines, but the strength of the team was pitching, led by starters Jim "Catfish" Hunter, Vida Blue, and handlebar-mustachioed reliever Rollie Fingers. But Finley soon sold off his stars, and the Athletics sank into ineptitude.

They played games in the late 1970s that drew fewer than 1,000 fans.

The team had no more sustained success until it was bought by the family of Walter Haas, the Levi's executive who became a model for professional sports owners. Under the Haas family's benevolence, the shrewd personnel moves of general manager Sandy Alderson, and the cool machinations of manager Tony LaRussa, the A's became Major League Baseball's best team from 1988 to 1990. Dave Stewart won 20 or more games four straight years, Dennis Eckersley was reborn as baseball's eminent closer, Rickey Henderson returned to his hometown to steal bases and runs, and hitting giants such as Jose Canseco and Mark McGwire drove opposing pitchers into deep depression. Oakland was upset by the Dodgers in '88 and the Reds in '90 but flattened the Giants in 1989's "Bay Bridge Series," which was interrupted by the 7.1-magnitude Loma Prieta earthquake.

Alas, the A's didn't have enough money to retain the superstars, and the team hit the rocks again in the 1990s as ownership passed to local businessmen Steve Schott and Ken Hofmann. Before long, Oakland had traded McGwire to St. Louis, given up (once again) on Rickey

Insiders' Tip

If you're going to the Oakland Coliseum or the Arena for a game, consider taking BART, the Bay Area Rapid Transit system. You can park in Richmond, at the northwest tip of what is commonly called the East Bay, and take a train to the Coliseum's doorstep. Call (415) 992-2278 for schedules and directions.

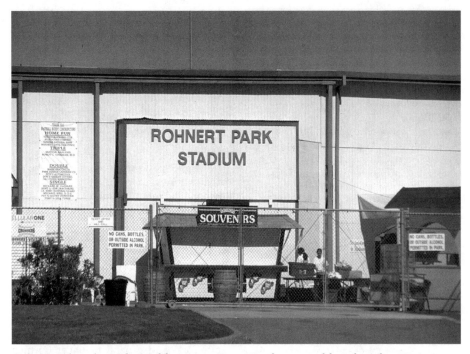

Rohnert Park Stadium is home of the Sonoma County Crushers, part of the Independent Western Baseball League. PHOTO: TINA LUSTER-HOBAN

Henderson, and watched Sandy Alderson leave to take a post with Major League Baseball.

The recently renovated Network Associates Coliseum remains a delightful place to watch a ball game. The music is way ahead of the standard play list, there is a play room for bored kids, and rainouts are nearly as rare as no-hitters. (There were only 11 rain checks issued between 1978 and 1996.) The stadium lies south of downtown Oakland, right off I-880. The cheapest A's ticket is $3.00; the most expensive is $30.00, and all of them are half-price if you are younger than 15 or older than 60.

Sonoma County Crushers
Rohnert Park Stadium, 5900 Labath Ave.,
Rohnert Park
(707) 588-8300
www.crushersbaseball.com
KBBF 89.1 FM

There may not be anyone named Bonds or Grieve on the field, but fans in Sonoma County have discovered what their ilk around the country already knew: Minor-league baseball is a heck of a lot of fun. The unaffiliated Crushers, 1998 champions of the independent Western Baseball League, play on a one-time cow pasture developed into a cozy, 4,150-seat stadium. (From U.S. 101, go west on the Rohnert Park Expressway.) Both the team and the league got going in 1995.

On 45 home dates between late May and early September, the Crushers host teams from places like Chico, Salinas, and Bend, Oregon. A Crushers ticket can be had for $5.00 to $13.00—quite a bargain for an experience that includes a field-adjacent barbecue deck, a giant Korbel champagne bottle that "explodes" upon every Crushers home run, and quite possibly the greatest name in the history of sports mascots: the Abominable Sonoman.

Football

San Francisco 49ers
3Com Park at Candlestick Point, off U.S. 101, about 1.5 miles south of I–280
(415) 656–4900
www.sf49ers.com
KGO 810 AM

Despite their recent implosion, the 49ers retain a firm grip on the hearts and minds of Northern California. The caps, the T-shirts, the bumper stickers, and the bar decorations are there to make sure you don't forget, not even for a minute, that the Wine Country is Niners country. It wasn't always this way, of course. The team had its core following for decades, but it wasn't until the harmonic convergence of Bill Walsh and Joe Montana that the serious adulation began.

The 49ers got their start in the All-America Football Conference in 1946, then became one of three AAFC teams (the Browns and Colts were the others) to join the NFL in 1950. Since then, Hall of Famers and perennial all-pros have regularly graced the gridirons of Kezar Stadium and Candlestick/3Com Park. There was quarterback Y.A. Tittle, with his balding head and golden arm. There was Hugh McElhenny, one of the finest open-field runners in history. There was halfback Joe Perry, an unlikely blend of power and speed. Throw in Leo Nomellini, Bob St. Clair (who actually ate, and eats, raw meat), and John Brodie. Though blessed with plenty of attractions, San Francisco had no championships. From 1946 through 1980, the 49ers had no NFL title banners to fly.

That changed when Walsh, the academic head coach, and Montana, the uncanny quarterback, arrived in 1979. The 49ers were in the Super Bowl by January 1982, and they'd be back four times in the next 13 seasons. During this era, even a down year usually amounted to an 11–5 record, an NFC West title, and a loss in the conference championship game. Along the way, Montana was replaced by scrambling Steve Young, now also retired from the game. Wide receiver Dwight Clark was replaced by Jerry Rice, maybe the best player ever to wear an NFL uniform. Battering-ram safety Ronnie Lott was replaced by Tim McDonald. Even Walsh was replaced with protege George Seifert, who was in turn supplanted by Steve Mariucci in 1997. Through it all, the team hardly missed a beat—until 1999, when it sank to the bottom of the NFL. They took another hit in 2001, when Jerry Rice defected to the Oakland Raiders.

The 49ers want a new, state-of-the-art stadium, not to mention an integrated commercial mega-complex, at the existing site of 3Com Park. And they want taxpayers to shoulder about $100 million of the project through bonds. Proposition D made that money available in 1997, and Proposition F changed the local zoning code. Both passed by the slimmest of margins in a highly charged election.

The aftermath was not pretty, as a front-office feud among longtime owner Eddie DeBartolo, his sister Denise DeBartolo York, and general manager Carmen Policy resulted in Policy's departure for the NFL's new Cleveland Browns franchise. Dwight Clark soon left the Niners' front office to join him. All this played out against the backdrop of Eddie's plea-bargain in a federal court case involving a riverboat casino licensing scheme.

A few end notes: 49ers tickets are about $50, but good luck purchasing one. The games have been sold out since 1981. Allow at least 90 minutes to 3Com Park from either Napa or Santa Rosa, progressively longer from points farther north. And for heaven's sake, bring a jacket and a thermos of something hot.

Oakland Raiders
Network Associates Coliseum,
off I–880, about 5 miles south of I–980
(888) 447–2433
www.raiders.com
The Ticket, 1050 AM/KVON 1440 AM

That wasn't a tremor you felt in June 1995, it was the earth shifting back onto its proper axis upon the Raiders' return to Oakland—the first time a pro sports franchise had come back to a city it once fled. To the citizens of Oakland and its working-class satellites such as Hayward and San Leandro, there never was a doubt about the return of their not-so-prodigal son, Al Davis. Los Angeles just never seemed right for the team that is symbolized by a surly, one-eyed pirate.

So far, however, the homecoming has produced more political than playoff contention. The hastily brokered deal that brought the Raiders back to town has left the city of Oakland responsible for unsold "personal seat licenses," and this is a city with little financial cushion. Still, the East Bay fans have waited a long time for the return of "Raidah football," as Davis might say, and they are generally forgiving.

Oakland was one of the eight original American Football League franchises and has proven to be quite successful. The Raiders, as they will tell you themselves at every opportunity, have the best record in all of professional sports since 1963, claiming 3 Super Bowl victories and 12 AFL/AFC West titles (the team spent 13 years in Los Angeles, 1982–94). The team's pinnacle was 1972 to 1976, when the blustery John Madden coached at least seven Pro Football Hall of Fame players: center Jim Otto, guard Gene Upshaw, tackle Art Shell, wide receiver Fred Biletnikoff, kicker George Blanda, linebacker Ted Hendricks, and corner-back Willie Brown (not to be confused with San Francisco's iconoclastic mayor of the same name). The '76 team shook off three consecutive losses in the AFC championship game to overwhelm Minnesota 32–14 in Super Bowl XI. The Raiders also captured the Lombardi Trophy in January of 1981 and 1984.

Stars of the 1980s included soft-spoken quarterback Jim Plunkett, relentless defensive end Howie Long, and incomparable running back Marcus Allen. Davis' never-ending search for the right head coach continued in 1998, when he brought in young Jon Gruden, an offensive whiz kid from the Philadelphia Eagles. (But he's more than a whiz kid, he's also beautiful. He made *People* magazine's "50 Most Beautiful People in the World" list in 2001. Go figure.) The team finished 8–8 in '98 behind a defense that

ranked as one of the league's best before suffering key injuries in the second half of the season and hovered right around 500 in '99, too. Tim Brown is still one of the NFL's most exciting receivers, and in 2000 the team also included quarterback Rich Gannon and a promising kicker named Sebastian Janikowski, a draft pick from Florida State.

The Raiders' rich on-field history notwithstanding, the best reason to come to Oakland on an autumn Sunday always has been the spontaneous circus that erupts in the parking lot and the cheap seats. It's a freak show of the highest order—not as physically dangerous as the version at the Los Angeles Coliseum, but more entertaining. Expect to see Darth Vaders, Grim Reapers, dangling bronco effigies, and more Harley-Davidsons and pirate tattoos than you can shake a cutlass at. Tickets are $41, $51, and $61.

Finally, take note that the Raiders moved their summer training camp to Napa in 1996. They practice on a field behind the Napa Valley Marriott Hotel at 3425 Solano Avenue, which runs parallel to Highway 29. Those sessions are closed to the public, but the team has an annual fan day in July—and perhaps a couple of open workouts—at Memorial Stadium, which is near the intersection of Jefferson Street and Pueblo Avenue.

Basketball

Golden State Warriors
The Arena in Oakland, off I–880,
about 5 miles south of I–980
(510) 986-2222
www.nba.com/Warriors
KNBR 680 AM

Careful observers will note that the Warriors and their NBA neighbors, the Sacramento Kings, were absent from the Wine Country, Bay Area, American, and world-sports landscapes for much of the so-called 1998–99 season—along with the rest of the near-moribund, salary-heavy league. The owners and players had the decency to resolve their bitter labor strife in time to jury-rig a 50-game schedule from January to June of 1999. Roughly 200 free agents hopped from team to team as the post-Michael Jordan epoch got started. The Warriors joined the fray.

Golden State rid itself of Latrell Sprewell, the troubled superstar guard. The Warriors added veterans John Starks, Terry Cummings, and Jason Caffey and had high hopes for first-round draft choice Antawn Jamison.

Born in Philadelphia in the 1940s, they moved west, becoming the San Francisco Warriors from 1962 to 1971, before floating across the bay to Oakland to become Golden State. They played a few games in San Diego early on, and they played all their 1996–97 home games in San Jose while the Coliseum Arena was being renovated. Now they are back in Oakland and looking to overcome a string of aggravating seasons.

The team that brought Wilt Chamberlain from Philadelphia in 1962 has won only one NBA title on the West Coast. That came in 1975, when superstar Rick Barry and a gang of overachievers shocked the Washington Bullets in a four-game sweep. Big-time performers such as Nate Thurmond and Cazzie Russell came before 1974–75, Bernard King and World B. Free after, but no other Warriors team has gone all the way. Golden State's frustration during the 1980s is summed up by the trade that sent workhorse center Robert Parish to Boston for the draft pick used on Joe Barry Carroll.

Things seemed to be looking up under coach Don Nelson in the early 1990s, but the situation blew up when Nelson feuded with star forward Chris Webber in 1994–95. Webber demanded a trade, and the Warriors obliged. Three months later Nelson was gone too, and the team was left to pick up the pieces. Can Golden State's fortunes turn? The team may have taken a step in the right direction when owner Christopher Cohan hired respected coach P. J. Carlesimo in 1997. Cohan's move proved less than brilliant as the team struggled to an ugly 19–63 record, a statistic bound to be rendered academic when Sprewell grabbed Carlesimo by the throat during a December practice session and was suspended without pay for the remainder of the season. The news dominated all accounts of the Warriors' progress, or lack of it. Warriors tickets range from $10 to $113.

Sacramento Kings
ARCO Arena,
near the northeast corner of I–5 and I–80
(916) 928-6900
www.nba.com/Kings
KHTK 1140 AM

Game after game, ARCO Arena is filled to the rafters with screaming, maniacal Kings fans. Finally, they've got something to shout about. In their first 13 seasons in Sacramento the Kings never had a winning season. But the love of hoops was unconditional here. Sellouts are practically a Sacramento city ordinance.

Existing franchises in various sports, including the Raiders and the A's, certainly have taken notice, making overtures to Sacramento in the recent past regarding possible moves. (Sacramento has been the Kings' home since 1985, but they've moved before—from Rochester, Cincinnati, and Kansas City.) Los Angeles-based developer Jim Thomas has headed a four-man ownership group since 1992, and he would like to add a championship one day. It's not as outlandish as it once sounded. Chris Webber, a powerful rebounder and scorer, has blossomed at the other end of Jason Williams' improbable no-look passes. With Vlade Divac and Nick Anderson adding veteran leadership, the Kings have become part of the NBA elite.

ARCO Arena is just north of Sacramento. From the Wine Country, take I-80 to Sacramento and turn off on I-5 north. Take the Del Paso Road exit and follow the signs. Tickets range from $10 to $115 per game, though all but the cheapest seats are snapped up by season-ticket holders. In fact, if you're after Kings tickets you are encouraged either to book weeks in advance or befriend a lonely corporate CEO.

Hockey

San Jose Sharks
San Jose Arena, off I-880
Ticket Master
(415) 421–8497, (408) 287–4275
www.sj-sharks.com
KXBX 1270 AM

The Sharks made a reputation as giant-killers as they knocked off high-ranked opponents, Detroit and then Calgary, in the opening rounds of the 1994 and 1995 NHL playoffs. But the problem for San Jose has been getting to the playoffs. The Sharks have been known as the bottom feeders of the Western Conference, though Coach Darryl Sutter's 1999–2000 squad was eminently respectable.

San Jose Arena is a tidy venue smack dab in the middle of a tidy city, and professional hockey has been an incongruous hit in Silicon Valley. To get to the arena, exit I-880 at Coleman Avenue, turn left on Coleman, right on Julian, and follow the parking signs. The Sharks began play in 1991, and the arena opened two years later. Recently, general manager Dean Lombardi has assembled a solid cast that includes right wing Owen Nolan and center Vincent Damphousse.

Be advised that San Jose is about 40 miles south of San Francisco or Oakland, so getting there and back from the Wine Country takes an investment of a full day or a long evening. Sharks tickets range from $18 for the most distant upper-reserved seats to $102 for sideline club seats. Many others are in the $35 to $72 range.

Insiders' Tip

We can't emphasize this enough: If you intend to drive from the Wine Country to major-league sporting events in San Francisco and Oakland be prepared to spend a lot of time in traffic getting to and from your destination. Leave early and please be patient.

Soccer

San Jose Earthquakes
Spartan Stadium, off I-280
(408) 985–GOAL
www.sjearthquakes.com
KLIV 1590 AM

When Major League Soccer officially set up shop in spring of 1996, the fledgling league chose San Jose as the site of its inaugural game. The city had everything MLS was looking for: an established soccer tradition, a first-rate stadium, and a well-run organization headed by transplanted Englishman Peter Bridgwater. More than 31,000 fans crammed into Spartan Stadium on April 6, 1996, and the Clash (as they were then known) did not disappoint, leaving with a 1-0 victory over D.C. United.

Hope springs eternal in the heart of Silicon Valley for a team led by defender John Doyle and goalkeeper Joe Cannon. Midfielder Eddie Lewis was named to the U.S. National Team for '99 while gifted forward Ronald Cerritos played for El Salvador. In 2000 they meshed under the tutelage of Bay Area favorite Lother Osiander. The Earthquakes won the MLS Cup in 2001 over the L.A. Galaxy, on the winning goal of Cerritos.

Spartan Stadium is on the San Jose State University campus, accessible by

I-280 in the heart of San Jose. Exit at Seventh Street, turn right on Seventh, and proceed about 1.5 miles to the stadium. (And please note the distance caveat stated at the end of the Sharks' summary.) Adult tickets range from $13 for behind-the-goal seats to $20 for the "premier" category. (Gold Club seats at midfield are sold out.) There are discounts for kids younger than 14 and seniors older than 60, beginning at $7.00 for the cheap seats. The Major League Soccer schedule runs from March through October.

Golf

**The Napa Championship Presented by Beringer—Senior Golf Championship
Silverado Country Club and Resort,
1600 Atlas Peak Rd., Napa
(707) 252-8687, (800) 286-GOLF
www.silveradoresort.com**

The PGA Senior Tour returned to Napa's Silverado Resort in October 1999 for the Transamerica, a tournament that in 11 years has raised more than $1.5 million for Napa Valley charities such as the Queen of the Valley Hospital Foundation and local Boys and Girls Clubs. The splendid 6632-yard, par 72 course, with its 1857 Colonial clubhouse, consistently lures the biggest names on the Senior Tour. Recent participants include Arnold Palmer, Lee Trevino, Chi Chi Rodriguez, Dick Stockton, Jim Colbert, and Tom Weiskopf.

Sponsorship changed after the 2001 event, won by Sammy Rachels after a final-round 69 for a 14-under-par 202 total. But the action for charity goes on in 2002 under the Beringer banner.

The weeklong event includes two practice rounds (free to attend the first day, $5.00 the second), a two-day Pro-Am competition ($13.00 each day to attend), and three rounds of serious golf ($18.00 the first day, $20.00 for each of the latter two). You also can choose from a series of packages that include subsequent admission to the tournament grounds and clubhouse. They run from $13 to $105. All of the noted prices are at the gate; you can save by ordering early. Parking runs $4.00 for a daily pass or $10.00 for a tournament pass. Silverado is northeast of downtown Napa, off Highway 121.

Motor Sports

Don't be surprised if the still air of your summer evening is suddenly torn apart by the growl of a 750-horsepower engine, the scent of ripening grapes replaced by a whiff of high-octane fuel. Love 'em or hate 'em, racing machines are here to stay in Wine Country. This section is divided by venue.

**Calistoga Speedway
Napa County Fairgrounds,
1435 N. Oak St., Calistoga
(707) 942-5111**

Calistoga is a gathering point for devotees of sprint cars, those miniature, winged beasts that evolved from old Indy 500 roadsters. Pound for pound, sprint cars pack as much power as modern-day Indy cars, and they seem to be as loud. Two features that separate sprint cars from the pack are the wings and the tires. Each vehicle has a billboard-size wing on top of its roll cage and a smaller one on the nose. They produce downward force, which helps the car grip the track; the larger one also happens to provide handy space for advertising. Sprint cars have fatter tires on the outside wheels to help them roll into corners. In fact, it is a rarity for any two tires on one car to be of the same size.

Calistoga Speedway's half-mile dirt track hosts approximately seven sprint-car nights a year: four sanctioned by the Northern Auto Racing Club and a three-day event put on by the World of Outlaws. The NARC nights tend to be in early May, Memorial Day weekend, and July 4th weekend. The World of Outlaws event is Labor Day weekend. A typical program might include four 10-lap heat races, a feature-inversion dash, a 12-lap semi-main event, and a 25-lap feature event. Tickets run about $15 for NARC races and $80 for the Outlaws' three-day package.

Sears Point Raceway
Hwys. 37 and 121
(800) 870–RACE
www.searspoint.com

Which event drew the largest crowd in the history of Northern California sports? It wasn't the 49ers vs. Dallas in the 1994 NFC Championship Game or one of the A's-Giants World Series contests in 1989. It was the NASCAR Winston Cup stock car race that drew 102,000 in May 1996. That event was staged at Sears Point.

If it's nitro-burning, rubber-ripping, and asphalt-grabbing, chances are you'll find it here. This might be the world's busiest raceway, with an average of 340 days a year of activity including 50 of 52 weekends. Much of that is devoted to the resident Russell Racing School, but there is plenty of competition among a variety of internally combusting machines.

Besides the twisting, 12-turn, 2.52-mile road course and the quarter-mile drag strip, Sears Point offers 700,000 square feet of coexisting shop space and posh, tower VIP seats. The facility is in a beautiful corner of lush rolling hills at the southern tip of Sonoma County. If you just want a look, it's open to the public free of charge on weekdays. If you want to get truly revved, race tickets range from $15 to $100, with many in the $15 to $25 range.

A comprehensive $35 million modernization project that was expected to last about two years finally got underway in late 2000. The first phase of the upgrade adds 34,000 new seats, additional garages for competitors, a pedestrian tunnel, new shops, and a landscaping beautification that creates more shaded picnic areas. Some of the racetrack's many twists and turns are also being reconstructed.

Petaluma Speedway
Petaluma Fairgrounds, 100 Fairgrounds Dr.
(707) 762–7223
www.petalumaspeedway.com

Check the notes about sprint cars listed in the Calistoga Speedway section and apply them here. NARC stages two events on Petaluma's three-eighths-mile, semi-banked track over the July 4th weekend and in early October. The fairgrounds are just west of U.S. 101 on E. Washington Street. If you have to ask how far away it is, maybe this sport isn't for you. A 1996 survey showed that sprint-car fans traveled an average of 82 miles to each event.

Marathons and Running Events

Vineman Marathon
Northern Sonoma County
(707) 528–1630
www.vineman.com

This popular event—in its 13th year—attracts more than 2,000 participants from throughout the world. It is set mostly on the backroads of northern Sonoma County, with the swimming portion held in the Russian River at Guerneville. The full course includes a 112-mile cycle, 26.2-mile run, and 2.4-mile swim. A Half Vineman is also featured.

Sutter Home Napa Valley Marathon
Calistoga to Napa
(707) 255–2609
www.napa-marathon.com

Hey, if you're gonna torture yourself, you might as well do it in Eden. This is an unbeatable course: 26.2 miles due south along the Silverado Trail, hills hugging the left side of the road, and a yellow sea of blooming mustard to the right. Only the last half-mile, the approach to the finish line at Vintage High School, is within any city limits. And after three moderate hills in the first 6 miles, the course offers a gently rolling descent.

The Napa Valley Marathon usually takes place the first Sunday in March. The 2002 edition was the 24th annual. You can park at Vintage High and take a shuttle bus to the start line (just south of Calistoga on the Silverado Trail) but be punctual—the last bus leaves at 5:30 A.M. Weather can vary, of course, but bet on lifting fog and temperatures in the mid-40s at start time (7:00 A.M.), progressing to warm sunshine later in the morning. Early entry costs $60, and it jumps to $75 on prerace Saturday.

The Relay
Calistoga to Santa Cruz
(415) 508–9700
www.TheRelay.com

The marathon doesn't present enough of a challenge for you? Try The Relay, a 199-mile trek that winds through seven counties and 36 cities from Calistoga to Santa Cruz, past cow pastures and redwoods and across the Golden Gate Bridge. The first Relay attracted exactly nine teams in 1995, but it has mushroomed to thousands of runners since then.

Everything about this race is unique, except for sore feet and sweaty bodies. Start times are staggered at the Calistoga Mineral plant. Teams of 12 competitors split up 36 3-to-7-mile legs, with vans leapfrogging runners to their next start position. The race heads south on the Silverado Trail, with competitors running through the night and the first finishers reaching the Pacific early the next morning. Several Silicon Valley companies have gotten involved, presenting more peculiarities. This was the first race in which runners wore bar codes and got scanned at checkpoints. The Relay's home page even offers a three-dimensional preview of each leg.

The Relay is run under a full moon in September or October. The entry fee is $40 per runner, climbing to $50 in August. Individuals looking for a team have two options: Find one yourself at the Web site, or mark the appropriate box on your application and organizers will place you.

Bicycle Road Races

Cherry Pie Criterium
Napa Valley Corporate Park, Napa
(707) 224–2369, (707) 258–0663

The carbo-loading comes after the race at this event. Besides the $1,500 or so in prize money—including $600 for the Pro I-II division—the top three finishers in each class are awarded fresh cherry pies. The 2002 Cherry Pie is the 27th annual. The 1-mile course, which includes one modest hill, is bounded by Napa Valley Corporate Drive, Napa Valley Corporate Way, and Trefethen Way. The simplest

way to find the start/finish line is to look for the famous Grape Crusher statue south of Napa. Between 300 and 350 racers split up into 11 divisions, including a recumbent category. It is run the second or third Sunday in February.

Napa Grand Prix
First and Main Sts., Napa
(707) 963–7736

This criterium (a timed road race, with the winner determined by number of laps completed) got its start only recently—in 1994—but its following is on the upswing. Hoping for a breeze off the Napa River in early August, the restaurants of downtown Napa put extra tables on the sidewalk so their customers can sip cool drinks and watch the colors go blurring by. The Master's race is a U.S. Cycling Federation district championship, and there are several other divisions including a 90-minute Pro race that draws about 80 riders. The 0.7-mile course is bounded by First, School, Second, and Main Streets.

Petaluma Criterium
8375 Lancaster Dr., Rohnert Park
(707) 795–6670
www.rahul.net/kpapai/westcoast

Sonoma County's West Coast Cycling Team organizes this race, which is held at Oakmead Business Park on the southeast end of town, just off Lakeville Highway (a.k.a. Highway 116). The 0.7-mile course offers great spectator viewing, and all races last approximately one hour. The race is generally held in early May, and the entrance fee is between $15 and $20—the 2003 event will be the 15th. Expect 300 to 350 riders.

Wine Country Cycling Classic
Graton and Santa Rosa
(707) 528–3283
www.socobikes.com

What started as the Santa Rosa Criterium in 1984 has become a two-day road event, the largest of its kind in Northern California. The Classic takes place in late March or early April and includes a total field of nearly 1,500 riders. The first day features the Graton Road Race, staged on an 11-mile course that presents four short, rolling climbs and one certified calf-burner. The pro division race is 88 miles long and pays about $4,000. Graton is 3.5 miles north of Sebastopol, just west of Highway 116.

As many as 5,000 spokeheads turn out to watch the action on the second day on a flat, fast 0.7-mile course in downtown Santa Rosa. The racing is only part of a day of festivities that often includes a live band. The Senior I/Pro division competes for 90 minutes and splits about $3,500. The starting/finish line is on Sonoma Avenue. Take the Downtown Santa Rosa exit from U.S. 101 and head east on Third Street to Santa Rosa Avenue. Turn right and proceed two blocks. Dave Walters, who organizes the Classic, also stages a weekly criterium every Tuesday night from April through August. The first race starts at 6:00 P.M. at Corporate Center Industrial Park. Call for directions.

Horse Jumping

Napa Valley Fairgrounds
1435 N. Oak St., Calistoga
(707) 942–5111
Carousel Show Management stages hunter-jumper horse shows here in mid-July and early October. The five-day event in July includes the Napa Valley Classic, probably the biggest one-day event of its kind in this part of California. Local merchants set up wine- and food-tasting stalls outside the jumping area. Admission is $25, and some $10,000 is generated for the Hospice of Napa Valley. The October show is a four-day event that includes the Northern California Hunter Jumper Association medal finals. There are separate awards for juniors, amateurs, and ponies. Admission is free.

Sonoma County Fairgrounds
Hwy. 12, east of U.S. 101, Santa Rosa
(707) 545–4200
www.sonomacountyfair.com
Carousel also organizes two three-day events at the Sonoma County Fairgrounds, which are off Highway 12, not

more than a mile east of U.S. 101. The first show is in May, the second over Labor Day weekend. The latter includes the Carousel medal finals and an evening event under the lights. There is no charge for either show.

Horse Racing

Sonoma County Fairgrounds
Hwy. 12, east of U.S. Hwy. 101, Santa Rosa
(707) 545–4200
www.sonomacountyfair.com
If the hoofbeat of the thoroughbreds should happen to draw your attention in midsummer, heed the call to the colors. What you'll find at the Sonoma County Fair from late July through early August is one of the country's most entertaining 12-day horse racing meets. Top jockeys such as Russell Baze, Dennis Carr, and Rafael Meza guide the trainees of Jerry Hollendorfer, Brent Sumja, Lloyd Mason, and others as thousands cheer home the world's greatest four-legged athletes. Wagering on the competition is optional. First post is 1:15 P.M.

The Jockey Club
1350 Bennett Valley Rd., Santa Rosa
(707) 524–6340
www.sonomacountyfair.com/jockey.asp
This is where Wine Country's wise guys and other hip handicappers amuse themselves when the shed rows across the street aren't booked with blood stock. It's a year-round off-track concession offering races live via satellite TV from major courses in California (e.g., Golden Gate Fields, Bay Meadows, Santa Anita, Hollywood Park, Del Mar), New York, and Florida.

Three bucks gets you through the door and into a well-kept room stocked with eight projection big-screen TVs, 70 monitors, a full bar, and complete food and beverage services. Friendly clerks will take your wagers, or you may purchase a voucher and have at the auto-tote self-serve screens yourself. Either way, remember: There's a winner in each race.

Top jockeys and their four-legged athletes compete at the Sonoma County Fairgrounds in July and August.

College Sports

With only three four-year colleges inside its borders, the expansive Wine Country isn't exactly a hotbed of collegiate sports. Again, the Bay Area might be the place to turn if you really feel like waving a pom-pom and belting out fight songs. Here is a brief look at your options.

Sonoma State University
1801 E. Cotati Ave., Rohnert Park
(707) 664–2701
www.sonoma.edu/athletics

With a couple of players in the NFL, including Pro Bowl guard Larry Allen of the Dallas Cowboys, the NCAA Division II Cossacks had reached a respected place among small football programs. That came to an end in 1997, when the university dropped football in the face of formidable travel expenses.

Sonoma State still has plenty of athletics, including seven women's and five men's teams (the student body is 60 percent female). Soccer is king and queen there: The women, who made it to the Division II championship game in 1998, have enjoyed great success in the '90s, winning six straight Northern California Athletic Conference titles from 1990 to 1995 and a national championship in 1990. The men won five of seven NCAC titles between 1990 and 1996. The Cossacks jumped to the California Collegiate Athletic Association in the 1998–99 sports year.

Pacific Union College
1 Angwin Ave., Angwin
(707) 965–6344
www.puc.edu

Tiny PUC has to scramble to come up with funding for sports, but the NAIA Division II school does what it can. It fields men's and/or women's teams in soccer, volleyball, tennis, cross-country, basketball, golf, and softball, with all but tennis staged on campus. The Pioneers have produced recent California Pacific Conference champions in women's basketball and men's golf.

University of California
2223 Fulton St., Berkeley
(800) 462–2327
www.calbears.fansonly.com

Known primarily for its academics and tradition of radical politics, Cal also has a rich sports heritage, with Rose Bowl victories dating back to 1921 (28–0 over Ohio State). The Golden Bear's football program, which produced such stars as Craig Morton, Steve Bartkowski, Wesley Walker, and Chuck Muncie, has seen better days. Coach Bruce Snyder took the Bears to strong conference finishes and a Citrus Bowl victory in the early '90s, but since then the program has floundered.

Bears basketball experienced a recent renaissance, begun by phenomenal point guard Jason Kidd (now an NBA star) in the early 1990s. In 1996–97, first-year coach Ben Braun took over a team in disarray (and headed for NCAA probation, thanks to the misdeeds of his predecessor Todd Bozeman), lost leading scorer Ed Gray at the end of the Pac-10 schedule, and still managed to invade the NCAA tourney's Sweet Sixteen. There, the Golden Bears fell in a close game to North Carolina.

Ironically, Braun's team signaled another resurgence in late '98 by extending its record to 9-1 for the 1998–99 season with a 78-71 victory over the Tar Heels. That squad was denied Big Dance access, but showed the selection committee by winning the lower-visibility NIT tournament. The Bears came back to earth in 1999–2000.

Stanford University
Stanford Ticket Office, Stanford
(415) 723–1021, (800) 232–8225
www.stanfordfanz.net
KVON 1440 AM

Stanford is acclaimed for its squeaky-clean (well, at least by today's standards) sports programs, but it still manages to attract professional-caliber talent. Historically, the Cardinal (singular, please) has been something of a quarterback factory, producing NFL passers from Frankie Albert to John Brodie to Jim Plunkett to John Elway. Lately, the basketball team has ascended under professorial coach Mike Montgomery. In 1998, Arthur Lee, Mark "Mad Dog" Madsen, and a group of no-names made it to the Final Four, where they lost their semifinal game in overtime to eventual champion Kentucky. That run led to a preseason No. 1 ranking in more than one poll for 1998–99. The 1999–2000 school year was even dizzier, as Madsen led the hoops teams to national contention while Tyrone Willingham's football team earned a Rose Bowl berth.

In the mid-'90s, Tara VanDerveer's women's basketball program earned most of the acclaim. The Cardinal women, building on the legacy of Jennifer Azzi and showcasing the graceful Kate Starbird (Class of '96) were an annual powerhouse that captured two Division I women's hoops titles early in the decade.

Kidstuff

Napa County

Sonoma County

Mendocino County

Lake County

Outside the Wine Country

You've just exited your tenth tasting room of the day and have an impressive collection of souvenir glasses, coasters, and corkscrews from an assortment of winery gift shops. The kids are bored, but with energy still left to burn. If you don't find a suitable diversion for them soon, you'll have a full-blown mutiny on your hands.

No need to worry—you don't have to change your plans and head to Orlando. If the adults are even the slightest bit flexible, any family can find common ground in Wine Country. That might not be the first impression you get from perusing this chapter. Why? Because most of the reliable kid pleasers are just as popular with adults and are profiled accordingly in other sections of the book. For example, our Attractions chapter is rife with amusements for the prepubescent set, from the Pedals Past Bicycle Museum in Calistoga to Safari West wildlife preserve, outside of Santa Rosa.

Our Parks and Recreation chapter has more great outdoors destinations for kids, plus fun diversions like horseback riding, swimming, and bowling. Add to those the wet activities in our On the Water chapter, and don't forget the professional and minor league athletic events you'll find if you turn to the Spectator Sports section.

But even after all that, we were left with a few places and events that begged for inclusion. Here they are—family-oriented attractions, including a handy selection of book and toy stores. It's everything you need to prevent boredom, even among an age group that prides itself on being bored.

Napa County

Napa Skate Park
Pearl and Clinton Sts., Napa
(707) 257–9529

If they're bouncing off the walls, just put a skateboard or a scooter under their feet and give 'em a gentle nudge. The skate park is just about what you'd expect: a cemented city block with an assortment of hills, dips, ramps, and pathways. This is a free, do-it-yourself attraction. Bring your own gear, supervise your own children, bandage your own knees. Roller skates and roller blades are welcome too.

John F. Kennedy Memorial Regional Park
Streblow Dr. off Hwy. 121, Napa
(707) 257–9529

The largest of Napa's municipal parks at 340 acres, Kennedy has four group picnic areas, hiking and jogging trails, volleyball courts, a lighted baseball diamond, and a multiuse ball field. It also has a duck pond and playground for the really young

ones, plus a boat ramp for family outings. It's a tranquil, breezy setting adjacent to the Napa River.

Paradise Miniature Golf
640 Third St., Napa
(707) 258–1695

What would a family road trip be without a few rounds of miniature golf? Paradise is in the heart of Napa (which some would say is in the heart of Paradise). It has a 19-hole course and a snack bar with candy and soft drinks. A couple of favorites: the 5th hole, with its grand loop-the-loop and, best of all, the 17th— the Valley Fog Hole—which tests your bad-weather vision as well as your hand-eye coordination. The cost is $3.50 for adults, $2.00 for kids 12 and younger, and $3.00 for members of the "senior tour." Paradise is open from 3:00 to 7:00 P.M. Monday through Friday and 11:00 A.M. to 7:00 P.M. on Saturday and Sunday during the summer; it's open weekends only in the off-season.

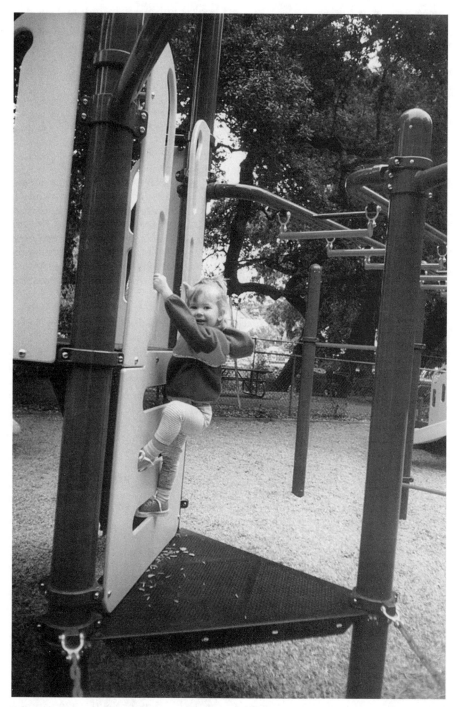

Calistoga's Pioneer Park has been improved with new playground equipment, making it popular with both locals and visitors with children. PHOTO: AHUVA SIMON-SA'AR

Carolyn Parr Nature Museum
3107 Browns Valley Rd., Napa
(707) 255-6465

This modest facility a mile west of Highway 29 is sponsored by the Napa Valley Naturalists. People come here to see the museum's dioramas, which show five habitats: grassland, chaparral, marshland, riparian, and woodland/forest. Inside each diorama are examples of native plants and animal specimens, from raccoons and wood ducks to king snakes and badgers. There is an extensive raptor display and a special kids' section with such hands-on items as pelts and skulls. Adults enjoy the Carolyn Parr museum too, but the small scale seems ideally suited to children. Admission is free. The museum is open from 1:00 to 4:00 P.M. Saturday and Sunday and for group tours by appointment (50 cents per head). It is at the entrance to Westwood Hills Park, a 111-acre green space with picnic facilities and a self-guided nature trail.

Learning Faire
964 Pearl St., Napa
(707) 253-1024

This Napa toy store, under the same ownership for more than 20 years, prides itself on selectivity. All products are prescreened for safety, and they sell nothing that promotes violence. Learning Faire stocks Brio, Thomas wooden trains, Legos, plenty of other toys, and lots of games, puzzles, crafts, books, cassettes, and CDs. There are hands-on stations and the occasional market-research play day—when manufacturer reps bring new toys for kids to sample.

Fun & Games
3646 Bel Aire Plaza, Napa
(707) 257-1468

Tradition is important to the folks at Fun & Games. They stock no video games, no electronic games, and no weaponry. Instead you'll find marbles, Wiffle bats, and a colorful variety of yo-yos. (The store even hosts yo-yo events that draw nationally prominent, um, yo-yoers.) Fun & Games focuses on a handful of children's

book publishers, including Scholastic and Random House. You'll find puzzles, timers, and games sitting out, waiting for tiny hands. And they have plenty of travel games, perfect for the drive home to Phoenix.

The Toy Cellar
Vintage 1870, 6525 Washington St., Yountville
(707) 944-2144

Sprawling Vintage 1870 tends to be a lot more popular with moms than juniors. The antidote? Let them roam around The Toy Cellar with its books and Brio trains, its Beanie Babies and Playmobil, its Steiff bears and model rockets, its LGB German trains and old-fashioned metal jack-in-the-boxes. Meanwhile, Dad can pop down to the wine cellar (see our Shopping chapter).

Crane Park
Crane Ave. and Grayson Ave., St. Helena
(707) 963-5706

St. Helena families and kids of every stripe gather at this well-kept sanctuary. The 10-acre park has two baseball diamonds, horseshoe pits, lighted bocce courts and tennis courts, substantial picnic set-ups, a playground, and volleyball pits. On summer Fridays the Farmers Market is here.

Smith's Mount St. Helena Trout Farm and Hatchery
18401 Ida Clayton Rd., Calistoga
(707) 987-3651

Smith's has been raising trout for private ponds for almost 60 years now. On weekends they open up their ¾-acre lake to the public, and locals have learned that it's one of the best diversions in the area for children. The proprietors provide poles and bait, and they even clean and bag the trout for you afterward. All you do is bait, cast, and reel. You pay only for the fish you take—$3.00 to $5.00, depending on size. From Highway 128 in Knights Valley, just north of Calistoga, go 7 miles north at the big sign for Smith's. On Saturdays and Sundays from February through October, the fun lasts from 10:00 A.M. to 5:00 P.M.

Sonoma County

Southern Sonoma

The Clubhouse Family Fun Center
19171 Sonoma Hwy., Sonoma
(707) 996-3616

When's the last time you paid $4.00 for 18 holes of golf? If you think miniature golf is a breeze of a game, just watch as your 10-year-old marks down all the low scores and comes in with a free game for whacking his ball on the 18th just right. The course is laid out to look like historic Sonoma, with ponds, fountains, and a lifelike City Hall. Not just for kids, it's a great place for dating teens. The Clubhouse also features a wide variety of the latest video games as well as sports games like air hockey, basketball, and football video games. To put an extra spin on a great family day, have a hot dog at the pond-side picnic area. The course and game room are open Monday through Thursday from noon to 8:00 P.M., Friday and Saturday to 10:00 P.M., and Sunday from 10:00 A.M. to 9:00 P.M. The rate for anyone older than five is $4.00 a game; kids younger than five play free. Special packages are available for family groups and birthday parties.

Train Town
20264 Broadway, Sonoma
(707) 938-3912
www.traintown.com

It's difficult to say who gets the most fun out of this train ride, kids or adults. The whole layout is so cleverly crafted that it's a marvel of dedication to the art of the train buff. The miniature train travels through scenic landscapes of trees, lakes, bridges, a 140-foot-long tunnel and a small-scale replica of a turn-of-the-century Sonoma Valley town called Lakeville. While adults may feel they have arrived in Lilliput, kids seem right in tune with the tiny country they travel through. Midway along, the best part for many kids is the petting zoo. For five minutes the train stops and everyone hauls out to pet llamas, horses, and miniature goats and to feed the ducks and geese. Back at the station there's a carousel ride ($1.00) and some interesting mechanical exhibits (see our Attractions chapter). Trains operate 10:00 A.M. to 5:00 P.M. every day in summer. Winter hours are 10:00 A.M. to 5:00 P.M. Friday through Sunday. At other times of the year, Engineer Kermit makes his own decisions on operating hours—it often depends on school schedules and rain—and will stick the "Open" sign out when he's there. Trains leave every 30 minutes. Adult fare is $3.75; kids and seniors go for $3.25.

Morton's Warm Springs
1651 Warm Springs Rd., Kenwood
(707) 833-5511
www.sterba.com/kenwood/morton/facility.html

One of the last of the natural mineral-water swimming holes, Morton's has three beautiful pools—for toddlers, for kids, and for the family. More fun can be had at the volleyball and basketball courts, horseshoe pits, baseball field, bocce ball court, and game room with all the latest video games. There are 11 naturally landscaped picnic areas (one by a stream) with barbecue pits and shaded tables. Morton's is well-known locally as a family gathering place and for hosting family and corporate picnics of up to 2,400 people. Parking is available at no extra charge. The snack bar is conveniently close to the pools with ice-cold drinks and a wide selection of hot dogs, hamburgers, chips, and all those picnic eats that make a family day so much fun. Morton's Warm Springs is open from the first weekend in May through most of September, from 10:00 A.M. to 7:30 P.M. on weekends and from 10:30 A.M. to 6:00 P.M. on weekdays. The pool is open a half-hour later. Weekday admission is $4.50 for adults and $4.00 for children; on weekends, it's $6.00 for adults and $5.00 for children for a full day of activity.

Early Work
141 Kentucky St., Petaluma
(707) 765-1993
www.earlywork.com

Early Work was formerly a shop for teachers looking for educational materials, but it is now open to the public. It's a great favorite with children because of its selection of creative toys and learning materials. There's something for everyone here, from age 1 to 100. Toys and books cover art, science, math, and language. There's an event schedule that changes from month to month—call the store for times or check their Web site.

Jungle Vibes
163 Kentucky St., Petaluma
(707) 762–6583, (800) 804–0007
www.junglevibes.com

They call it a nature and science store, but it's really an adventure where nature and science meet world culture. At this unique Petaluma store walking in the door is like entering another country. Imagine strolling from vendor to vendor amid gondolas and giant baskets heaped high with handmade textiles and artifacts. The sound of foreign tongues and the smell of strange new fruits converge. A taste of adventure and multicultural exploration goes a long way in our busy lives, and Jungle Vibes is set to help the community explore the world, using nature and science toys and books to complement an authentic collection of ethnic arts and sounds. This is the place to expand your child's world.

Victoria's Fashion Stables
4193 Old Adobe Rd., Petaluma
(707) 769-8820
www.fashionstables.com

No, it's not related to that tantalizing fashion catalog. This place is pure, clean barnyard fun, featuring good stuff for good kids—small, medium, or large.

For the little ones, there's a petting zoo along with pony rides. This isn't your average petting zoo, though. You'll start by seeing clucking chickens and waddling ducks, proceed to greeting pygmy goats, potbellied pigs, and baby horses, and then go on to a lesson in how to milk a cow. Pony rides are suitable for even very small children—the staff will walk beside the horse and even hold junior steady if necessary. A half-hour of pony riding will cost $15, or the pony ride can be combined with the petting zoo for $20 (for one to two children). Older children will enjoy horseback riding. These are well-mannered horses, not simply trained to ride in-line. The price of trail rides, English or Western, is $30 for a half-hour, up to $60 for two hours. Those who have paid for rides or the zoo can picnic at no extra charge (barbecue grills are available). The stables are open every day except Tuesday. Appointments are preferred though drop-ins can usually be accommodated. Every October, there's a pumpkin patch here. Victoria's also operates a day-use and over-night campground, with fishing nearby. Wait, there's more: a horse and carriage service for weddings.

Wildlife Natural History Museum
201 Fair St., Petaluma
(707) 778-4787
www.sonic.net/~museum

Exhibits at this unique museum include a saltwater tidepool, African and North

American wildlife (appearing in their natural habitats), exotic live animal displays, and hands-on participation. Live animals include chinchillas, iguanas, pythons, and other snakes. Funded entirely by local contributions, this museum is part of Petaluma High School and is operated by students under the supervision of a science teacher. It's the largest museum on a high school campus in the United States, with 9,000 square feet of exhibit space and a $3 million inventory that includes 100 live animals. Almost 8,000 school kids come to see the museum each school year. Unfortunately, the budget to allow for public viewing is small, and the museum is open to the public only on the first and third Saturdays of the month during the school year. Admission for kids younger than 12 is $1.00; anyone older pays $2.00.

Cal Skate
6100 Commerce Blvd., Rohnert Park
(707) 585–0500
www.calskate.com

Kids of all ages love to rollerskate here. The arena is open from 9:30 A.M. to 8:00 P.M., and it offers special sessions—such as the tiny tots session for kids eight and under. There is also plenty of open skating. Adult prices are $3.50 to $4.75.

Scandia Family Fun Center
5301 Redwood Dr., Rohnert Park
(707) 584–1398
www.scandiafunland.com

There's fun for everyone here: miniature golf, batting cages, go-carts, a video arcade, an Indy raceway, Tidal Wave bumper boats, and a snack bar. It opens every day at 10:00 A.M. and stays open until 11:00 P.M. on weekdays and midnight on weekends. Prices vary by attraction.

Toobtown
6591 Commerce Blvd., Rohnert Park
(707) 588–8100

This one is for children 2 to 12 and younger. Toobtown offers unlimited play in a four-story tube structure, plus a dinosaur-bounce and fun in the gym, three bumper boat rides in a pond, and lots of rides on horses and tortoises and spaceships. Socks are required by the dress code. Hours are 10:00 A.M. to 8:00 P.M. Sunday through Thursday, 10:00 A.M. to 9:00 P.M. on Friday and Saturday. Weekday prices are $4.95; it's $6.95 on the weekend.

"Please, mom, can we go to the petting zoo?" PHOTO: JOHN NAGIECKI

A boy enjoys the bumper boats at Scandia Family Fun Center in Rohnert Park. PHOTO: TINA LUSTER-HOBAN

Copperfield's Books
2316 Montgomery Dr., Santa Rosa
(707) 578-8938
650 Fourth St., Santa Rosa
(707) 576-7681
www.copperfld.com

Voted best kids' bookstore by an independent Sonoma County readers' poll, Copperfield's keeps up a steady stream of events to get kids interested in reading. Book promotions are unusual: For the Cat in the Hat program, kids had a chance to get their picture taken with the Cat himself. Family Fun Night brought out Curious George and provided an opportunity to help the man in the yellow hat find his curious companion. Occasional get-togethers with balloons and storytelling give book reading a party atmosphere. (See the Bookstores section of our Shopping chapter for more on Copperfield's.)

Howarth Park
630 Summerfield Rd., Santa Rosa
(707) 443-3770

One of 27 parks in Santa Rosa, Howarth is the big one, a 152-acre retreat into the world of nature. There's a 25-acre lake where families can rent canoes, rowboats, paddleboats, and sailboats and even take sailing lessons. Kids and parents also can fish for trout, bluegill, and bass throughout the year. In another part of the park, a simulated steam train follows a quarter-mile track over a bridge and through a tunnel. But wait, there's more: a carousel, pony rides, and Old Man Olson's farm, where kids can pet a variety of barnyard animals. Bring a picnic and have a great day! The park is open from 6:00 A.M. to 9:00 P.M. in summer and 6:00 A.M. to 6:00 P.M. in winter. Boat rentals (fishing is optional and subject to state regulations) and amusement rides are in operation Tuesday through Sunday from 11:00 A.M. to 5:00 P.M. during summer and on weekends in spring and fall.

Petrified Forest
4100 Petrified Forest Rd., Santa Rosa
(707) 942-6667
www.petrifiedforest.org

The trees died a few million years ago, but they remain alive forever as stone sculptures of what they used to be. Paths wind in and out through the fossilized forest (see our Attractions chapter). Visitors can take a quarter-mile loop that requires about 20 minutes to stroll. Summer hours are 10:00 A.M. to 4:30 P.M. Admission is $4.00 for adults, $3.00 for youngsters ages 12 through 17, and $2.00 for kids ages 6 to 11. Seniors 60 and over pay $3.00. Almost as interesting as the forest is the museum and gift shop, where you can buy all kinds of good stuff—stones you've never seen before and pieces of wood turned to stone. There's also a good selection of books.

Redwood Empire Ice Arena
1667 West Steele Ln., Santa Rosa
(707) 546-7147
www.snoopyshomeice.com

Charles Schulz, famous for his Peanuts cartoons, grew up in Minnesota and never lost his love for ice skating. The rink he built in Santa Rosa is a beautiful venue compared to the outdoor rinks he knew in his youth. A full range of skating is offered, with mornings reserved for programs and classes (many world champions have trained here). The arena is open daily, but hours vary. The cost is $5.50 for adults and teens and $4.50 for children younger than 12. Aside from the ice arena, there's a wonderful Peanuts Gallery gift shop that's appealing to all ages (see our Shopping chapter). You can also buy skates here, both ice and roller. (For more information on the arena and the Charles M. Schulz Museum next door, see our Attractions chapter.)

Riley Street Art Supplies
103 Maxwell Ct., Santa Rosa
(707) 526–2416
www.rileystreet.com

This is a great place to pick up childrens' craft supplies, including face-painting kits, tempera paints, tattoo books, how-to-draw books, and build-your-own foam dinosaur kits. For one week each July (exact dates vary), a kids' art camp is held at the store from 9:00 A.M. to 1:00 P.M. at a cost of $120 per child. Youngsters get professional instruction in whatever medium is suitable for their age. This is a premier shopping spot for professional artists and craftspeople.

Santa Rosa Junior College Planetarium
2001 Lark Hall, 1501 Mendocino Ave.,
Santa Rosa
(707) 527–4371
www.santarosa.edu

Star-studded shows feature various astronomical phenomena, with the night sky projected (with special effects) onto the dome, using state-of-the-art equipment. Offered only during the school year, shows are scheduled at 7:00 and 8:30 P.M. on Fridays and Saturdays, and at 1:30 and 3:00 P.M. on Sundays. Cost is $4.00 for adult general admission and $2.00 for students and seniors, all on a first-come, first-served basis. Children younger than five are not admitted.

Snoopy and Charlie Brown of "Peanuts" fame are forever young in this commemorative statue in Santa Rosa's Railroad Square. The late cartoonist Charles Schulz lived in Santa Rosa for most of his career. PHOTO: JEAN SAYLOR DOPPENBERG

Northern Sonoma

Windsor Waterworks & Slides
5225 Conde Ln., Windsor
(707) 838–7360
www.windsorwaterworks.com

The excitement begins 42 feet up, where you can pair up with a friend or go it alone on the big double-tube river ride. Or maybe you'd rather plunge down the speed slide for the thrill of a lifetime. Want more? Try King Richard's run, a giant of a slide, with double tubes that propel you through a tunnel of fun. The height requirement for those thrill rides is 45 inches. But the little ones (at least 36 inches tall) haven't been forgotten. There's a special body flume just for them. Between rides, there's time to swim, play volleyball, pitch horseshoes, or take a whack at Ping-Pong. Bring a picnic, or grab a pizza pocket or hot dog at Friar Tuck's. It's open 11:00 A.M. to 7:00 P.M.

from May through September (weekends only until June 15). Adults and teens pay $13.25 for full use of the park, kids ages 4 to 12 are $12.25, and those younger than 4 are free. There is another option: an afternoon splash special running from 4:00 to 7:00 P.M. is only $9.75 per person.

The Toyworks
103-B Plaza St., Healdsburg
(707) 433–4743
2759 Fourth St., Santa Rosa
(707) 526–2099
6940 Sebastopol Ave., Sebastopol
(707) 829–2003
www.sonomatoyworks.com

A store of educational toys, Toyworks claims 13,000 different items, from European toys, Lego blocks, and science and nature items to educational books and Lionel trains. Store hours are 10:00 A.M. to 6:00 P.M. Monday through Saturday and Sunday from 11:00 A.M. to 5:00 P.M.

Lake Sonoma Fish Hatchery
3333 Skaggs Springs Rd., Geyserville
(707) 433–9483

Here's a chance to peek in on all phases of fish life, depending on the season. In summer you'll see the small, young fish; later in the season, from late October through March, you'll be able to watch the coho salmon and steelheads returning to spawn and climbing the fish ladder. The coho salmon will die after spawning, but the steelheads will live to return to the sea. Once the eggs have been laid and fertilized, the fish hatchery starts collecting the eggs once a week—each Thursday at 10:30 A.M.. Summer hours here are 9:00 A.M. to 5:00 P.M. daily; winter hours are 9:00 A.M. to 4:00 P.M., Wednesday through Sunday. There is no charge. Visitors also will enjoy a display of Native American artifacts, plus information on local geology.

West County/Russian River

Pet-a-Llama Ranch
5505 Lone Pine Rd., Sebastopol
(707) 823–9395
www.pet-a-llama.com

You only need to look into a llama's soulful, gentle eyes and stroke its long, softly curving banana ears, to fall in love. The llama's long eyelashes are to be envied; their arched necks give them dignity. The place to get acquainted with these exotic animals is at Pet-a-Llama Ranch, where two dozen of them live and entertain visitors. School groups come during the week to learn about the animals' habits, to get up close and personal with them, and give them a snack. Saturday and Sunday, though, is open house from 10:00 A.M. to 4:00 P.M. from April to December. Kids will get a kick out of feeding them (it's 50 cents) and listening to the manager of the ranch tell what llama life is all about—where they come from, what they eat, and how they're used as pack animals in their native South America.

J's Amusements
16101 Neeley Rd., Guerneville
(707) 869–3102

This small, affordable park is reminiscent of the amusement parks of yore—before the high-tech world invaded them. Rides include the tilt-a-whirl, go-carts, Roundup, bumper cars, water slides, and a roller coaster. No admission fee is charged. You pay as you enjoy the individual rides—most are $1.50, bumper cars cost $2.25, and $6.00 gets you unlimited use of the water slide. Summer hours (mid-June to mid-September) are 11:00 A.M. to 11:00 P.M. In winter the park is open on weekends from 11:00 A.M. to 10:00 P.M. Saturday and 11:00 A.M. until 6:00 P.M. on Sunday.

Mendocino County

Pomo Cultural Center
Marine Dr., Lake Mendocino, Ukiah
(707) 485–8285, (707) 485–8685 (gift shop)

The round shape of the center is modeled on the Pomo tribe's ceremonial dance house, where cultural knowledge was passed down through the generations. Kids will be intrigued with the games the Pomo played, will learn how clam shells were used as money, and will have the chance to hold animal skins in the wild animal exhibit. The gift shop, operated by the Pomo, has a fascinating collection of items made by local Native Americans. Admission is free. The museum is open from 9:00 A.M. to 5:00 P.M. Wednesday through Sunday, June through October and is closed in winter (see our Attractions chapter).

Mendocino Coast
Recreation and Park District
213 E. Laurel St., Fort Bragg
(707) 964–9446
www.mcn.org/1/mcrpd/mcrhmpg1.htm

This county recreation program provides fun for kids the whole summer long. An indoor swimming pool is available for recreational swimming and for swim classes. Day use of the pool is $2.00 for kids, $3.00 for adults, and $2.50 for seniors. A multiuse gymnasium provides a wide variety of other athletic activities including roller skating, available at $2.00 (75 cents for skates). Schedules vary by week and month, so it is necessary to call or drop by for activity information. A complete schedule is available by mail.

California Western Railroad
(Skunk Train)
Laurel St. Depot, Fort Bragg
(707) 964–6371
www.skunktrain.com

The "Skunk" got its name from the odor of earlier gas engines, but today the train is moved by steam (or sometimes diesel fuel). It will take you all the way to Willits and back, but when you're traveling with kids, a more intelligent choice might be the trip to Northspur, at the halfway mark. There you can find food treats, cold juices, and soft drinks; then take the return trip on the next train. Fare for the full round-trip is $39 for adults and $22 for children ages 3 to 17. The one-way trip is $31 for adults and teens, $18 for children. Reservations are recommended. (For more on the Skunk Train, see our Attractions chapter.)

Triangle Tattoo Museum
356-B N. Main St., Fort Bragg
(707) 964–8814
www.triangletattoo.com

Here are some amazing examples of skin art among various peoples of the world and an opportunity to see the tools used and learn how tattooing is done. (See our Attractions chapter for more information.) The museum is open noon to 6:00 P.M. from Sunday through Thursday, noon to 8:00 P.M. on Friday and Saturday. Admission is free, and tours are given upon request.

Lake County

Outrageous Waters
Hwy. 53 & Old State Hwy. 53, Clearlake
(707) 995–1402, (877) WE–BE–FUN

The newest way to beat the heat in Lake County is to make the long slide into a pool at this water park. Next to the slides is a fun center with volleyball courts and a video arcade. A grand prix race track is the latest addition, featuring 15 cars with 9-horsepower engines maneuvering a professionally banked concrete track. Hardball and softball batting cages round out the energy-burning attractions. Outrageous Waters also has a food concession, storage lockers and a kiddie pool for those not ready to take the plunge. The park is open from noon to 7:00 P.M. daily in the summer, and Friday, Saturday, and Sunday in the off season. The water park is closed after summer, but the Fun Center is open all year. Admission is $13.95 for adults, $9.95 for children shorter than 48 inches (children three and under are free) and $3.95 for seniors 55 and older. ID-bearing Lake County residents get a discount, and the whole world gets one after 4:30 P.M.

Lakeside County Park
Park Dr. near St. Francis Dr., Lakeport
(707) 262–1618

Lake County's biggest neighborhood park (53 acres) has a lot to offer: three baseball diamonds, two volleyball courts, a picnic area, and a playground. Of course, Clear Lake is right there, so it's possible the kids won't see dry land until it's time to leave. The park has two boat ramps as well.

The Book Stop
305 N. Main St., Lakeport
(707) 263–5787

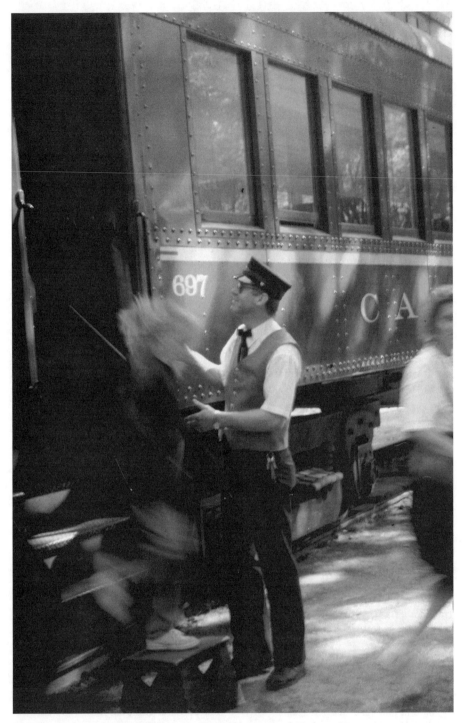

Kids leap for joy after riding Mendocino County's old-time Skunk Train. PHOTO: JOHN NAGIECKI

Lake County's most comprehensive bookstore (see our Shopping chapter) is also a haven for tykes of all ages. One of the store's five rooms is the Nature and Discovery Shop. The bustling shop offers videos, science-oriented material, physics-based games, puppets and stuffed animals, puzzles, magnetic games, toy airplanes, posters and prints, paper dolls, children's literature and, perhaps most crucial, the largest selection of Beanie Babies in Lake County. The Book Stop almost always has a few hands-on demonstrations to keep the kids from tearing up those valuable first editions.

Outside the Wine Country

Six Flags Marine World
Marine World Parkway, Vallejo, Calif.
(707) 643–6722
www.sixflags.com/marineworld

Yes, it falls outside our "official" boundaries, but rare is the Wine Country parent who hasn't succumbed to the splashy fun of Marine World. Now run by the Six Flags Corporation, the park has occupied its present 160-acre spot since 1986. It's one of those places that is impossible to conquer in a day, though you can certainly try. The long bill of shows includes performances by whales and dolphins, sea lions, tigers, lions, and humans on water skis. The ongoing attractions are too numerous to mention—among them are Shark Experience, Walrus Experience, Butterfly World, Elephant Encounter, the Primate Play Area, and the Animal Nursery. And don't miss two recent additions: a 10-story roller coaster called Roar and the V-2 Vertical Velocity Spiral Coaster, one of only three like it in the world. One-day tickets are $43 for adults and teens, $25 for children 4 through 12, and $33 for seniors 60 or older (children 3 and under get in free). Two-day passes are available at significant discounts. Parking is $10 per vehicle. From Napa, go south on Highway 29, then east on Highway 37 for just more than a mile. Days and hours of operation vary by season, so call ahead.

Daytrippin'

Northern California is brimming with intriguing destinations, so it's understandable that Wine Country visitors might want to veer off the wine trail long enough to experience another taste of the Golden State. That's fine with us—we respect your right of wanderlust and encourage you to broaden your travel horizons. Fortunately, several exceptional locations are within a few hours' drive of Napa or Santa Rosa.

To the south, the Marin Headlands, part of the Golden Gate National Recreation Area, offers scenic drives and hikes and the best views (usually above the fog) of the Golden Gate Bridge and San Francisco. Nearby Sausalito is a charming burg, with bayside dining and interesting shops. Across the bay, Berkeley is still funky, and further east the Gold Country towns of the Sierra foothills are rich in history. All of these are suitable excursions, and so are the three areas outlined below.

Depending on where you start, the spots we're recommending may be enjoyed as day trips, but if you have the time, plan for an overnight or weekend getaway. And don't forget to toss handfuls of baguette from your car every mile or two, so that you can be sure to find your way back to Wine Country.

Point Reyes National Seashore

Just southwest of Wine Country, Point Reyes offers miles of windswept beaches and magnificent palisades. Walk along cliffside trails (not too close to the edge, please), roll down lofty dunes, explore tidal marshes, and wander through a foggy forest. You're equally likely to bump into a tule elk, a sea lion, or a cow.

Dividing Point Reyes from the bulk of Marin County is the long, skinny arm of Tomales Bay and the infamous San Andreas Fault—the active demarcation line between the Pacific and North American tectonic plates. Point Reyes is moving away from the rest of the mainland, heading toward Alaska at the rate of 2 inches a year.

To get to the park, take Petaluma–Point Reyes Road southwest from Petaluma for about 20 miles. A good place to start your excursion in the 71,000-acre park is the Bear Valley Visitor Center, a big barn of a building just off Highway 1 near Olema. Close to the center you'll encounter Morgan Horse Ranch, Kule Loklo, and several hiking trails. Morgan Ranch is the only working horse-breeding farm in the national park system. Kule Loklo is a re-creation of a Miwok village, with traditional domed shelters. If you visit in July, you might get to witness the

Insiders' Tip

Built 307 steps below the visitor center at the southern tip of the peninsula, the Point Reyes Lighthouse invites you to walk down for a closer look. But beware! The return climb up the narrow stairs is an aerobic challenge not intended for the meek of heart. If you decide to venture down, pace yourself on the return and use the rest platforms provided by the park service along the staircase.

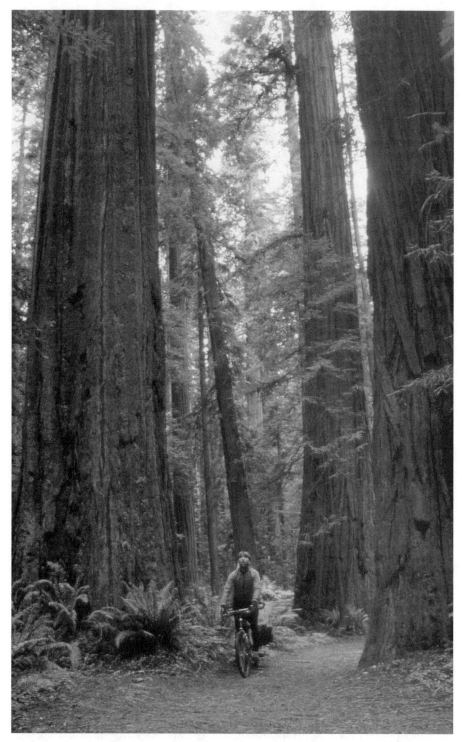

A bike rider rolls through a majestic grove along the Avenue of the Giants. PHOTO: SIRI MING

The beach at Point Reyes invites a romantic stroll. PHOTO: JOHN NAGIECKI

annual Native American Celebration, during which Miwok-descended basket makers, stone carvers, singers, and dancers bring the exhibit to life.

While some visitors simply want to flop down on the pearly sand for a good read or nap, others come to explore the diversity of fascinating natural attractions. Limantour Estero is an estuary where most of the bird-watchers flock; McClures Beach has excellent tide pools; the windy Great Beach, one of the longest in the state, gets high marks from beachcombers; and Drakes Beach (which, like Drakes Bay and Drakes Estero, is named for Sir Francis Drake, the English privateer who supposedly landed here in 1579) is a Northern California rarity: a safe swimming beach. Of course, hiking routes abound, including 70 miles of trails in a big chunk of park set aside as wilderness area.

Probably foremost among attractions is Point Reyes Lighthouse, built about 1870 to help prevent the many shipwrecks that had plagued the treacherous, rocky shoreline for centuries. It is also one of California's best spots for whale watching.

In the fall, gray whales migrate from Alaska to their breeding grounds in Baja, California. In spring, they return north with their young. The peak watching season is Christmas through the end of January, when it's not uncommon to see 100 or more spouts rise in a day. During this busy migration period, the park service runs a shuttle from Drakes Beach to the lighthouse.

In the southern end of the park, near the time-warped town of Bolinas, is the Point Reyes Bird Observatory—the first of its kind when founded in 1965. A rest stop on the western migratory superhighway, the aviary plays host to an incredible diversity of bird species, one of the largest in the continental United States. Nearly 350 varieties regularly show up in the Audubon Society's annual Christmas bird count. The observatory offers classes, interpretive exhibits, and a nature trail.

Even the villages are pretty here. Point Reyes Station and Inverness, in particular, have remained undisturbed by the masses of visitors. Note that the local microclimate is highly unpredictable—except at the actual Point, which is the foggiest place on the West Coast. For more up-to-date information, look for a copy of *Coastal Traveler*, a free quarterly published by the *Point Reyes Light*, the area's Pulitzer Prize-winning newspaper, or call the Point Reyes National Seashore at (415) 663-1092.

The Big Trees

California's legendary redwood forests have inspired poetry and major awe (and more than a little avarice) during the last 200 years. Though they are often confused with their inland cousin, the giant sequoia, the redwood—or coastal redwood as it is called—is a variety unto itself, with a coastal range that extends from Monterey to southwest Oregon. Santa Rosa considers itself the capital of the Redwood Empire, and several Wine Country parks are home to these noble giants (see our Parks and Recreation chapter). But if you really want to behold these extraordinary trees in all their grandeur you have to drive north to Humboldt County. There you will find the last large stands of California's coast redwoods.

Sequoia sempervirens covered some two million acres when Archibald Menzies first gave them botanical classification in 1794. The state government created several parks around individual groves in the 1920s, but by 1965 logging had reduced the redwood ecosystem to about 300,000 acres. This prompted the U.S. government to consolidate various state, federal, and private holdings into Redwood National Park in 1968.

More land was added to the park in 1978, after bitter wrangling between environmental and pro-industry groups and deterioration of virgin growth due to upstream logging along Redwood Creek. The 110,000-acre national park is the destination of many visitors, along with three remaining state parks: Jedediah Smith Redwoods, Del Norte Coast Redwoods, and Prairie Creek Redwoods. All four parks are adjacent and, in fact, comanaged by the National Park Service and the California Department of Parks and Recreation. The national park is a World Heritage Site, the only one on the Pacific coast of the United States. Prairie Creek, meanwhile, is home to the last herds of Roosevelt elk in California.

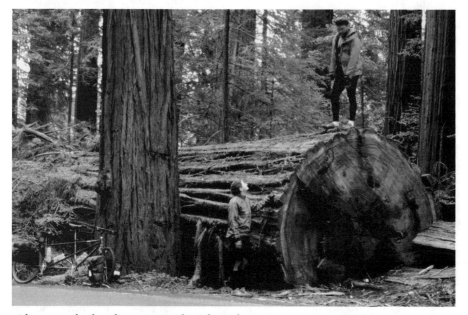

A large coastal redwood measures nearly 15 feet in diameter. PHOTO: JOHN NAGIECKI

The 7,500-acre Headwaters Forest Reserve is the most recent entry in the list of protected ancient groves. The reserve, made famous by the tree-sitting, old-growth activist Julia Butterfly, came into being as part of a $480 million controversial deal struck between the U.S. government and the Pacific Lumber Company.

Farther south, between Garberville and Ferndale, is the famed Avenue of the Giants, a 33-mile stretch of roadway that parallels U.S. 101 and offers up the most majestic succession of trees on the planet. The Avenue follows the Eel River and cuts through 51,000-acre Humboldt Redwoods State Park, the largest state park in Northern California. Along the road you'll encounter a hollow redwood (The Chimney Tree), a redwood trunk made into a domicile (One-Log House), and a redwood you can bisect without leaving the car (Shrine Drive Thru Tree, one of the state's oldest surviving tourist attractions).

What are the big groves like? It's like walking into one of Europe's grandest old cathedrals, only with better ventilation. The huge trunks absorb every trace of sound, with the exception of the occasional notes of a Swainson's thrush or Wilson's warbler that float down from the branches above. The forest bed, soft with many layers of needles, crunches under your feet, and the lush fern understory lends a primordial feel to the place that goes to the bone.

The trees are indeed ancient, with the oldest dated at approximately 2,200 years. And big? Three of the six tallest trees in the world, including the grand-champion, 368-foot Howard Libby Redwood, are in the national park. What is the secret to their great size? Moisture, and lots of it. The 50 to 80 inches of annual rainfall that drenches coastal California quenches most of the redwood's tremendous thirst, while fog, almost a daily occurrence, keeps the trees damp and cool when the rains subside.

All the attractions mentioned here are accessed via U.S. 101 between Garberville and Crescent City, just south of the Oregon border. From Wine Country, simply continue north on U.S. 101 through Mendocino County; Garberville is about 10 miles past the county line. Admission to the state parks is $6.00, which will get you into all of them. There is no charge to enter the national park. Camping and hiking options abound. For more information, call the northern parks at (707) 464-6101 or Humboldt Redwoods State Park at (707) 946-2409.

Insiders' Tip

"Tahoe" is a Washoe Indian word for "lake," but the magnificent body of water on the California-Nevada border has gone by many other names since the arrival of Europeans. First it was Mountain Lake, then Lake Bonpland. And from 1852 to 1945 it was called Lake Bigler, after John Bigler, a California governor who had Confederate ties during the Civil War.

Lake Tahoe

Nature has lavished on Lake Tahoe the bluest waters, the most majestic pines, the most handsome mountains, and the most brilliant cloud-studded skies you'll find anywhere—all that and keno, too! Mark Twain was the first travel writer to tour the Lake of the Sky. His awestruck descriptions have since been quoted by a thousand equally dumbfounded travel writers who can scarcely describe the indescribable. Photos simply don't capture this cobalt-blue beauty, nor do paintings. The colors are right, but oddly, they seem too perfect, too vivid.

Tahoe lies half in California and half in Nevada (the South Shore is a two-hour

Emerald Bay is a popular destination for boaters on Lake Tahoe. PHOTO: KRISTIN MARKGRAF

drive from Sacramento, on U.S. 50), which gives impetus for pilgrimages by a swarm of weekend gamblers. They head for our neighbor state and hope Lady Luck will smooch the slot machine or gaming table they've selected.

But Tahoe's best bet is the lake itself. Twelve miles wide and twenty-two miles long, it offers all the water-oriented fun one would expect from the largest alpine lake in North America (in the Western Hemisphere, only Lake Titicaca is larger). Look out across the waters, and you'll see colorful hot-air balloons rising from a barge in the middle of the lake just as the sun makes its appearance over the edge of the Sierra Nevada Mountains.

Two-masted sailboats cut a leisurely path across the waves, while yachts hurry on their way. Couples in canoes or kayaks paddle through the shallow waters. Anglers, waiting patiently for the trout to find them, sit in their fishing boats, unimpressed by the brave soul hovering above them, dangling from a rainbow-hued parasail.

At 97 percent pure—the same as distilled water—Lake Tahoe is as clean as it is beautiful. Fortunately, the Sierra Club and other environmental groups are fighting

to keep it that way. All of this is available at a price, mainly from the beaches of the city of South Lake Tahoe or at Kings Beach on the north shore. In addition, the *M.S. Dixie II* takes passengers on two, sometimes three, cruises a day—an afternoon run that crosses the lake to Emerald Bay (with its turquoise waters), and a morning cruise that features a big breakfast while following the shoreline. Prices are $20 for a basic cruise, $25 for a brunch cruise, and $35 for a dinner cruise.

For a look at the lake as a whole, nothing beats the spectacular 72-mile perimeter drive. It takes about five hours (with scenic stops) on a good weather day. Plan to begin your drive early. In summer, pack or buy a picnic lunch for a brief sojourn in an adjacent park. In winter, include a midday pit stop at a ski area. Options exist for numerous side trips while traveling the highway that circles North America's second-deepest lake (maximum depth: 1,645 feet). If all the water were somehow released from the lake—and if water behaved very differently than it does in real life—it would cover the entire state of California to a depth of 8 inches.

Heading clockwise from South Lake Tahoe, you'll soon climb a steep grade to a

The tram at Heavenly Valley on the south shore of Lake Tahoe rewards visitors with a sterling view of the water and surrounding mountains. PHOTO: LOREN DOPPENBERG

point overlooking the breathtaking vistas of Emerald Bay State Park. Below is the 39-room Vikingsholm Castle, a 19th-century mansion built by Laura Knight, who fell in love with Norway and sent craftsmen there to copy museum pieces for her home. Tours are available to those who walk the half-mile down the hill, which is the only visitor access except by boat. Vistas along the entire west shore are so stunning, you'll be hauling your Nikon out of the car every few minutes. Heading northeast, you'll pass what has essentially always been the residential zone of Tahoe. San Francisco's early social elite spent their summers here, and millionaires put up huge estates. Hollywood has come calling more than once, and one of these homes figured prominently in the filming of *The Godfather, Part II.*

Tahoe's oldest permanent settlement is Tahoe City, on the northwest shores of the lake. Three shopping complexes and several condominium projects give this town a year-round population of 2,000. Near the site of the bridge over the Truckee River

(called Fanny Bridge because of the people hanging over its floodgates), there's a wonderful collection of Indian lore at the Gatekeeper's Museum. Tahoe City is also the take-off point for three-hour rafting trips down the Truckee River, and it is a favored location for fishermen who head out to deep water with a guide in search of mackinaw and cutthroat trout.

The lake's north shore abounds with interesting geological formations—immense boulders and tiny carnelian stones. Along the north shore you'll cross the state line into Nevada, where gambling is legal. One of its more famous casinos, the Cal-Neva, once belonged to Frank Sinatra. Those were the days when Hollywood luminaries filled the lobby. At the northeast corner of the lake, you'll find Incline Village, with its shopping center, fine art galleries, craft shops, restaurants, and, for culture vultures, drama, opera, Shakespeare, and mime, courtesy of the North Tahoe Fine Arts Council.

South of Incline Village lies one of Tahoe's best beaches—Sand Harbor State

Beach, strewn with giant boulders, the refuse of Tahoe's ice age. Paths climb to the top of one of the granite outcroppings, allowing a view down into turquoise waters so clear that submerged boulders as high as a house can be seen in full detail. Facilities for picnicking and barbecuing in a wooded setting are unusually pleasant. Also on the east shore you'll find Ponderosa Ranch, developed at the time the TV show *Bonanza* was popular. Some consider it corny, but kids have plenty of room to run around, and anyone who used to watch the show will recognize Ben Cartwright's office and accouterments.

Most of Tahoe's east shore is privately owned, but there is a small area (recognizable by a proliferation of parked cars) where sun worshippers thread their way down a footpath through the forest and spread out nude on the massive rocks to achieve that all-over tan. Zephyr Cove, meanwhile, is where you set sail on the *M.S. Dixie*. It's near the state line.

And there are other options for side trips. At Incline Village, for example, there's a junction with Highway 27 that will take you to Reno or to Virginia City, a lively ghost town recalling days when silver taken from its mines built San Francisco and made millionaires whose names are still familiar. Its wooden plank streets and weathered buildings are surprisingly authentic, though the usual tourist shops line the street as well. (Look to the buildings' upper stories for a true feeling of the Old West.) Reno, calling itself the "biggest little city in the world," is rife with sleek, splashy gambling casinos. The city has achieved a modest fame among nearby California cities for its inexpensive hotel rooms. Recently it has also become home to the National Bowling Association, which is quartered in a massive complex of bowling lanes and offices.

In winter, some of the best skiing in the world can be had at South Lake Tahoe—specifically at Heavenly Valley. If you're not on hand during the winter months, take advantage of the tram anyway; ride to the top of the mountain and take a stroll along the path that skirts the rim. It's a breathtaking view, and you can sip wine and have lunch at the summit's inviting patio. Be sure to bring along a panoramic camera to freeze-frame the magnificent scenery for later enjoyment.

Real Estate

Napa County
Sonoma County
Mendocino County
Lake County

The red-hot real estate market in the San Francisco Bay Area, which had surged over the past few years, cooled down by several degrees in 2001. Home prices and rental rates that had escalated almost beyond belief in 1999 and 2000 finally stabilized during the downturn in the national economy in 2001. Mind you, prices didn't drop much—they just didn't skyrocket higher.

One of the most visible factors that contributed to the market leveling off in 2001 was the loss of jobs in the high-tech world and the sinking of many dot-com businesses. Just south of San Francisco, Silicon Valley had been the incubator for scores of Internet startup companies. Many of these went belly-up in 2000 and 2001, along with a proliferation of interactive media companies that had settled in downtown San Francisco, in an area dubbed "Multimedia Gulch."

Though some high-tech companies in Wine Country experienced financial setbacks and cut staff, the agricultural base of our four-county area remains strong and profitable. Our real estate market reflects this more stable and diverse environment.

Our goal with this chapter is to give you a glimpse of the market in each of the four counties. We'll quote some average prices and provide some broad descriptions. Take this information as a starting point on your real estate search, but be sure to rely on your real estate agent for the most up-to-date prices and details. (Also see our Area Overview chapter for more county demographic information.)

Napa County

Like everywhere else in the greater San Francisco Bay Area, Napa Valley's real estate prices rocketed into the stratosphere over the past couple of years. Make no mistake about it: You pay dearly for quality of life here. If you fall in love with our postcard scenery, robust lifestyle, and small-town sense of community, you won't be the first. More and more people want to relocate here, retire here, or commute from here (to the Bay Area), yet the supply of homes is tightly limited. And if you're from outside California, be prepared for sticker shock.

Here's a bit of recent history: In the first six months of 2000, Napa Valley home prices increased by more than 21 percent. In August 2000, the median price of an existing house sold through the Multiple Listing Service was $285,000, up more than $50,000 from the previous year. (Median price means that half of the sales were at a higher price and half were lower.) In late 2001, the median price was hovering around $315,000—an increase of $30,000. Today, single-family homes listing for under $200,000 are a distant memory, while listings for million-dollar homes are setting records.

With the median income for a Napa household around $36,000, the median-priced home is now beyond the reach of many. It's no surprise that a good percentage of our newest property owners are not from around here. In fact, realtors estimate that nearly a third of all buyers of Napa County properties in 2000 were well-heeled folks from outside our region.

Be that as it may, bargain prices (if you can call them that) may still be found in American Canyon, just south of Napa. But as you head north on Highway 29, the meter on home costs begins to spin faster. As a general rule, Yountville is more expensive than Napa, the Oakville-Rutherford area is more expensive than Yountville, and St. Helena is the most expensive town in the valley. The price tags drop again in Calistoga, down to about the Yountville level. Along the way, you will find every sort of residence imaginable: new tract homes, spectacular Victorians, modest 1940s bungalows, mountaintop castles, Tuscan-inspired villas, and prefab structures.

But what you will see most as you travel Highway 29 is vineyards. That's because the whole of Napa County is a designated agricultural preserve, a decision ratified by the county Board of Supervisors in 1968. The designation put development decisions in the hands of the board and set a 20-acre minimum for any new subdivision of land—a dimension that later increased to 40 acres, and more recently to 160.

At the ballot box, voters took the plan a step further with Measure J in 1990, giving themselves the power to vote down any exceptions to the rule regarding minimum subdivision acreage. At times it's been a frustrating situation for developers, but most residents are pleased with the valley's farsightedness. The Ag Preserve designation protects the vineyards and keeps the scenery uncluttered, and those are the twin engines that drive Napa's megadollar tourist economy.

Before getting into specific areas, we can make a couple of generalizations about the valley. First, a dictum that applies here and just about everywhere else in the world: Property values tend to be directly related to elevation. In other words, the rich folks live on the hilltops. That can be traced to the days when people disposed of their garbage by throwing it out the window. Second, the really ritzy places tend to be large holdings in the country.

In Napa, most of the Victorian splendor is in Old Town—located among the letter streets south of Lincoln Avenue between California Boulevard and Jefferson Street—and the Napa Abajo/Fuller Park area. Fuller Park, in fact, is a Historical Preservation District. As such, it is eligible to receive economic incentives from the city for refurbishment. The boundaries of the preservation district are ragged, but it is bordered more or less by Jefferson, Third, Brown, and Pine Streets.

Another desirable locale, and much more expensive, is Silverado Country

Club, where, in late 2001, some of the massive homes (2,000 to 5,000 square feet) had listing prices ranging from $650,000 to as much as $1.3 million. Condominiums at Silverado had price tags from $498,500 to $765,000, while the final subdivision being built at the country club (called the Highlands) had asking prices in the neighborhood of $600,000 to $800,000.

St. Helena is the burg that best typifies the Wine Country dream: charming, early-century stone-front buildings, modest scale, vineyard views, and well-kept flower gardens. Accordingly, the prices tend to be sky high here, especially on the west side. Calistoga offers more of a mixed bag, but it does have some wonderfully restored old houses, especially on Cedar and Myrtle

Classic barns such as this are among the outbuildings included on some Wine Country properties. PHOTO: JOHN NAGIECKI

Streets just northwest of Lincoln Avenue. But country estates are considered the true gems, especially if they have significant acreage.

Which brings us to the price of vineyard land. Perhaps you've fantasized about owning a hobby vineyard, investing in a few acres of grapes and living the life of a gentleman farmer. Are you sitting down? Your name may not be Gallo or Gates, but you will still need a sizable bankroll to enter into the grape-growing business here. Vineyards in Napa Valley represent some of the most valuable agricultural land in America, and the price of the terra firma generally corresponds to the prevailing market price of the grape variety flourishing upon it and how much the growing techniques on each acre have been modernized.

Thanks to a healthy economy and the loyalty of wine lovers everywhere, prices for Napa Valley Cabernet Sauvignon grapes increased more than 40 percent over the past decade; Chardonnay prices were up 22 percent in the same period. That's why one vineyard property recently sold for a whopping $100,000 per acre,

double what a typical acre of disease-resistant grape land sold for throughout much of the 1990s. If you're willing to buy a lower-quality parcel (less fruit density, old trellises, and no developable homesites), expect to pay at least $50,000 per acre. If your fantasy includes building a modest winery on that property, be prepared to wait about two years for approval of the use permits, at a cost of nearly $1 million. And that's all before you begin construction. You want a tasting room, too? Good luck. Napa County officials are starting to say "no" to many new winery proposals, especially those with big plans for tasting rooms and event centers.

Rentals

In late 2001, rent on a two-bedroom apartment in Napa was averaging about $1,100 to $1,300 per month; its St. Helena equivalent is fetching $1,450. The typical two-bedroom house in Napa can set you back about $1,300 per month; the price goes up to $1,500 and beyond for a three-bedroom, two-bath domicile, depending on location. A similar home in St.

Helena starts at about $1,600, while some with more amenities rent for well over $2,000 per month.

At the north end of the valley, rents are moving gradually upward but are not yet at the St. Helena level. In Calistoga, a studio apartment, if you can find one, might be around $750; a two-bedroom apartment is just shy of $1,000. Two-bedroom homes may be had for $1,110 to $1,250 per month.

Property Rentals Only Inc.
2005 Delpha Dr., Napa
(707) 252–6147
www.prorent.com

You can usually find 25 to 50 rental listings posted outside the Property Rentals Only office. If anything piques your interest, the company will hand you an application. You can then take the stack of paperwork they offer, drive by selected properties, and mark those that you feel may be appropriate. The majority of PRO's buildings are in Napa, but they handle Yountville, St. Helena, and Calistoga too. All they charge is a $20 fee for a credit check.

Real Estate Companies

Prudential California Realty
2015 Redwood Rd., Napa
(707) 259–4900
www.prudentialnapa.com

Prudential has been in Napa Valley for more than 10 years, and broker Ed Wickman now oversees this redefined office. (His wife, Sally, manages the place.) With more than 20 Realtors, Prudential California covers all of Napa County and all sorts of property. It also has a full-time commercial department, not to mention three outposts in neighboring Solano County.

Century 21 Alpha Realty
1290 Jefferson St., Napa
(707) 255–8711

With 15 Realtors working the county, Century 21 has been one of the valley's premier offices since the early 1970s. Helen Johnson's crew focuses primarily on residential property, but also ventures into commercial space, acreage, and investment property. More services in the

Century 21 portfolio: property management and real estate license training.

Coldwell Banker Brokers of the Valley
1775 Lincoln Ave., Napa
(707) 258–5200
1289 Main St., St. Helena
(707) 963–1152
6505 Washington St., Yountville
(707) 944–0421
www.cbnapavalley.com

This is the county's biggest real estate office based on several parameters, not the least of which is its 69 Realtors (56 in the Napa office alone). The company covers the entire county and all variety of property, though it is particularly strong in the realms of vineyard and residential holdings. The latter extends to houses, condos, mobile homes, farms, and ranches. (The St. Helena office is known for properties valued at $500,000 or more.) Coldwell Banker also has the advantage of "preview" listings: expensive pieces that are advertised nationally or even internationally.

Continental Real Estate
743 First St., Napa
(707) 257–1177

Shane (one name suffices, a la Cher) is the sole proprietor of this business, and she's a busy gal. She made more than 60 sales totaling in excess of $12 million in 1998, making her the most productive Realtor in the county, according to independent research. Do-it-all Continental covers the whole valley but concentrates on Napa city. Shane also offers notary, appraisal, and consulting services.

RE/MAX Napa Valley
780 Trancas St., Napa
(707) 255–0845
1309 Main St., St. Helena
(707) 968–9600
www.remax-napavalley-ca.com
www.nvplatinum.com

There is plenty of experience at work here. RE/MAX has 32 agents, with a grand total of more than 400 years of combined experience, working the length of the valley. They handle various residential and high-end listings of vineyard acreage and estate homes. (If you want a serious case of house envy, gaze at their property board.) Morgan Lane has 36 Realtors in Yountville, St. Helena, and Sonoma, covering all of Napa and Sonoma valleys. The company also is an official affiliate of Sotheby's, and as such has access to high rollers from San Francisco to Singapore and readers of publications such as *The New York Times* and *The Wall Street Journal.*

Arroyo Real Estate
1540 Railroad Ave., St. Helena
(707) 963–1342
www.arroyorealestate.com

This is a small company that goes for luxury. Arroyo's three Realtors are long-time residents of Napa Valley. The firm's realm stretches from Yountville to the north end of the county, and the listings are exclusive—fine country homes, vineyard estates, and similarly desirable acreage.

Frank Howard Allen Realtors
1316 Main St., St. Helena
(707) 963–5266
www.winecountrygroup.com

One of Sonoma's most respected real estate offices moved into Napa Valley in 1998. They'll help you locate your dream home in either county. The St. Helena site has five Realtors, including a woman who once was mayor of the town (plus her son and daughter-in-law). Frank Howard Allen handles a mix of residential, vineyard, and undeveloped land.

Up Valley Associates
1126 Adams St., St. Helena
(707) 963–1222, (800) 326–6073
www.napavalleyrealestate.com

Up Valley has four brokers and two agents who cover the entire county, though they focus on, well, the name tells the story. The company does a little bit of everything, and they are also the exclusive Wine Country representative of Christie's Great Estates. Most of the Realtors have been with the office since it adopted its name in 1979. As one of them said, "We're all really old." In other words, they can offer you a wealth of helpful experience.

commercial properties, including large developments and subdivisions. Still, they stress that no job is too small.

Silverado Realty
1561 Third St., Ste. B, Napa
(707) 252–4755
www.silveradorealtyinc.com

Silverado does country, residential, and income property in Napa, including Silverado Country Club. The country club alone has many properties from which to choose. The office started in 1970 and has two Realtors.

Morgan Lane
1932 Sierra Ave., Napa
(707) 252–2177, (800) 511–1030
1109 Jefferson St., Napa
(707) 254–1100
6795 Washington St., Yountville
(707) 944–8500
1350 Main St., St. Helena
(707) 963–5226
www.morganlane.com

This company doesn't want to exclude anyone, but it is clearly known for its

Pacific Union
1508 Main St., St. Helena
(707) 967–1340
www.pacunion.com

This team of 16 agents, a satellite office of the larger San Francisco-based real estate company, handles just about everything, from homes to land and other income property up and down the valley. They specialize in luxury estates and vineyard parcels. A recent listing: 700 acres of prime planted vineyards with plenty of room to build a winery with an asking price of $20 million.

California Properties
13 Angwin Plaza, Angwin
(707) 965–2485, (800) 788–0410
www.napavalleyrealestate.net

Connections? What can you say about a company whose lineup includes the former proprietor of historic Alta Vineyards and the director of the St. Helena Hospital Men's Chorus? California Properties, which started in St. Helena in 1983, has four Realtors who serve most of Napa County. They stick primarily to residential property but also handle a few vineyard sales.

Beck & Taylor
1406 Lincoln Ave., Calistoga
(707) 942–5500
www.naparealty.com

Robert Beck's small shop is a general brokerage, but it has some specialties that set it apart in Calistoga. Beck & Taylor handles substantial property management and commercial space. In addition, one of its Realtors concentrates on the sale and purchase of bed and breakfast inns around Northern California. The company generally covers the entire Napa Valley.

Calistoga Realty Co.
1473-C Lincoln Ave., Calistoga
(707) 942–9422
www.calistoga-realty.com

This is Calistoga's largest real estate company, with four licensed Realtors and an office manager. They handle Napa Valley down to Yountville plus Knights Valley and a few other corners of Sonoma County. Cal-

istoga Realty carries more listings than anyone in the immediate area, primarily residential and small land parcels.

Real Estate Publications

Wine Country Weekly Real Estate Reader
1921 Jefferson St., Napa
(707) 258–6150
www.rereader.com

This is far more than a series of property listings. The *Reader's* editorial format offers a comprehensive look at the four-county real estate market, and beyond, highlighted by short articles on home-buying tips or new tax laws. It also lists a selection of open houses in the Wine Country and includes at least 10 pages of classified ads. The *Reader's* sharpest focus is on estate vineyards, wineries, and farm and ranch property. The paper is distributed throughout the Wine Country, not to mention real estate offices, BART stations (rapid transit outposts), and supermarkets in nine Bay Area counties.

Distinctive Properties of Napa Valley
P.O. Box 2849, Yountville 94599
(707) 257–0803, (707) 944–0384
www.distinctiveproperties.com

When it comes to depth of listings, *Distinctive Properties* is the bible of Napa Valley. Make that the bibles: There are two versions of the publication. One is a monthly printed in black and white (inside, anyway) on newspaper stock. The monthly lists 500 to 600 different properties from the southern to northern tip of the valley, with a handy price index on page 6. The other edition is a slick, color quarterly that focuses on estates, vineyards, and executive homes that go for $300,000 or more. Both publications are free, distributed throughout Napa and Sonoma valleys and around the Bay Area. David Barker has published *Distinctive Properties* since 1987.

The Real Estate Book of Napa County
4086 Byway East, Napa
(707) 253–1284
www.realestatebook.com

This is a small, free booklet that has been publicizing a wide range of Napa and

Lake County properties for about seven years. *The Real Estate Book* is distributed mainly in those two counties and to a lesser extent in Sonoma, Solano, and Marin Counties. Each issue includes listings from anywhere between 30 and 75 different real estate companies.

Sonoma County

The real estate market in Sonoma County made national headlines in 2000. For example, in its May issue that year, *Forbes* magazine listed the Santa Rosa area among the top three dynamic economic regions in the nation. A year later, Sonoma County ranked No. 6 on the same list. To help meet the explosion in housing demand, builders have been constructing new homes in Sonoma County, but not without resistance. Many residents have become increasingly fearful of losing their open spaces and associated quality of life and have been doing something about it. A county-wide sales tax was recently approved by county voters for use in preserving open space—the first of its kind in the nation—and most municipalities have instituted voter-approved growth restrictions. The towns of Rohnert Park and Sonoma passed such initiatives on the 2000 ballot, joining the ranks of Santa Rosa, Petaluma, Windsor, Healdsburg, Sebastopol, Cotati, and Cloverdale, which already have such restrictions on the books.

Much of the county's growth is centered around the city of Santa Rosa. With a current population of about 147,600, it is the county's largest city. Here, as in most cities, home seekers will find neighborhoods of high-priced, handsome Victorian homes, a score of new modern housing developments (some still in progress), and a wide variety of medium and lower-priced homes. In general, median prices in the northwest sector of Santa Rosa are about $299,000; in the southeast, $333,000; in the southwest, $283,000; and $390,000 in the northeast.

In towns to the north on the U.S. 101 corridor home prices vary. Median prices are $385,500 in Heraldsburg and $280,000 in Cloverdale. An interesting real estate situation exists in the town of Windsor. Until the late '80s, it was a sleepy village, but then it was "discovered" by housing developers. They just kept building and building. As a result, almost everything in the town is of recent origin. Now incorporated, this is a fast-growing city—second only to nearby Cloverdale—with median home prices at about $339,000.

The area around the town of Sebastopol on the edge of Apple Country is, in a way, an anomaly in the county—a place where many homes are set on large acreage. People who live here like the idea of country living with amenities such as extra guest houses and plenty of room for dogs to run and horses to graze. Because of the super-large lot sizes, Sebastopol has among the highest housing prices in the county. Estate-size lots, rambling homes, and mini-ranches will often push or top the $1 million mark. The median home price is $460,475.

The southern reaches of Sonoma County are just 45 minutes from the Golden Gate, assuming, of course, there is no traffic on U.S. 101, which there usually is. Though San Francisco-bound commuters live in all parts of the county, most live in the southernmost reaches—a fact that has influenced average home prices there. Median home prices in the border towns of Petaluma and Sonoma during 2001 ranged between $405,000 and $440,000—in 2000, the prices ranged between $379,000 and $390,000.

There is little residential property along the Sonoma Coast, which is one reason median home prices near $584,000. The large, modern Sea Ranch development at the northeastern edge of the county offers homes on sites that range from a quarter-acre to three or more acres. Some of the oceanfront lots go for as much as $600,000. For people who love the ocean, life along the Sonoma Coast is indeed soul satisfying. Fortunately, it can also be rented. (See Rentals on the following pages.)

One thing is certain: Wherever you choose to settle down in Sonoma County, there is no shortage of well-qualified Realtors and brokers to clear a path for you. The firms we have selected to highlight for this guide are among the best. But there are 100 or more other excellent agents and brokers who are familiar with their territory. The publications listed will help you find one that suits you.

We remind you that local chambers of commerce are also helpful clearinghouses of information. Often, you can get more specifics about locations and individual agencies through them. The Sonoma Valley Chamber of Commerce is at 645 Broadway, Sonoma. Call (707) 996-1033 for assistance. Also, the North Coast Builders Exchange in Santa Rosa, (707) 542-9502, can help with information for individuals hiring contractors or building custom homes.

Rentals

Understand that the high-priced housing market makes renting as tough, if not tougher, than buying. Some rentals rose as much as 150 percent in 2000. In such a volatile market, it's hard to identify an average price. Expect rental prices for apartments and duplexes in Sonoma County to be anywhere from $700 (if you're lucky) to $1,500. The average apartment rent in Sonoma County in mid-2001 was $1,087. The rent for a three-bedroom, two-bath midpriced apartment is about $1,500. You can generally find lower rents in the outlying areas. Guerneville, for example, offers rentals as low as $500, but they are hard to find. In Santa Rosa, where good jobs can be found, a newer, three-bedroom house will rent for a minimum of $1,300, while a simple two-bedroom house in the older section of town rents from $900 to $1,400. In the city of Sonoma, the favorable climate and pleasant ambiance have attracted retired folks. They come with their retirement funds and live in homes that cost upwards of $350,000. The rental picture reflects those real estate values.

Sonoma Management
662 Broadway, Sonoma
(707) 938-3177
www.sonomamanagement.com
Robert and Sylvia Bernard have operated this full-service rental agency since 1982,

serving those moving to Sonoma from all walks of life. The office is in an historic home built more than 100 years ago. The Bernards provide listings throughout Sonoma Valley with no fee charged to the renter-client.

The Rental Connection
1220 Fourth St., Santa Rosa
(707) 575-9652
www.rentalconn.com
Owner Cathy J. Romero provides a rental listing service that covers all of Sonoma County. Prospective renters pay a $50 service fee that gives them one month of access to a comprehensive list of rental properties tailored to their needs. The listings divide the county into 17 areas to offer thorough coverage in a convenient format.

West County Property Management
6380 Vine Hill School Rd., Sebastopol
(707) 823-5700
Jim and Lynn Eis provide long-term rental services at no cost to the client. Rental prices vary, but you can bet that they will get snapped up quickly.

D&G Property Management
14080 Mill St., Guerneville
(707) 869-0623
http://riverhomes.com/dandg
This firm offers permanent rentals in western Sonoma County. Studio apartments start at $500. You can expect to pay anywhere from $800 to $1,400 for a two-bedroom, one-bath unit, but a four-bedroom home might go as high as $1,800. Although much of D&G's clientele is looking for residential property, the company also offers business and commercial sites.

Vacation Rentals

If you are interested in a short-term rental for a vacation stay, Sonoma County has agencies that can help. Russian River Vacation Homes, Russian River Getaways, Sea Coast Hide-a-Ways, and Rams Head Realty all offer vacation rentals. See our Hotels and Motels chapter for more details on these and other Wine Country agencies specializing in vacation homes.

Real Estate Companies

Prudential California Real Estate
101 Golf Course Dr., Rohnert Park
(707) 588–8900
326 Healdsburg Ave., Healdsburg
(707) 433–4150
16316 Main St., Guerneville
(707) 887–2204
www.pruweb.com

An award-winning team of seasoned pros covers everything from mobile homes to ranches and wineries in Sonoma County. Additional offices serve Northern California, but the Prudential is hooked into a network that is not just national but worldwide. Comprehensive relocation services can help you make the transition wherever you come from.

Frank Howard Allen Realtors
423 First St. West, Sonoma
(707) 938–8400
9200 Sonoma Hwy., Kenwood
(707) 833–2881
905 E. Washington St., Petaluma
(707) 762–7766
2245 Montgomery Dr., Santa Rosa
(707) 523–3000
332 Healdsburg Ave., Healdsburg
(707) 431–9446
6876 Sebastopol Ave., Sebastopol
(707) 824–5400
www.fhallen.com

Frank Howard Allen Realtors has two corporate-owned offices and numerous independently owned firms operating as licensees. They handle all types of real estate, including residential, commercial, vacation, and business properties. In Napa and Sonoma Counties, they specialize in wineries and vineyards. The Sonoma offices boast about one-third of the company's nearly $1 billion in total annual sales. In business more than 85 years, this is one of the Bay Area's largest independent, locally owned and operated real estate firms. Special relocation services can be arranged and coordinated from Frank Howard Allen's administrative offices in Novato.

Coldwell Banker
333 S. McDowell Blvd., Petaluma
(707) 762–6611
50 Enterprise Dr., Rohnert Park
(707) 586–4500
790 Sonoma Ave., Santa Rosa
(707) 527–8567
www.coldwellbanker.com

Claiming to be the nation's largest full-service real estate company, Coldwell Banker in Sonoma County handles all types of properties including homes, ranches, mobile homes, and land and investment property. Coldwell offers a free national relocation service, as well as a buyer-seller coupon booklet that gives discounts at Sears on home improvement items. Ask for their Best Buyer Guidebook to help find and finance your dream home. All Coldwell Banker offices are independently owned and operated.

RE/MAX Central
320 College Ave., Santa Rosa
(707) 524–3500
371 Windsor River Rd., Windsor
(707) 837–7800
www.santarosa-homes.com

RE/MAX has experts in transactions involving dwellings, business property, commercial developments, and agricultural real estate. Each RE/MAX office is independently owned and operated, assuring the dedicated service of personnel with local knowledge about the areas they cover.

Century 21
561 Broadway, Sonoma
(707) 938–5830
616 Petaluma Blvd. South, Petaluma
(707) 769–9000
1057 College Ave., Santa Rosa
(707) 577–7777
107 North St., Healdsburg
(707) 433–4404
114 Lake St., Cloverdale
(707) 894–5232
www.century21.com

If you're attracted to a name you've seen elsewhere, Century 21 has a presence on the real estate scene that's recognized nationwide for its reliability and attention to clients. With offices covering strategic points in Sonoma County, Century 21 specialists offer knowledge of local residential markets. They try to tune into individual needs in a real estate area that is unusually diverse.

Griewe Real Estate
141 E. Napa St., Sonoma
(707) 938–0916
www.griewerealestate.com

This independently owned firm started business in 1990 under the ownership of Jim and Linda Griewe and serves all of Sonoma Valley. Griewe is intimately familiar with the area and has a reputation for excellence and integrity. Griewe sale signs hang in front of many homes in the Sonoma Valley, but they also deal in vineyard properties. Services include multiple-listing service, computer search programs, and relocation services.

Morgan Lane
500 Broadway, Sonoma
(707) 935–5777
www.morganlane.com

With seven offices throughout Sonoma County, Morgan Lane covers properties across Wine Country, as far north as Boonville in Mendocino County. (See previous listing under Napa County Real Estate Companies.)

Coralee Barkela & Company
1815 Fourth St., Santa Rosa
(707) 833–5700, (707) 542–9200
www.coraleebarkela.com

Coralee Barkela has been a top real estate professional in Sonoma County since the early 1970s, and in 1997 she opened her own office. With the help of five agents, her company covers all of Sonoma County.

Highly knowledgeable about grape culture and wine making, she concentrates heavily on ranches and vineyards as well as high-quality residential properties.

Pacific Union Residential Brokerage
640 Broadway, Sonoma
(707) 939–9500
www.pacunion.com

Originally a Bay Area company specializing in commercial and estate-type property sales, Pacific Union now serves residential clients throughout the Sonoma Valley. The agents are all highly seasoned professionals, most of them brokers in their own right, with an average of 12 years of experience. Relocation services are offered.

Broadway Realty
654 Broadway, Sonoma
(707) 996–1072

Robert and Sylvia Bernard, longtime owners of Sonoma Management (see previous listing in Rentals), expanded to join 35-year veterans Mori & Perkins Real Estate and form a company that encompasses both enterprises. This is a real family business—Bill Mori is Sylvia's uncle, and the property where the Broadway offices are located has been in the family since Sylvia's grandfather bought it 60 years ago. These are people who know Sonoma very well, with some 50 years of experience all told, and they serve a diverse clientele throughout the Sonoma Valley. They are capable of selling everything from residences to vineyard acreage in an area they know thoroughly.

Mid-Towne Realty, Inc.
709 Healdsburg Ave., Healdsburg
(707) 433–6555
www.midtownerealty.com

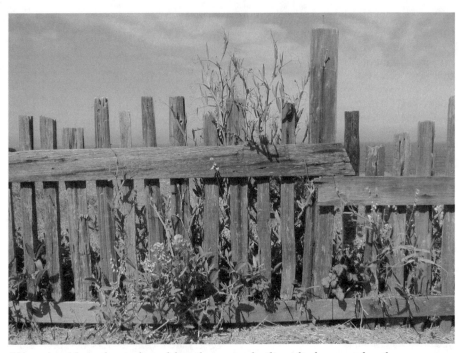

Old weathered fences that mark ranch boundaries are a familiar sight along coastal roads. PHOTO: JOHN NAGIECKI

This local, professional, and independent firm has been in business for more than 30 years. In addition to serving clientele in the Healdsburg community, the office also handles Russian River properties, both for sales and rentals. Relocation services are provided to purchasers from other areas.

North County Properties
21069 Geyserville Ave., Geyserville
(707) 857–1728

Karen and Doug Waelde, a husband and wife team, have been in the real estate business for 17 years in Healdsburg and (for the last few years) in Geyserville, a favorable location between two beautiful wine appellations—Dry Creek Valley and Alexander Valley. They cover the area between Santa Rosa and Cloverdale, including the town of Windsor. It's a piece of countryside they know as well as they know their own back yard. The Waeldes are there to negotiate purchase and sale of residential property, vacation property

(second homes), farms, ranches, mini-ranches (from 2 to 200 acres), and vine-yards, and they are particularly pleased to offer expertise to first-time buyers.

Sea Ranch Realty
Sea Ranch Lodge, Sea Ranch
(707) 785–2494, (888) 732–7262
www.888searanch.com

Sea Ranch is a private community that extends 10 miles along the Sonoma Coast. Sea Ranch Realty provides infor-mation on existing home sales or build-ing opportunities. Offices are right on-site at the lodge, and the company offers homes on ocean bluffs or grassy meadows.

Real Estate Publications

For more information about the Sonoma County real estate market, check the real estate section in the Friday edition of *The Sonoma Index-Tribune* or the *Santa Rosa Press-Democrat*'s Saturday and Sunday real estate sections. You can also pick up the following free publications at area grocery stores, drug stores, or newspaper racks.

Distinctive Properties
www.buycoastal.com

Sponsored by the participating real estate firms, this publication comes out every other month in black and white, with a color version published quarterly. It covers only Sonoma and Napa Counties. Distribution is primarily in supermarkets, but locations that display free literature are also used as outlets. Range of properties included varies from mobile homes to million-dollar estates.

The Press Democrat Real Estate
Network Magazine
www.pressdemocrat.com

This publication, issued every other month, covers all Wine Country counties. Primarily black and white, with a few color photos, it presents advertising by individual real estate firms. Distribution is free at magazine racks at supermarkets, drug stores, and individual real estate offices. Properties are listed primarily by individual real estate firms, but the magazine additionally provides maps and graphs and an indexed location guide. Residential property listings range from $95,000 fixer-uppers to $2.5 million spreads.

The Prudential California Realty:
A Presentation of Wine Country Properties

This colorful quarterly presentation covers Sonoma Valley and the four Prudential California Realty offices. In addition to availability at Prudential offices, the magazine-format publication can be found at wineries, supermarkets, and drug store racks. All types of property, including commercial, are covered in a wide price range.

Real Estate in the Wine Country

This glossy real estate magazine, published weekly, colorfully presents properties in all four counties of Wine Country. It's available at supermarkets, drug stores, and any available public-literature distribution point. Individual real estate firms

advertise in the publication and present a full range of properties from mobile homes and residential ranches to acreage and vineyards. Residential properties range from fixer-uppers starting in the low $100,000 category to estates costing $850,000 and up.

Mendocino County

The rugged Mendocino coast stretches 120 miles along the Pacific from its southern point at Gualala to the King Mountain range on the north. Each of the small towns and hamlets that dot the coastline has its own unique identity and charm. And each has a different set of real estate values.

If you long for a view of the sea, it will cost you. But what it costs depends on where you want to settle. Fort Bragg, with a population of about 6,000, is basically a lumbering and fishing community, though tourism is becoming a factor. Most of Fort Bragg's homes are long established, but there is some new construction going on. A new housing development is slowly making an appearance, with the builder preferring to work on contract, one home at a time. Average price of single-family dwellings in the area is $200,000, though ocean views can go as high as $450,000.

Eight miles south in tiny Mendocino (population 1,000), the cost of housing rises steeply. A two-bedroom home in the village, without a view of the water, will likely be priced at $325,000. Add an ocean view, and the price would rise to $500,000 on average—these addresses top out in the millions.

In the inland valleys, a few modest-sized towns and hamlets cling to U.S. 101—Hopland, Ukiah, and Willits. The landscape is agricultural, and it is prime grape-growing territory. Nestled in the valley below the spectacular Coast Range is Ukiah, county seat and Mendocino's largest city (population 15,500). It's a blend of businesses, recreational opportunities, affordable housing, verdant vineyards and orchards, and untamed wilderness. The city's west side includes hundreds of historic homes and buildings shaded by a lush canopy of mature trees. Norman Crampton's *100 Best Small Towns* in 1993 named Ukiah the No. 1 small town in California.

Overall, housing in the Ukiah area presents the best of two worlds. In town one is close to everything—quiet, family-oriented neighborhoods are the city's primary feature. Just minutes from the city limits is the Yokayo Valley countryside. Dotted with orchards and vineyards, rolling green hills, and stands of oak and redwood, one can get away from it all and still be a quick 10-minute drive from the town's amenities. Average price for a three-bedroom home is $150,000, average home rental runs $900 a month, and apartments rent for $500 on average.

Known mainly as a railroad hub and lumber community, the town of Willits, 25 miles north of Ukiah, is at the western edge of the Little Lake Valley, 1,350 feet above sea level. The chaparral and oak glades characteristic of the southern part of the county give way here to thick redwood and fir forests that stretch to the Oregon border.

With a population of 5,000, the town itself is not very large; however, the surrounding area includes a surprising number of homes, bringing the greater Willits population to nearly 15,000. Home prices are more modest here, running between $85,000 to $200,000 for a three-bedroom home.

You'll find other information about the Mendocino market in the real estate pages of the *Fort Bragg Advocate-News.* Chambers of commerce often prove to be valuable resources as well. The Greater Ukiah Chamber of Commerce is at 200 S. School Street. Call (707) 462-4705 for assistance.

Rentals

Frontier Realty Property Management
218 S. Humboldt St., Willits
(707) 459-1525

The oldest property management firm in Willits, Frontier has been in business since 1977. They serve Willits and Mendocino County only.

Vacation Rentals

If your stay will be short and oriented toward fun, or if you want a change of pace, you may want to rent a vacation home. Coast Getaways and Mendocino Coast Reservations offer vacation rentals. Details about these and other vacation rental agencies in Wine Country can be found in our Hotels and Motels chapter.

Real Estate Companies

Wally Johnson Realty
3810 Eastside Calpella Rd., Ukiah
(707) 485-8700, (800) 289-8542
www.wjrealty.com

Realtor Wally Johnson has served the Ukiah area since 1990, dealing in homes, income property, lots, and land sales as well as quality manufactured homes. He is a member of the Mendocino County Board of Realtors.

E.S. Wolf & Company
514 S. School St., Ukiah
(707) 463-2719
www.eswolf.com

This broker deals entirely in large properties—ranch lands, vineyards, and large estates. It is also the exclusive Mendocino representative for Sotheby's International Realty, handling the local end of that firm's national and international dealings.

Pacific Properties
36 South St., Willits
(707) 459-6175, (800) 767-9546

This is the largest independently owned and operated real estate office in Willits, with eight agents specializing in residential and county properties.

Mendo Realty
690 S. Main St., Fort Bragg
(707) 964-3610
1061 Main St., Mendocino
(707) 937-5822
www.mendorealty.com

The Mendocino coast's oldest real estate firm, Mendo Realty covers the coast from Gualala to Westport. Most of their representatives have a lengthy tenure and they have accumulated firsthand knowledge of area history and trends in residential properties as well as commercial, business, ranch, and timber acreage.

Sea Cottage Real Estate
45120 Main St., Mendocino
(707) 937–0423, (800) 707–0423
www.seacottage.com

The first certified residential specialist on the Mendocino coast, this firm has been in business since 1979. With six agents, Sea Cottage covers the entire Mendocino coast.

Lake County

Mount St. Helena is only 4,300 feet high, but when it comes to the real estate landscape, it might as well be Everest. The southern slopes of the mountain fall away to Napa Valley and its $315,000 median-priced home. The northern slopes level off into Lake County, where bargains, relatively speaking, abound. Though Lake County was mildly affected by the feeding frenzy in the Wine Country real estate market of the last several years, home prices here did not shoot up at the same rate.

In late 2001, the median price for a home in Lake County was estimated at $150,000, edging upward to $180,000 for properties nearest Napa County. But because of its isolation from major job centers and the long and sometimes hair-raising commute to and from Napa and Sonoma Counties, it's unlikely that bargain hunters will overrun Lake County any time soon.

Lake and Napa Counties are roughly the same size in acreage, yet Lake's population is only about 58,300—smaller than the city of Napa. It is a truly rural environment—ranchland sprinkled with pickup trucks and the occasional double-wide trailer. As such, there is far less glitz and glamour than in Napa, and the word "fixer-upper" is seen more frequently in listings for homes here. It is still possible to buy a home in Lake County for under $100,000, but it may be a fixer, exceptionally small, or quite old—in some cases, all

three. Chances are it's a double-wide in a good or even excellent location. But for many folks searching for a part-time vacation home, these may be ideal investments.

There is very little here in the way of subdivided development. About the only major subdivision is the gated community of Hidden Valley Lake, and it has room to nearly double its current configuration. Middletown, the community closest to Napa Valley, is in high demand, but finding desirable properties between Middletown and the Napa County line is becoming increasingly difficult. And like just about anywhere else in the our four-county region, it is the country estates, and the big homes with sweeping views of Clear Lake, that fetch the highest selling prices.

Million-dollar homes are rare but their counterparts in Napa or Sonoma Counties are listing for twice that, or more. Homes situated around Buckingham Golf and Country Club in Kelseyville are commanding prices in the high-$300s. Also in Kelseyville, a four-bedroom, two-bath house on 2.5 acres with a barn and other usable outbuildings may have an asking price of $275,000. A three-bedroom, two-bath home in nearby Soda Bay with a view of Clear Lake might go for $168,000. In Lakeport, smaller homes (two bedroom, one bath) begin in the mid-$90s and go on up to $120,000.

Rentals

Like house prices, monthly rentals in Lake County are about half what you'd pay in Napa and Sonoma Counties. A two-bedroom house in Kelseyville fetches $525 per month; a larger three-bedroom, two-bath home in Lakeport goes for $700. Large furnished homes in Westlake, a gated community in north Lakeport, are much pricier—about $1,100 per month. In Nice, a nice two-bedroom, two-bath home runs about $600.

As in other parts of Wine Country, apartments are hard to come by in Lake County. But when you can find them, you'll think you've stumbled into a time warp. Rents can be $425 for a one-bedroom unit, reaching $750 for a three-bedroom unit. A two-bedroom house with a view of Clear Lake may fetch $750 and up.

Real Estate Companies

Neft & Neft Realtors
21162 Hwy. 29, Middletown
(707) 987–3630, (800) 200–0374
www.neftrealtors.com

David Neft is a genetically programmed Realtor, having inherited the business from his property-handling parents in 1978. His office has four Realtors and listings throughout the county, though it concentrates on Middletown, Cobb Mountain, and Hidden Valley Lake. Neft & Neft has always been known for facilitating the first-home American dream, but it is branching out to include sales of commercial vineyards and acreage.

Century 21 House of Realty
19851 Hartman Rd., Middletown
(707) 987–3800, (800) 373–3888

This office has been tackling the southern Lake County real estate market since 1984. Its five Realtors concentrate on Cobb, Middletown, and Hidden Valley Lakes.

Insiders' Tip

Before making an offer, make sure your dream house won't be under water in the next "100-year flood" (which seems to come every other winter lately). The city or county should be able to tell you whether your prospective domicile rests in a recognized flood zone.

Century 21 Vintage Horizon
1175 N. Main St., Lakeport
(707) 263–4235, (800) 300–1289

This Lake County office has been in place for more than 20 years, so they have plenty of experience around the lake and throughout the county. There are about 10 Realtors and they handle everything from residential property to exclusive acreage.

Shore Line Realty
13725 E. Hwy. 20, Clearlake Oaks
(707) 998–1137, (800) 998–1130
1556 New Long Valley Rd., Spring Valley
(707) 998-2211
9945 E. Hwy. 20, Glenhaven
(707) 998-3366
375 S. Main St., Lakeport
(707) 263–4104, (888) 770–0428
www.ngl.net/shoreline

Shore Line's broker and six agents together have more than 100 years of experience as licensed Realtors. The business itself has been operating in Lake County since 1981. They do all types of property, but offer several specialties within the office—such as commercial and income-producing property (lakefront resorts included) and vineyards or undeveloped hillside.

Coldwell Banker
190 S. Main St., Lakeport
(707) 262–1000, (800) 598–3865
21037 Calistoga Rd., Suite 8, Middletown
(707) 994–4920
14085 Lakeshore Dr., Clearlake
(707) 994-3662
www.coldwellbanker.com

Coldwell Banker's 14 Realtors handle all of Lake County. The office trades heavily in residential property but also has a commercial division called T&C Properties—a sideline that makes use of broker Robert Dunk's accounting background.

CPS Country Air
808 Lakeport Blvd., Lakeport
(707) 263–2620, (800) 637–0947
9730 Soda Bay Rd., Kelseyville
(707) 277–9255

Hwy. 175 and Golf Rd., Cobb Mountain
(707) 928–5113
www.cpsrealestate.com

With three offices and 18 certified Realtors, CPS enjoys Lake County's largest market share. The office specializes in residential sales and rental property and covers the entire county.

United Country Noble Realty
9739 Soda Bay Rd., Kelseyville
(707) 277–7477, (800) 350–6597
200 Lakeport Blvd., Lakeport
(707) 263–1818, (800) 350–5948

6222 E. Hwy. 20, Lucerne
(707) 274–5528, (800) 474–5528
3654 E. Hwy. 20, Nice
(707) 274–5576, (800) 815–5568
www.noblerealty.com

If you look at volume of sales in Lake County during the last decade or so, Noble probably rests at the top of the heap. The company has 22 Realtors and several satellite offices around Clear Lake, but the main office is in Lucerne. Noble handles the entire county and all sorts of property, with its largest share in land, including vineyards. May Noble started the business in 1968.

Retirement

In much the same way thousands of visitors flock to Wine Country for the vino, the cuisine, and the general ambience that surrounds it, retirees have discovered that this four-county region with its mild winters and laid-back ways makes an ideal place to spend their golden years.

Wine Country has become a happy haven for retirees, those young-at-heart oldsters who are aging with grace and style. They're a lively lot, this new breed of senior citizens. Forget the orthopedic shoes—these seniors are filling closets with footwear appropriate for hiking, tennis, golf, biking, boating, and walking. In their former lives they were businesspeople, teachers, salespeople, lawyers, and homemakers. Now they've turned the rooms that were formerly for children into offices, darkrooms, hobby centers, and exercise rooms. They're signing up for classes for everything from painting to wine tasting. And they have become volunteers—those essential citizens who move the wheels of progress in hospitals, learning centers, churches, libraries, and civic organizations.

In short, Wine Country is a place well geared to the 65-plus segment of our population (and those other lucky dogs who have been able to hang up the work togs at a younger age). In this chapter, you'll find living accommodations and lifestyle options for the affluent, the middle-of-the-roaders, and those of lower income (though Wine Country can never really be considered inexpensive). Residential developments restricted to the older-than-55 crowd are an option seized by many, with some featuring a club-like style of living. Adult-only mobile-home parks offer a popular choice, and in some areas, city government has provided cozy, subsidized cottages for low-income seniors, though this option usually entails a waiting list. For older folks who want to (or must) cut down on the working side, there are complexes of apartments that offer individual living with one to three meals a day. And for some who need watchful care, Wine Country has that covered too.

We start the information rolling with listings of area senior services, which have grown right alongside the growth of the Wine Country's senior population.

Senior Services

We hope that most seniors who visit or choose to live in our region are spending their retirement years actively pursuing good health and happiness. Everyone, however, needs a little help and guidance from time to time to lead a satisfying life, and seniors are no different. Here are a few connections that should make it easier for seniors to find their way around in new territory.

Napa County

The Volunteer Center of Napa County
1820 Jefferson St., Napa
(707) 252–6222, (707) 963–3922

The Volunteer Center does all sorts of good work in the county, and its Senior Services Program, funded by the Area Agency on Aging (serving Napa and Solano Counties, see listing in this section) and the United Way, is foremost on the list. Especially valuable is the Senior Guide it publishes each year. It's a well-organized 15-page catalog of write-ups and phone numbers, with suggestions on topics ranging from health services and home care to housing and transportation.

Comprehensive Services for Older Adults
900 Coombs St., Ste. 257, Napa
(707) 253–4625, (888) 619–6913

This program, administered by the Napa County Health and Human Services Agency, offers in-home care to the aged, blind, and disabled who can't afford to fend for themselves. The manifold services include household tasks and shopping, nonmedical personal care when needed to ensure safety, alcohol and drug counseling, adult protective services, and psychiatric case management for seniors 62 or older who suffer from mental illness or Alzheimer's disease. Comprehensive Services also assists with procurement of food stamps and Medi-Cal (state-subsidized medical insurance) benefits.

Senior Class
Queen of the Valley Hospital,
1000 Trancas St., Napa
(707) 253–9000

Queen of the Valley has targeted older adults for health promotion and education with this membership program since 1986. Members are offered a variety of classes, lectures, and health screenings, conducted by the hospital's able team of healthcare professionals. It's $15 to join and $10 a year thereafter, though nobody is turned away. (For more on Queen of the Valley, see our Healthcare chapter.)

Napa Valley Dining Club
1500 Jefferson St., Napa
(707) 253–6112, (800) 788–0124

This service cooks up hot, nutritious meals for people 60 years or older on a donation basis. When needed, the club will even transport guests to one of six Napa County sites or deliver food to homes. Call one day in advance for reservations.

Adult Day Services of Napa Valley
3295 Claremont Way, Ste. 3, Napa
(707) 258–9087

The frail elderly and younger functionally impaired adults are the focus of this organization. Daily hot lunches, caregiver respites, social activities, and transportation assistance are all provided.

Napa Valley Committee on Aging
1500 Jefferson St., Napa
(707) 224–5121

This is a referral service for seniors seeking in-home care or housekeeping. The committee also offers handyman service for minor home repairs. (The fee is negotiable.)

Garden Haven
2447 Old Sonoma Rd., Napa
(707) 253–3425

Even the most devoted caregiver needs an occasional break, and here is a day center you can trust to watch over your elderly relative or friend, especially if they suffer from Alzheimer's or dementia. Activities include music, exercise regimens, crafts, cooking, and gardening. Wheelchairs are welcome. The center is open Monday, Tuesday, Thursday, and Friday from 10:00 A.M. to 3:00 P.M. The cost is $12.50 per day.

Napa-Solano Area Agency on Aging
1443 Main St., Napa
(800) 510–2020

People 55 and older who are mentally and physically fit, and who are looking for a little extra cash, are encouraged to get in touch with this agency. They'll help you find part-time employment.

Sonoma County

Council on Aging
730 Bennett Valley Rd., Santa Rosa
(707) 525–0143
www.councilonaging.com

This is the overall program that provides many of the benefits that are incorporated in member organizations such as the senior centers listed subsequently. Council on Aging provides dining rooms with a hot, healthy noontime meal at 10 locations in Sonoma County. The Meals on Wheels program delivers hot meals seven days a week to the homes of temporarily or chronically homebound seniors. Legal consultation services are provided, as well as money management programs, health insurance counseling, and door-to-door transportation for seniors with doctor visits. The council offers an excellent Senior Resource Guide available at senior centers or by calling the listed number.

Weathered barns and decades-old vineyards are some of the many rural charms that attract retirees to Wine Country. PHOTO: JOHN NAGIECKI

American Association of Retired Persons
P.O. Box 662, Santa Rosa 95402
(707) 527-7282
www.aarp.org

AARP is a senior advocacy organization for people who have reached 50 years of age. Its mission is to promote the welfare and status of the country's elder population, and some of this work is carried on through local chapters. The agenda is likely to be the same for the different chapters—there's always a monthly meeting (call the numbers listed to find out which day and time), educational opportunities, insurance advantages, and travel information.

Meetings usually include speakers involved with state or local government, health organizations, Medicare, or widowhood. Some chapters organize social activities. The Santa Rosa chapter, for instance, has an annual picnic in July, featuring hot dogs and a potluck assortment of foods furnished by members. A nominal membership fee is charged ($12 per year), but anyone older than 50 is welcome to attend meetings.

AARP Senior Community Service Employment Program
2050 W. Steele Ln., Ste. E-1, Santa Rosa
(707) 525-9190

Partially government-sponsored, this is an AARP program to help low-income seniors get back into the work force through on-the-job training with organizations such as the American Red Cross and Goodwill Industries. It is also an employment office that can find jobs in the private sector after training.

AARP 55 Alive/Mature Driving
980 Ninth St., Ste. 700, Sacramento 95814
(916) 446-2277

Sonoma County: Call (888) 227-7669 and leave your zip code and phone number, and an instructor will contact you. There is an $10 charge for the two-day course—four hours each day.

North Bay HI-CAP
55 Maria Dr., Ste. 837, Petaluma
(800) 303-4477

The North Bay Health Insurance Counseling and Advocacy Program (HI-CAP) covers six counties north of the Golden Gate Bridge (including all four in Wine Country). The center offers one-on-one counseling by trained volunteers registered by the California Department of Aging. They provide independent, unbiased information on health insurance, including Medicare and supplemental programs. They also help clients sort out their medical finances and make sure they are being billed appropriately for Medicare. There is no charge for this service.

Petaluma Ecumenical Project
1400 Caulfield Ln., Petaluma
(707) 762-2336

In 1977 three local ministers came together to find a way to provide low-cost housing for seniors. With community backing, the Petaluma Ecumenical Project sought out suitable building sites and developed architectural plans. The group has built and manages nine projects and is now supported by 11 churches and AARP contributions.

Jewish Seniors Program
3855 Montgomery Dr., Santa Rosa
(707) 528-4222
www.jcagency.org

The wide spectrum of entertainment and educational opportunities offered through this program includes musical events, folk dancing, autobiographical writing, book discussion, parties, and trips. Want to learn Yiddish? That's an option too! The group welcomes participants from all denominations.

Sons In Retirement
Sonoma
(707) 938-2643
www.sirinc.org

To join, you must simply be retired; there is no minimum age. Members meet once a month for lunch and to hear a speaker. Other than that there are few requirements, although you're expected to attend the meetings: Sonoma County has five groups of 125 each, offering various forms of entertainment—golf, bowling, computers, photography groups, and travel excursions, to mention a few. Bus tours to Reno or Lake Tahoe are frequent, and trips as far afield as Yellowstone and Canada are possible. SIR headquarters is in Sacramento.

Mendocino County

Multipurpose Senior Services Program
487 N. State St., Ukiah
(707) 468-9347

The Multipurpose Senior Services Program is a nonprofit community agency that strives to meet the needs of people with disabilities so that they can remain in their own homes and live an independent life of dignity. Some of the home-care services that MSSP helps obtain include personal care, home repairs, house cleaning, shopping, transportation, and home-delivered meals. The agency serves Ukiah, Willits, Hopland, Potter Valley, and the Fort Bragg/Mendocino area, plus Lake County.

Lake County

Community Care
14642 Lakeshore Dr., Clearlake
(707) 995-7010

Community Care helps anyone older than 18 with disability or illness, but it is seniors who have come to rely on the program most. A nonprofit agency funded by a variety of sources, Community Care seeks to arrange affordable, competent help for people trying to live independently at home. At no charge, the agency's Multipurpose Senior Services Program serves frail elderly people (65 or older) who are Medi-Cal recipients.

Senior Health
922 Bevins Ct., Lakeport
(707) 263-1090

This function of the Lake County Health Department offers free general health assessments for area seniors, including a nutritional analysis. The department also screens for blood pressure and hearing and will run blood tests for a small fee.

Senior Centers

They're social centers, educational resources, service sources, and just plain fun places for seniors with leisure time. Most of the centers publish newsletters so everyone can find out what's in store. All have an extensive, varied program of activities, and all offer services such as blood pressure and hearing testing, legal counsel, and tax assistance on a regular basis.

Napa County

Senior Citizens Center
1500 Jefferson St., Napa
(707) 255-1800

Older residents get one-stop shopping at this office. Nearly 60 clubs and organizations—including the Senior Friendship Club and Napa Grange—use the center as a meeting place. It's open Monday through Friday, from 8:00 A.M. to 4:00 P.M. Activities range from dances, bingo, and potluck dinners to arts and crafts and pancake breakfasts. Friday mornings welcome a diversity of guest speakers for Senior Seminars. Call for a monthly schedule of events.

Berryessa Senior Citizens
4380 Spanish Flat Loop Rd., Berryessa
(707) 966-0206

The highlands surrounding Lake Berryessa sound like a nice place for retired folks—and, well, they are. The center has a strong lineup of health, educational, social, and recreational programs. If you call for a monthly schedule, you'll discover potluck meals, bingo, crafts, Adventure College classes, trips, dances, and more.

Sonoma County

Southern Sonoma

Vintage House
264 First St. East, Sonoma
(707) 996-0311

Staffed largely by senior volunteers, Vintage House is open Monday through Friday, serving more than 1,000 individuals each month with up to 70 classes and activities, most of them free or low-cost. The choices include art classes, line dancing, tap dancing, international folk dance instruction, canasta, bridge in several forms, exercise classes, and French, Italian, and Spanish at levels for beginner, intermediate, and advanced speakers. The Vintage House Singers, a choral group, is coached by a professional music director and performs twice a year. The Department of Motor Vehicles has a representative visit each month to administer driving tests, and the tax man cometh during his season. Lunch is served Tuesday, Thursday, and Friday in the dining room for a small fee.

Lucchesi Park Senior Center
(Petaluma Community Center)
211 Novak Dr., Petaluma
(707) 778-4399

This facility largely houses the recreational part of Petaluma's senior program—the local meal program is now administered by the adjacent Petaluma People Services

Center. Line dancing events draw 25 to 40 participants each week, and ballroom dancing attracts 100 or more. Group exercise goes over big, along with the computer classes, eclectic discussion groups, art instruction, and creative writing classes. Many daytrips and extended trips are sponsored. The center also sponsors flu shots and blood pressure testing.

Rohnert Park Senior Center
6800 Hunter Dr., Suite A, Rohnert Park
(707) 585–6780

Active seniors as well as disabled persons who can manage on their own are welcome here to chat, play cards, and watch the once-a-month movie. General activities include line dancing, duplicate bridge, basketry, Spanish classes, a craft shop, and a billiards table. Every other month an early-evening dance (held the second Tuesday of each month from 1:00 to 4:00 P.M.) brings out a lively crowd. In fact, it has grown so popular that the center had to move it to a larger facility—the Community Center on 5401 Snyder Lane. According to the director, seniors often claim this is the best center around, and it draws older folks from as far away as Ukiah. A noon meal is served daily.

Santa Rosa Senior Center
704 Bennett Valley Rd., Santa Rosa
(707) 545–8608

Dancing is big here—afternoon ballroom dancing once a week, line dancing, and tap dancing. Bingo, bridge, whist, chess, and pinochle games are lively, and there are three billiards tables. Watercolor painting classes are a big draw, and there's creative writing, a poetry group, and Spanish instruction. The drama group puts on shows, and a choral group attracts those who like to belt out a tune. There are also clinics for blood pressure, allergy screening, chiropractic evaluations, and even toenail clipping. Once a month the Friendship Club organizes a potluck lunch. Meals are served Monday to Friday at 4:00 P.M. The Council on Aging also uses the center kitchen to prepare meals for delivery to the homebound.

Northern Sonoma
Windsor Senior Center
9231 Foxwood Dr., Windsor
(707) 838–1250

This center is surrounded by roses—45 varieties, in fact, in a lovely garden. In the artistic category, classes are available in oil and pastel painting and sculpture. Card players have a choice of pinochle or bridge, and seniors can learn to play the guitar, study genealogy, or join in a quilting bee.

For the athletic, the bocce ball court is an attraction, as is the horseshoe pit. But most popular of all is the swimming pool: Windsor tends to be hot in summer, and the pool is a terrific place to cool off. It is outfitted for the disabled, who can be lowered from wheelchair to water by a special lift device.

Healdsburg Senior Center
133 Matheson St., Healdsburg
(707) 431–3324

Lunch is served here Monday through Friday, and a bus service is available to bring seniors to the center as well as to take them to shopping areas and other destinations around town. Crafts are popular here, with a group meeting once a week to work on a variety of handcrafts including the art of flower arranging. An unusually talented group of woodworkers has been awarded several honors for items created at the center. Bingo brings the lucky and unlucky to play each Thursday. Department of Motor Vehicles testing also is provided.

Cloverdale Senior Multi-Purpose Center
Second and Commercial Sts., Cloverdale
(707) 894–4826

Weekly blood-pressure screenings, visits by an optometrist, and hearing-aid maintenance are among the services offered in Cloverdale. Line dancing is offered one day each week, and an instructor comes in to help seniors create an autobiographical record of their lives. A newsletter keeps seniors apprised of coming attractions at the center, where lunch is served every weekday.

West County/Russian River

Sebastopol Burbank Senior Center
167 N. High St., Sebastopol
(707) 829–2440
www.seb.org/comm/seniorctr.html

This center receives laudable backing from the community, and several stores and bakeries bring in day-old products to distribute among the members. In addition, lunch is served in the dining room each weekday, and home-delivered meals are dispatched to those who cannot come in. Card games and bingo are regular sources of entertainment, and every once in a while, there's a special program by a harp and flute duo. Through a coalition of other senior service groups, a lively travel program has been developed in Sebastopol. Not only do seniors make short local trips—say, to Lake Tahoe, the San Francisco Zoo, the Golden Gate Bridge, and the Sonoma County Fair—but they have also taken journeys as far afield as Alaska and the Panama Canal.

Russian River Community Senior Center
15010 Armstrong Woods Rd., Guerneville
(707) 869–0618

Both on-site lunch and Meals on Wheels are provided from this center, and because this is a rural area, limited transportation is provided. Afternoon field trips and picnics are ideally suited to this vacation spot with its many scenic locales. Writing autobiographies and exercise classes are among indoor activities.

Mendocino County

U.S. 101

Ukiah Senior Center
499 Leslie St., Ukiah
(707) 462–4343

A lot happens here, and it would be hard not to have fun. There's line dancing, ballroom dancing, and dancing classes, plus a Saturday night dance to practice your lessons. You can play bingo, pinochle, bridge, Scrabble, or chess; learn to knit or crochet; or practice t'ai chi. The exercise class is on Tuesday, Wednesday, and Thursday. Legal help, tax assistance, and health screenings are available. Oh yes, lunch is served in the dining room each weekday.

Willits Senior Center
1501 Baechtel Rd., Willits
(707) 459–6826

A noon meal is served at the center and delivered to shut-ins. Seniors enjoy movies and bingo twice a week and a dance once a month. Breakfast is served once a month, and special weekend dinners are staged monthly. A worthy program at Willits is Extra Hands—a plan to hire people to do chores like gardening, cleaning house, and shopping for seniors who find these activities difficult. Drivers are provided to take people to medical appointments. The center is fortunate: there are 100 volunteers to help. Some funds are created by a thrift shop run by the seniors themselves. Says the director, "They have made the shop look like a real department store."

Mendocino Coast

South Coast Senior Citizens
140 Main St., Point Arena
(707) 882–2137

Arts and crafts occupy part of the daily schedule in Point Arena. An abalone breakfast is served on the second Sunday a month, and a spaghetti dinner is served on the fourth Friday. Monthly bus trips are scheduled to visit various spots and happenings. The dining room here provides a noon meal twice a week and provides transportation so seniors can get to the center. Delivered meals also are provided on the same days.

Fort Bragg Senior Center
490 N. Harold St., Fort Bragg
(707) 964–0443

Seniors enjoy bingo twice a week and can take a course in writing provided by the College of the Redwoods staff. From time to time a four-week improvisation class gives seniors a chance to practice acting, and occasionally a professional writer comes to tell seniors how they can learn to write and sell their output. A hot meal is served here each weekday from 11:30 A.M. to 12:30 P.M., with transportation provided.

Lake County

Highlands Senior Service Center
14773 Lakeshore Dr., Clearlake
(707) 994-3051

Highlands does a little bit of everything. It provides free legal assistance, money management advice, and medical transportation at 16 cents per mile. (They'll haul you as far as 300 miles.) The center also screens and hires people to provide in-home support services such as shopping, maintenance, and things of that nature. It also stages a blood pressure clinic on the second Monday and last Wednesday of each month. Meals are in the dining room at noon, for a suggested donation of $2.50; Highlands' Meals on Wheels program caters to the homebound.

Live Oaks Senior Center
12502 Foothill Blvd., Clearlake Oaks
(707) 998-1950

Experienced folks are treated well in Clearlake Oaks. This center is open daily from 8:00 A.M. to 2:00 P.M., with lunch served about noon. They do blood-pressure testing every Tuesday, a birthday lunch one Friday a month (presents included), and a health clinic on the third Wednesday of each month. Live Oaks also offers HMO information and counseling, loans equipment to the handicapped, and even sells fishing licenses to low-income, high-energy seniors.

Lakeport Senior Center
527 Konocti Ave., Lakeport
(707) 263-4218

Drawing much of its funding from the Older Americans Act of 1965, this center keeps things peppy. The agenda includes bingo every Wednesday, exercise classes, and crafts. You can even kick up your heels for line dancing. The hearing-aid technician comes once a week, the podiatrist once a month. The center also serves Sunday breakfast monthly.

Upper Lake Senior Outreach
9410 Mendenhall Ave., Upper Lake
(707) 275-3513

Here's a portion of what the elderly can expect in Upper Lake: information referral, shopping assistance, employment screening, and escorts (not that kind). The center directs people to food sources if necessary and sets up a health clinic every Thursday. A small group of interfaith volunteers helps out with driving duty and chores.

Retirement Housing Options

In the city of Sonoma, more than one-third of the population is older than 60, and the situation is similar in most of southern Sonoma County. This means a wide assortment of housing arrangements for retired folks in that area.

A retired couple takes a leisurely stroll on a poppy-edged pathway. PHOTO: SONOMA INDEX-TRIBUNE

Many retirees, of course, are simply absorbed into the general population. However, some choose to buy a home in one of the many active adult communities, which are not much different from any other residential area except that residents must have reached a certain age to live there. Usually there is a clubhouse and limited activities for homeowners. But mainly, there are no children.

Among the most popular of these communities in Sonoma are Temelec, Chantarelle, and Creekside. By far, the largest of these adult communities is Oakmont. It lies between Valley of the Moon and Santa Rosa but is actually within the Santa Rosa city limits. Its population runs to 5,000, with amenities including two golf courses, bowling greens, several activity rooms, and a sizable shopping center within the complex. It is possible to rent as well as buy at Oakmont.

Other popular options in Sonoma are adult mobile-home communities that limit residency to those over 55. These are generally operated by an on-site manager. They are practical, fairly inexpensive, and surprisingly spacious and appealing. A few worthy of mention are Pueblo Serena, Seven Flags, and De Anza Moon Valley. Residents own their own home but pay a monthly rental fee to the landowner for the lot. In Sonoma, this lot-rental fee has been regulated by city government and is rather low. A point of caution, however: In negotiating for the purchase of a home, it is wise to inquire as to whether you're permitted to rent out your home in case you choose to be absent for a length of time.

Although southern Sonoma County remains the setting for a large portion of Wine Country's adult mobile-home parks, they also are popular in other areas, partially because they are an inexpensive alternate to home ownership. Many are subject to rent control, which is adjusted annually by city government, and buyers should keep in mind that if rent control should cease, their home may be sitting on expensive property, making it difficult to sell and not so easy to move elsewhere.

With Wine Country in general showing every sign of becoming Northern California's retirement zone, senior housing facilities across the region are expanding to meet the demand. This is particularly true in the area of independent-living apartment complexes that provide housekeeping, meals, and laundry services, while allowing for complete freedom of movement and individuality. Following are listings for this type of retirement-living option (with a couple of other independent-living choices thrown in) within our four-county area.

Napa County

The Meadows of Napa Valley
1800 Atrium Pkwy., Napa
(707) 257-7885
www.meadowsofnapavalley.org

Three levels of personalized care are offered at this 20-acre residential retirement community. The apartments are available in one- and two-bedroom floorplans, augmented by the assisted living program and a skilled nursing center with rehabilitation services in a home-like setting. There's also a gift shop and beauty/barber shop on-site.

Aegis of Napa
2100 Redwood Rd., Napa
(707) 251-1409
www.aegisal.com

Studio apartments, one-bedroom flats, and shared suites are offered at this community, along with "Life's Neighborhood," an Alzheimer's program. This facility's "Small Indulgences" program helps family caregivers by keeping track of each resident's favorite foods, flowers, and special treats.

Silverado Orchards
601 Pope St., St. Helena
(707) 963-3688

In a quiet, green setting between St. Helena proper and the Silverado Trail is this popular retirement community. Silverado Orchards has 80 units all together—small studios, deluxe studios, one-bedroom apartments, and a couple of two-bedroom units. It's an active population that takes advantage of the immediate area's pleasant walking routes, plus twice-a-week exercise classes. They get a wealth of musical presentations in the multipurpose room. Because the proprietors are Seventh-day Adventists (the community itself is strictly nondenominational), residents can choose vegetarian meals if so desired.

Woodbridge Village
727 Hunt Ave., St. Helena
(707) 963–3231

Several years ago this HUD-supported retirement complex won an award for best landscaping in St. Helena, and the park-like grounds have only improved since then, the managers say, thanks in part to some resident green thumbs. Woodbridge is a series of tidy one-bedroom, one-bathroom apartments, most of them grouped into fourplexes. Vineyards remain on one side of the property. HUD defines a senior as anyone age 62 or older.

Rancho de Calistoga
2412 Foothill Blvd., Calistoga
(707) 942–6971

Yes, it's a mobile-home park, but if all of them looked like this, they would have a very different reputation. Centuries-old oak trees tower over the big lawn area out front, and the whole community is full of flowering plants. Rancho de Calistoga has a total of 184 lots. It also has a clubhouse, recreation building, pool, and spa. Oh, and activities? They include bingo twice a month, bridge, poker, exercise classes, quilting, potlucks, and Wednesday-morning brunch. The park is meant for seniors 55 and older.

Sonoma County

Westlake Wine Country House
800 Oregon St., Sonoma
(707) 996–7101
www.westlakecompany.com

Billed as a "luxury congregate retirement facility," Westlake Wine Country offers one- and two-bedroom suites, fully carpeted (bring your own furniture), with a small kitchen, private deck, or balcony and three meals a day in a rather elegant dining room. Having guests? You can use

one of the smaller dining rooms suitable for up to a dozen. You can also rent rooms for your guests in the complex for a nominal fee. The Westlake van takes residents to shopping or medical appointments, or you can use a parking space for your own car.

Westlake House Springs
4855 Snyder Lane, Rohnert Park
(707) 585–7878
www.westlakecompany.com

Although the Springs enjoys country views of rolling green farmlands, the property is near shopping, one block from a large medical complex, and a short putt to the nearest golf course. This complex is owned by the same company as Sonoma's Westlake Wine Country (see previous listing), with accommodations slightly upgraded in price and style. You can participate in a wide range of activities, both in-house and away—wine-and-cheese socials, book reviews, college courses, pool tournaments, movies, swimming, library visits, exercise, and game-room fun. The complex consists of 176 apartments and 190 residents.

Valley Orchards Retirement Community
2100 E. Washington St., Petaluma
(707) 778–6030

No medical or nursing service is provided here, the manager says, "but from time to time the resident may contract for outside assistance for bathing or personal care, which makes it a good bit cheaper than assisted living." Valley Orchards provides three meals a day, utilities, cable TV, transportation three days a week, housekeeping once a week, bathroom and bedroom laundry, 24-hour emergency assistance, and yard maintenance. Valley Orchard's 104 units are split between large studios and one- and two-bedroom apartments.

Friends House
684 Benicia Dr., Santa Rosa
(707) 538–0152
www.friendshouse.org

A Quaker institution, Friends House is composed of four interrelated programs for the older person: independent-living apartments and houses, an adult day-care center, an assisted-living facility, and a skilled-nursing facility. A large part of the six-acre Friends House site contains 60 garden apartments. People live in their own homes with their own belongings and garden space. One- and two-bedroom apartments are available, and recently some three-bedroom, two-bath homes were added to accommodate couples who want more space within the Friends House community. New residents must pay an entrance fee, and a monthly assessment covers housekeeping services. The dining room offers meals to residents for an additional charge. Cultural activities include visits to symphony performances, art galleries, libraries, and sporting events.

Renaissance at The Lodge at Paulin Creek
2375 Range Ave., Santa Rosa
(707) 575–3722, (800) 900–HOME
www.renaissancesl.com

The Lodge is set in parklike grounds with inviting courtyards. Apartments are sunny and bright, with the charm of designer fabrics, art reproductions, and handmade quilts. They range from studios to three-bedroom, two-bath units. Some dining options are offered—you can either be served graciously in the dining room or serve yourself casually from the salad and hot entree buffet. Amenities include a pool, fitness trail, billiards room, an opportunity to garden, and a calendar of day trips.

Mendocino County

Redwood Meadows
1475 Baechtel Rd., Willits
(707) 459–1616

In a lovely setting with walkways and green belts, Redwood Meadows is a senior apartment community open to active, independent seniors older than 55. The community center houses a game room, craft room, and community lounge. Because it is right next door to the Willits Senior Center (see previous listing), the amenities of that group are easily accessible. Meals are not served, but the dining

room is a center for potlucks, parties, movies, lectures, and other social events. Small pets are allowed.

The Woods
43300 Little River Airport Rd., Little River
(707) 937–6132, (800) GO–WOODS
www.ncphs.org

Quality manufactured homes nestled among redwoods, pines, and rhododendrons make up this residential community for seniors. The Woods is on 37 sunbelt acres connected by winding roads that lead walkers to a heated indoor pool and spa, the clubhouse, library, and art room. State park beaches and golf courses are minutes away. Assisted-living facilities are also available.

Redwood Coast Seniors
490 N. Harold St., Fort Bragg
(707) 964–0443

This organization maintains a list of Fort Bragg senior housing. Entries are all clean, well-maintained apartments or detached houses, with rents on a sliding scale according to income.

Lake County

Autumn Village
14930 Burns Valley Rd., Clearlake
(707) 995–1650

This community is divided into two complexes, with 40 one-bedroom apartments on one end and 22 on the other. Autumn Village has a reputation for tidy grounds and well-maintained units. It features bingo on Saturday, movies each Wednesday evening, and a potluck dinner on the third Thursday of the month. On Monday morning from 9:00 to 11:00 A.M., many of the women get together for crafts, sewing, and chitchat.

Highlands Village
6215 Old Hwy. 53, Clearlake
(707) 994–7538

A HUD-subsidized establishment, Highlands Village is open to seniors 62 and older who are eligible for public assistance. Dotted with gardens, the complex has 39 units, 38 of which are one-bedroom apartments. (Four are units for the disabled.) The laundry and recreation rooms are centrally located. Highlands Village has a tenants' association that schedules dinners, bingo every Tuesday, and numerous other activities.

Educational Opportunities

Several agencies and area schools offer opportunities for inquisitive, mature men and women to prove there is no age limit to new intellectual experiences. In addition to the resources listed, many senior centers throughout Wine Country offer classes in writing, foreign languages, computer skills, and other subjects.

Napa County

Napa Valley College Community Education
2277 Napa-Vallejo Highway, Napa
(707) 253–3070

North Bay Driving School
1878 El Centro Avenue, Napa
(707) 252–2066

Pacific Union College Extension, Angwin
(707) 965–6311, (800) 862–7080

Sonoma County

Petaluma Adult Education Center
200 Douglas Street, Petaluma
(707) 778–4633

Sonoma State University Gerontology Program
1801 E. Cotati Avenue, Rohnert Park
(707) 664–2411

Lewis Adult Education Center
2230 Lomitas Avenue, Santa Rosa
(707) 528–5421

Santa Rosa Junior College
1501 Mendocino Avenue, Santa Rosa
(707) 527–4011

New Vista Adult Education School
6980 Analy Avenue, Sebastopol
(707) 824–6455

Insiders' Tip
The California Department of Fish and Game offers a reduced-fee sport-fishing license for those aged 65 and older.

Lake County

Yuba College
15880 Dam Rd. Ext., Clearlake
(707) 995–7900

Konocti Adult School
9625 Adams St., Lower Lake
(707) 994–7142

Volunteer Opportunities

A number of programs are available that put to use the skills, talents, and personalities of older individuals who choose to work full- or part-time for little or no remuneration. Here are a handful of options.

Retired and Senior Volunteer Program
264 First St. East, Sonoma
(707) 996–4644
17A Fourth St., Petaluma
(707) 762–0111
1041 Fourth St., Santa Rosa
(707) 573–3399
413 North State St., Ukiah
(707) 573–3399 (ext. 215)
RSVP provides volunteer opportunities in more than 400 community agencies for people older than 60. This is an umbrella agency through which most volunteers work, whether they restock library shelves or send out mailing for Pets Lifeline.

Service Corps of Retired Executives
777 Sonoma Ave., Ste. 115-B, Santa Rosa
(707) 571–8342
www.score.org
Members of SCORE are retired business executives who volunteer their time and

expertise without charge to advise and help people who are running or starting a new business. Sponsored by the Small Business Administration, it's open to any retired executive in any field of business.

Foster Grandparent Program
15000 Arnold Dr., Eldridge
(707) 938–6201
413 N. State St., Ukiah
(707) 462–1954

The Foster Grandparent Program is a nationwide volunteer program for those 60 years or older who choose to make a lasting connection with children with special needs (whether mental or physical). Forty hours of orientation are required to acquaint the grandparent with the facility and the child, but the rewards go both ways. The child forms a permanent loving attachment, and the grandparent/senior learns to know the child as a person in a close-knit relationship. It's not an easy commitment. The pair spends four hours a day together, five days a week. There is a modest stipend that goes with the work, in addition to transportation and lunch.

Education and Child Care

The public school systems here are solid. The rates of high school seniors matriculating to universities, though they vary from district to district, are frequently higher than national and state averages. Post-secondary school students have a choice of at least two four-year universities: one state school and a small, private Adventist college on top of a mountain. We profile those universities later in this chapter, after we examine the public school systems, private schools of various philosophy and grade range, and two-year junior colleges. There's also a sampling of other institutions of higher learning. At the close we briefly cover child-care options—perhaps the most important section for those who are visiting the Wine Country for a short time.

Public Schools

Napa County

Anyone who questions Napa County's commitment to education would do well to look at the many charitable events devoted to private or public schools, some of them featuring ultrapremium wines generously donated by the biggest names in the valley for live and silent auctions. A recent fundraiser for Trinity Grammar and Prep School in Napa raised $60,000 in one afternoon. Among the big names donating items for auction were—in addition to scores of Napa Valley wineries—the Oakland Raiders, Sears Point Raceway, the Petrified Forest, and the Winchester Mystery House in San Jose. A baseball bat signed by Barry Bonds also went up for bid.

But Calistoga really goes all out. Every year, a special evening is set aside for an auction with generous donations from local vintners, restaurants, and dozens of sponsors. In 2000, about $180,000 was raised to benefit the Calistoga Joint Unified School District; in 2001, the tally dropped a bit, to $146,000, but was no less impressive. The money is used for field trips, art projects, and computer purchases, among other things.

In 2001, there were 19,100 pupils enrolled in Napa County public schools, dispersed among five districts: Calistoga Joint Union, Napa Valley Unified, St. Helena Unified, Howell Mountain, and Pope Valley.

Bilingual education is one of the many hot-button issues facing California schools. As with many areas of the state, a large immigrant population—in this case, almost wholly from Mexico—mingles with those of us who migrated earlier. Figures from a recent report about the Napa Valley Unified School District revealed that more than 24 percent of students are learning English as a second language and the percentage of Hispanic students has almost doubled in the past decade, to 32.6 percent. Muddying the issue in 1997 was Proposition 227 and its wake of legal challenges. Passed in 1998, Prop. 227 effectively prohibited bilingual instruction in California's public schools. One Napa County school with a highly regarded dual-immersion program—where all students spend periods of time learning in both English and Spanish—suddenly was faced with the prospect of English-only instruction. The former Westwood Elementary School beat the system by becoming a charter school, and the institution was renamed the Napa Valley Language Academy in 1999. Dual-immersion language instruction continues there, and most classes have two teachers. One speaks only English, and the other only Spanish. In 2000, the school received a $150,000 state grant to build a science and arts facility.

On the academic side, Napa County's chartered performance remains relatively strong. SAT I scores are always well above the state average, and participation is usually high. In other testing, Napa County's students traditionally rank high on their Academic Performance Index (API) scores, with pupils in all grades showing improvement on the Stanford 9 tests that surpassed goals set for them by the State of California. In addition, a recent report about the Napa Valley Unified School District showed that three out of four high school graduates went on to college in 2001.

Other success stories abound: Ten school campuses in Napa County have recently received California Distinguished School Awards after evaluation of their curricula, test scores, school environments, parental participation, and special programs.

Progress has also been achieved through the New Technology High School, a Napa facility where students spend most of their time on-line or in-lab, with minimal teacher supervision. New Tech (www.techhigh.napanet.net), named a U.S. Department of Education Demonstration School for its technological advances, graduated its first senior class of future Silicon Valley moguls in 1998. Meanwhile, the only Waldorf-method charter school in Napa Valley opened in 2000.

Sonoma County

Sonoma County's schools have consistently ranked in the top half of the state, although they're funded at less than the state average. Thirty-eight of the county's schools have been named California Distinguished Schools, and four have been recognized as National Blue Ribbon schools. Within Sonoma County's 40 school districts, 154 schools serve students from kindergarten through 12th grade. There are 91 elementary schools, 18 junior high schools, 15 high schools, 23 special alternative schools, and 11 charter schools. Enrollment in 2001 was nearly 72,600, which represents approximately 90 percent of the county's student population.

The growth in diversity among Sonoma County students is significant. Today, local schools are educating the most culturally, socially, academically, and linguistically diverse student population in the county's history. More than 7 percent of the county's students are limited in their ability to speak English, 8 percent are enrolled in programs for gifted students, and nearly 4 percent attend alternative programs such as independent study, home study, or continuation school.

Schools recognize an obligation to offer opportunities for success for all kids. Secondary school students receive the majority of efforts in this direction, because of larger student populations at the higher grade levels. For example, for those who can't keep up, schools allow a home study arrangement. This demands that at least one parent be a stay-at-home presence. Students meet with teachers at specified intervals to review their progress.

Teenage parents also are offered a safety net. In the Petaluma School District, for instance, teens can leave infants and toddlers in a district-operated child-

Insiders' Tip

In 1995 Santa Rosa-area schools began an "open enrollment" program, permitting students to transfer to any participating school that has the room to accommodate them. In 1999-2000, more than 900 Santa Rosa students participated in the program, as did students from Sebastopol, Forestville, and Sonoma.

care center for the morning while they pursue their academic studies. The public school system also is working to address the needs of teens who have problems with alcohol or other drugs. Through programs such as Clean and Sober, the dropout rate for Sonoma County, at 2.8 percent, is considerably lower than the state average of 4.4 percent, and it continues to go down.

While attending to the needs of students with special needs, Sonoma County schools also consistently score in the top third of the state for every grade level and subject tested through the California Assessment Program. Average SAT scores for the county are usually higher than state and national averages. In 2000 Sonoma County high schools graduated 3,430 students, and more than 1,500 of them completed the requirements for admission into California's university and state college systems.

And things just keep getting better. New magnet programs are under consideration. Local districts are consistently tracking forward with school improvements, made possible by the passage of several multimillion-dollar community bond issues. New schools are being built, and older schools are being modernized and retrofitted for earthquake security. New libraries are being installed, and a system amphitheater is being built so students can perform outdoor plays.

Mendocino County

The size of this county is so immense and the geography so diverse—with its various communities separated by forests, mountains, and winding roads—that schools within the system operate almost independently of each other, relying on guidelines from the central offices of the county superintendent of schools. There are 12 districts that include 27 elementary schools, 15 middle schools, and 21 high schools (including continuation high schools). There are also 6 charter schools in the county. Enrollment in 2001 was about 15,200.

Still, academic standards are high, with most schools posting average SAT scores at or slightly above national levels. About 35 percent of students go on to college, generally of the two-year community type. Special emphasis is put on vocational job training, with programs specifically aimed at jobs like firefighting (Mendocino County is heavily forested) and agriculture (since the area is mostly rural). This sort of training starts as early as grade nine for those who have no plans to go on to college and can benefit from learning a vocation.

There are other special programs. Preschool classes are offered, as well as classes for those for whom English is a second language. In addition, a staff member regularly makes the county circuit (racking up 100,000 miles a year) to assist with home-study programs and teach life skills to disadvantaged young people. The high school in Ukiah, the county seat, has classes at Juvenile Hall for young people who have run afoul of the law, as well as a Clean and Sober program for students with alcohol or drug problems.

Athletic programs are available, usually including basketball, baseball, softball, soccer, track, volleyball, and cheerleading and in some districts swimming, golf, and tennis. Fort Bragg High School is proud of its exemplary drama program that has given students an opportunity to work with acting and stage management. It has been extremely popular. Mendocino High School has an outstanding program called Windows to the Future, initiated in 1991, that links traditional studies in arts and sciences with computer technology. And here's a major advantage to having a widely scattered county population: Class sizes in Mendocino County schools are generally small, often having fewer than 20 students per teacher.

Lake County

In rural counties such as Lake, a school is more than a place to send your child for six hours a day. It's often the center of the community—a meeting hall and polling place and local playground, especially in unincorporated areas. (Lake County has only two incorporated cities.) The homecoming parade goes right down the center of town, and the big football game draws distant neighbors who don't get enough opportunities to bump into one another.

Lake County is divided into seven school districts: Kelseyville Unified, Konocti Unified, Lakeport Unified, Middletown Unified, Lucerne Elementary, Upper Lake Union Elementary, and Upper Lake Union High School. Among them, they served just over 10,000 students in 2000-2001. Transportation is a challenge in Lake, with some pupils riding buses for hours each day. The transportation must be subsidized, of course, and that cuts into teacher salaries. The county's wage schedule is below the state average; then again, low housing costs certainly offset the difference.

Five Lake County schools—Lucerne Elementary, Riviera Elementary, Middletown Middle (it only sounds redundant), Kelseyville High, and Middletown High—have been recognized in recent years as Distinguished Schools by the state of California. Middletown Middle School has a "Mac Lab" for its students' regular use and

has developed a Student Court program in collaboration with the California State Bar Association. Kelseyville High School is in the top 10 percent in the state in placing students in vocational education classes. And several of the districts employ the Success for All reading system. Devised at Johns Hopkins University, it's an intensive program that is particularly effective in teaching disadvantaged children.

Private Schools

A wide variety of private schooling options exists in Wine Country. Individual school listings follow the geographical order for each county explained in How to Use This Book.

Napa County

Justin-Siena High School
4026 Maher St., Napa
(707) 255-0950
www.justin-siena.napanet.net

Justin High School for boys was founded by the Christian Brothers of the San Francisco District in 1966, Siena High School for girls by the Dominican Sisters of San Rafael that same year. In 1972 the two schools merged to form Justin-Siena, a private, Catholic, coeducational high school that now serves about 615 students in grades 9 through 12. Justin-Siena is widely regarded as one of the finest secondary educational facilities in Northern California. Ninety-seven percent of graduates go on to college, two-thirds of those to four-year institutions. The average SAT score for graduates attending a four-year college is 1,140. The high school has a strong college preparatory curriculum and Honors programs in English, science, math, and foreign languages.

The student body tends to be active outside the classroom. The sports program has been quite successful; the school won 13 league championships in 1997–98, and the golf team won the Northern California championship. Justin-Siena also requires 100 hours of community service for graduation, including an annual Just-In Service day that involves all students and staff in a full day of activity. The school has two gymnasiums and more than 120 computers with Internet access. In addition to a classical liberal arts curriculum, the school offers courses in drama, photography, jazz band, dance, choral, history of film and literature, and environmental ecology.

Kolbe Academy
1600 F St., Napa
(707) 256-4306
www.kolbe.org

"Absurdly simple" is how Kolbe's administrators describe the school's philosophy. It's a small Ignatian school (a total of 20 to 30 students in grades 1 through 12) that, unlike most modern Jesuit institutions, returns to the methods and objectives of Ignatius of Loyola, who founded the order in the 1600s. Kolbe has three main goals: to help the student to speak, to write, and to act, and these are accomplished through a regimen of imitation and repetition. Oral presentations play a large role in the educational process here. Every Friday, for example, students deliver five-minute presentations; audience members, in turn, are graded on the questions they ask. There is a heavy emphasis on drama as well. Every pupil at the academy gets into character at some point.

The Oxbow School
530 Third St., Napa
(707) 255-6000
www.oxbowschool.org

Further evidence of Napa's quest for consideration as a world-class arts hub is the Oxbow School, founded by Ann Hatch (who previously founded the Capp Street Project artist-in-residence program in San Francisco) and wine luminary Robert Mondavi. Set on three acres within a looping bend of the Napa River, the school offers a one-semester fine arts program for high school juniors or second-semester seniors. Students live in dormitories and earn marks through the portfolios they assemble. The focus is on studio art in four domains: drawing and painting, printmaking, sculpture, and new media (which include photography, video, and digital art). The Oxbow School takes only 48 students per semester. Admission is competitive and expensive ($13,500 for the 2000–2001 school year), though a need-blind admissions policy welcomes students regardless of their ability to pay.

Napa Adventist Junior Academy
2201 Pine St., Napa
(707) 255-5233

Having celebrated its 50th anniversary recently, Napa Adventist Junior Academy (NAJA) has a lot to be proud of. Take the award-winning music program, for instance. Children learn the Kodaly Program in grades 1 through 4. Grades 4 through 6 have recorded a pair of compact discs—one Christian, the other Christmas songs—and grades 7 through 10 often perform at music festivals. The entire school is wired for the Web, and the older kids play a variety of after-school sports. (NAJA, which resides on a 10-acre campus, is kindergarten through 10th grade—the traditional Adventist structure.) The approximately 200 students come from as far away as Vacaville and Sonoma, eager to reap the Christian education that the school promises.

St. John's Lutheran School
3521 Linda Vista Ave., Napa
(707) 226-7970

This Christian-based school (in the Lutheran Church's Missouri Synod) was founded in 1937. It now sits in a pleasant grove of cedars north of Redwood Road. The approximately 275 students, ranging from preschoolers to eighth graders, are encouraged to develop beliefs and behavior consistent with Lutheran teachings, and to pass each grade with the requisite skills in communication, critical thinking, and analysis. St. John's offers some sports activities, a bit of arts and crafts, and after-school care.

Casa Montessori School
780 Lincoln Ave., Napa
(707) 224-1944

"Respect" is the buzzword at this small (approximately 60 pupils) Napa school.

Everyone must be treated with courtesy, and that goes for students as well as teachers. It is an ungraded elementary school, which means the kids progress at their own rate. The scope is preschool (age three) through sixth grade, but students can go far beyond that level if abilities dictate. In fact, administrators stress that most Casa students function about two years above the norm. How does the school do it? Part of the answer is self-correcting material—books, puzzles, and games that allow youngsters to work independently.

St. Apollinaris Elementary School
3700 Lassen St., Napa
(707) 224-6525

The largest Catholic elementary/middle school (kindergarten through eighth grade) in Napa Country is in north Napa, near Trower Avenue. The academic program is rigorous, and there is a lineup of after-school sports for the more than 300 students who attend. The school was founded in 1959.

Foothills Adventist Elementary School
711 Sunnyside Rd., St. Helena
(707) 963-3546
www.napanet.net/~foothilo

In 1902 the Elmshaven Seventh-day Adventist Church built a one-room schoolhouse for its pupils. That school, Foothills Elementary, now supports more than 175 students (grades K through eight) and is sponsored by four Adventist churches. Foothills balances religious training with lessons in reading, writing, math, social studies, science, technology, physical education, and music. Most noteworthy is the school's outdoor education programs. Describing the world of nature as "God's second book," Foothills offers memorable field trips. Primary kids might spend a day combing tide pools at Point Reyes or climbing Mount St. Helena. The middle school pupils, meanwhile, might go to Catalina Island Marine Institute for five days of oceanography and marine studies or to the Marin Headlands Institute for a week of ecological training.

St. Helena Montessori School
1328 Spring St., St. Helena
(707) 963-1527

This is Napa County's only Catholic Montessori facility, though it isn't affiliated with any one church. It's part of the Association Montessori Internationale, and its teachers must be accredited by that Amsterdam-based organization (founded by Dr. Maria Montessori in 1929). The school has about 75 pupils ranging from 2 1/2 to 12 years (sixth grade), and they are continually challenged to expand their abilities, though in a generally noncompetitive atmosphere. The youngest ones do tumbling and gymnastics, the elementary schoolers receive training in computers and foreign language, and all are exposed to the Orff-Schulwerk systematic music program.

St. Helena Catholic School
1255 Oak Ave., St. Helena
(707) 963-4677

This school has been providing a Catholic education to Napa Valley residents since 1963. The sisters still aim for a well-rounded education for their economically and ethnically diverse student body. With 130 to 135 kids spread between kindergarten and eighth grade, multi-age classrooms are the norm (except for the kindergartners). The Boys and Girls Club of St. Helena meets on campus in the afternoon, making it easy for Catholic School kids to take part.

Sonoma County

Old Adobe School
252 W. Spain St., Sonoma
(707) 938-4510
www.wco.com/~kenwood/oldadobe

As the name suggests, Old Adobe School got its start in a historic adobe building—one believed to have been built by Gen. Mariano Vallejo 200 years ago. It has since relocated to its present location on the grounds of the First Congregational Church. Founded by John Larson, a single parent who saw a need for a school that could offer children quality instruction, the school features an unpressured environment, and high regard for the individual child.

Old Adobe is private, nonprofit, and has no religious affiliations. It is managed by a board consisting of parents, teachers, the school director, and involved community members. It includes preschool as well as kindergarten (ages two through six), with extended day care available for both classes. While separate age levels are given different instruction, there is frequent opportunity for children to interact with older or younger students during outside time and music time. The teaching philosophy can be summed up by a conversation between Alice in Wonderland and the Cheshire Cat. "Could you please tell me which is the right way to go?" asked Alice. "That depends entirely on where you want to get to," replied the cat. Each child is encouraged to develop and express his total self, learning, discovering, and creating while growing. Cooperation rather than competition is stressed.

St. Francis Solano School
342 W. Napa St., Sonoma
(707) 996–4994
www.saintfrancissolano.org

The school's roots trace back to Presentation Academy, founded in 1882 as an adjunct of the Sisters of Presentation Convent in Sonoma. Many years after the convent school had closed for lack of financial support, wine patriarch Samuele Sebastiani funded a new school for the St. Francis parish. Today, St. Francis Solano School is housed in a building next to the church. In 1996–97 the school underwent a $1.2 million remodeling to meet city requirements for earthquake safety and to reshape and modernize classrooms and offices.

The school is currently a diocesan school, and enrollment is around 350 students in kindergarten through eighth grade. Uniforms are required. Significant parental commitment (of both the financial and the hands-on varieties) is required, and upper-grade students are required to perform service hours. The school's reputation for academic excellence is well established, with its middle school students consistently winning national and state honors in competitions. Other values emphasized at St. Francis Solano include community service, the gospel message, social justice, and moral values.

The Presentation School
276 E. Napa St., Sonoma
(707) 996–2496
www.presentationschool.com

Believing Sonoma Valley needed more educational opportunities, several local families—led by Nancy and Don Sebastiani of the well-known winery family—founded the Presentation School in 1997. The K-8 school opened in temporary quarters at the Sonoma Community Center with an enrollment of 150 students. Presentation School takes its name from Sonoma's original Presentation Academy, established in 1882 by the Sisters of Presentation from San Francisco. An independent Catholic school, Presentation's philosophy is, through education, "to build community, to proclaim the gospel message, and to reach out to the world in service." Its core curriculum, in addition to traditional subjects, includes religious studies, language arts, music, and physical education. With a limit of 20 students per grade, Presentation School offers "individualized instruction in a challenging, enriching, and nurturing environment." Students are required to wear uniforms.

St. Vincent de Paul High School
849 Keokuk St. (at Magnolia), Petaluma
(707) 763–1032
www.sonic.net/~svhs

This Catholic high school run by the St. Vincent de Paul parish takes pride in its prep school academic environment. It has won top national awards for physics and biology instruction, and 95 percent of the school's graduates go on to college. With an enrollment of slightly more than 400, the school places an emphasis on Christian values and academic excellence and attracts students, both Catholic and non-Catholic, from all over southern and central Sonoma County. St. Vincent's also has a full interscholastic athletic program for boys and girls and has won many league championships in the last decade in volleyball, football, and baseball. Students are not required to wear uniforms. The parish also runs a small K-8 grade school.

Adobe Christian Preschool/Daycare
2875 Adobe Rd., Petaluma
(707) 763-2012
Adobe school offers preschool and daycare for children from two to five years old, in a strong Christian environment. The curriculum stresses language development through the study of Bible literature and exploration of science and nature through gardening, animal care, and nature study. There is also music, gymnastics, and computer play. The school's philosophy emphasizes enabling each child to experience the joy of playing, working, and learning with others. Child care is available from 6:30 A.M. to 6:00 P.M.

Ursuline High School
90 Ursuline Rd., Santa Rosa
(707) 524-1130
www.ursulinehs.org
This Catholic school was started in 1880 in downtown Santa Rosa, but has been at its present location since 1957. The current population is more than 400 girls, who are required to wear uniforms. It's a college preparatory school—99 percent of the students go on to postsecondary school and 85 percent of those graduate from four-year colleges across the country. SAT scores average 590 in verbal and 570 in math—higher than both state and national averages.

Aside from strong academic requirements, students must also perform community service. Seniors must complete a special community research project focused on developing solutions to a local problem—performed with the help of a local mentor. Before graduation students must appear before a board to defend their project. The program has inspired many Ursuline students to become community leaders. The boys' school, Cardinal Newman High School, is just down the road, and although Ursuline freshmen and sophomores do not commingle, the girls in their junior and senior years share social activities with the boys of Cardinal Newman.

Cardinal Newman High School
50 Ursuline Rd., Santa Rosa
(707) 546-6470
www.cardinalnewman.org
Students here adhere to the principle of education for "mind, body, and spirit." Unlike Ursuline High School—its girls' school counterpart—Cardinal Newman does not require uniforms for its 450 male students, but it does promote the same ideal of service to the community. Cardinal Newman is well known for its emphasis on sports, and the Santa Rosa school has had great success in basketball and football. However, there are plenty of other sports to choose from—baseball, wrestling, swimming, water polo, tennis, soccer, cross-country skiing, and track, to name a few. The school has a tradition of academic excellence, with more than 95 percent of students enrolling in four-year universities or two-year community colleges upon graduation.

St. Luke Lutheran School
905 Mendocino Ave., Santa Rosa
(707) 545-0526
www.stluke-lcms.org
St. Luke serves the educational needs of Sonoma County children—from preschool through eighth grade—in a nurturing environment geared to touch and change young lives spiritually, academically, emotionally, socially, and intellectually. Faculty strive to provide a positive atmosphere in which students develop self-discipline, learn to understand what it means to be a child of God, and engage in healthy relationships with their teachers and peers. Any necessary discipline is approached in a dignified manner.

Stuart School
431 Humboldt St., Santa Rosa
(707) 528-0721
Believing that "success is the strongest foundation for academic growth," Stuart School works with children from prekindergarten through eighth grade and

has done so since 1977. The downtown location is convenient for working parents and gives students opportunities for library and museum visits and athletic activities in the nearby park. The faculty have extensive credentials, and they stress fundamental education built on phonics, vocabulary, reading, composition, science, math, and yes, recess! Believing that active kids are better students, every class has plenty of moving-around time.

Jacquelyn Giovanniello, who started the school in 1977 with her husband Ralph, holds a bachelor of music degree, two master's degrees, and a Ph.D. in Education. She was named Outstanding Educator for 1995–96 by the California League of Middle Schools. Ralph has served as superintendent in three school districts.

Merryhill Country School
4044 Mayette Ave. (Infants through junior kindergarten), Santa Rosa
(707) 575-7660
4580 Bennett View Dr. (K-6), Santa Rosa
(707) 575-0910
www.nobellearning.com

The preschool program at Merryhill provides youngsters with a stimulating and creative environment. Focus is on activity-based learning, which includes counting, sorting, graphing, and playtime learning with paints, puppets, and music. The program for kindergarten through sixth grade is a strong, skills-based curriculum in math, literature, science, the visual arts, computer skills, and Spanish. Parent involvement is considered one of the significant reasons that children succeed. The school is supervised from 6:30 A.M. to 6:00 P.M. daily.

The Bridge School
1625 Franklin Ave., Santa Rosa
(707) 575-7959

Offering a nurturing and educationally stimulating environment, this school's goal is to combine social development with academic growth. To that end, three programs are offered: Full Day Extended Care allows kids to experience this fun world from 7:30 A.M. to 5:30 P.M. Monday through Friday; Program Two offers either morning or afternoon half-day care; and Program Three is a flexible two- or three-day half-day program. Director Julie Day has a B.A. in child development, and her focus emphasizes the importance of allowing children room for individual creativity within a safe and nurturing environment. She has created parenting clubs and informative newsletters in an attempt to bridge the programs between school and family. Her combination of professional expertise and warm heart give The Bridge its unique difference.

Little Angels Children's Center
4305 Hoen Ave., Santa Rosa
(707) 579-4305

Offering both day care and preschool, Little Angels aims to help children acquire readiness skills, increase their ability to express themselves, learn to get along with others through work and play, and accept responsibilities within a group setting. Although the school is owned and operated without church support, there are Bible stories, songs, and prayers. Other than that, the philosophy is to encourage children's eagerness, curiosity, and motivation.

Mendocino County

Mariposa Institute
3800 Low Gap Rd., Ukiah
(707) 462-1016

With a successful record covering nearly 30 years of hands-on education for children from first through fifth grade, Mariposa School follows a tradition of social and academic learning in multiage classrooms. Youngsters pursue an academic program that integrates art, music, drama, Spanish, and social skills development. The country setting itself is beautiful—a place where children can play and learn amid oak woodlands.

Cozy Corner Children's Center
530 S. Main St., Ukiah
(707) 462-1251

Children in this school are mainly ages 2 through 5, though children up to age 12 are welcome. Half-day or full-day sessions are available, and drop-ins are accepted. The strong point here is the loving and nurturing environment, but teachers work with youngsters on academic readiness as well as learning to use the five senses. A dandy creative play area is augmented by a computer room to advance technological skills. The school usually has about 25 youngsters attending.

Melville Montessori School
4015 Second Gate Rd., Willits
(707) 459-3100

Although this is a Montessori school, it operates more on the American Montessori plan, according to Athena Melville, a founder of the school in 1980. Its program is more holistic, covering every aspect of the child, not just the intellect. Emphasis is on impressive and expressive areas. The philosophy mixes dance, singing, making music, and having fun with a concentration on history, English, science, the humanities, and mathematics. Melville likes the idea of children teaching younger children, saying both older and younger students learn from the practice. Each Monday is "suggestion pig" day, when they break out the pig and see what suggestions have been dropped in by students. (Rulings are on a majority basis.) With fewer than 24 students total in kindergarten through grade 12, the pupil-teacher ratio remains low at about 12 students per teacher. The school invites visitors on a drop-in basis, from 9:00 A.M. to 3:00 P.M. on school days.

Deep Valley Christian School
8555 Uva Dr., Redwood Valley
(707) 485-8778
www.jps.net/bburn/dvcs.htm

Not sponsored by any specific religious organization, Deep Valley Christian School is committed to developing the best in every child, utilizing a back-to-basics curriculum that emphasizes individual responsibility. The student population runs to about 350 (grades K–12), with average SAT scores well above state and national levels. Situated in beautiful Redwood Valley, a region of vineyards and oaks, the school is growing so rapidly that new buildings are being added to house a science lab, computer lab, and gym. The athletic program includes both junior varsity and varsity football teams, volleyball, basketball, and track. A great deal of pride is also taken in the music program at Deep Valley—especially the band. There are about 30 students to a class at the high-school level, and the school receives the strong support of parents, who are required to put 25 hours of volunteer time into school activities each year.

Lake County

Zemorah Christian Academy
16174 Main St., Lower Lake
(707) 994-4206

Zemorah is Christian, but nondenominational. If you agree with the mission statement, you're free to sign up your kids. The K-through-12 school seeks to build "godly Christian character traits" such as discipline, honesty, and kindness. It also has a strong phonics program—kindergartners are usually reading within nine weeks. Zemorah has music and drama programs and a full computer network. (The kids start learning the keyboard in first grade.)

Hilltop Christian Academy
40th St. and Snook Ave., Clearlake
(707) 994-3125

This accredited, 12-grade facility is part of the School of Tomorrow, a national aggregation of 7,000 institutions. In 1997 the School of Tomorrow recognized Hilltop as a Quality School, its second-highest commendation. Hilltop teaches all the basics—math, English, etc.—with Biblical concepts. The student body is between 65 and 70.

Westlake Seventh-day Adventist Christian School
6585 Westlake Rd., Lakeport
(707) 263-4607

This small Adventist school is in a perfectly peaceful setting, amidst oak trees at the Nice-Lucerne Cutoff. There are only two teachers and 20 to 40 students, but that doesn't negate extracurricular activities. The lower grades might make pizza or cookies one day, and the upper grades have been known to hold a three-day "outdoor school" in Southern California. Founded in 1942, Westlake serves school-age children, grades one through eight.

Two-Year Colleges

Napa County

Napa Valley College
2277 Napa-Vallejo Hwy.
(Hwy. 221), Napa
(707) 253–3000, (800) 826–1077
www.nvc.cc.ca.us

Napa Valley College dates back to 1942 and has occupied its current site—180 tree-lined acres near the Napa River—since 1965. It's a two-year community college with about 9,000 students and associate degree programs in a spectrum of fields, including business administration, healthcare, and, not surprisingly, viticulture and wine technology. On-campus facilities include a Child and Family Studies and Services complex and an Olympic-sized swimming pool. The school has an Upper Valley Campus on the outskirts of St. Helena and a Small Business Development Center in Napa. It also shares a guaranteed transfer agreement with the University of California at Davis, Sacramento State University, and Sonoma State University. And in case you were interested, it's the sister college of Launceston College in Tasmania.

Sonoma County

Santa Rosa Junior College
1501 Mendocino Ave., Santa Rosa
(707) 527–4011
www.santarosa.edu

The scholarship program at Santa Rosa Junior College is unique in all of America because of an association with the county-based Exchange Bank. In 1948 the bank's president, Frank P. Doyle, set up a trust that in the 1950–51 school year paid out $19,475 in scholarships to 95 students. In 2000–2001, dividends from the trust awarded more than $4.6 million in scholarships to approximately 4,000 students. Located on more than 100 acres, the college has a full-time enrollment of almost 7,000. Emphasis centers on general education, transfer education for students headed to four-year institutions, and occupational education in the fields of dental hygiene, radiologic technology, respiratory therapy, and many other areas.

The college's athletic teams (nicknamed the Bear Cubs) are part of the Bay Valley Conference, with the exception of the football team, which plays in the Nor-Cal Conference. Intercollegiate competition for men and women is offered in baseball, basketball, cross-country, football, golf, gymnastics, soccer, swimming, tennis, track and field, volleyball, water polo, and wrestling. A recent addition to Santa Rosa Junior College is an 87-seat planetarium. It has a dome 40 feet in diameter and 27 feet high. (See our Kid-stuff chapter; see our Arts and Culture chapter for information on theater troupes and events at the school.) An additional 40-acre campus in east Petaluma offers occupational training, national park ranger training, police and fire technology, and public safety.

> ### Insiders' Tip
> Napa Valley College and Santa Rosa Junior College both offer several courses— semester-long and shorter—in viticulture and winemaking. SRJC also offers classes such as Wine Industry Event Planning, Wine Marketing Fundamentals, and Media in the Wine and Vineyard Industry.

Empire College
3035 Cleveland Ave., Santa Rosa
(707) 546–4000
www.empcol.com

Empire College offers four specialized associate degrees—in accounting, office technology, legal office administration, and medical assistance. It also offers certificates to those studying to become legal secretaries, medical administrative/clinical assistants, medical transcriptionists, bookkeepers, and travel and tourism agents. A state-accredited college, Empire has operated since 1961 and now has some 500 students.

Mendocino County

Mendocino College
1000 Hensley Creek Rd., Ukiah
(707) 463–3073
www.mendocino.cc.ca.us

The campus of Mendocino College occupies 126 acres and serves a rural area that encompasses 3,200 square miles. The school has additional educational centers at Willits and at Lakeport in Lake County. Founded in 1972 as a junior college, Mendocino provides the first two years of study for a four-year degree or confers an associate degree with vocational training in a wide variety of fields. There are programs in horticulture, agriculture, administration of justice, business administration, computer and information sciences, and premed and prenursing, to name a few.

Construction projects have been ongoing since 1985, when the Lowery Library building was completed and the college moved into its permanent facility. Other campus buildings include the classroom/office building, horticulture center, and a child-care center. One of the most stunning buildings is the Center for Performing Arts, with its 400-seat theater and recording studio that houses programs in theater arts, music, arts, and textiles. The physical education program and the college's sports activities take place in an $8.2-million complex.

Both the Willits and Lake County centers provide administrative services and classrooms, plus counseling and financial aid assistance. Mendocino College has an additional facility at Point Arena, 50 miles southwest of Ukiah, which serves as a field laboratory for science classes in marine biology, geology and meteorology.

College of the Redwoods
1211 Del Mar Dr., Fort Bragg
(707) 962–2600
www.redwoods.cc.ca.us

The main campus of College of the Redwoods is at Eureka in Humboldt County. This is a two-year community college offering associate degrees, career training, and enrichment classes to residents of the north coast. Students receive top academic instruction in science, mathematics, and humanities courses, which transfer to Humboldt State University and other four-year colleges and universities across the nation.

The Fort Bragg site is beautiful, with low-lying buildings of natural-finish wood, an unobstructed view of the ocean, and a student population of 1,200. This campus is well known for courses in fine woodworking. It has a one-year program (though many sign up for a second year); its fame is such that students come to Fort Bragg from all over the world to study cabinetry and furniture-making. The college also offers a program that links art with computer technology to provide for study in photo transfer work and graphics communication. College of the Redwoods has no athletic program.

Lake County

Yuba Community College
15880 Dam Rd., Clearlake
(707) 995–7900
www.yuba.cc.ca.us

Since 1972 Lake County has been home to the secondary campus of Yuba College, a community college based in Marysville (to the east in Yuba County). The Clearlake campus offers a dozen different degree certificates, specializing in business and vocational fields such as welding, food services, computers, and income tax preparation. It also has the only program in Northern California to study water and wastewater treatment. Yuba College has between 1,200 and 1,500 students in Lake County, some 300 of whom attend full-time during the day. The faculty is composed of six full-time and numerous part-time teachers drawn from the business community. The school is currently trying to raise funds for a Performing Arts Center to enhance the 11-acre campus.

Mendocino College (Lake Center)
1005 Parallel Dr., Lakeport
(707) 263–4944
www.mendocino.cc.ca.us

Mendocino College, centered in Ukiah, also has a satellite at a leased facility in downtown Lakeport (see previous listing for Mendocino College in this chapter). It used to be that you couldn't get your two-year degree without attending at least some classes at the main campus, but that is no more. The Lake Center now offers most, but not all, of the certificate programs found in Ukiah, including business office technology (with subcategories in legal assistance and medical assistance), small business management, child development, and psychology. Students get library services through an arrangement with the Lake County Library, and would-be astronomers make use of the Lake County Observatory/Planetarium on Mount Konocti. The college has about 1,000 students in Lakeport, counting both full- and part-time attendees.

Four-Year Colleges and Universities

Napa County

Pacific Union College
100 Howell Mountain Rd. North, Angwin
(707) 965–6311, (800) 862–7080
www.puc.edu

PUC is a small (just more than 1,600 students), private, Seventh-day Adventist college surrounded by 1,800 acres of crops and forest on top of Howell Mountain, where it has been since 1906. The views are fabulous, and the education is highly regarded. *U.S. News & World Report* ranked the school the top liberal arts college in California in 1998, and *The Right College* places it in the top 10 in the nation for the percentage of male graduates who enter medical school. The student-faculty ratio is an appealing 12-to-1.

Pacific Union is most definitely a unique experience. The student body is ethnically diverse, the cafeteria is vegetarian (in line with Seventh-day Adventist practice), and the Abroad Program offers overseas study, including full-year programs in Argentina, Austria, France, Kenya, and Spain. Service is a big part of a PUC student's commitment. Many strike out on yearlong missions, and even more are actively involved with local homeless shelters, prison ministries, and the like. The college offers associate, bachelor's, and master's degrees in 19 academic

Insiders' Tip

Isn't it time you thought about enrolling your 10-year-old in college? Sonoma State University's EXCEL program offers a variety of interesting, one-day Saturday classes for kids of various age groups (typically, grades 4-6 or 6-10). A recent example: Junior prosecutors and defenders develop their cases and present evidence at A Day in Court. EXCEL programs run in spring and summer only. For more information, call Sonoma State's Extended Education office at (707) 664-2394.

departments. The 50-plus areas of study include all the usual subjects, plus such extras as digital media technology, fashion merchandising, and medical technology. Pacific Union is on the quarter system.

Sonoma County

University of Northern California
1304 Southpoint Blvd., Ste. 220, Petaluma
(707) 765–6400
www.uncm.edu

This new university, established in 1993, welcomes students from around the world. It aspires to become a premier engineering and scientific university with substantial programs in the liberal arts. Students enjoy small classes with ample individual attention from professors dedicated to quality teaching. About 50 full-time equivalent students attend the university, more than half of which are in graduate studies. Interdisciplinary studies are encouraged, and all academic programs emphasize the importance of effective communication for success in the modern world. The university focuses on programs in biological technology,

and its early degree programs include the B.E., M.S., and Ph.D. in Biomedical Engineering and the B.A. in Engineering and in Languages and Linguistics.

Sonoma State University
1801 E. Cotati Ave., Rohnert Park
(707) 664–2880
www.sonoma.edu

This university was established on 270 acres of farmland in 1960. Today it offers undergraduate liberal arts and science curricula and 13 master's degree programs to a student population of about 7,000. Its computer engineering graduates walk directly into high-paying jobs, and similar results are expected for those completing the new wine business program. The school's Sonoma Plan is considered a model nursing program throughout America. In the fall of 2000, the university unveiled a new three-story, 215,000 square foot Jean and Charles Schulz Information Center. This elegant structure—named in honor of the renowned Peanuts cartoonist and his wife—is home to both the university library and the campus information technology department.

The Everett B. Person Theatre is a popular arts venue on the Sonoma State University campus in Rohnert Park. PHOTO: TINA LUSTER-HOBAN

Performing arts get top billing at the campus, with plays from the pens of local writers and international favorites performed year-round, along with dance recitals and musical concerts (see our Arts and Culture chapter). Sonoma State ranks high in sports among the 23 campuses of the state system, particularly in men's and women's soccer, volleyball, women's basketball, and baseball. In all, the university has 16 intercollegiate teams. Its outdoor swimming pool is open to faculty, staff, and students and has access for the disabled.

Other Institutes of Higher Learning

Napa County

The Culinary Institute of America at Greystone
2555 Main St., St. Helena
(707) 967–1100
www.ciachef.edu

This learning institution devoted to the gustatory arts is one of the perks of living in Wine Country.

It is the only center in the world dedicated exclusively to continuing education for professionals in the food, wine, health, and hospitality fields—and it's a beauty.

It all began some years ago, when executives of the Culinary Institute of America, that factory of chefs in Hyde Park, New York, looked at some 50 potential sites to establish a West Coast center for continuing education. Their logical choice was Greystone, the majestic winery built in 1888 and used by the Christian Brothers to make sparkling wine from 1950 to 1989. After a massive gift from the Heublein Corporation (then owners of the property) and a $14 million renovation, the CIA opened for business in Napa Valley in 1995.

Inside, the facilities are almost as impressive as the 22-inch-thick tufa stone walls that frame Greystone's exterior. The third story is an immense teaching kitchen with 15,000 square feet of undivided floor space, 35-foot ceilings, and

> **Insiders' Tip**
> Even lifelong cooks who know their way around a good meatloaf and a hundred uses for cream of mushroom soup will enjoy a short course presented by Gourmet Retreats at Casa Lana, a Calistoga company that offers cooking classes in a professionally equipped kitchen. A variety of options are available, including a three-hour mid-week session limited to 8 to 12 students that runs about $65. All materials are provided, and graduates of the class get printed recipes and the leftovers. Call (707) 942-0615 or (877) YOU COOK to inquire about the details.

clusters of exquisite Bonnet stoves. In the middle of the space is a dining area where students sample the various assignments they and their cohorts have handed in.

The building also houses the EcoLab Theater, a 125-seat amphitheater used for cooking demonstrations and lectures; the Wine Spectator Greystone Restaurant (see our Restaurants chapter for more on that); The Campus Store with its preponderance of cooking equipment, books, and uniforms; and the DeBaun Food and Wine Museum, which displays a changing collection of wine-related artifacts. Outside the old winery are garlic and onion beds, seven terraces of herbs, an edible flower and herbal tea garden, and, off-site, 15 acres of Merlot grapes and an organic fruit and vegetable garden.

Courses vary in length from three days to the 30-week, two-semester Baking and Pastry Arts Certification Program. (The average class duration is one week.) The faculty is drawn from three sources: the small but talented core of resident instructors, visiting teachers from Hyde Park, and guest instructors.

Sonoma County

Western Institute of Science and Health
130 Avram Ave., Rohnert Park
(707) 664–9267, (800) 437–9474
www.westerni.org
The Western Institute of Science and Health offers an Associate of Science program for physical therapist assistants and helps its students find employment in hospitals, outpatient clinics, public schools, and home-health agencies. The institute teaches students, through academic courses and clinical internship experiences, how to effectively treat patients who suffer from physical impairment. Graduates must pass a state examination given by the Physical Therapy Examination Committee before they may practice in California.

New College of California
99 Sixth St., Santa Rosa
(707) 568–0122, (888) 437–3460
www.newcollege.edu/northbay/campus.htm
This alternative college's main campus is in San Francisco, where students can earn undergraduate and graduate degrees in subjects that range from women's spirituality to poetics. The north bay campus—located in a quaint brick building off Railroad Square—offers both BA and MA degrees in the subjects of culture, ecology, and sustainable community. The BA degree is a one-year weekend "completion" program designed for students who are working and unable to attend traditionally scheduled classes. Applicants must have already acquired at least 45 units from another institution to enter the program. Along with core seminars and an academic journal, students complete a senior thesis and independent study or internship. The college states

that its program focuses on "the capacity to think globally and systematically, the capacity to clarify value conflicts as well as one's own motivations and learning styles, and the ability to plan and carry out a creative project which has been perceived in terms of its impact on the social ecology."

Mendocino County

Dharma Realm Buddhist University
City of Ten Thousand Buddhas,
5251 Kindness Ave., Ukiah
(707) 468–9112
www.drba.org
State-approved Dharma Realm University offers year-round education to qualified students, with programs leading to bachelor's, master's, and doctoral certificates. The emphasis is on Buddhist study and practice, including loyalty, felicity, humanness, and righteousness. Students are given the opportunity to develop their innate wholesome wisdom. At the same time, high standards of academic excellence are maintained. Degrees are currently offered in Buddhist studies and practice, translation, and Buddhist education. Full scholarships are available to qualified students.

Child Care

Whether you're visiting for a few days or putting down roots for a several years, finding qualified child care can be a daunting task. There are scores from which to choose, no matter where you're located in Wine Country, and each differs from the next in small ways. Some centers are church-affiliated, others purely secular; some are in charming, turn-of-the-century Victorians, others in office complexes; some provide transportation, others leave that to you; some accept infants, others don't; some are low-tech, others have computers; some aren't really "centers" at all, but licensed homes.

Each county has at least one organization that will help you sort out all the factors, free of charge. They are able to quote prices, describe individual providers, and refer you to ones in which you might be interested. Here they are, by county.

Napa County

Community Resources for Children
5 Financial Plaza, Ste. 224, Napa
(707) 253–0376 (general information),
(707) 253–0366 (referrals),
(800) 696–4CRC
www.crcnapa.org

This nonprofit agency, funded primarily by the California Department of Education but supplemented by federal and private contributions, is an important friend to Napa County families. Community Resources for Children (CRC) is contacted most often for its free referrals to child-care centers and in-home providers. It does a lot more than that, though. It gives financial assistance to qualifying families, trains prospective child-care providers, advocates for children and families in the community, provides low-cost car seats to eligible families, and maintains a lending library of toys, videos, books, and educational resources. CRC can help you find a continuing day-care center or a one-day baby-sitter. Se habla español.

Sonoma County

Community Child Care Council
396 Tesconi Ct., Santa Rosa
(707) 544–3077
www.sonoma4cs.org

This service (known as 4Cs) helps parents find a suitable system of child care by providing names of licensed centers or homes near the parents' home or workplace. To assure that parents get the best from their search, the council provides a list of questions parents should ask when they call—such as what educational training is offered, whether the staff has CPR training, and any special programs offered. Another list indicates things parents should look for when they visit the facility. No recommendations are offered, but lists of licensed care centers and homes are extensive.

If parents prefer someone unlicensed to come into their home, such as a nanny or au pair, the council will give advice on that as well. It also can help with co-op parent participation, preschool planning, and organizing play groups, in which parents and children meet in one another's homes on a rotating basis.

River Child Care Services
16315 First St., Guerneville
(707) 869–3613
www.sonic.net/~rccs

This service covers the area along the Russian River and West County as far as the coast, providing information on

Insiders' Tip

TrustLine is a powerful resource for those wanting to hire a nanny or license-exempt child-care provider. All child-care providers listed with TrustLine have submitted their fingerprints to the California Department of Justice and have no disqualifying child-abuse reports or criminal convictions, and they are all in good standing with the Immigration and Naturalization Service. It costs the provider $90 to be registered. Nannies and baby-sitters placed through an employment agency must be listed on the TrustLine registry. For more information, call (415) 882-0234 or the TrustLine provider check at (800) 822-8490. For further details, visit www.trustline.org.

choosing child care and offering lists of licensed providers and home-based care. In addition to long-term regular care, they also can advise on baby-sitting services. The organization can provide parents with important information about prospective providers, such as methods of discipline used (spanking is not allowed), what happens if the provider is ill or the child is ill, and where meals are eaten.

River Child Care Services offers a list of workers interested in caring for children on a family-by-family basis. However, a referral does not imply a recommendation or a guarantee of quality. A brochure they publish gives some good hints on interviewing candidates by phone.

Mendocino and Lake Counties

North Coast Opportunities, Inc.
413 N. State St., Ukiah
(707) 462–1954

156 Humboldt St. South, Willits
(707) 459–2019
155 Cypress St., Ft. Bragg
(707) 964–3080
14130 Lakeshore Dr., Clearlake
(707) 994–4647
850 Lakeport Blvd., Lakeport
(707) 263–4688

This valuable, not-for-profit organization is dedicated to offering referrals and resources to families in the largely rural and dispersed counties of Mendocino and Lake. Anyone who calls is given a free referral to one or more state-licensed child-care facilities. North Coast Opportunities also offers child-care subsidies, support services for both parents and providers, and a helpful food and nutrition program. If you have a general question about the service, call the Parent-Child Information Center at (707) 467–3211.

Healthcare

Walk-In Prompt-Care Centers

Hospitals

Hospice Care

Alternative Healthcare

The last thing you want to worry about while visiting Wine Country is a health crisis of some sort, but rest assured you'll be treated well by experts if it becomes necessary. No matter where you roam in this region, you're never too far from a clinic or hospital that can patch you up and have you back sipping Sauvignon Blanc in no time flat.

Considering that most of our region is rural, the population relatively sparse, and the towns small to midsize, healthcare is amazingly accessible and the quality is excellent. Hospital staffs (from the doctors on down to the volunteer helpers) are "small-town friendly" and more easy-going than their big-city counterparts. But their dedication to medicine is just as serious.

On the local level, zealous hospital benefactors have pitched in to provide state-of-the-art equipment and medical instruments. Several hospitals in the area have been competing keenly with one another for many years to acquire the best equipment, services, and physicians—leading to improved healthcare for all. Some of Northern California's finest doctors have traditionally gravitated by choice to this less stressful environment, while still providing the kind of technically current surgical and medical expertise that normally exists only in larger metropolitan areas.

However, the nationwide nursing shortage and other healthcare industry crises have also impacted our medical facilities locally, with scaled-back services and shorter hours of operation at many places. The smaller community hospitals in particular have been hard hit by financial constraints and in response have reduced their services and trimmed staffs. Yet the larger facilities are expanding services, building new wings, and acquiring new and better equipment. Along the way, they are receiving accolades for their skills and expertise.

Twenty-four-hour emergency service is available throughout much of the area, so when you gash your finger while trying to master that new corkscrew from Dean & DeLuca, help is close at hand.

Walk-In/Prompt-Care Centers

Napa County

ExpressCare
Queen of the Valley Hospital
1000 Trancas St., Napa
(707) 257-4008

This walk-in center, an adjunct of Queen of the Valley's emergency room, is open from 9:00 A.M. to 9:00 P.M. daily and can address a variety of non-lethal illnesses, allergies, and injuries. (As the ExpressCare brochure says, "There is no such thing as a little emergency.") Board-certified physicians are on hand to treat you, and they will make referrals or deliver follow-up care if needed.

Upper Napa Valley Urgent Care
1370 Railroad Ave., St. Helena
(707) 963-4399

Upvalley residents gained a little peace of mind when this clinic opened in St. Helena in 1999. Urgent Care treats all nonlife-threatening ailments, including pain, migraine headaches, asthma, rashes, infections, allergies, and Homer Simpson-style, self-inflicted boo-boos. Appointments are preferred, but walk-ins are accepted too. The clinic is open Monday through Friday from 9:00 A.M. to 5:00 P.M., and on Saturday from 10:00 A.M. to 2:00 P.M.

Queen of the Valley Hospital provides quality medical and emergency care for visitors and residents of Napa. PHOTO: TINA LUSTER-HOBAN

Sonoma County

Rohnert Park Healthcare Center
1450 Medical Center Dr., Rohnert Park
(707) 584–0674

Operated by the St. Joseph Health System—Sonoma County, this handy walk-in clinic is open 8:00 A.M. to 9:00 P.M. daily for treating minor injuries and illnesses. Health education, infusion services, and related services are also available.

Lake County

Sutter Lakeside Hospital
Urgent Care Center
5176 Hill Rd. East, Lakeport
(707) 262–5008

Sutter Lakeside has an urgent care center available for those who need nonemergency treatment, but have no primary care physician. There are two ways to end up here: Make an appointment, or go to the emergency room and get screened by a trained nurse who refers you here. The urgent care center is open 9:00 A.M. to 9:00 P.M. daily.

Hospitals

Napa County

Queen of the Valley Hospital
1000 Trancas St., Napa
(707) 252–4411
www.thequeen.org

Queen of the Valley might be best known as the hospital that posts a hotel-trained concierge in the front lobby. It's a well-respected facility with 162 beds. QVH has a community cancer center, a high-end imaging department, home-care services, maternity services (including an intensive-care nursery), occupational health services, a regional heart center where open-heart surgeries are performed, and a respiratory-care department. It also features an upgraded Vascular and Interventional Radiology Lab, an expanded maternity unit, and improved MRI technology.

Queen of the Valley is the designated trauma center for Napa County, with a 24-hour emergency room. It also offers the Queen's Carriage, a van that serves outpatients from Yountville to American Canyon.

A couple of QVH services stand out. The Acute Rehabilitation Center offers comprehensive physical, occupational, and speech therapies for people who have experienced trauma (such as a stroke or spinal cord injury). And the hospital's community pharmaceutical services provide infusion capability, clinical monitoring, and computerized pumps for patients at home. Queen of the Valley is part of the St. Joseph Health System, which emphasizes dignity, service, justice, and excellence.

St. Helena Hospital
650 Sanitarium Rd., Deer Park
(707) 963–3611,
TTY/TDD: (707) 963-6527
www.sthelenahospital.org

The address may conjure up lightning storms and strange goings-on in the basement, but don't be alarmed. This full-service community hospital, off the Silverado Trail about 3 miles northeast of St. Helena, dates back to the 1800s, when a sanitarium was a health resort.

St. Helena Hospital has 192 licensed beds and 36 beds for residential health-enhancement programs. It also has a wide range of specialties, including cardiac surgery, cardiovascular rehabilitation, pulmonary rehabilitation, mental health services, oncology, obstetrics, pain rehabilitation, and preventive medicine. And it not only offers many services but also performs them well.

A member of the Adventist Health network of facilities, St. Helena is known for its sleep disorders clinic and, especially, its cardiovascular lab—a major heart center for Northern California. If you want a state-of-the-art, peephole view of someone's arteries, this lab is the place to go. In fact, in 2001 the hospital received a five-star rating for excellence for its coronary bypass surgery program and treatment of heart attacks. Add to the mix hospice services (through a joint venture with

Queen of the Valley Hospital) and extensive adult mental health services, both inpatient and day treatment. The hospital's Health Center offers community classes on relevant fitness topics such as smoking cessation and weight loss.

Finally, St. Helena has a Women's Center in downtown St. Helena, providing mammography, bone density testing, a health resource library, and a wide range of health education classes and support groups. The Women's Center is at 1299 Pine Street; call (707) 963-1912.

Sonoma County

Sonoma Valley Hospital
347 Andrieux St., Sonoma
(707) 935-5000
www.svh.com

When Sonoma Valley Hospital was created in 1944, the vision was to combine the best of medicine with a warm and caring staff. Since that date, tremendous advances in research and diagnosis have changed the face of medicine. But Sonoma Valley Hospital remains a warm, caring, family-oriented hospital with the same small-town spirit that permeates the community

from which it draws its patients.

Today's 83-bed facility serves 40,000 people in Sonoma Valley. The credentialed medical staff totals 136 active, consulting, and courtesy physicians involved in 25 different disciplines. The intensive-care unit has six private rooms staffed by experienced critical-care nurses. A full range of cardiopulmonary testing equipment is available, along with cardiac rehab programs. A Birth Center provides a comfortable, homey place where labor, delivery, recovery, and postpartum phases all take place in one room with the family at hand. Recently a state-of-the-art system was installed linking doctors instantly to patient information and test results.

Petaluma Valley Hospital
400 N. McDowell Blvd., Petaluma
(707) 778-1111
www.stjosephhealth.org

With 82 beds and 30 medical specialties from cardiology to urology, this facility, operated by the St. Joseph Health System—Sonoma County, is a busy place. The attractive two-story, 20-year-old hospital is also a genuine community resource. There's a full-service emergency department with a physician on duty 24 hours a day and a helipad for emergency helicopter air transport. The pharmacy is open and staffed seven days a week, 24 hours a day. Other features available to the community include home healthcare, a hospice, and an electronic telecommunications system called Lifeline that provides 24-hour emergency access to anyone who might need quick response at home.

Petaluma Valley has a number of educational programs that offer assistance in quitting smoking and living with cancer. The hospital also offers consultation for diabetics. Other services include counseling on nutrition, food allergies, dialysis, and pregnancy. Visitors are always welcome to tour Petaluma Valley Hospital.

Santa Rosa Memorial Hospital
1165 Montgomery Dr., Santa Rosa
(707) 546-3210
www.stjosephhealth.org

Memorial Hospital opened its doors in 1950 under the guidance of the Sisters of

St. Joseph, founders of eight other hospitals on the West Coast since 1920. All services and programs are guided by the healing mission of the Sisters—service, excellence, justice, and dignity for all members of the community. The hospital is the "flagship" facility for the St. Joseph Health System–Sonoma County, which operates several clinics and acute-care facilities throughout the region.

In 2000, Memorial Hospital was named the designated trauma center for Sonoma, Lake, and Mendocino Counties, making it the busiest and best-equipped hospital of its kind north of the Golden Gate. Rescue helicopters bring the most severely injured right to the facility's rooftop.

In addition to cutting-edge surgical facilities and medical equipment, 192-bed Memorial Hospital has some unique services including the Mobile Health Clinic, which serves children 16 and younger from low-income families that have difficulty locating affordable healthcare. Care is provided by medical professionals who speak English and Spanish. The hospital also established a clinic for students at Elsie Allen High School—one of only 50 such school-based clinics in California—to treat minor illnesses or injuries, administer immunizations, and provide counseling for emotional problems.

The Family Birthing Center offers a soothing decor of pastel colors and wall-coverings inspired by Impressionist painters. Windows open onto a garden patio where new mothers and the family can stroll. Top-notch medical equipment helps ensure safe delivery, with operating rooms available should Caesarian delivery be necessary. To give new parents extra peace of mind, the hospital now partners with University of California–San Francisco Medical Center to operate an intensive-care nursery for ill newborns on-site.

In 2000, the St. Joseph Health System added another dimension to its services: A Palliative Care unit, across the street from Santa Rosa Memorial Hospital. One of only two units of its kind in California, this acute-care service focuses on end-of-life pain management and improving the quality of life for those with life-threatening illness.

A lifesaving helicopter arrives at the helipad at Santa Rosa Memorial Hospital, the designated regional trauma center for Sonoma, Lake, and Mendocino Counties. PHOTO: JEAN SAYLOR DOPPENBERG

Sutter Warrack Hospital
2449 Summerfield Rd., Santa Rosa
(707) 542–9030

Built in 1960, Warrack is a 69-bed hospital with four operating rooms. Its primary services cover intensive and coronary care, pediatric surgery, and diagnostic imaging. Emergency care is available 24 hours a day, with a physician always on duty.

Sutter Medical Center of Santa Rosa
3325 Chanate Rd., Santa Rosa
(707) 576–4000

This hospital was established in 1866 and has provided advanced healthcare services for Sonoma County and the adjoining communities for 132 years.

As a teaching institution affiliated with the University of California at San

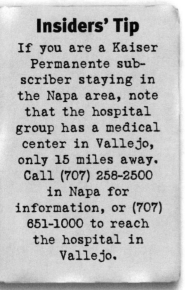

Insiders' Tip

If you are a Kaiser Permanente subscriber staying in the Napa area, note that the hospital group has a medical center in Vallejo, only 15 miles away. Call (707) 258-2500 in Napa for information, or (707) 651-1000 to reach the hospital in Vallejo.

Francisco School of Medicine, Sutter is regionally recognized for its wide range of specialty services, including a high-risk maternity department, newborn intensive-care unit, and an emergency trauma care program. It offers other special services too. The facility's major expansion in 2001 was to its cardiovascular services. The newly constructed Heart Center provides a complete range of cardiac services, from open-heart surgery to cardiac rehabilitation.

The Emergency department provides specialized care 24 hours a day.

North Coast Health Care Center
1287 Fulton Rd., Santa Rosa
(707) 543-2400
www.stjosephhealth.org

Operating in five locations (four in Santa Rosa and one in Petaluma), the North Coast clinics offer a wide range of services, both inpatient and outpatient.

Two locations have hospital facilities for medical and surgical patients, with a specialty of orthopedic surgery. Some of the other services in its facilities include physical and speech therapy and rehabilitation from brain injuries, strokes, spinal cord injuries, and comas. Home healthcare and preemployment physicals are also offered.

Healdsburg General Hospital
1375 University Ave., Healdsburg
(707) 431-6500

Today's Healdsburg General is a far cry from the World War I-era, wood-frame building that burned to the ground in the 1930s. Amazingly, there was no loss of life, although patients had to be carried one-by-one down flights of stairs from surgery. Rebuilt during World War II when medical staff was virtually unavailable, the hospital was mainly operated by the director of nursing, who coped with staff shortages by hiring schoolgirls to do nursing chores while she slept on a gurney (on call) at night.

Today's hospital is a beautiful modern facility with 15 beds. Services include 24-hour emergency care, physical therapy and occupational medicine services, same-day surgery center, and a new respite care service.

Palm Drive Hospital
501 Petaluma Ave., Sebastopol
(707) 823-8511
www.palmdrivehospital.com

Palm Drive's future as a small community hospital has been tested during the past few years. Currently it has 55 beds and one operating room, and its emergency room is staffed 24 hours a day.

Mendocino County

Ukiah Valley Medical Center
275 Hospital Dr., Ukiah
(707) 462-3111
www.uvmc.org

A member of the Adventist Health Corporation, this 116-bed hospital has offered a full spectrum of outpatient treatment and surgery since its inception in 1956, when it was known as Hillside Hospital. In 1979 it joined the 18-hospital Adventist Health group. This affiliation provides the advantage of being connected to a network of locations so that patients can be transferred quickly, by helicopter if necessary, to whichever Adventist Health hospital specializes in treating the particular problem.

The Adventist's university at Loma

Linda is famed for being on the cutting edge of cardiac expertise, knowledge, and treatment. Hence, Ukiah Valley offers a high-quality cardiac specialty department.

Frank R. Howard Memorial Hospital
Madrone and Manzanita Sts., Willits
(707) 459-6801
www.howardhospital.com

Affiliated with the Adventist Health group since 1986, Frank R. Howard Memorial Hospital has been a part of the Willits community for 74 years. Willits is a small community (population 5,000) and also serves as a gateway to wide-open spaces to the north. That means the hospital serves a population in a wide area of wilderness and ranch and forest land as far north as the Oregon border. There is 24-hour emergency service. While the hospital is small (just 28 beds), its connection with the Adventist group gives it wide latitude in serving patients through larger hospitals in the group.

Redwood Coast Medical Services
46900 Ocean Dr., Gualala
(707) 884-4005

In a town too small to accommodate a hospital, this federally qualified medical-service facility fills a gap with medical specialists that include an ophthalmologist, cardiologist, oncologist, and orthopedist. The office is open from 8:00 A.M. to 6:00 P.M. Monday through Friday and from 9:00 A.M. to 1:00 P.M. on Saturday. However, doctors are on duty 24 hours a day to treat injuries and medical emergencies for visitors and residents alike and can be reached for services after Redwood Coast closes.

Mendocino Coast District Hospital
700 River Dr., Fort Bragg
(707) 961-1234

Its garden setting makes this lone hospital on the Mendocino coast very attractive. Created by the cities of the coastal community in 1971, it still maintains an attitude that locals call "neighbors taking care of neighbors." Patients from large cities often remark on this small-town support and warmth and on how amazingly caring the hospital personnel can be. With 54 beds, two operating rooms, and an outpatient surgery area, services offered include critical-care facilities, 24-hour emergency service, laboratory services, radiology, and cardiopulmonary care.

A very active ambulance service travels to coastal areas as far away as Westport, 16 miles north.

Lake County

Redbud Community Hospital
18th Ave. and Hwy. 53, Clearlake
(707) 994-6486
www.adventisthealth.org

Squeezed, as many smaller hospitals are these days, by spiraling insurance and equipment costs, Redbud Community (established 1968) became part of the large Adventist Health network (see the previous listings for St. Helena Hospital, Ukiah Valley Medical Center, and Frank R. Howard Memorial Hospital). Anything but a hostile takeover, the deal was approved by 89 percent of Clearlake voters in 1996.

Insiders' Tip

Need some information on a medical condition affecting you or a family member? The Redwood Health Library, a community service of the Petaluma Healthcare District, is a consumer health library—a medical library designed for public use. It is located at 314 Western Avenue in Petaluma; call (707) 778-9114 for more information.

Redbud is a 40-bed facility with 24-hour emergency care. It also offers nuclear medicine, mammography, cardiopulmonary care, CAT and MRI imaging techniques, obstetrics and gynecology, an intensive care unit, and extensive outpatient services.

Sutter Lakeside Hospital
5176 Hill Rd. East, Lakeport
(707) 262–5000
www.lakeside.sutterhealth.org

Lakeside Community Hospital was Lake County's first major infirmary, established as a 30-bed unit in 1945. The private facility was donated to the community by the family of Dr. Neal Woods in 1966, when it was deeded to the nonprofit Lakeside Community Hospital corporation. In 1978 the hospital moved from its original structure to a 32,000-square-foot facility on adjoining property, toting all its supplies and equipment—not to mention 14 patients—up the hill. Lakeside added a new wing in 1986, and in 1992 it joined Sutter Health, a nonprofit organization operating across Northern California.

Today the hospital provides a broad range of services, including a 24-hour emergency department that, combined with the urgent-care center, treats 25,000 patients a year; an intensive-care unit; a full array of medical imaging diagnostics, including CAT scans, MRIs, and mammography; a cardiac rehabilitation center; home medical services; and an obstetrics wing. Sutter Lakeside also has added four outpatient centers offering obstetric and gynecological, internal medicine, pediatric, and family-care services. Despite the arrangement with Sutter Health, a local board of directors plots the hospital's course.

Hospice Care

Napa County

Hospice of Napa Valley
3299 Claremont Way, Napa
(707) 258–9080, (800) 451–4664

If the time comes to end the aggressive search for a cure and to focus instead on comfort and symptom alleviation as death approaches, hospice care is the appropriate choice. Hospice of Napa Valley, a nonprofit organization and a joint community service of St. Helena Hospital and Queen of the Valley Hospital, has been serving the county since 1979.

The hospice's provisions include round-the-clock, on-call nursing; short-term respite to reduce caregiver stress; medical equipment; oxygen; and intermittent visits from team members. That team includes a medical director, the patient's physician, registered nurses, medical social workers, home-health aides, chaplains, bereavement counselors, and volunteers. Hospice of Napa Valley accepts patients regardless of ability to pay. Grief education and counseling services are also available to community members.

Sonoma County

Hospice of Petaluma
416 Payran St., Petaluma
(707) 778–6242

Memorial Hospice
821 Mendocino Ave., Santa Rosa
(707) 568–1094
www.stjosephhealth.org

Working in tandem as part of the St. Joseph Health System—Sonoma County, these agencies provide support and care for persons facing life-threatening illnesses so that they may live as fully and comfortably as possible. Hospice of Petaluma (working with Memorial Hospice of Santa Rosa) benefits the community served by Petaluma Valley and Santa Rosa Memorial hospitals. A counseling and social work staff offer emotional support, counseling, and information about community resources. A hospice chaplain provides spiritual support. Nursing services include expert pain and symptom management, home visits, and 24-hour on-call family assistance. Trained volunteers provide companionship for family members. After the fact, there also is grief counseling, support, and education.

Safety in Numbers

Call 911 during any medical emergency. If an ambulance is not what you need, consider one of the following numbers. In the first group are lines that apply throughout the Wine Country. They are followed by county-specific numbers.

Throughout Wine Country
Poison Control Center
(800) 876–4766

National HIV and AIDS Information Service
English: (800) 342–2437;
Spanish: (800) 344–7432;

California HIV/AIDS Hotline
(800) 367–2437

Crisis Line for the Handicapped
(800) 426–4263

California Smokers Helpline
(800) 662–8887

Centers for Disease Control and Prevention (Sexually Transmitted Disease Hotline)
(800) 227–8922

Medical Board of California (Central Complaint Unit)
(800) 633–2322

Mental Health Referral Service
(800) 843–7274 or (800) 448–3000

Dental Referral
(800) DENTIST

Napa County
Suicide Prevention
(707) 963–2555, (866) 289–8888

Napa County Health and Human Services Department
(707) 253–6052

Napa Valley AIDS Project
(707) 258–2437

Napa County Alcohol and Drug Services
(707) 253–4412

Napa Emergency Women's Services
(707) 255–6397

Napa Walk-In Center
(short-term crisis counseling)
(707) 224–4309

Sonoma County
Sonoma County Department of Health Services and Center for HIV Prevention and Care
(707) 565–7373

Suicide Prevention
(707) 576–8181

Crisis Line for the Handicapped
(800) 426–4263

Department of Alcohol and Drug Programs
(800) 879–2772

Mendocino County
Mendocino County Health Department
(800) 734–7793, (707) 463–4461

Mendocino County Suicide Prevention
(800) 575–4357

Community Care AIDS Project of Mendocino and Lake Counties
(707) 462–3041

Lake County
Lake County Health Department
Clearlake: (707) 994–9433
Lakeport: (800) 794–9291

Lake County Mental Health Department (Suicide Prevention)
(800) 900–2075
Clearlake: (707) 994–9437
Lakeport: (707) 263–1170

Lake County

Hospice Services of Lake County
1717 S. Main St., Lakeport
(707) 263–6222, (800) 900–8820

Lake County citizens suffering from heart disease, cancer, AIDS, and end-stage Alzheimer's have been turning to this state-licensed hospice since 1979. It's a nonprofit organization committed to the medical, nursing, psychological, emotional, and spiritual needs of the terminally ill and their families. The goal is to keep subjects at home and to provide comfort care rather than a curative treatment approach to the disease, when that is what the patient wishes.

The patient's personal physician must authorize hospice care. Bereavement counselors offer grief support before the death and for up to one year afterward at no charge. The organization denies care to no one, regardless of a patient's ability to pay.

Alternative Healthcare

Alternative forms of treatment and prevention proliferate and thrive in this region. Why? First of all, this is the Wine Country, where health and quality of life are paramount. And second, this is California, where people tend to be open-minded in their decision making.

So if you're in search of a less traditional cure for what ails you, you're in luck. Within a short drive you can find homeopaths and naturopaths, Ayurvedics and herbalists, acupuncturists and acupressurists, chiropractors and yoga gurus, reflexologists and hypnotists—and practitioners of Reiki, rolfing, and biofeedback. You can even find a few shaman healers if you try hard enough. The Sonoma County phone book alone lists 65 acupuncturists, 46 hypnotists, 12 homeopaths, and a couple hundred chiropractors. If you want to verify a license, call the Medical Board of California at (916) 263-2635.

Now get out there and heal thyself.

Media

If you want to forget about the world while you're visiting the Wine Country, go right ahead. But if after a few days you sense that your news gland is beginning to atrophy and needs feeding, just look around you. Wine Country has access to most major print and broadcast information sources. You can pick up the San Francisco *Chronicle*—the nation's 10th-largest newspaper—practically anywhere in the four-county region. You'll also find the *New York Times* and *Wall Street Journal* in many tourist-oriented towns. And some hotels and cafes and all libraries have computers on hand for you to access the Internet, in case you happened to lose your laptop.

Along with these big city dailies are a host of small-town papers. The people who read the *Cloverdale Reveille, Middletown Times Star,* or the *Sonoma Index-Tribune* are interested in reading about the latest local initiatives or who won this year's pie-baking contest at the Gravenstein Apple Fair rather than the scoop on Washington's scandal du jour. Along with the local papers are regional TV and radio stations, and other specialized publications covering niche markets.

Daily Newspapers

Napa County

The Napa Valley Register
1615 Second St., Napa
(707) 226–3711
www.napanews.com
Napa County's only daily dates back to 1863, though it has gone through a few changes of ownership since Abe Lincoln's administration. The paper is now a member of the Pulitzer Community of Newspapers. It had been the second-largest community paper in the Scripps chain (after Tucson's *Arizona Daily Star*) before Pulitzer gobbled up that group. Current paid circulation is about 20,500.

The *Register* ably handles the entire county, nodding to St. Helena and Calistoga in its "Upvalley" section. The paper uses wire-service reports but does a lot of local reporting, such as a multifaceted 1997 series about the valley's farmworkers that garnered much acclaim.

The *Register* is an afternoon paper during the week, switching to morning delivery on Saturday and Sunday. Also worth noting here is its monthly news-rack supplement: *Inside Napa Valley,* a tourist-aimed tabloid with better-than-expected features on art, food, wine, and coming events. The supplement is free.

Sonoma County

The Press Democrat
427 Mendocino Ave., Santa Rosa
(707) 546–2020
www.pressdemocrat.com
For many Sonoma County residents, as well as readers in adjoining counties, the morning *Press Democrat* is the paper for local, national, and international daily news, with a circulation of about 93,000 (104,000 on Sundays).

The *P.D.,* as locals call it, is owned by the *New York Times* now but has been serving the Sonoma County area since 1857. Although the paper's name includes the word Democrat, the editorial stance is more middle-of-the-road.

A strong sports section features popular columnists such as Bob Padecky and Lowell Cohn. On the entertainment scene, local residents keep abreast of what's going on about town through a lively entertainment section called "Q."

Columns by Chris Coursey and Gaye LeBaron also offer colorful, behind-the-scenes coverage of Santa Rosa people, places, and happenings.

Mendocino County

Ukiah Daily Journal
590 S. School St., Ukiah
(707) 468–0123
www.ukiahdailyjournal.com

This newspaper's roots go back to 1860, when it was called the *Redwood Journal.* Former editor Robb Hicken plowed his way through 137 years of back issues to come up with a complete history of the paper, and in mid-1997 he published a three-page supplement to the *Daily Journal* to give readers a look at what was important news for Ukiah in other times. (A few copies are still available.) With a circulation of 8,500, the *Daily Journal,* now edited by K.C. Meadows, covers local and county news that the metropolitan dailies don't. Coverage includes sports, society news, club activities, high school events, and news from Mendocino College, located in the Ukiah foothills.

Other Newspapers

Napa County

Napa County Record/Positive Living
1320 Second St., Napa
(707) 252–8877

The *Record* started as a monthly paper in 1946, went weekly, and in 1996 switched back to monthly, where it now comfortably abides. Distributed free on the last Friday of every month, it's a family-oriented community paper that covers topics such as business, automobiles, and hunting and fishing. *Positive Living* has two special editions: a program-style section dedicated to Symphony on the River (see our Festivals and Events chapter) and a seniors section that prints in February, July, and October (the last one focusing on the local Senior Games). *Positive Living* sponsors an internship at New Technology High School, allowing students to design a page in the paper each month during the school year.

St. Helena Star
1328 Main St., St. Helena
(707) 963–2731
www.sthelenastar.com

St. Helena's well-preserved Victorian charm even extends to its newspaper, the *Star,* which has been a family-owned broadsheet weekly since it was founded in 1874. The paper attempts to stay within the city limits, plus Angwin and its Howell Mountain environs.

The paper astutely covers the important local issues—growth, tourism, elections—and its wine coverage is getting more comprehensive. (There is a special wine edition every October.) George Starke, whose column concentrates on the human side of the wine industry, has ruffled a few feathers by breaking news on the buying and selling of vineyards. But even the editors will admit that the feature best known for reeling in readers is the precious Police Log. You don't really know St. Helena until you have studied this compendium of barking dogs, double-parked cars, and nosy neighbors.

The Weekly Calistogan
1328 Main St., St. Helena
(707) 942–6242

This might be the only newspaper in the nation whose motto is longer than some of its features. And we quote: "Published at the Head of the Napa Valley, a Beautiful and Fertile Section of Country, Possessing a Climate that for Health and Comfort is Not Surpassed on Earth." Amen.

The *Calistogan* is co-owned with the *St. Helena Star* and, like that paper, comes out each Thursday. When publisher Paul Krsek shut down the *Weekly Calistogan* office and moved the staff to St. Helena (to share space with the *St. Helena Star*) in 1999, locals worried they were about to lose an institution founded in 1877. But the paper is still afloat, and Randy Johnson's coverage of the local sports scene is about as thorough as you'll find in a small-town paper.

Sonoma County

The Sonoma Index-Tribune
117 W. Napa St., Sonoma
(707) 938–2111
www.sonomanews.com

Established in 1879, the twice-weekly *Sonoma Index-Tribune* has been in the same family since 1884. Current publisher Robert Lynch leads the family's third generation to own and operate the paper. His son, Bill, is editor and CEO. Bill's brother, Jim, is the chief financial officer.

Serving the Sonoma Valley—a region approximately 18 miles long that extends from San Pablo Bay north to Kenwood—the paper publishes every Tuesday and Friday, with a paid circulation of 12,500. The *Index-Tribune* is an award-winning community newspaper, covering all aspects of local news—schools, city government, the fire and water boards, the wine business, prep and youth sports, adult recreational sports leagues, even bake sales and spaghetti dinners. If something is happening in Sonoma Valley, you'll find it in the *Index-Tribune*. The Friday issue also includes the latest in local entertainment and covers the local theater scene.

In May 1997, the *Index-Tribune* received five awards for excellence in the annual California Newspaper Publishers Association Better Newspapers Contest, including a coveted honor in the general excellence category.

Four times a year, the newspaper publishes *Sonoma Valley Magazine* as a supple-

The Sonoma Index-Tribune *has been owned by the same family since 1884.* PHOTO: SONOMA INDEX-TRIBUNE

ment to the newspaper. It includes a variety of features and special stories on local people and institutions. The newspaper also publishes a number of supplemental journals, including the annual *Sonoma Valley Almanac* and the *Sonoma Valley Guide,* distributed each month to dozens of local hotels, motels, restaurants, and wineries.

The newspaper's editorial policy leans toward community "boosterism," and the paper often leads the charge in support of local school bond elections and fund-raising for local service projects. In mid-1997 the *Index-Tribune* published an illustrated, hardcover history of the community called the *Sonoma Valley Story.* It covers the history of the community from before the Spanish missionaries arrived up to the present day.

Argus Courier
830 Petaluma Blvd. North, Petaluma
(707) 762–4541
www.arguscourier.com

Published each Wednesday, this publication (recently purchased by the *New York Times*) has been in business since 1855, making it the oldest paper in Sonoma County. Publisher John Burns and managing editor Chris Samson focus on Petaluma community news and information on arts and entertainment. Circulation is 8,500. About 12,000 nonsubscribing Petalumans receive a free weekly shopper each Wednesday.

The Community Voice
5625 State Farm Dr., Rohnert Park
(707) 584-2222

The *Community Voice,* published every Wednesday, is the local newspaper for residents of Rohnert Park and Cotati. It tells them what is going on in their schools and neighborhoods. Columnists write up the news about anniversaries, birthdays, and other small-town happenings. The paper's well-designed sports section covers local recreational activities—especially youth sports—with the intensity that city papers use to cover the major leagues.

The newspaper works closely with the Rohnert Park and Cotati chambers of commerce, is involved in promoting local business, and beats the drum for many local events and institutions, including the local professional baseball team, the Crushers (see our Spectator Sports chapter). There is also a reporter covering Sonoma State University.

North Bay Bohemian
50 Mark West Springs Road., Santa Rosa
(707) 527-1200
www.metroactive.com/sonoma

Before becoming the *Bohemian* in 2000, this free weekly tabloid was known as the *Sonoma County Independent*—and before that it was the *West Sonoma County Paper.* In 1994 the paper joined a Bay Area group of alternative weeklies, Metro Newspapers. Formerly serving only Sonoma County, the *Bohemian* now covers Marin and Napa Counties, featuring news stories relating to civic issues—from an indy perspective—as well as a reliable culture and entertainment department. This weekly comes out each Thursday, with numerous distribution points in the three counties. On top of all this, there's great photography.

Sonoma County Herald-Recorder
1818 Fourth St., Santa Rosa
(707) 545-1166
www.dailyjournal.com/public/home/home_pub.cfm

Published twice a week with a readership of 5,000, the *Herald-Recorder* covers real estate, business, and legal news, with statistical information from the *Recorder's* Office and County Clerk plus news affecting local attorneys and real estate interests. The publisher is Christine Griego. The paper has been published since 1899.

Sonoma-Marin Farm News
870 Piner Rd., Santa Rosa
(707) 544-5575
www.sonomacountyfarmbureau.com

The Farm Bureau has been distributing its monthly agricultural newspaper to the ranchers of Sonoma County and adjoining Marin County for 22 years. Editor Laurie Ferguson focuses on different laws and regulations that affect farm lands and disseminates information on wetlands and tree ordinances that apply to vineyards and dairy and cattle ranches. There is also general farming and viticulture news. Circulation is 3,200.

North Bay Business Journal
5464 Skylane Blvd., Ste. B, Santa Rosa
(707) 579–2900
www.NorthBayBusinessJournal.com

The *Business Journal* publishes strictly business news, focusing on new startups, expansions of existing firms, and information on relocations. Circulation is more than 10,000. Usually the 40-page-plus journal will include a profile of a top-level executive, describing his company, its history, and anticipation of future progress. Published weekly, it covers Sonoma, Marin, and Napa Counties. They also print a monthly wine industry *Business Journal.*

Healdsburg Tribune and Windsor Times
5 Mitchell Ln., Healdsburg
(707) 433–4451

The *Tribune* has had different owners since its inception more than 130 years ago—it recently became a part of the Sonoma West Publishers newspaper group, which also publishes the *Sonoma West Times & News* (see below). The present editor, Ray Holley, puts out a well-rounded weekly, covering all the news of Healdsburg and Geyersville: community affairs and events, legal matters, and local personalities.

The paper also prints occasional special sections. Holley also edits the *Windsor Times.* This, too, is strictly locally oriented—and owned by the Sonoma West Publishers. Both the *Healdsburg Tribune* and *Windsor Times* print on Wednesdays. Together, the newspapers' circulation is approximately 9,000.

Cloverdale Reveille
207 N. Cloverdale Blvd., Cloverdale
(707) 894–3339
www.thegrid.net/reveille

This community newspaper is published on Wednesdays and covers community and school news. Records stacked away in old files indicate the *Reveille* was first published in 1879. Present circulation of the *Cloverdale Reveille* is 2,400. Editor Bonny Hanchette is proud of the role of small newspapers in relaying local news to readers. "It's a special field that fills a niche that the larger mediums don't," she says.

Bodega Bay Navigator
1580 Eastshore Rd., Bodega Bay
(707) 875–3574

A weekly newspaper established in 1986, with a circulation of 1,400, the *Bodega Bay Navigator* comes out on Thursdays and is distributed through most of West County. Publisher and editor Joel Hack focuses on both community news and global issues and has printed some controversial or unusual stories that other small papers often shy away from. For example, the *Navigator* has published stories on teen pregnancy services, violence, and the plight of the Navajo nation.

Sonoma West Times & News
130 S. Main St., Suite 114, Sebastopol
(707) 823–7845
www.sonomawest.com

Locally owned and intimately focused, this paper covers Sebastopol and the Russian River area. Publisher Rollie Atkinson says the *Times & News* is "about our families, our towns, about the guy next door." Those towns are primarily Sebastopol, Bodega Bay, and Guerneville. Look for the paper each Wednesday.

Mendocino County

Fort Bragg Advocate-News
450 N. Franklin St., Fort Bragg
(707) 964–5642
www.advocate-news.com
Mendocino Beacon
(707) 937–5874
www.mendocinobeacon.com

Publisher Sharon Brewer and managing editor Katherine Lee handle both of these weeklies. Both papers trace their roots to the heydays of the lumbering industry that gave birth to the towns. The *Mendocino Beacon-News* came first in 1877, followed by the *Advocate News* in 1889—both are now owned by the Donrey Media Group. Early news coverage focused on forests and shipping and sawmills. Today the slant is local with a strong appeal to tourists. The *Advocate* and *Beacon* are based in Fort Bragg, which has a population of 7,000; the *Beacon* serves the village of Mendocino, with its population of

1,000. Each covers news of the community, the arts, school affairs, and local personalities. One of the most popular features in both papers is the calendar of events.

Independent Coast Observer
38500 Hwy. 1, South, Gualala
(707) 884–3501
www.mendonoma.com

Stephen McLaughlin has been publishing and editing this weekly paper for nearly 30 years. It covers the coastal area from Jenner to Elk. This is strictly a visitors' publication, offering news of upcoming events, art exhibits (with a rundown on some of the artists), and reviews of musical groups performing in Mendocino and elsewhere in the area. There are 3,000 copies printed each week and distributed to restaurants along the coast. A free supplement, *Destination Mendonoma,* is published once a year, in May.

Anderson Valley Advertiser
12451 Anderson Valley Rd., Boonville
(707) 895–3016
www.pacificsites.com/~ava

The *AVA*'s banner displays three quotes. "Peace to the cottages! War on the palaces," from the French Revolution. "Be as radical as reality," from Lenin. And Pulitzer's: "Newspapers should have no friends." Published weekly by Bruce Anderson, a "socialist unabashed," the *AVA* comes out on Wednesdays and covers news of Anderson Valley, an area largely devoted to farming and vineyards. But Anderson also gives in-depth coverage to political matters in the valley, particularly to the activities of the board of supervisors, and often challenges political policies. Because some of his views incite strong reactions, he claims to get more mail than the big daily newspapers in the area. Circulation of this paper is 3,000.

Lake County

Middletown Times Star
21159 Calistoga St., Middletown
(707) 987–3602

This weekly paper ignores those faraway urban metropolises—and by that we mean Santa Rosa and Napa. The *Times Star* has no Associated Press wire and no grand yearnings. The 128-year-old publication covers the issues important to Middletown and southern Lake County—things like tourism, logging, agriculture, and the Geysers. It publishes every Thursday, and many of the locals turn immediately to Sharon Dawson's humor column. Also popular: the event listings and the wide variety of opinions on the editorial page.

Clear Lake Observer-American
14913-B Lakeshore Dr., Clearlake
(707) 994–6444

This is a paper that gets high marks for its strictly local news. In fact, the California Newspaper Publishers Association gave it a general excellence award in 1996, calling it the best biweekly paper in the state.

The *Observer-American,* published Wednesday and Saturday, covers Clearlake, Clearlake Oaks, Lower Lake, and Middletown, paying practically no attention to the "civilized" world. It has been providing solid, balanced reporting for 60 years, going after nuts-and-bolts issues such as Lake County's water and sewer systems. Case in point: A few years ago, rumors circulated that raw sewage was being dumped into Clear Lake. The paper investigated and found that the runoff in question was actually percolating from local ponds. It was, they discovered, cleaner than the lake water.

Lake County Record-Bee
2150 S. Main St., Lakeport
(707) 263–5636
www.record-bee.com

The *Lake County Bee* was founded in 1873, the *Lakeport Press and Record* in 1925. Those two oldtimers have since been merged into the *Record-Bee,* which publishes five times a week (Tuesday through Saturday). Though traditionally devoted to the immediate community, the paper recently changed its focus to place a greater emphasis on state and national news. The *Record-Bee* is owned by Media Newsgroup Inc., which also owns the *Clear Lake Observer-American.*

Magazines

Wine Country Living
489 First St., Sonoma
(707) 935–0111
www.winecountryliving.net

This magazine underwent a name change from its former moniker, *Appellation,* but it's still a four-color publication that publishes every two months and has a circulation of about 100,000. Its primary function is to document what most of what one would probably call The Good Life as it is lived up and down the wine regions of the western United States. What it does best is show people having a swell time with a bottle of wine, with the pages filled with food (including recipes and restaurant reviews), wine, travel destinations, personality profiles, and general finery. There's also a terrific Wine Country map.

Sonoma Business
3565 Airway Dr., Santa Rosa
(707) 575–8282
www.sonomabusiness.com

Norman Rosinski publishes and edits this glossy monthly magazine, impressive with its well-designed cover and artistic inside pages. It has provided 25 years of business intelligence in Sonoma County. It covers technology, real estate, and wine and other industries. An annual issue identifies the top 500 industries in the county, ranked by gross revenues. The magazine's annual wine issue also doubles as the official program of the Sonoma County Harvest Fair. Circulation is more than 7,000.

Other Publications

Lake County Visitor
P.O. Box 2692, Clearlake
(707) 995–1725

This tabloid-sized publication comes out once a year, right around New Year's Day. Published by Shelley Graphics, it's basically a countywide tourist guide that includes a calendar of events and suggestions for things to do and see. You can find it at the Lake County Visitor Center and the various chambers of commerce.

Insiders' Tip

A discount of $50 on a hot-air balloon ride! Don't underestimate the savings of coupons. Pick up copies of the many complimentary advertising handouts that proliferate in Wine Country and check out the deals. Hey, $50 is 50 bucks.

Radio Stations

KVON-1440 AM

Between bouts of revelry, even Napa Valley tourists sometimes crave a direct line to the outside world. They often turn to Napa's KVON for news, opinion, and information. This has been a full-time news and talk station since the early 1980s, making it one of the most established info stations in Northern California. KVON is a past recipient of the National Association of Broadcasters' "Crystal Award."

KVYN-99.3 FM

This Napa station is self-described as Hot Adult Contemporary. It's an upbeat mix of pop, rock, dance, alternative, and ballads, mostly from the '80s and '90s. KVYN is music-intensive but, as an affiliate of ABC News, it has its talkative side too.

The station offers local news, sports, and weather to residents and tourists.

KXBX-1270 AM

This is a mature station, both in terms of its own age (it has been around since the 1940s) and the lifestyle of its listeners. KXBX plays adult standards and offers plenty of talk programming, including a call-in health show with a local pharmacist and a Saturday-morning food-and-travel show. The station's main morning guy, Bill Moen, was a San Francisco institution for 32 years.

KXBX-98.3 FM

An adult contemporary station out of Lakeport, KXBX is the most listened to frequency in Lake County. It has been broadcasting since the early 1980s. The station is heavily into promotion and giveaways, and it sponsors a 10-week summer concert series in Lakeport. It's the sister station of KXBX-AM.

Station List

Adult Contemporary

KSAY-98.5 FM
KTDE-100.5 FM
KUIC-10.5 FM
KVYN-99.3 FM
KWNE-94.5 FM
KXBX-98.3 FM
KZST-100.1 FM

Christian

KLVR-91.9 FM
KNDL-89.9 FM
KPRA-89.5 FM

Country

KFGY-92.9 FM
KRPQ-104.9 FM
KUKI-103.3 FM

Jazz

KJZY-93.7 FM

News, Talk, Sports

KDAC-1230 AM
KPMO-1300 AM
KSRO-1350 AM
KVON-1440 AM
KZYZ-91.5 FM

Oldies, Standards

KMFB-92.7 FM
KXBX-1270 AM

Public Radio

KRCB-90.9 and 91.1 FM
KZYX-90.7 FM

Rock

KGRP-100.9 FM (Classic rock)
KLLK-96.7 FM (Alternative)
KMGG-97.7 FM (Rock oldies)
KMHX-104.1 FM (Alternative)
KNTI-99.5 FM (Light rock)
KRSH-98.7 FM (Classic rock and blues)
KSXY-95.9 FM
KXFX-101.7 FM, 1250 AM

Spanish

KBBF-89.1 FM
KRRS-1460 AM
KTOB-1490 AM

Television

Station List

ABC: KGO Channel 7 (Napa, Sonoma, Mendocino, Lake)
CBS: KPIX Channel 5 (Napa, Sonoma, Mendocino, Lake); KOVR Channel 14 (Lake)
NBC: KNTV Channel 3 (Napa, Sonoma, Mendocino, Lake)
FOX: KTVU Channel 2 (Napa, Sonoma, Mendocino, Lake); KTXL Channel 12 (Lake)
PBS: KQED Channel 9 (Napa, Sonoma, Mendocino, Lake); KRCB Channel 22 (Sonoma)
UPN: KBHK Channel 44 (Napa, Sonoma, Mendocino) and Channel 11 (Lake)
Independents: KFTY Channel 50 (Sonoma, Mendocino)

Local Broadcast Channels

KFTY Channel 50 (Independent)
533 Mendocino Ave., Santa Rosa
(707) 526–5050
www.newschannel50.com

Started in 1981 by Wichard Brown, then owner of the *Marin Independent Journal*, this station is now owned by Ackerley Broadcast Group, a Seattle-based advertising, sports, and entertainment conglomerate. KFTY serves the six counties just north of San Francisco (or, as they term it, "north of the Gate"). General programming includes news, movies, sitcoms, and public interest programs, with a special 30-minute North

Bay news program Monday through Friday at 7:00 P.M. and a one-hour news program at 10:00 P.M.

This station is intensely community-oriented and sponsors the Luther Burbank Rose Parade (see our Festivals and Annual Events chapter) each spring, along with a health, fitness, and safety series at the end of June.

KRCB Channel 22 (Public TV)
5850 Labath Ave., Rohnert Park
(707) 585-8522

This public television station was started in December 1984 and now reaches the counties of Sonoma, Napa, Mendocino, and Lake, plus portions of Alameda, Marin, Solano, and Contra Costa Counties. It even broadcasts to San Francisco.

Programming is typical public television fare: *Sesame Street, Nova, This Old House,* news programs, a North Bay Journal featuring regional business news, and *Expressions,* which features local artists. It has pledge drives and an auction in November (its affiliate, KRCB-91.1 FM, is also listener-supported).

Cable TV

Napa County
Sonoma County

AT&T Broadband
(800) 945-2288, (888) 824-8047
www.broadband.att.com, www.home.att.com

If you live in one of these two counties, this is your cable TV provider. AT&T has the monopoly in a huge chunk of Wine Country, and reviews of its service are mixed. But there's no sign it will change anytime soon. AT&T offers standard cable and digital services in several packages. Digital packages begin at about $45 and go up to $75. Basic cable begins at about $37; add an "All-Star" package of several premium movie channels and the monthly bill jumps to around $67.

Mendocino County

Adelphia Communications
1060 N. State St., Ukiah
(707) 462-8737
1260 N. Main St., Fort Bragg
(800) 626-6299

Adelphia provides two different levels of basic cable TV service with slightly varied channel lineups to customers in Ukiah, Willits, and Fort Bragg. Basic service runs about $28 per month; their digital service adds about 19 more channels to the basic lineup.

Central Valley Cable
38951 S. Hwy. 1, Gualala
(707) 884-4111

This cable TV provider services the coastal region of Mendocino County, including Gualala, Point Arena, and Manchester, with some service to Sea Ranch residents in northern Sonoma County. Their basic cable service offers about 51 channels to subscribers; digital service is not an option at this time.

Lake County

Mediacom
13221 E. Hwy. 20, Clearlake Oaks
(707) 998-1516, (800) 832-4440
www.mediacomcc.com

Mediacom is the name in cable for almost all of Lake County. The company offers 21 channels for $17.89 a month in its Limited Basic package—primarily local network and independent stations, plus C-SPAN and The Weather Channel. For $35.16 per month you can upgrade to the Basic Plus package, a 51-channel stable that adds standbys such as the Discovery Channel, Arts & Entertainment, ESPN, Cable News Network, Nickelodeon, and the Nashville Network. Four premium channels also are available. Mediacom offers several FM radio stations free to its cable customers.

Worship

Napa County
Sonoma County
Mendocino County
Lake County

Every now and again some wise guy offers a variation on a witticism we've heard too many times before: "Give the United States a good shake-up, and everything loose will land in California."

We might not like the word "loose," but we are proud of the open-minded climate that has brought a wonderful diversity to California. It manifests itself in many ways—including the way we worship. Here in Wine Country, where a certain sense of spontaneity dominates the culture, an amazingly eclectic assortment of houses of worship has taken root and prospered. In Sonoma County alone, with a thinly spread population of about 458,600 (no larger than a good-sized American city), the Yellow Pages list nearly 80 different faiths.

That would be in line with figures gathered at the turn of the century, when it was revealed that Sonoma County had more churches than any other county in the state except San Francisco. The zeal of the early religious organizers and preachers sustained the pioneers and laid a firm foundation for the church-building of the future. Although the earliest religious activity had been the domain of the Spanish missionaries—particularly under the direction of Fr. Jose Altimira, who established the mission in Sonoma—that system broke down when the young republic of Mexico secularized the missions in the 1830s, leaving a religious vacuum (see our History chapter). But when the first American families started to move into the Sonoma and Napa valleys early in the 1860s to establish farms and businesses, organized religion moved apace. Some of the churches built in those times remain. Many have been designated historic landmarks, their congregations dedicated to keeping the coffers filled and the clapboard freshly painted.

Napa County

The story of spirituality in Napa County—or, more accurately, of European-rooted religion—is sprinkled with visionaries, hard knocks, and roustabouts. Fittingly, the tale more or less begins with the Gold Rush. Among the starry-eyed prospectors who gravitated to California in 1849 was James Milton Small, an ordained minister of the Cumberland Presbyterian Church. In the fall of 1850, Small gave up on gold and moved to Napa to save souls, preaching to early settlers in the dining room of a boarding house.

Three years later the national Presbyterian Board of Missionaries sent the Rev. J. C. Herron from Philadelphia to the Napa Valley. He sermonized in the old Court House, a trying experience according to the record of an original church member: "The inside appearance of the Court-room was rather sorry for a place of worship, especially when Court had been held there the preceding day. . . . No carpets and no curtains, no paint, no finish of any kind had been wasted on this public hall. No lamps, or even candle-sticks were there . . . The upper part of the building was used for public offices, and a jail; and it was not at all an uncommon thing for the nervous and timid ones of the congregation, during service, to be annoyed by the rattling of chains and other discordant sounds proceeding from the prisoners' apartments."

It was in reaction to such conditions that the Presbyterians built the first church in Napa city in 1855, at a time when white settlers were true pioneers. After the congregation moved its facilities a couple of years later, the old edifice was reduced to service as a paint shop. In 1858 it was purchased by a group of Black Methodists, who splintered from their white congregation, moved the structure

The Sea Ranch Chapel is a tiny, nondenominational sanctuary for reflection and spiritual renewal. Built in 1985, the chapel has a cedar roof with a distinctive bronze spire that offers inspiration in a peaceful setting. PHOTO: JEAN SAYLOR DOPPENBERG to Washington Street, and called it the African Methodist Church. That church is gone, but a bell purchased for $600 by the main Presbyterian congregation in 1868 announces the hour of prayer even today, at the First Presbyterian Church at 1333 Third Street in Napa. (It was "warranted for one year.") Rev. Richard Wylie was the pastor of First Presbyterian when that bell was acquired, and he remained in the pulpit until 1921—a remarkable tenure of 54 years, minus a couple of years he spent in Europe recuperating from illness. One of Wylie's successors, Rev. Lee Vernon, had a 16-year run (1937–1953), during which he was well known for broadcasting "Religious News of the Week" for KVON on Sunday afternoons.

Soon after the original Napa temple had been raised, the Presbyterians built a church in St. Helena. On July 26, 1873, somebody tried to burn it down, fastening bags saturated with coal oil up the length of the belfry rope and setting them ablaze. The fire was discovered and dampened before any real damage was done, but the relief was short-lived: The building was destroyed by fire in February 1874. Two years before that, a Presbyterian church had been erected in Calistoga.

Rev. S. D. Simonds is said to have been the first Methodist Episcopal preacher to reside in Napa Valley. That was about 1851. A year later Rev. Asa White delivered a sermon in a grove of redwood trees known as Paradise Park. The grove was part of the Tucker farm, about halfway between St. Helena and Calistoga, and it became the site of the first church in Napa Valley in 1853. The 700-square-foot temple was called the White Church—either because of its color (it is reported to have been the only painted edifice in the valley) or in honor of Asa. The White Church burned down in the early 1900s.

The Methodists built a separate church in Napa in 1856. The Rev. James Corwin, besides his evangelical duties, happened to be engineer at a sawmill north of St. Helena. The owner of the mill, Erwin Kellogg, donated use of his facility long enough for the Rev. Corwin to cut the logs and have them hauled to Napa for the new church. The Methodists also laid the foundation for a church in Calistoga in 1868, but construction didn't go much further. The railroad wanted the land, you see, and there wasn't much the railroad didn't get. Sam Brannan donated another site to the congregation, and the church, Calistoga's first, was completed in 1869. It also served as the local primary school for a year.

The Napa Collegiate Institute, a private Methodist college, was founded in Napa in 1860. The name was changed to Napa College in 1890, and by 1896 financial difficulties had forced the California Conference to move the school to Santa Clara. There it was known as the University of the Pacific, forerunner to the school of the same name that now is located in Stockton.

In 1917 a new Methodist church opened in Napa. During the dedication service, it was reported that $31,000 had been raised for building the church—$5,000 short of the total cost. Addressing the congregation, Bishop Adna Leonard said, "A collection is now in order. This is a courteous congregation. I am going to ask you to remain until the benediction is reached." Leonard's lock-the-doors-until-we're-solvent strategy worked. He marked pledges on a blackboard and eventually reached the $36,000 goal. That building stands today, a registered landmark of English Gothic architecture. The downstairs pews date to 1895. The organ, fashioned by the Wicks Organ Company of Highland, Illinois, is only 20 years old, but is worth noting. It was tonally designed for the building and made to fit within the existing organ chamber. As for the trees in the parking lot, they were planted by Boy Scout Troop No. 2 many years ago.

The Christian Church appeared in the valley in 1853, when J. P. McCorkle preached under a madrone tree in Yountville. His flock founded a church in Browns Valley in 1865, then moved to Napa in 1870, setting up shop in the building that previously had housed the town's first newspaper, the *Napa Reporter*. Later that year they purchased land at the corner of Pearl and Randolph Streets and built a proper church. (The American Legion Post is there now.)

The Roman Catholics held occasional services in Margaret McEnerny's boarding house on Main Street in Napa in the mid-1850s. (The priest would ride over from the Sonoma Mission.) When those attending Mass outgrew Mrs. McEnerny's parlor, services were moved to a warehouse next door, then to the second floor of a building on the southwest corner of First and Main Streets. Finally Napa merchant George Cornwell, a non-Catholic, donated land on Main Street, and St. John the Baptist Church was erected in 1858. It's not the St. John's you see today, however. Father Slattery built a beautiful Gothic church in 1881, which is where noted French-born, English-adopted author Hilaire Belloc married in 1897, having followed his heart across the Atlantic. Unfortunately, that church was leveled in the 1960s. The current edifice was built in 1957.

One of the most colorful religious figures of early Napa Valley was Father Peter Deyaert, a Belgian priest whose far-flung parish covered Napa and Lake Counties and portions of Solano and Sonoma. A contemporary, Frank Leach, described him thus: "Father Deyaert . . . was exceedingly popular with all classes. He was fond of outdoor life, especially in trampling the neighboring hills and shooting quail. . . . He would frequently go into saloons, not to scold or preach to those who happened to be in there, but simply to be social." For many years, Father Deyaert's grave was in the St. John's schoolyard.

The first Catholic Church in St. Helena was built in 1866; actually, it was the remodeled home of a Mrs. Sheehan at Oak Avenue and Tainter Street. When the local parishioners got a new church in 1878, they paid $72 for the old bell from the Napa Courthouse. It became the first bell in St. Helena. Separate Catholic parishes were formed in Calistoga in 1915 and Yountville in 1920.

The Seventh-day Adventist Church held its first meetings in 1873, in tents at the site of what is today known as Fuller Park in Napa, and a church was dedicated in the winter of 1873-74. That building still stands, after many alterations, on the corner of Church and Second Streets, though the Adventists moved out in 1958. Also in 1873, the Seventh-day Adventists held a bustling one-week camp meeting—their second in California—in a shady grove at the confluence of Conn Creek and the Napa River, about a mile northeast of Yountville. Sixty-three tents were neatly arranged around thoroughfares—Present Truth Street, Law and Order Street, etc. On Sunday, nearly 1,500 people pushed in and out of the big evangelistic tent, and afterward 29 were baptized in the river. One of them was Moses J. Church, who founded the city of Fresno and was a seminal figure in the irrigation of the San Joaquin Valley.

In 1877, Dr. Merritt Kellogg was busy laying the groundwork for what would become the St. Helena Sanitarium. One of his builders, Frank Lamb, remembered hearing Ellen G. White remark at an Adventist meeting in Oakland, "We are going to have a health institution on the Pacific coast." The famed mystic (her visions in the 1860s called Adventists to adopt the message of health reform) didn't know exactly where, but "we had to go across water to get to it." Kellogg, in need of funding, immediately invited White and her husband to St. Helena for a view of his site. White said she had seen the terrain in her visions; this must be the place. She purchased eight acres next to Kellogg's and helped turn the area into an Adventist stronghold.

The history of Calistoga, meanwhile, is inexorably entwined with the Church of Jesus Christ of Latter-Day Saints, for Sam Brannan, that iconoclastic founding father and California's first millionaire, was a Mormon. After sailing around the Cape with a church group in the 1840s, Brannan hung onto the collected tithings. He wanted San Francisco to be the center of Mormon culture, not Salt Lake City. Brigham Young saw otherwise, and he eventually excommunicated Brannan for absconding with those funds. (He just as easily could have done it in response to Sam's legendary drinking and philandering.)

The first LDS church in the valley was in St. Helena, adjacent to where that town's current Mormon church stands on

Spring Street. One curious note concerning the denomination: Lilburn Boggs, who issued the infamous Mormon Extermination Order as governor of Missouri, is buried at Tulocay Cemetery in Napa.

Other early arrivals included Christ (Episcopal) Church, organized in 1858. One of the church's earliest rectors was Rev. William Goodwin, inventor of the dry plate used in early photographic processes. Goodwin, it's said, helped make a multimillionaire out of George Eastman.

It wasn't just proper townsfolk who received the Lord's word, either. The Oat Hill Quicksilver Mine, in the rocky mountains east of Calistoga, offered diggers weekly church and Sunday school. Nor was worship confined to English speakers. Second-language services are a common occurrence today, but they aren't a recent invention. St. John Evangelical Lutheran Church gave sermons in German in the early 1900s. And even before that, in 1879, Napa was one of only two California cities to have a Chinese mission. Five evenings a week, local Chinese laborers were given instruction in English and Christianity, first in the chapel of the sponsoring Presbyterian Church, then in an old brick building on Franklin Street that was rented for $50 a year.

By 1963, Napa County counted some 37 separate churches, representing 20 denominations. Today, it's more like 70 churches and 40 denominations, not to mention the many spiritual individualists who defy traditional classification.

Sonoma County

A zealous young Spanish priest, Father Jose Altimira, was the first to bring Christianity to these parts. He came to what is now Sonoma County in 1823 to establish the Mission San Francisco de Solano, northernmost in a chain of missions spaced along California's coast. Despite the overthrow of the Spanish rulers in Mexico, Altimira was nothing if not enthusiastic, and he convinced his colleagues in the church that the area would be a better climate than San Francisco for the Native American converts.

Altimira's mission building was not impressive—a flimsy wooden structure that was swept twice by fire before achieving its present, fireproof adobe state. The Catholic Church's plan was to convey missions to the Native Americans they converted and trained, and within six years, Altimira claimed 1,000 converts.

The mission would not last (the Mexican government issued a decree in 1834

The Church of the Oaks, an historic building, is still in use in Cotati. PHOTO: TINA LUSTER-HOBAN

A Russian Orthodox priest arrives at historic Fort Ross to perform an annual consecration rite. PHOTO: JOHN NAGIECKI

that all church properties were to be "secularized," or confiscated), but the influences of this early presence of organized religion are still evident today.

A small Russian Orthodox chapel was built on the coast in western Sonoma County about the time the Spanish secularized their missions. The small wooden chapel was a part of the Russian American Company's settlement at Fort Ross (see History chapter). The Russians abandoned the fort in 1841, taking all the icons from the chapel with them, leaving behind only a large bell, candelabra, candlestand, and a lectern.

The chapel successfully withstood the ravages of time until the 1906 earthquake caved in its walls and reduced its foundation to rubble. The California legislature granted funds to rebuild the church in 1916, and timbers from some of the other remaining original buildings were used to reconstruct the chapel. All went relatively well until 1970 when an intense fire com-

pletely destroyed the structure, even reducing the bell and other Russian relics to puddles of molten metal. All has since been restored—even the bell has been recast—and the chapel is now open to visitors year-round.

The Russians had come and gone by the time other church activity began to stir in the established city of Sonoma. In approximately 1859, Congregationalists founded Cumberland Presbyterian College, a learning center where services were also sometimes held. But some distance from the village there lived a rancher named Edwin Sutherland who decided he would start his own church under the protecting branches of a large live oak tree on his property. He had five children, his sister across the road had six, and with the children of a few neighbors he established the Big Tree Sunday School in his own backyard.

Sutherland had a strong bass voice and his wife was a soprano, and thus a small

Saddle of Faith

One of the most persistent of the rugged western individualists was the circuit-riding preacher.

It was said that whenever a new territory was opened up, the first to arrive were the whiskey seller and the missionary. Often the circuit-rider's pulpit was under a tree or in a saloon, for a church was definitely not one of the first structures in a new settlement. The God of the American West, it was said, did his good work from the saddle. The territories these men served were sometimes as wide as the West itself. Methodist bishop John Asbury traveled 270,000 miles in ministering to his western flock. Father Francis de Smet covered more than 180,000 miles.

One of the first circuit riders to approach Sonoma County was Isaiah L. Hopkins, a Southern Methodist who served his apprenticeship as a junior preacher riding what was known as the Bodega Circuit. His territory is an example of the dedication required—it included Petaluma, Santa Rosa, Healdsburg, Mark West, and Macedonia, and on as far as Sebastopol. In 1857 it was reported of Hopkins' work that "many souls were converted and brought into the Church." He received $75 for his services that year.

"A wine producing community such as Sonoma County was by no means favorable for the morals of the youth who lived there," proclaimed Presbyterian circuit-rider C. H. Crawford. "The greatest drawback to church work I found was rum power. Men were bold and impudent under the influence of 'Old Tanglefoot.'" Sunday was the drinking and gambling day of the week. Naturally, there were those who did not drink, and God-fearing families who conducted themselves morally in immoral surroundings. But it required the courage of a grizzly bear and plenty of divine grace to stand up and say it.

Besides strong drink, the circuit-riders fought irreverence. According to an account of the day, itinerant preacher Brother Iry Taylor walked past a saloon one Sunday morning and found a man by the name of "Kentuck" mocking a church service. To Taylor's horrified eyes, four young men came forward and knelt at the bench and received crackers and whiskey, in mockery of the communion.

These were no namby-pamby preachers, but men of strong opinion, strongly voiced. Circuit-riding Brother John McCorkle of the Christian Church ("Bro Mac") usually preached his sermons under an oak tree to an audience that might include gamblers and prostitutes as well as professionals. He was a fiery speaker, able to rouse a crowd, and people loved to gather around. No preacher, however, attained the

Before the erection of places like the United Methodist Church in St. Helena, the circuit riders preached throughout the area. PHOTO: TINA LUSTER-HOBAN

notoriety of Episcopalian Reverend D'Estaing, who, convinced Santa Rosa was dangerous territory, preached his sermons with a gun on his hip (much to the chagrin of his flock). Attendance dissipated, and Rev. D'Estaing was defrocked by the Diocese. Rumors persisted that he may have actually shot someone.

Many preachers were indistinguishable from the gamblers they spoke to—a long black coat, white shirt, and string tie were the trademark of both. Sometimes they appeared in the jeans of the sturdy farm folk they came to enlighten. It was said of Bro Mac, who preached to crowds while dressed in homespun Kentucky trousers, that his audience "was made up of every walk of life—the rancher, the coquette, gamblers and horse racers." He was a compelling speaker who seldom made speaking errors although he was said to be illiterate.

Another wandering preacher was described as long-legged, cadaverous, and melancholy, wearing a black, wide-brimmed, low-crowned hat. He sported a scraggly beard of the variety known as a Galway choker. He carried a large Bible under one arm and used the other to wave a horsewhip. In one boot was a Bowie knife; a rim-fire revolver was hidden in the other. It was all, he said, "to discourage over-familiarity."

Whatever role these free spirits played in the epic drama of the taming of the West, they were tough of fiber and filled with the vigorous juice of life. They were nonconformists bringing the good news to an often bad-tempered lot.

choir was formed to augment the teaching. One can only imagine the inspiration of hearing those hymns wafting across the meadow on a summer breeze. Still, a church must be for all seasons, not just for balmy Sunday mornings. Within three years, Sutherland began forming a church in the village. It would be called the First Congregational Church of Sonoma. That church still stands today, though in a different location, at 252 W. Spain Street. The choir there is one of the best in Sonoma. Still, one wonders if music could ever sound quite the same as it did on those Sunday mornings under the live oak.

Conducting church services outside was actually not uncommon in those days of circuit-riding preachers. As early as 1852, on a ranch 6 miles from what would become Santa Rosa, the circuit-riding Rev. Stephen Riley helped form a congregation of Baptists, using the home of rancher Martin Hudson as a Sunday morning place of worship. When the congregation grew too large for the Hudson home, preacher and flock moved outdoors to the banks of a river, under the spreading branches of a large live oak. Winter rains

and wandering cattle, however, helped take the luster off outdoor worship, and the congregation raised enough money to build a proper church, the Lebanon Baptist, which eventually merged with the First Baptist Church.

For years, one of the lesser known secrets about First Baptist Church was that it had been built out of a single 3,000-year-old redwood tree. The tree, 275 feet high and 18 feet in diameter, came from a ranch near Guerneville. The congregation had been unaware of the church's unique status until 1900, when a member, attorney Thomas Butts, told his story. He had been employed by a Guernevillle mill at the time the tree was felled. The mill's owner, knowing the intended purpose of the tree, personally monitored every step of the milling process to ensure the wood wasn't mingled with other lumber.

In 1939 Robert Ripley, a church member, featured the church in his "Believe It Or Not" column and gave it instant fame. For many years, the Church Of One Tree, at 492 Sonoma Avenue in Santa Rosa, housed the Robert Ripley Museum. Although it started as a Baptist church,

A Russian Orthodox choir sings at the historic Fort Ross chapel. PHOTO: JOHN NAGIECKI

One Tree became a church for many faiths, and on any given Sunday as many as 5,000 people worshipped there—as many as 10 services were offered there each week. Finally it was necessary to break up the flock. Two of today's Baptist congregations in Santa Rosa, the Community Baptist Church at 1620 Sonoma Avenue and the First Baptist Church at 3300 Sonoma Avenue, trace their roots to the church Ripley attended.

Members of a Petaluma Baptist church achieved fame of a different sort by installing a certain bell in their belfry, the legend of which still lingers. Having learned of a bell for sale in San Francisco, a committee was dispatched to purchase what was said to be the sweetest-sounding instrument in the land. On arrival, they learned the bell had been used by vigilantes during Gold Rush days to announce the hanging of another lawless

rascal, but the group bought it anyway for $550. It is said the bell's tolling could be heard for 12 miles.

The sexton took to ringing the bell whenever the Union Army had a victory— a source of annoyance to Southern sympathizers who had paid liberally for its purchase. One morning in 1864, the bell disappeared, but by nightfall 40 Union loyalists had found it and hoisted it again to the church tower with the American flag flying above it. The next morning, the bell sounded only once and never rang clear again. It had cracked during the changing of hands.

The 1870s and 1880s saw tremendous expansion of church activity in Sonoma County. Denominations sprang up like dogs to the dinner bell, including Methodists, Baptists, Presbyterians, Episcopalians, and a sizable number of fundamentalist groups.

In the early days of frontier religion, most congregations were served by a circuit rider, a pastor who tended many flocks and spent most of his life on horseback. Pity the Rev. Isaac Owen, a Methodist minister, whose circuit included 10 congregations from Sonoma to Bodega and everything else up to the Russian River. One of the most renowned preachers of Sonoma County was the Rev. James Woods, who established a Presbyterian church in Healdsburg in 1858. His first congregation included Cyrus Alexander, who owned the entire valley north of Healdsburg and was himself a minister. In fact, it was Alexander who proposed that if the church could raise $1,000, he would put up $800 to secure the Methodist property on the plaza, which was up for sale. The lot was eventually purchased and the church was renovated and occupied.

The church remained there until 1932, when the Presbyterians and Methodists decided to join forces; one church had the building, the other had a large congregation. Together they created the Federated Church, which stands today at 555 Monte Vista Avenue in Healdsburg. At about the same time, the Church of Christ established a congregation in Healdsburg, followed by the Seventh-day Adventists and the Episcopalians.

In Cloverdale, the American Home Mission Society founded a First Congregational Church in 1868. The Catholics started making a place for themselves in Cloverdale as early as 1870, holding Mass in the Cloverdale Hotel, a hostelry of some 30 rooms. Various priests served the church, coming from other parishes. In 1879, a Scotsman named Peter Donohue opened a railroad line and took considerable interest in building a Catholic church. The original church cost about $4,000 and was a rustic frame building. In 1962, the new Cloverdale St. Peter's was built at 491 S. Franklin Street. The church has changed considerably from the days when missionaries came barefooted to say Mass; nowadays, three Masses are said each Sunday and two daily.

In Santa Rosa, the first semblance of a Catholic church (a wooden building with eight pews) was erected in 1860 on a lot donated by one of Gen. Vallejo's relatives, Julio Carrillo. For the next 15 years, a priest came up from Marin County once a month to offer Mass at St. Rose. Finally, in 1876, a new parish formed that included Sebastopol, Healdsburg, Cloverdale, and Guerneville. The parish's most popular priest was Fr. John Conway, loved for his sense of humor. He stayed for 37 years.

Today, St. Rose parish serves as the mother church in Santa Rosa, with a seating capacity of 500. The church that was built in 1900—while Fr. Conway was there—still stands as a historic monument, but it is empty and unused, declared unsafe in earthquake conditions. Still grand, it is now surrounded by a new church that wraps around it like a boomerang. The new building at 398 10th Street is stunning, with walls of colored glass. From inside, many portraits of Christ become brilliant when the sun shines through the windows.

Churches that once fell neatly into a half-dozen denominations—mainly Methodist, Baptist, Catholic—have now splintered into dozens of churches. It started during the Civil War when Southern Methodists and Southern Baptists started their own congregations to denote their sympathies with the South. Today there are American Baptists, Independent Baptists, Fundamental Baptists, and GARBC

Insiders' Tip

Twice each year, on Memorial Day and the Fourth of July, the Russian Orthodox Church conducts services at the chapel at Fort Ross. The events generally feature the extraordinary voices of a Russian choir from San Francisco and a colorful procession to the nearby cemetery to consecrate the graves of the old Russian settlers.

Baptists. We have various branches of Presbyterians including Korean Western. We have Buddhist and Soto Zen centers, and we have Pentecostal, Orthodox Eastern, New Age churches, and a group called Metropolitan Community, plus a Church of God of Prophecy and the Foursquare Gospel.

If it is a similar upwelling of faith and devotion that resides in all these houses of worship, rest assured that the North Coast allows each of its citizens a unique way of describing it.

Mendocino County

A rough bunch of citizens populated the Mendocino Coast in 1854. The Gold Rush had waned and lumber was the new booming industry in need of lots of strong backs. Single men by the hundreds poured in from everywhere to work in the mills. After a hard day's work battling logs, lumberjacks sought entertainment, and they found it on the east end of the town of Mendocino, a wild, wide-open district that

gained the name Fury Town for its typical mood on a Saturday night (see History chapter). Saloons and bawdy houses lined the streets. "Big River Bits" (the local name for $20 gold pieces) were stacked on gambling tables.

This was a hard-living breed, and any parson who sought to bring religion to them necessarily possessed a rare courage and tenacity. In 1854, the first Protestant services in this infant village on Big River took place in the cookhouse of the Mendocino Lumber Company. The first ministers who came to preach in Mendocino on an itinerant basis were Methodists, and it was four years before visiting ministers of any other persuasion showed up. When no preacher was available, Mendocino pioneer Peter Kelley, who was an ordained minister from Prince Edward Island, took over.

By 1859, eight determined members from the community applied to the Presbyterian denomination for status as an established congregation, and a mere nine years later they had built a church. It was a

St. Anthony's Catholic Church is a familiar sight in Mendocino for locals and visitors. PHOTO: BILL HOBAN

lovely little white church, in the Gothic style, designed by the same architect who designed the State Capitol in Sacramento. Today, the Mendocino Presbyterian Church is one of the first structures to catch your eye as you enter the village of Mendocino.

It was often rough going for the little congregation. Harmony did not always prevail. One account tells of a confrontation in which the president of the Board of Trustees punched the pastor in the nose. Rugged pioneer personalities sometimes clashed. At one point a schism split the congregation, and attendance declined to the point that the Presbytery considered dissolving it. But the group rode out the rough times, and in 1967 the church celebrated its first 100 years.

Now a California Historic Landmark, the church also is listed in the Federal Registry of Historic Places. From its original eight charter members, it has grown to a membership of 230—this oldest of California's still-active Presbyterian churches is still vigorous and young. Guided tours are conducted on Saturdays between 10:00 A.M. and noon, from July 4 through Labor Day.

Perhaps the first church to be established in Fort Bragg was the First Baptist Church at the corner of East Pine and North Franklin Streets. Like most early churches, the congregation first met at a home in nearby Caspar, beginning in 1878. By 1887 a formal church with a handsome, tall steeple was under construction on land donated by the Fort Bragg Lumber Company.

That church is still there, though it would be hard to identify it. In 1911, the building was put on rollers, pushed farther back on the lot, and turned to face east instead of south. A new church was built right on top of the old. The original church now serves as a social room and Sunday school. One of the grand features of this early church was a beautiful, 1,200-pound bell, purchased in England and shipped around Cape Horn. It was said the bell rang so clearly you could hear it all the way to Caspar—several miles to the south—on a windy day. But by 1932 the clapper had worn out and had to be replaced—unfortunately by a clapper so heavy it cracked the bell. Another clapper, furnished by the fire department, would fit only upside down. At last the bell came down and was set behind the church, where weeds soon overgrew it. Rescued by a church member who was a Daughter of the Golden West, it is now proudly displayed in front of the church with a plaque on it. The present church holds 300 people and is a rare example of a Protestant church built in the California Mission style.

Another of Fort Bragg's oldest churches is St. Michael's and All Angels Episcopal Church at 201 Fir Street. It came into being in 1911 at the instigation of a number of women in town who had become seriously annoyed by the proliferation of saloons and brothels. They advised their husbands that it was time to erect a church, and so they did. Built of local heart redwood at a cost of $3,600, the church could seat 200 worshipers. A dramatic rose window, created by Charles Stevenson, a local artist of some acclaim, features a portrait of St. Michael with his hands outstretched. The window is so beautiful that it's kept lighted at night for round-the-clock enjoyment.

The First Methodist Church at 270 N. Pine Street in Ukiah originally served two congregations—one dating to 1850, the other to 1857. In 1926, they united and built a new church. When fire ravaged that building, they put another right on top of it—a brick building with grounds that spread out over a full city block. (They're still finding rubble from the old church under the sanctuary.) Its steeple stands out as you come into town on U.S. 101.

From the beginning, the great fame of this church came from the vesper chimes played high in the steeple. Every day someone mounted the stairs to play the chimes at 5:00 P.M., a welcome signal to office workers across town that it was time to go home. The chimes wore out (as chimes will), but have been replaced by a programmed version.

Perhaps the most beautiful of Mendocino's spiritual centers is the Sagely City of Ten Thousand Buddhas, set among 488 acres of groves and meadows in Ukiah's lovely Valley at Talmage. The campus consists of 70 buildings, including the Dharma Realm Buddhist University (see our Education and Child Care chapter), on approximately 80 landscaped acres. An atmosphere of quiet peace pervades the City of Ten Thousand Buddhas. Everyone shares a common goal: the sincere pursuit of spiritual truth and value, along with a desire to become wiser and more compassionate. All residents, whether students, faculty, administrators, or staff workers, observe a basic ethical code that prohibits killing, stealing, sexual misconduct, false speech (lying, lewd speech, cruel words, and gossip), and intoxicants. They strive to free their thoughts, words, and deeds from any fighting, greed, selfishness, self-seeking ambition, and lying.

Incorporated in the United States in 1959, the Dharma Realm Buddhist Association seeks to spread the teachings of the Buddha in America. In 1966 the Most Venerable Master Hsuan Hua set up a center for Buddhist study in San Francisco. It has been moved to the Ukiah Valley to become one of California's foremost Buddhist centers. Serious-minded individuals from all walks of life may attend intensive recitation or bowing sessions and meditation retreats. The Dharma Realm Buddhist Association offers daily and weekly lectures and ceremonies, classes, vegetarian meals, and celebrations of Buddhist holidays.

Lake County

Times change but Lake County remains a bucolic and loosely populated domain. Back in the pioneer days it could be downright primitive. Spreading the gospel in such conditions was hard and time-consuming work, performed (as in other Wine Country locales) by circuit-rider ministers who got to know every pothole and muddy quagmire in the land (see this chapter's Close-up, "Saddle of Faith"). At the same time, the rural nature of the area made a house of worship that much more important to the community. The church was a place for weddings, christenings, baptisms, funerals, political meetings, puppet shows, and coffee socials. The

young people's society encouraged chaperoned courting and, in effect, shaped the county by bringing together important families.

The first denomination to organize within the bounds of the county was the Methodist Episcopal Church. The California Conference of the M.E. Church established a Clear Lake Circuit in 1857, and followers met in the schoolhouse in Big Valley. The first Methodist church in Lakeport opened in 1870. Big Valley finally got its Methodist church in 1897, but services were discontinued 19 years later. John Hendricks, who owned the surrounding land, bought the church, tore it down, and built a granary in its stead. In Upper Lake, Methodist camp meetings sometimes lasted two weeks. Interested parties would flock to the area in ranch wagons and cook beef or mutton in a barbecue pit. The ministers often wound up with 50 to 60 converts.

Another early Methodist church, this one in Scotts Valley, had an unusual floor plan: All seats faced toward, and the rostrum and pulpit away from, the entrance. "This was quite a shock to anyone coming to church here for the first time," wrote Alice W. Deacon in her book *Scottslandia*. "One had to go past the pulpit and down the aisles with the eyes of everyone upon him. This convenient arrangement saved everyone from looking back to see who each arrival was."

The Methodists also built a wooden church in the southern part of the county in 1871, when the village of Guenoc was relocated and redubbed Middletown. When they replaced the Church of the Pioneers in 1890, they placed the old structure on rollers and moved it by horsepower to the edge of town. The procession took a week. In 1918 a fire wiped out practically all of Middletown, but not the old church, which by then had become a private residence. The neglected building was finally done in by a storm in 1948. Its 1890 replacement, made of stone, survives today.

A predominately Irish gathering celebrated the first Holy Mass in Lake County in a Big Valley schoolhouse. In 1867 the Catholic Church established a mission farm in Big Valley, under the guidance of Father Luciano Osuna. It was called St. Turibius Mission, though it's not known whether the site was named for the Bishop of Astorga, Spain (c. 450) or the Archbishop of Lima, Peru, who helped spread Catholicism during the Spanish conquest in the early 1600s.

In any case, the mission held 160 acres of fertile valley land on the south shore of Clear Lake, and that soon grew to 225 acres (at least 80 of which were under cultivation). There was an Indian rancheria with a schoolhouse and wooden living quarters, and the tribal people were paid for their work. Father Luciano converted nearly the entire tribe of Pomos living around Clear Lake. He baptized 567 people between 1867 and 1878; most of them were Indians and a few were Russian. The U.S. government made the Indian school at St. Turibius a contract day school from 1888 to 1900. In 1915 the church at the mission was moved to the Finley Rancheria, which had just been created by the U.S. Indian Bureau.

The conversion of indigenous peoples has remained an interesting sidelight to worship in Lake County. The American Indian Full Gospel Assembly Church was built about 1945 by making an addition to Harry's Garage on the Big Valley Rancheria. Average attendance was about 40. Eight years later the Big Valley Pomo Indian Association granted the church a plot of land for a new structure. It's now known as the Big Valley Community Church.

Jumping back in time again, Catholic churches were soon erected in Kelseyville (St. Peter's in 1870), Lakeport (Immaculate Conception of the Blessed Virgin Mary, 1871), Lower Lake (St. Joseph's, 1881), and Sulphur Banks (St. Anthony's, 1909). St. Joseph's was equipped with an exquisite, hand-carved altar, fashioned in Napa Valley by Swiss and Italian craftsmen. St. Anthony's was erected to serve the mine workers at Sulphur Banks. The bricks used in construction, almost certainly tainted with mercury, were obtained from old mine furnaces at $5.00 a load. St. Peter's still stands in Kelseyville. They added an entrance room, tower, and steeple in 1913 and wrapped the bottom

Insiders' Tip

As Lake County debated whether to make Lakeport or Lower Lake the permanent county seat in 1870, the Baptist church in Lakeport was used as a courtroom.

portion of the building in a concrete block skirt between 1955 and 1960. Nevertheless, some of what you see is more than a century old.

When the Catholics needed a new Lakeport church in 1916, they bought the property of the dilapidated Benvenue Hotel on Main Street, between Seventh and Ninth Streets. The fathers lived in the old hotel while constructing the church, which was in the Mission style with a stucco exterior.

Siblings John and Lee Gard owned most of Kelseyville, and they were friends of all denominations. John donated land for the Catholic and Methodist churches, Lee for the Presbyterian. The First Presbyterian Church of Clear Lake opened in Kelseyville in 1874. "It was pronounced bold by friends, hazardous by the indifferent and a failure in advance by the critical," wrote Slocum, Bowen & Co. in their *History of Lake County* (1881). The Presbyterians abandoned the brick, semi-Gothic church when they moved to a new location in 1883.

The Episcopal Church established Trinity Mission in Lakeport in 1876. The missionaries held regular services at Lakeport, rotated among three other sites in the county, and made occasional trips to Ukiah. Meanwhile, the American Sunday School Union appointed Rev. Will E. Read as its missionary for the Northern District of California in July 1880. Read commenced his work in Lake County about a year later. He stayed through the summer of 1881 to organize Sunday schools, supply literature, and offer moral support. In Slocum's history, he's described as "an earnest, eloquent preacher, a zealous, indefatigable worker."

Often, the problem in Lake County has been getting enough bodies in the pews each Sunday. A note in the Methodist Church record from 1906 states, "A siege of measles in early summer followed by a long spell of excessive heat have caused some falling off in attendance during the summer." In 1922 the Methodist, Presbyterian, and Christian churches in Kelseyville were all in dire financial straits. When a minister wasn't available at one of the churches, the congregation simply attended another. So Rev. Story, a Methodist, with the help of the high school principal, initiated a federation called the Kelseyville United Community Church. Two years later the Methodists withdrew, but in 1929 their church and manse were destroyed by a fire. The Presbyterians were without a minister at the time, so they invited Rev. John Anderson and his Methodist flock to share their sanctuary (the then-new stucco building now known as Social Hall). On New Year's Day, 1930, the two denominations reunited as the Kelseyville Federated Church. The federation lasted until 1948, and church membership grew during that time.

As a final note, on May 15, 1971, the Middletown Methodists opened the cornerstone of their Church of the Pioneers. Trustees chiseled away at the stone and mortar to reveal a 1-foot by 8-inch by 4-inch copper box. It was a time capsule, and inside was a copy of the *Middletown Independent* dated October 7, 1893. The hole was enlarged to accommodate a larger, stainless steel box filled with contemporary items. If you're around in 2071 (the 200th anniversary of the church), you can make your way to Middletown and watch it unsealed.

Index

About the Authors

Jean Saylor Doppenberg

A 14-year resident of Wine Country, Jean grew up on the outskirts of Des Moines, Iowa, surrounded by cornfields, not grapevines. She worked in the newsroom of the *Des Moines Register* for more than a decade, writing everything from obituaries to restaurant reviews. After visiting San Francisco and Wine Country in the early 1980s, Jean returned in 1988 and settled in Santa Rosa. She has completed courses in winery public relations and wine marketing, and has written for a publication that covers the business end of the wine industry. In addition, she has co-authored another guide to Wine Country and has written freelance articles for the local hospitality and wine industries.

John Nagiecki

A former Colorado ski instructor and bicycle racer, John has led bicycle tours through the national parks and other popular destination areas in the West. In 1985 his journeys brought him to Wine Country, where he escorted groups of vacationing cyclists from wineries to restaurants and inns. He occupies his non-biking hours with freelance writing, editing, and photography assignments. His work has appeared in the *Seattle Times, San Francisco Examiner, San Jose Mercury News, E Magazine, The Ecologist,* and other national and international publications. He co-authored *Road Biking Northern California* (2002) by The Globe Pequot Press.